Managing Crises

Managing Crises
Responses to Large-Scale Emergencies

Edited by

Arnold M. Howitt and Herman B. Leonard
Harvard University

with David Giles
Harvard University

A Division of SAGE
Washington, D.C.

CQ Press
2300 N Street, NW, Suite 800
Washington, DC 20037

Phone: 202-729-1900; toll-free, 1-866-4CQ-PRESS (1-866-427-7737)

Web: www.cqpress.com

Cover design: Tony Olivis
Composition: BMWW

13 12 11 10 09   1 2 3 4 5

Library of Congress Cataloging-in-Publication Data

Howitt, Arnold M.
  Managing crises : responses to large-scale emergencies / Arnold M. Howitt,
Herman B. Leonard.
    p. cm.
  ISBN 978-0-87289-570-6
  1. Emergency management—United States.   2. Crisis management—United States.
I. Leonard, Herman B.   II. Title.

  HV551.3.H68 2009
  363.34'560973—dc22

                                                                        2008055443

For Maryalice and Kathy

Contents

Exhibits

Part III. Adapting to Novelty

Preface

Devastating crisis events of massive size, which we refer to as *landscape-scale disasters*, have been occurring with distressing regularity—notably the tsunami that hit South Asia at the end of 2004, thought to have taken over 300,000 lives (more than two-thirds of them in the first hour, principally in one location); Hurricane Katrina on the Gulf Coast of the United States; the earthquake in Pakistan in late 2005; Cyclone Nargis in Myanmar; and the devastating snowfalls and Wenchuan earthquake, both in China in 2008. Smaller-scale emergency events, like any number of serious transportation accidents or the 2008 Mumbai terror attacks, directly affect a smaller number of people than do large natural disasters, but they nonetheless create—indeed, are sometimes designed to create—high levels of fear and disruption. Such events frequently dominate the headlines and force us to think about whether we as individuals and society as a whole are prepared for disaster and ready to cope with the consequences. Perhaps because these events are so salient, how effectively we handle them often becomes a defining characterization of both our values and our competence.

What can we do in advance to prepare to respond to major emergency events? What forms of organization are most likely to be helpful and effective? What approaches to training and equipping responders and codifying procedures have the best chance of achieving productive results? What kinds of behavior are most valuable and effective "in the moment"—that is, during rapidly unfolding, urgent, and high-consequence events?

These are complex questions, and they yield no simple answers. A great many good treatments of emergency management describe methods of organization, training, and response procedures. They range from highly technical manuals focusing on specific kinds of events (such as wildland fires or floods) or on specific forms of response (such as search and rescue following earthquakes) to broader treatments on how to organize the response to a major event through more general approaches such as the incident management system. In these works, readers will find descriptions of historical events, well-developed theories of how responses should be designed and executed, and cogent advice about both preparation and response. In our research and teaching about crisis management, we often use materials of this kind, and we are grateful to have them. We find, however, that the descriptions of events provided in these treatments tend to be relatively spare, so that they constitute illustrations rather than the central subject of the work. Given that these works are principally concerned with developing more general frameworks, their use of compressed examples seems fair enough—but it often leaves us wanting richer, more complete descriptions of the events to inform and expand our thinking and make our teaching more salient. For students (and teachers) who never have experienced disaster situations firsthand, it may be hard to identify with the conditions that prevail or the challenges faced by those enmeshed in such events—and we find that deeper, more comprehensive descriptions can help all of us get a more vivid sense of these dramatic circumstances.

On the other hand, we can also find quite detailed treatments of individual crisis events, with rich, comprehensive descriptions of how the events unfolded, the sequence of both the damage and the emergency response, and the flow of consequences emanating from the disaster. These accounts—written from first-person or journalistic perspectives—frequently provide an excellent understanding of the evolution of the events. But they typically do not illustrate or provide much data about the relationship between the emergency organization structures and concepts of emergency management, on the one hand, and the performance and effectiveness of the response, on the other.

This book—a case-based examination of crisis and emergency management—attempts to fill the gap between these genres by providing detailed cases about specific emergency events in the context of discussions about concepts, terminology, hypotheses, and theories about emergency management. In our teaching, we find that the depth of the event descriptions in the cases we have included in this book bring these historical events alive in the classroom, galvanizing both our own and our students' interest. But we also find that we need to put these cases in a teaching context in which we examine well-organized ideas about how emergencies differ from one another, what kinds of responses are necessary, and how different forms of organization and behaviors (or the lack thereof) contribute to successful (or less successful) performance and results. In that way, we can draw more deeply on the rich material these cases provide to guide the work of future emergency managers and, more broadly, to inform both their colleagues in government and the citizens who support their efforts.

There are several ways that instructors and students can use the case studies presented in this book in a classroom, but two are probably most common. First, the cases can be used as detailed illustrations of concepts and theories that already have been presented to students to show how they play out in specific circumstances. Most of the teaching in this approach then focuses on the abstract concepts, with some class time allocated to explore how they are demonstrated or illustrated by the events of the associated cases. (This is sometimes referred to as a "deductive" approach, where concepts are developed from first principles and then conclusions are deduced or applied to illustrations.) In teaching the "wisdom of crowds" concept, for example, which can be illustrated by the case describing the U.S. Centers for Disease Control and Prevention (CDC) Team B, "CDC Develops Its 'Team B'" (Case 11), the discussion will first focus on the theoretical underpinnings of the "wisdom of crowds" idea. Once that has been fully developed as a concept, the discussion will turn to the Team B case: "How does the CDC's experience with Team B illustrate the advantages and the difficulties of a 'wisdom of crowds' approach?"

The alternative—which is the approach that we use in most of our teaching—is to begin by discussing the case itself, drawing out its potential implications for the concepts and theories, which will be examined in detail only after the event-based discussion. In this approach, the case is central to the discussion, but the *ideas* are central to the learning. (This is sometimes referred to by case-based instructors as an "inductive" approach; the ideas and commentary about the ideas emerge from the cases.) In the class session about the CDC and Team B, the class focuses on the case without first concentrating on the concepts. An instructor may begin by asking students to examine the sequence of devices used by the CDC at different times in different circumstances. "How did the problems they were confronting differ from one another? Why did they use different approaches to Team B in these different circumstances? How well did they work? For which kinds of challenges is the Team B approach most likely to be useful?" Students can thus explore the issues in the case, forming their own ideas and impressions about what worked and what did not. After working on the events in the case, the class can turn back to the conceptual issues: "What does this tell us about the general idea of the 'wisdom of crowds' approach?" Collateral readings about the concepts may be assigned along with the case study or can be introduced after the case has been discussed.

Using either approach, both the concepts and the case examples can be examined in detail. To aid this process, we have provided some additional material. Introductions to each of the five sections of the book highlight and succinctly develop the main analytic themes of the sections. Brief introductions to each case study set up its key issues, and suggested discussion questions guide the students' reading of each case. In addition, lists of key actors and chronologies of the main events are presented at the end of each case for student reference during and after reading. A concluding chapter summarizes the major themes of the book and places them in the perspective of two modes of response, which we term *routine emergencies* and *crisis emergencies*. Also, teaching notes and PowerPoint lecture slides created by the authors are available from CQ Press to assist faculty in the classroom use of these case studies.

Perhaps the essential point: using a well-developed set of principles and a collection of detailed case examples together, an instructor and class can produce a much richer, more complete, more interesting, and ultimately more satisfying examination of the key features of crisis management and leadership. That was our fundamental purpose in developing these cases for our own teaching and the primary reason for collecting these cases to share with other faculty and their students. We hope that this book helps you understand the nature of these critical events better and helps you figure out how better to prepare for and respond to those that still lie in our collective future.

Acknowledgments

Early in our careers as faculty members teaching about public management and leadership, we became intrigued by cases about crisis situations because they offered a degree of clarity about success and failure that is unavailable in cases about more ordinary circumstances. Two decades later, in the late 1990s, we became more focused on the management problems of effective emergency response. We began working together on crisis management issues in 2001. Together we founded a Harvard Kennedy School research and teaching program— Emergency Preparedness, Crisis Management, and Disaster Recovery. Today that program is deeply involved in a number of executive education initiatives; a diverse set of research projects; advisory work in several cities; and, most pertinent here, curriculum development.

As we look toward publication of this volume, we recognize with gratitude how many people and institutions have provided support and encouragement as these case studies were written, tested in the classroom, and revised. We can say—with no reservations whatsoever—that this book would never have been produced without their involvement.

Perhaps our greatest debt is to the "sources": the many officials, responders, journalists, and other participants and observers who granted personal interviews to the case writers. Generous with their time and patient in working with the researchers, these people were also, in most cases, very candid and helpful in securing additional information. Almost to a person, they were motivated by a desire to help others learn from their experiences and improve the emergency management system. All of us involved in producing this book thank them for their willingness to participate.

We owe another enormous debt to the extremely talented case writers who researched and wrote these studies. We commissioned each of these cases, helped define their scope and focus in concert with their authors, and worked with the authors in revising drafts, but the case writers conducted their research and writing very independently. The results on view in this book are attributable to these authors' incredibly dedicated work:

- Howard Husock, now vice president of policy research at the Manhattan Institute and director of its Social Entrepreneurship Initiative, was for many years the director of the Harvard Kennedy School Case Study Program. His thoughtful advice and firm editorial hand are visible in most of the cases in this volume, and he is the author of one of them.
- Esther Scott is the editor at the case program.
- Pamela Varley is a senior case writer.
- Kirsten Lundberg, after her years at the case program, is now director of the Knight Case Studies Initiative at the Columbia University School of Journalism.
- Susan Rosegrant, also a longtime staff member at the case program, now teaches writing at the University of Michigan's Residential College and works at the university's Institute for Social Research.
- John Buntin, formerly at the case program, is now a staff writer for *Governing* magazine and a coauthor of *Governing States and Localities* and author of the forthcoming *L.A. Noir: The Struggle for the Soul of America's Most Seductive City.*
- David Tannenwald, a recent Harvard College graduate, wrote his case as an undergraduate research assistant.

- Jerry Williams, since retiring as national director of the Fire and Aviation Management Program at the U.S. Forest Service, has conducted research on wildland fire policy.

Another indispensable partner was David Giles, a senior research associate in our Program on Emergency Preparedness, Crisis Management, and Disaster Recovery. He helped us abridge longer versions of the cases, perceptively provided editorial advice, and dealt with the multitude of tasks and relationships essential to move from manuscript to published book. He is equally adept at creative intellectual work and the exacting tasks of formalizing or creating footnotes and proofreading—all of which made a significant difference in the quality of this volume. Throughout, too, he has worked on several separate research projects with energy, intellectual vigor, and persistent good humor.

Others in the Program on Emergency Preparedness, Crisis Management, and Disaster Recovery have also been valued colleagues: Doug Ahlers, Arrietta Chakos, David Tannenwald, Jerry Williams, Carolyn Wood, and Tom Wooten.

Both Harvard Kennedy School and Harvard University as a whole are incredibly stimulating and highly supportive environments for research and teaching. We have been fortunate indeed to spend our student days and professional lives at this university. It is impossible to name every colleague who has contributed ideas or asked searching questions on the matters at hand, but we especially wish to thank Doug Ahlers, Graham Allison, Alan Altshuler, Max Bazerman, Robert Behn, Robert Blendon, Hannah Riley Bowles, Ashton Carter, Jack Donahue, Amy Edmondson, David Ellwood, Richard Falkenrath, David Gergen, Richard Hackman, Frank Hartmann, Philip Heymann, James Honan, Juliette Kayyem, David Luberoff, Leonard Marcus, Judith McLaughlin, Matthew Meselson, Steven Miller, Joseph Nye, Tony Saich, Terry Scott, Jessica Stern, Christopher Stone, Guy Stuart, and Peter Zimmerman.

We thank our close Chinese faculty colleagues as well, particularly Xue Lan and Peng Zongchao of Tsinghua University, Zhong Kaibin of the China National School of Administration, and Zhang Qiang of Beijing Normal University, who have been instrumental in launching our China Crisis Management research and executive education program.

Our case study development took off during the four years that one of us (Howitt) directed the Executive Session on Domestic Preparedness (ESDP), sponsored at Harvard by the Office of Justice Programs, U.S. Department of Justice. He cofounded this program with Richard Falkenrath, who left Harvard to serve as a senior director at the White House National Security Council, then deputy director of the Homeland Security Council, and now deputy commissioner for counterterrorism of the New York City Police Department. Falkenrath ignited Howitt's interest in emergency preparedness and crisis management, for which Howitt is very grateful. Juliette Kayyem, now Massachusetts deputy secretary of public safety and homeland security adviser to the governor, was a challenging and congenial intellectual partner during the remaining three years of the project. Other stimulating ESDP research and staff colleagues include Gregory Koblentz, Rebecca Storo, Robyn Pangi, Kendall Hoyt, Kerry Fosher, Laura Donahue, Patricia Chang, and Gavin Cameron.

The practitioner members of ESDP—most senior officials in local, state, or federal government agencies—were an incredible group to work with over four years. Among them, Thomas Antush, Joseph Barbera, Hank Christen, Rebecca Denlinger, Peter LaPorte, Marcelle Layton, Paul Maniscalco, Gary McConnell, Andrew Mitchell, Leslee Stein-Spencer, Darrel Stephens, Patrick Sullivan, Ralph Timperi, A. D. Vickery, and Frances (Winslow) Edwards deserve special thanks. We've also had the privilege of working with seasoned and dedicated practitioners in many other venues. Among these, we are particularly grateful to Christopher Combs, Gary Margolis, Joseph Pfeifer, Marc Rounsaville, James Schwartz, and Jerry Williams.

Theodore C. Sorensen has repeatedly given the gift of his time as a guest faculty member in our Leadership in Crises executive education program; he is inspiring as both a teacher and practitioner of crisis management.

We have benefited tremendously from and gratefully acknowledge intellectual and institutional support from several research centers at Harvard Kennedy School and especially from their faculty directors: Alan Altshuler and Edward Glaeser of the Taubman Center for State and Local Government, Graham Allison of the Belfer Center for Science and International Affairs, Anthony Saich of the Ash Institute for Democratic Governance and Innovation, and David Gergen of the Center for Public Leadership. Special thanks also go to David Luberoff and Sandra Garron, our longtime colleagues at the Taubman Center.

We have thankfully worked with a dedicated and talented team at Harvard Kennedy School Executive Education, including Jane Latcham, Christine Letts, Kristi Scafide, Maryellen Smyth, and Peter Zimmerman. Extra special thanks goes to Annette Wilson, our coconspirator in so many training endeavors. Likewise, we thank our colleagues in the Ash Institute/Asia Programs—Julian Chang, Jessica Eykholt, Laura Ma, and Kathy O'Brien—and at Tsinghua University, Meng Bo. David Gergen, Leonard Marcus, and Donna Kalikow have our sincere thanks for their support of case development as a component of the National Preparedness Leadership Initiative. At the Harvard Kennedy School Case Study Program, we have had consistent administrative support from Howard Husock, Mary Flaherty, Anne Drazen, and Leslie Adkins-Shellie, as well as those staff writers already mentioned. Joseph Zolner at the Harvard Graduate School of Education has provided invaluable backing in launching the Crisis Leadership in Higher Education program.

A number of teaching venues have provided us with the opportunity to test these cases and, in turn, get ideas for future case development. Harvard Kennedy School attracts superb participants to its executive education programs, mainly senior officials from federal, state, and local governments in the United States and other countries, as well as individuals from nongovernmental organizations and business firms. Not passive consumers of the case studies, these "students" have probed and commented vigorously in discussions inside and outside the classroom. First and foremost, we have taught these cases in Leadership in Crises, our original and most frequently offered program, and in the National Preparedness Leadership Initiative, sponsored at Harvard by the U.S. Centers for Disease Control and Prevention. A new program, Crisis Leadership in Higher Education, in collaboration with colleagues at the Harvard Graduate School of Education (HGSE), debuts in 2009, following in the footsteps of earlier presentations in HGSE programs for university leaders. Shorter modules on crisis management have been included in several other Harvard Kennedy School executive education programs aimed mainly at officials from the United States, including the Senior Executives in State and Local Government and the Leadership for State Health Officials programs. We have also taught these cases in Harvard Kennedy School international executive education programs, including a one-week version of Leadership in Crises for participants from South and Southeast Asia at the Lee Kuan Yew School of Public Policy at the National University of Singapore. With colleagues from Tsinghua University, we have taught China Crisis Management in Beijing. Shorter modules on crisis management have also been included in Harvard Kennedy School's China's Leaders in Development Program, the Leadership Enhancement and Development Program for Hong Kong, the Beijing Executive Public Management Training Program, the Taiwan Executive Leadership Program, and the Pakistan Executive Leadership Development Program. Leonard has taught this material at the Australian–New Zealand School of Government and in two Harvard Business School programs: the South Africa Senior Executive Program and the Senior Executive Program for the Middle East. Howitt has taught a version of Leadership in Crises at the Cascade Center for Public Service at the University of Washington, Seattle; one-day courses at annual meetings of the National Conference of State Legislatures and the Conference of Minority Transportation Officials; and a graduate course, Crisis Management and Emergency Preparedness, at the Harvard Extension School.

Overall, nearly 2,000 executive education participants and other students have read and discussed the cases in this volume. Through discussion and criticism, they have helped us frame and refine our thinking about the events depicted, develop more general ideas about the leadership and management processes of emergency preparedness and response, and gain confidence in the value of our approach to the critical questions and issues faced by practitioners of emergency management.

Financial support for these case studies has come from the Office of Justice Programs, U.S. Department of Justice; the U.S. Centers for Disease Control and Prevention; the New England University Transportation Center, a U.S. Department of Transportation program; the Robert Wood Johnson Foundation; and the Taubman Center for State and Local Government at Harvard Kennedy School. We also acknowledge financial support for related research from Dean David Ellwood's Acting in Time project at Harvard Kennedy School, which has informed our thinking for some of the analytic material in this book, and from the Harvard China Fund, to launch our parallel research and teaching in China. We deeply appreciate the faith in our work that such support indicates but proclaim with more than normal vehemence the usual disclaimer: These case studies do not necessarily reflect the views of any of these funders or of Harvard University; any errors of commission or omission are ours and ours alone.

The President and Fellows of Harvard College (the Harvard Corporation), which owns the original copyrights to these cases, has graciously permitted us to seek their publication.

The following reviewers provided feedback on the proposal for this volume and helped shape its development: John Donaldson, Liberty University; Herbert Gooch, California Lutheran University; Jamie Mitchem, California University of Pennsylvania; Tim Murphy, Findlay University; Bill Newmann, Virginia Commonwealth University; Bill Parle, Oklahoma State University; Scot Phelps, Metropolitan College of New York; Eugene Rovai, University of California-Chico; Steven Stehr, Washington State University; and Robert Whelan, University of New Orleans.

Our partners at CQ Press have been an extraordinary group to work with: supportive, extraordinarily patient, persistent in pressing us to finish, and endlessly helpful in maneuvering through the myriad steps remaining when we thought (and wished) we were almost there. Charisse Kiino has championed this book from the beginning; Julie Nemer has edited our copy with painstaking intelligence; and Allison McKay and Anne Stewart have been extraordinary in turning the manuscript into printed pages. To all of them, sincere thanks!

Our children and grandchild—Mark, Alexandra, Molly, and Matt and Melissa Howitt and their daughter, Allison; and Dana and Whitney Leonard—light up our lives even when the matters claiming our professional attention are grim. Maryalice Sloan-Howitt and Kathryn Angell are our treasured life partners. With great love, we dedicate this book to Maryalice and Kathy.

Finally, as academics who do not work in the trenches of emergency response, we want to express our admiration, respect, and gratitude to the many thousands of men and women in the United States and around the world who go to work every day willing to place themselves in harm's way—and who, not infrequently, directly insert themselves between us and the perils that would otherwise befall us. It is no exaggeration to say that they provide a fundamental building block of civilization by standing ready to help others, even at the risk of their own lives. That they deserve our thanks goes without saying. We hope to do more in this book by calling attention to the substantive tasks of their profession, conveying the difficult challenges they face, and showing the courage and skill they need to cope with those demands. It is a most fitting tribute, we feel, to help a new generation begin thinking about how to make the emergency management profession and system even better in the future.

Arnold M. Howitt and Herman B. "Dutch" Leonard
Cambridge, Massachusetts
January 2009

Part I   Prepared for the Worst?
The Dilemmas of Crisis Management

In the brief history of the twenty-first century, a number of searing events have focused attention on society's capacity to respond to emergencies—some naturally occurring, some the result of human agency.[1] These include:

- *natural catastrophes* such as the Asian tsunami in 2004, Hurricane Katrina in the United States in 2005, the wildfires in Greece in 2007, and the Sichuan earthquake in China in 2008
- outbreaks of *new, threatening diseases* such as severe acute respiratory syndrome (SARS) in 2003 and the perceived threat of avian influenza
- *technology failures and industrial accidents* such as mine cave-ins in the United States in 2006 and regularly in China, and major transportation disasters such as the foundering of an Egyptian ferry in stormy seas that took the lives of more than 1,000 people in 2006
- *terrorist attacks* such as the fateful 9/11 assaults on the World Trade Center towers and the Pentagon, the anthrax-laced letters that closely followed in 2001, the train bombings in Madrid in 2004, and the London subway and bus bombings in 2005

Disasters—some more dire than these—have always plagued human society. But the scale, density, and interconnectedness of modern life magnify the impact of present-day catastrophes. The relative ease of modern transportation means that some potential emergencies—most notably, emergent infectious diseases or terrorism—can travel very rapidly within a single country or across national boundaries, as SARS did from China to other countries in Asia and then to Canada. Of course, those immediately in the path of a major emergency are severely affected, but others linked by family or social ties or by connections to disrupted economic networks experience the disaster indirectly. Many individuals who suffer no harm directly may nonetheless live in fear that future catastrophes will affect their families; others empathically identify with the pain of victims. Society, moreover, pays high

---

[1]This discussion draws on Arnold M. Howitt and Herman B. "Dutch" Leonard, "Beyond Katrina: Improving Disaster Response Capabilities," *Crisis/Response Journal* Pt. 1: 2, no. 3 (June 2006): 52–53; Pt. 2: 2, no. 4 (September 2006): 54–56; "Katrina and the Core Challenges of Disaster Response," *Fletcher Forum of World Affairs* 30, no. 1 (winter 2006): 215–220.

monetary costs—through public budgets and charitable and personal resources—in reconstructing damaged physical infrastructure, struggling to restore community vitality, and rehabilitating disrupted lives.

Interconnectedness has also increased both the visibility and the potential political impact of modern disasters. The near omnipresence of contemporary communications media means that we learn faster and in greater detail about most disasters. Videos and photos are quickly flashed even from remote areas, and the immediacy and visual impact of human tragedy seen on television or the Internet accentuate the emotional effects. The effectiveness of response is also visible. In some cases, resourcefulness, heroism, and resilience are prominent. In others, lack of preparedness, poor communications among emergency responders, and weak coordination expand the consequences and increase the pain that catastrophe imposes on society. In the face of disaster, elected leaders must increasingly explain why serious emergencies that might realistically have been prevented occurred on their watch or why their jurisdictions failed to respond effectively to emergencies that occurred through no fault of their own, while political rivals try to hold them accountable both for failures of prevention and for how well response and recovery efforts were conducted.

A Distinctive Public Management Problem

Many people have come to see connections, too, among disaster types, noting important similarities in terms of what society must do to get ready for and respond to major threats. In the United States, the idea of "all hazards" emergency preparedness has been official doctrine for over half a century, but the reality at all levels of government has fallen short of the ideal. Far more must be done to ensure that overall capacity is adequate; that small and large jurisdictions are protected; and that different agencies and professional groups, as well as different levels of government, collaborate in building response capabilities, work together in the event of disaster, and coordinate action effectively under the stress of dangerous events.

To develop robust response capabilities we must see emergency preparedness as a distinctive problem of public management that requires different approaches than other management tasks with which we tend to be more familiar. Effective emergency management is not a matter of administering *routine operations* or service delivery, where the key problem is matching the supply of service in time and space to a more or less continuous, although varying, flow of demand from citizens or organizations. It is not *project management,* where a unique capital facility or operational activity is conceived, planned, and executed on schedule. Nor is it an *overhead* or *staff function* like budgeting, human resources, planning, or policy development that, on behalf of senior executives or legislative overseers, supports, analyzes, and critiques operations.

Instead, emergency management demands different capabilities. It requires readiness, as near to instantaneous as possible, for a wide range of contingencies that happen only episodically—or not at all—in a particular place. Responders thus must plan for events whose precise nature (timing, type, location, and specific requisites of response) can only be loosely predicted and for which prior training, experience, and drill may not have been appropriate or adequate. The effort required by emergency conditions will certainly involve those who think of themselves as emergency responders (for example, firefighters and law enforcement and emergency medical personnel). But, under severe circumstances, it may also involve others whose normal activities and professional identities do not center on disaster management. These may include, for example, personnel in public health, transportation, public works, social services, and schools, as well as a variety of private-sector entities. Ideally, all these individuals and the professions they represent will be ready for the contributions they will need to—or could usefully—make in the event of catastrophe.

Emergent Views of Preparedness and Response Capacity

In the United States, elected officials and the public pay intense attention to emergency management mainly when highly visible events are handled poorly and concerns are then raised about the adequacy of disaster preparedness for future contingencies.

In 1992, quite notably, the massive destruction caused by Hurricane Andrew in Florida and the subsequent weak performance of the Federal Emergency Management Agency (FEMA) led to major reforms in FEMA's organization and leadership (and probably contributed to the defeat of George H. W. Bush in the presidential election that immediately followed the storm). Nearly a decade later, the 9/11 terrorist attacks stimulated renewed scrutiny of the adequacy of emergency management at all levels of government and led to the reorganization of federal agencies into the Department of Homeland Security. During roughly the same period, the appearance of West Nile virus in New York City in 1999, the threat of bioterrorism dramatized by the anthrax attacks in 2001, and SARS in Asia and Canada in 2003 focused attention on the potential widespread outbreak of an emergent infectious disease, concern that intensified in the next several years with the possibility that A(H5N1) avian influenza might spark just such a pandemic. Yet it was nature's fury in Hurricane Katrina, which lashed the gulf coast in late August 2005, that most vividly exposed serious weaknesses in U.S. emergency response capabilities.

A Bottom-Up System
Of course, not all emergencies pose challenges of the magnitude of a Hurricane Katrina, nor require an extraordinary commitment of resources from every level of government. In the United States, as in most countries, the initial—and usually major—responsibility for

disaster response rests with local authorities. This bottom-up system of emergency management has a long history and continues to make sense in most circumstances. Because local governments are proximate to disaster sites and have at least some emergency capacity, they can respond quickly to initial alerts. They have detailed knowledge of local conditions and, in many cases, have agreements for mutual aid to secure additional help rapidly from nearby jurisdictions.

Aid from state or national sources is provided mainly when local capability is inadequate or has been exhausted. State government may have important specialized resources and capabilities, but because its resources may be farther away, it is usually less able to respond immediately (its resources may have to travel a considerable distance to get to a disaster site). Federal government responders are likely to be even more distant—hence, much slower to arrive on a significant scale—and lack both local knowledge and integration with local and state responders. FEMA, with relatively few deployable staff, has historically played a much larger role in pre-event planning and post-event recovery than in the management of a disaster-in-progress. Other federal agencies have more operational resources but are generally deployed as backup. Notwithstanding the reorganization of emergency response at the federal level as a consequence of the establishment of the Department of Homeland Security, the bottom-up system remains the normal model of disaster response.

Core Challenges of Large-Scale Disaster Response

Quite clearly, however, the normal model was inadequate to handle the results of an event of the scale of Hurricane Katrina. It is thus worthwhile to look at a number of *core challenges* that figure in major disasters of various types. These challenges tend to recur and thus are critical design parameters for the emergency management system.

Routine and Crisis Emergencies: Recognizing
Novelty and Effectively Improvising Necessary Responses

Emergency responders ready themselves for a wide range of urgent circumstances. These involve high stakes, danger, and outcomes that are critically contingent on responders' own effective action. Although quite demanding, many of these situations can be regarded as *routine emergencies,* not because they are in some sense "easy" but because the predictability of the general type of situation permits agencies to prepare in advance and take advantage of lessons from prior experience. Such anticipatable events are routine for both the agencies and individuals concerned. Response organizations develop contingency plans, train personnel, practice their skills, and ready or stockpile necessary resources so that they are ready when such predictable challenges occur. For example, when forecasters predict that hurricane winds will make landfall, emergency organizations in areas where hurricanes are common launch a range of programmed actions to protect property, provide temporary shelter and supplies, make rescues as needed, and provide emergency medical care and other assistance. Public health agencies and medical care providers, similarly, have annual routines to get ready for and deal with the problems of flu season. In a fast-moving routine emergency, individual responders can rely on this preparation and on their own near-instantaneous recognition of complex patterns to size up cause and effect and trigger swift implementation of the appropriate protective measures.

The capacity to treat a wide range of contingencies, including quite severe ones, as *routine* constitutes an enormous source of strength for emergency response personnel and organizations. They have thought through how to act. They are equipped. They have trained and practiced. Their leaders' judgment has been honed by experience. In moments when delay may literally make a difference of life or death, they don't need to size up the situation for an extended period, plan their response from scratch, assemble people and resources, and divide up roles and responsibilities. Responders are ready, in multiple dimensions of the term.

But not all emergencies fit the mold. Katrina was not merely another hurricane; SARS was not just another wave of influenza. Such *crisis emergencies* are distinguished from more common routine (although possibly very severe) emergencies by significant elements of *novelty.* These novel features may result from threats never before encountered (for example, an earthquake in an area that has not experienced one in recent memory or an emergent infectious disease like avian flu); from a more familiar event occurring at an unprecedented scale, outstripping available resources; or from a confluence of forces, which, although not new, in combination pose unique challenges. Katrina was a crisis primarily because of its unusually large scale and the novel mixture of challenges that it posed, not least the failure of the levees in New Orleans. SARS was novel not only because it was caused by a new bug but also because its pattern of infectiousness departed from the norm. It should be clearly noted, however, that novelty, from this perspective, is *subjective.* It is something new from the perspective of the jurisdictions, organizations, and individuals involved in response and possibly—but not necessarily—from the experience or point of view of other jurisdictions, organizations, or individuals. A severe fire in a chemical plant may pose novel conditions to the firefighters confronting it, even though other fire departments in other states may have previously encountered these conditions.

An important consequence flows from considering novelty to be the defining feature of a crisis. Because of the novelty, predetermined emergency plans and response behavior that may function quite well in dealing with routine emergencies are frequently grossly inadequate or even counterproductive. That proved true in New Orleans, for example, in terms of evacuation planning, law enforcement, rescue activities, sheltering, and provisions for the elderly and infirm. SARS defeated the normal precautions that hospitals take to prevent the spread of respiratory infections, resulting in the contamination and shutdown of several hospitals in Toronto.

By contrast with routine emergencies, therefore, crises require quite different capabilities. In crises, responders must first quickly *diagnose* the elements of novelty (for example, in New Orleans, the widespread need for assisted evacuation, the likely consequences when the levees failed, and the unexpected use of the convention center for sheltering immobile refugees). Then they need to *improvise* response measures adequate to cope with the unanticipated dimensions of the emergency (for example, quickly procuring vehicles for evacuation, making emergency repairs to the levees, and providing food and law and order in an unprepared shelter). These measures, born of necessity, may be quite different from or exceed in scale anything responders have done before. The responders must be creative and extremely adaptable to execute improvised tactics. Equipping organizations to recognize the novelty in a crisis and improvise skillfully is thus a far different (and far more difficult) matter than preparing them mainly to implement preset emergency plans.

Many crisis situations occur suddenly and are unavoidably noticeable as something novel: a major earthquake, the landfall of a major hurricane, a bomb blast. But some forms of crisis do not arrive suddenly. They fester and grow, arising from more ordinary circumstances that often mask their appearance. We term such situations *emergent crises*—a special and especially difficult category. When SARS emerged in south China in winter 2002–2003, it appeared first as a series of unexplained deaths in a region that has, annually, many unexplained deaths. The famous 1979 nuclear accident at the Three Mile Island power plant in Pennsylvania started as a simple pump failure, out of which spun an escalating series of failures and mistakes until a major crisis was underway.

Emergent crises pose special challenges for responders in terms of recognizing novelty because they look much like routine emergencies in their early stages, only later revealing their unusual characteristics. By then, responders may well have committed to treating the situation as they would a routine emergency and could be slow to see the new features that require different forms of response—so slow that the emergency may by then be difficult to control.

Scalability and Surge Capacity

In many disasters, responders must cope with far greater numbers of endangered people or more extensive damage than is typical of a routine emergency. Crisis impacts may occur very intensively in a delimited area, as was true of Katrina, or be spread across a wide geographical region, as proved the case with SARS. To scale up operations to handle this surge of demand, emergency agencies require access to resources in larger quantities than they normally do and frequently to specialized equipment or personnel. If an emergency lasts for days or weeks, there also must be enough people and resources to cope with exhaustion of the personnel.

No local jurisdiction—or even state—could bear the expense of keeping these assets in reserve for a large-scale disaster that might never occur there. When such an event strikes, therefore, it is virtually inevitable that the jurisdictions affected will have to import and effectively absorb support from surrounding areas or—in very severe circumstances, such as Katrina—from around the nation.

Some emergency professions have incorporated the idea of *surge capacity* into their regular operating patterns. In firefighting, most jurisdictions already have mutual aid agreements with neighboring communities that enable any of them to expand the available workforce and equipment. In case of a major fire, each community can draw on its neighbors' resources, so no community has to invest in firefighting capacity sufficient to counter a worst-case scenario. Mutual aid agreements are regularly invoked, and firefighters from different locales both exercise together and gain experience in confronting real fires. At an even higher level, very specialized resources may be maintained on a regional or state basis. Not all emergency professions, however, have adopted such practices.

As Katrina revealed, it is a very complex matter to address the need for reserve or surge capacity in large-scale disasters, in which many kinds of emergency response functions, equipment, and personnel must be mobilized. The sudden need for many vehicles to evacuate autoless, elderly, ill, or partially disabled people from New Orleans in the wake of Katrina indicates the critical need for the right kind of resources, in sufficient amounts, to be available in timely fashion. Some of these resources can be provided for in advance. Improved plans can and should be put in place to provide surge capacity for transport, food and water, medical facilities, and personnel. The task requires careful advance assessment of potential needs, detailed logistical planning for transporting resources to disaster sites (or moving people away from disasters to shelter and care), and procedures for operational integration of personnel and materiel from many sources. Given the cost of acquiring and maintaining this capacity, different levels of government must work out in advance how the emergency plans of each align to provide for sudden surges in demand for response and relief capacity. This may well involve arrangements that take advantage of private-sector capabilities for providing supplies and aid.[2] In effect, these actions will be moving a potential element of crisis novelty into the realm of routine preparedness.

There are, moreover, political dimensions to the problem. By definition, surge capacity is likely to be unused most of the time. Difficult trade-offs must be made between local (and thus more rapid) availability of resources and the high costs of sustaining them when no emergency is visible on the horizon; what some see as a strategic reserve, others regard as waste or inefficiency. Maintaining sufficient capacity to respond to large-scale disasters requires maintaining political support for emergency preparedness budgets, notwithstanding competing, often compelling demands for funds from stakeholders concerned with quite

---

[2]As the case study "Wal-Mart's Response to Hurricane Katrina" (Case 9 in this book) suggests.

different issues, e.g., education, local public works, or housing. In the American federal system, moreover, debate about how much responsibility and burden should be assumed by each level of government is also likely to be endemic.

Developing and Maintaining Situational Awareness

The novel circumstances of a crisis may also generate unexpected demands for resources (or predictable demands for which the resource supply remains inadequate) that make improvised scale-up essential. It is critical, therefore, that responders (both individuals and organizations) develop and maintain *situational awareness.* That is, they need to gather and assimilate key facts, often under conditions of great confusion and uncertainty, and assess how they are positioned to deal with the emergency. The response to Katrina reflected numerous examples of situational *un*awareness: failure to expedite the evacuation of New Orleans sufficiently in advance of the storm, failure to anticipate the substantial number of individuals who could not self-evacuate because they lacked cars and access to transit or were confused or too physically infirm to manage, slow or inadequate response to the breach of the levees, and lack of awareness of the conditions faced by people sheltered in the New Orleans Superdome and in the convention center.

Press and official comment in the aftermath of Hurricane Katrina often focused on whether key officials had received or reached out for timely and sufficient information about these conditions. Who knew what about the developing crisis, and when did they know it? As important as good intelligence about an emergency is, however, robust situational awareness involves far more. Decision makers must also be able to project forward the implications of the information they have gathered, so they can anticipate the likely consequences of a still-moving situation. With such anticipation comes at least some possibility of changing the future before it arrives. Projecting likely consequences also provides responders with a way of tracking actual results against what they expected, thus providing a check on how well they understand what is truly happening. Finally, situational awareness involves being able to generate possible alternative courses of action and assess which of them holds the most promise of dealing with emergency conditions. Major shortcomings of situational awareness during the Katrina crisis resulted less from information about conditions being unavailable or not reaching senior officials and more from leaders failing to project the likely consequences of the developing situation or generate feasible measures to counter the impacts of the storm and levee failure; thus, they fell short in different dimensions of situational awareness.

Integrated Execution in Real Time

In a major disaster, as local agencies confront extraordinary operational demands, emergency responders from adjoining jurisdictions, the state, and far-flung locations are likely to converge on the scene. Many will be self-dispatched rather than answering requests for assistance. Not only must they perform useful tasks themselves, they must also avoid interference or conflict with or endangerment of others. This demands skillful coordination of aid workers, equipment, and organizations across professions, agencies, jurisdictions, levels of government, and the public and private sectors—even though many of these people and organizations will have had little or no prior experience working together.

This need was recognized by Congress in the 2002 statutory requirement for a National Incident Management System (NIMS), a flexible template for leading crisis operations that enables organizations to frame and rapidly implement response actions under enormous pressure. The underlying model for NIMS—called the Incident Command System (ICS) or Incident Management System (IMS)—was initially devised during the 1970s in California to fight wildland fires and has since spread to many other states and some other emergency professions. In response to the congressional requirement, the Department of Homeland Security has initiated a staged deployment of NIMS, aiming at full utilization by all emergency response organizations, across professional disciplines and levels of government.

IMS has important strengths in organizing emergency response. It factors critical emergency tasks, establishing a clear division of labor and assignment of functional responsibility. It unambiguously defines the chain of command, provides a manageable span of control for each function, and establishes a resource-allocation decision-making structure, which is critically important to avoid disputes about "who's in charge" and to enable rapid deployment and direction of personnel and equipment. It systematically promotes information flows up, down, and across the organization—and to the public. As a result, IMS is highly flexible in response to incident type, scale, and location. It has been applied successfully to wildland and urban fires, industrial explosions, earthquake response, hospital emergency room operations, and hostage scenarios.

However, as Katrina revealed, even a basic diffusion of NIMS was not completed in many jurisdictions that had not previously used the system or by professional disciplines that had been unaware of or unenthusiastic about NIMS. Nor were the procedures for federal operations, on one hand, and intergovernmental collaboration, on the other, that were nominally in place in the then-new National Response Plan adequate or effectively applied to coordinate federal agencies with each other or with state and local responders. NIMS implementation has now gone further, and a new National Response Framework is currently being implemented to remedy some of these difficulties. The effectiveness of recent efforts, however, has not yet been tested by dire events similar to Katrina.

Operational versus Political Leadership

Widespread deployment and skillful use of NIMS is a necessary but not sufficient condition for integrated crisis response. IMS has proved to be a highly effective technical system when the goals to be achieved are relatively unambiguous. For example, in dealing with the typical urban structural fire—even a very severe one—there is generally firm consensus on the priorities and constraints of action: save lives, protect property, but don't unduly risk the lives of responders. This agreement enables firefighting professionals, clear about the ends they are seeking, to focus mainly on the means they will use.

IMS functions best when it is directed at a well-defined, reasonably consistent, or clearly prioritized set of purposes. By contrast, where goals are unclear or in conflict—when difficult, controversial trade-offs must be made—IMS lacks the political and moral authority to make the hard choices that present themselves. Even in the fire service, IMS has worked less well when there has been contention about either the goals of the response or the priorities among several objectives. When a dozen major forest fires menaced southern California in autumn 2003,[3] the strategy developed by professional firefighting organizations was subjected to severe criticism by local, state, and federal elected officials who disagreed with both the professionals and one another about the objectives and technical means of fighting the fires. There was no adequate institutional forum in which these elected officials could engage the issues, with one another and with the firefighting professionals, so they could be resolved. The emergency response nearly faltered because of this discord.

If a pandemic flu, bioterrorist attack, or nuclear plant disaster occurred, do the responders in command of NIMS—police commanders, fire chiefs, or public health directors—have legitimate authority to decide which areas should get resources and which should not, perhaps even to make choices that in effect determine who will live and who will die? Do they have the community standing and ability to mobilize public support behind a difficult decision? Can they—should they—hold to their decisions if elected leaders challenge them?

We invest elected leaders with the authority to make key decisions about values and priorities for society and to rally their communities behind their choices, much as President George W. Bush and New York's Mayor Rudolph Giuliani did in the 9/11 crisis. But in a future emergency that cuts across organizational, jurisdictional, and level-of-government boundaries—particularly if the government has been partially disabled by the crisis, as it was during and after Katrina—it may be unclear who has this authority and difficult to assemble them in the heat of the moment. It is precisely for such complex situations that NIMS is designed, but the model does not include an effective way to coordinate political leaders and operational commanders, especially when multiple jurisdictions are involved.

So, as NIMS develops as an emergency response system, we must create parallel structures for making critical decisions that the public will regard as legitimate and compelling. The temporary emergency operations structure of NIMS must be paired with institutions that do have ready connections to key stakeholders and legitimate decision-making authority.

---

[3]This situation is described in the case study "The 2003 San Diego Firestorm" (Case 7 in this book).

The United States has not yet fully thought through this need and invented the emergency policymaking institutions it requires. That is a step that must still be taken.

Handoffs across Boundaries

As action in a crisis scales up and becomes more complex, leadership or certain responsibilities may need to be transferred from those initially in charge to others with different skills or broader authority and resources. Yet frequently this evolution of crisis response produces substantial friction between organizations or jurisdictions, even when emergency plans or statutes theoretically provide for such transitions. During Katrina, these frictions became readily apparent as the city and mayor clashed with the state and governor, as both criticized the federal response, and, ultimately, as voices in other agencies within the federal government criticized FEMA's performance in leading the federal response.

The mere existence of laws, emergency plans, or NIMS does not ensure that responsible officials will know or play their roles effectively or that conflicts will not arise in interpreting the rules. In the midst of a crisis, the leaders of individual agencies or political jurisdictions may find it personally or politically difficult to recognize or acknowledge that exigent events surpass their ability to cope with the crisis; they may, in fact, resist turning full or partial responsibility over to others better situated to deal with circumstances.

Although no advance preparation can fully mitigate such reactions, addressing the possibilities inherent in disaster scenarios can reduce the chances of hesitation or paralysis in crisis. Institutionally, within jurisdictions and across levels of government, senior officials should address the conditions and procedures under which handoffs would be made. Key officials must also consider their personal as well as institutional preparedness. Preparedness requires anticipation of the potential need for such handoffs and readiness to make (or accept) transfers of responsibility when the initial allocation is unworkable in the face of a particular disaster. Newly elected or appointed officials need to think through their substantive functions and moral responsibilities as crisis leaders in advance rather than addressing their obligations for the first time in the midst of catastrophe.

Improving Disaster Response

The case studies that follow afford the student an opportunity to see the strategic and tactical issues of modern emergency management described not in the abstract but in the rich detail of actual events. These accounts of major emergencies provide insight into the perspectives of the emergency responders, other professionals, elected leaders, private- and voluntary-sector personnel, and citizens who lived through these events. They offer the chance for readers to consider and discuss how unfolding events appeared to those who lived through them and what imperatives they felt. What choices did these people see or create? How did they interact and coordinate with peers and personnel in other agencies or at other levels of government? What obstacles did they confront, and how did they seek to overcome them? What successes and failures did they experience?

Most important, what lessons might we draw from these experiences that could prove useful in improving the emergency response system and in educating policymakers and citizens about system needs? The subject matter is fascinating, the events are absorbing, and the need for thoughtful construction of a better emergency management system in the United States and elsewhere is compelling.

1   Hurricane Katrina (A): Preparing for the "Big One" in New Orleans

Esther Scott

Hurricane Katrina, which raged through New Orleans and other parts of the Gulf Coast in August 2005, revealed deep problems in U.S. emergency preparedness and crisis management capabilities. The storm's destructive winds and rain were followed by the rupture of the levees holding back the waters of Lake Pontchartrain, flooding most parts of the city, destroying property, and threatening lives. While the majority of New Orleans residents were able to evacuate the city, substantial numbers of poor, autoless, elderly, disabled, or institutionalized individuals and their families were left behind in harrowing conditions. Video and photographs flashed across the country and the world: hurricane victims clinging to rooftops, awaiting rescue; bodies floating in the flood waters. Thousands sought shelter in the city's convention center and domed stadium, where crowding, insufficient food supply, and inadequate sanitation made life miserable and dangerous. In the aftermath, large numbers of residents were displaced far from New Orleans or returned to find their homes severely damaged or uninhabitable.

In the three subcases of this case study, we see how governments at the local, state, and federal levels prepared for the on-rushing hurricane and learn how emergency responders and relief workers performed in the aftermath. Subcase A of the case study focuses on the preparations that preceded Katrina's initial landfall in Florida; Subcase B looks at the period immediately before, during, and after the storm hit New Orleans; and Subcase C chronicles what happened to the city and its people after the levees were breached. The story of the preparation for and emergency response to Hurricane Katrina provides a dramatic illustration of the severe challenges that a natural disaster can pose for responders even when the general threat is familiar and some preparations have been made.

Discussion Questions

- Notwithstanding extensive efforts, the advance preparations taken by New Orleans, the state of Louisiana, and the federal government proved inadequate to meet the full challenges of Hurricane Katrina. To the extent that these preparations could have been improved, what steps should have been taken?
- What factors constrained the authorities' ability to take these steps before the hurricane?

This is an abridged version of a case written by Esther Scott for Arnold M. Howitt, executive director of the Taubman Center for State and Local Government, for use at the John F. Kennedy School of Government, Harvard University. Funding for the case was provided by the National Preparedness Leadership Initiative. Kennedy School of Government Case Program, C15-06-1843.0 and C15-06-1844.0. Copyright © 2006, 2007 by the President and Fellows of Harvard College.

- Does the Hurricane Katrina story exhibit the distinguishing features of a crisis, as defined in the introductory essay preceding the case study?
- How might the emergency response during and after Katrina struck New Orleans have been improved?
- Were the core challenges of crisis response, described in the introductory essay, confronted in this case?

On Tuesday, August 23, 2005, meteorologists at the U.S. National Weather Service (NWS) spotted a tropical depression in the southeastern Bahamas, the twelfth in a busy hurricane season in the Atlantic. The following day, as it strengthened into a tropical storm, weather officials gave it a name—Katrina—and closely tracked it as it turned into a hurricane, crossing south Florida and then moving into the Gulf of Mexico. There, fed by the gulf's warm waters, Katrina grew into a monster: a Category 5 hurricane—the most intense on the scale used by the NWS—with winds gusting past 170 miles per hour and an unusually wide span extending over 100 miles from its center. Katrina appeared to be heading next for the Florida Panhandle, but on Friday it made what a Louisiana official later called "one of the most dramatic shifts in weather history."[1] It turned westward and appeared to take dead aim at one of the most storied, and fragile, cities in the United States—New Orleans.

The specter of a major hurricane striking low-lying New Orleans had long hung over the historic city of almost half a million people. The catastrophic results of a direct hit had been predicted by computer models, described in emergency planners' scenarios, and imagined in harrowing detail in the press. Now, after years of dodging its fate, New Orleans seemed about to encounter the long-dreaded "Big One," as it was sometimes called. Weather officials did not mince words. "This is really scary," said Max Mayfield, director of the NWS's National Hurricane Center, on Saturday. ". . . This is the real thing."[2]

With landfall on the southeastern coast of Louisiana predicted for early Monday morning, August 29, city and state officials swung into action, following the roadmaps laid out in their various emergency response plans: activating emergency operations centers; putting emergency responders on alert; issuing advisories and evacuation notices to the public; pre-staging equipment, supplies, and crews; and opening emergency shelters. The Federal Emergency Management Agency (FEMA) kept close tabs on activities at the state and local levels and mounted the largest operation to pre-position food and supplies for storm victims in its history.

---

[1]Col. Jeff Smith, Louisiana Office of Homeland Security and Emergency Preparedness, testimony before the House Select Committee to Investigate the Preparation for and Response to Hurricane Katrina (hereafter, House Select Committee), December 14, 2005.

[2]The *Times-Picayune* (New Orleans), Web ed., August 27, 2005.

Only a few days later, most of these plans would be in a shambles, and the response to Hurricane Katrina already rated as perhaps the worst in U.S. history. But in the hours before the storm struck, those charged with preparing for it and dealing with its aftermath appeared confident that they had done their homework. Many of them had worked together on emergency response plans and exercises, readying themselves for just such an event, and their preparations seemed commensurate with the challenges Katrina would pose. "We've planned for this kind of disaster for many years because we've always known about New Orleans and the situation," Michael Brown, director of FEMA, told a television reporter the day Katrina came ashore. ". . . We were so ready for this." [3]

Background: New Orleans and the "Big One"

New Orleans has variously been likened to a soup bowl, a cereal bowl, a punch bowl, a fish bowl, and even a bathtub—all metaphors to describe its precarious relationship with two large and looming bodies of water: the Mississippi River to the south and the broad but shallow Lake Pontchartrain to the north. (See Exhibit 1A-1 for a map of metropolitan New Orleans.) Except for the oldest parts of the city (including its legendary French Quarter) most of it was below sea level and in constant danger that the water would "slosh" over during a storm and "fill the bowl."

Greater New Orleans, which comprised the city proper and its surrounding parishes, was protected by an elaborate 475-mile-long system of levees, floodwalls, canals, bridges, floodgates, and pumping stations, intended to both hold back and channel the waters. [4] A key part of the system was a complex chain of levees, floodwalls, and canals along Lake Pontchartrain (see Exhibit 1A-2), which had been built in the aftermath of Hurricane Betsy in 1965, a calamitous Category 3 storm that swamped parts of New Orleans and neighboring St. Bernard Parish, leaving eighty-one dead and thousands homeless. But, as many noted, this system—called the Lake Pontchartrain and Vicinity Hurricane Protection Project—was designed to withstand the effects of a composite hurricane, known as the "standard project hurricane," which was roughly the equivalent of a Category 3 storm. This meant, as Louisiana's leading newspaper, the *Times-Picayune*, pointed out, that there was "currently . . . no defense against a surge from a major storm," that is, a Category 4 or 5 hurricane. [5]

---

[3]Nicole Gaouette, Alan C. Miller, Mark Mazzetti, Doyle McManus, Josh Meyer, and Kevin Sack, "Katrina's Aftermath: The Response," *Los Angeles Times*, September 11, 2005, A1.

[4]Louisiana is divided into sixty-four parishes, which are roughly comparable to counties in other states. Levees are generally earthen mounds, while floodwalls are large slabs of concrete and steel, sometimes perched atop a levee. John Cloud, "Mopping up New Orleans," *Time*, September 19, 2005, 54.

[5]John McQuaid and Mark Schleifstein, "In Harm's Way," *Times-Picayune*, first in a five-part series, "Washing Away," June 23–27, 2002. Available at www.nola.com/hurricane/?/washingaway.

Exhibit 1A-1   Metropolitan New Orleans and Lake Pontchartrain

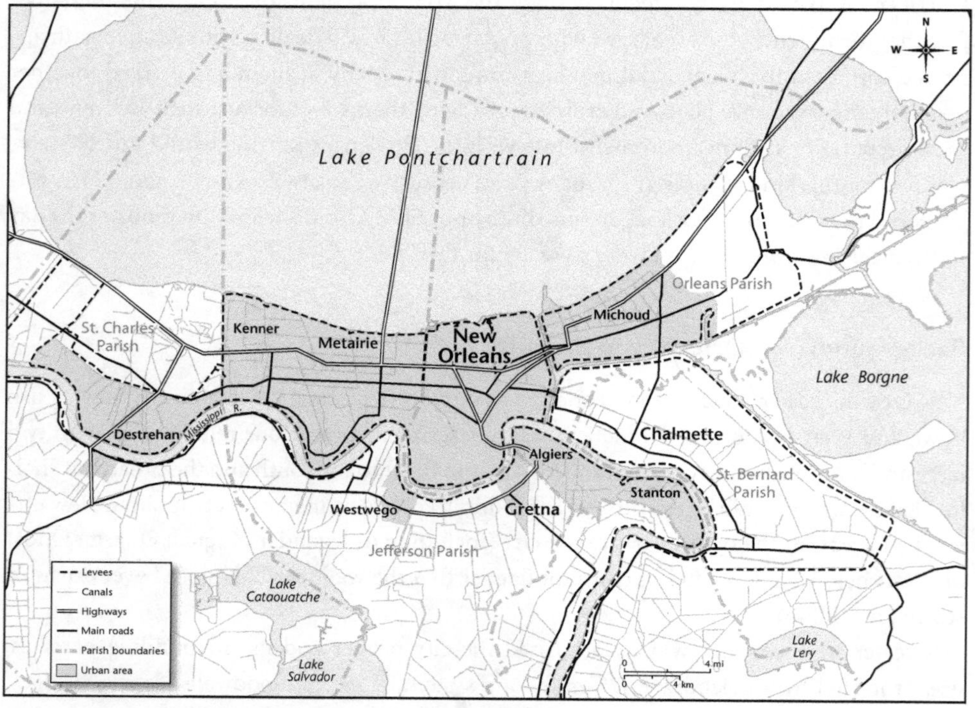

Source: New Orleans Hurricane Impact Study Area, Lousiana State University Hurricane Center

New Orleans's vulnerability to flooding had, moreover, been exacerbated by the very defenses that had been erected to protect it from a storm surge. The levees and floodwalls that kept the waters at bay also walled out the silt that renewed and rebuilt the Mississippi Delta land. Consequently, the city and its suburbs had begun to subside, a process hastened by heavy development on soil that had been drained and subsequently compressed.[6] This, combined with coastal erosion and rising sea levels, helped put the Crescent City (an allusion to the semi-circular shape of New Orleans along the banks of the Mississippi) on the short list of major disasters waiting to happen.

Anticipating the "Big One"
In the decades since Betsy had pummeled the city, the state of Louisiana and the U.S. Army Corps of Engineers (which was responsible for the design and construction of the levee sys-

---

[6]Ibid.

Exhibit 1A-2   Greater New Orleans levees, floodwalls, and canals system

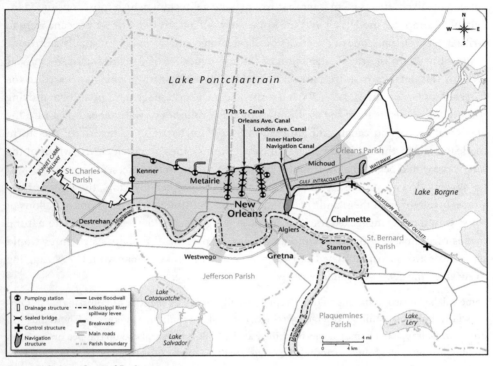

Source: U.S. Army Corps of Engineers

tem) had put forward various proposals to strengthen the Pontchartrain levees or otherwise improve New Orleans's defenses against floods.[7] But, primarily because of budget shortfalls and competition from other priorities, the protections afforded by the levee system had not been upgraded to withstand the force of a severe hurricane. Major improvements to the existing system, such as raising levees that had settled over time, were delayed as well due to lack of funds.[8] During these years, New Orleans faced few serious hurricane threats, although there had been a couple of near misses with Hurricane Georges in 1998 and Hurricane Ivan in 2004. But with hurricane activity in the Atlantic picking up in the mid-1990s,

---

[7]The Army Corps was generally responsible for the construction of the flood protection infrastructure, and local governments were responsible for its upkeep. In Louisiana, local levee boards, whose members were appointed by the governor and parish governments, and water and sewer boards were charged with operating and maintaining the flood protection system. The Army Corps, however, operated and maintained the Mississippi River levees.

[8]Nicole C. Carter, "New Orleans Levees and Floodwalls: Hurricane Damage Protection," CRS Report for Congress, received through the CRS Web, Congressional Research Service, order code RS22238, September 6, 2005, 4; available at www.fas.org/sgp/crs/misc/RS22238.pdf.

hurricane experts and emergency planners cast a worried eye on the slowly sinking city and studied the likely effects of an intense storm making a direct hit, which most considered inevitable. Computer models all told the same story—if a Category 4 or 5 hurricane were to strike it, New Orleans, one of America's most celebrated cities, would be virtually destroyed.

Possibly the most graphic depiction of the consequences of a major hurricane in New Orleans was detailed in a five-part series entitled "Washing Away," which appeared in the *Times-Picayune* on June 23–27, 2002. It presented a worst-case scenario of a storm moving toward New Orleans from the south, pushing huge volumes of water ahead of it into the area's waterways and canals and, ultimately, Lake Pontchartrain; as the eye of the storm made its way northward (and just east of New Orleans), the counterclockwise winds of the hurricane would begin to blow from the north across the swollen lake, sending waves of water surging down into the city. Eventually, they would either "overtop" the levees or, far worse, break through them and create a gap or breach through which billions of gallons of water would pour unchecked into "an area averaging 5 feet below sea level with no natural means of drainage."[9] Between wind and water, 90 percent of the city's structures would likely be destroyed. An estimated 200,000 people who did not evacuate would be "struggling to survive," the *Times-Picayune* wrote with eerie prescience.

Some will be housed in the Superdome [a sports facility owned by the state of Louisiana]. . . . Others will end up in last-minute emergency refuges that will offer minimal safety. . . . Thousands will drown while trapped in homes or cars by rising water. . . . Survivors will end up trapped on roofs, on buildings or on high ground surrounded by water, with no means of escape and little food or fresh water, perhaps for several days.[10]

The death toll, according to some sources, could range from 25,000 to 100,000. "Filling the bowl," the *Times-Picayune* noted in its "Washing Away" series, was rated "the worst potential scenario for a natural disaster" in the United States by emergency officials.[11] It stood at or near the top of the Federal Emergency Management Agency's list of most worrisome, and probable, disasters, along with a few other familiar, grim scenarios, such as an earthquake in San Francisco.

Planning for the "Big One"

It was New Orleans's preeminence among potential disaster sites that prompted FEMA to sponsor an initiative that would lead to the development of comprehensive plans for responding to a catastrophic hurricane in the city. In July 2004, the project brought together officials from all thirteen southeast Louisiana parishes, most of Louisiana's state agencies,

---

[9]Although a levee failure could happen, a Louisiana State University engineer told the *Times-Picayune* in 2002, it was "not something that's expected."

[10]McQuaid and Schleifstein, "Washing Away."

[11]Ibid.

and fifteen federal agencies for an eight-day workshop that focused on dealing with the consequences of the hypothetical Hurricane Pam, a "strong, slow-moving Category 3 storm" that unleashed tornadoes and dumped 20 inches of rain on metropolitan New Orleans.

The workshop culminated in the draft "Southeast Louisiana Catastrophic Hurricane Functional Plan," released in August 2004, which covered fourteen different areas of response, some highly detailed, others sketchy in parts, with the particulars "to be decided" at a later time. Although the plan was envisioned as a response to a catastrophic event, some of the components did not address the most dire scenarios. For example, the section on "unwatering" (that is, draining the flooded city) "assumed there are no levee breeches [sic]. This is the worst case situation."

After the initial July 2004 session, there were three more workshops, involving fewer participants, to do some additional planning on specific areas. But, as one FEMA official later told the *New York Times,* "funding dried up" for more follow-ups to Hurricane Pam, leaving plans in some key areas unfinished.[12] Even without the comprehensive document envisioned in the Hurricane Pam exercise, however, officials at the state, local, and federal levels could turn to their own plans, which were designed, and in some cases explicitly tailored, to help them prepare for and respond to a major emergency, such as Katrina.

Getting Ready: State and Local Emergency Response Plans

In Louisiana, the Emergency Assistance and Disaster Act of 1993 parceled out the general duties and powers of state and local officials—who would be on the frontlines of the response to Katrina—in the event of a disaster or emergency. Under its provisions, the governor was authorized to, among other things, declare a state of emergency; "direct and compel the evacuation of all or part of the population from any stricken or threatened area"; "commandeer or utilize any private property" if necessary; and "[p]rescribe routes, modes of transportation, and destination in connection with evacuation." The state law conferred many of the same emergency powers on parish presidents and the chief executives of municipalities, including the authority to declare emergencies and order evacuations.

In accordance with the Emergency Assistance and Disaster Act, the Louisiana Office of Homeland Security and Emergency Preparedness (LOHSEP), housed in the state's Military Department and headed by the state adjutant general (who was also head of the Louisiana National Guard), was responsible for preparing and implementing the state emergency operations plan. The law also required each parish president to establish an office of homeland security and emergency preparedness, which would work with LOHSEP to develop local emergency plans.

---

[12]Scott Shane and Eric Lipton, "Storm and Crisis: Federal Response," *New York Times,* September 2, 2005, A1.

The State Plan

Given the state's vulnerability to Gulf Coast storms, it was not surprising that Louisiana's emergency operations plan had two supplements devoted solely to hurricane emergencies, one each for the southwestern and the southeastern sections of the state. Their focus was on getting residents out of harm's way as a hurricane approached. The Southeast Louisiana Hurricane Evacuation and Sheltering Plan, which included metropolitan New Orleans, was intended to provide, in its words, "an orderly procedure" for the thirteen area parishes—home to a population of almost 1.7 million (in 1999)—"in response to a catastrophic hurricane." The plan did not, however, "replace or supersede any local plans" or "usurp the authority of any local governing body."

After a chaotic evacuation that jammed the state's highways in advance of Hurricane Ivan in 2004, Louisiana Governor Kathleen Babineaux Blanco had ordered state police and transportation officials to retool the evacuation plan for southern Louisiana. The new plan called for residents to evacuate in three phases, according to geographical area: those living in areas unprotected by levees would leave first, 50 hours before the onset of tropical storm winds; those living in levee-protected areas that were nonetheless considered vulnerable to Category 2 or higher storms would evacuate 40 hours before onset; finally, those living on the east bank of the Mississippi River in metropolitan New Orleans (within the protection of the levee system but vulnerable to a slow-moving Category 3 or higher storm) would leave 30 hours before onset. (See Exhibit 1A-3 for the evacuation map.) In the event of a mandatory evacuation, when authorities would "put maximum emphasis on encouraging evacuation and limiting ingress," evacuation routes could be "augmented" by turning the inbound lanes of some highways into outbound ones—often referred to as a "contraflow" pattern.

The state plan assumed that the "primary means of hurricane evacuation will be personal vehicles," although school and municipal buses and other government-owned vehicles "may be used" to evacuate those who had no means of transportation. It would be the responsibility of the parishes to mobilize transportation and establish "staging areas," where residents needing help could go to be taken to shelters. Hospitals and nursing homes were required to prepare their own state-approved "pre-determined evacuation and/or refuge plans." The state plan also assumed that shelters would not be opened in "risk area parishes"; instead, "host parishes" (those out of harm's way) would be required to open designated shelters to receive evacuees.[13] For those who did not evacuate, parishes within the risk areas were responsible for setting up "last resort refuges"; unlike shelters, which offered food and bedding, refuges were bare-bones facilities, with "little or no water or food and possibly no utilities." They were intended, the state plan noted, "to provide best available survival protection for the duration of the hurricane only."

---

[13]The Red Cross no longer opened shelters in risk areas in the event of a catastrophic hurricane.

Exhibit 1A-3   Louisiana emergency evacuation map

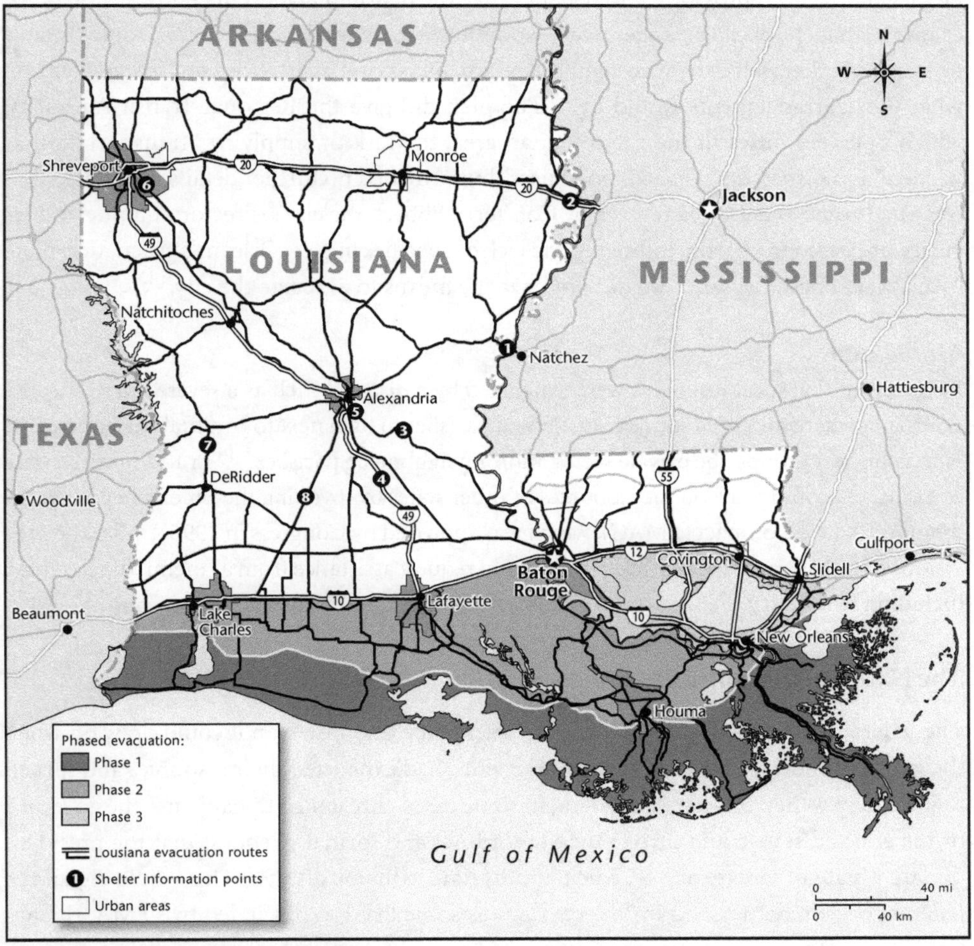

Source: Louisiana Department of Transportation

The City Plan

As with the state, the city's emergency plan had a special supplement—in this case, an "annex"—devoted to hurricanes. It, too, focused on evacuation issues, although there were sections on "recovery" and "mitigation" as well. Management of evacuations was the responsibility of the mayor, to whom state law delegated the authority to order evacuations, "in coordination with" both the director and the shelter coordinator of the city's Office of Emergency Preparedness.

The annex to the city's emergency plan described a "Hurricane Emergency Evacuation Standard Operating Procedure" that was "designed to deal with all case scenarios of an evacuation in response to the approach of a major hurricane towards New Orleans." The annex itself, however, provided few specifics on how it would achieve its ends. It noted, for example, that "[s]pecial arrangements" would have to be made to evacuate people "unable to transport themselves or who require specific life saving assistance," but it was silent on what those arrangements would be.[14] The plan did give the Regional Transit Authority, which operated buses in the metropolitan area, the task of supplying "transportation as needed" and dispatching "evacuation buses" but provided no further details. Later, after Katrina had come and gone, a remark by Col. Terry Ebbert, the city's director of homeland security, appeared to explain, indirectly, the lack of specifics in New Orleans's evacuation plan. "We always knew," he said, "we did not have the means to evacuate the city." [15]

Mutual Aid

In the event that local resources were exhausted by a disaster, such as a severe hurricane, the Louisiana emergency operations plan advised parishes to turn next to "mutual aid agreements with volunteer groups, the private sector and/or neighboring parishes." [16] In addition, the state of Louisiana could draw on the resources of other states by invoking the Emergency Management Assistance Compact (EMAC), which was approved by Congress in 1996. Under the provisions of EMAC, a disaster-stricken state could request assistance from a "menu" of resources, including temporary shelters, cargo aircraft, helicopters, and National Guard troops.[17]

The National Response Plan

The federal government, too, had its own emergency response plan it could draw on when the first responders, state and local governments, had exhausted their resources and turned to it for help. When this happened—or, in some cases, threatened to happen—the governor of the affected state could invoke the Stafford Act and formally request that the president declare a state of emergency or, when appropriate, a major disaster. This would signal the federal government to send in "the cavalry," as some liked to put it, led by FEMA, the nation's "chief steward of disaster response. . . ." [18]

---

[14]According to "A Failure of Initiative," final report of the House Select Bipartisan Committee to Investigate the Preparation for and Response to Hurricane Katrina (hereafter, House Select Committee report), February 15, 2006, the city had established a "Brother's Keeper" program, in conjunction with local churches, that would help match riders with drivers in the event of an evacuation. The plan estimated that about 100,000 residents did not have "means of personal transportation."

[15]Susan Glasser and Michael Grunwald, "The Steady Buildup to a City's Chaos," *Washington Post,* September 11, 2005, A1.

[16]As quoted in "The Federal Response to Hurricane Katrina: Lessons Learned," report to President George W. Bush (hereafter, White House report), February 23, 2006, Chap. 2: 6.

[17]House Select Committee report, 31. According to the House Select Committee report, EMAC built on a regional compact created by Florida and sixteen other states as a result of dissatisfaction with federal and state responses to the catastrophic Hurricane Andrew in 1992.

[18]White House report, Chap. 2: 8.

A relatively small agency (in 2005, it had roughly 2,500 employees), FEMA did not itself provide disaster assistance but managed "the operational response, relief and recovery efforts" of the federal government, assigning tasks to agencies and departments and coordinating their work.[19] It also drew on state and local governments, private contractors, volunteers, and the National Guard to supply equipment and workers in its relief efforts.[20] After the September 11, 2001, terrorist attacks, the federal emergency preparedness and response apparatus was overhauled, and FEMA became part of a massive new agency, the Department of Homeland Security (DHS), created by Congress in 2002. Under the new organization, FEMA was housed in the department's Emergency Preparedness and Response Directorate, and its head became an undersecretary of homeland security, reporting to the DHS secretary.

The National Response Plan

Along with establishing a new emergency management structure, the federal government, in compliance with a mandate in the 2002 Homeland Security Act, embarked on an ambitious overhaul of its existing emergency response plans. The result—the National Response Plan (NRP), officially adopted in December 2004—was designed primarily for use in what it termed an "Incident of National Significance." This was defined as "an actual or potential high-impact event that requires a coordinated and effective response by [an] appropriate combination of Federal, State, local, tribal, nongovernmental, and/or private sector entities in order to save lives and minimize damage, and provide the basis for long-term recovery and mitigation activities."

As the White House–led inquiry into the federal response to Hurricane Katrina later noted, the NRP was not clear as to how and when an incident of national significance was to be declared,[21] but once invoked, it set in motion a complex array of "incident management activities" led by a number of agency and multiagency coordinating entities. At the federal headquarters–level, the DHS Homeland Security Operations Center and its "component element" the FEMA National Response Coordination Center were responsible for coordinating "incident information-sharing, operational planning, and deployment of Federal resources. . . ." The Interagency Incident Management Group, composed of senior federal department and agency officials, was expected to provide "strategic incident management planning and coordination" and to act as an "advisory body" to the DHS secretary. At the local level, the "joint field office," which would be set up near the incident itself, was responsible for coordinating "operational Federal assistance activities to affected jurisdiction(s). . . ." The

---

[19]Ibid., Chap. 2: 6.

[20]David Kirkpatrick and Scott Shane, "Ex-FEMA Chief Tells of Frustration and Chaos," *New York Times,* September 14, 2005, A1.

[21]The NRP stated in one section that the DHS secretary was responsible for making the declaration and in another that all presidentially declared emergencies and disasters under the Stafford Act were automatically considered incidents of national significance.

joint field office was headed by a *principal federal official* (PFO), "personally designated" by the secretary of DHS.[22] (See Exhibits 1A-4 and 1A-5 for organization charts.)

The actual delivery of federal resources and assistance was organized according to fifteen emergency support functions (ESFs), each headed by one or more primary departments or agencies (or, in one instance, the Red Cross), with other agencies designated to play a supportive role (see Exhibit 1A-6). In the event of an incident of national significance, representatives from the appropriate ESF agencies would sit in at national and regional coordination centers and the joint field office.

Dealing with Catastrophes

Appended to the NRP were seven "incident annexes," each dealing with a specific kind of event (for example, biological incidents, nuclear/radiological incidents, and catastrophic incidents). This last annex dealt with incidents, either "natural or manmade," that resulted in "extraordinary levels of mass casualties, damage, or disruption severely affecting the population, infrastructure, environment, economy, national morale, and/or government functions." The severity of these consequences was expected to draw an unusually forceful response from the federal government. The process of obtaining federal assistance in most incidents was often described as a "pull system," in which a state or local government whose resources had been overwhelmed by a disaster essentially asked the president to send help. By contrast, the catastrophic annex was characterized as a "push system," in which the federal government would take the initiative in the face of circumstances so devastating that state and local governments, as the White House report put it, became "victims themselves, prohibiting their ability to identify, request, receive, or deliver assistance. This is the moment of catastrophic crisis. . . ."[23]

Although the NRP catastrophic incident annex outlined "an overarching strategy" and "guiding principles" for a "proactive" federal response, it did not provide a specific plan of action to deliver on that promise. That was to be left to the Catastrophic Incident Supplement, which would present a "more detailed and operationally specific" roadmap for federal responders. A draft of the supplement had been prepared, but final approval and promulgation were still pending in late August 2005, as Hurricane Katrina boiled up the Gulf Coast.

Although parts of the NRP had been used "to various degrees and magnitudes" in thirty "Stafford Act events," Katrina, as the White House report put it, was its first major test. As it turned out, not everyone viewed it, or DHS, as a helpful addition to the federal government's response arsenal.

---

[22]The PFO is not to be confused with the *federal coordinating officer* (FCO), who was designated by FEMA to manage an incident under the Stafford Act. Unlike the PFO, whose role was primarily one of coordination, the FCO was in charge of federal response operations and had the authority to obligate funds. House Select Committee report, 189.

[23]White House report, Chap. 2: 7.

Exhibit 1A-4   National Incident Management System framework

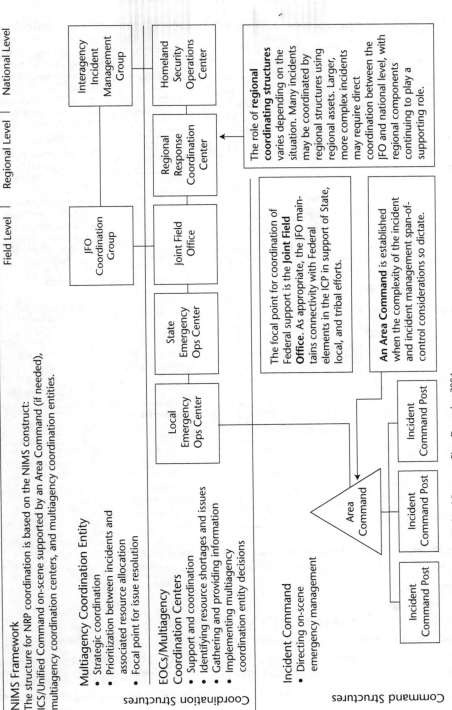

Source: Department of Homeland Security, National Response Plan, December 2004.

Note: EOCs, emergency operations centers; ICP, incident command post; ICS, Incident Command System; JFO, joint field office; NIMS, National Incident Management System; NRP, National Response Plan.

Exhibit 1A-5   Sample Joint Field Office organization during natural disasters

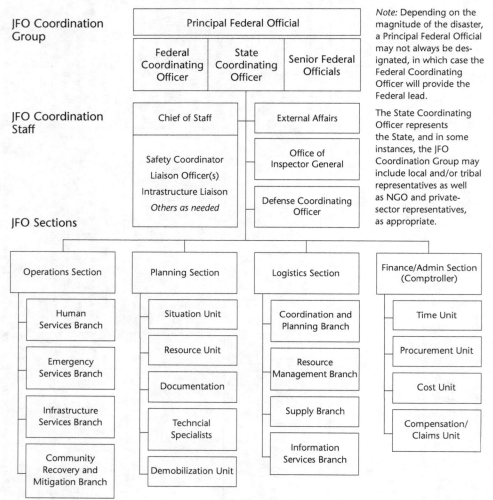

Source: Department of Homeland Security, National Response Plan, December 2004.

Note: JFO, joint field office; NGO, nongovernmetnal organization.

Trouble in the Federal Emergency Management Agency

Despite the NRP's depiction of a "cohesive, coordinated, and seamless framework for domestic incident management," beneath its confident prose lay a turbulent drama of bureaucratic displacement and discontent. The integration of FEMA into the fledgling DHS had not gone smoothly. FEMA's director, Michael Brown, who assumed the job and the new

Exhibit 1A-6   Emergency support functions

	ESF	Primary Department or Agency
ESF #1	Transportation	DOT
ESF #2	Communications	DHS (IAIP/NCS)
ESF #3	Public Works and Engineering	DOD (USACE) and DHS (FEMA)
ESF #4	Firefighting	USDA (Forest Service)
ESF #5	Emergency Management	DHS (FEMA)
ESF #6	Mass Care, Housing, and Human Services	DHS (FEMA) and American Red Cross
ESF #7	Resource Support	GSA
ESF #8	Public Health and Medical Services	HHS
ESF #9	Urban Search and Rescue	DHS (FEMA)
ESF #10	Oil and Hazardous Materials Response	EPA and DHS (U.S. Coast Guard)
ESF #11	Agriculture and Natural Resources	USDA and DOI
ESF #12	Energy	DOE
ESF #13	Public Safety and Security	DHS and DOJ
ESF #14	Long-Term Community Recovery and Mitigation	USDA, DOC, DHS (FEMA), HUD, Treas, and SBA
ESF #15	External Affairs	DHS (FEMA)

Source: "The Federal Response to Hurricane Katrina: Lessons Learned," report to President George W. Bush, February 23, 2006.

Note: DHS, Department of Homeland Security; DOC, Department of Commerce; DOD, Department of Defense; DOE, Department of Energy; DOI, Department of the Interior; DOJ, Department of Justice; DOT, Department of Transportation; EPA, Environment Protection Agency; ESF, emergency support function; FEMA, Federal Emergency Management Agency; GSA, General Services Administration; HHS, Department of Health and Human Services; HUD, Department of Housing and Urban Development; IAIP, Information Analysis and Infrastructure Protection; NCS, National Communications System; SBA, Small Business Administration; Treas, Department of the Treasury; USACE, U.S. Army Corps of Engineers; USDA, Department of Agriculture.

title of undersecretary for emergency preparedness and response in February 2003, had vowed to make sure that "FEMA remained FEMA," in the words of one account, and not lose its identity and mission in the huge new department.[24] Although Brown succeeded in keeping the agency's name, his determined efforts to hold on to its traditional roles and responsibilities alienated those who were seeking to "create a unified DHS brand. . . ."[25] When it came time to put together the NRP, DHS Secretary Tom Ridge did not turn to

---

[24]Michael Grunwald and Susan Glasser, "Brown's Turf Wars Sapped FEMA's Strength," *Washington Post*, December 23, 2005, A1. Brown, a lawyer by training, had earlier served as FEMA's general counsel and then deputy director. Previously, he had held positions in city and state government in Oklahoma and, most recently, had served as commissioner of the International Arabian Horse Association.

[25]Ibid.

FEMA, even though it had overseen the development of its predecessor, the Federal Response Plan. Instead, he gave the job to James Loy, head of the Transportation Security Administration within DHS. Brown did not disguise his disdain for the resulting document.

Brown was not alone in his concerns about the direction DHS was taking. Others in FEMA worried that the new preoccupation with terrorism came at the expense of natural disaster preparedness and response. The numbers seemed to confirm their fears. By 2005, as *Time* magazine reported, nearly three-fourths of every dollar the federal government gave in grants to state and local emergency response organizations was "earmarked for terrorism."[26] Brown and others also complained about the "DHS tax," which they argued siphoned off FEMA funds to other areas within the department; in a 2005 memo, Brown maintained that his agency had lost almost $78 million from its operating budget base since joining DHS.[27] More disturbing perhaps was DHS Secretary Ridge's decision in late 2003 to move control of federal preparedness grants from FEMA to another rival office in DHS—the Office of Domestic Preparedness. This upset FEMA staff members, who believed that separating emergency response from preparedness would disrupt their "relationships with first responders" and degrade emergency response operations.[28] But there was worse to come. When Michael Chertoff succeeded Ridge as DHS secretary in February 2005, he endorsed a plan that would move what remained of FEMA's preparedness mission to a new directorate within DHS. These developments were blamed for what some called FEMA's "brain drain," the steady exodus of some of its "top disaster specialists, senior leaders, and experienced personnel. . . ." By August 2005, FEMA had "about 500 vacancies and eight out of its ten regional directors were working in an acting capacity."[29] Brown expected to follow suit. When his appeal to reconsider the plan to eliminate FEMA's preparedness mission was rebuffed, he decided, according to the *Washington Post,* "to submit his resignation after Labor Day."[30] Before he could act on that decision, however, Hurricane Katrina made its ominous appearance in the waters of the Gulf of Mexico.

---

[26]Mark Thompson, "Why Did FEMA and Its Chief, Michael Brown, Fail Their Biggest Test?" *Time,* September 19, 2005, 39.

[27]Grunwald and Glasser, "Brown's Turf Wars Sapped FEMA's Strength." DHS officials, according to the House Select Committee report, "vigorously" disputed this claim.

[28]Grunwald and Glasser, "Brown's Turf Wars Sapped FEMA's Strength"; House Select Committee report, 154. The National Emergency Management Association sided with FEMA on this issue and on its argument that DHS was emphasizing terrorism readiness to the detriment of other kinds of hazards.

[29]House Select Committee report, 152, 157.

[30]Grunwald and Glasser, "Brown's Turf Wars Sapped FEMA's Strength"; House Select Committee report, 154. The National Emergency Management Association sided with FEMA on this issue and on its argument that DHS was emphasizing terrorism readiness to the detriment of other kinds of hazards.

Hurricane Katrina (B): The Looming Storm

Hurricane Katrina made its first landfall in south Florida on Thursday, August 25, 2005, as an unusually destructive Category 1 storm. As it churned into the Gulf of Mexico, few doubted that it would become more deadly, and state and local governments up and down the Gulf Coast went on alert. Initially, it appeared that the storm's path might take it to the Florida Panhandle, but, in the words of one account, it shifted dramatically on Friday afternoon, moving roughly "150 miles west in a matter of hours." [1] Late that night, the National Hurricane Center advised that computer models were pointing to landfall "between the eastern coast of Louisiana and the coast of Mississippi."

All through the following day, the storm grew stronger and the forecast grimmer. Weather officials confidently predicted that Katrina would strengthen into a Category 4 storm, and possibly into a rare Category 5; it also appeared increasingly likely that it would strike at, or close to, New Orleans. Landfall was expected late Sunday night or early Monday morning. As Katrina intensified, officials in New Orleans, Baton Rouge (the Louisiana state capital), and Washington, D.C. dusted off their emergency plans, activated their emergency operations centers, and prepared to meet the full force of the monster storm.

Saturday, August 27

In Metropolitan New Orleans

At the local level, early action on Hurricane Katrina varied from parish to parish. Some parishes, like St. Tammany, St. Charles, and the low-lying Plaquemines, issued mandatory evacuation notices on Saturday morning; others, like Jefferson and St. Bernard Parishes, went with voluntary or recommended evacuations. (See Exhibit 1B-1 for a map of the parishes.) In New Orleans, Mayor Ray Nagin (a former cable company executive who had been elected in 2002) called for a voluntary evacuation as well, although he couched his recommendation in urgent terms. "This is not a test. This is the real deal," he declared at a joint Saturday afternoon news conference with Governor Kathleen Blanco. Nagin strongly encouraged the city's residents to leave town.[2]

---

[1] Col. Jeff Smith, Louisiana Office of Homeland Security and Emergency Preparedness, testimony before the House Select Committee to Investigate the Preparation for and Response to Hurricane Katrina (hereafter, House Select Committee), December 14, 2005.

[2] *Times-Picayune,* Web ed., August 27, 2005.

Exhibit 1B-1 New Orleans area parishes

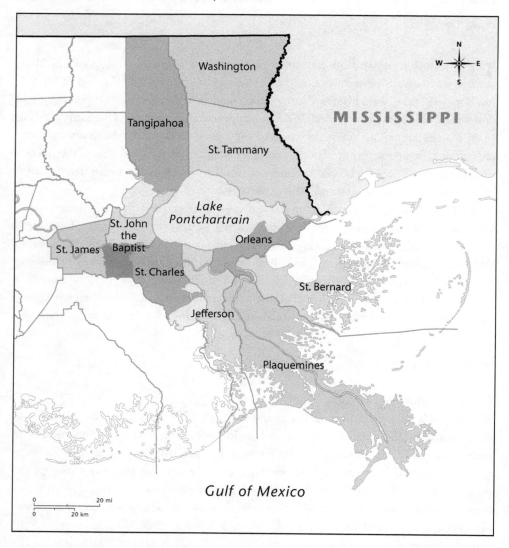

Nagin had reason to be concerned that citizens would not necessarily take his warnings to heart. Perhaps lulled by years of relatively little hurricane activity and a few near-misses, a significant portion of the population seemed unlikely to evacuate despite the threat of a major storm. A 2003 Louisiana State University poll indicated that 31 percent of New Orleans residents would opt to stay in the city even if a Category 4 hurricane were to strike.[3] This tendency to play "hurricane roulette," as it was sometimes called, was not limited to New Orleans; it was noted as well by Mississippi Governor Haley Barbour, who spoke of "hurricane fatigue" among evacuation-weary residents of the Gulf Coast.[4]

But, at least in the case of New Orleans, the roulette was sometimes played of necessity by the poor and disabled, who often did not have the means to leave the city. New Orleans had a large number of residents who fell into these categories: 28 percent lived below the poverty line (compared to 9 percent nationwide), and 24 percent of its adults were disabled (compared to 19 percent across the United States).[5] An analysis of 2000 census data indicated that a large percentage of the city's poor did not own cars. According to one Brookings Institution study, a little over 123,000 New Orleans residents lived in households with no access to a car; of these, almost 47 percent fell below the poverty line.[6]

Still, Nagin did not call for a mandatory evacuation from New Orleans on Saturday. Early that morning, the state had decided to recommend that its new phased evacuation plan for southeast Louisiana be implemented. The *Times-Picayune* reported that during his afternoon press conference with Blanco, Nagin indicated that "he would stick with the state's evacuation plan and not officially call for residents to leave until 30 hours before expected landfall, allowing residents in low-lying surrounding areas to leave first."[7]

Nagin did, however, announce that the Superdome—a state-owned sports facility located near the city's Central Business District—would open on Sunday as a shelter of last resort for people with special needs; the following day it would be declared open to the general population as well. He advised those seeking shelter there to bring their own food and drink and other comforts, such as folding chairs. "No weapons, no large items," he said, "and bring small quantities of food for three or four days, to be safe."[8]

In Baton Rouge

Governor Blanco (like Nagin, a Democrat serving her first term in office) had already declared a state of emergency in Louisiana on late Friday, which cleared the way for evacuation and other emergency procedures that would follow the next day. Early on Saturday morning, the Louisiana Office of Homeland Security and Emergency Preparedness

---

[3]Peter Applebome, Christopher Drew, Jere Longman, and Andrew Revkin, "A Delicate Balance Is Undone in a Flash, and a Battered City Waits," *New York Times*, September 4, 2005, 25.

[4]"A Failure of Initiative," final report of the House Select Bipartisan Committee to Investigate the Preparation for and Response to Hurricane Katrina (hereafter, House Select Committee report), February 15, 2006, 114.

[5]Applebome et al., "Delicate Balance."

[6]Alan Berube and Steven Raphael, *Access to Cars in New Orleans*, Brookings Institution, Washington, D.C., September 15, 2005. The total population of New Orleans, according to 2000 census data, was roughly 485,000.

[7]*Times-Picayune,* Web ed., August 27, 2005.

[8]Ibid. The Superdome was designated as a special needs shelter in the state's emergency response plan.

(LOHSEP), which would lead the state's response to Katrina, activated its emergency operations center in Baton Rouge.

State agencies began stockpiling supplies and equipment and moving "key assets" out of harm's way. The Department of Wildlife and Fisheries pre-positioned roughly two hundred boats—many of them small—both within the metropolitan area and on its outskirts to be ready to begin search and rescue efforts once the storm blew over.[9] The Louisiana National Guard had begun to mobilize as well—2,000 guardsmen were called to active duty on Friday and another 2,000 on Saturday.[10] "Never before in Louisiana's history," Maj. Gen. Bennett Landreneau, the state's adjutant general and head of LOHSEP, later testified, "had so many National Guardsmen been called up before a hurricane."[11]

Amid the bustle of preparations for the storm, the increasingly ominous reports emanating from the National Hurricane Center prompted Blanco to take an unusual step that Saturday: she formally asked President Bush to declare a state of emergency in Louisiana under the provisions of the Stafford Act. That night, Bush, who was vacationing at his ranch in Crawford, Texas, signed the emergency declaration for Louisiana; he would do the same the following day for Mississippi and Alabama, whose coasts were also in Katrina's path, at the request of their governors. It was rare, Blanco pointed out, for a president to declare an emergency before a storm had even made landfall. "At the highest levels of our nation," she said, "they believe this is a very serious storm."[12]

In Washington, D.C.

There could be little doubt that the Federal Emergency Management Agency (FEMA) was taking the storm very seriously. The agency, Michael Brown later testified, "pushed forward with everything it had in order to be ready to help the states respond after landfall."[13] In fact, said William Lokey, who served as FEMA's federal coordinating officer in Louisiana for its Katrina response, the agency "pre-positioned more commodities and staged more rescue and medical teams than ever in our history. . . ."[14]

FEMA also conducted daily video teleconferences with the affected states from its National Response Coordination Center in Washington to discuss preparations; meteorologists

---

[9]"Hurricane Katrina: A Nation Still Unprepared," report of the Senate Committee on Homeland Security and Governmental Affairs, May 2006, Chap. 21: 5, 9. New Orleans itself, the report noted, had few assets to contribute to the search and rescue effort—the city police department owned five boats; the fire department had none.

[10]House Select Committee report, 67. The National Guard's local ranks were thinner than usual, with 3,200 of its members deployed to Iraq. Scott Shane and Thom Shanker, "When Storm Hit, National Guard Was Deluged Too," *New York Times*, September 28, 2005, A1.

[11]Maj. Gen. Bennett C. Landreneau, statement before the Senate Homeland Security Committee, February 9, 2006.

[12]Jan Moller, "Revised Contraflow Starts Off Smoothly," *Times-Picayune*, August 28, 2005, 1.

[13]Michael D. Brown, statement to the House Select Committee investigation, September 27, 2005.

[14]William Lokey, testimony before the House Select Committee investigation, December 14, 2005.

from the National Hurricane Center also joined these sessions to update officials on Katrina's progress. The video teleconference conversations were crisp and matter-of-fact, with a "can-do" tone, but as the Saturday briefing drew to a close, Brown spoke to participants with some urgency about the potentially catastrophic storm that was brewing in the gulf. Addressing his FEMA staff, he said, "This is our chance to really show what we can do based on the catastrophic planning that we've done, based on the teamwork we've developed around here. This is our chance to really shine." Brown urged FEMA officials to do "whatever it takes to get it done. . . . [I]f you lean forward and get right to the edge of the envelope, you're not going to hear me screaming about it."

The Military

Various branches of the military also made their preparations for the storm. Historically in the United States, the primary military responder to domestic crises was the state National Guard. In Louisiana, the 4,000 National Guardsmen called to active duty before Katrina struck were a visible presence in the lead-up to the storm, helping to ready and supply the Superdome and other state shelters, assisting in law enforcement and traffic control, and in some cases providing medical personnel.[15] Blanco, as well as the other Gulf Coast governors, could also ask other states to send their National Guard troops under the provisions of the Emergency Management Assistance Compact, which Congress had approved in 1996. Although there were discussions with nearby states about what forms of assistance might be needed, Louisiana limited its requests in advance of the hurricane to aircraft and aviation forces to help with poststorm search and rescue efforts.[16]

In contrast to the National Guard, the federal military role in domestic disaster response was limited, largely because of "traditional reliance on local control," according to the House Select Committee report. The Department of Defense (DOD) viewed itself as a "resource of last resort" in matters of "civil support," usually responding to a disaster only at the request of a "lead federal agency," most typically, FEMA.[17] In addition, the military was barred by federal law from engaging in law enforcement activities at home. If, however, the military wished to be "forward leaning," in the words of the House Select Committee report, it could designate a *defense coordinating officer* (DCO), essentially a liaison to a state's emergency operations center, prior to a formal request for aid from FEMA. This was what the Northern Command (NORTHCOM) chose to do for Alabama, Mississippi, and Louisiana on August 26, the day Katrina struck south Florida. Two days later, DCOs were deployed to Mississippi and Louisiana.

---

[15]House Select Committee report, 67.

[16]Ibid., 66; Landreneau, statement, February 9, 2006.

[17]House Select Committee report, 39–40. FEMA, however, normally sought federal forces only at the request of the state.

Saturday Night

As night fell, Katrina continued to grow and intensify over the warm waters of the Gulf of Mexico and to set its course inexorably for New Orleans. But despite the warnings from Nagin and Blanco and news stories on the dangers that the hurricane posed, there was evidence that the message to get out of town was not getting through to some residents. One state representative, the *Times-Picayune* reported, had seen a crowd of seven hundred people at a Little League game at 7:00 p.m. who seemed unconcerned or unaware that a major hurricane was fast approaching.[18]

At the National Hurricane Center, however, all eyes were on Katrina. Around 7:30 on Saturday night, the center's director, Max Mayfield, took the unusual step of calling the governors of all three states in the hurricane's path to warn them of "the severity of the situation." After talking with Blanco, Mayfield, at her suggestion, called Mayor Nagin as well. As Nagin later related their conversation, Mayfield told him that "in his over 30 years experience in watching hurricanes, he had never seen a storm or conditions like this. I immediately called my staff and visited every television station in the city to alert the citizens to stress the need for evacuation."[19] He did not, however, issue a mandatory evacuation. His legal staff, the *Times-Picayune* reported, was looking into "whether [the mayor] can order a mandatory evacuation of the city, a step he's been hesitant to do because of potential liability on the part of the city for closing hotels and other businesses." But, Nagin told one local TV station, "come the first break of light in the morning, you may have the first mandatory evacuation of New Orleans."[20]

Meanwhile, at 10:00 p.m., Central Daylight Time, the National Hurricane Center upgraded its hurricane watch to a hurricane warning for the North Central Gulf Coast, including "the city of New Orleans and Lake Pontchartrain." The warning predicted "coastal storm surge flooding of 15 to 20 feet above normal tide levels," and as high as 25 feet in some spots. "The bottom line," the hurricane center's advisory concluded, "is that Katrina is expected to be an intense and dangerous hurricane . . . and this has to be taken very seriously."[21]

Sunday, August 28

Evacuating New Orleans

At 9:30 on Sunday morning, Nagin did what no previous mayor of New Orleans had done—he ordered a mandatory evacuation of the city. According to Nagin's later testimony,

---

[18]Moller, "Revised Contraflow Starts Off Smoothly."

[19]Mayor Ray Nagin, testimony before the House Select Committee, December 14, 2005. In his testimony, Nagin said that he himself had called Mayfield at Blanco's urging.

[20]Bruce Nolan, "Katrina Takes Aim," *Times-Picayune*, August 28, 2005, 1.

[21]*Times-Picayune*, Web ed., August 28, 2005.

he had issued the order after a "statewide conference call," but he had also been urged to do so by no less than President Bush, who, at Michael Brown's urging, had phoned him and Blanco earlier that morning. Later that same morning, Nagin and Blanco called a press conference to announce the evacuation order. "[W]e are facing a storm that most of us have feared," the mayor declared. The storm was now a Category 5, he continued, with sustained winds of 150 and wind gusts of 190 miles per hour. The storm surge, he warned, "most likely will topple our levee system. . . . So that's why we're ordering a mandatory evacuation." [22] Blanco invoked the president to drive home the urgent need for residents to flee the city.

To help get the word out about the evacuation, the *Times-Picayune* reported, Nagin ordered police and fire crews to drive through the city's neighborhoods that day "with bullhorns, directing people to leave." He also announced that, using the powers granted to him by state law, he was authorizing the police to commandeer private buildings and vehicles—including boats—"as they see fit." [23] As Sunday wore on, it appeared that residents of metropolitan New Orleans were heeding the dire warnings of their leaders and taking to the roads in huge numbers. For the most part, the traffic, although glacially slow, kept moving; however, there were later reports that some people were unable to get out of the city because of gridlock. In all, some 1.2 million residents left the area before Katrina made landfall—a figure that state officials later pointed to with pride. The governor's revised evacuation plan had been "executed almost flawlessly," said LOHSEP Deputy Director Col. Jeff Smith in his testimony, enabling 90 percent of residents in the affected parishes to flee in the space of about 40 hours. "I don't know of any other evacuation that has occurred," Smith continued, "with that many people under these circumstances . . . in that short of a time period." [24]

But even with over a million evacuated, tens of thousands remained behind—an estimated 70,000 in New Orleans itself. "We begged all those people to get out," Blanco said later.[25] But there were constraints, she maintained, on what the state could do to make people leave. The "word 'mandatory,' " she argued, "doesn't mean any more than us getting up [and] saying, get out." Officials would not resort to strong-arm tactics. "[I]n the United States of America," Blanco declared, "you don't force people [out of their homes], you urge them to leave." [26]

The Last Resort

For those who could not or would not evacuate New Orleans, there were two options: staying home or seeking shelter in the designated refuge of last resort, the Superdome. At 8:00 on Sunday morning, the Superdome was opened only for people with special needs. Later

---

[22]Ibid.

[23]Ibid.

[24]Smith, testimony, December 14, 2005.

[25]Sam Coates and Dan Eggen, "In New Orleans, a Desperate Exodus," *Washington Post,* September 1, 2005, A1.

[26]House Select Committee report, 114, 110.

that day, when the facility was opened to the general population, people began streaming in. Those who could not get there on their own power could go to one of twelve staging areas in the city where they could board buses that would take them to the sports facility. Once there, they were screened by a contingent of about two hundred National Guard members and New Orleans police officers before being allowed to enter the shelter.[27] Estimates varied as to the number of people at the Superdome when Katrina struck; the White House report put the figure at 10,000–12,000, including 300–500 with special needs, while one FEMA official guessed 15,000.

According to the *Times-Picayune,* the Louisiana National Guard had delivered enough food and water to the Superdome to supply 15,000 people for 3 days. But Marty Bahamonde, a FEMA public affairs officer who was in the city to do advance work for Brown (he was, as he later noted, the only FEMA official deployed to New Orleans itself ahead of the storm), painted a different picture. On Sunday evening, he testified, members of the National Guard told him that they expected 360,000 "meals ready to eat" (MREs) and fifteen trucks of water to arrive later that night; instead, however, only 40,000 MREs and five trucks of water were delivered. Earlier that day, Bahamonde recalled, as thousands flocked to the Superdome seeking shelter, the city's homeland security director "asked the maintenance staff to gather up all of the toilet paper in city hall and any other commodities they could find" and bring them to the Superdome. "I specifically note this," Bahamonde said, "because it told me that supplies at the Dome might be a serious issue." [28]

Special Needs and Medical Care Facilities

In the frantic hours before Katrina made landfall, both the state and the city worked to transport special needs residents to shelters outside New Orleans. Just how many people with special needs lived in New Orleans was a matter of some debate, but the city itself put the figure at roughly 1,000.[29] According to Nagin's testimony, about four hundred of these were evacuated to a state shelter—one of four that Louisiana had set up for people with special needs—outside the risk area. In addition, another two hundred were transported by bus from the Superdome to hospitals in Baton Rouge.[30] Because of "traffic congestion," according to later testimony, some six hundred special needs residents remained in the

---

[27]Ibid., 117.

[28]Marty J. Bahamonde, testimony before the Senate Homeland Security Committee, October 20, 2005.

[29]House Select Committee report, 278. Neighboring Jefferson Parish, with an "equivalent population," the report noted, counted 45,000 special needs patients within its precincts. As the report pointed out, *special needs* was variously defined by the state and by the parishes. In New Orleans, individuals with chronic diseases, requiring "intermittent or occasional assistance," who were dependent on electricity for medical treatments or refrigeration of medications, were considered eligible for admission to special needs shelters; people with acute illnesses were not. According to the director of the city's health department, New Orleans did not maintain a list of its special needs residents for evacuation purposes.

[30]Ibid., 279.

Superdome,[31] where there was little medical care available beyond what could be provided by National Guard personnel and the city.

Those who were in medical or nursing facilities would also ride out the storm in the city. Most of greater New Orleans's sixteen acute care hospitals chose not to evacuate their patients. Although required by state law to have evacuation plans, hospitals generally "sheltered in place" during hurricanes, citing time and money as major barriers to transporting their often frail charges to facilities outside the risk area.[32] Many of the city's sixty-three nursing homes chose to do the same. According to the House Select Committee report, only nineteen nursing homes evacuated their residents before the storm.

A Worsening Outlook

Throughout Sunday, the reports on Katrina's progress grew steadily more worrisome. At 10:00 a.m., the National Weather Service issued a warning that described the consequences of the storm—now hovering in the Category 4–5 range—in the starkest terms. Katrina, it said, was "a most powerful hurricane with unprecedented strength" that could render most of the New Orleans area "uninhabitable for weeks . . . perhaps longer."[33]

By mid-day on Sunday, the National Hurricane Center was forecasting that Katrina's eye would pass just east of Lake Pontchartrain; if it maintained its intensity, it would generate a storm surge of about 12.5 feet in the massive lake. "The big question is going to be, will that top some of the levees," Mayfield said in the video teleconference. Although the current track of the storm suggested "minimal flooding" in New Orleans itself, he explained, if the storm's track were to "deviate just a little bit to the west," it would make "all the difference in the world" and lead to the overtopping of some of the levees. It was as yet impossible to predict whether this would happen, Mayfield concluded, "but that's obviously a very, very grave concern."

The gravity of the impending crisis permeated the conversation during the August 28 video teleconference, the last that would be held before Katrina made landfall. This time the briefing was attended by U. S. Department of Homeland Security (DHS) Secretary Michael Chertoff, who spoke from the department's Homeland Security Operations Center, and by President Bush and his deputy chief of staff, Joe Hagin, from Crawford, Texas. The president underscored the federal government's commitment to come to the aid of the states that lay in the path of the giant hurricane. "I want to assure the folks at the state level," he said, "that we are fully prepared to not only help you during the storm, but we will move in whatever resources and assets we have at our disposal after the storm."

---

[31]City of New Orleans Health Department, response to Senate Homeland Security Committee, January 31, 2006.

[32]House Select Committee report, 268.

[33]National Weather Service, see www.srh.noaa.gov/data/warn_archive/LIX/NPW/0828_155101.txt.

But Brown himself sounded uncertain about some aspects of preparedness, particularly in New Orleans. "They're not taking patients out of hospitals," he fretted, "[not] taking prisoners out of prisons, and they're leaving hotels open in downtown New Orleans. So I'm very concerned about that." He worried, too, about the advisability of designating the Superdome as the refuge of last resort. The facility was "12 feet below sea level . . .," Brown said. "I don't know whether the roof is designed to . . . withstand a Category 5 hurricane." In addition, he expressed doubts about whether there would be enough federal medical and mortuary teams inside the Superdome. "I'm concerned," he told those in attendance, "about . . . their ability to respond to a catastrophe within a catastrophe." [34]

Once again, Brown spoke of his gut feeling that "this [storm] is a bad one and a big one," and once again he encouraged his FEMA team to cut through red tape to speed the government's response. "I want that supply chain jammed up as much as possible," he said. "Just keep jamming those lines as much as you can with commodities." He reiterated his plea for FEMA officials to "get to the edge of the envelope. . . . Go ahead and do it," he urged. "I'll figure out some way to justify it. . . . Just let them yell at me."

Hunkering Down

By early evening, the first tentacles of the coming storm had reached the Gulf Coast, lashing it with heavy rains and high winds. At about 7:00 p.m., the buses taking residents to the Superdome ceased operations as the weather worsened.[35] The Coast Guard closed down ports and waterways along the coast; state police shut down the contraflow pattern at 5:00 p.m. and prepared to close down interstate highways once conditions grew too dangerous for motorists. Mayor Nagin had called a 6:00 p.m. curfew and, for once, most residents seemed to have obeyed. Even bars in the French Quarter, famed for their studied indifference to hurricane warnings and curfews, shut down, and the streets of the normally bustling quarter were deserted. Boarded up and battened down, the city waited tensely as Hurricane Katrina barreled up the coast for its rendezvous with New Orleans.

Monday, August 29

Katrina Comes Ashore

Hurricane Katrina made landfall in Plaquemines Parish shortly after 6:00 a.m. Central Daylight Time, but the effects of the huge storm—its hurricane-force winds extended outward

---

[34]Quotations in this and the following paragraph from Margaret Ebrahim and John Solomon, Associated Press, "Video Shows Bush Warned before Katrina Hit," *Dallas Morning News,* March 2, 2006.

[35]House Select Committee report, 65.

for over 100 miles from its center—had been felt long before then. Later, the National Weather Service determined that Katrina came ashore somewhat weaker than predicted, as a strong Category 3 storm (the same strength as envisioned in the Hurricane Pam exercise) rather than Category 4 or 5. But for those in the storm's path, this distinction meant little as Katrina ravaged the Gulf Coast on its journey northward. With sustained winds of 115 miles per hour and gusts as high as 130, it knocked down power lines, leaving almost 3 million people without electricity; it also toppled telephone poles and cell towers, wiping out both wireline and cell phone service to millions. At the Superdome, the thousands waiting out the storm were shocked and frightened when winds tore off a portion of the roof, forcing the National Guard to move people off the field and up into the seating area to get away from the rain that began pouring in. When the power failed, the uneasy evacuees sat sweltering in the heat with only dim emergency lights to illuminate the vast sports facility.

Yet, despite Katrina's violent assault, initial reports from New Orleans that day indicated that the city had once again escaped the devastation that so many had forecast and feared. It appeared to be the coastal towns of Mississippi—Gulfport, Waveland, Biloxi, and others—that had sustained the greatest destruction from the storm. In New Orleans, the worst damage was in eastern sections of the city, which bore the brunt of the storm. There were reports of major flooding in the Lower Ninth Ward and neighboring St. Bernard Parish, with water standing 8–10 feet deep, but much of the rest of the city appeared to be relatively dry. (See Exhibit 1B-2 for a map of New Orleans neighborhoods, which are all in Orleans Parish.) Among longtime New Orleans residents, the *Washington Post* reported, there was "a palpable relief" that although the city had suffered significant damage, it had "avoided a far worse catastrophe."[36]

At that day's noontime video teleconference with FEMA and state officials, there was less sense of relief, with information only just beginning to trickle in. Brown, who spoke from the Louisiana Emergency Operations Center in Baton Rouge, continued to talk of the need "to push the envelope" and maintain urgency. "I know there is this natural tendency, once it makes landfall to [think], 'Whew, we dodged that one.' Well, there's still a lot of work to do, so keep it up. . . ." Still, officials spoke with some confidence as they discussed preparations. Jeff Smith, LOHSEP's deputy director, praised FEMA for its "outstanding coordination and support." In turn, Brown complimented the state. There was "a lot of great work going on down here in Louisiana," he observed. Addressing Governor Blanco, who, along with Governor Barbour, joined the conference by phone, Brown added, "You have a really good team, and they're just doing an excellent job."

---

[36]Peter Whoriskey and Sam Coates, "Amid the Devastation, Some Feel Relief," *Washington Post,* August 29, 2005, A1.

Exhibit 1B-2   Orleans Parish neighborhoods

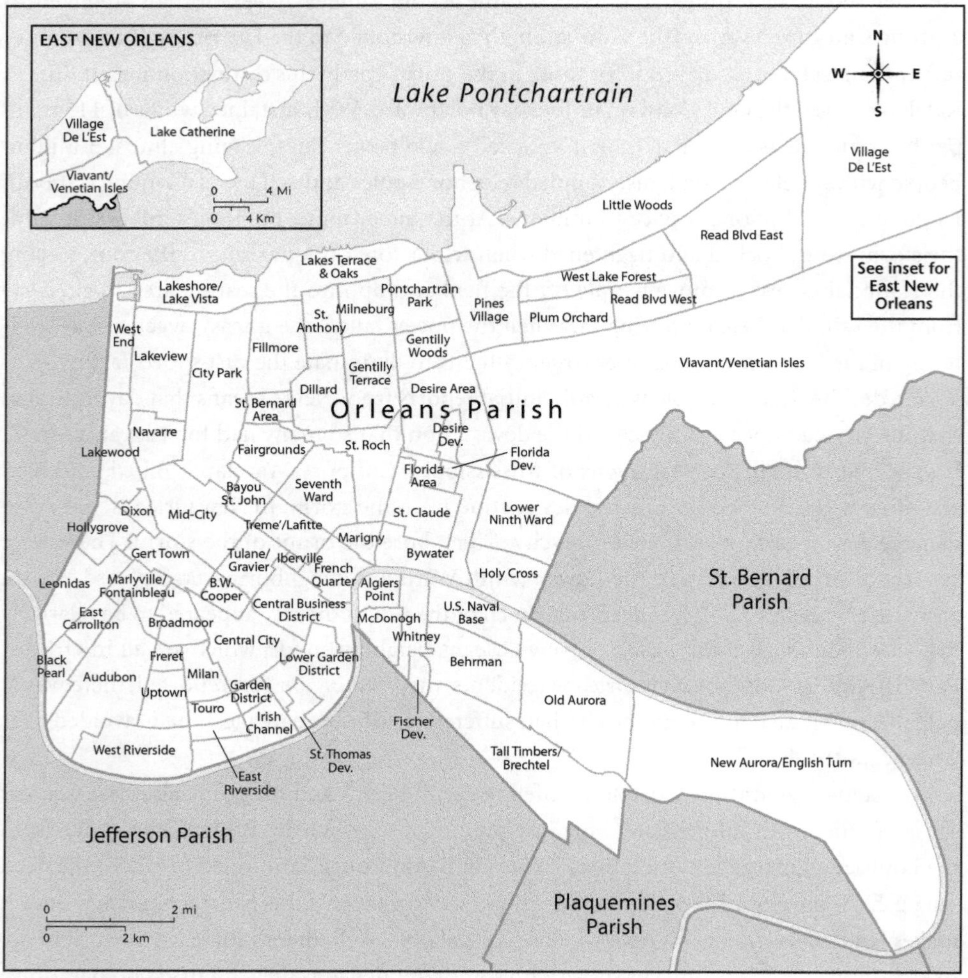

Source: Greater New Orleans Community Data Center

A Breach in the Levees

Amid the words of encouragement and determination, however, an ominous note was struck when White House Deputy Chief of Staff Joe Hagin asked about the status of the levees. "We keep getting reports in some places that maybe water is coming over the levees," Blanco replied. "We heard a report unconfirmed. I think we have not breached the levee . . . at this point in time. That could change." In fact, the first report of a breach had come hours earlier, at 9:12 a.m., when the National Weather Service issued a flash flood warning due to a breach

Exhibit 1B-3   Metropolitan New Orleans elevations

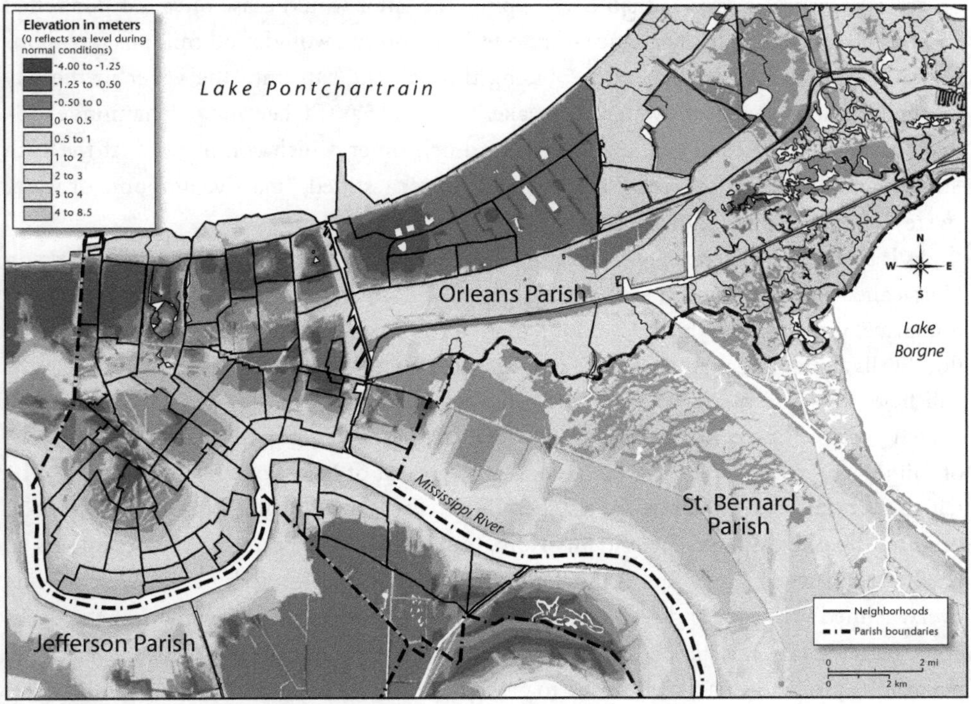

Source: Greater New Orleans Community Data Center, August 30, 2005.

along the Industrial Canal, which bordered the Lower Ninth Ward.[37] As the day progressed, sporadic reports began filtering in to the DHS Homeland Security Operations Center (HSOC), some mentioning rising waters or overtopped levees or levee breaches. Perhaps because of the spottiness of these messages from the field, HSOC reported to senior DHS staff at 6:00 that evening that preliminary reports "indicate the levees in New Orleans have not been breached; however an assessment is still pending."[38]

But in New Orleans itself, the grim possibility was already established fact. Marty Bahamonde, the FEMA public affairs officer, had remained in the city during the storm. After traffic jams prevented him from getting out on Sunday, he rode out the hurricane in New Orleans's emergency operations center (EOC) in City Hall. It was there at 11:00 a.m. on Monday that "the worst possible news came into the [city] EOC," he later recalled. "I stood

---

[37]White House report, Chap. 4: 3.
[38]Ibid.

there and listened to the first report of the levee break at the 17th Street Canal." [39] A levee breach was far more serious than overtopping; the latter would cease once the storm had passed and the waters had a chance to recede, but a breach would send millions of gallons of water from Lake Pontchartrain coursing through the gap until the water in the city reached the same level as the water in the lake.[40] Around 5:00 that evening, Bahamonde took two tours of the stricken area by Coast Guard helicopter, which confirmed that the 17th Street Canal had been breached and that, as he later testified, "massive amounts of water [were] being deposited into the city by the levee break." [41]

As it turned out, there were three large breaches, all of them in the Lake Pontchartrain Hurricane Protection Project area: the 17th Street Canal, the Industrial Canal, and the London Street Canal. (See Exhibit 1B-3 for a map of city elevations.) All three breaches were in floodwalls along the canals, and some of them were huge—the length of three or more football fields in some places. Possibly the most calamitous of these—the 17th Street Canal breach—was estimated to be 450–500 feet wide. By Monday night, the effects of "hundreds of millions of gallons" of water per second gushing out of Lake Pontchartrain began to be felt all over the city.[42] Water began rising in the streets at the rate of a foot or more every 20 minutes, by one estimate.[43] Residents riding out the storm in their homes scrambled to reach their attics and rooftops as the floodwaters surged in. The city's pumps were quickly overwhelmed, its water and sewage systems swamped. As Tuesday dawned over the darkened, battered city, the stark truth was apparent to all who were there—the worst-case scenario, long predicted, had at last come to pass; the bowl that was New Orleans was filling up with water.

---

[39]Bahamonde, testimony, October 20, 2005. Bahamonde did not recall who made the report.

[40]House Select Committee report, 142.

[41]Bahamonde, testimony, October 20, 2005, 3.

[42]Mark Schleifstein, "Flooding Will Only Get Worse," *Times-Picayune,* National Web ed., August 31, 2005.

[43]Christopher Rhoads, "Cut Off: At Center of Crisis, City Officials Faced Struggle to Keep in Touch," *Wall Street Journal,* September 9, 2005, A1.

Hurricane Katrina (C):
Responding to an Ultra-Catastrophe in New Orleans

In the early morning hours of August 29, 2005, Hurricane Katrina—a storm whose size and ferocity made it an instant legend—slammed into the southeastern shore of the United States, cutting a wide swath of destruction through the Gulf Coast towns of Mississippi and Louisiana. Despite the enormous damage it inflicted, however, it initially appeared that the storm had not delivered a knockout punch to New Orleans, the fabled city of nearly half a million whose vulnerability to a major hurricane had long worried emergency response officials. As the hurricane blew itself out and weakened into a tropical storm, however, it soon became apparent to the tens of thousands who had not evacuated New Orleans that something was going very wrong. By late Monday, almost every part of the city had begun to flood, and the waters were rising with frightening rapidity. The storm surge had opened three major breaches in the floodwalls, allowing water from Lake Pontchartrain to pour unchecked into the city's streets.

The rising floodwaters sent people who had stayed in their homes during the storm racing to their attics and rooftops, where they waited anxiously for rescue, or wading out into the flooded streets in search of shelter. Thousands flocked to the Superdome, a state-owned sports facility, where as many as 15,000 people had already sought refuge from the storm. Others gathered on dry sections of the highway or at the hastily opened Convention Center on high ground. With the power out and temperatures soaring into the 90s, the need for food, water, shelter, and medical care was acute. Bodies were seen floating in the fetid water, and looters were reported moving in packs through the flooded city.

As federal, state, and local emergency officials converged on New Orleans, they faced the task of responding to what some would later label the "most destructive natural disaster in American history."[1] Still, many of the challenges confronting officials had been foreseen and even tackled in disaster planning exercises; some had been addressed in emergency response plans.[2] But as the days dragged on, it became increasingly apparent that almost every aspect of the response was falling far short of what was needed. As public outrage grew, fed by TV footage of distraught storm victims, emergency response officials and political leaders—all the way up to President George W. Bush—found themselves scrambling to cope with what Secretary of Homeland Security Michael Chertoff called the "ultra-catastrophe" that Katrina had visited on New Orleans.[3]

---

[1] "The Federal Response to Hurricane Katrina: Lessons Learned," report to President George W. Bush (hereafter White House report), February 23, 2006, Foreword: 1.

[2] For a detailed account of hurricane planning for New Orleans, see Part A of this case.

[3] "Chertoff: Katrina Scenario Did Not Exist," CNN.com, September 4, 2005.

Monday, August 29

The Bowl Begins to Fill

Within a few hours after Katrina made landfall, at around 6:00 a.m. on Monday, the Lower Ninth Ward, in the eastern part of the city, and neighboring St. Bernard Parish began flooding—the result, it was later determined, of a major breach in the Industrial Canal. The rest of the city appeared to be relatively dry, at least through the morning hours, but at around 11:00 a.m. there was an ominous report of a major breach in the 17th Street Canal, eventually estimated to be 450–500 feet wide. Soon thereafter, as the *Times-Picayune* reported the following day, residents of the Lakeview neighborhood, close to Lake Pontchartrain, "watched in horror as the water began to rise." Even after the storm passed and skies cleared, the paper went on, the water "continued to rise one brick every 20 minutes, . . . continuing its ascent well into the night." A third major breach, at the London Street Canal, sent more water flowing into the city.

The surging floodwaters trapped the estimated 70,000 people who had not fled New Orleans in advance of the hurricane. Of these, somewhere between 12,000 and 15,000 had taken shelter in the Superdome, which the city had designated as a refuge of last resort during the storm. There, they had a harrowing time of it as first the power went out—knocking out the air conditioning and leaving the vast facility dimly lit by emergency lights—and then a section of the roof tore off in the winds, exposing the frightened occupants to the rain; the plumbing failed as well on all but the first floor. Conditions were even more serious for the many thousands who had decided to ride out the storm in their homes. By early afternoon on Monday, the *Times-Picayune* was reporting that people were "waiting on roofs and clinging to trees. . . ."

The situation was made more desperate by the almost complete collapse of the communications system of the city. Phone lines and cellular towers had been toppled by wind and floodwaters, as had the towers that supported the radio system used by police, fire, and other emergency officials; many 911 emergency call centers went down as well. As a result, victims were unable to call for help, emergency responders on the street could not communicate with dispatchers, and emergency operations centers could not communicate with either.[4]

Getting Out the Word

Despite what the Senate Committee on Homeland Security and Governmental Affairs (which conducted a later inquiry into the response to Katrina) termed a "communications void," information about the increasingly dire situation in New Orleans did manage to filter up to the state emergency operations center (EOC) in Baton Rouge, where state and federal

---

[4]"Hurricane Katrina: A Nation Still Unprepared," report of the Senate Committee on Homeland Security and Governmental Affairs (hereafter Senate Committee report), May 2006, Chap. 18: 5.

officials had gathered, including Michael Brown, head of the Federal Emergency Management Agency (FEMA), which would spearhead the federal government's response to Katrina. Reports made their way as well to the Homeland Security Operations Center (HSOC) at U.S. Department of Homeland Security (DHS) headquarters in Washington, D.C. The data coming in were sporadic and sometimes contradictory, especially early on, when reports of breaches were difficult to confirm, but they did indicate major flooding in the city and the likelihood of levee breaches. Still, a 6:00 p.m. situation report issued by the HSOC stated that "[p]reliminary reports indicate the levees in New Orleans have not been breached," although, it added, "an assessment is still pending."

At about the same time that the HSOC was issuing its situation report, more definitive information was being gathered on conditions in New Orleans. Marty Bahamonde, a FEMA public affairs official, then the sole representative of the agency on the ground in New Orleans, had toured the city by helicopter at around 5:00 p.m. on Monday. Later, he recounted what he had witnessed:

[A]s far as the eye could see in either direction was completely covered with water. There was no dry land. . . . And as we got back to the city, it became obvious . . . that there [were] literally hundreds of people on rooftops, standing in balconies in apartments, and that there was a desperate need for a rescue mission because it was now getting dark.[5]

Bahamonde's observations were bundled into an HSOC spot report, completed at 10:30 that night. The spot report noted, among other things, that there was a "quarter-mile breach" in the 17th Street Canal, that an "estimated ⅔ to 75% of the city is under water," and that "a few bodies were seen floating in the water. . . ." Although the spot report was "widely distributed by e-mail," according to the Senate Committee report, few DHS officials later recalled seeing it; DHS Secretary Chertoff, who did not use e-mail, was not apprised of the contents of the report that night.[6]

At the White House

The spot report did not arrive by e-mail at the White House Situation Room until 12:02 a.m. Late August was a quiet time at the White House. President Bush was on vacation at his ranch in Crawford, Texas; Vice President Richard Cheney, White House Chief of Staff Andrew Card, and White House Homeland Security Advisor Frances Fragos Townsend were all on vacation as well. That left Ken Rapuano, Townsend's deputy, as the most senior official on hand with homeland security responsibilities, and he had left the Situation Room at 10:00 p.m.[7]

---

[5]As quoted in ibid., Chap. 4: 6–7.

[6]Ibid., Chap. 19: 7.

[7]"Additional Views Presented by the Select Committee on Behalf of Rep. Charlie Melancon and Rep. William J. Jefferson," February 15, 2006, 27–28.

While it was not clear who at the White House finally read the spot report, or when, Bahamonde's eyewitness account, according to Rapuano, was not viewed as conclusive evidence of a levee breach, in part because it had not been confirmed by an earlier report from the Army Corps of Engineers. It was not until 6:30 on Tuesday morning that White House officials considered they had confirmation of breaches in the levee system after receiving an updated situation report from HSOC.[8]

Other Channels

Bahamonde's account did, however, make its way to White House officials through other channels. After completing his flights over New Orleans, Bahamonde had called FEMA Director Michael Brown in Baton Rouge to relay his observations. Brown's response, as Bahamonde later recalled, had been to thank him and say that he would "call the White House." Later, in testimony before the Senate Committee on Homeland Security and Governmental Affairs, Brown did not "recall specifically" whom he had spoken to, but assumed that it was Deputy Chief of Staff Joe Hagin, who was with the president in Crawford. He did not remember if he also called his immediate superior, DHS Secretary Chertoff, that evening, but added pointedly, "I need[ed] to get things done, and the way I get things done is I request it from the White House and they happen." Calling Chertoff, he said, "would have wasted my time. . . ."

Brown, who had been unhappy over FEMA's diminished role in DHS, had made no secret of his disdain for the department, its leader, and the National Response Plan (NRP) that DHS had recently authored—or of his wish to circumvent all three. That had been, Brown testified, his modus operandi in managing earlier disasters. In 2004, he said, when a series of hurricanes struck Florida, "I specifically [told] both [Andrew] Card and Joe Hagin . . . that the best thing they could do for me was to keep DHS out of my hair." The department merely added "additional layers," he told members of the House Select Committee (which was also investigating the response to Katrina) and hampered FEMA officials' ability to act decisively. However, Brown insisted, Chertoff and others at DHS were kept fully apprised of the situation in New Orleans through the daily video teleconferences that FEMA hosted, as well as regular situational reports. But Brown made clear to whom he felt answerable. "In terms of my responsibility," he said, "much like I had operated successfully in Florida [during the previous year's hurricanes], my obligation was to the White House and to make certain that the president understood what was going on and what the situation was, and I did that."

Nevertheless, as a number of observers noted, both the White House and Secretary Chertoff seemed slow to "grasp the gravity of the situation" unfolding in New Orleans, in the words of the Senate Committee report, possibly lulled by the first HSOC report stating

---

[8]"A Failure of Initiative," final report of the House Select Bipartisan Committee to Investigate the Preparations for and Response to Hurricane Katrina (hereafter, House Select Committee report), February 15, 2006, 142, 141.

that the levees had not been breached. Bush later spoke of a "sense of relaxation" on Monday after learning that Katrina had not hit New Orleans directly and of having "dodged a bullet." That day and the following day, he kept to his schedule, traveling to Arizona to celebrate Sen. John McCain's (R-Ariz) birthday, giving a speech on the government's new Medicare prescription drug benefit, and making an appearance at a naval base in San Diego. On Tuesday, when FEMA convened its video teleconference session, no one from the White House was on hand.[9]

Meanwhile, Chertoff was also on the road, traveling to Atlanta to attend a conference on avian flu. Chertoff, a former prosecutor and federal judge who had been appointed DHS secretary in February 2005, acknowledged in testimony before the House Select Committee that he was not, in the committee's words, "a hurricane expert" nor much experienced in dealing with disasters.[10] Katrina provided him with a memorable baptism.

Options

Although the president had already declared both Louisiana and Mississippi major disaster areas, Chertoff could, under the NRP, take matters a step further by declaring Katrina an incident of national significance, defined as "an actual or potential high-impact event that requires a coordinated and effective response" at all levels of government. What's more, Chertoff could invoke the NRP's Catastrophic Incident Annex, which applied to disasters that resulted in "extraordinary levels of mass casualties, damage or disruption severely affecting the population, infrastructure, environment, economy, national morale, and/or government functions." To date, an incident of national significance had never been formally declared, nor had the Catastrophic Incident Annex been invoked. In fact, the NRP was not entirely clear as to when and how an incident of national significance was to be designated, but in the case of Katrina, Chertoff initially made no declarations of any kind.

Tuesday, August 30

Things Fall Apart

By Tuesday, New Orleans was, in the words of the *New York Times,* "a shocking sight of utter demolition," with "vast stretches" of the city engulfed by water, sometimes up to the roofs of three-story houses.[11] Mayor Ray Nagin estimated that 80 percent of the city was flooded; the only remaining dry land, according to the *Times-Picayune,* was "a narrow band from the French Quarter and parts of uptown, the same small strip that was settled by" the city's

---

[9]Senate Committee report, Chap. 15: 4–6; Chap. 19: 2.

[10]House Select Committee report, 132.

[11]Joseph Treaster and N. R. Kleinfield, "New Orleans Is Inundated as 2 Levees Fail," *New York Times,* August 31, 2005, A1.

founder in 1718. The water continued to rise into Tuesday night at the rate of 3 inches per hour. "Truth to tell," said the city's director of homeland security, "we're not too far from filling in the bowl." [12]

The widespread flooding and accompanying loss of communications were devastating to the city's governing and law enforcement capacity. The police department's headquarters and six of its eight district stations were swamped with water on Monday morning. Later that day, both police and fire officials lost their radio communications systems when the backup generators for their radio towers were engulfed in floodwaters; the police system was inoperative for the next 3 days. [13] Many first responders in the city were reduced to communicating over a few mutual aid channels, which led to heavy congestion and frequent delays. [14]

Meanwhile, the city's leaders found themselves marooned in a hotel with almost no way to talk to the outside world. Nagin and a group of officials—including Police Chief Edwin P. Compass III—had decamped to the Hyatt Regency, which the mayor thought would be "better served with power and food than the city command post" in City Hall. [15] But when first the phone lines and then the police radio system went down, the mayor and his staff found themselves gradually enveloped in "information darkness." So, too, did those who had remained at the EOC in City Hall. It would not be until Wednesday that the group at the Hyatt was finally able to make "its first outside call in two days." [16]

In the meantime, the lack of communications and the absence of an organized law enforcement presence on the streets led to a growing sense of anarchy in the city. Looting was reported to be widespread as many stranded residents broke into stores in search of food, water, diapers, and other necessities. But some looters were more opportunistic, helping themselves to televisions, computers, and jewelry, as police stood by helplessly or, in some instances, joined in the looting themselves. [17]

Search and Rescue

What police actions could be organized in chaotic New Orleans were directed to search and rescue efforts, which both Mayor Nagin and Louisiana Governor Kathleen Blanco made their number one poststorm priority. At the local level, police and firefighters "waded through water and climbed to roofs" to rescue trapped residents, as the *Times-Picayune* reported, aided by "an armada of Louisiana sportsmen in flat-bottom boats, who responded

---

[12]Quoted in Dan Shea, "Under Water; Levee Breach Swamps City from Lake to River," *Times-Picayune,* August 31, 2005, 1.

[13]House Select Committee report, 164.

[14]Senate Committee report, Chap. 18: 5.

[15]Quoted in Christopher Rhoads, "Cut Off: At Center of Crisis, City Officials Faced Struggle to Keep in Touch," *Wall Street Journal,* September 9, 2005, A1.

[16]Ibid.

[17]*Times-Picayune,* Web ed., August 30, 2006.

to an appeal for help."[18] But the city had few resources to bring to the search and rescue effort. According to the Senate Committee report, the police department owned only five boats and the fire department had none. To supplement their tiny fleet, police and fire officials "had to commandeer and hotwire boats to improvise rescue missions."[19]

Louisiana pitched in with over two hundred boats manned by the Department of Wildlife and Fisheries (DWF), which was the state's designated first responder for search and rescue operations. DWF officials, who had regularly trained for this mission, kept at it day and night in the first days following the hurricane. Hampered, like other responders, by a nonfunctioning communications system, DWF agents working at night were guided by "the cries for help" in the darkened city, illuminated only by the eerie glow from fires that firefighters—lacking sufficient water power—were helpless to extinguish.[20] The Coast Guard, too, launched a massive search and rescue effort. Like the DWF, the Coast Guard had pre-positioned "personnel and assets" close enough to the affected area to be able to launch a quick response. Within 12 hours of landfall, the House Select Committee report noted, the Coast Guard had assigned twenty-nine helicopters, eight fixed-wing aircraft, and twenty-nine cutters to the New Orleans area to "support rescue operations."[21]

As the lead agency for urban search and rescue under the NRP, FEMA had established twenty-eight teams of state and local responders trained in urban search and rescue techniques, which it could deploy anywhere in the country. But, as one FEMA official later pointed out, these teams were not trained for water rescue, and when the three that had been pre-positioned in Shreveport, Louisiana, in advance of the storm arrived in New Orleans, they came without boats.[22]

Altogether, over 60,000 people were rescued from the floodwaters that engulfed New Orleans. When he testified before the House Select Committee in December 2005, Col. Jeff Smith, deputy director of the Louisiana Office of Homeland Security and Emergency Preparedness (LOHSEP), pointed with considerable pride to that figure. "How quickly," he asked, "should you be able to pluck over 62,000 people out of the water, off rooftops, and out of attics and move them to safety? Louisiana did it in five days. This averages 12,000 rescued per day. This is nothing short of outstanding."

The Shelter Crisis

Unfortunately for the tens of thousands of people heroically rescued by the DWF or the Coast Guard or other groups, however, there proved to be no good place for them to go.

---

[18]Ibid.

[19]Senate Committee report, Chap. 21: 2.

[20]*Times-Picayune*, Web ed., September 7, 2005.

[21]House Select Committee report, 69.

[22]Senate Committee report, Chap. 21: 1–5. Later in the rescue effort, FEMA was able to assemble eight teams with training in water rescue to help out in the city.

They were unceremoniously dropped off at a number of collection points—many of them highway overpasses—where they waited in vain to be picked up and taken to shelter. At one of these—an overpass at Interstate 10 sometimes referred to as the cloverleaf—a large crowd gathered, some left there by rescue crews, some arriving on their own power, many bringing only the clothes they were wearing. Eventually, the crowd would swell to over 5,000.

Others were taken to the Superdome, which, as a refuge of last resort, officials had expected to be emptied out once the storm had blown over. Instead, the population in the facility began to grow after the hurricane departed as those already in residence were joined by people who had been rescued or who had made their way there on their own. Before long, the population ballooned to well over 20,000. By Tuesday night, the Superdome was a house of horrors: the plumbing had failed completely, and the stench of human waste permeated the darkened, sweltering building. Because not enough supplies had been stockpiled in advance, food and water ran low. Marty Bahamonde who, along with a four-member emergency response team from FEMA, stayed at the Superdome for 3 days, recalled the ordeal in his Senate testimony. "Each day," he said, "it was a battle to find enough food and water and get it to the Superdome. It was a struggle meal-to-meal. . . ."

As yet, however, there appeared to be no quick way—and no existing plan—to evacuate the thousands of people at the Superdome or at the highway overpasses or at yet another venue on high ground, the Ernest N. Morial Convention Center, which Nagin had ordered opened sometime on Tuesday to accommodate the rapidly growing number of people seeking shelter. Unlike the Superdome, there were no police or National Guard on hand and no food or water at the convention center.[23] Despite the complete lack of basic amenities, an estimated 20,000 people, including tourists apparently steered there by their hotels, eventually gathered there.

Meanwhile, efforts to plug one of the worst levee breaches, in the 17th Street Canal, had thus far failed. The Army Corps of Engineers had tried dropping sandbags into the canal and lowering large concrete barriers, but had been unable to close the yawning gap in the floodwall. As a result, said one Army Corps engineer on Tuesday night, water would "continue to flow down into the center of town."[24]

A Second Evacuation

By Tuesday evening, evacuation had moved to the top of the priority list for city and state officials. After touring the Superdome that afternoon, Blanco appeared disturbed by what

---

[23]House Select Committee report, 118. In a prepared statement quoted in the report, Nagin said that the growing demand for shelter "required us to open the Convention Center as another refuge." Elsewhere in its report, however, the House Select Committee maintained that evacuees themselves went to the convention center seeking dry ground and broke into the locked facility.

[24]Quoted in Robert Travis Scott, "Late Blanco Statement," *Times-Picayune,* Web ed., August 30, 2005.

she had witnessed. "It's a very, very desperate situation," she told reporters. "It's imperative that we get [the people in the Superdome] out."[25]

The evacuation effort began with a search for buses to transport many thousands of people out of the city. Sometime on Tuesday, Nagin called the governor's chief of staff to say that his "No. 1 priority" for help from the state was buses. New Orleans itself did not appear to have any buses of its own available to evacuate residents from its flooded streets and fetid shelters. The city's school buses had been parked in an area that flooded during the storm, rendering them useless. The same was believed to be true for Regional Transit Authority (RTA) buses, which the city tried to obtain for evacuation purposes; it later emerged that two hundred of them had been safely parked on high ground, but RTA officials did not convey this information to the city.[26]

The state began its own effort on Tuesday to line up buses from other school districts and churches to help with its evacuation effort, but that ran into a roadblock the following day when some school systems, troubled by reports of lawlessness in New Orleans, began to balk. Finally, on Wednesday, Blanco, exercising her emergency powers, signed an order commandeering the school buses; even so, they did not begin to arrive in New Orleans until Thursday.[27] At the same time, the governor sought help from the federal government in rounding up enough buses to meet the huge need. According to Blanco, she had asked Michael Brown for five hundred buses as early as Monday. He had agreed, she later reported, but no buses arrived on Tuesday or the next day, even though Blanco had repeated her request to Brown and, eventually, to White House Chief of Staff Andrew Card. It was not until the early morning hours of Wednesday that FEMA officially requested the buses from the U.S. Department of Transportation.[28] Once the order for buses was received, one FEMA official noted, a multiagency effort was mounted to charter over 1,000 buses to help evacuate residents. "In 96 hours," he said, "we built a transportation system equal to the capability of the Greyhound Bus Company."[29] For many, however, the agency's failure to provide buses in the first 48 hours after landfall was the more noteworthy, and deplorable, event.

A Shaky Command

FEMA's slowness to act on the request for buses was never entirely explained, although difficulties in communications between agency officials at the beleaguered Superdome and in the state EOC in Baton Rouge were believed to have contributed to the problem. But perhaps equally important was the growing sense of disarray among those who were expected

---

[25]Quoted in ibid.

[26]Senate Committee report, Chap. 22: 5.

[27]Ibid., Chap. 22: 6.

[28]Ibid., Chap. 22: 5.

[29]William Lokey, testimony before the House Select Committee, December 14, 2005.

to lead the disaster response. In Michael Brown's view, much of the blame for this lay with the state of Louisiana. In his September 27 testimony before the House Select Committee, Brown maintained that his "biggest mistake" in the response to Katrina was "not recognizing by Saturday that Louisiana was dysfunctional."

The state's disorganization, Brown maintained, made it impossible to set up a unified command at the EOC in Baton Rouge. He was dismayed by the "lack of coordinated response," as the *New York Times* put it, from Blanco and Maj. Gen. Bennett Landreneau, the adjutant general of the Louisiana National Guard and head of LOHSEP. Brown told the *New York Times* that he had asked them, "What do you need? Help me help you," but that their response "was like, 'Let us find out,' and then I never received specific requests for specific things that needed doing." Blanco angrily disputed Brown's charges, and members of her staff complained about FEMA's insistence on receiving itemized requests from the state. "It was like walking into an emergency room bleeding profusely," said one, "and being expected to instruct the doctors how to treat you." [30]

Making a Declaration

As the growing distress of New Orleans began to be reported extensively in the media, the White House announced that President Bush would cut short his vacation by 2 days and return to Washington on Wednesday. In addition, on Tuesday night, Chertoff formally designated the hurricane an incident of national significance—the first declaration of its kind. This action set in motion a number of mechanisms laid out in the NRP. It activated the Interagency Incident Management Group, made up of senior-level officials from relevant federal agencies to act as an advisory body to the DHS secretary. It also prompted the appointment of a *principal federal official* (PFO), whose role was to provide "a primary point of contact and situational awareness locally" for the DHS secretary.

To the surprise of many—including the appointee—Chertoff named Brown as his PFO for Hurricane Katrina. For one thing, the PFO was supposed to have received special training for the post, which Brown had not had. But more crucially, the PFO, under the provisions of the NRP, did not have "directive authority" over other federal and state officials on the scene, including the *federal coordinating officer* (FCO), who was appointed by FEMA (and therefore ultimately answerable to Brown) to oversee the agency's response to a specific disaster. Chertoff later testified that he had named Brown as PFO because he was his "battlefield commander." This led the House Select Committee to conclude that Chertoff "was confused about the role and authority of the PFO." [31]

---

[30]David Kirkpatrick and Scott Shane, "Ex-FEMA Chief Tells of Frustration and Chaos," *New York Times*, September 15, 2005, A1.

[31]House Select Committee report, 135.

Brown regarded his appointment as PFO with dismay. It added "another layer of bureaucracy," he maintained in his House testimony, and worse still, tethered him to Chertoff. The main task of the PFO, he pointed out, was to provide "information to the [DHS] secretary, which then takes away from my operational responsibilities[.]" Brown had been accustomed to bypassing Chertoff, but the White House had begun to make it clear that this practice would have to stop. During a conversation with Andrew Card about a Katrina-related request, he was told, " 'Mike, we are going to have to follow the protocol. We are going to have to follow the chain of command.' . . . And I took that to mean . . . if you really need something, you need to go back to Chertoff. . . ."[32]

For his part, the DHS secretary indicated a growing impatience with Brown's elusiveness. Starting late Tuesday morning, Chertoff told the House Select Committee, and "rising in crescendo through the afternoon and late afternoon, I made it very clear to the people I was speaking to and communicating through [at FEMA] that I expected Mr. Brown to get in touch with me because I insisted on speaking to him." While some questioned Chertoff's subsequent decision that night to name Brown as PFO, it was possible that the move reflected a wish to put his freewheeling undersecretary on a tighter leash.

Depending on how the NRP was interpreted, Chertoff's declaration was considered belated or redundant or inadequate. It stopped short of invoking the NRP's Catastrophic Incident Annex—but, in any event, it seemed to promise, along with Bush's return to the White House, a more coordinated and intensive response to Katrina's victims from the federal government. "I anticipate this is going to be a very, very substantial effort. . . . We have a substantial challenge, but . . . we're going to do what it takes," Chertoff said at a news conference the following day.[33]

Wednesday, August 31 to Thursday, September 1

Descent into Hell

Despite reports that President Bush was mobilizing "one of the biggest relief efforts in history,"[34] the miserable conditions facing stranded residents in New Orleans continued largely unmitigated throughout Wednesday and most of Thursday, with neither the promised supplies of food and water nor the buses needed for evacuation showing up in sufficient numbers. Thousands of people trapped in their homes still waited for rescue, while tens of thousands sweltered in hot, squalid shelters or broiled in the sun on highway overpasses. As wretched as life was for those in the Superdome and even at the I-10 cloverleaf

---

[32]Michael Brown, deposition before the House Select Committee, February 11, 2006.

[33]Josh White, "Bush Mobilizes a Huge Recovery Effort," *Washington Post*, September 1, 2005, A20.

[34]Peter Baker, "Vacation Ends, and Crisis Management Begins," *Washington Post*, September 1, 2005, A1.

(where there were some supplies of food, water, and medicine, albeit grossly inadequate), the plight of those who had gathered at the Ernest Morial Convention Center was far worse. Nagin had apparently neglected to tell state officials that he had opened the facility for evacuees,[35] and although a huge crowd of roughly 20,000 had massed there, no one appeared to notice them. They continued to languish there through Wednesday and into the following day without food or water, and with only news reporters and television cameras to witness their growing desperation.

By Thursday, TV news shows were beaming grim footage from the convention center: the image of an elderly woman, for example, dead in her wheelchair outside the facility, with a note on her lap giving her name—one of "a half-dozen corpses . . . slumped in lawn chairs or covered with makeshift shrouds"; a day later, the *New York Times* reported, her body still lay there, exposed to the harsh sun.[36] Television viewers tuning into CNN were treated to the spectacle of "hundreds of disheveled residents," in the words of one account, "huddled around the convention center, including a visibly frightened group chanting, 'Help, help, help.' . . ." Soon after, Nagin chimed in with his own plea. "This is a desperate SOS," he said in a statement to CNN. "Right now we are out of resources at the convention center and don't anticipate enough buses. We need buses. Currently the convention center is unsanitary and unsafe. . . ."[37]

Lawlessness in the City

As Nagin's statement indicated, evacuees in the convention center faced not only hunger and thirst but an anarchic environment in the absence of police or National Guard troops. Reports of violence were chilling. No less than the chief of police, Edwin Compass, warned that "armed thugs," in the words of the *New York Times*, had "taken control of" the convention center and were preying on the people there—including "stranded tourists"—and on neighboring streets. "We have individuals who are getting raped," he said during an interview. "We have individuals who are getting beaten."[38]

Tales of violent crime were not limited to the convention center, however. Nagin talked of people who "have been in that frickin' Superdome for five days watching dead bodies, watching hooligans killing people, raping people."[39] There were also disturbing stories of

---

[35]Senate Committee report, Chap. 19: 11.

[36]James Dao, Joseph Treaster, and Felicity Barringer, "New Orleans Is Awaiting Deliverance," *New York Times*, September 2, 2005, 15; Joseph Treaster, "First Steps to Alleviate Squalor and Suffering at Convention Center," *New York Times*, September 3, 2005, 16.

[37]Marc Sandalow, "Anarchy, Anger, Desperation; Sharp Criticism of US Reaction and Failure to Prevent Disaster," *San Francisco Chronicle*, September 2, 2005, A1.

[38]Joseph Treaster and Deborah Sontag, "Despair and Lawlessness Grip New Orleans as Thousands Remain Stranded in Squalor," *New York Times*, September 2, 2005, A1; Dao et al., "New Orleans Is Awaiting Deliverance." Compass maintained that thugs had repelled eight squads of police officers sent to secure the convention center.

[39]David Carr, "More Horrible than Truth: News Reports," *New York Times*, September 19, 2005, C1. In a September 6 appearance on the *Oprah Winfrey* show, Compass said, "We had little babies in [the Superdome], some of the little babies getting raped."

sniper fire aimed at helicopters airlifting patients out of hospitals, of attacks on National Guard troops patrolling the Superdome, and, later, of the body of a seven-year-old girl whose throat had been slit. Danger lurked outside the shelters as well. Two evacuees told of "pirates" seizing boats used to rescue residents, threatening them with firearms and forcing them into the floodwaters.[40]

The reports of the most lurid crimes, including Nagin's and Compass's allegations, ultimately proved either untrue or unconfirmed, and the press was roundly criticized later for passing them along uncritically. But there was enough evidence of looting, and either the absence or the collusion of the police, to convey a sense of peril and vulnerability to the city's traumatized population—and to scare off some of the people who were rushing to their rescue.

By Wednesday, Nagin had ordered the city's 1,500 police officers to turn from search and rescue to "stopping the looting,"[41] but by then it was apparent that the police force itself was in disarray. Many officers had lost their own homes in the flooding, and many were overwhelmed by the chaos enveloping the city. "Dozens of officers turned in their badges or fled without a word," the *Times-Picayune* reported. "Some joined in with looters and marauders, plunging an already jittery situation into moments of complete societal breakdown."[42] Reports of rampant looting also spurred a change of heart in Blanco, who had initially made search and rescue her number one priority, followed by levee repairs. On August 31, she announced that 200 state police troopers and 350 additional Louisiana National Guardsmen would be deployed to New Orleans. "We will do what it takes," she declared, "to restore law and order."[43]

The Medical Emergency

While TV cameras were trained on the distraught denizens of the convention center, news of another distressed population began filtering into the press: the patients and staff of the city's hospitals. Most of New Orleans's hospitals and nursing homes had not evacuated their patients ahead of Katrina's onslaught. As elsewhere in the city, they had lost power early, and their backup generators had either flooded or run out of fuel; many facilities were surrounded by water and approachable only by helicopter or boat. While limited supplies of food and water had been delivered by helicopter, these were running low, and there were reports that some hungry hospital workers were "feeding themselves intravenous sugar solutions." Doctors were

---

[40]Dao et al., "New Orleans Is Awaiting Deliverance."

[41]Robert McFadden and Ralph Blumenthal, "Bush Sees Long Recovery for New Orleans," *New York Times,* August 31, 2005, A1.

[42]Michael Perlstein, " 'I Told Them the Worst Is Yet to Come'; Most Officers Working on Adrenaline, Little Else," *Times-Picayune,* September 4, 2005, A2. According to a September 28 report in the *New York Times,* an estimated 15 percent of the police force—250 officers—would later face investigation for "absences without permission."

[43]Ed Anderson, Michael Perlstein and Robert Travis Scott, "We Will Do What It Takes to Restore Law and Order," *Times-Picayune,* September 1, 2005, 5.

"working by flashlight," using manual ventilators on patients, and "waiting helplessly for news from outside."[44] Early efforts to come to the assistance of hospitals had been hampered by reports of gunfire aimed at helicopters attempting to drop off supplies or airlift patients. The head of one private ambulance service told a reporter that medics trying to reach hospitals by boat had been shot at as well.[45]

By Thursday, the situation grew desperate. "Beside himself after failing to get through to city and state officials," the *Times-Picayune* reported, "the chief of trauma at Charity Hospital [a public facility] called a news conference . . . to beg for help. Charity was nearly out of food and power for its generators and had been forced to move patients to higher floors to escape looters prowling the hospital. . . ."[46] A doctor at Pendleton Memorial Methodist Hospital reported similarly perilous conditions in an e-mail: 130 patients in need of care, over 500 "non-patient refugees" who were "very close to rioting for the balance" of food and water available in the facility, "dehydrating" staff, "snakes in hospital," and temperature at 110 degrees.[47]

The transportation needed to remove patients from hospitals was, as the Senate Committee report noted, already "tied up in search and rescue efforts," and there was not enough to go around. The director of the Louisiana Department of Health and Hospitals, Dr. Jimmy Guidry, described being besieged with calls from hospitals, "saying, . . . 'We've got to get them [the patients] out of here.' . . . [A]nd I'm beating my head to try to get the help. And you've got search and rescue that's trying to get people out of water and rooftops and out of hospitals. And that's all . . . competing needs for the limited assets."[48]

Anger Grows

By midweek, state and local leaders in Louisiana appeared at times exhausted and discouraged. "The whole situation," Blanco said on *Good Morning America* on Wednesday, "is totally overwhelming."[49] In New Orleans, cries for help were turning into cries of outrage, many of them aimed at the federal government and at FEMA in particular. "This is a national disgrace," Terry Ebbert, director of homeland security in New Orleans, declared. "FEMA has been here for three days, yet there is no command and control. We can send

---

[44]Felicity Barringer and Donald McNeil Jr., "Grim Triage for Ailing and Dying at a Makeshift Hospital," *New York Times,* September 3, 2005, A13.

[45]Sam Coates and Dan Eggen, "A City of Despair and Lawlessness," *Washington Post,* September 2, 2005, A1. The reports of gunfire later came into question. While one man was arrested for shooting at a helicopter on September 5, many officials, the *Washington Post* reported on October 5, came to believe that at least some of the gunfire was most probably intended to alert rescuers to the presence of people needing help.

[46]Jed Horne, "Help Us, Please; after the Disaster, Chaos and Lawlessness Rule the Streets," *Times-Picayune,* September 2, 2005, A1.

[47]House Select Committee report, 286–287.

[48]Senate Committee report, Chap. 24: 5.

[49]Quoted in Dan Balz, "A Defining Moment for State Leaders," *Washington Post,* September 1, 2005, A13.

massive amounts of aid to tsunami victims [in Asia], but we can't bail out the city of New Orleans." [50] There was a sense of betrayal that the federal government had not come to the city's aid. The Hurricane Pam exercise of 2004 (which brought state, local, and federal emergency officials together to devise a plan specifically to respond to a major hurricane in New Orleans) appeared to have created the expectation of a rapid, although not immediate, influx of federal assistance. The Hurricane Pam exercise had "predicted a massive federal response within two days," according to Ebbert, and, consequently, the city's plan, he told the *Washington Post,* was to "hang in there for 48 hours and wait for the cavalry." [51]

Some observers also noted the contrast between the responses to Katrina and to earlier hurricanes. "The scene [in Louisiana and Mississippi] was starkly different than in Florida a year ago after Hurricanes Charley and Frances roared in," wrote the *Wall Street Journal.* "Then, federal agencies pulled off a tour-de-force rescue, quickly pouring in billions of dollars to help distressed residents," supplementing that aid when two more storms followed. "President Bush visited the scene within 48 hours," the *Wall Street Journal* continued (at that point, Bush had not yet gone to New Orleans), and his brother, Florida Governor Jeb Bush, "took personal responsibility for managing the relief effort." While there were "delays and frustrations, FEMA generally received high marks." [52]

The failure to muster a show of federal responsiveness prompted bitter remarks from New Orleans area leaders. Possibly the most memorable of these came from Nagin during an appearance on a local radio talk show on Thursday afternoon. Referring to the president's recent flyover inspection of the devastated Gulf Coast, he said, "They don't have a clue what's going on down here. They flew down here one time two days after the doggone event was over, with all kinds of goddamn excuses. Excuse my French, everybody in America, but I am pissed." Contrasting the response to another notable disaster, Nagin declared, "After 9/11 we gave the president unprecedented powers, lickety-quick, to take care of New York and other places." Nagin brushed aside promises of troops and supplies. "They're not here," he declared. "It's too doggone late. Get off your asses, and let's do something and let's fix the biggest goddamn crisis in the history of this country." [53]

A Struggling Federal Emergency Management Agency

Nagin's remarks, which were replayed across the country, focused attention on FEMA and its apparent inability either to provide evacuees with adequate supplies of food, water, and

---

[50]Josh White and Peter Whoriskey, "Planning, Response Are Faulted," *Washington Post,* September 2, 2005, A1.

[51]Quoted in Susan Glasser and Michael Grunwald, "Steady Buildup to a City's Chaos," *Washington Post,* September 11, 2005, A1.

[52]Ann Carrns, Chad Terhune, Kris Hudson, and Gary Fields, "As U.S. Mobilizes Aid, Katrina Exposes Flaws in Preparation," *Wall Street Journal,* September 1, 2005, A1.

[53]As quoted in *Times-Picayune,* Web ed., September 2, 2005.

medicine or to assemble enough transportation to remove them from squalid shelters and hospitals. At one level, the reason for the agency's faltering response was a straightforward one. "Despite all of our efforts and despite the fact that we pre-positioned more commodities and staged more rescue and medical teams than ever in our history," said William Lokey, FEMA's federal coordinating officer for Louisiana, in testimony before the House Select Committee, "as a result of the catastrophic size and scope of Katrina, our initial response was overwhelmed."

Defenders of the federal response pointed out that with communications in New Orleans destroyed and many roads into the city in poor condition, it was not easy to keep supplies moving and reaching those in need. But it did not escape the notice of critics that Wal-Mart, for example, did not appear to be experiencing this difficulty.[54] "On Thursday morning," the *Times-Picayune* pointed out, a crew of journalists, who had also figured out how to haul themselves and their equipment into the city, "saw a caravan of 13 Wal-Mart tractor trailers head into town to bring food, water and supplies to a dying city."[55]

FEMA's failure to match Wal-Mart's performance was attributed to a number of problems. For one, its logistics system worked poorly. "FEMA has a logistics problem . . . ," Brown later acknowledged. "I can point out where the stuff is, and I can point out where it's supposed to go to; I can't always tell you that it actually got there."[56] FEMA was plagued as well by a shortage of drivers to transport supplies and people and by a shortage of supplies to transport; although it had pre-positioned an unprecedented volume of supplies, it was not "robust" enough, as Lokey put it, "for the catastrophe at hand."[57] The bureaucracy of FEMA also seemed to interfere with the smooth delivery of supplies. Despite Brown's urging FEMA staff to "push the envelope" and cut red tape in prestorm meetings, there were numerous tales of trucks being halted or diverted or refused entry by agency workers. The problem, Brown explained in his House testimony, lay with "disaster assistance employees," a "cadre" of part-time workers the agency hired to provide "surge capacity" in times of disaster. They tended to be sticklers for detail, he said, and too far removed from the leadership of the agency to "understand that the guy at the top—at the time, me—doesn't care." In his later testimony, Brown described himself as constantly prodding the system to move supplies along. "I continued to do operations as best I could all along . . . ," he said. "And I would continually ask questions: Are things happening? Are things happening? Are things happening?" But, he acknowledged to the House Select Committee in February, "I remained frustrated throughout the entire process that the requests that we were working on were not

---

[54]For more on Wal-Mart's response to Katrina, see Case 9 in this book.
[55]*Times-Picayune,* "An Open Letter to the President," September 4, 2005, A15.
[56]House Select Committee report, 322.
[57]White House report, Chap. 4: 7.

being filled timely." In a rueful nod to his earlier criticism of Blanco and Louisiana state government, Brown said, "We were dysfunctional, too. . . . I couldn't make things happen."

Disconnect

FEMA's perceived shortcomings in responding to Katrina were exacerbated in the public eye by an apparent lack of awareness of some of the most shocking scenes coming out of New Orleans. On Thursday, at a time when images of thirsty, hungry, and distraught evacuees were dominating the nation's TV screens, Chertoff remarked that "it is a source of tremendous pride to me to work with people who have pulled off this really exceptional response." [58] More embarrassing perhaps was his reply to repeated questions that day on National Public Radio's *All Things Considered* about the plight of evacuees at the convention center. Asked about "thousands of people at the convention center in New Orleans with no food, zero," Chertoff responded that "we are getting food and water to areas where people are staging." Then he remarked, "The one thing about an episode like this is if you talk to someone and you get a rumor or you get someone's anecdotal version of something, I think it's dangerous to extrapolate it all over the place." When the interviewer, Robert Siegel, pressed the issue, pointing out that experienced reporters had witnessed the scene in person, Chertoff answered, "Well, . . . actually I have not heard a report of thousands of people in the convention center who don't have food and water."

By this time, Brown had concluded that FEMA was overmatched by the tasks it faced and that it was time to call in the army.

Turning to the Department of Defense

As Brown recalled in his February House testimony, as early as Tuesday, August 30, he began talking to White House officials, primarily Deputy Chief of Staff Joe Hagin, about asking the Department of Defense (DOD) to assume responsibility for FEMA's logistics mission. "I was asking for a hostile takeover," he said. "I wanted them to come in and run logistics, to run distribution . . . because we knew it was beyond our capacity to do that."

Brown may have spoken to the White House of his wish to hand over logistics to the DOD; however, there was, according to the Senate Committee report, "scant evidence" that he or anyone from FEMA discussed this with Pentagon officials until Thursday, September 1. That day, FEMA's acting director of the response division spoke with the agency's acting director of operations about the need for DOD's help with "commodities, supplies, and logistics." After discussions between FEMA and DOD, and within DOD, the Pentagon agreed to take on the job. The logistics mission assignment was written up on Friday, September 2, and approved the following day.

---

[58]Quoted in Amanda Ripley, "How Did This Happen?" *Time* magazine, September 12, 2005, 52.

Calling in the Military

FEMA was not the only entity seeking to tap the resources of the military. The state of Louisiana—overwhelmed by the challenges of caring for and evacuating tens of thousands of people in the New Orleans area—began an urgent quest for troops from fellow states and the federal government.

By long tradition in the United States, it is the National Guard, not federal forces, that states first call on to help out in times of disaster. Unlike active-duty troops, which are, with certain exceptions, forbidden by statute to engage in domestic law enforcement activities, National Guardsmen can take on policing duties as well as provide a workforce for an array of tasks, from rescue operations to distribution of supplies. In advance of Katrina, Louisiana had activated 4,000 National Guard troops; by Tuesday, August 30, that number had risen to about 5,800.

As the crisis in New Orleans deepened, it quickly became evident that the Louisiana National Guard was spread too thin to maintain law and order, assist with search and rescue efforts, and—which soon became a high priority—help evacuate the huge crowds at the Superdome and the convention center. On Tuesday afternoon, after visiting the Superdome, Blanco told Maj. Gen. Bennett Landreneau (adjutant general of the Louisiana National Guard) to "ask for all available assistance from the National Guard and the United States Government, specifically federal military assistance." [59]

As Blanco's instructions indicated, there were two avenues the state could pursue to supplement its own National Guard forces: it could ask other states to send their National Guard troops, and it could ask the federal government to send its active-duty troops. The state sought both kinds of help, although later there were disputes about when this was done, what was said to whom, and what specifically was asked for. Early on, Blanco, in conversation with Bush on Monday afternoon, had made a sweeping request for assistance. "We need your help," she told the president, by her own account. "We need everything you've got." Blanco came away from the conversation convinced that Bush intended to "send all of the resources and assistance within the power of the federal government" to her stricken state. When the hoped-for, although unspecified, help was not forthcoming, Blanco eventually put a figure on what she wanted: 40,000 troops. [60]

National Guard Troops

Negotiations over National Guard troops were relatively straightforward, although here, too, there were some disagreements over the timing of the state's request. Under the provisions of

---

[59]Senate Committee report, Chap. 26: 51.
[60]Ibid., Chap. 26: 46, 59.

the Emergency Management Assistance Compact (EMAC), Louisiana could ask states to send National Guard resources—equipment and troops. A couple of hundred troops from three states trickled in on Tuesday, but the EMAC process (a state-to-state transaction) proved too cumbersome to handle the huge volume of requests for help coming from Mississippi and Louisiana in Katrina's devastating wake. Eventually, both states sought help from the National Guard Bureau in Washington, D.C., a DOD unit headed by Lt. Gen. H. Steven Blum.

Blum immediately began calling and e-mailing state adjutants general across the country, according to the Senate Committee report, asking in particular for "National Guard military police, engineers, and high water trucks." The results were impressive. Within 96 hours, over 30,000 National Guard troops were deployed to Louisiana and Mississippi from all fifty states plus two territories and the District of Columbia (see Exhibit 1C-1). But it took a while for the troops to appear in sufficient numbers for the distressed people of New Orleans to feel their presence. It was not until Thursday night, September 1, that, with the help of fresh National Guard reinforcements, the evacuation of the Superdome could finally begin.

Exhibit 1C-1   Activated National Guard personnel serving in Louisiana and Mississippi, 2005

Date	Number serving in Louisiana			Number serving in Mississippi		
	Louisiana National Guard personnel	National Guard personnel from other states	Total	Mississippi National Guard personnel	National Guard personnel from other states	Total
Aug. 30	5,804	178	5,982	3,822	16	3,838
Aug. 31	5,804	663	6,467	3,822	1,149	4,971
Sept. 1	5,804	2,555	8,359	3,823	2,861	6,684
Sept. 2	6,779	5,445	12,224	3,823	3,719	7,542
Sept. 3	6,779	10,635	17,414	3,823	6,314	10,137
Sept. 4	6,779	12,404	19,183	4,017	9,399	13,416
Sept. 5	6,779	16,162	22,941	4,017	10,999	15,016
Sept. 6	6,779	20,510	27,289	4,023	11,095	15,118
Sept. 7	6,779	22,589	29,368	4,023	11,388	15,411
Sept. 8	6,779	23,476	30,255	4,023	11,506	15,529

Source: Congressional Research Service, *Hurricane Katrina: DOD Disaster Response,* January 24, 2006, 12, reprinted in "Hurricane Katrina: A Nation Still Unprepared," report of the Senate Committee on Homeland Security and Governmental Affairs, Washington, D.C., May 2006.

Federal Troops

The effort to obtain federal active-duty troops proved far more challenging and time-consuming, in part because it was an inherently complex process, taking, according to the White House report, twenty-one steps from the time the request was made to actual delivery of military forces, and in part because of confusion and disagreements that dogged the quest for troops. The formal process called for the request for active-duty troops to be made through FEMA, but state officials largely bypassed this channel and made their requests directly either to the White House or to the military commander in the field, Lt. Gen. Russel Honoré, who, on Tuesday night, August 30, was appointed commander of Joint Task Force Katrina in Camp Shelby, Mississippi. The task force, according to the Senate Committee report, consisted of "all the active-duty military forces in the Gulf Coast region responding to Katrina." Nevertheless, it was days before they would make an appearance in New Orleans.

On Tuesday morning, Landreneau had spoken by phone with Honoré and, by his own account, "conveyed the Governor's desire for federal troops, in particular an Army division headquarters to plan, coordinate, and execute the evacuation of New Orleans." Honoré, however, maintained that the request for military forces did not come until the following day. Whenever the request was made, it did not yield results. Although Honoré himself visited the stricken city on Wednesday, he did not bring any troops with him.[61]

That day, Blanco also made an "urgent call" to the White House, according to a timeline she submitted to the Senate Committee, "in an effort to reach President Bush and express the need for significant resources." She was unable to reach Bush, but eventually spoke with both Chief of Staff Andrew Card and Homeland Security Advisor Frances Townsend. These conversations, however, also proved unsuccessful, in part, the Senate Committee report maintained, because "White House officials did not understand what the governor was requesting." Later, Blanco acknowledged that, initially at least, "I didn't give [Bush] a checklist or anything." She was criticized for the lack of specificity of her requests for help. Others asked her, she recalled, "Did you ask for this; did you ask for that? It got to be a very difficult little game."[62]

But, as the Senate Committee report pointed out, even after Blanco clarified her request, a major sticking point remained—the terms under which active-duty and National Guard troops would serve. Some officials—including Michael Brown—were arguing for the federalization of National Guard troops in Louisiana by invoking the Insurrection Act. Normally, National Guard forces were under the command of the governor, but the Insurrection Act would allow the president to place them, along with active-duty forces, under his command;

---

[61]Ibid., Chap. 26: 51, 59.

[62]Quoted in Karen Tumulty with Brian Bennett, "The Governor: Did Kathleen Babineaux Blanco Make Every Effort to Get Federal Help?" *Time*, September 19, 2005, 38; House Select Committee report, 222.

moreover, under the provisions of the act, both National Guard and active-duty troops could participate in law enforcement missions. Brown maintained that he was a "strong advocate" of federalization because of reports of violent crime that were rife in New Orleans at the time and because "I want[ed] active-duty troops that are ready, willing and able to kill in that area, because we can't do search and rescue with that kind of stuff going on."[63] Blanco, however, resisted federalization.[64]

Talks between Louisiana and White House officials about federalization dragged on inconclusively. Meanwhile, some Department of Defense officials argued against deploying active-duty troops at all, maintaining that enough National Guard forces were flowing into the region to satisfy the demand for military assistance. But Blanco disagreed and continued to press for federal troops to help make up the full complement of 40,000 troops that she felt was needed. On Friday, September 2, President Bush made his first appearance in New Orleans and met with Blanco, Nagin, and others aboard Air Force One to discuss the issue. Nagin recommended that Honoré be placed in charge of all troops, both National Guard and active-duty. The mayor also chided Bush and Blanco for haggling over command issues while New Orleans suffered: "I stopped everyone and basically said, 'Mr. President, Madame Governor, if the two of you don't get together on this issue, more people are going to die in this city, and you need to resolve this immediately.' "[65] Nagin's plea notwithstanding, the president and the governor, who continued to refuse to give up her authority over the National Guard, did not come to an agreement. That night, at 11:30 p.m., the White House faxed Blanco a new proposal: Honoré would take command of both National Guard and active-duty forces but in a "dual-hat" capacity; that is, he would report to Blanco for the National Guard forces under his command and to Bush for the active-duty forces under this command. The following morning, Blanco, in a phone conversation with Andrew Card, rejected the proposal. "The bottom line of it is," said Lt. Gen. Blum of the National Guard Bureau (who supported Blanco's position), "there were many offers and overtures made to the Governor on command and control, but they all centered on a Federal officer being in charge of the Governor's National Guard, and that was rejected."[66]

It was not until Secretary of Defense Donald Rumsfeld overruled military officials in the Northern Command on Saturday, September 3—amid mounting public criticism of the federal response to Katrina—that the way was cleared for deployment of active-duty forces.[67] At 11:00 that morning, President Bush announced that 7,200 U.S. Army and Marine

---

[63]Senate Committee report, Chap. 26: 49, 58.

[64]Mississippi did not seek active-duty federal troops, so the issue of federalization concerned Louisiana only.

[65]Senate Committee report, Chap. 26: 64.

[66]Ibid., Chap. 26: 67.

[67]Nicole Gaouette, Alan Miller, Mark Mazzetti, Doyle McManus, Josh Meyer, and Kevin Sack, "Put to Katrina's Test," *Los Angeles Times,* September 11, 2005, A1.

troops would be sent to Louisiana. By that time, there were over 17,000 National Guard troops in the state, with thousands more arriving every day, and the evacuation of the Superdome and convention center was well underway.

Friday, September 2 to Monday, September 5

Relief

With both National Guard troops and buses converging on New Orleans, the first concerted effort to evacuate the Superdome began on Thursday. It did not go smoothly. "When the first dozen buses finally arrived . . . ," the *Times-Picayune* reported, "shoving and fights broke out and trash cans were set ablaze as people jockeyed to get out of the fetid, stinking stadium in which they had been captive since entering the city's shelter of last resort four days earlier." [68] But by Friday, September 2, there were enough buses—a total of 822, by Landreneau's account—and workers on hand to begin to make a dent in the huge crowd of 23,000 evacuees. By the following day, the now-dilapidated sports facility was empty.

Meanwhile, troops and buses had also begun to appear at the convention center. According to Landreneau's Senate testimony, the site was "secured" shortly after noon on Friday, and food, water, and medical help arrived soon thereafter. The evacuation of the convention center began the next morning and was completed by 6:00 that evening. The population of the I-10 cloverleaf began to diminish as well, as buses came by to pick up evacuees who had been dropped off there by rescuers; their numbers dwindled from roughly 5,000 to 2,500 by mid-day Saturday, although more evacuees continued to show up there, as well as at the Superdome and convention center, in hopes of finding a way out of the ruined city. By the end of Saturday, September 3, according to the testimony of Philip Parr, a FEMA official, a total of 66,825 people had been "transported" out of New Orleans.

Hospitals began emptying out as well. "With hundreds of National Guard troops spreading out in the city streets," the *New York Times* reported, "it was finally easier for small boats to approach embattled hospitals, some of which were surrounded by six feet of flood-water. . . ." The "fleet of helicopters evacuating patients from rooftops" expanded as well, from a "handful of single-patient civilian ambulances" to "about 100 military medevac choppers." [69] But hospital patients faced a further ordeal—roughly 3,000 of them were transported to a makeshift hospital at Louis Armstrong Airport where, on early Friday morning, conditions were described as "extremely desperate." Later that morning, however, military transports and chartered commercial jets began arriving to move the patients out; by Friday afternoon, only a few hundred remained at the airport.

---

[68]Horne, "Help Us, Please."
[69]Barringer and McNeil, "Grim Triage."

The influx of National Guard troops also helped improve security in the city. "It was a relief," the *Times-Picayune* reported on Friday, "to see so many uniformed men bearing machine guns, patrolling expressways and major intersections." When the active-duty troops began arriving on Monday, they could not, by law, take on policing duties, but "their mere presence," the Senate Committee report noted, "had a reassuring effect" on the beleaguered citizens of New Orleans.[70]

Working Together

The arrival of federal troops under the charge of Lt. Gen. Honoré, however, added one more element to an already complex command situation. The NRP had envisioned the establishment of a unified command composed of "designated members" who would work together at a single location to "establish a common set of objectives and strategies and a single Incident Action Plan."[71] But even though a unified command was set up for the Katrina response—led by FCO William Lokey of FEMA and State Coordinating Officer Col. Jeffrey Smith of LOHSEP—it was routinely bypassed.

The command situation became further confused when Michael Brown was appointed PFO. Brown was slow to establish a joint field office (JFO), which the NRP envisioned as the "central location" for the coordination of federal, state, and local organizations; the JFO, situated in Baton Rouge, did not become operational until 12 days after Katrina struck.[72] As a result, the White House report noted, agencies "independently deployed resources, operated autonomously, and generated disparate reporting streams. . . ."[73]

Federal officials, particularly from FEMA, in part blamed Louisiana's "lack of emergency management capacity," as the Senate Committee report put it, and its unfamiliarity with the principles of the NRP and the National Incident Management System on which it was based for the failure to establish a unified command. But Louisiana officials argued that the problem lay with the federal government. "[A]nyone who was there," declared Col. Jeff Smith in his House testimony in December, "anyone who chose to look, would realize that there were literally three separate Federal commands." The first was the official unified command, initially established at the Baton Rouge emergency operations center and later moved to the JFO, which he and Lokey led. The second consisted of, essentially, the PFO. "The PFO in Katrina," Smith maintained, "went operational and began directing and guiding response operations and to a large degree left out the [FCO]." The third was Honoré, commander of Joint Task Force Katrina. "Whenever . . . Gen. Honoré came onto the scene," Smith

---

[70]Senate Committee report, Chap. 26: 68. The federal troops, according to the report, engaged in "door-to-door search and rescue, debris removal, and logistics support" (Ibid.).

[71]Senate Committee report, Chap. 27: 10.

[72]Senate Committee report, Chap. 27: 15.

[73]White House report, Chap. 4: 8.

observed, "he was also operating independently with little regard whatsoever for the Joint Field Office, which should have been the only unified command."

Nonetheless, critics acknowledged, the extreme situation in New Orleans at least in part justified the circumvention of the unified command system. "Some may forgive Honoré for bypassing this process," the House Select Committee wrote, "because it was broken and therefore unworkable after Katrina. . . ." Lokey, the FCO for Louisiana, also praised Honoré for "doing what had to be done to get things moving."[74] Honoré and his state counterpart, Landreneau, were also credited with working well together, despite having separate commands over federal and National Guard troops, respectively. It helped, the *Times-Picayune* pointed out, that Landrenau and Honoré had "some important personal ties. . . . Honoré, known as the Ragin' Cajun, is a Louisiana native and has known Landreneau for years."[75]

Winding Down

By Sunday, September 4, the *Times-Picayune* could write that a "semblance of post-storm order" had returned to "ravaged New Orleans," with most of the crowds of evacuees dispersed and troops and supplies continuing to stream into the city. By Monday, the paper reported that some areas were "overflowing with ice," a commodity hitherto in high demand but short supply. On Monday, too, the huge breach in the 17th Street Canal was finally plugged, and crews were planning to move on to repair the gap in the London Street Canal. Soon, the pumps began working to drain the city of its filthy floodwaters.

Search and rescue operations continued into a second week, and troops launched what amounted to the third evacuation of New Orleans—this time, to remove the estimated 5,000–10,000 people who had somehow managed to remain in their homes through both the storm and the ensuing catastrophic flooding.[76] Meanwhile, the grisly work of finding and counting the dead began. Initial predictions were grim. "Some computer models say 10,000," Nagin remarked on CBS television. "I don't know what the number is. But it's going to be big. And it's going to shock the nation."[77] The death toll, shocking as it was, would turn out to be far lower than Nagin predicted; by February 2006, it stood at about 1,300, with hundreds still missing.

While New Orleans confronted a years-long recovery and an uncertain future, government officials at all levels—but most particularly the federal—faced months of withering criticism for their perceived failure to provide more help more quickly to the stricken resi-

---

[74]House Select Committee report, 190.

[75]Bill Walsh, Robert Travis Scott, and Jan Moller, "Bush, Blanco Spar over Military, Visit," *Times-Picayune,* September 6, 2005, A6. Honoré's son was serving in Iraq at the time as a member of the Louisiana National Guard.

[76]Jeff Duncan, "Mayor Nagin Stays Optimistic and Defiant," *Times-Picayune,* September 7, 2005, A4.

[77]*Times-Picayune,* Web ed., September 6, 2005. Nagin was apparently referring to figures projected in earlier computer simulations.

dents of New Orleans. The harshest criticism fell on Brown, who was also the first and most visible political casualty of the Katrina response.[78] On September 9, a week after Bush had famously praised him for "doing a heck of a job, Brownie," the FEMA chief was relieved of his Katrina-related duties; a few days later, to no one's surprise, he resigned.

DHS Secretary Chertoff also bore a major share of the blame for the shortcomings of the relief effort, although he held on to his job. As critics grew more vocal and questions from the press more pointed, Chertoff tried repeatedly to explain why the federal government appeared unequal to the task of responding to Katrina's devastating aftermath. Essentially, he said, the government was caught off-guard by the "second catastrophe," or the "second wave," after the fury of the storm had spent itself—that is, the breaching of the levees. This was, he maintained, "breathtaking in its surprise."[79] True, he acknowledged in a press briefing, there had been "over the last few years, some specific planning for the possibility of a significant hurricane in New Orleans with a lot of rainfall, with water rising in the levees and water overflowing the levees. . . . And although the planning was not complete, a lot of work had been done."[80] In the case of Katrina, however, "[w]e didn't merely have the overflow, we actually had the break in the wall." The result was a "perfect storm" of catastrophes that "exceeded the foresight of the planners, and maybe anybody's foresight."[81]

---

[78]Another was New Orleans Police Chief Edwin Compass, who resigned in late September.

[79]NBC-TV, *Meet the Press,* September 4, 2005; CNN.com, September 4, 2005.

[80]Recall that the Hurricane Pam planning exercise assumed that the levees would be overtopped but not breached.

[81]CNN.com, September 4, 2005.

Key Actors in Hurricane Katrina

New Orleans Officials

P. Edwin Compass III, chief, New Orleans Police Department

Col. Terry J. Ebbert, director of Homeland Security, City of New Orleans

C. Ray Nagin, mayor, City of New Orleans

State Officials

Kathleen Babineaux Blanco, governor of Louisiana

Maj. Gen. Bennett C. Landreneau, adjutant general, Louisiana National Guard, and director, Louisiana Office of Homeland Security and Emergency Preparedness (LOHSEP)

Col. Jeffrey Smith, state coordinating officer, Louisiana Office of Homeland Security and Emergency Preparedness (LOHSEP)

Federal Officials

Marty Bahamonde, Federal Emergency Management Agency (FEMA) public affairs officer and only FEMA representative in New Orleans when Katrina hit

Lt. Gen. H. Steven Blum, chief, National Guard Bureau, Department of Defense

Michael D. Brown, director of FEMA and U.S. Department of Homeland Security (DHS) undersecretary for emergency preparedness and response; also initially named as the DHS principal federal official (PFO) for Hurricane Katrina

George W. Bush, president of the United State of America

Richard (Dick) Cheney, vice president of the United States of America

Andrew (Andy) H. Card, White House chief of staff

Michael Chertoff, secretary of homeland security

Joe Hagin, deputy White House chief of staff

Lt. Gen. Russel L. Honoré, commander of Joint Task Force Katrina (responsible for coordinating military relief activities along the Gulf Coast)

William M. Lokey, FEMA federal coordinating officer (FCO) for Louisiana

Max Mayfield, director of the National Hurricane Center, National Oceanic and Atmospheric Administration (NOAA)

Ken Rapuano, deputy assistant to the president and deputy White House homeland security advisor (most senior White House homeland security official on duty when Katrina struck)

Donald H. Rumsfeld, secretary of defense

Frances Fragos Townsend, White House homeland security advisor

Hurricane Katrina, 2005

Chronology of Events

Wednesday, August 24

A tropical depression that had emerged in the Bahamas a day earlier gathers strength. It is officially named Tropical Storm Katrina.

Thursday, August 25

Katrina makes landfall in southern Florida as a Category 1 hurricane.

Friday, August 26

Katrina shifts from its predicted course, redirecting itself toward New Orleans.

Louisiana Governor Kathleen Babineaux Blanco declares a state of emergency and activates an initial 2,000 Louisiana National Guardsmen.

Saturday, August 27

Katrina grows in strength, prompting increasingly dire forecasts and warnings.

The Louisiana Office of Homeland Security and Emergency Preparedness (LOHSEP) activates the state's emergency operations center (EOC), located in the state capital, Baton Rouge.

Louisiana recommends implementation of its phased evacuation plan for southeast Louisiana. St. Tammany, St. Charles, and Plaquemines parishes issue mandatory evacuations, while Jefferson and St. Bernard parishes issue voluntary/recommended evacuations. New Orleans Mayor Ray Nagin encourages city residents to leave, but does not issue a mandatory evacuation.

Governor Blanco asks President Bush to declare a state of emergency for Louisiana (Bush does so that night; the next day, he signs emergency declarations for the states of Alabama and Mississippi).

7:30 p.m.: Max Mayfield, director of the National Hurricane Center, takes the unusual step of calling the governors of Louisiana, Mississippi, and Alabama and Mayor Nagin to warn them of Katrina's severity.

10:00 p.m.: The National Hurricane Center upgrades it hurricane watch for the North Central Gulf Coast to a hurricane warning.

Sunday, August 28

8:00 a.m.: The New Orleans Superdome opens to people with special needs. Later on Sunday, the stadium opens to the general population.

9:30 a.m.: Mayor Nagin issues a mandatory evacuation of New Orleans.

In the early evening, Katrina's forward reach hits the Gulf Coast. Consequently, state police cease contraflow travel at 5:00 p.m., Mayor Nagin issues a curfew at 6:00 p.m., and buses carrying residents to the Superdome cease operations at 7:00 p.m.

Monday, August 29

6:00 a.m.: Hurricane Katrina makes landfall in Plaquemines Parish as a Category 3 hurricane. Initial reports indicate that much of New Orleans has been spared the worst.

9:12 a.m.: The National Weather Service issues a flash flood warning due to a reported breach along the Industrial Canal in the Lower Ninth Ward.

11:00 a.m.: The New Orleans EOC receives a report of a levee breach along the 17th Street Canal.

During a noontime video teleconference, FEMA Director Michael Brown cautions against easing up, but participants express confidence that the situation is largely under control. Governor Blanco acknowledges reports of levees either breaching or topping over, but states that she does not believe this to be the case.

5:00 p.m.: Marty Bahamonde, the only FEMA official to remain in New Orleans during the storm, tours the area by helicopter. He observes serious flooding caused by a breach in the 17th Street Canal.

6:00 p.m.: The DHS Homeland Security Operations Center (HSOC) reports that there is no indication of levee breaching, despite intelligence to the contrary. HSOC notes, however, that a final assessment is still pending.

10:30 p.m.: The HSOC completes a spot report that incorporates Bahamonde's observations regarding breaching and widespread flooding. Few DHS officials, however, recollect seeing the report that night.

Throughout the night, water continues to pour into New Orleans, threatening the remaining residents. The up to 15,000 people at the Superdome endure squalid conditions, while those remaining in their homes rush to their attics and rooftops to escape the rising water.

Tuesday, August 30

12:02 a.m.: The HSOC spot report arrives at the White House Situation Room. But it is unclear when and by whom the report is received.

6:30 a.m.: White House officials receive an updated situation report from HSOC and finally conclude that the levees have been breached.

By morning, most of New Orleans is under water. City government and emergency services are seriously hampered by damage to the power and communication systems.

New Orleans Fire and Police, along with area fishermen, the Louisiana Department of Wildlife and Fisheries (DWF), and the U.S. Coast Guard conduct search and rescue efforts. Rescued residents are dropped off on overpasses and other pockets of dry land and left to wait for further assistance. Others are brought to the Superdome, where conditions prove unbearable.

Mayor Nagin opens the Ernest N. Morial Convention Center as an additional shelter.

Governor Blanco seeks to contact President Bush to request extensive federal resources. She fails to reach him, but speaks with Andrew Card, White House chief of staff, and Frances Fragos Townsend, White House homeland security advisor. The conversation proves unproductive. (Later in the day, the White House announces that President Bush will cut short his vacation and return to Washington.)

Mayor Nagin asks Governor Blanco's office for help in obtaining buses for evacuating residents stranded in the city.

In the evening, Secretary Chertoff designates Katrina an incident of national significance, triggering a series of additional response measures, including the appointment of a principal federal official (PFO). Chertoff designates Michael Brown as the PFO, despite his already serving as FEMA director.

Also in the evening, Lt. Gen. Russel Honoré is appointed commander of Joint Task Force Katrina in Camp Shelby, Mississippi. He is charged with overseeing all active-duty military forces involved in the response to Katrina.

Wednesday, August 31

Conditions worsen for residents still stranded in New Orleans, especially at the convention center, where 20,000 people have gathered, despite there being no food, water, or security presence.

Residents and officials, including Mayor Nagin and Police Chief Compass, relate horrific stories of lawlessness and violence to the media. Many of the reports later prove to be erroneous, but they add to a sense of fear and complicate rescue efforts.

Mayor Nagin orders police officers to focus on preventing looting, but it becomes apparent that the police force is in disarray, with dozens of officers having left the city. Governor Blanco subsequently announces the deployment of 200 state police troopers and 350 Louisiana National Guardsmen to help with law enforcement in New Orleans.

Governor Blanco signs an order allowing the state to commandeer buses after some school districts refuse to supply vehicles to New Orleans.

FEMA formally requests buses form the U.S. Department of Transportation. (Governor Blanco had reportedly asked Michael Brown and Andrew Card for transportation resources as early as Monday.)

Thursday, September 1

Even though Wal-Mart trucks deliver food, water, and other supplies to the city, there are continued delays of similar federal deliveries.

Television footage documents the miserable conditions at the convention center. Mayor Nagin pleads on CNN for help, declaring, "This is a desperate SOS."

Hospitals and other health-care facilities also endure horrendous conditions. Failing to reach city or state officials, the chief of trauma at Charity Hospital calls a news conference begging for aid.

In an afternoon radio interview, Mayor Nagin lambastes federal officials for their failure to effectively respond. He compares the severity of Katrina to 9/11.

Efforts to involve the Department of Defense (DOD) take shape, as FEMA officials discuss obtaining the DOD's help with logistics and supplies. The Pentagon agrees to provide the requested support (formal arrangements are not completed until Saturday, September 3).

With the assistance of newly arrived National Guard troops, the evacuation of the Superdome begins in the evening.

Friday, September 2

President Bush arrives in New Orleans and meets with Governor Blanco, Mayor Nagin, and other officials. Nagin unsuccessfully pressures the governor and president to set aside their differences regarding the command of National Guard forces. He also suggests that Honoré be given command of all troops, including the National Guard. That evening, the White House proposes to Blanco that Honoré command all troops but report to Blanco in the context of the National Guard forces and to the president in the context of active-duty military.

The convention center is secured in the afternoon. Shortly thereafter, food, water, and other supplies begin arriving.

Saturday, September 3

In the morning, the evacuation of the convention center begins. It is completed by 6:00 p.m. that night. Residents who had been stranded on overpasses are evacuated throughout the day.

In a conversation with Andrew Card, Governor Blanco, with the support of Lt. Gen. Steven Blum, chief of the National Guard Bureau, rejects the president's proposal regarding troop command.

Secretary of Defense Rumsfeld overrules the objections of military leaders at Northern Command and allows for the deployment of active-duty forces to assist with response efforts.

Sunday, September 4
With most residents now evacuated and supply chains beginning to function, order is slowly restored to the city.

Monday, September 5
The massive 17th Street Canal breach is plugged and crews move on to repair the London Street Canal breach.

Friday, September 9
Michael Brown is relieved of his Katrina-related duties. He resigns from his post as director of FEMA just a few days later.

2 SARS in Toronto (A): Emergency Response System under Duress

Pamela Varley

The novel consequences of Hurricane Katrina were glaringly apparent soon after they occurred (although there was some delay in recognizing that the levees had broken). Katrina was a sudden crisis. Little or no doubt existed that extraordinary conditions were faced.

What happens, however, when the novel features of a crisis are not visible at the outset or soon thereafter? How do the challenges and tasks of responders differ when novel circumstances manifest themselves gradually rather than suddenly? Are there special features of a situation when responders initially think they are dealing with a routine emergency and thus lag considerably in perceiving that they face what we call an emergent crisis? Does this kind of situation require a different type of response than a routine emergency demands? If so, are there any unusual difficulties in switching from one mode of operation to another as the true conditions are discovered and appreciated?

In the following case study of Toronto's 2003 epidemic of severe acute respiratory syndrome (soon known worldwide as SARS), the medical community of the city misperceived the incipient epidemic as a routine wave of common influenza. Because it was more contagious than ordinary flu, however, SARS began to spread from patient to patient and among staff members within the hospital where the first patients came for emergency care. Soon it spread to other health-care institutions, carried by transferred patients. The delay in recognizing that they were dealing with something different—indeed new—put the Toronto medical community behind the curve in dealing with the very difficult demands of the SARS epidemic.

Not only was discovering how to deal with a new disease like SARS difficult in medical and scientific terms, but it was also very problematic to deal with the problem in the highly decentralized health-care system. In Canada, as in the United States, the health-care delivery system is a mixture of private and public institutions and personnel, loosely connected in routine service delivery and financially but not ordinarily ready and able to act in concert to deal with exigent circumstances. SARS, however, demanded urgent and coordinated action from health-care institutions throughout the system—small or large, well- or ill-equipped—to deal with this new disease. This required a good deal of improvisation—invention of new medical and organizational procedures; methods of coordinating; ways of dealing with resource and capacity shortages; and outreach across jurisdictional, government-level, and international boundaries.

This is an abridged version of a case written by Pamela Varley, case writer at the John F. Kennedy School of Government, Harvard University, for Arnold M. Howitt, executive director, Taubman Center for State and Local Government, Harvard University. It was funded by the National Preparedness Leadership Initiative, a project of the Centers for Disease Control and Prevention, U.S. Department of Health and Human Services, and by a grant from the Robert Wood Johnson Foundation. Kennedy School of Government Case Program C16-05-1792.0, C16-05-1793.0, and C16-05-1793.1. Copyright © 2005, 2007 by the President and Fellows of Harvard College.

Most of the public health professionals who had to deal with SARS had not previously considered themselves "first responders" like police, firefighters, or emergency medical technicians. But the circumstances of the SARS epidemic required that they learn how to function in a crisis, a mode of operation far different from what they normally experienced and how they were best equipped to perform. As the crisis stretched out over weeks and months, they also found that an extended crisis places enormous strains on any system and requires outside assistance and new ways of operating to meet the extraordinary demands of the crisis.

Discussion Questions

- What challenges for operational capacity did Toronto's SARS crisis create for the region's public health and hospital systems? In what ways were these challenges similar to and different from those created in the aftermath of Hurricane Katrina?
- How did the SARS crisis affect nonhealth emergency responders?
- What should jurisdictions outside the Toronto area have been doing as Toronto's SARS crisis deepened?
- What implications does Toronto's experience with SARS have for jurisdictions preparing for future incidents of emergent infectious disease or contagious agents loosed by bioterrorists?

When, on February 23, 2003, the severe acute respiratory syndrome (SARS) virus slipped into Toronto's Pearson International Airport aboard a commercial flight from Hong Kong, the illness was known only as a mysterious and virulent pneumonia[1] that was spreading in Mainland China's Guangdong Province. The person who unwittingly brought the disease to Toronto—setting off an outbreak that would infect 375[2] and kill 44—was a 78-year-old Toronto grandmother, Kwan Sui-chu, returning home from a 10-day trip to Hong Kong with her husband.[3] Two days after their return, Kwan began to feel sick. On February 28, she went to a doctor. But public health officials did not learn that the mystery pneumonia had entered their city until March 13. By that time, five other members of Kwan's family

---

[1] Pneumonia is not a single disease but a category of diseases. These diseases share symptoms—inflammation of the lungs and the collection of fluid in air passages—but these symptoms have a variety of causes.

[2] Because there was no definitive test to diagnose SARS, public health physicians labeled cases as "probable SARS" or "suspect SARS" (and in Ontario, there was a third category: "persons under investigation") based on clinical, laboratory, and epidemiological evidence. The convention, internationally, was to count only the probable cases for official record-keeping purposes. Thus, there were 375 probable SARS cases in the Toronto area between February and June 2003. Within the Toronto city limits, there were 199 probable SARS cases and 38 deaths.

[3] Official government documents about the SARS outbreak keep the names of all SARS patients and their relatives confidential. Local reporters were able to find out some of the names, however. In this case study, names are used, for the sake of clarity, if they have already been made public by the press.

Exhibit 2A-1   Acronyms

AIDS	acquired immunodeficiency syndrome
BiPAP	bilevel positive airway pressure
BLD	Bukas-Loob Sa Diyos Covenant Community
CDC	U.S. Centers for Disease Control and Prevention
ER	emergency room
GTA	Greater Toronto area
ICS	Incident Command System
ICU	intensive care unit
iPHIS	Integrated Public Health Information System
MAG	ministry action group
POC	Provincial Operations Centre
ProMED	Programs for Monitoring Emerging Diseases
PUIs	persons under investigation
SAC	Science Advisory Committee
SARS	severe acute respiratory syndrome
TB	tuberculosis
TPH	Toronto Public Health
WHO	World Health Organization

were visibly sick. Unbeknownst to public health or hospital staff, the virus had also spread to a group of patients and health-care workers at one of Toronto's community hospitals. By the time this group fell sick, the virus had moved on, silently infecting a new set of victims.

The Emergence of SARS

SARS made its quiet arrival in Toronto, Canada's largest city and its economic center, 3 weeks before the World Health Organization (WHO) officially identified the disease as something new and distinct from known types of pneumonia. (For a complete list of acronyms used in this case, see Exhibit 2A-1.) Public health experts later observed that it was Toronto's bad luck to be part of the first small cluster of SARS cases exported from China. Although SARS traveled via passenger jets to many cities around the world in the course of the outbreak, its arrival in most of these places came days or weeks later, giving them time to prepare. By contrast, SARS had killed two people and infected between twelve and twenty[4] others in Toronto before WHO issued its first global alert about the disease on March 12.

---

[4]These figures assume that SARS patients who had become symptomatic by March 16 or March 17 had been infected March 12 or earlier. The incubation period for the virus ranged from 1 to 12 days in Toronto, but the statistical average was 4.7 days. Jim Young, Ontario's public safety commissioner and, later, the co-chair of the province's emergency response to SARS, suspects that the number of people infected by March 12 was greater than twenty, but there is no way to know for certain.

The Chinese-Canadian Community

This is not to say that no one in Canada had been aware of the mystery illness before then. As early as January 2003, Chinese enclaves in Vancouver and Toronto had been hearing about the deadly new disease from panicky relatives in Mainland China.[5] And in early February, Toronto's *Sing Tao Daily,* a Chinese language newspaper, posited that an infected person from Asia might bring the disease to Canada. After all, tens of thousands of people traveled from Asia to Toronto's Pearson Airport every month. But Health Canada, the country's massive federal health agency, assured *Sing Tao* that the agency was on top of the situation and was "closely monitoring the spread of pneumonia" diseases globally.[6]

WHO, for its part, had been receiving unofficial reports of the virulent disease for a number of weeks. An e-mail message received on February 10, 2003, reported that more than one hundred people had died of the illness in a single week in Guangdong Province, where panic had become widespread. The Chinese Ministry of Health had previously refused to acknowledge the existence of the mystery disease, but on February 11, 2003, it notified WHO that an acute respiratory syndrome of unknown origin had struck the province. The official statistics, however, were far less dire than the rumors. The disease had killed five people, according to the Ministry, and infected another three hundred. Later, Chinese authorities acknowledged that these figures represented a significant undercount.

SARS Enters the Hospital System

The story of SARS's spread to Toronto began on February 21, when Dr. Liu Jianlun, a semi-retired respiratory specialist, flew to Hong Kong to attend his nephew's wedding. Liu, who had been treating severely ill pneumonia patients in Guangdong Province, had been bothered by respiratory symptoms for 5 days before his trip to Hong Kong, but paid them little heed. After checking into the Metropole Hotel, however, his condition dramatically worsened. The following day, he checked himself into a nearby hospital, where he died 10 days later, on March 4. But during his few hours in the Metropole, Liu had infected nine other hotel guests, including Kwan.[7]

Meanwhile, on February 25, 2 days after Kwan and her husband returned to the Toronto apartment they shared with their two grown sons, daughter-in-law, and 5-year-old grandson, Kwan developed a fever, sore throat, cough, and aches. On February 28, she went to see her primary care physician, who diagnosed flu, prescribed antibiotics, and sent her home.

---

[5]The first known case of SARS—thought to have crossed the species line from an animal—occurred in Guangdong province in November 2002. Most of the world's new infectious diseases originate in this part of China.

[6]The information in this paragraph is drawn from "SARS: Behind the Mask," CBS News Online, November 19, 2003.

[7]Carolyn Abraham, "How a Deadly Disease Made Its Way to Canada," *Globe & Mail,* March 29, 2003, A1.

But Kwan soon began to have trouble breathing, and on March 5, she died at home, tended by family. Because she had a history of heart disease, the local coroner identified her cause of death as a heart attack.

Following Kwan's death, her 38-year-old daughter, Cora, who was feeling unwell herself, became greatly concerned about her 43-year-old brother, Tse Chi Kwai, who had been their mother's primary caretaker during her illness. For several days, Tse had struggled with fever, cough, and respiratory symptoms. Although he had gone twice to see a doctor and was taking antibiotics, he was getting rapidly worse. Two days after the death of their mother, Cora persuaded him to seek medical care at a nearby community hospital, Scarborough-Grace.

The young triage nurse at the Scarborough-Grace Emergency Department took one look at Tse—feverish, shaky, and gasping for breath—and immediately escorted him into the emergency room (ER), which was, per usual, overwhelmed and understaffed.[8] The ER doctor recommended that Tse be hospitalized, but there were no beds available in the inpatient hospital wards—also a commonplace circumstance. Consequently, the ER staff moved Tse to the observation unit of the Emergency Department, where he spent the night on a gurney, just a few feet from other patients, some of them elderly. To ease his difficulty breathing, the ER staff placed a noninvasive BiPAP (bilevel positive airway pressure) ventilator over Tse's face. The BiPAP's forced air helped Tse to breathe but also probably aerosolized his virus-laden respiratory droplets, thereby dispersing them across a wider area.

Emergency Room Infection Controls

Later, these actions would face scrutiny. Why had a seriously ill pneumonia patient been placed so close to other patients? And why had BiPAP been used on an infectious patient lying chock-a-block with other patients in a confined area?

But the way the Scarborough-Grace ER handled Tse's case was characteristic of ER practices citywide. Many ERs had become the densely populated holding areas for patients; in some instances, a patient might have to spend up to 3–4 days on a gurney in an ER hallway before a bed became available. Moreover, there was generally very little space in the ER for isolating infectious patients, especially those with pneumonia, which was extremely common and, for the most part, easily treatable. And because pneumonia was, in general, not terribly contagious, hospital workers were not required to use special precautions or barrier infection controls (masks, goggles, gowns, and gloves) when treating pneumonia patients. Putting on and taking off such items was time-consuming. Wearing them was thought to be alienating to patients and, for staff, cumbersome and uncomfortable. Masks, in particular, caused breathing difficulties, dizziness, and rashes for many wearers. Even the most basic

---

[8]Romesh Ratnesar, Hannah Beech, and Steven Frank, "Tale of Two Countries," *Time* magazine, May 5, 2003, available at www.time.com/time/magazine/article/0,9171,1004759-5,00.html (accessed on August 27, 2008).

precautions against spreading infection, such as frequent hand washing, tended to be a low priority in the hectic ER atmosphere.

Dr. Brian Schwartz, director of prehospital care at Toronto's Sunnybrook & Women's College Health Sciences Centre, who played a key role in the response to the SARS outbreak, believes health-care workers should always wear masks when treating patients with febrile respiratory illness. He argues that medical workers have grown dangerously blasé about infection control, an attitude that may date to the eradication of smallpox in the western hemisphere in 1971 and U.S. Surgeon General William Stewart's declaration a year earlier that the nation was "ready to close the book on infectious disease as a major health threat." [9] According to Schwartz, anyone who seemed overly concerned about infection control risked eye rolling from colleagues. In the case of blood, that attitude had changed with the advent of acquired immunodeficiency syndrome (AIDS) in the 1980s. But "as an international medical community, we became very complacent with respect to respiratory illnesses, except in pockets where you might have TB (tuberculosis)," he says. "We [developed] an air of invincibility that is unwarranted." [10]

The ramifications of this attitude have been far-reaching, according to infection-control experts. For one, a generation of hospital emergency departments was designed and maintained with little regard for infection control. Allison McGeer, director of infection control at Toronto's Mt. Sinai Hospital, told a reporter that this state of affairs gave the SARS virus its first real opening in Toronto. "We could have gotten away without the full outbreak," she said, "if we had emergency departments that had higher air speeds of ventilation and negative air pressure,[11] if we had single rooms in our [ER] observation areas, if we had adequate hand washing facilities and training—and *time* for people to wash their hands." [12]

Public Health in Toronto and Ontario

In Canada, the primary responsibility for controlling infectious diseases belonged to local government. In Ontario alone, that meant thirty-seven local public health units, each governed by a medical officer of health[13] and a local health board. These included the nationally respected Toronto Public Health (TPH), Canada's largest public health agency.

---

[9]Commission to Investigate the Introduction and Spread of SARS in Ontario, *Interim Report: SARS and Public Health in Ontario* (Toronto, 2004), 35.

[10]Interview with Dr. Brian Schwartz, director of prehospital care at Toronto's Sunnybrook & Women's College Health Sciences Centre, 2004. Unless noted, subsequent quotations from Schwartz are also from this interview.

[11]*Negative air pressure* refers to a system by which the air in a room is sucked out, and fresh air pumped in, at a rapid rate.

[12]Quoted in *Toronto Observer,* October 22, 2003.

[13]In the United States, the administrators who lead local, state, or federal public health agencies typically have a masters-level professional degree but need not be medical doctors. In Canada, by contrast, public health—like neurology or pediatrics—is a medical specialty. Thus, the leaders of Canada's public health agencies at all levels of government are generally public health doctors.

Communicable disease control had once stood at the center of TPH's activities. Over time, however, it had moved to the side to make room for health promotion and disease-prevention programs, reflecting changes in the public health field at large.

TPH's Communicable Disease Control division employed 300 of TPH's 1,700 employees and was still the agency's largest single division. It received 40,000 communicable disease reports and oversaw three hundred minor disease outbreaks annually, each generally controlled in 2 or 3 days. But when SARS hit, the division lacked the legal authority or the staff resources to promote compliance with Ontario's minimum mandatory infection-control requirements in institutional settings such as hospitals and long-term care facilities.[14] Moreover, there had historically been few well-developed relationships between the TPH and the hospitals' infection-control staffs.[15]

It was not clear what role the Ontario Public Health Department (a division of the provincial Ministry for Health and Long-term Care) was supposed to play in the event of a communicable disease emergency. Some public health experts were under the impression that if an outbreak overwhelmed the resources of the local public health unit or if it spread beyond the boundaries of a single local jurisdiction, the provincial Public Health Department was supposed to take charge.

But Ontario Public Health was small (TPH was fifteen times larger) and by reputation weak, in terms of its statutory authority, its resources, and the skill level of its staff. Ontario Public Health was not widely viewed as a helpful or galvanizing force in Ontario by the local medical officers of health, nor was it held in high esteem in the public health field outside Ontario. Several of Ontario's medical officers of health later reported that they had long found the agency resistant to sharing information with the field and to approaching issues in an open, collegial fashion. As a result, relations between Ontario Public Health and the public health units were generally wary and strained at the moment that Tse walked into the Scarborough-Grace Emergency Department on that fateful Friday, March 7.

Is It Tuberculosis?

On Saturday, March 8, after Tse had spent 12 hours on an emergency room gurney, his condition was visibly declining and he was placed in the Scarborough-Grace intensive care unit (ICU). ICU Director Sandy Finkelstein examined the patient later that day, noting that Tse was dangerously ill and that his mother, who had also been sick with respiratory symptoms, had just died. Finkelstein was puzzled by Tse's condition, but his first instinct was to check

---

[14]In fact, Toronto's largest teaching hospitals had significant resources and had more infection-control expertise than TPH itself did.

[15]This had just begun to change in late 2002, when TPH established the Pandemic Influenza Steering Committee that included representatives from the hospital-infection control field. These burgeoning new relationships, according to Dr. Barbara Yaffe, then director of the TPH Communicable Disease Control, proved valuable during the SARS outbreak.

for the possibility of tuberculosis (TB), an illness common in Tse's Toronto neighborhood of Scarborough, home to many immigrants. The doctor ordered TB tests and immediately moved Tse to an isolation room in the intensive care unit.[16]

By this point, Kwan's husband, Tse's wife, and Tse's two siblings all had fevers, coughs, and labored breathing. Finkelstein ordered x-rays for the four, checking for TB. As a matter of protocol, the Scarborough-Grace Hospital notified TPH of a possible TB cluster within a family on March 9. This raised no special alarm—some 400 TB cases are reported in Toronto each year—and TPH referred the case to its TB unit for investigation and follow-up, the usual procedure.

Although Finkelstein's TB concern proved wrong, it had been a lucky instinct that he pursued it. Even a remote chance of TB—unlike pneumonia—required the isolation of the patient and the use of special infection-control precautions by health-care workers and visitors. As a result, hospital staff, other patients, and visitors were all much better protected from SARS once Finkelstein had made his tentative diagnosis and moved Tse into an isolated room. Meanwhile, members of the TPH staff asked the rest of Tse's extended family to stay home until the tentative TB diagnosis was either confirmed or ruled out, to avoid spreading it to others.

Or Is It Bird Flu?

On Monday, March 10, Agnes Wong, a nurse and patient care manager in the Scarborough-Grace ICU, returned to work after an off-duty weekend. During her days off, she had enjoyed a favorite pastime, reading Chinese language newspapers. One story in particular had haunted her, that of a young family in Hong Kong that had contracted avian flu during an early 2003 visit to Fujian Province.

On returning to work, Wong learned about Tse, who was extremely sick with a tentative diagnosis of TB. "Somehow I connected this event with the other event I'd read about in Hong Kong," Wong later told a *Toronto Sun* reporter. "I asked the nurse to check their traveling history." When Wong learned that Tse's just-deceased mother had, in fact, recently returned from Hong Kong, she became more and more persuaded that Tse's illness might be bird flu. Wong took her hunch to Finkelstein and the hospital's infection-control division.[17]

As Tse's condition worsened, Finkelstein considered what other disease he and his family might have contracted, including bird flu. Certainly from a clinical perspective, Tse's illness appeared to be progressing far too quickly to be TB. What's more, the Vancouver Public Health Department was now reporting a mysterious respiratory case too. Vancouver's patient had also stayed at the Metropole Hotel in Hong Kong.[18]

---

[16]Tanya Talaga and Kevin Donovan, "Why SARS Alert Was Late," *Toronto Star,* September 22, 2003, A1.

[17]Quotations and information from Michele Mandel, "Our Christmas Angels: Mandel Grace ICU Doc Isolated First SARS Case," *Toronto Sun,* December 21, 2003, 36.

[18]The patient recovered, and the disease did not spread to anyone else.

The WHO Alert

On Wednesday, March 12, WHO issued a global alert about outbreaks of atypical pneumonia[19] in Viet Nam, Hong Kong, and Guangdong Province. It appeared that the same disease had broken out in all three locations, but even this much was uncertain. Only sketchy information was available from public health authorities in mainland China, but in Hanoi and Hong Kong, there had been significant outbreaks of the respiratory syndrome among health-care workers in hospitals treating patients with the disease. In Hanoi, twenty hospital staff had become sick, and in Hong Kong, twenty-six had developed fever and respiratory symptoms.

Traditionally, information about a WHO alert passed through several levels of government to medical practitioners in Canada. WHO notified the federal government, which notified state or provincial governments, which notified local jurisdictions, which notified local hospitals and doctors. In addition, some local officials and doctors might see word of the WHO alert on television or in the newspaper. But some Toronto doctors say they first learned of the WHO alert from ProMED (Programs for Monitoring Emerging Diseases), a relatively new Internet service that disseminated infectious disease alerts to an international network of subscribers. The ProMED subscribers received word of the WHO alert on the evening of March 12. This was faster than the traditional news media could manage, and much faster than the traditional government chain of communication. Doctors and other health experts on the front lines of the SARS battle came to rely on ProMED to learn the most current information about the disease and the outbreak.

Toronto Goes Public

On Thursday, March 13, the day after the WHO alert, Tse died of respiratory failure at Scarborough-Grace. When Tse's younger brother and sister arrived to view his body, hospital staff were appalled at how sick they both appeared and sent them directly to the Scarborough-Grace Emergency Department. An Emergency Department physician placed a call to Andrew Simor, microbiologist-in-chief at Sunnybrook and Women's College Health Sciences Centre, and asked whether Sunnybrook had an isolation room free and could take one of the Tse siblings. Simor agreed, and—mindful of the WHO alert—stipulated that the patients go straight into an isolation room upon arrival.[20]

In the meantime, Finkelstein's TB tests for Tse and his family came back negative. Finkelstein phoned Allison McGeer, director of Mt. Sinai's Infectious Disease Department, the largest in the area. McGeer agreed to admit Tse's sister, as well as his young widow and

---

[19]*Atypical pneumonia* refers to a subset of pneumonia diseases marked by a particularly rapid onset and severity of symptoms.

[20]*Globe & Mail*, March 29, 2003.

baby.[21] Kwan's husband, too, was sick by this point, and he was soon admitted to Mt. Sinai as well.

Late Thursday afternoon, Simor, McGeer, and Irving Salit, director of the Infectious Disease Division of the University Health Network, held a teleconference to discuss treatment for the new patients. The first two Toronto residents to contract this virulent pneumonia had both died. Now there were four more cases, three of them critical. They decided on an aggressive course of treatment—a complement of three broad-spectrum antibiotics and two anti-virals.

After a teleconference with McGeer Thursday night, the Toronto and Ontario Public Health departments decided to hold a press conference on Friday night, March 14, to inform the public about the cluster of cases and to urge anyone who had been in contact with the family or had suspicious symptoms to call a TPH hotline, which TPH hastily established Saturday morning. McGeer also notified Health Canada, the U.S. Centers for Disease Control and Prevention (CDC), and WHO.

The Race to Understand SARS

In Hong Kong, meanwhile, tests run to determine whether the new outbreak of atypical pneumonia was actually an incarnation of the old bird flu virus had come back negative, as did tests for several other recognized types of atypical pneumonia. That meant the disease was new and its cause was unknown. Health officials knew it was crucial to identify it as quickly as possible. Without knowing the cause, it was impossible to make a definitive diagnosis, develop vaccines to fend off the disease, or design better medicines to treat it.

WHO moved quickly. On Saturday, March 15, the organization named the disease severe acute respiratory syndrome (SARS) and declared it "a worldwide threat." It also announced criteria for identifying a probable or suspect SARS case.[22] In addition, WHO set up a network of eleven leading laboratories in nine countries to expedite the discovery of the SARS causative agent and to develop an accurate diagnostic test. In parallel, an international network was set up to pool clinical knowledge of the symptoms, diagnosis, and management of SARS. A third network was established to study SARS epidemiology.

In Toronto, Dr. Donald Low, Mt. Sinai's microbioligst-in-chief, made sure Tse was autopsied. He then gathered and sent as many disease specimens as possible from the autopsy and

---

[21]The baby was not sick, which created a dilemma—what should be done with the child when there were, at the moment, no healthy adults in the family to take care of him? As a stopgap measure, Mt. Sinai admitted the child "for observation."

[22]If WHO was to keep track of a disease worldwide, it was important that everyone use the same definitions. Even though WHO did not have the authority to require other countries to use the WHO definitions, most countries did use the WHO definition or a close variation.

from Tse's ill relatives to the Ontario provincial laboratory, the National Microbiology Laboratory in Winnipeg, and the CDC's laboratory in the United States. Mt. Sinai's infectious disease research group collected detailed clinical information about the signs and symptoms of the disease in Toronto's six cases. On Sunday night, March 16, Mt. Sinai sent these clinical data to ProMED and sent a copy to the CDC. "So as of Sunday night, we had the feeling we were doing a pretty good job," says Low. "Things were going along tickety-boo." [23]

The Lull before the Storm

As of Saturday, March 15, there was still no discussion within Toronto's infectious disease and public health circles that SARS might sweep through Toronto's hospital workers, as it had in Hong Kong and Hanoi. When told of a large SARS outbreak among patients and health-care workers at Hong Kong's Prince of Wales hospital, Low assumed there had been an egregious breach of safety precautions and infection-control standards.

Over the next few days, this confident mood held steady, but there were a few worrisome developments. First, a primary care physician who had seen Tse and his wife for about 15 minutes in an outpatient clinic was now home sick with pneumonia. She was quickly diagnosed with SARS and hospitalized. Second, on Sunday, March 16, Joseph Pollack, 76, came to the Scarborough-Grace Hospital ER for the third time in 10 days, this time very sick and gasping for breath. He had first come to the ER on March 7 with heart arrhythmia. A few days later, he returned with a fever and pneumonia, but was not deemed sick enough for hospitalization and was sent home. Upon arrival on March 16, however, he was immediately placed in an isolation room in the ICU. The ER staff checked his recent history and ascertained that on March 7, Pollack had spent 12 hours lying on a gurney next to Tse. "So now we've got another case that's outside the family, and evidence of transmission in the hospital setting, which is a bit more disconcerting," says Low. After all, he adds, "We were trying to wrap this thing *up*."

In Retrospect, a Crucial Juncture

After the fact, some critics remarked that if the Scarborough-Grace Hospital had temporarily isolated itself at this point, the magnitude of the SARS outbreak in Toronto would have been vastly reduced. Richard Schabas, chief-of-staff at York Central Hospital and Ontario's former chief medical officer of health, puts it this way: "One of the things you would

---

[23]Interview with Dr. Donald Low, microbioligst-in-chief, Mt. Sinai Hospital, Toronto, 2004. Unless noted, subsequent quotations from Low are also from this interview.

think you would do in a situation like that . . . is you would put a wall around that hospital. At the very least, you'd stop transferring patients from that hospital to other hospitals."[24]

A sharply critical *Toronto Star* article, written several months after the SARS outbreak, echoed this sentiment, noting that in a similar situation a hospital in Hanoi had closed immediately. Hanoi's outbreak was limited to 63 cases and 5 deaths, compared to the Toronto area's 375 cases and 44 deaths.[25]

Hindsight is always 20/20, counter the decision makers who were on the scene at the time. All that had apparently happened at Scarborough-Grace, by that point, was that SARS had passed in the ER from Tse to an elderly and susceptible man lying right next to him. It wasn't a good thing, but it didn't indicate a virus running amok, either.

Moreover, closing a hospital is tantamount to declaring the hospital too overwhelmed to continue its normal functions. In addition to the stigma, it is very expensive for a hospital to curtail its revenues in this way, and many Ontario hospitals were already running significantly in the red.[26] A hospital shutdown also cuts off an avenue of medical care from many patients. Emergency patients have to go to another hospital. Patients already in the hospital can no longer enjoy the visits of family members and friends. Patients who require specialized care can no longer be transferred to the appropriate facility. In other words, a hospital shutdown is disruptive and inconvenient to staff, doctors, patients, and patients' families.

Health-Care Workers in Trouble

By Thursday, March 20, however, things took an abrupt turn for the worse. Scarborough-Grace nurses and hospital workers began to straggle into the Scarborough-Grace Emergency Department complaining of high fevers. The following day, March 21, Pollack died—the city's third SARS fatality. With Scarborough-Grace workers continuing to turn up at the hospital ER, there was an active discussion in Toronto about whether Scarborough-Grace should close. The hospital management resisted closing completely, but it did shut down its Emergency Department and intensive care unit to new patients. That evening, hospital staff began appearing at the ERs of other Toronto hospitals and in the hospitals of neighboring jurisdictions. By Sunday, March 23, twelve members of the Scarborough-Grace staff had been diagnosed with probable SARS.

On Sunday, under growing pressure from the Ontario Health Ministry, Scarborough-Grace closed altogether. At the same time, Toronto Medical Officer of Health Sheela Basrur

---

[24]Interview with Dr. Richard Schabas, chief-of-staff, York Central Hospital, and former chief medical officer of health for the Province of Ontario, 2004. Unless noted, subsequent quotations from Schabas are also from this interview.

[25]Kevin Donovan, "Crucial SARS Experts Fail To Testify," *Toronto Star,* October 5, 2003, A1.

[26]Karen Palmer, "Hospital Crisis Feared," *Toronto Star,* June 21, 2003, B2.

and her executive team issued a public appeal to all hospital staff and all other people who had visited Scarborough-Grace Hospital on or after March 16 to (1) contact the TPH and (2) put themselves in self-quarantine for a period of 10 days from the date of their most recent exposure to the hospital. "We recognized that that was a pretty broad sweep, a big extension of quarantine—that it might affect thousands of people," says Basrur. "But I think at the outset, given the tremendous number of unknowns we were facing, it was the only reasonable thing to do." [27]

Compounding the problems was the fact that there were very few hospital isolation rooms available. In general, Toronto's hospitals ran very close to full capacity, which allowed for almost no surge capacity in an emergency; the need for isolation rooms made the problem that much harder. No one knew what the magnitude of the SARS outbreak would be at its peak. Hospital-based infectious disease doctors McGeer and Simor began to discuss the dramatic possibility of calling in the military to set up a mobile hospital where all the SARS patients in the city could be treated. But on Sunday, the West Park rehabilitation and long-term-care facility offered at least a temporary solution—it would revive its twenty-five-bed TB hospital, long shut down, to create a SARS facility. With help from staff at Scarborough-Grace and Mt. Sinai hospitals, West Park readied the facility in less than 6 hours—a feat likened to a miracle. There was a catch, however. Collective bargaining agreements precluded hospital workers from being transferred to the facility against their will. By this time, doctors, nurses, and other hospital workers were very frightened of catching SARS, and West Park was able to find enough staff to care for only fourteen patients.

Could the spread of SARS have been anticipated? In retrospect, physicians realized that there had been some intimations of coming trouble earlier in the week, but no one had picked up on them. Low, for instance, recalls that on Tuesday, March 18, while visiting Scarborough-Grace, a nurse had remarked to him that Pollack's 73-year-old wife, Rose, was running a fever. "I remember thinking 'Well, that's not good,'" Low says, but, on the other hand, many things could explain a fever. Rose Pollack was not suffering any respiratory symptoms, the sine qua non of the SARS illness. The following day, another nurse casually remarked to Low that she herself, who rarely fell sick, had run a fever the night before but it had broken and now she felt fine. This remark, too, made him vaguely uneasy, but, after all, hadn't the nurse said she was fine? "These things just didn't gel at that time. It was still early," he says; then he adds, "In outbreaks, there's quite a denial component. The psychology is really to try to minimize it. You're trying to say, 'We've got this under control.'"

---

[27]Interview with Dr. Sheela Basrur, Toronto Medical Officer of Health, 2004. Unless noted, subsequent quotations from Basrur are also from this interview.

Resurrecting an Age-Old Strategy: Quarantine

Before the illness that had killed Kwan and Tse had been identified as probable SARS, the TPH had informally tried to halt the spread of the disease by asking family members to stay home and avoid exposing others. But once the disease was tentatively identified as SARS, TPH and, in particular, its Communicable Disease Control Division had to face an uncomfortable fact. For the first time in decades, Toronto was confronting a disease of unknown biological cause that was potentially fatal and perhaps highly contagious and for which there was no immunization available and no cure. This meant that contemporary approaches to preventing the spread of contagious illness (immunizing against the flu, for example, or, in the case of AIDS, providing condoms, clean needles, and public education) would not be sufficient. Instead, TPH leaders, in line with recommendations from WHO, decided they must resort to the old-fashioned techniques of isolating those with probable or suspect SARS in the hospital (as the hospitals were already doing) and quarantining those who had been exposed to the disease.

Quarantine, however, had not been used in Toronto in at least 50 years—that is, not during the working lifetime of anyone presently working for TPH. The TPH leadership had to come up to speed quickly on how to run a quarantine program, train staff, and educate the public about why a quarantine was necessary and what it entailed.

The idea behind a quarantine was deceptively simple. When a person was diagnosed as a possible SARS case, the first task for the TPH was to determine how long the person had been infectious and then to review this infectious period with the patient (and sometimes with close family or friends). The goal was to get the patient to remember every place he or she had gone while infectious and every person with whom he or she had had sufficient contact to transmit the disease.[28] Then each of these exposed individuals was contacted and placed under quarantine for the incubation period of the disease (the length of time between infection and the first sign of symptoms). The incubation period was thought to be between 2 and 10 days for SARS. If no symptoms appeared after 10 days, the person was considered safe from contracting the disease at that point. If SARS symptoms did appear, the person was hospitalized in an isolation room. If indeterminate symptoms appeared— just a cough, for instance—the person remained in quarantine until the symptoms expanded to meet the criteria of SARS, disappeared, or took the shape of a recognizably different ailment. While under quarantine, the person had to remain home and avoid all contact with other household members. TPH's job was to call each person under quarantine daily to check on his or her health status and to ensure that the person was complying

---

[28]However, it was not clear how much contact was, in fact, sufficient. Overall, the disease behaved like a droplet-spread illness that needed quite close contact to spread, but in some anecdotal cases, it seemed to have spread with more remote contact, and scientists were not sure why.

with quarantine rules. Hospital workers who were considered contacts (but not close contacts) of a SARS patient were to be placed on work quarantine; this meant that they observed quarantine procedures at home, traveled alone to and from work, and followed full infection-control procedures at work.

A Snowballing Crisis

Between the morning and evening of March 26, the number of SARS cases suddenly shot up from eighteen to forty-nine. By Wednesday evening, every isolation room in the city was occupied; ten Scarborough-Grace staff members were awaiting hospital admission, and other sick hospital workers were at home, waiting to be seen.

That same day, Mt. Sinai Hospital doctors concluded that one of their ICU patients, a liver transplant recipient who had been transferred a day and a half earlier from Scarborough-Grace, almost certainly had SARS as well. For 31 hours, he had been treated at Mt. Sinai without infection-control precautions. As a consequence, Mt. Sinai announced that it would transfer the patient to Toronto General and close its Emergency Department and ICU for 10 days. All hospital workers who had been exposed to the patient were instructed to quarantine themselves. During Mt. Sinai's shutdown, the patient's doctor, seven health-care workers from the Mt. Sinai ICU, and six members of the patient's own family developed SARS symptoms. This was a serious blow given Mt. Sinai's leading role in infectious disease work and the desperate need for SARS hospital beds. Sunnybrook stepped into the breach and announced that it would convert forty standard hospital rooms to isolation rooms over the next 48 hours.

By this point, says Low, no one was denying that Toronto was in trouble. In fact, he and others now feared that SARS was a virulent and highly contagious disease. "I thought that it was only going to be a matter of time before it would spread out into the community in Toronto. Then it would be Ottawa, Hamilton—other communities," he explains. "I thought that at the end of the day, we'd be recognized as the epicenter for SARS in North America."

SARS in Toronto (B):
The Public Health Fight to Contain the Disease

On March 26, 2003, Ontario Premier Ernie Eves declared the severe acute respiratory syndrome (SARS) outbreak an emergency under the province's Emergency Management Act. Emergency responders launched an intensive effort to isolate everyone with the disease, to quarantine everyone who had been exposed to it, and to protect hospital workers from contracting it. After a month-long battle, culminating in a tense Easter-week vigil, the public health community heaved a collective sigh of relief, convinced that SARS was all but extinguished in Toronto. Unfortunately, they were wrong.

Ontario's Role

Between March 13 and March 26, Ontario Public Health and the larger Ontario Ministry of Health and Long-term Care, both headquartered in Toronto, were well aware of the SARS outbreak, but had played a backstage role in it. The ministry had leaned on the Scarborough-Grace Hospital to close on March 23 and had declared SARS a reportable illness under the province's Health Protection and Promotion Act on March 25. (This required hospitals and health-care providers to report any and all cases of SARS to their local public health department. It also allowed public health units to track infected people and issue isolation and quarantine orders to prevent the spread of the disease.) The ministry had also collected SARS data from Toronto Public Health (TPH) and public health units from several adjoining communities and had passed it on to Health Canada, which in turn passed it on to the World Health Organization (WHO). Once hospital workers began to come down with SARS, Colin D'Cunha, Ontario's chief medical officer of health and public health commissioner, began participating in a daily telephone conference with decision makers in the affected public health units and infectious disease experts from area hospitals.

On March 25, Ontario Public Safety Commissioner Jim Young, who believed he should be playing a role in the outbreak both as safety commissioner and as the province's chief coroner, asked D'Cunha if he might join these teleconferences, and D'Cunha readily agreed. Young had, in the past, managed such provincial emergencies as plane crashes, ice storms, and power failures. From this vantage point, what he heard made him nervous. Everybody was doing his or her best to think constructively about the problem, he says, but in his view, the group was neither bold enough nor quick enough in its decision making: "What you have to do in an emergency is—you have to have structure enough to make decisions quickly. You can't sit there and ponder decisions all day. You have to have a meeting, make decisions, let everybody go out and do them, and then have another meeting. . . . It seemed to me the situation was getting a whole lot worse, not better." [1] Not only was the number of people visibly sick with SARS growing, but also there was an unknown number of people infected but not yet symptomatic.

After sitting through a second group conference call the following day, Young suggested to D'Cunha that they urge their respective ministers (the solicitor general in Young's case, and the health minister in D'Cunha's) to advise Ontario Premier Ernie Eves to officially declare the outbreak an emergency, as per the Emergency Management Act. Doing so would give the province the flexibility to take swift and decisive action if necessary—for example, confining individuals who refused to abide by quarantine orders, closing down borders, commandeering buildings, and handing down orders to doctors and to hospitals. D'Cunha was quick to agree.

It did not prove difficult to persuade the solicitor general, the health minister, or Premier Eves to take this action. They were elected officials, laymen without expertise in infectious diseases. Faced with the spread of a mysterious, often fatal illness, no one wanted to under-react. Health Minister Tony Clement recalls thinking, "If they're going to accuse me of anything after this is over, it's better to say, 'He did too much' rather than 'He did too little.' So I was very quick with my recommendation to the Premier that we declare the state of emergency." [2]

Who's in Charge?

On March 26, Health Minister Clement announced that Premier Eves had formally declared the SARS outbreak an emergency. This automatically activated the Provincial Operations Centre (POC), a well-equipped central gathering area that facilitated information exchange and cooperative decision making among the twelve Ontario ministries deemed pertinent to the emergency at hand. But who should manage the emergency day by day and moment by moment?

All things being equal, this responsibility should have fallen to the Health and Long-term Care Ministry. But Allison Stuart, then director of the ministry's Hospitals Division, characterizes the ministry's emergency plan as "a patchwork quilt, with no overall sense of strategy." [3] Moreover, Stuart adds, although the ministry had created an internal *ministry action group* (MAG), which was to take action on behalf of the ministry in a crisis, it had never made

---

[1]Interview with Jim Young, Ontario public safety commissioner, 2004. Unless noted, subsequent quotations from Young are also from this interview.

[2]Interview with Hon. Tony Clement, minister of health, Province of Ontario, 2004. Unless, noted, subsequent quotations from Clement are also from this interview.

[3]Interview with Allison Stuart, director, Hospital Division, Health and Long-term Care Ministry, 2004. Unless noted, subsequent quotations from Stuart are also from this interview.

the group a priority. The MAG was, for the most part, made up of a rapidly changing stable of junior staff members, reluctantly pressed into service and uncertain what they were supposed to do. The MAG's meeting space—small, ill equipped, and located about a half hour subway ride from Queens Park, the seat of provincial government in downtown Toronto—was hardly adequate for dealing with a real emergency. In addition, despite having managed many kinds of emergencies in the past, Young had never managed a public health emergency. Nor was he an expert in infectious diseases or public health matters.

Premier Eves therefore decided to make Young and D'Cunha co-chairs of the emergency response, in charge of developing a workable decision-making system under the mantle of the POC. They would report to Health Minister Clement, who would report to Eves. This kind of joint management approach "can work," Young muses, "or can *not*-work. The major problem with it is—what if your approaches are different and you've got different personalities? And how do you break ties [in the event of a disagreement]?" Although Young says that the arrangement initially worked well, conflicts emerged over time.

Opening Salvos in the War on SARS

As soon as Eves had declared a provincial emergency on March 26, Young called a 7:00 p.m. meeting of the frontline decision makers in the SARS outbreak. He asked the group to explain to him where the outbreak stood. "Initially," recalls Toronto Medical Officer of Health Sheela Basrur, "there had been an assumption by those who were relatively new to the situation—in other words the provincial folks—that we could establish a planning structure, get some advice, consider what the best approach would be, and then issue something as guidance to local hospitals." But the reaction from the local public health and hospital personnel was fast and adamant: this would not be sufficient. "Something had to be done *tonight* for *tomorrow*, because we did not know how far this had spread, and the fish were already swimming away from the net," Basrur explains.[4]

So the group sat together until 4:00 a.m., hammering out a set of emergency operating instructions for Toronto area hospitals. One of the group's first decisions was to make these mandatory directives rather than advisory guidelines. That way, all hospitals, doctors, and health-care workers would be following the same procedures. "If you sent out 'guidelines' to 100 hospitals and 100 hospital administrators and then 100 doctors got ahold of them, there'd be 400 ways of doing it by the end of the day—if they did it at all," Young explains.

It was somewhat blurry under provincial law whether the province actually had the legal authority to issue mandates to the hospitals. "The hospitals aren't owned by municipalities, they aren't owned by private industry. They're stand-alone nonprofits," says Young. But this

---

[4]Interview with Dr. Sheela Basrur, Toronto Medical Officer of Health, 2004. Unless noted, subsequent quotations by Basrur are also from this interview.

did not deter him: "The funding for them, almost entirely, comes from the province. . . . You assume you have the legal responsibility and ability to do it, but if it's hazy, you err on the side of doing what you have to do anyway, and then you let the courts sort it out afterward. Did we have the authority? I'd like to think we did."

The group agreed to impose a rather draconian set of restrictions on all the hospitals in the Greater Toronto Area (GTA; this included York, Durham, and Peel counties) plus Simcoe County, just north of the GTA. The directives were faxed or e-mailed to the forty-four hospitals in these affected areas on the morning of March 27.

The First Set of Directives
Under the directives, each hospital was required to invoke its Code Orange emergency plan—that is, to activate a preexisting blueprint for closing down the hospital to all but essential care. The hospital could continue to receive patients needing urgent medical care, but many elective services would be either suspended or limited to the most serious medical conditions.

There were a number of additional directives aimed at infection control:

- Hospital access was restricted to staff with identification and patients needing emergency care. Visitors were not permitted to enter except in certain specific cases—for instance, the parents of an admitted child or the partner of a woman giving birth.
- Everyone entering the hospital was to be screened; that is, staff members were posted to take temperatures and to ask about recent health symptoms and possible contacts with people at high risk of having SARS.
- Every hospital was to create a SARS unit. This meant emptying an existing ward and ensuring that each room had a negative pressure ventilation system or the equivalent.
- All hospital personnel were to wear an N95 mask, isolation gown, gloves, and protective eyewear or face shield. (N95 masks are designed to filter out smaller particles than standard surgical masks and are said to be 95 percent effective in screening out airborne viruses. They had not often been used in health-care settings, however, except in caring for tuberculosis (TB) patients.)
- Part-time staff members who had worked at Scarborough-Grace after March 16 were prohibited from working their scheduled shifts in other hospitals.
- Patient transfers from outside the area into Toronto area hospitals were stopped, and transfers from one hospital to another in the GTA and Simcoe were limited to urgent cases.

Four days later, on March 31, the provincial decision makers decided to extend the screening and other infection precautions to all 160 hospitals in the province. Only the hospitals in the GTA and Simcoe County were instructed to implement the more extreme Code Orange provisions, however.

A Jury-Rigged Management Group:
The Provincial Operations Centre Executive Committee

Because the Health Ministry MAG was deemed incapable of serving as an executive decision-making body in the provincial emergency response to SARS, Young and D'Cunha created and co-chaired a group they called the POC Executive Committee, which was initially made up of key provincial and municipal decision makers in the response effort (or their designees). The Executive Committee began as a group of about eight people: hospital doctors treating SARS patients, infectious disease and emergency medicine experts, and representatives from TPH. Over time, however, its membership swelled to two dozen and came to include infection-control nurses, broader representation from local public health agencies, assorted academic experts, occupational health doctors, and family physicians. Because many of its members were also managing the outbreak response, the POC Executive Committee quickly developed a modus operandi that allowed its members to participate but also attend to other pressing duties. The committee met each morning at 10:00 a.m.[5] to review the events of the previous 24 hours, raise concerns, and, when necessary, make a major decision about the course of the emergency response.

Early on, for example, the committee debated whether the province should try to contain the SARS disease in a single designated hospital. Proponents of the idea argued that it would be easier to bring the disease under control in a single hospital, while opponents noted that it would expose SARS health-care workers to a concentrated risk that was, at present, dispersed more democratically among a number of city hospitals. In the current anxious climate, moreover, there was an excellent chance that the health-care staff would refuse to work there, raising the specter of inciting a union battle in the midst of a health-care emergency. In addition, some argued that creating a designated SARS hospital would give the other non-SARS hospitals a false sense of security. If a SARS patient were mistakenly admitted to a hospital that was not on guard against SARS, the undetected spread of the disease would begin all over again. In the end, these latter arguments won the day.

Information and Advice

Ontario Public Health possessed neither expertise in the infectious disease field nor in-house capacity for epidemiological analysis, two areas of major importance in the SARS outbreak. Young and D'Cunha set out to fill these gaps as best they could.

---

[5]The meeting time was later changed to 1:00 p.m.

The Science Advisory Committee

Young created the ad hoc Science Advisory Committee (SAC) by asking Mt. Sinai's infectious disease expert Dr. Don Low to send out an SOS to his infectious disease colleagues across the country, requesting that they come to Toronto to help turn the daily arrival of new bits and pieces of information into practical advice about how to stop SARS from spreading. Over time, the group grew to include experts in public health, emergency medicine, and family medicine. The SAC met daily and reported to Young.

The Epi Unit

D'Cunha, meanwhile, created within Ontario Public Health a temporary Epi Unit, which reported to him. The staff consisted primarily of a rotating group of epidemiologists volunteered by public health units in communities not yet affected by SARS and four federal field epidemiologists.

The SARS Operations Centre

Young also created a temporary SARS Operations Centre within the Hospitals Division of the Ontario Health and Long-term Care Ministry. This center had responsibility for writing and disseminating special emergency infection-control directives to hospitals and other health-care facilities based on recommendations handed down from the SAC. It was also responsible for managing the logistics of the outbreak, for example, providing help in rounding up N95 masks for hospitals and doctors.

A Word about the Incident Command System

Students of emergency management may note that the organization of the SARS response effort borrowed several concepts from the *Incident Command System* (ICS), an organizational template for managing a broad array of emergencies.[6] For example, ICS calls for a clearly identified *incident commander* or for multiple commanders working closely in a *unified command structure*. Young and D'Cunha arguably fit this description—two commissioners managing the emergency response together. As specified in the ICS, they brought in

---

[6]The ICS (used in the United States and Canada) features a preestablished organizational template that has the advantage of being simple, consistent, and flexible and thus is adaptable to emergencies of varying sizes and types. Emergency response is managed by either a single incident commander or a joint unified command team that oversees four major sections: the Operations Section, which manages all tactical activities; the Planning Section, which gathers and evaluates current and forecast information so that the command group can create and update the Incident Action Plan; the Logistics Section, which provides ongoing support for the responders, from managing resources to arranging for medical care; and the Finance/Administration Section, which keeps track of the money and time spent on the emergency response. ICS, which was originally created to eliminate chaotic management in the case of large fires that cut across two or more jurisdictions, is not without its critics, however. They charge that it is not a good one-size-fits-all solution for all emergencies.

outside experts to advise them in making decisions, via the SAC and the Epi Unit. Young says that he used ICS principles "as was practical," but notes that the ICS model was not familiar to many in the health-care system and that the health-care system was not organized to operate in line with the model. For instance, ICS calls for a single, clear chain of command linking every frontline responder straight up to the incident commander(s), but this was impossible to establish under provincial law and practice. The frontline activities of the responders were all carried out by a combination of doctors, hospital personnel, and staff members of the local public health units. The doctors were not, in a day-to-day way, accountable to anyone, and the hospitals were ultimately governed by private boards of directors. Local public health units, likewise, had their own internal hierarchies and were ultimately accountable to their local medical officers of health and boards of health.

Thus, although Young created the SARS Operations Centre to write the emergency directives for hospitals and other medical institutions and clinics, there was no mechanism to ensure that they did, in fact, comply, beyond their own self-interest in remaining on the safe side of the law with respect to medical malpractice. In the absence of any legal authority (or organizational capacity) to proceed differently, the SARS emergency response relied on the existing and highly decentralized medical and public health systems to carry out the outbreak response.

The Cost of Missed Cases

On March 28, 2 days after Eves declared a provincial emergency, the staff at York Central Hospital made a dismaying discovery. James Dougherty, a 77-year-old cardiology patient, had been transferred from the Scarborough-Grace Hospital to York Central on March 16 for dialysis treatment. He had arrived with a low fever and respiratory trouble—symptoms that, at the time, doctors assumed were by-products of the heart attack. But by March 28, Dougherty was near death with a virulent pneumonia and York Central doctors concluded that he had SARS. Further investigation revealed that a week before his heart attack, on March 7, Dougherty had come to the Scarborough-Grace Emergency Department with congestive heart failure and had spent the night on a gurney in the observation unit across from Tse Chi Kwai and Joseph Pollack. After his March 14 heart attack, Dougherty had spent 2 days in the Scarborough-Grace cardiology ward without infection precautions, followed by 12 days at York Central, also without infection precautions.

This news meant that the Scarborough-Grace infection-control unit and TPH had not, in fact, tracked down every hospital patient who had been exposed to Tse. In addition, it wasn't until 14 days into his second hospitalization that Dougherty's SARS case was finally recognized. Once the diagnosis was made, York Central immediately closed down its Emergency Department and ICU and more than 3,000 staff members, patients, and visitors were placed under quarantine.

Over the next several weeks, public health officials tallied the effects of the Dougherty case. At Scarborough-Grace, Dougherty spread SARS to an estimated twenty-one contacts (including the liver transplant recipient who was transferred from Scarborough-Grace to Mt. Sinai on March 25, forcing the 10-day shut-down of the Mt. Sinai Emergency Department and ICU), and at York Central, he infected an estimated fifteen people. "In hindsight," said Dr. Allison McGeer, Mt. Sinai Hospital's director of infection control, the Dougherty case "was the worst miss of the early days of the investigation." [7]

Another early miss also proved consequential for many weeks to come. When Joseph Pollack was rushed to the Scarborough-Grace Emergency Department on March 16 with an advanced case of pneumonia, his wife Rose had accompanied him. Although Joseph was quickly identified as a probable SARS patient, no one thought to worry about Rose, who was feverish but not otherwise symptomatic. She too had been infected with SARS, however, and was highly infectious. While checking her husband in at the registration desk, she infected three ward clerks. She then infected five more people in the waiting room, along with a security guard, three nurses, and a housekeeper. In the end, public health workers calculated that Rose Pollack infected a total of twenty-four people. She and Dougherty were the first SARS patients identified as *super-spreaders*,[8] and their cases revealed a frustrating truth about the disease—because SARS symptoms were extremely general, it was particularly hard to diagnose, especially in its early stages before all symptoms were manifest.

The Diagnosis Dilemma

Researchers did not isolate the SARS virus until April 16. Even though this discovery paved the way for the rapid development of a laboratory test for SARS, the test was not reliable for patients in the early stages of the disease. Thus, doctors were forced to rely on a combination of the patient's clinical symptoms and the epi link—the moment of contact with a person or place that could have exposed the patient to SARS.

As soon as WHO had identified SARS as a new infectious disease and global threat, the organization developed diagnostic criteria for making both probable and suspect SARS diagnoses. The WHO criteria for a suspect SARS were as follows:

---

[7]Quoted in Romesh Ratnesar, Hannah Beech, and Steven Frank, "Tale of Two Countries," *Time* magazine, May 5, 2003, available at www.time.com/time/magazine/article/0,9171,1004759,00.html [accessed August 27, 2008].

[8]The term *super-spreader* was imprecise but referred to a SARS patient who was thought to excrete the virus in unusually large quantities, thus infecting an unusually large number of people. Some epidemiologists, after the fact, questioned whether the notion of the super-spreader might not be entirely myth. The explanation, instead, might be that the hospital environment was especially conducive to the spread of SARS for a number of reasons: warm, humid air in a relatively contained environment; close contact among health-care workers and SARS patients at their sickest; high-risk procedures that put health-care workers in direct contact with respiratory secretions; and SARS patients in proximity to susceptible fellow patients.

- The patient must have had SARS symptoms after February 1, 2003.
- The patient must have had a fever of 100.4°F or higher and one or more respiratory symptoms (for example, cough, shortness of breath, or difficulty breathing).
- In addition, the patient must have had either close personal contact with a diagnosed SARS patient or a recent history of travel to an area reporting SARS cases (an epi link).

The criteria for a probable SARS case included all the suspect criteria plus *one* of the following:

- The patient must have a chest x-ray finding of pneumonia or respiratory distress syndrome.[9]
- The patient's death must be due to an unexplained respiratory illness, with an autopsy examination demonstrating the pathology of respiratory distress syndrome without an identifiable cause.

Other symptoms sometimes associated with SARS according to WHO included headache, muscular stiffness, loss of appetite, malaise, confusion, rash, and diarrhea. For purposes of developing an official disease count, WHO used only the probable SARS numbers from each country.[10]

The official definition used in Canada was the same as the WHO definition except that, instead of a chest x-ray finding of pneumonia or respiratory distress syndrome, Health Canada required a clinical finding of severe progressive pneumonia. Although this disparity had little effect in the early days of the outbreak, it later proved consequential.

The problem with both the WHO and the Health Canada definitions, says Ian Johnson, a member of the Epi Unit, was that they assumed that everyone who was infected with SARS would be symptomatic. But what if some of the people infected with the virus never became sick themselves but spread the disease to others? Most infectious diseases included such asymptomatic carriers. If this were true of SARS, then it would not be possible to find the epi link in every case; a person might catch SARS from someone who appeared perfectly healthy. Thus, Johnson explains, public health personnel now had to start monitoring for cases of SARS-like illnesses that did not even have an epi link.[11]

On the other hand, to consider every pneumonia patient a possible SARS case would overwhelm the hospital system and confuse efforts to distinguish SARS from other kinds of pneumonia. Ontario therefore created a third category, persons under investigation (PUI), which primarily consisted of people with all the clinical symptoms of SARS but no

---

[9] *Respiratory distress syndrome* refers to a syndrome of life-threatening progressive pulmonary insufficiency in the absence of a known pulmonary disease.

[10] Over time, a number of suspect cases evolved into probable cases.

[11] Interview with Dr. Ian Johnson, professor, University of Toronto, and epidemiology director of the Epi Unit, 2004.

apparent epi link. In addition, a person with an epi link and just one SARS symptom was often categorized as a PUI.

Despite the fail-safe PUI category, it was still easy to miss SARS cases, doctors noted. One of the most confounding situations arose when a doctor believed a pneumonia patient not only had no epi link to SARS but that his or her pneumonia symptoms had a very likely alternative cause. Such was the case with Dougherty, whose respiratory symptoms were initially assumed to be part of his congestive heart condition.

Finding the Epi Link

For several reasons, it was often very difficult to find the epi link. First, the primary source of information was necessarily the patient's own memory. Public health staff thus had the challenge of questioning patients—who were often woozy with fever and struggling to breathe—about everything they had done and every person they had been near for the 10 days preceding the first onset of symptoms.

What's more, the links frequently proved extremely difficult to uncover. For example, in mid-April, health authorities in Manila, the Philippines, announced that a 46-year-old Toronto woman, Adela Catalon, had brought SARS to the country when she arrived from Canada to visit her ill father and attend a wedding. Becoming increasingly ill during her stay, she went to the hospital, where she was diagnosed with SARS. She died just 10 hours after checking in, but not before having potentially exposed many people, including the five hundred guests at the wedding she had come to attend.[12]

Although Ontario public health authorities at first disputed the Philippines's claim, TPH eventually did find a link between Catalon and the Toronto SARS pool. Just before her departure, Catalon reportedly helped care for the ill 69-year-old mother of her roommate. That 69-year-old woman was later diagnosed with SARS and died on April 25, 11 days after Catalon had died in the Philippines. Published reports indicate that the roommate's mother may have contracted SARS at the Lapsley Family Clinic in late March from a member of the Samson family. Some seventeen members of this family reportedly contracted SARS from the family patriarch, 82-year-old Eulialo Samson, who was not diagnosed with SARS until a few days after his death on April 1. Samson and his son had contracted SARS on March 16 in the Scarborough-Grace Emergency Department from Rose Pollack, who was seated near them in the waiting room.

A Shifting Approach to Diagnosing SARS

Through the month of April, the number of probable, suspect, and PUI cases mushroomed. While public health officials continued to believe that it was disastrous for a SARS case to

---

[12] *Toronto Star,* "Adela Catalon," September 27, 2003, H3.

go undiagnosed, they also saw the downside to casting too wide a net for SARS. If the child of a health-care worker under quarantine came down with the flu, for example, and public health doctors decided to consider it a possible SARS case, the diagnosis could close down an entire school for days. If a hospital patient acquired pneumonia and doctors diagnosed possible SARS, it could close the hospital ward and send hundreds of health-care workers into quarantine. If it was crucial not to miss cases, it was almost as important not to bend over backward to diagnose the disease when the chances were remote.

Thus, in mid-April, D'Cunha began to stress the need to pay strict attention to the SARS criteria listed in the Health Canada SARS definition. In addition, with the support of the POC Executive Committee, he created a provincial adjudication program, in which questionable or conflicting local diagnoses were subject to the review of one of several provincially designated experts, who would look at the patient's case file and make a final judgment call.[13]

The Month of April: Long Hours, Camaraderie, and a Large Dose of Exasperation

During the month of April, the emergency response to SARS settled into a basic modus operandi, buoyed by a high level of expertise, professionalism, and earnest good-will among the participants but hobbled by limited information, inadequate staff resources, and unworkable systems for the exchange of vital incoming information about the behavior of the disease. Within this basic context, each of the major organizational players in the response— TPH, the Epi Unit, the SAC, and the GTA hospitals—faced a particular set of challenges and frustrations.

The Toronto Public Health and the Problem of Overwhelm

The tasks that fell to the local public health units during the outbreak were all extremely labor-intensive, especially for the TPH because most of the SARS caseload was in Toronto. For example, a TPH staff member had to investigate every potential SARS case in an effort to find the epi link. In some cases, the link was obvious, but others required intensive investigations that could last many days. In the course of the outbreak, TPH investigated 2,000 potential cases, with the average epi link investigation taking 9 hours to complete.

Once a patient had been identified as a possible SARS case, the TPH had to come up with a list of every person who might have been exposed to the patient since the onset of his or her symptoms. In the course of the outbreak, more than 26,000 people were identified as

---

[13]Some public health units objected to this move, which they regarded as an unlawful usurpation of their authority.

contacts. If the contact had no SARS symptoms but had been exposed to the SARS patient less than 10 days before, the virus might be incubating in the body of the contact person. Thus, the contact had to go into quarantine for the remainder of the 10-day period. That meant getting the person a mask and thermometer and calling once or twice a day to make sure the person was complying with the quarantine and to check on his or her health status.

As a practical matter, TPH caseworkers found that they also had to help people under quarantine in a number of other respects, such as arranging psychological support for the severely anxious and depressed and helping quarantined parents find childcare. If an employer refused to allow an employee to comply with quarantine, TPH had to call the employer to advocate on the employee's behalf.

TPH leaders, meanwhile, had to determine how to keep track of assorted details of every possible SARS case and each of his or her possible contacts. Finding the existing software for reporting infectious diseases in Ontario too limited for the task at hand, TPH tried devising a new Excel template. When this proved inadequate, too, TPH asked its internal computer experts to devise a viable tracking system; they did so, but they were not able to complete it until late April. In the meantime, TPH resorted to old-fashioned paper files. As Basrur explained:

We had flip charts and color-coded [P]ost-its as one of the key ways in which we shared information and passed it on between shifts. It [was] absolutely manual—highly visual. Expeditious, but not efficient, if you know what I mean, when it comes to such things as reporting to the Ministry or to the media what was our total number of cases, how many were in hospital, how many were in ICU, how many were on ventilators. At one point, it was practically a matter of counting stick men every single time they called us up to ask for more recent numbers, and that's no way to run a public health unit.[14]

Given the amount of work involved and given the burden to those under quarantine, there were questions early on about which categories of people should be placed under quarantine. Everyone at TPH agreed on the need to track down the contacts of all the probable and suspect SARS cases, but what about the PUI's? Did all their contacts have to be quarantined as well? As Dr. Barbara Yaffe, director of the TPH Communicable Disease Control division explains, "We decided to err on the side of caution. So if there was any doubt that the person was a case, we kept investigating very carefully to figure out if they were or they weren't. In the meantime, we had to deal with them as if they were, and deal with their contacts as if they were the contacts of a case."[15]

Similar questions arose with respect to the degree of exposure needed to spread SARS. It seemed clear that the virus was at least primarily spread by droplets; an airborne virus would

---

[14]Quoted in Kelly Krowe, "Indepth: SARS. Behind the Mask," Canadian Broadcasting Company News Online, November 19, 2003, available at www.cbc.ca/news/background/sars/behindthemask.html (accessed August 27, 2008).

[15]Interview with Dr. Barbara Yaffe, director of the TPH Communicable Disease Control division, 2004. Unless noted, subsequent quotations from Yaffe are also from this interview.

have spread the disease far more widely and quickly. Droplets were heavy enough that they could travel only about 3 feet before falling to the ground. They could also land on flat surfaces and be spread by the hands. That meant that close contact between people was generally necessary to spread the disease. But there were also examples of disease transmission that seemed to have occurred after a more remote level of contact. In terms of identifying people who should be quarantined, this uncertainty posed a dilemma. The members of a SARS patient's household should clearly be quarantined. But what about someone who had walked through a hospital at a time when SARS was spreading unchecked among the health-care workers? Early on, TPH decided to quarantine anyone with a plausible level of contact, but it later adopted a middle-ground position—active surveillance for low-likelihood contacts. That meant allowing such people to go about their regular lives but monitoring them closely for SARS-type symptoms. Still, there were 13,374 people under quarantine in Toronto over the entire course of the outbreak—as many as 8,000 at once during the outbreak peak.

Although TPH leadership and staff worked long hours with unstinting effort, for which they received wide praise, there were simply not enough trained people available to deal with the outbreak, nor was the old-fashioned paper information system really viable. As a result, a frustrated public reported many grievances: people spending hours on hold when trying to call TPH for information, people under quarantine never receiving a call or being called repeatedly, and grieving relatives of deceased SARS victims receiving calls asking about the patient's condition. And then there were the SARS-exposed individuals who were not contacted soon enough to prevent the possibility of further spreading the disease.

In fact, a number of Toronto residents figured out they had been exposed to SARS and placed themselves under quarantine, not at the request of TPH but because they had heard about the protocols from TV news reports and decided to do the responsible thing.[16] There were also a few infamous examples of noncompliance—in particular, a Hewlett-Packard employee who scoffed at the idea that he might be infected and went to work, persuading his wife to cover for him on the phone when public health workers called. Not only did he have a fatal case of SARS, but he infected a co-worker who also died.

Although it created an overwhelming workload, most people in the public health field agreed that, given what was known at the time, there had been little choice but to use quarantine in Toronto. There was one prominent exception to this viewpoint, however. Dr. Richard Schabas, chief-of-staff at the York Central Hospital and Ontario's former chief medical officer of health, declares:

Quarantine was abandoned by public health a hundred years ago because it doesn't work. When it comes to quarantine diseases, there are two categories. There are those diseases where quarantine is ineffective because the disease is too infectious—like measles or influenza. And then there are diseases

---

[16]The impression of widespread cooperation and compliance with the quarantine in Toronto was later a topic of some wonder among officials at both WHO and the CDC. There was no way to calculate the actual compliance rate; estimates ranged from 50 to 90 percent.

where quarantine is unnecessary because the disease isn't sufficiently infectious—your standard garden-variety pneumonias. Why would you put immense effort into a control measure which doesn't work for any other infectious disease? You might as well bring out the leeches.[17]

Schabas argues that epidemiologists should have been able to see that the outbreak was almost entirely hospital-based and focused their resources there, not exhausted themselves trying to halt the small amount of community spread. Even after the fact, Schabas's view was well out of the mainstream, however; and certainly at the time, the TPH leadership did not doubt the need to use quarantine, however arduous and imperfect it was.

The Epi Unit and the Bad Information Reporting System

One of the greatest challenges to developing infection-control protocols for SARS was the lack of clear information about the disease and how it spread.[18] For example, the operating assumption was that everyone infected by the virus got sick—but was that really true? Might there not be people who were infected but asymptomatic, and might they not still spread the disease? Was SARS spread only by droplets, and was the virus transmitted only through respiratory secretions or also through fecal matter? Was the maximum incubation period 10 days, or was it really 12? Were some SARS patients super-spreaders (people who were highly infectious because their secretions contained an unusually large volume of the virus), and, if so, did they have identifiable characteristics?

The job of the Epi Unit was to provide the answers to these kinds of questions by analyzing statistical data about the behavior of the disease. In addition, the Epi Unit was to provide authoritative data about all SARS cases in Ontario. It was information and analysis that many agencies and interest groups desperately wanted, including Health Canada, WHO, the SAC, scientific researchers, provincial politicians, and the media.

This would have been challenge enough to an established epidemiology office working with the latest and most flexible computer software. In Ontario, the Epi Unit had to be created from scratch in the midst of the outbreak. "This fact, in and of itself, is stunning," stated the interim report of the province's post hoc analysis of the SARS response effort. "[Y]ou cannot, in the event of an outbreak, suddenly hire your whole work force, implement your computer system, and then implement the processes and the legislative frameworks in which to produce a coherent surveillance system," pointed out an anonymous observer quoted in the report.[19]

---

[17]Interview with Dr. Richard Schabas, chief-of-staff, York Central Hospital, and former chief medical officer of health for the Province of Ontario, 2004. Unless noted, subsequent quotations from Schabas are also from this interview.

[18]The information in this section was largely drawn from "Problem 13: No Provincial Epidemiology Unit" and "Problem 14: Inadequate Infectious Disease Information Systems," in *SARS & Public Health in Ontario, Interim Report,* 2004, Toronto.

[19]"Problem 13," 96, 98.

The Epi Unit staff included a revolving pool of epidemiologists on loan from the local public health units, which necessitated the constant training of incoming epidemiologists and created problems with consistency in the work produced.[20] But the biggest problem for the Epi Unit leaders concerned the hopelessly antiquated system for reporting data from the province's thirty-seven public health units to the Epi Unit. This Reportable Disease Information System was a DOS-based system that dated from the late 1980s and worked only for specific, known diseases.[21] By the time the Epi Unit was up and running, each public health unit affected by SARS had come up with its own means of recording patient data using Excel spreadsheets, which they e-mailed to the Epi Unit. There were several problems with this: the data were inconsistent from one public health unit to another, the information that the unit was trying to record often did not fit the design of the Excel template, and the spreadsheets did not track changes in a patient's condition. Thus, the only way to see, for example, whether the diagnosis of a particular patient had changed from suspect to probable SARS was to rifle through past spreadsheets. Even worse, the sheets did not record enough detail about patients to allow epidemiologists to do the kind of analysis urgently required by the SAC and Health Canada.

In collaboration with Health Canada, therefore, the Epi Unit devoted a great deal of energy to bringing in the more state-of-the-art Integrated Public Health Information System (iPHIS), which was ready for use in mid-April. By then, TPH and other public health units were at their busiest, however, and did not feel able to make the switch. What's more, although the iPHIS system would have allowed for better analysis of SARS, it did not have the capacity to track quarantine contacts—an important need as far as the local public health units were concerned. Further, TPH was well along in developing its own system, which TPH leaders insisted would be superior to iPHIS. In the end, the Epi Unit quietly hired a group of caseworkers to go back out to the community and re-research every SARS case to capture the data the Epi Unit needed, a time-consuming process that raised hackles among hospitals and public health units.

The Science Advisory Committee and the Lack of Data

The SAC was created out of Young's conviction that Ontario should take advantage of any new discoveries about SARS gleaned from research scientists or from the behavior of the

---

[20]Early on, the managers of the Epi Unit tried to get the Ontario Public Health Branch staff to assist the Epi Unit, but they were turned down on the grounds that the staff was too busy working on other projects. According to the province's later analysis, there was an odd dynamic in play, in which the Epi Unit volunteers worked long hours at a frantic pace while the Public Health Branch staff worked their usual 8:30 a.m. to 4:30 p.m. schedule at a deliberate and unhurried pace on non-SARS matters.

[21]The inadequacy of this system was no secret to the Public Health Branch or to the local public health units. D'Cunha had tried and failed to obtain provincial funding to upgrade it in 2000. A 2003 provincial report had also noted the inadequacy of the system in reporting information about the West Nile virus. Provincial Auditor of Ontario, *2003 Annual Report,* available at www.auditor.on.ca/en/reports_2003_en.htm [accessed August 27, 2008].

disease in the outbreak itself. Young reasoned that a group of infectious disease experts would be able to interpret the new information and then recommend the best possible outbreak policies.

When Low and others put out a call to infectious disease experts around the country to come and help Ontario, many responded, in some cases spending weeks away from their work and home. After the fact, the provincial analysis of the outbreak praised the group's good-will, camaraderie, and civic-mindedness, but argued that because the SAC had been created without the advantage of emergency planning ahead of time, it had been created without thought to important topics: Should other areas of expertise be represented on the committee, and if so, which areas; who, exactly, should the committee report to; and what kinds of questions should the committee take up (and what kinds should it not)?

Over time, the membership of the SAC did broaden to include, in particular, public health doctors and (after some campaigning) primary care physicians—but not without first incurring bad feeling among those left out. Committee members also expressed confusion over whether they were reporting to Young or D'Cunha, both of whom were members of the committee.

There was in addition some doubt about the purview of the SAC and about how it should prioritize its tasks. For example, in addition to recommending directives to hospitals, the committee was lobbied to send out guidance to long-term care facilities and primary care physicians. The committee also received questions from hospital administrators confused about aspects of the directives that had been sent out and inquiries from the media. It was impossible to do everything, and it was especially impossible to do everything all at once, even though committee members reportedly often put in 14- and 16-hour days.

In addition, except for three or four core members, the SAC members could not serve on the committee for more than a week or so because they had work and personal demands elsewhere. The turnover meant there was a continual need to bring new people up to speed, explains Sunnybrook's Dr. Brian Schwartz, director of prehospital care, who co-chaired the SAC from beginning to end. "There was a learning curve—and in an outbreak, you don't have time for that." In addition, Schwartz says, many of the experts had a tendency to offer information in all its complexity, but were reluctant to make hard-and-fast recommendations. Schwartz, with his background in emergency medicine, pushed them to do so, but he believes it would have been better to have had a preestablished roster of experts who were trained in emergency decision making and who were willing to help out in the case of such an event.[22]

To the committee members, themselves, the great frustration was the lack of daily-breaking epidemiological data and analysis on which to base their recommendations. "Put yourself in the position we were in, in the second week of April," explains Schwartz. "We do not yet know the results of the protection measures [in the hospitals] and the quarantine

---

[22]Interview with Dr. Brian Schwartz, director of prehospital care at Toronto's Sunnybrook & Women's College Health Sciences Centre, 2004. Unless noted, subsequent quotations from Schwartz are also from this interview.

measures and all the other things we were doing. We don't know whether it's working or not. We still aren't sure whether [SARS transmission] is *airborne*." It was crucial to know, yea or nay, in order to decide whether to stay the course or take a new, more draconian approach.

After-the-fact analyses cited several reasons for the information problem, including D'Cunha's insistence on reviewing all data from the Epi Unit so that he could ensure its accuracy before passing it on. This, reportedly, became quite a bottleneck, although D'Cunha steadfastly denied that it caused any significant delays. He was, however, adamant that his department not release flawed data. At one point, for instance, he explained to the SAC that patients were sometimes double-counted—once in the city or region in which they lived and once in the city or region in which they were hospitalized—and he insisted that such errors be corrected. "One of the things we said was, we'd rather have flawed data than no data," comments SAC co-chair Schwartz. "At least we'd have *something* to work with, even if some patients were counted twice. And Dr. D'Cunha's retort was, 'Well, no, we can't do that.'"

When the SAC was able to have direct contact with the Epi Unit, Schwartz adds, the exchange was generally very useful. On several occasions, however, D'Cunha directed the Epi Unit leaders to cancel scheduled presentations to the SAC. Such episodes enraged SAC members. In mid-April, the SAC wrote an official letter of complaint and, at one point, even threatened to disband. Young and a high-level Health Ministry official tried to intervene to speed up the flow of data to the SAC, with mixed results. As Young puts it, "You see, the problem we ran into is—how do I fix that? They're my committee, but he's got the information. . . . We tended to find ways to fix it by going around the edges and developing side pathways—stuff that you shouldn't do in an emergency."

Resorting to Side Pathways

The frustration, from many quarters, at not having the newest and best data led to assorted efforts to circumvent the official reporting structure and recreate the data from scratch, leading to some of the most unpleasant tensions in the outbreak response.

The Epi Unit, frustrated at not getting the detailed information it needed through regular channels, decided to hire caseworkers to collect all the information they could on the SARS cases again, one at a time. But the Epi Unit was not alone. D'Cunha's staff, the SAC, Health Canada, and the POC all ended up calling hospitals, public health units, and patients or their relatives to get data. Not only did this result in assorted discrepancies, but already-overloaded hospitals and public health units were flooded with calls for information on specific cases. Under increasing pressure from WHO, however, Health Canada pressured D'Cunha, who in turn pressured the Epi Unit staff and his own staff. Sometimes five different people would be asked to get the same information, and all would call the public health unit, insisting that the matter was extremely urgent. "I had people coming into my office *crying* about being harassed," says TPH's Yaffe.

The Hospitals and the Problematic Directives

According to an article in the *Toronto Star*, the Ontario Health Ministry sent out more than fifty bulletins and directives to hospitals and other medical settings during the outbreak.[23] The system for developing the directives began with deliberations by the SAC. The SAC then made a recommendation and passed it along to Young, who passed it on to the SARS Operations Centre, which was supposed to take the SAC's advice and write it up as a clear workable directive. Any big changes were sent to Schwartz or his SAC co-chair for approval, then on to Young and D'Cunha for their signatures, up to Health Minister Clement for final approval, and then back to the SARS Operations Centre for dissemination.

From the perspective of the hospitals, these directives were overly long and complicated—not at all what was needed in an emergency. Some members of the SAC and the Health Ministry conceded the point, but said they were doing their best, given the circumstances. Even more exasperating to the hospitals, however, was the fact that, based on new information and complaints from the field, the SAC and SARS Operations Centre re-issued directives. The new version would be sent out without summaries of what changes had been made, so hospital personnel had to spend hours wading through them all over again. In retrospect, Young notes, a simple expedient might have been to highlight the changes, but he adds that in the press of the moment no one thought to do this.

Hospital administrators, in addition, complained that some of the directives were simply impossible to fulfill, such as the one that required all hospital personnel to use N95 masks. Unbeknownst to the SAC or the Health Ministry, there were not enough N95 masks available for all GTA hospital workers to use them. And although the hospitals were eventually able to get the masks—by cleaning out the supply of stored N95 masks all across North America—there was a second problem. The Ontario Labor Ministry required that these particular masks be "fit-tested," an elaborate procedure requiring trained personnel and special testing equipment. The SAC and Health Ministry had not known about this occupational safety requirement when they adopted the directive.

Schwartz says that despite these difficulties, he stands by the N95 requirement. "My feeling as a front-liner was—get the damn masks out there. Even if you're not exactly sure how to use it, even if it's not perfectly fit-tested, it will provide you a level of protection. Better than nothing—and better than the surgical masks." That the provincially required masks were not available to them made some health-care workers extremely uneasy, however, especially as they watched their colleagues with SARS growing sicker and sicker. Some filed union grievances about having to work without the N95 masks.

Former Ontario Chief Medical Officer of Health Schabas argues that the whole notion of sending out detailed directives during the outbreak was benighted from the beginning:

---

[23] *Toronto Star*, 2003.

Hospitals are large and complex and, for the most part, very sophisticated organizations. . . . [The provincial leaders of the response] were dealing with institutions that in many cases had far more expertise than they did at the [Health] Ministry. Basically, the Ministry's approach was to deal with the hospitals like they were small children. . . . And of course as a result, they had to change their policies every few *hours* because people found flaws in them.

They should have issued general guidelines and left it to the hospitals how they implemented them—and they should have had the capacity to respond to questions and to troubleshoot. That's not what they did—and so there was tremendous wasted effort, tremendous ill will created between the hospitals and the Ministry.

The Weekend from Hell

In the week before Easter Sunday, April 20, the emergency responders endured the two most dispiriting and frightening developments in the outbreak. The first was the discovery of an undetected cluster of SARS cases, not in a hospital but at large in Toronto; the second was the infection of eleven health-care workers at Sunnybrook Hospital.

The Cluster in the Bukas-Loob Sa Diyos Covenant Community

On Friday, April 11, TPH discovered that SARS had been spreading just outside the radar of the public health surveillance system, within a five-hundred-member, mostly Filipino, charismatic Catholic group called the Bukas-Loob Sa Diyos Covenant Community (BLD). As of April 11, TPH reported, there were ten probable and nineteen suspect SARS cases in the BLD. In addition, two community-based doctors who had treated some of these patients had also acquired SARS. Although TPH had been following most of these cases individually, it had taken some time to see the connections among them.

The two cases that began the cluster were those of Eulialo Samson, who had fatefully gone to the Scarborough-Grace Emergency Department on March 16 with a knee injury, and his son, who had accompanied him. There they had contracted SARS from Rose Pollack, who was sitting nearby in the waiting room. Eulialo Samson was not diagnosed with SARS until after his April 1 death, but in the meantime, he had infected seventeen members of his extended family. At least one of those family members had attended two large BLD events: a March 28 religious service attended by 500 people and a March 29 religious retreat attended by 225. In addition, an April 3 funeral visitation service for Samson had been attended by a combination of BLD members and family members who had been infected with SARS.

TPH authorities found it impossible to reconstruct which specific BLD members had been exposed to SARS, given the large numbers of people at each gathering, and by April 13, they reluctantly decided they had to quarantine the entire BLD community. But TPH leaders were not confident that they could get the word of the quarantine out to everyone in the

BLD fast enough and persuasively enough to avoid a major spread of the disease during Easter weekend, April 18–20. Family visits during the holiday had the potential to disperse the disease widely. Officials also worried that some of the rites of Easter in Catholic and Protestant churches might facilitate its spread, for instance, drinking wine from a common cup or kissing the crucifix on Good Friday.

Health Minister Clement appealed to the local Catholic archbishop for help in encouraging BLD members to observe the quarantine. He also asked the archbishop (and some Protestant church leaders) to substitute bows and other noncontact rituals for the traditional rites. Church leaders pledged their help, but the leaders of the outbreak response were still on tenterhooks. They worried that this could be the moment they had fought hard to avoid, the moment when a disease that was still traceable, and therefore still controllable, spilled out of control. "We were on the razor's edge," says Clement.

The Sunnybrook Intubation Fiasco

In the midst of the BLD anxiety, the leaders of the emergency response learned, to their horror, that at the Sunnybrook Hospital, eleven health-care workers—who had taken pains to follow infection control precautions—had contracted SARS during a particularly difficult intubation procedure.[24] Although the health-care workers present had worn the requisite N95 masks, goggles, gloves, and gowns, doctors speculate that the techniques and specific circumstances of the procedure (it took place in crowded quarters and lasted a total of 4 hours) led to the aerosolization of the patient's secretions, which increased the virus's ability to spread.

Three days later, the health-care workers began to get sick. By the end of the Easter weekend, four were diagnosed with probable SARS and another eight with suspect SARS. On April 20, Sunnybrook closed its Emergency Department and ICU for 10 days—a blow to morale in the medical community because Sunnybrook was a flagship hospital with the largest trauma center in Canada. It had played a leadership role in the outbreak and had treated about half of the area's SARS patients.

To the SAC advisors, the episode was especially devastating. They had banked on the idea that these precautions were—if anything—cautious to a fault. Now they began to fear that there might be nothing that health-care workers could do to stay safe. "We thought we'd see health care workers walk out of the hospitals—because we weren't protecting them," says Low.[25]

---

[24]*Intubation* in this context refers to the insertion of a tube down a patient's trachea to clear the airway.

[25]Interview with Dr. Donald Low, microbioligst-in-chief, Mt. Sinai Hospital, Toronto, 2004. Unless noted, subsequent quotations from Low are also from this interview.

Bracing for the Worst-Case Scenario

The BLD outbreak demonstrated that Toronto's contact tracing and quarantine efforts were not fool-proof; the Sunnybrook episode demonstrated the shortcomings of the new hospital safeguards. Were these cases aberrations, or was the emergency response, more broadly, failing to stop SARS? The data needed to answer that question were not yet available. Thus, on April 22, Health Minister Clement called a meeting with the SAC to ask the scientific experts some distressing questions: If their best efforts failed, if SARS continued to spread, what was the worst-case scenario? What dire and extreme choices might he and Premier Eves be forced to face? "You hope for the best, but plan for the worst—that was my motto during this whole thing," Clement says.

The SAC laid out a shocking picture. In the absolutely worst-case scenario, SARS would turn out to be a highly contagious disease, impossible to contain, that would begin spreading uncontrolled in the community until it infected everyone. Given the projections at the time of a 10 percent mortality rate, that would mean 1 million people dead in Ontario and 3 million dead in Canada before the virus burned itself out.

In terms of the government response, if the disease began spreading out of control in the Toronto area, the government might have to close down all nonessential venues for public mixing, such as movie theaters and sports arenas. In the worst-case scenario, the province might have to quarantine the entire GTA in an effort to save the rest of Ontario and Canada.

A Sigh of Relief

Once Toronto had gotten through the Easter weekend, however, the situation brightened considerably. The BLD community did in fact comply with the city's quarantine order; the outbreak did not, after all, slip out of control. Nor did health-care workers walk out en masse. SAC members and provincial authorities candidly expressed their distress and bewilderment at the fact that health-care workers were still getting SARS and vowed to redouble their efforts to understand why. In support of that effort, Health Canada requested assistance from the Atlanta-based Centers for Disease Control and Prevention (CDC).[26]

On SAC's recommendation, the province issued new protective regulations, for example, the use of face shields in place of goggles and the wearing of double gloves, double gowns, and double masks when caring for SARS patients, so that the top layer could be shed as the worker left the patient's room. SAC stopped short of mandating stryker space suits for high-risk procedures such as intubation, suctioning, bronchoscopy, or the use of BiPAP masks.

---

[26]Nothing conclusive came out of the CDC consultation, but the CDC did heighten SAC's consciousness about the importance of individuals' removing protective clothing correctly to avoid becoming infected from the protective gear itself. The CDC recommended removing the gear in a strict order, interspersed with frequent hand washing.

The best news, however, was that data were now available that indicated that in the previous 2 weeks, there had been only one new case identified as probable or suspect SARS in the GTA. The outbreak was dying out; the end was in sight. The emergency response group heaved a collective sigh of relief—but not for long.

Blind-Sided: WHO Cautions against Travel to Toronto

On Wednesday, April 23, WHO issued a global advisory against all nonessential travel to the City of Toronto. Local and provincial health officials were dumbfounded. *Why*—when SARS had been almost entirely confined to Toronto-area hospitals? And *why now*—when the outbreak was nearly over?

WHO had issued SARS travel advisories to only four other cities or regions: Hong Kong, Beijing, and two provinces in mainland China (Guangdong and Shanxi). Although the purpose of the alerts was pragmatic—to minimize the spread of SARS to other regions and to other nations—any city or region named in such an alert regarded it as a tremendous blow, sure to exact a heavy penalty in lost revenue from foreign visitors.

What's more, for a wealthy industrial nation like Canada, inclusion in a WHO travel advisory was a significant embarrassment. The government of such a nation was expected to have the public health sophistication to rein in infectious diseases expeditiously. After all, Canada, by many widely accepted measures, offered some of the best-quality health care in the world. It was accustomed to advising the WHO, not receiving its injunctions. And Toronto was the nation's largest city, its thriving economic center. How could Toronto be placed in the same category as struggling, poverty-ridden Guangdong Province in China?

Complaints about Political Leadership

The indignation of the health authorities on learning of the WHO travel advisory was immediately matched by that of local, provincial, and federal politicians of every stripe. "I've never been so angry in all my life," said Toronto Mayor Mel Lastman. "Let me be clear: It's safe to live in Toronto. . . . It's safe to visit this city. . . . This isn't a city in the grips of fear and panic."[27] Federal Health Minister Anne McLellan telephoned WHO Director General Gro Harlem Brundtland to argue that the advisory was unwarranted and should be rescinded immediately. Brundtland refused to do that, but did agree to listen to Canada's arguments at a WHO review of the decision the following week.[28] The next day, Canadian

---

[27]Quoted in Nicolass Van Rijn, "Britain Warns Its Citizens Not to Travel to Toronto," *Toronto Star*, April 24, 2003, A1.

[28]*Ottawa Citizen*, April 25, 2003.

Prime Minister Jean Chretien called Brundtland personally, to reiterate McLellan's call for an immediate end to the advisory. He also put in a similar call to the deputy secretary-general of the United Nations, Louise Frechette.[29] (WHO and the UN stuck to their guns, however, and WHO Communicable Disease Director David Heymann later called Canada's April lobbying effort "very inappropriate."[30])

But the sudden visibility of political leaders seemed to remind local reporters of their prior invisibility. Except for Ontario Health Minister Tony Clement, elected leaders had played almost no role during the first month of SARS. Chretien, followed by other federal officials and later by Ontario Premier Eves, did troop into Toronto's Chinatown in the second and third weeks of April to eat in local restaurants and assure a jittery public that these establishments were perfectly safe. But reporters observed pointedly that during the darkest hours of the SARS outbreak—when the leaders of the emergency response had been sick with worry at the thought of an uncontrolled community outbreak and an angry walk-out by health-care workers—the top political leaders of the city, the province, and the country were nowhere to be found. In fact, during Easter week, Prime Minister Chretien had been in the Dominican Republic on a golfing holiday. The parliament was likewise in vacation mode, enjoying the Easter recess. Ontario Premier Ernie Eves was golfing in Arizona, and had, since the start of the outbreak, not deemed SARS the kind of emergency that required the interruption of the Ontario legislature's 4-month recess.

Toronto Mayor Mel Lastman had been receiving arduous medical treatment for hepatitis C, which made him a more sympathetic figure, but in the course of excoriating the WHO travel advisory, Lastman mortified partisans and enemies alike by appearing to be befuddled on international news broadcasts. He made an especially serious gaffe during an appearance on CNN, when, apparently trying to diminish the stature of the WHO, he remarked, "I don't know who this group is. I've never heard of them before."[31] The tactic, if such it was, backfired. "There's a vastly greater chance of dying from embarrassment in this city over the performance of our political leaders than there is from succumbing to SARS," wrote *Toronto Star* columnist Jim Coyle on April 26, 2003. With respect to Lastman, in particular, Coyle continued, "To admit, as he has, to not even knowing what WHO is demonstrated a degree of ignorance inconceivable in any newspaper-reading adult. For that admission to come from the leader of a cosmopolitan metropolis is mind-boggling. To have gone on CNN and admitted as much is just plain stupid—a credibility-destroyer that was total."[32]

For their part, the politicians insisted that they had been taking the high road by stepping back and letting the professionals handle the situation—that they did not want to exploit

---

[29]Oakland Ross, "City's Next Battle on Public Relations Front," *Toronto Star,* April 26, 2003, A9.

[30]Martin Regg Cohn, "WHO Rebukes Canada for SARS Lobby," *Toronto Star,* June 17, 2003, A1.

[31]"SARS according to Mayor Mel," *Globe & Mail,* April 26, 2003, A8.

[32]Jim Coyle, "True Leaders During Crisis Aren't Elected," *Toronto Star,* April 26, 2003, A18.

SARS for political capital or increase public alarm. In fact, their biggest role came later, with a partisan federal versus provincial (and Liberal versus Tory, respectively) tussle over who was going to foot the bill for the SARS emergency response and how much of the economic loss suffered in the GTA would be offset by government spending.

The Cavalry Rides to Geneva

After receiving Canada's enraged response to its Toronto travel advisory, WHO did agree to hear an appeal of its decision on April 30. The Canadian delegation came armed with facts and figures and suggested that WHO had probably not seen the best and most current data from Toronto, and thus it did not understand that SARS was well in-hand in the city, that there had been no new transmissions of the disease in the previous 10 days. Clement recalls, "When we gave them the numbers on the decline in new cases, and when we gave them the information on how we were handling the cases in the hospitals, what they said to us was, 'OK, what about the border issue?'"

The Border Issue

According to Clement, it rapidly became clear to the delegation that the WHO's primary concern with respect to SARS was to prevent the disease from traveling to developing countries that had little public health infrastructure. The WHO's sudden focus on Toronto, in fact, may have resulted from the claim of the Philippine government that Adela Catalon had brought SARS to Manila from Toronto.[33]

On March 27, well before the Catalon incident, WHO had called on the federal government in Canada to institute health screening of all passengers aboard international flights out of Toronto's Pearson International Airport. Ontario officials had urged their federal counterparts to comply, but federal officials were reportedly not convinced of the efficacy of airport screening. Instead, they arranged for the distribution of information cards at the airport, asking passengers with SARS symptoms to put off traveling and see a physician. To WHO, which favored the use of questionnaires to identify potential SARS carriers along with infrared scanners to detect passengers traveling with a fever, the Canadian information cards were anemic indeed. Clement recalls WHO officials asking, "Why are we getting better compliance on border control from Asia than we are from North America?"

In Geneva, Clement and his delegation colleagues were able to broker a deal. Health Canada committed itself to carrying out a set of specific, robust airport screening measures, and WHO rescinded its advisory on April 30, 1 week after issuing it.

---

[33]Whether Catalon really had SARS was in sharp dispute at that time, and the question was never completely resolved even though TPH did eventually find a clinical link between Catalon and other SARS patients in Toronto.

It's Over!

Back in Toronto, meanwhile, leaders of the emergency response to SARS were worn out, dispirited by the WHO advisory, and eager to put this difficult chapter behind them. Luckily, the prospects of doing so appeared promising—there had been 10 consecutive days without a new probable SARS case. Once the city had gone 20 consecutive days without a case—two incubation periods—the epidemiologists believed it would be safe to declare the outbreak at an end.

On May 9, Toronto's Basrur jubilantly told the press that the outbreak was over. On May 14, WHO removed Toronto from its list of areas with recent local transmission, and on May 17, Ontario Premier Eves formally ended the province's declared emergency and dismantled the POC. That same day, the Ontario Health Ministry ended Code Orange for GTA hospitals, so they could return to their full complement of health-care services. But the post-SARS celebration was brief.

"Falling Apart before Our Eyes"

On Friday, May 18, Maurice Buckner, a 57-year-old double-lung transplant recipient at St. John's Rehabilitation Hospital, went home for the Victoria Day long weekend. Almost immediately, he became feverish and exhausted. In alarm, his wife took him to the Emergency Department of Toronto General Hospital. Doctors there stabilized him and sent him back to St. John's, where he developed pneumonia symptoms. But one Toronto General doctor, fearing SARS, ordered a bronchoscopy and tested Buckner's respiratory secretions for signs of the SARS virus.

On May 22, that test came back positive. When TPH received this grim report, it immediately sent an envoy to St. John's, where investigators discovered a cluster of four patients with probable SARS. At 9:00 p.m. that night, according to the Canada Press, "a clutch of ashen-faced public health officials" gathered at the headquarters of TPH to report this dispiriting piece of news to the public.[34] They did not yet have the answer to the crucial public health question: Where had this cluster come from?

At first, public health workers held out the hope that the St. John's outbreak would turn out to be a small and isolated incident. They learned that Kitty Chan, the mother of St. John's leg surgery patient Hubert Chan, had recently returned with her husband from a trip to Hong Kong, where the couple spent part of each year. Both Kitty Chan and Hubert Chan were now sick with probable SARS. Had Kitty brought SARS back from Hong Kong and

---

[34]Canadian Press, "Strange twists during SARS four-month outbreak," July 6, 2003, available at www.ctv.ca/servlet/ArticleNews/print/CTVNews/20030706/sars_review_030706/20030706/?hub=Health&subhub=PrintStory [accessed August 27, 2008].

infected her son, who had, in turn, passed the disease to others at St. John? But the answer was no. Kitty Chan and her husband had returned from Hong Kong on April 22 and had immediately placed themselves in a 10-day self-quarantine, just to be on the safe side. After that, they went to visit their son, who was, at the time, at North York General Hospital. On May 9, he was transferred to St. John's, and on Mother's Day, May 11, Kitty Chan visited him there. Over the next 2 or 3 days, both Kitty and Hubert became feverish and weak with respiratory symptoms. Kitty Chan was admitted to Centennial Hospital soon thereafter.

Another of the St. John's SARS cluster had also been a patient in North York's orthopedic ward. On May 23, two TPH doctors and Low headed to North York General and asked to look at the medical charts of all the pneumonia patients. They soon discovered that there were a large number of pneumonia cases—perhaps twenty—clustered in the orthopedic ward. Even as they sat in North York General poring over the charts, they learned that members of the hospital staff had just turned up in the Emergency Department with suspicious symptoms. It was all too familiar. "The day we sat in that conference room, I remember, it was really quite surreal, because things were falling apart before our eyes," Low recalls. That night, at TPH's instigation, North York General closed down. TPH announced that anyone who had visited St. John's between May 9 and May 20 or North York between May 13 and May 23 must go into quarantine. The outbreak was back.

SARS II

Call it SARS II, or call it the moment when Toronto realized that SARS I had never actually ended; either way, the second go-round of the outbreak had a very different character from the first. (See Exhibit 2B-1 for an epidemiological curve of the entire Toronto SARS outbreak.) "Phase One was sort of a rah-rah kind of outbreak," explains Low. "And Phase Two—everybody was sick of it. They didn't want it. It was a mistake. People were fed up with SARS. It was a failure. It was a very different atmosphere than the first wave."

For all that, the actual containment of the second outbreak was smoother and more efficient than the first, public health experts agree. Working with better information about SARS and having learned from the experience of SARS I, hospitals and public health departments had clearer protocols from the start. In fact, once the second outbreak was detected, it took only 1 week to halt nearly all transmission of the disease, and WHO removed Toronto from its list of active SARS outbreak areas on July 2. But 118 people became sick during SARS II, and 13 of them died. Thus, the city was much-occupied with figuring out what had gone wrong—what had allowed the resurgence of SARS when it had been all but extinguished in late April?

By mid-June, with the help of epidemiologists from the CDC, TPH doctors believed they had worked out the basics of the link between SARS I and SARS II. According to the CDC

Exhibit 2B-1   Epidemiological curve of the Toronto SARS outbreak*

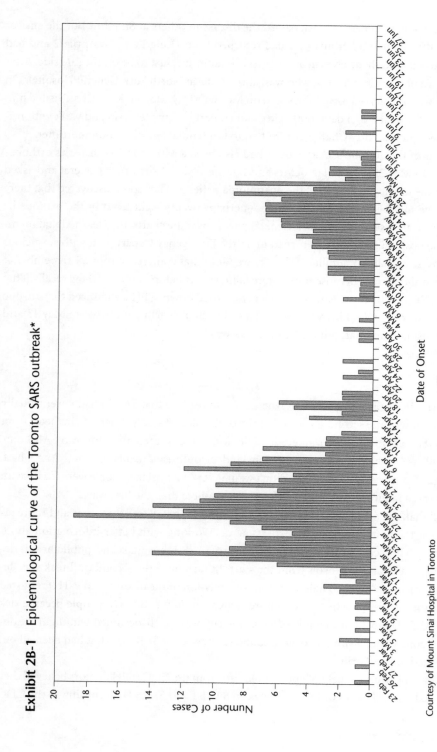

Courtesy of Mount Sinai Hospital in Toronto

*Date that symptoms of illness began for each person diagnosed with probable SARS in the Toronto area between February and June 2003.

report, the chain of infection went all the way back to Tse, who had passed the disease to James Dougherty, who had spent the night of March 7 on a gurney near Tse's in the Scarborough-Grace Emergency Department. When Dougherty was re-admitted to Scarborough-Grace on March 14 with a heart attack, he spent 2 days in the Scarborough-Grace cardiac unit without being recognized as a SARS patient and without being isolated. There he is believed to have passed SARS to a female heart patient who returned home on March 17, where she developed respiratory symptoms but was never diagnosed with SARS. She passed the virus to her daughter, who was a nurse at North York General. The nurse began to feel sick on March 30, but did not immediately stop working. The CDC was not sure how she could have come into contact with Lewis Huppert, a 99-year-old North York patient with a fractured pelvis because she was not assigned to his ward. But epidemiologists believed that, somehow, she did pass the disease to him.

Huppert developed pneumonia symptoms on April 2, but doctors assumed he had aspiration pneumonia, which is common in elderly, bedridden patients. Especially confusing, Huppert's symptoms seemed to abate when he was given a round of antibiotics.[35] By April 19, however, he was worse again, with a fever and diarrhea. On May 1, Huppert died. Meanwhile, other patients in the orthopedic ward began to develop pneumonia symptoms. So, too, did Huppert's wife, daughter, son-in-law, and granddaughter—all of whom came, at some point, to the North York Emergency Department as patients. None of the four was diagnosed with SARS, and none was hospitalized.

A junior doctor at North York and a number of nurses were convinced that the family had SARS, however. They finally insisted on a meeting with hospital management on May 20 to press the issue. North York's management team reportedly tried to calm the group and repeated the common wisdom that the SARS outbreak was over.

Political Pressure?

Once the news of the missed SARS cluster became public, there was much public speculation about whether the WHO travel advisory had led to direct or indirect political pressure on doctors, hospitals, and public health personnel not to find any more SARS cases. For one thing, the WHO travel advisory had resulted in an abrupt shift in public rhetoric about SARS. Before the advisory, the rhetoric had been cautionary (some said alarmist) warnings to the public and exhortations to stay home if suffering from flu-type symptoms. Afterward, the rhetoric was reassuring and stressed that the outbreak was well in-hand and the city safe. Some remarked wryly that the city and province had gone directly from panic to denial with no stop in between.

What's more, a late May dustup over Health Canada's diagnostic criteria for SARS fed the picture of a nation trying to minimize its SARS profile through a bit of fancy footwork. The

---

[35] Antibiotics should have no effect on a viral disease like SARS.

issue erupted when Low and TPH doctors were deciding how to diagnose the cluster of cases at North York General in late May. The dilemma was whether they should be labeled probable SARS or suspect SARS. In terms of stopping the spread of the disease, this distinction did not matter because all the cases would be isolated and handled with the same barrier infection precautions. But only the probable SARS tally was reported to the WHO. Infectious disease and public health doctors had actually paid little attention to the Health Canada definition until mid-April when D'Cunha had begun pushing for a more exacting diagnosis of SARS in an effort to cut down on the false-positive diagnoses of the disease. But the Health Canada definition of probable SARS was stricter than the WHO definition and, in Low's opinion, stricter in a way that made no sense.[36]

When asked by a radio journalist on May 28 to characterize the scope of the North York outbreak, Low publicly criticized the Health Canada definition, arguing that it led to a significant undercount of probable SARS cases. His comments set off an international media uproar. WHO expressed indignation at being given a deceptively low SARS count from Canada. Health Canada expressed indignation at Low, saying that this was the first the agency had heard of the problem. "By the end of the day, I was ready to leave town," Low recalls. "But within 24 hours, Heath Canada had changed the definition," bringing it in line with the WHO language. Under the new definition, there were not just a handful but forty-three probable SARS cases in the GTA.

Infectious disease experts and public health doctors at all levels of government resolutely denied that there was any political pressure not to find SARS cases after the WHO advisory. "It is an urban myth. It did not occur," says Young. According to Yaffe, TPH, for its part, "remained vigilant for any new cases of SARS and did not let down our guard." In the case of hospital physicians, the pressure not to find SARS cases—to the extent that it existed— was subtle and internal, according to Low. "I don't think anybody tried to hide a case they thought in their hearts was SARS," he says. But, for all kinds of reasons, doctors ardently wanted to believe that SARS had gone for good. And given the general nature of SARS symptoms and the prevalence of pneumonia among hospital patients, it was not difficult to find ample evidence for an alternative diagnosis. There was a climate, he explains, in which "subconsciously, people were more apt to say 'no' as opposed to 'yes.'"

Exit Strategy

None of that would have mattered, however, if Ontario had consciously developed an outbreak "exit strategy" back in April, Low continued, voicing the common wisdom of the emergency responders in retrospect. On May 14, the day WHO removed Toronto from the list of

---

[36]Recall that the Health Canada definition required a clinical finding of severe progressive pneumonia, while the WHO definition required only an x-ray finding of pneumonia or respiratory distress syndrome.

areas with local SARS transmission, "everybody should have gone into their hospitals and identified everybody over the next week that had febrile respiratory illness with pneumonia. [You then assume] that person has SARS until proven otherwise, and therefore you don't allow [any further] transmission to occur."

This was, more or less, what happened at the end of SARS II, although Low says that the second time around, the province and the hospitals erred on the side of extreme caution. Many precautions remained in place long after the threat of SARS had passed. "We just kept everything in place until there was absolutely no possible way in the world that we could ever have missed a case. And then," he adds, "we added a buffer of two to three months."

SARS in Toronto (C): Epilogue

SARS infected and killed more people in Toronto than it did anywhere else in the western industrialized world, and it was brought to heel in Toronto later than in any other place except Taiwan. Federal and provincial postmortem analyses of the Toronto SARS outbreak painted a picture of a system under significant duress because of a 20-year erosion of investment in the public health system, which consequently meant that many of the building blocks for an effective emergency response were not in place when SARS hit. These reports praised the Herculean efforts of the city, provincial, and medical community, but called for extensive improvements in the country's public health infrastructure.

Others interpreted the situation quite differently. "You would have thought that of all the cities that were hit by SARS, that Toronto was the one that should have handled it the best," says Dr. Richard Schabas, the former provincial chief medical officer of health. "In fact, you can make the argument that maybe we handled it the worst." The heart of Toronto's problem, he claims, was a series of wrongheaded decisions and judgments by the leaders of the outbreak response.[1]

No matter what the ultimate assessment, it was unnerving for observers of the outbreak response to realize that SARS was only moderately contagious compared to other communicable diseases. If the local, provincial, and federal governments had struggled this hard to control a moderately infectious disease in Toronto, how would they fare in the face of something more deadly and more infectious—a true pandemic, say, or a bioterror attack?

Opposing Assessments

Even granting that Toronto had a heavy dose of bad luck in facing the SARS virus before the world was on guard against the disease, almost everyone involved in the SARS outbreak in Canada acknowledged that aspects of the emergency response went awry. Learning the right lessons from the Toronto SARS outbreak, however, is tricky because mistakes and lapses were made at every level. Doctors missed SARS cases when they mistook them for different kinds of pneumonia. People who had been exposed to SARS were sometimes contacted too late to keep them from spreading the disease. Doctors, bureaucrats, and politicians wanted to believe the SARS outbreak was over before it was. Were these errors at the heart of what went wrong, or were systemic problems with preparedness at the heart?

---

[1] Interview with Dr. Richard Schabas, chief-of-staff, York Central Hospital, and former chief medical officer of health for the Province of Ontario, 2004. Unless noted, subsequent quotations from Schabas are also from this interview.

The Schabas Critique

For his part, Schabas believes that commonsense leadership judgments were at the heart of the difficulty. His has been a sometimes abrasive and lonely voice of criticism, and some have questioned his credibility because he has a record of criticizing the Progressive Conservative Party, which was in control of Ontario government during the SARS outbreak. Schabas's views do, however, make a provocative counterpoint to the conventional wisdom, and even his detractors have admitted that he has made some good points. For example, there is general agreement with Schabas that at the apparent end of SARS I all Greater Toronto area (GTA) hospitals should have instituted a pneumonia surveillance protocol, observing strict infection controls and closely watching every pneumonia case to be sure there were no stealth cases of SARS in the system that could rise up to continue the outbreak.

According to Schabas, there was, first, an underreaction in the failure to follow the commonsense precaution of halting all patient transfers out of Scarborough-Grace as soon as it was clear that a patient with an unknown virulent disease was being treated there. Then there was a wild overreaction in the decision to close down the hospital system and institute mass quarantine, setting off "public panic." Both those initiatives were so extreme that people did not have the energy or clarity to focus in on the few things that were really most important. "All you need to stop SARS is to identify cases, put them in private rooms, and nurse them with a mask," he says.

Schabas's critics say that his arguments are willfully simplistic, on the one hand, and reflect the advantage of 20/20 hindsight, on the other. At the time, the health community did not know how contagious SARS was or the circumstances under which it could spread. Yes, in retrospect, it turned out that it was not very contagious and that it was mostly droplet-spread by people in hospitals. Although ultimately there was little community spread, there *might* have been—and the responders had to act on that possibility. According to Ontario Public Safety Commissioner Jim Young, co-director of the provincial response to the SARS outbreak, "Richard was on one side saying, 'This isn't the pandemic.' There were others coming to me and saying, 'It is.' When you're in the middle of something like this, you're getting contrary advice from different people. I didn't feel that we could take the chance." [2]

Schabas counters that simply by graphing the incidence of new cases—creating an epi curve—the responders should have been able to see pretty quickly that SARS was not terribly contagious.

The fundamental problem, in my view, was that people jumped to conclusions about SARS. . . . From the very beginning, there was this perception that this was a highly infectious pandemic disease. . . . All efforts were put into . . . "controlling this disease"—forgetting the fact that if it *was* a highly

---

[2]Interview with Jim Young, Ontario public safety commissioner, 2004. Unless noted, subsequent quotations from Young are also from this interview.

infectious disease, we didn't have a hope in hell of controlling it. But they did not put sufficient effort into understanding what was going on—into challenging their basic assumptions about this disease and collecting and analyzing the data.

Basically, according to Schabas, there were just two critically important pieces of data: the date that each diagnosed probable SARS patient got sick and the likely route of transmission. By about April 10, the pattern was clear enough to Schabas that he sat down and wrote an editorial arguing that the reaction to SARS was overblown—that the disease was not terribly infectious after all. As a confirming piece of evidence, he adds, Hanoi had brought its outbreak under control quickly and had posted its epi curve on the World Health Organization (WHO) Web site by the end of March. "Hanoi had a nice curve that went up and came down, and it was over. And I said to people, if you can control an infectious disease in Hanoi, I mean, how hard can it be? And I'm not being disparaging to the Vietnamese. It's true."

The Government-Sponsored Reports

Meanwhile, both the federal government of Canada and the provincial government of Ontario commissioned after-the-fact studies of the emergency response to SARS in order to learn for the future and, in the case of the Ontario study, to identify the things that went wrong and led to SARS II.

Federal Health Minister Anne McLellan established the National Advisory Committee on SARS and Public Health in May 2003. The report of that committee, titled *Learning from SARS,* summarized the committee's viewpoint as follows:

Although the toll of the epidemic was substantial, thousands in the health field rose to the occasion and ultimately contained the SARS outbreak in this country, notwithstanding systems and resources that were manifestly sub optimal. The challenge now is to ensure not only that we are better prepared for the next epidemic, but that public health in Canada is broadly renewed, so as to protect and promote the health of all our present and future citizens.[3]

Of the committee's seventy-five recommendations, the biggest called for the creation of a Canadian Agency for Public Health—a sort of "CDC North"—that would be led by a chief public health officer. The committee also recommended the infusion of $700 million of new federal spending for public health by the year 2007 and called on federal and provincial/territorial governments to work jointly to address the country's shortage of public health nurses, public health doctors, microbiologists, and infection-control experts. In addition, it

---

[3]National Advisory Committee on SARS and Public Health, *Learning from SARS: Renewal of Public Health in Canada* (Ottawa: Health Canada, 2003), 12.

called on Canada to take a lead role in advocating international standards for issuing travel advisories and warnings.

The interim version of the report commissioned by Ontario, *SARS and Public Health in Ontario*, was more detailed in its analysis of what went wrong and more passionate in tone. While the federal report characterized systems and resources as "manifestly sub optimal," the provincial report stated that "SARS showed Ontario's central public health system to be unprepared, fragmented, poorly led, uncoordinated, inadequately resourced, professionally impoverished, and generally incapable of discharging its mandate." [4] The Ontario report, however, like that of the National Advisory Committee, made a point to praise the heroic efforts of the health-care and public health workers and their medical advisers.

In addition to endorsing the recommendations made in the federal report, the Ontario report included a separate set of recommendations with respect to the province's own public health system. It called for the creation of a provincial Centre for Disease Control, independent of the Ministry of Health, to support the chief medical officer of health. This Ontario Centre for Disease Control, it said, should have "a critical mass of public health expertise, strong academic links and central lab capacity." [5]

"The SARS crisis exposed deep fault lines in the structure and capacity of Ontario's public health system," the report stated and, in its aftermath, the province faces "a clear choice":

If it has the necessary political will, it can make the financial investment and the long-term commitment to reform that is required to bring our public health protection against infectious disease up to a reasonable standard. If it lacks the necessary political will, it can tinker with the system, make a token investment, and then wait for the death, sickness, suffering and economic disaster that will come with the next outbreak of disease. [6]

---

[4] Commission to Investigate the Introduction and Spread of SARS in Ontario, *Interim Report: SARS and Public Health in Ontario* (Toronto, 2004), 1.

[5] Ibid., 3.

[6] Ibid., 24, 217.

Key Actors in SARS Outbreak in Toronto

Public Officials in Spring 2003

Sheela Basrur, MD, Toronto medical officer of health

Tony Clement, Ontario Ministry of Health and Long-term Care

Colin D'Cunha, MD, Ontario chief medical officer of health and public health commissioner

Ernie Eves, Ontario premier

Allison Stuart, director, Ontario Health and Long-term Care Ministry's Hospitals Division

Barbara Yaffe, MD, TPH communicable disease control director

Jim Young, MD, Ontario public safety commissioner

Medical Experts

Sandy Finkelstein, MD, Scarborough-Grace intensive care unit director

David Heymann, WHO communicable disease director

Ian Johnson, MD, professor of public health, University of Toronto, and the Epi Unit's epidemiology director

Donald Low, MD, Mt. Sinai microbiologist-in-chief

Allison McGeer, MD, Mt. Sinai infection control director

Irving Salit, MD, University Health Network Infectious Disease Division director

Richard Schabas, MD, former Ontario chief medical officer of health and York Central Hospital chief-of-staff

Brian Schwartz, MD, Sunnybrook pre-care director

Andrew Simor, MD, Sunnybrook microbiologist-in-chief

Agnes Wong, Scarborough-Grace intensive care unit patient care manager

SARS Patients

Kwan Sui-chu, 78

Liu Jian Lun, 64

Tse Chi Kwai, 43

Joseph Pollack, 76

Rose Pollack, 73

James Dougherty, 77

Adela Catalon, 46

Eulialo Samson, 82

Nestor Yanga, 54

Maurice Buckner, 57

Kitty Chan, 66

Hubert Chan, 44

Lewis Huppert, 99

SARS Outbreak in Toronto, 2003

Chronology of Events

February 21

Kwan Sui-chu is infected with the SARS virus in Hong Kong's Metropole Hotel.

February 23

Kwan returns home to Toronto.

February 25

Kwan begins to feel ill.

February 28

Kwan goes to see her primary care physician, who prescribes antibiotics.

March 5

Kwan dies at home.

March 7

Kwan's son, Tse Chi Kwai, goes to the Scarborough-Grace Hospital Emergency Department with a severe case of pneumonia.

A Vancouver citizen, who had also stayed at the Metropole Hotel, returns home from Bali very sick and is rushed directly from the plane to isolated care at Vancouver General Hospital.

March 8

Tse is tentatively diagnosed with tuberculosis and placed in an isolated room in the intensive care unit.

March 9

Scarborough-Grace Hospital notifies Toronto Public Health of a possible cluster of tuberculosis cases in an extended Scarborough family.

March 10

Scarborough-Grace Patient Care Manager Agnes Wong raises the possibility that Tse might have bird flu, at the time considered a possible cause of the "mystery pneumonia" in China's Guangdong Province.

March 12

The World Health Organization (WHO) issues a global alert about outbreaks of atypical pneumonia in Viet Nam, Hong Kong, and Guangdong Province.

March 13

Tse dies at Scarborough-Grace Hospital.

March 14

Toronto and Ontario public health officials hold a joint press conference to alert the public to the fact that two members of a Toronto family have died and another four are sick as a result of contracting a mysterious, virulent pneumonia—perhaps the same one circulating in China and Viet Nam.

March 15

WHO names the new disease severe acute respiratory syndrome (SARS), declares it a world-wide threat, and releases diagnostic criteria for it.

The primary care physician who saw Tse and his wife in her outpatient clinic is diagnosed with SARS.

March 16

Joseph Pollack, 76, a cardiac patient who spent 12 hours on a gurney next to Tse's in the Scarborough-Grace Emergency Department on March 7, is rushed to the Scarborough-Grace Emergency Department and swiftly diagnosed with SARS.

March 20

Scarborough-Grace health-care workers begin to appear at the hospital's Emergency Department with high fevers.

March 21

Pollack dies at Scarborough-Grace.

Scarborough-Grace shuts down its emergency department and intensive care unit.

March 23

Scarborough-Grace closes to all new hospital admissions and places sharp restrictions on day patients and visitors.

March 25

Ontario Health Minister Tony Clement declares SARS a reportable disease under provincial law.

March 26

The SARS caseload in the Greater Toronto area rises from eighteen to forty-nine during this single day.

Mt. Sinai Hospital discovers that an undetected SARS patient spent 31 hours in its intensive care unit without being isolated. The hospital closes its emergency department and intensive care unit for 10 days and orders all exposed hospital workers to quarantine themselves.

Ontario Premier Ernie Eves declares a provincial emergency.

March 27

On the recommendation of an ad hoc group of frontline public health and infectious disease experts, the Ontario Health Ministry requires all greater Toronto hospitals to invoke their Code Orange emergency plans, closing down the hospitals to all but essential care. The ministry also issues a set of directives to the hospitals for improving infection controls.

Public Safety Commissioner Jim Young creates a SARS Operations Centre within the Health Ministry to translate the hospital policy recommendations of the Science Advisory Committee into hospital directives.

Young asks Don Low, microbiologist-in-chief at Mt. Sinai Hospital, and others to recruit infectious disease experts from across Canada to form a Science Advisory Committee.

WHO calls on Health Canada to institute health screening of all passengers aboard international flights out of Toronto's Pearson International Airport.

March 28

York Central Hospital discovers that James Dougherty, an undetected SARS patient, spent 12 days in its hospital without being isolated. York Central closes its emergency department and intensive care unit and sends 3,000 staff, patients, and visitors into quarantine.

A person with undiagnosed SARS attends a religious service of the Bukas-Loob Sa Diyos Covenant Community (a mostly Filipino religious group), where 500 people had gathered.

March 29

A person with undiagnosed SARS attends a Bukas-Loob Sa Diyos Covenant Community religious retreat attended by 225 people.

March 31

Ontario extends the infection control directives (but not Code Orange) to all Ontario acute-care hospitals.

Colin D'Cunha, Ontario chief medical officer of health, asks Bill Mindell, medical officer of health in the York region, to create a temporary Epi Unit in the Ontario Public Health Branch.

April 2
Experts believe Lewis Huppert, 99, a patient at North York Hospital, had SARS and not aspiration pneumonia, as doctors had initially believed.

April 11
Toronto Public Health discovers SARS spreading within the Bukas-Loob Sa Diyos Covenant Community.

April 12
Eleven health-care workers at Sunnybrook and Women's Health Care Centre are infected with SARS during a difficult intubation procedure.

April 13
Toronto Public Health quarantines the entire Bukas-Loob Sa Diyos Covenant Community.

April 15
Eleven health-care workers at Sunnybrook and Women's Health Care Centre begin to show symptoms.

April 20
Sunnybrook Hospital closes its Emergency Department and intensive care unit for 10 days.

April 23
WHO issues a worldwide advisory warning against nonessential travel to Toronto.

April 30
A delegation of health officials from Toronto, Ontario, and Canada meets with WHO officials in Geneva to try to persuade them to rescind the travel advisory.

Canada agrees to put in place rigorous airport screening of passengers traveling internationally and WHO agrees to lift the advisory.

May 9
Toronto Public Health declares the SARS outbreak over.

May 14
WHO removes Toronto from its list of areas with active SARS transmission.

May 17
Ontario Premier Eves ends the province's formal emergency.

May 20
A group of North York General nurses and other health-care workers holds a meeting with hospital management expressing concern over a possible SARS cluster in the hospital.

May 22
Maurice Buckner, 57, a patient at St. John's Rehabilitation Hospital, tests positive for the SARS virus. Toronto Public Health doctors diagnose three other St. John's patients with probable SARS. Toronto and Ontario public health officials announce the cluster of four cases.

May 23
Toronto Public Health and Mt. Sinai's Low discover a large cluster of patients with suspect or probable SARS at North York General.

May 28
Low publicly criticizes the Health Canada definition of probable SARS, saying it had led to a pronounced undercounting of cases compared to the WHO definition.

May 29
Health Canada brings its definition of probable SARS in line with the WHO definition.

July 2
WHO once again removes Toronto from the list of areas with active SARS transmission.

Part II   Structuring Crisis Response

The introduction to Part I identified several core challenges of disaster response. Several of these are highly pertinent to the issues posed by the case studies in Part II:

- *Scalability and surge capacity.* Disasters are generally much larger than the emergencies that jurisdictions deal with on a regular basis and therefore demand more complex forms of organization and levels of resources that greatly exceed the ordinary.
- *Maintaining situational awareness.* Responders need to gather and assimilate key facts—often under conditions of great confusion and uncertainty—and assess how they are positioned to deal with the emergency. They must also use this information to anticipate how the emergency is likely to develop going forward, assess what options they have for managing it, and put selected actions into play effectively.
- *Integrated execution in real time.* As local agencies confront extraordinary operational demands, emergency responders from adjoining jurisdictions, the state, and far-flung locations are likely to converge on the scene. Not only must they perform useful tasks themselves, they must also avoid interference or conflict with and endangerment of others, even though many of these people and organizations will have had little or no prior experience working together.

Over time, much has been learned about how to design response organizations and the responses themselves to provide efficient and effective action when emergencies arise. One particularly effective mechanism for organizing response is the *Incident Command System* (ICS) or *Incident Management System* (IMS). As we mention in the introduction to Part I, this mechanism arose out of wildland firefighting in the 1970s (drawn from organizational and decision-making models widely used in military planning and operations). Over the past several decades, it has spread to related professional disciplines such as structural firefighting, emergency medical services, and emergency management. As a result of a congressional mandate in the Homeland Security Act of 2002, IMS has now become the basis for the National Incident Management System (NIMS), a national system that all emergency organizations in the United States are required to adopt and use.

In the case studies that follow, readers can judge the ways in which the emergency challenges identified here tested responders in several critical situations. They can also assess whether and how well IMS works in coping with these severe challenges. In the Los Angeles riots of 1992, city, county, state, and federal responders operated without benefit of such a system. By contrast, in dealing with the Baltimore tunnel fire of 2001, city firefighters organized the response using the IMS principles that they routinely used in their work and, as the response grew, used them to coordinate with other city responders and organizations from outside the city. In an at least equally complex situation, firefighters from Arlington County led the emergency response to the terrorist attack on the Pentagon on 9/11, organizing their efforts in a unified command that encompassed numerous organizations from other jurisdictions and levels of government. Before engaging these case studies, however, it is worthwhile to consider how and why IMS developed and what its key features are.

Development of the Incident Command System Structure

Wildland or forest firefighting has a number of characteristics that made it a natural host for the development of such a system. Wildland fires have become larger and more threatening to inhabited areas. They come in many different sizes. Nearly always, they start off relatively small, so the larger ones have grown progressively through many stages. Organizations that contend with such fires need to operate at different scales and to change scales smoothly and easily (both when scaling up and scaling down). Putting out forest fires often involves engagements of extended duration, which implies that simply deploying and hoping that logistics (such as supplying food and replenishing supplies and equipment) will take care of itself is likely to result in poor performance.

As a consequence of these imperatives, in the 1960s and 1970s wildland firefighting evolved a succession of models for organizational design that have matured into today's IMS. The characteristics of wildland firefighting shaped the development and structure of IMS, and today's archetypal system thus embodies some characteristics that are better suited to large-scale, long-duration actions than to "short and sharp" emergencies. This sometimes causes tensions when NIMS seems to require that some emergency organizations, whose more typical engagements are of shorter term and smaller scale, nonetheless have to conform to a model that permits scaling to a very large and very long-term deployment. As a consequence, there is ongoing debate about whether NIMS needs to allow more variability in its application to different emergency response organizations.

One important feature of ICS (as it is typically termed in wildland firefighting) is that it is designed to be assembled from the bottom; that is, the first responders to an accident, emergency, or disaster scene are supposed to set up a small incident command system, and as additional responders join the effort, command is handed up to successively more senior, experienced, and higher-level commanders as they arrive on the scene. This results in what might be described as a self-assembling hierarchy, and one of the design features of ICS is that it maintains the same structure and nomenclature as the organization scales up.

This also permits responses to be assembled from the top down, however. If a large deployment is needed, an ICS command team can be deployed to establish a headquarters operation. As operational response units deploy, they can then be told to establish communication with the headquarters (sometimes referred to as "overhead") organization that will help plan, organize, and direct their work while coordinating it with the work of other response groups.

Often, the system will grow in both directions at once. Self-assembling hierarchies of responders organize themselves in various impact locations, and a headquarters unit deploys to spread its wings over them and provide resources, planning, and coordination.

Organizational Units

For a deployment of significant scale, the standard incident command model generally begins with a designated *incident commander* (IC), who has a small staff that includes a public information officer, a safety officer, and a liaison officer. The IC oversees four functional organizational units that conduct the work of planning, supplying, operationally directing, and keeping track of the response activities. Through a series of meetings and briefings, which are largely standardized, these units keep each other and the IC informed about the situation and their projected activities and needs. The IC generally chairs these meetings, coordinating the work of the units; working toward a common understanding of the situation, goals, options, and chosen operational directions; and resolving conflicts that arise among these functions.

Exhibit II-1 shows a standard organizational chart for an ICS command structure. Each functional unit (Operations, Planning, Logistics, and Administration/Finance) has its own chief, and each chief has his or her own staff (whose size varies depending on the scale and complexity of the deployment). The operations chief (referred to as ops chief or just ops) is the person most directly responsible for formulating and communicating instructions about the current operational cycle, which, depending on the nature of the operation, may range from a few hours to a day but is generally 12 or 24 hours. The ops chief gets updates about the situation, keeps track of where his or her responders are deployed, and makes tactical and operational adjustments in the disposition of resources currently in the field, giving instructions about what is to be done now and what is to be done in the more or less immediate future.

The planning chief (or plans chief) is responsible for formulating the engagement plan for the next operational cycle (with an eye to the cycles beyond, as well, including the eventual demobilization of the response effort). He or she (and his or her staff) must track the current situation and try to project what it will look like at the end of the current operational cycle, so he or she can plan the deployment for the next cycle. What additional resources will be needed and where? Which of the current resources must be taken out of

Exhibit II-1   Basic functional structure of Incident Command System

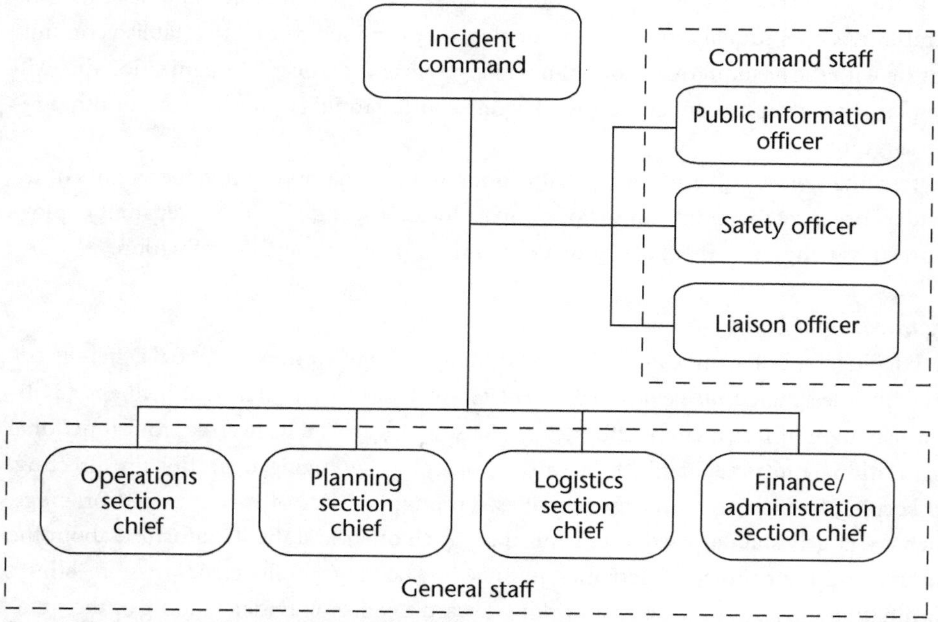

Source: U.S. Department of Homeland Security, *National Incident Management System,* draft, August 2007, 52.

service and given a rest period? What approach to the situation will be most likely to be effective? Should there be a change in strategy? Or do things seem to be working well and merely need to be continued? The Plans section works on forward-looking strategy and, in consultation with the IC and Operations, determines the plan for the next period. It then deduces the implications for what and who will be needed where and when. Because Operations will inherit and manage the plan when the new cycle begins, Operations has a keen interest. There tends to be a good deal of interaction among the ops chief, the plans chief, and the IC.

The Logistics group is charged with ensuring that the plan is implementable. Once strategy has been reviewed and set, tactics have been determined, and resource needs have been established for various locations, Logistics works to get the needed supplies, equipment, and support staged and moved into position for action. How many lunches will we need, and how do we get them to the right place? If we need additional people and/or equipment, where will they come from, how soon can they get here, and what transport resources are needed to move them? Where and in what quantities are shelter and sanitary facilities needed for responders whose daily shifts are coming to an end?

Again, there are important interactions between these functional areas that must take place successfully for things to work out well. Logistics must have a good understanding of the plan to be able to mobilize and position the required resources. Just as important, Plans needs to be aware of the logistical constraints—what will actually be available—so that the plan can be built around a realistic understanding of the resources that will be on hand.

Finally, Finance/Administration works to keep track of resource utilization, recording whose resources are being used; making sure that orders that are placed stay within budgeted limits (and the authority of those placing the orders); and, quite important, tracking who is supposed to pay for the people, equipment, supplies, outside contracts, and so on.

Processes and Procedures

In addition to the structure of the system and the roles played by people in various positions within that structure, ICS systems are characterized by a set of processes and procedures through which information about the situation is assembled and analyzed, predictions are made about how things will evolve, options are developed and decided on, and plans are formulated. Regular briefings and cycles of planning and problem solving are the hallmark of ICS in action. Especially in large ICS organizations, which might be overseeing a range of subunits below them, effective communication within the staffs of each functional area, across units, and between headquarters units at different levels is critical to the success of the operations.

ICS is not always used, and it is not always deployed effectively. When it is used well in circumstances for which it is appropriate, it can produce the remarkable capability to swiftly create an organization that can swing rapidly into action. It is not unusual for a headquarters unit deployed to manage a wildland fire to be established in a matter of hours and have the capability to organize, oversee, and direct thousands of firefighters more or less immediately. The ability to go from an empty room, with a pallet of supplies (phones, easels, pens, fax machines, and laptop computers, all in boxes) to a functional headquarters unit commanding thousands of responders operating in field units in a matter of hours—the ability to have an "organization in a box" and unpack it rapidly—is remarkable to watch. It takes a great deal of prior planning, practice, and training to make this work.

Lessons from Incident Command

The cases that follow feature quite different illustrations of ICS (or its absence). In examining these cases, think about which kinds of situations the incident command process is best suited to handle and what kinds of leadership are needed to make it function effectively. When riots broke out in Los Angeles after the announcement of the "not guilty" verdict in the trial of the police officers who beat Rodney King, the response was not formally organized along ICS lines, and coordination within and across agencies was generally poor—although there were also episodes of excellent performance by various units. By contrast, when a train derailed deep inside a rail tunnel in Baltimore in July 2001, ICS contributed to the ability of a variety of agencies to coordinate and bring their different but relevant expertise to bear on the situation. And in the terrible events at the Pentagon on September 11, 2001, an ICS combining federal, state, and local authorities was rapidly established and functioned continuously for 3 weeks, adapting (and shifting command influence across agencies) as the circumstances and challenges evolved from rescue to crime investigation to recovery.

3   The 1992 Los Angeles Riots (A): The Rodney King Case and Verdict

Susan Rosegrant

The rioting that engulfed Los Angeles in late April 1992 imposed horrible costs in human life and property destruction and deeply wounded the spirit of the city. By many measures, it was the worst U.S. civil disorder of the twentieth century. While the roots of these events were complex, the city's preparation for the possibility of widespread anger in the wake of the jury verdict in the Rodney King case and its emergency response once the rioting began were arguably responsible for letting an extraordinarily tense situation get severely out of control. In reconsidering the response strategy and execution, this case study raises important questions about planning for and managing the actions of widely dispersed responders operating in the face of significant danger and uncertainty.

When the riots broke out after a predominately white jury acquitted four police officers who had been accused of using excessive force in the videotaped beating of motorist Rodney King, the city was largely unprepared. Its emergency plan for civil disorder, developed in the aftermath of the Watts riots in 1965, was skeletal. It had neither been fleshed out with detailed contingency plans nor extensively exercised. Few resources were mobilized in anticipation of the imminent King case verdict. In the event, slow initial response by police, including the retreat of some units in the face of large threatening crowds, left significant areas of the city with little law enforcement presence. Widespread rioting, looting, and arson took place in several areas of the city over the next several days, and a number of brutal attacks on civilians were filmed by news crews from helicopters and played repeatedly on local and national television networks. Poor coordination between the Los Angeles police, firefighters, and the Los Angeles County Sheriff's Department repeatedly hobbled response efforts. In a number of areas, fire officials refused to send firefighters except when accompanied by a sizable police presence for protection, and as a result many fires burned unchecked. The deployment of National Guard units, called out by the governor to restore order, was also slowed by equipment and transportation difficulties and lack of coordination with local personnel. Order began to be restored with the arrival of 2,000 National Guard troops near the end of the second day of rioting and with the arrival of an additional 2,000 National Guard troops and nearly 2,000 federal law enforcement personnel by the end of the third day, but it was not fully restored until 4,000 federal troops activated under the Insurrection Act began to arrive on the fourth day.

Throughout these chaotic events, the response was plagued by poor planning and coordination among different agencies within city government and across jurisdictions: the city,

This is an abridged version of a case written by Susan Rosegrant for Richard Falkenrath, assistant professor of public policy, and Arnold M. Howitt, executive director of the Taubman Center for State and Local Government, for use at the Executive Session on Domestic Preparedness, John F. Kennedy School of Government, Harvard University. Funding for the case was provided by the Office of Justice Programs, U.S. Department of Justice. Kennedy School of Government Case Program, C16-00-1586.0, C16-00-1587.0, and C16-00-1588.0. Copyright © 2000, 2007 by the President and Fellows of Harvard College.

county, state, and federal governments. Different agencies had different organizational structures for coordinating response, used different means of communication, and sometimes disagreed about legal authority in specific situations. Notwithstanding these difficulties, however, there were examples of quite effective work by a number of units. Often, this arose through effective improvisation as on-site commanders figured out how to adapt successfully to chaotic conditions and developed ways of coordinating with units from other agencies.

Subcase A describes the events leading up to the verdict in the Rodney King case and the ways in which the city did and did not get ready for the possible reaction to the jury's decision. Subcase B covers the early stages from the outbreak of the rioting to LA Mayor Tom Bradley's decision to request state assistance from Governor Pete Wilson by calling out the National Guard. Subcase C recounts the difficulties encountered effectively deploying the National Guard, and Subcase D describes how federal assistance was secured and how, ultimately, order was restored to Los Angeles. As you read through the description of these events, think about the challenges of operating with multiple units of different types from different jurisdictions and with different responsibilities in a highly fluid situation.

Discussion Questions

- What kinds of prior preparation might have improved Los Angeles's early response to the rioting?
- As the situation intensified and its geographic scope expanded, what problems were created by the arrival and operations of so many emergency responders?
- How did responders establish a chain of command, both *within* their own organizations and *across* different organizations and professional groups? To what extent was this successful? In what ways did it fall short?
- Did new coordination issues arise as operations to deal with the crisis became more complex with the arrival of the National Guard and other responders from outside the area and extended over a longer period time?
- Which aspects of the response(s) to the LA riots seem to have been most effective? What would have enabled them to be more effective? What forms of command and coordination among different units does this suggest that we need to construct?

In the middle of the night in early March 1991, white police officers from the Los Angeles Police Department beat a black man named Rodney King while trying to arrest him after he was stopped for speeding. A videotape of the altercation, taped by a nearby resident and soon broadcast worldwide, turned Rodney King's arrest into a national symbol of police brutality and provided what most people believed was solid proof of misconduct by the four police officers eventually charged. More than a year later, as an almost all-white jury considered the evidence against the officers, Los Angeles awaited what almost everyone—including Los Angeles Mayor Tom Bradley and most members of the Los Angeles Police Department—had concluded would be at least one or two guilty verdicts.

But on April 29, 1992, the suburban jury acquitted three of the four police officers of all charges in the case and deadlocked on one charge against the remaining officer. The acquittals shocked Los Angeles and triggered outrage in the city's African American community. Neither the mayor, the Los Angeles Police Department (LAPD), nor the Los Angeles County Sheriff's Department, however, appeared able to respond effectively during the early hours of unrest, and what began as an outbreak of anger and frustration quickly escalated into one of the deadliest and most costly civil disturbances in U.S. history. During the 6 days of rioting, desperate officials ultimately called in not only thousands of California National Guard troops but also soldiers from the army and the marines to quell the violence. The riots' grim toll—54 people dead and more than 2,000 injured, and damages in the county estimated at between $800 million and $1 billion—raised serious questions about how the city had been caught so unprepared, why local law enforcement officers had been unable to regain control, and why the mutual aid system that pulled in resources from the region and the state had functioned so poorly.

Behind the "Thin Blue Line"

When LA police officers arrested Rodney King on March 3, 1991, relations between the city's black community and the police were already strained—in fact, they had been so for decades. Contributing to this tense relationship, some critics claimed, was the unusual degree of autonomy that the LAPD enjoyed, causing it to become arrogant and to lose touch with some of the communities it was supposed to serve. Since an amendment to the City Charter in the 1920s, the police chief had civil service status and could be fired only under extraordinary circumstances.[1]

By the mid-1960s, the LAPD's mostly white force was known for aggressive policing that included stopping and searching individuals merely because they looked suspicious—a policy that led many blacks to conclude they were being targeted because of their race. By the middle of 1965, following several incidents in which police had clashed with black residents, tensions were running particularly high in the city's economically stressed and mostly black inner-city neighborhoods. On August 11, the arrest of a black motorist by a white California Highway Patrol (CHP) officer in Watts drew an angry crowd and soon escalated out of

---

[1]The only charges that could lead to dismissal were high crimes and misdemeanors, insubordination, or incapacitation. No chief had been fired since the charter was approved.

control. The Watts riots that followed—6 days of violence, looting, and arson—resulted in at least 34 deaths, 1,032 injuries, and a torched central Watts business district. Many observers suggested that more community outreach might have lessened the hostility and friction that ultimately erupted in the devastating civil disturbance. The LAPD leadership, however, focused not on prevention but on what it saw as its own flawed response, concluding that deploying massive force at the outset could have controlled the riot and vowing not to make the same mistake again.[2]

After the Watts riots, the LAPD attempted to improve its relations with the black community. Tom Bradley, a former LAPD lieutenant elected in 1973 as the city's first African American mayor, made it clear he expected full integration of the police department.[3] In addition, Edward Davis, police chief from 1969 to 1978, instituted several community-oriented policing programs, including team policing, an approach in which officers were responsible for a specific neighborhood or section of the city. But even though most observers believed the team policing effort helped cut crime and improve relations between the LAPD and minority communities, it was short-lived. Mayor Bradley, concerned that specialized units were pulling too many officers off regular street patrol, and new Police Chief Daryl Gates, citing cost-cutting pressures and a general lack of support for the initiative among the department's rank and file, joined in dismantling the team policing approach.[4]

The Los Angeles Police Department and Rodney King's Arrest

By the early 1990s, conditions in some Los Angeles neighborhoods were reminiscent of the period preceding the Watts riots. The city was experiencing its worst economic downturn since the Depression, brought on in part by deep cuts in federal defense spending and an exodus from the city of auto makers and other manufacturers. The impact of the recession was particularly severe in South Central Los Angeles, an almost 40-square-mile area encompassing Watts and other economically depressed areas of the city (see Exhibit 3A-1 for a map of Los Angeles Police Department bureaus, including the area known as South Central).[5] In 1990, more than a third of South Central's 630,000 residents were living below the poverty line. Most families with the means to leave the area already had, depleting the black middle class that had served as a stabilizing force during previous decades. Arriving in their place were recent immigrants from Central America and Mexico, many of them illegal aliens. By

---

[2]Soon after, the department invested in two armored personnel carriers for use in possible future outbreaks.

[3]Mayor Bradley had faced racism within the LAPD head-on, having struggled against the racial barriers of the 1950s to achieve the position of lieutenant within the department.

[4]Some of Davis's other community policing programs remained intact.

[5]The city of Los Angeles occupied 479 and the county occupied 4,079 square miles.

Exhibit 3A-1   Map of Los Angeles Police Department Bureaus and South Central Los Angeles*

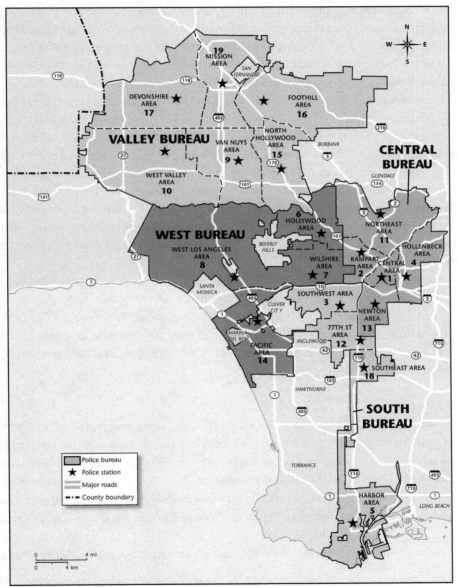

Source: LAPD/PRD/GIS Mapping, February 2, 2005, www.lapdonline.org/our_communities.

*The area that comprises south central Los Angeles—although not exactly defined—corresponds roughly with the LAPD South Bureau's divisions of Southwest, 77th Street, and Southeast, plus the Central Bureau's Newton Street Division.

1990, Latinos accounted for 49 percent of the population of South Central, while blacks made up 43 percent.

The rates for violent crime and gang activity had risen along with unemployment, fueled in part by the crack cocaine epidemic of the mid-1980s. In an effort to get tough, Police Chief Daryl Gates, in April 1988, had instituted Operation Hammer, an aggressive program to arrest gang members by conducting street sweeps through South Central. Operation Hammer, however, led to increased charges of police harassment and racism.[6]

In certain respects, the LAPD had changed since the Watts riots. The once largely white force had become integrated in the wake of Tom Bradley's election in 1973, and the percentage of black officers had grown to approximate the percentage of blacks in the city's population. Yet many African Americans still believed that police were disrespectful of, or even abusive toward, blacks. Within the department, meanwhile, the goal of doing more with less had become a bitter reality. Like other city agencies, the LAPD had felt the bite of Proposition 13, a landmark state initiative passed in June 1978 that reduced property taxes by two-thirds and curtailed the ability of local governments to raise taxes, thus severely limiting the local tax base available to support services such as schools, police, and fire protection.

Since the passage of Proposition 13, Los Angeles voters had approved only a few tax increases to support new hiring or equipment for the LAPD.[7] Although in 1990 the department had a peak workforce of about 11,000, including almost 8,400 sworn officers, that translated to only 2.4 officers per 1,000 residents, an extremely low ratio for a major metropolitan area. Washington, D.C., by contrast, had 7.81 officers per 1,000 residents, and New York had 3.67.[8]

The Arrest

In the early hours of March 3, 1991, CHP officers pursued a speeding vehicle on the Foothill Freeway at the northern edge of Los Angeles, a chase that ended when the car screeched to a stop with its path blocked on Foothill Boulevard. The two CHP officers had been joined by three LAPD cars, an LAPD helicopter, and police from the Los Angeles Unified School District.[9] According to official reports, the car's two passengers quickly got out and lay on the ground as instructed. But when the driver, Rodney King, finally emerged from the car,

---

[6]Lou Cannon, *Official Negligence: How Rodney King and the Riots Changed Los Angeles and the LAPD* (Boulder, Colo.: Westview Press, 1999), 17.

[7]Ironically, despite negative attitudes toward the police, residents from poor areas like South Central were more likely to support tax increases to pay for better police protection than were wealthier Angelenos, who were more insulated from the impact of crime.

[8]William H. Webster and Hubert Williams, *The City in Crisis: A Report by the Special Advisor to the Board of Police Commissioners on the Civil Disorder in Los Angeles* (Los Angeles, Calif.: October 21, 1992) Vol. 2, App. 15–16.

[9]By the time the arrest was completed, there were twenty-five law enforcement officers present.

his bizarre behavior and spotty compliance with police orders led officers to suspect he was drunk, if not high on phencyclidine (PCP).[10]

LAPD Sergeant Stacey Koon, the ranking officer at the scene, quickly took control of the arrest.[11] After King threw off officers who attempted to hold him down and handcuff him, and after darts from Koon's electric stun gun failed to keep King down, Koon ordered officers to use their metal batons. The violent and apparently unrestrained effort to subdue and arrest King after he charged one officer—in particular, the more than two dozen baton swings by Officer Laurence Powell, including a blow to King's head—sickened some officers at the scene. Yet the arrest probably would have triggered nothing more serious than a departmental review, except for one fact. The incident, beginning with King's charge toward Officer Powell, had been captured on videotape by George Holliday, a resident in a nearby apartment building awakened by the sound of the sirens.

One day later, Holliday took his video to a local Los Angeles TV station, and that night, a 68-second segment showing the Rodney King beating was broadcast for the first time.[12] Within hours, Holliday's video of the beating was the featured story in Los Angeles and a lead news story nationwide, as public leaders and private citizens alike spoke out against the apparent instance of police brutality.

Chief Gates, who was horrified by the scene depicted on the tape and who did not want the entire department tarnished by the incident, appeared to have concluded that the officers were guilty, and he announced March 7 that they would be prosecuted. On March 14, just 11 days after King's brutal arrest, a grand jury returned indictments against Laurence Powell, Stacey Koon, and two other officers involved in the beating, Theodore Briseno and Timothy Wind.[13] The disclosure that Powell appeared to have joked about the beating in a radio message afterward, as well as the release March 18 of a tape transcript from earlier on the night of King's beating in which Powell made a derogatory remark about African Americans, further fueled charges of racism and police brutality. According to a survey of registered Los Angeles County voters conducted a month and a half after the arrest, 81 percent of respondents thought the officers were guilty.[14] In the months leading up to the trial,

---

[10]The drug PCP had been known to give its users almost superhuman strength and the ability to ignore pain, making some suspects who had taken the drug particularly difficult to arrest. King later admitted to having drunk alcohol before the car chase, but it was never proved that he had drugs in his system.

[11]Koon later testified that he feared a CHP officer who had drawn her gun would end up shooting King or being shot by her own weapon if he didn't intervene.

[12]Holliday sold the tape to a local TV station after his district police station showed no interest in reviewing it. In the wake of the video fallout, both the LAPD and the Los Angeles County Sheriff's Department initiated formal policies to accept for review and possible action all tapes of law enforcement activity submitted by citizens.

[13]All four officers were accused of assault with a deadly weapon and assault under color of authority. In addition, Koon and Powell were charged with filing false police reports, and Koon was charged with being an accessory after the fact.

[14]Cannon, *Official Negligence*, 83.

eventually set for the following March, public condemnation of the officers' behavior never wavered.

The Christopher Commission and Latasha Harlins

Even before the Rodney King beating, the relationship between Mayor Bradley and Chief Gates had been a cool one. The disclosure of the violent arrest, however, was a turning point. Bradley was deeply offended by the videotape and what it appeared to indicate about attitudes within the LAPD. While Bradley saw the entire incident as a dangerous blow to racial unity in Los Angeles, he also saw it as a chance to force Gates from office and to bolster his faltering support among his own liberal and black constituency.[15]

On April 1, 1991, Bradley appointed the Independent Commission on the Los Angeles Police Department, chaired by prominent attorney Warren Christopher, to provide an unbiased investigation of Gates's leadership, focusing in particular on the policies, attitudes, and practices within the LAPD that bore on the use of excessive force. The goal, in Bradley's words, was to "restore the public's confidence" in the police.[16]

One hundred days later, on July 9, the so-called Christopher Commission released its report. Among its recommendations were the appointment of an inspector general within the Police Commission; better officer training; beefed-up discipline (including expulsion) of those problem officers who had received repeat charges of improper tactics; and a fundamental shift in training, rewards, and culture to encourage community-based policing. Most eagerly awaited, however, was the commission's assessment of Gates. After concluding that the chief had failed to foster a departmental culture that barred excessive force or that sufficiently curbed and punished officers who broke that rule, the report recommended that Gates resign.

Gates had already been chief for 13 years and had begun to broach the subject of his own retirement. But the Christopher Commission report seemed to fuel his defiance, and he declared that only when voters approved a charter change to limit the chief's term would he resign. In addition, Gates rejected those among the LAPD's top leadership, such as Assistant Chief David Dotson, director of the Office of Administrative Services, who had spoken critically to the commission about both the department and Gates. Increasingly, the sense of being under attack appeared to cause Gates to turn inward, trusting ever fewer people within

---

[15]Bradley had barely won reelection to a fifth term in 1989. While supporters attributed the slim margin of victory to the fact that the mayor did not campaign aggressively, some critics said support among Bradley's liberal backers had eroded because he had neglected the needs of poor areas like South Central in his eagerness to woo affluent developers.

[16]Cannon, *Official Negligence,* 121.

his own organization. The chief did, however, begin to execute most of the Christopher Commission's recommended changes.

Events outside of the LAPD's control, however, were conspiring to ratchet up tension in South Central and other areas with significant black populations. In particular, the seething antagonism that had existed for years between the black and Korean American communities was coming to a boil. Over the previous two decades, Koreans had purchased hundreds of liquor and convenience stores in inner-city and majority black neighborhoods that had been abandoned by other merchants in the wake of the Watts riots. In 1991, Korean immigrants ran some 3,300 convenience and liquor stores in greater Los Angeles and 350 stores in South Central alone.[17] Although many Korean-run stores prospered, armed assaults and shoplifting were frequent problems. Partly as a result, some Korean store owners had come to view all black customers as potential criminals, while African Americans complained of being charged too much and of being treated with contempt.

In March 1991, less than 2 weeks after the beating of Rodney King, a Korean shopkeeper shot and killed a 15-year-old black girl, Latasha Harlins, after a fight over a container of orange juice. The shopkeeper, Soon Ja Du, claimed that Harlins was trying to rob her, but her version of the incident was not supported by the scene captured on the store's own security camera. Du was charged with murder, and given the existence of the tape, which showed Du shooting an unarmed Harlins in the back of the head as she attempted to walk out of the store, most observers predicted a swift guilty verdict and a substantial prison sentence when the case went to trial.

The trial, however, did not conclude as expected. Although a jury returned a generally respected verdict of voluntary manslaughter, in November 1991, a novice judge gave Soon Ja Du a suspended 10-year prison sentence and placed her on 5 years probation.[18] The surprisingly light sentence, which many observers viewed as being blatantly biased toward the defendant, not only exacerbated tensions between Koreans and blacks; it convinced many in the city's African American community that the U.S. legal system was unjust.

People of California v. Powell

On November 26, 1991, less than 2 weeks after Du's controversial sentencing, the judge responsible for trying the Rodney King case made a surprising announcement. A change of venue from Los Angeles County had already been granted, apparently due to fears about the

---

[17]Ibid., 113–114.

[18]Du also had to do community service and pay a $500 fine and restitution to the victim's family for medical and funeral expenses. Harlins's enraged family refused to accept the restitution.

impact the trial could have on an already tense city, as well as concern that the police officers could not get a fair trial due to extensive pretrial publicity.[19] Instead of moving the trial
to an area untouched by city politics and outside of the Los Angeles media market, however,
Judge Stanley Weisberg announced that the case would be heard in neighboring Ventura
County in the largely white town of Simi Valley, a community whose residents included a
high concentration of Los Angeles law enforcement officers.[20]

For the four officers charged in *People of California v. Powell*, the new venue appeared to
be a miraculous break. Indeed, the makeup of the twelve-person jury ultimately seated on
March 2, 1992, only confirmed the location's benefits for the defense. The members of the
jury, all non-Hispanic whites except for one Latino and one Filipino American woman, almost uniformly revealed a conservative and pro-police orientation on their questionnaires.
Nevertheless, prosecutors chose not to speak out strongly against either the venue or the
jury pool, perhaps believing that the videotape was sufficiently compelling to overcome
these obstacles.

Almost lost in the predictions of guilty verdicts were the comments of a few black leaders who noted the dangerous similarity between the economic and social conditions in
South Central and what they had been prior to the Watts riots of 1965. Patricia Moore, a city
councilwoman representing Compton, a city with a large African American constituency
south of Watts, observed that, if the eventual verdict was seen as unfair, "this community,
and possibly the nation, will see upheavals as never before."[21]

On Thursday, April 23, 1992, after a twelve-and-a-half-week trial, the jury in *People of
California v. Powell* began its deliberations. Largely unrecognized, however, was the fact that
the evidence before the jury was not as one-sided as many observers believed. Most media
reports had glossed over the fact that King had only recently been paroled from prison after robbing a convenience store; had driven at dangerously high speeds while being pursued
by the CHP; and had been drinking in violation of his parole, having a blood alcohol content that was still well over California's legal limit several hours after the beating. Because
the prosecution deemed King an unreliable witness, in part because he continued to give
conflicting accounts of the beating, he was not called to the stand during the trial. Moreover,
although Officer Laurence Powell was known to have made racist remarks and had been

---

[19]Critics of the change of venue noted that, in recent decades, almost no trials had been moved in California
and that the ubiquitous videotape of the beating made it unlikely that potential jurors anywhere in the country
would be unaware of the incident.

[20]Some observers later speculated that Weisberg, whose wife was ill, made the venue decision based on the fact
that it was an easy commute.

[21]Quoted in Rene Lynch, "Minority Leaders Say Verdict Seen as Racist Could Blow Lid off Powder Keg," *Daily
News*, April 5, 1992; also quoted in Cannon, *Official Negligence*, 160.

accused in the past of unprofessional conduct and of using excessive force, the other three officers were well regarded.[22]

Ironically, it was the very videotape that constituted the prosecution's main evidence that ultimately undermined the case in important ways. First, the ubiquitous airing of the video had almost guaranteed a jury that was tilted toward the defense because potential jurors who had already concluded from watching the video that the officers were guilty were excused from duty. Those jurors who remained, therefore, were automatically less receptive to the prosecution's evidence. Even more important, however, the tape shown to the jurors was more complete than the one most people had seen on TV and placed the beating, although still brutal, in a broader context—3 seconds at the beginning showed King charging toward Officer Powell. Faced with the unedited video, jurors, already inclined to be supportive of the police and suspicious of the media's version of events, found it easy to believe the officers' claims that the beating arose from difficulties in arresting a dangerous, erratic, and resistant suspect.

Preparing for a Verdict: The Emergency Operations Organization

Mayor Bradley and Police Chief Gates, like most others following the trial, believed that at least Laurence Powell, if not all the officers, would be found guilty of excessive force. This strong belief in a guilty verdict, probably more than anything else, colored the city's and the LAPD's approach in preparing for the trial's conclusion. If the jury ruled as expected, Gates and others reasoned, there was little reason to anticipate a major disturbance. "If we were not prepared for any one thing, we were not prepared for four not-guilty verdicts," said then LAPD Commander Bayan Lewis. "We did not plan for a worst-case scenario." [23]

Bradley and Gates, as director and deputy director of the city's Emergency Operations Organization (EOO), respectively, were the leaders of the city's emergency preparedness structure. The three arms of the EOO—the Emergency Operations Board, the Emergency Management Committee, and the Emergency Operations Center—were charged not only with overseeing the response to city emergencies, but also with planning and training activities in preparation for a possible crisis (see Exhibit 3A-2 for an EOO organization chart). The EOO had a small permanent staff located in the office of the city administrative

---

[22]Stacey Koon's reputation for even-handed professionalism, for example, was cemented in many officers' minds when he gave mouth-to-mouth resuscitation to a black transvestite prostitute with bleeding mouth sores who had collapsed in the 77th Street Police Station. The man, who died despite Koon's efforts, was later found to have AIDS. Cannon, *Official Negligence*, 28.

[23]Ibid., 264.

Exhibit 3A-2   Emergency Operations Organization chart, City of Los Angeles

Director
Mayor

City Council

EMERGENCY OPERATIONS BOARD
DEPUTY DIRECTOR AND BOARD CHAIRMAN
Chief of Police
EMERGENCY OPERATIONS COORDINATOR AND BOARD VICE CHAIRMAN
City Administrative Officer
LEGAL ADVISOR
City Attorney
BOARD MEMBERS

General Manager Fire Department
General Manager Building & Safety
General Manager Personnel Department
Chief Public Works Division

General Manager Department of Recreations and Parks
General Manager Department of Transportation
General Manager Department of General Services
General Manager Department of Water and Power

EMERGENCY MANAGEMENT COMMITTEE
COMMITTEE CHAIRPERSON AND BOARD EXECUTIVE ASSISTANT
Chief Administrative Analyst, Office of the City Administrative Officer
COMMITTEE MEMBERS
(staff representing)

Department of Airports
Animal Regulation Department
Building & Safety Department
Chief Legislative Assistant
City Administrative Officer
City Attorney
City Clerk
Community Redevelopment Agency

Environmental Affairs
Fire Department
Department of General Services
Harbor Department
Information Services Department
Library Department
Office of the Mayor
Personnel Department

City Planning Department
Police Department
Department of Public Works
Department of Recreation & Parks
Department of Transportation
Department of Telecommunications
Department of Water and Power

American Red Cross
Los Angeles Unified School District

U.S. Coast Guard
Southern California Gas Company

Los Angeles County CAO
U.S. Army Corps of Engineers

EMC SUBCOMMITTEE

Budget
Communications
Computerization
Damage Assessment
Dehydrated Foods
EOC Facilities

Legislative
Master Plan
Media Task Force
Policies and Procedures
Recovery and Reconstruction
Task Group on Hazardous Materials

Shelter Management
Training
Transportation
Utilities
Volunteers

Note: CAO, Chief Administrative Office; EMC, Emergency Management Committee; EOC, Emergency Operations Center.

Source: William H. Webster and Hubert Williams, *The City in Crisis: A Report by the Special Advisor to the Board of Police Commissioners on the Civil Disorder in Los Angeles* (Los Angeles, Calif.: October 21, 1992) , 48, Fig. 3-1.

officer, and many city departments had one or two staff members devoted full-time to the organization.

The Emergency Operations Board, which reported directly to Bradley and was chaired by Chief Gates, comprised the general managers of eight agencies whose involvement was key to any emergency response, including the Los Angeles City Fire Department and the Transportation, Building and Safety, and Water and Power departments. Although only the eight general managers were voting members, board meetings were sometimes attended by dozens of department representatives. The board typically met once a quarter to consult on broad issues of coordination.

The Emergency Management Committee, on the other hand, chaired by Shirley Mattingly, director of emergency management and coordinator of the EOO, was a much larger group of staff-level representatives from all city departments, as well as some state, county, and nongovernmental organizations.[24] The committee and its subcommittees met at least monthly to discuss practical and logistical aspects of planning, coordination, and response.

Finally, during a major event, representatives of the city departments involved in a response came together to coordinate operations at the Emergency Operations Center (EOC), located in a subbasement of City Hall East, across the street from police headquarters. Although the EOC was the emergency center for the entire city, responsibility for running it rested with the LAPD, specifically its Tactical Planning Section. Unlike the EOO, however, there were no staff members permanently located at the EOC, nor were there high-level officers responsible for managing the center. Instead, a cadre of trained officers at the rank of lieutenant or lower reported to the center whenever Gates or some other top LAPD official activated the EOC.

According to then EOO Coordinator Mattingly, the EOO ran a major exercise in the EOC at least once a year. In addition, the LAPD typically activated the center several times a year to deal with both planned events, such as the visit of a major dignitary, and the area's many natural disasters, including brush fires and floods.

On paper, Bradley, as mayor and head of the EOO, shared responsibility with Gates for riot preparation and response. In practice, however, Mattingly explains, the board and its staff were the experts on emergency preparedness, and Bradley counted on them and on the LAPD, in particular, "to figure out what needed to be done and to do it."[25]

According to former Fire Chief Donald Manning, however, the Emergency Operations Board didn't convene any special meetings during the trial, nor did the board discuss in detail during a regularly scheduled meeting the possibility of a riot. Similarly, Shirley

---

[24]Although the EOO organization chart listed the city administrative officer as the official coordinator of the EOO, Mattingly had assumed that responsibility on his behalf.

[25]Interview with Shirley Mattingly, director of emergency management, April 7, 2000. Unless noted, subsequent comments by Mattingly are also from this interview.

Mattingly says, there was no coordinated planning among the representatives on the Emergency Management Committee for how to train for a possible civil disturbance or how to prioritize competing tasks. Although in theory the committee should have taken an active role in such planning, its efforts were focused on more routine earthquake and generic emergency preparedness, for which Los Angeles planners had won considerable recognition.[26] "The attitude in Los Angeles at the time was that we had been through the riots in the '60s, and as a society we had come a long way," recalls Mattingly. "There was no way that something like that, particularly racially motivated, could occur in Los Angeles in the '90s."

In any event, most observers say, the real responsibility for riot preparation lay with the LAPD, which would be the lead agency in any response. Gates, however, also failed to request a plan, either in his role as head of the board or as police chief. When questioned about the department's preparation, Gates claimed to have had a plan to handle a possible outbreak. The so-called plan, however, was simply a twenty-nine-page segment of the LAPD Tactical Manual, written after the Watts riots, as well as the "standing plans" of each police division. By contrast, when the Olympic Games were held in Los Angeles in 1984, the LAPD had created a highly specific and successful plan for handling emergencies.

Preparing for a Verdict: The Los Angeles Police Department

As a few days passed without a jury decision, some observers, particularly within the black community, began to worry that the officers might be found innocent after all and that such a verdict would set off angry and violent demonstrations. But even if Gates and the rest of the LAPD hierarchy had been convinced that such a disturbance was likely, other institutional factors lessened the ability and motivation of the top command staff to prepare.

Under the Law Enforcement Division of the California Office of Emergency Services (OES), law enforcement agencies could call on the state's mutual aid system for help if a situation escalated beyond their control or appeared likely to do so. Gates, therefore, could have arranged in advance of the verdict to have backup forces alerted and available from a range of local and state agencies. State mutual aid was coordinated on a regional basis, and in the case of Los Angeles, such requests for help would have been handled through Los Angeles County Sheriff Sherman Block, the coordinator for Region I, covering Los Angeles and Orange counties.

It was a point of pride with Gates, however, that the LAPD could handle any situation on its own. The aversion to mutual aid, observers said, arose both from a sense of superiority on the part of the LAPD and from the fear that other agencies would burden the LAPD with

---

[26]Even though earthquake planning included a small civil disturbance component, Mattingly says, it was not comprehensive enough to apply to a full-scale riot situation.

frequent requests for help. Even before Gates, the LAPD had had a reputation for not requesting mutual aid. When the Watts riots first erupted back in 1965, for example, not only did then Police Chief Parker not ask for help but he refused the Sheriff's Department's offer of three hundred deputies. The eventual deployment of the California National Guard to help control the riots had rankled some LAPD leaders ever since.

To make matters worse, Chief Gates and Sheriff Block, both of whom were often described as egotistical, had developed a testy relationship over the years. "Daryl Gates considered himself the chief law enforcement officer in the County of Los Angeles, but by law, Sherman Block, the sheriff, was the chief law enforcement officer in the county," explains Bayan Lewis, then commanding officer of the LAPD's Uniformed Services Group. "So there was this infighting between the two major agencies."[27]

Internal problems within the LAPD also hampered preparation. Gates, facing ongoing pressure from Bradley and others to resign, appeared to have distanced himself from running the department and had not met with his staff at all during April. Although the chief had not set a date for retirement, his imminent departure had transformed department dynamics, with some assistant and deputy chiefs disillusioned, others trying to win approval as possible successors, and others on their way out. Indeed, by the time of the jury's deliberation, the leadership of the LAPD was in a state of near paralysis. "The general attitude was not to act decisively," one critic later remarked. "The prevailing attitude was that if you don't make any decisions, you can't get hurt."[28]

Below Gates there would normally have been three assistant chiefs, who in turn oversaw nine deputy chiefs (see Exhibit 3A-3 for an LAPD organization chart). Several top positions were vacant, however, and Gates was not on speaking terms with some key aides. Assistant Chief Robert Vernon directed the Office of Operations, probably the most important office within the LAPD. Vernon was on reasonably good terms with Gates; however, the assistant chief had learned he wasn't among the finalists for Gates's job and had announced he would resign in early June. To use up accumulated vacation time, Vernon left on April 24, with no replacement yet named, even though a verdict in the case was imminent. As a result, the office that oversaw almost 90 percent of police officers and detectives, including the Headquarters Bureau and the four geographical bureaus, was without a leader as the jury continued its deliberations.[29]

---

[27]Interviews with Commander Bayan Lewis, Uniformed Services Group, March 27 and June 30, 2000. Unless noted, subsequent comments by Lewis are also from these interviews.

[28]Comment by Hubert Williams, former chief of the Newark, New Jersey, Police Department and co-author of *The City in Crisis*, an analysis of the police response to the riots. Quoted in Cannon, *Official Negligence*, 267.

[29]Vernon actually did return the day the riots began, but when Gates refused his phoned offers of help, Vernon left for vacation on the second day of the disturbance.

Exhibit 3A-3 Organization of the Los Angeles Police Department

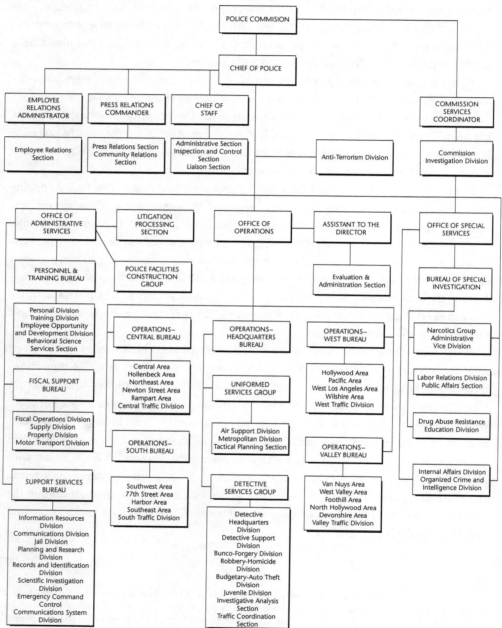

Source: *Manual of the Los Angeles Police Department,* Los Angeles, Calif; reproduced in William H. Webster and Hubert Williams, *The City in Crisis: A Report by the Special Advisor to the Board of Police Commissioners on the Civil Disorder in Los Angeles* (Los Angeles, Calif.: October 21, 1992), 58, Fig. 4-1.

Maintaining a Low Profile

A final factor strongly influenced the LAPD's level of preparation. Mayor Bradley and Chief Gates didn't agree on many things, but both had reached the conclusion that the LAPD should not make a public show of mobilizing. Gates doubted that violence would occur; but even more important, he didn't want the police to appear overly aggressive, given the nature of the ongoing trial and the recent criticisms by the Christopher Commission. This sense of cautiousness had already seeped through the department—LAPD arrests had dropped significantly during the previous year as police changed tactics and avoided problematic arrests that might lead to discipline or a charge of excessive force.

Bradley and other black leaders, such as Councilman Mark Ridley-Thomas and Representative Maxine Waters (D-Calif.), meanwhile, opposed a highly mobilized LAPD both because they feared the police might overreact and create another Rodney King–like incident and because they worried that the mere sight of riot-ready police could incite a violent reaction among already tense residents.

Bradley realized any verdict might spur some protests, but he felt they would be best managed through outreach. As part of an effort dubbed Operation Cool Response, Bradley planned to meet with church and community leaders at the First African Methodist Episcopal Church in South Central as soon as the verdicts were announced. In addition, the mayor's office prepared talking points to guide community leaders and officials in dealing with the public. Finally, contingents from local churches were to spread out through the community to defuse tension.[30]

Against this backdrop, those individuals within the LAPD who believed it essential to prepare for a possible disturbance faced an almost complete absence of departmental support. In the last weeks before his vacation and retirement, Assistant Chief Robert Vernon made an effort to increase police readiness. On April 10, he brought together high-level officers from the department's eighteen divisions to discuss emergency plans and suggested that the department declare a citywide tactical alert to coincide with the verdict's announcement. Vernon reportedly dropped the idea, however, after some of the officers complained an alert would be unnecessarily provocative.[31] The meeting's effectiveness was also probably lessened by Gates's directive to Vernon that the gathering and any subsequent riot preparation be hidden from the press. "Make sure they understand I don't want to put the LAPD in the position of predicting a riot," Gates instructed Vernon, according to the assistant chief's later account in *L.A. Justice: Lessons From the Firestorm*.[32] As a result, most

---

[30]Webster and Williams, *City in Crisis,* Vol. 1, 19.

[31]Representatives from three divisions, including 77th Street, the South Central area with the city's highest murder rate, didn't even attend the meeting.

[32]Robert Vernon, *L.A. Justice: Lessons from the Firestorm* (Colorado Springs, Colo.: Focus on the Family Publishing, 1993), 160.

divisions not only kept planning to a minimum, they did not even inform officers through-out the division that riot preparation was taking place.[33]

Lieutenant Michael Hillmann, whom Gates had recently named as interim commander of the elite Metropolitan Division (Metro), was even more concerned than Vernon. Unlike most of the LAPD's leadership, Hillmann felt conditions were ripe for a riot, and he urged preparation for a strong but restrained Metro response in the event of a disturbance. On his own, he borrowed extra bullet-proof vests and helmets from another police force, worked out a tactical plan for Metro, which included the Special Weapons and Tactics (SWAT) and Crisis Negotiating teams, and ran secret civil disturbance training sessions outside of the city during part of the week that the jury was deliberating.

But when Hillmann asked Deputy Chief Ronald Frankle, the commanding officer of Headquarters Bureau, in late April for permission to deploy Metro during daylight hours on the date the verdict would be announced and to have the department's two armored per-sonnel carriers on hand, the deputy chief turned him down. Frankle didn't want Metro squads armed in riot gear on the streets when Gates and other leaders had made it clear that the department should keep a low profile. Instead, then Commander Bayan Lewis, who oversaw Metro, scheduled the division to report at 6:00 p.m. Like most LAPD officers, Lewis believed that if riots occurred at all, they wouldn't start until night, as had been the experi-ence during Watts and most other urban disturbances. Hillmann received another blow when he learned that a request from Metro the previous month to obtain nonlethal foam-rubber bullets for training and riot use had also been rejected on the grounds that the bul-lets were risky and insufficiently tested.[34]

Although Bayan Lewis had not pushed for a daylight Metro deployment, he, like Hill-mann, took the riot risk seriously and tried to get the LAPD ready to respond. Lewis set up the department's emergency mobile fleet—four large vans that carried the communications and other equipment necessary to establish emergency field command posts.[35] In addition, Lewis distributed a list of city gun stores to all eighteen LAPD divisions, along with an ad-visory that warned officers to guard the stores if rioting broke out. Lewis also borrowed more than three hundred sets of riot helmets and flak vests from the California Army Na-tional Guard and asked a personal friend at National Guard headquarters in Sacramento to unofficially alert leaders that if "things went bad" in Los Angeles, the LAPD might need help. The warning, however, appeared to fall on deaf ears. "They said, 'Well if they call, they call,'" Lewis says. "And that was our contact with the Army National Guard."

---

[33]Cannon, *Official Negligence,* 268–270.

[34]The LAPD later approved the use of rubber bullets by Metro. Ibid., 274.

[35]As with the armored personnel carriers, however, the vans were not sent to the likely areas of unrest ahead of time.

An Unexpected Verdict

At 1:00 p.m. on Wednesday, April 29, after 7 days of deliberation, Judge Stanley Weisberg announced that the jury had reached its verdicts and that the results would be read in 2 hours. The pause was intended not only to give reporters a chance to congregate but also to allow police and other emergency agencies an opportunity to prepare.

Within the previous week, in a nod toward preparedness, Gates had approved $1 million for police overtime in preparation for the verdict. But that Wednesday, the LAPD was ill-prepared for an emergency. Two-thirds of the department's patrol captains had begun a 3-day training seminar that day in Ventura, almost an hour and a half outside of central Los Angeles. In addition, despite knowing when the verdict would be announced, the LAPD decided the risk of trouble was too low to justify holding officers over at the normal shift change. As a result, almost half of the LAPD's eighteen stations changed shifts at 3:00 without retaining extra officers, leaving 838 police on duty when the verdicts were announced, only about 150 more than would normally have been on duty at that time.[36]

At about 3:15 p.m., the verdicts were revealed to a packed courtroom of astonished reporters. Except for a single charge against Powell of excessive force, on which the jurors had deadlocked, the four officers were acquitted of all charges. Chief Gates was probably as shocked by the verdicts as anyone else in the city, but he did not declare a tactical alert or take other immediate preparatory action, other than to activate the city's EOC.[37] Under the "activation," however, as one analysis later noted, "all that appears to have happened was the doors were opened, the lights turned on and the coffee pot plugged in."[38] Not until an hour and a half later, at 4:45 p.m., did EOO personnel try to assemble the representatives of the city agencies that constituted the Emergency Operations Board, who were supposed to gather at the EOC to coordinate the city's response to the emergency. "The EOC should have been in full operation when the verdicts were read," declares then Los Angeles City Fire Chief Donald Manning.[39]

Gates's understated reaction to the verdict was mirrored by other top LAPD officials, none of whom stepped forward in the initial hour after the verdict to demand decisive

---

[36]The afternoon shift was the largest. Fewer than half as many officers were typically on duty during the day shift.

[37]President George Bush was reportedly stunned by the verdicts and within an hour had begun looking at the possibility of bringing a federal civil rights case against the four officers. Federal prosecutors began presenting evidence to a grand jury on May 7, just 8 days after the original verdicts were released. The resulting two-count federal indictment charged three of the officers with using unreasonable force and Stacey Koon with failing to control the officers under his supervision. On April 17, 1993, two of the officers, Briseno and Wind, were acquitted, but Koon and Powell were both found guilty and sentenced to 30 months in prison, with a mandatory $50 fine.

[38]Quoted in Webster and Williams, *City in Crisis*, Vol. 1, 106.

[39]Interview with Fire Chief Donald Manning, March 28, 2000. Unless noted, subsequent quotations from Donald Manning are also from this interview.

action. At the 77th Street Station in South Central, however, where many residents in the surrounding neighborhoods had been hostile and belligerent all day, there was no sense of complacency. Lieutenant Michael Moulin, the watch commander, remembered telling the incoming shift that "it was going to be a horrible day in the history of Los Angeles, a day on which many of them could well lose their lives."[40]

Within minutes of the verdicts, angry groups began to form in the 77th Street Division and elsewhere in South Central. About an hour later, in an incident that was afterward identified as the start of the riot, a group of young black men stole bottles of malt liquor from a Korean American–owned store, hitting the owner's son in the head with a bottle and smashing the door as one man cried, "This is for Rodney King."[41] Mayor Bradley, meanwhile, appeared on television 2 hours after the verdict to express his disbelief and anger. "My friends, I am here to tell the jury . . . our eyes did not deceive us. We saw what we saw, and what we saw was a crime. No, we will not tolerate the savage beating of our citizens by a few renegade cops." Bradley cautioned, however, "We must not endanger the reforms we have achieved by resorting to mindless acts. We must not push back progress by striking back blindly."[42]

Bradley's strong words shocked many who were involved in the emergency response, and some claimed that the mayor had tacitly given approval to the people of Los Angeles to riot. "I think Mayor Bradley was probably the finest mayor the city of Los Angeles has ever had," says former Fire Chief Donald Manning. "But at that moment, his emotions got in control of his normal, very reserved self, and it added fuel to the situation." Philip Depoian, however, then special councilor to the mayor and a police department liaison, says that Bradley's speech was appropriate and that the mayor never regretted his words. "What he was trying to do for his citizens was say, 'Hey, I understand your frustration. I'm an African-American man, I'm a former police officer, and I saw what happened a year ago,'" Depoian explains. "But this was a man of law. That was the basis of his life, and he would never have done anything that would inflame the situation."[43]

In any event, by 5:30 p.m., the sort of mindless acts that Bradley had cautioned against were well underway.

---

[40]Quoted in Cannon, *Official Negligence*, 280.

[41]After the verdicts were read, protests and violence broke out in other locations across the country, including San Francisco, Las Vegas, Buffalo, Atlanta, and New York City, but none approached the scale or intensity of the Los Angeles riots.

[42]Quoted in Cannon, *Official Negligence*, 284.

[43]Interview with Philip Depoian, special councilor to the mayor, April 19, 2000. Unless noted, subsequent quotations from Depoian are also from this interview.

The 1992 Los Angeles Riots (B):
The Flawed Emergency Response

Police Chief Daryl Gates and most members of the Los Angeles Police Department (LAPD) were taken by surprise by the acquittals in the Rodney King beating trial. Even more surprising, however, was the speed with which the black community's anger spread and grew. In South Central Los Angeles, rage over the acquittals soon turned into violent acts, and as calls reporting incidents of looting and attacks began peppering the 77th Street Station, the police appeared powerless to stop the mounting disturbance.

At 5:23 p.m., just down the street from where the young men had smashed the liquor store door, police chased and arrested a black youth after seeing him swing a bat to break the windshield of a car with two white men inside. Television crews, alerted to the growing unrest, had rushed to the area, and as a camera crew began to film the arrest, police later recalled, a gathering crowd appeared to respond to the attention, chanting, "Rodney King, Rodney King, Rodney King." [1]

Police Chief Gates, ensconced at the LAPD Parker Center headquarters, was still denying that a serious problem existed, declaring at 5:38 that "If we have disturbances, we are prepared." In the 77th Street Division, however, the situation was quickly spiraling out of control. Down the street from the earlier arrest, police caught near the intersection of Florence and Normandie by an angry, rock-throwing crowd radioed for help and were joined by eighteen patrol cars and more than thirty officers. As police made a few arrests, the mood grew uglier. One police and four television helicopters hovered overhead as police tried to stave off the advancing crowd. Perhaps due to fears of appearing overly aggressive, observers later reported, the cornered police appeared oddly passive. Without question, they were also unprepared—many officers lacked helmets and bulletproof vests, and the individual canisters of tear gas strapped to their belts were not suitable for crowd control. "We had not trained to use tear gas in crowd situations," recalls then Commander Bayan Lewis, head of the LAPD Uniformed Services Group.[2] "As a matter of fact, I can't remember when we ever used tear gas in crowd situations." [3] At 5:43, 5 minutes after Gates had declared the LAPD prepared, ranking officer Lieutenant Michael Moulin ordered a retreat.

---

[1] Lou Cannon, *Official Negligence: How Rodney King and the Riots Changed Los Angeles and the LAPD* (Boulder, Colo.: Westview Press, 1999), 283.

[2] Interview with Commander Bayan Lewis, Uniformed Services Group, March 27, 2000. Unless noted, subsequent quotations from Lewis are also from this interview.

[3] In any event, the commanding officer at Florence and Normandie, Lieutenant Michael Moulin, lacked the authority to call for the use of tear gas. (According to LAPD policy, only an officer holding the rank of commander or higher could authorize its use.) Cannon, *Official Negligence,* 275.

With the police gone, a growing mob of angry blacks began attacking cars of whites, Latinos, and Asians who were driving through the area. Most of the officers who had retreated expected to be sent back to the scene after recruiting additional reinforcements. After all, LAPD doctrine stated:

The *primary responsibility* of the . . . Field Commander during the initial stages of an unlawful assembly or riot is the *rapid assembly of sufficient forces to immediately confront the participants.* In the case of an unlawful assembly, a dispersal order must be issued. If the dispersal order is ignored, or in case of riot, law violators must be *quickly overwhelmed and arrested.*[4]

Lieutenant Moulin, however, acting under ambiguous orders from his superior, 77th Street Division Commander Captain Paul Jefferson, concluded that it would be impossible to retake the increasingly violent intersection without far more officers than he had at his disposal.[5] "There was no plan that I knew of," Moulin later told a reporter. "I had never seen a plan."[6] According to a police dispatcher, the crowd, by just before 6:00, had grown to "approximately five hundred male blacks throwing bottles at passing cars."[7] Instead of returning to the scene, Lieutenant Moulin began to set up a staging area at an almost 10-acre municipal bus yard located at 54th and Arlington streets, a little more than 2 miles away from the Florence-Normandie intersection—a secure area where additional officers could congregate. Had the Metropolitan Division (Metro), with its Special Weapons and Tactics (SWAT) teams and its civil disturbance training, been readily available in concentrated tactical squads equipped with riot gear, as Metro's Lieutenant Michael Hillmann had requested, Moulin's decision might have been different. As it was, Metro was unprepared for action, with many officers, including the new commander, off-duty and others out of the city.

The decision to abandon the intersection was a defining moment in the growing disturbance. When police failed to return, gang members and other residents began looting area businesses and liquor stores. A few officers made forays on their own into what increasingly appeared to be a riot zone, heroically assisting motorists and pedestrians under attack. But after the officers themselves barely escaped, Moulin at 6:20 ordered a temporary halt to all rescue efforts.[8]

---

[4]Quoted in William H. Webster and Hubert Williams, *The City in Crisis: A Report by the Special Advisor to the Board of Police Commissioners on the Civil Disorder in Los Angeles* (Los Angeles, Calif.: October 21, 1992), Vol. 1, 121. Emphasis in original.

[5]Moulin and Jefferson later gave different accounts of their meeting. According to Moulin, although he asked Jefferson to declare a tactical alert, Jefferson made no immediate decision and, instead, told Moulin to go back, assess the intersection, and then set up a staging area nearby for officer reinforcements. Jefferson, on the other hand, said that he told Moulin to retake the intersection. Cannon, *Official Negligence,* 292.

[6]ABC-TV, "Anatomy of a Riot," *Nightline,* May 28, 1992.

[7]Quoted in Cannon, *Official Negligence,* 292.

[8]Looting was beginning to break out in other areas of the city, but Florence and Normandie was the hub of violent incidents, driven by a small group of individuals.

The absence of police was not only obvious to people already on the streets; it could be seen by those at home watching the live coverage provided by television helicopters still hovering over the scene. Indeed, many officials involved in the emergency response believed that the constant coverage of rioters apparently unchecked by an official response fueled the looting and rioting like gasoline thrown on a fire. "A lot of the time you had people who really didn't care about the trial, but who were opportunists," says Terrance Manning, a Los Angeles City Fire Department battalion commander (and son of former Chief Donald Manning). "They see, gosh, these people are looting and running around with TVs, and nothing is happening to them. So all of a sudden they start breaking out incredibly fast." He adds, "The Watts riots went slow, slow, slow, while this went from nothing to full-fledged within an hour and a half." [9]

Los Angeles County Sheriff Sherman Block, who had begun to mobilize additional deputies immediately after the verdicts were read, later declared that sheriff's deputies would have been on the scene if he had realized the LAPD had abandoned the area. "A show of force at that location at that time might not have stopped everything, but certainly would have had a significant impact," Block told the Los Angeles County Board of Supervisors 1 week after the riots broke out. [10]

The Crisis Deepens

As the situation on the streets worsened, and as Lieutenant Moulin struggled to set up the staging area, the 77th Street Division received no instructions from headquarters or the city's Emergency Operations Center (EOC); also, officials at Parker Center were not receiving many reports from the field, instead getting most of their information from television and radio. Other than his brief remarks at 5:38, Gates had stayed in his office and at 6:30 left for a political fund-raiser outside of Los Angeles. [11]

The chief appeared unaware of the seriousness of the disturbance, despite an increasingly hostile protest outside Parker Center and despite a message to the EOC from an intelligence officer that the Florence-Normandie area was "out of control." [12] "It is not at all uncommon," Richard Andrews, then director of the state Office of Emergency Services (OES) explains, "not just in riots but in natural disasters, for people to seriously underestimate initially how

---

[9]Interview with Terrance Manning, battalion commander, Los Angeles Fire Department, March 28, 2000. Unless noted, subsequent quotations from Terrance Manning are also from this interview.

[10]Quoted in Cannon, *Official Negligence,* 350.

[11]The fund-raiser was part of an effort to defeat Charter Amendment F, an amendment spurred by the Christopher Commission report, whose provisions included limiting the tenure of the police chief to two 5-year terms, making it easier to remove the chief, and increasing the mayor's and City Council's involvement in choosing the chief.

[12]Cannon, *Official Negligence,* 299.

bad the situation is." [13] Adds Bayan Lewis, "Gates thought we had some sporadic problems, but [his attitude was], 'By God, get in there and deal with it. It's not going to take the chief of police of the city of Los Angeles to run this operation, and if it does, I've got the wrong people below me.' So there was no centralized direction."

Shortly after the chief left, rioters and protesters stormed the front of Parker Center, opening a new front in the disturbance and erasing any hope that the riots' violence and destruction would be limited to South Central. According to Bayan Lewis, officers had debated whether to let the large group vent its anger against the police or to drive it off, with the risk that rioters might pillage the downtown area. When police finally pushed the demonstrators away about an hour later, the crowd went on to burn a guard shack on the police parking lot, break ground-floor windows of hotels and the Los Angeles Times building nearby, and damage other civic center buildings before the police regained control. One Metro platoon of about fifty officers was sent to help defend Parker Center; the officers were tied up there for hours and unavailable for deployment in South Central. At 6:45, in response to a flood of 911 emergency calls, a lieutenant at Parker Center finally declared a tactical alert, a step that many observers believed Gates should have taken much earlier. The move put affected areas on alert to have a reserve officer force available and to be prepared to send officers to other areas as needed. It also improved radio communication by barring all but emergency messages.

Back at Florence and Normandie, meanwhile, seven television helicopters were recording scenes of destruction, as shocked pilots decried the lack of a police presence. "I can't believe the cops are looking at this and not doing something," one local anchorwoman exclaimed.[14] Police had made no attempt to close the routes leading into the intersection, and in the absence of such traffic control, local television and radio stations tried to alert motorists to the danger. Inevitably, not everyone got the word.

At 6:46, a white man named Reginald Denny drove a truck full of sand into the intersection. Black rioters pelted the truck with rocks, then pulled Denny from the cab and brutally attacked him—a chilling scene captured by the helicopter cameras above and televised live as it occurred. During the entire event, police were nowhere in sight.[15] According to many observers, the live shots of Denny's attack, which highlighted the absence of police, were not only shocking; they sent a strong message to viewers that anarchy ruled on the streets of Los Angeles. However, neither Gates, on his way to the fund-raiser, nor Mayor Tom Bradley,

---

[13]Interview with Richard Andrews, director, Office of Emergency Services, March 27, 2000. Unless noted, subsequent quotations from Andrews are also from this interview.

[14]Quoted in Marc Lacey and Shawn Hubler, "Rioters Set Fires, Loot Stores; Four Reported Dead," *Los Angeles Times*, April 30, 1992.

[15]Denny eventually was rescued and driven to a nearby hospital by four African Americans who had watched the attack on television. The four were among a number of Good Samaritans who risked their own lives to rescue victims of mob violence.

attending the Operation Cool Response rally at the First African Methodist Episcopal Church in South Central, saw the televised coverage of the Denny attack. Nor was there a television set at the staging area where Moulin was trying to organize a plan.

A Leadership Vacuum

In the wake of the attack on Reginald Denny, a combination of inadequate communications technology, poor planning and training, absentee leaders, and apparent indecisiveness continued to blunt the LAPD's response to the city's growing turmoil. Conditions at the city's EOC across from Parker Center were symptomatic of the overall collapse of order. The center was supposed to operate as the city's main information conduit, not only managing information for the LAPD response but also coordinating the involvement of other agencies. But experienced officers from the LAPD did not arrive until hours into the disturbance, and representatives from other agencies either had little training or lacked the authority to make decisions.

The EOC's scanty technological capabilities were another problem. The center had very few computers, the radio system was old, and there were only a few trunk lines out, making it impossible to communicate effectively with the staging area, police stations, the sheriff's EOC, Parker Center, and other city agencies.[16] According to Bayan Lewis, "The EOC immediately became kind of an isolated island of non-information." Given the lack of good outside information, Lewis says, officers in the EOC relied disproportionately on what they could glean from the live television coverage of the riots. Accordingly, Lewis recalls, the EOC tended to direct whatever resources it could muster to locations being featured on television, even when other areas of the city might have had equal or greater needs.

Internal communications at the center were also flawed. The EOC relied on a cumbersome system of passing information to a central site for review by way of handwritten notes, which staffers would then prioritize and send by runners to the appropriate city agency representatives within the main room or in one of the connected satellite rooms for action. Not surprisingly, the handwritten system became so overloaded and bogged down that many requests were never delivered. Critics later estimated that only a quarter of incoming requests were actually processed during the first night of the riot.[17]

At the staging area at 54th and Arlington streets, meanwhile, the situation was chaotic. Commander Bayan Lewis, who had arrived at the bus yard from Parker Center at about 7:00, began to set up the staging area as a full-fledged field command post and asked the Tactical Planning Section to send over two mobile telephone vans carrying high-quality radio

---

[16]Cell phones in 1992 were not yet ubiquitous in Los Angeles and were not commonly used within the LAPD.
[17]Webster and Williams, *City in Crisis,* Vol. 1, 112.

communications equipment.[18] When the vans were halfway to the command post, however, a mob heaved rocks and bottles at them and the drivers refused to continue without a separate police escort. The inability to bring in extra communications equipment was a serious setback. There was no dedicated phone line to the EOC, and police couldn't call out on most of the bus station's telephones because they were limited to an internal transit communications system. Apparently oblivious to these limitations, Lieutenant Moulin had directed local 911 calls to be sent directly to the command post, further tying up the few phones that were available. In fact, hours into the riot, officers at the command post ended up sending runners to carry information to and from the EOC because it was so difficult to establish communication by phone.[19]

In addition, the LAPD's outdated radio communications system forced officers to rely more on the few cellular phones they could locate than on radio contact. Although Moulin put out an emergency request for one hundred handheld radios, he received only seven.[20] To make matters worse, there were no computers available. Indeed, because police had set up the command post so precipitously, they didn't even have a television set, which meant they were generally less well informed than the average Los Angeles resident sitting at home watching the news.

Despite these many inadequacies, the bus station, due to its proximity to the riot center, became the emergency response center for the entire South Bureau, including 77th Street. When Lieutenant Moulin had first arrived to set up the staging area, the lot had been clogged with hundreds of buses. As officers from 77th Street and other divisions congregated at the post during the early hours of the riot, buses were still being directed out of the congested center, blocking the influx of emergency vehicles and adding to the commotion. The lack of normal operating procedures soon further incapacitated the post. No one had thought to assign someone to collect patrol car keys from officers as they reported for duty. As a result, police who went back out in a different car often did so with their own keys in their pockets, leaving locked cars behind. The stranded cars were not only useless; they worsened the immobilizing congestion of the yard.

More serious even than all these problems, some officers later recalled, was the inability of leaders at the command post to implement a plan. As Lewis began setting up the post at 7:00 p.m., about an hour and 15 minutes after Lieutenant Moulin first ordered the retreat, some 480 officers had congregated at the yard. The goal, Bayan Lewis says, was to send out four cars at a time, with at least ten officers and a sergeant in command. Yet many officers remained stranded and idle at the post.

---

[18]The *LAPD Tactical Manual* directed field commanders to establish temporary field command posts to mobilize for an emergency, such as a civil disturbance.

[19]A dedicated line was finally set up a couple of days into the riot.

[20]Cannon, *Official Negligence,* 310.

At 8:00 p.m., Deputy Chief Ronald Frankle finally ordered the mobilization of the LAPD, which immediately changed the officer shifts from 8 to 12 hours, recalled off-duty police, and revoked all leave. But neither that nor the arrival at the command post 1 hour later of Deputy Chief Matthew Hunt, the head of the LAPD's South Bureau, appeared to help much. Retaking the streets without more officers was probably already impossible, Lewis says. But Hunt and his subordinates did not even attempt basic riot-control measures, such as blocking access to the most disrupted area, establishing a perimeter around it, and then establishing order in the enclosed area one section at a time as additional officers arrived. "It's important to keep in mind that this was basically the fastest moving, most violent riot in U.S. history," notes Richard Andrews, then director of OES. "There had really been nothing quite like this."

Exacerbating the problem, many officers later said, was the order from headquarters that police should maintain a strong visible presence without making arrests because to do so would further tie up limited officer resources. As a result, live news programs continued to show apparently powerless police parked in cars or driving by slowly as looters broke store windows and filled their vehicles with stolen goods.[21]

When Chief Gates finally arrived at the post after 10:00, he "took Hunt absolutely apart in public," according to Bayan Lewis. "Since I'd been through it, I kind of thought that fellow members of the top command knew what to do," Gates later remarked. "They didn't." [22] Adds former Fire Department Chief Donald Manning, "We all know that a plan that people don't know about is as bad as no plan at all—in fact, it's probably worse. In this case, I think Daryl believed that they had a plan. He may well have believed that his people were fully trained in it. In the real world, they weren't." [23] Although the LAPD later attempted to isolate the Florence-Normandie area, the effort came too late to be effective.

Even the specially trained Metro, with its elite SWAT teams, was finding it hard to mobilize and launch the kind of quick and forceful response for which it was renowned. Once the riot developed, Metro simply couldn't concentrate the forces necessary to combat and control the situation. Almost a third of the division was off-duty at 6:00, one platoon was in the San Fernando Valley, and one lost precious time going to the defense of Parker Center, leaving only eighty-two officers to report to South Central.[24]

Metro's Lieutenant Michael Hillmann, following normal protocol, set up a Metro command within the larger post, and on his own instructed the platoon reporting from San Fernando to "engage the rioters." [25] The LAPD, however, had already lost control. The looting

---

[21]The no-arrest edict was lifted later that night after more officers were mobilized.

[22]Quoted in Cannon, *Official Negligence*, 327.

[23]Interview with Fire Chief Donald Manning, March 28, 2000. Unless noted, subsequent quotations from Donald Manning are also from this interview.

[24]Cannon, *Official Negligence*, 316.

[25]Ibid., 317.

and violence earlier had remained centered in the 77th Street and Southwest LAPD divisions, but after 7:00, the riots began to spread west and north, and at 7:30 the first reports arrived of the fires that would soon be burning over a large part of South Central. At about 8:15, the shooting of an 18-year-old—probably an instance of wild gunfire rather than a purposeful slaying—produced the first death of the riot.

Fighting Fires: Implementing the Plan

Unlike LAPD officers, Los Angeles firefighters had generally been well liked in the communities in which they operated, and during the 1980s they had been able to work in relative safety throughout the city, including in the more violence-prone areas such as South Central, where the department had two battalions.[26] The Los Angeles Fire Department, the nation's third largest, with 2,855 uniformed personnel, 337 civilian workers, and 411 paramedics, operated the city's ambulance service as well, and ambulances were based in about half of the city's 102 fire stations.[27]

Even before the Rodney King beating incident, however, the department's previous immunity from attack had begun to fray, and it had become official policy for firefighters and paramedics to wear body armor to every shooting, stabbing, or assault call. In early April 1992, with the trial of the police officers underway, Fire Chief Donald Manning undertook additional precautions. He created an ad hoc fire department committee to prepare contingency plans for a possible disturbance, and the department held a number of meetings—both internally and with outside agencies—to address issues such as tactical operations and personnel security. Assistant Fire Chief Robert Ramirez also met with LAPD commanders to confirm that police would provide protection to firefighters if the streets grew dangerous.[28]

The afternoon of the verdicts, Chief Manning left work at the end of the day expecting controllable demonstrations at most, despite the surprise outcome. But as he listened to radio reports of the growing unrest, Manning returned to his office at about 7:00 and re-called his staff.

Meanwhile, Deputy Chief Donald Anthony, commander of the Bureau of Fire Suppression and Rescue (the firefighting arm of the department) began to implement the emergency plan that the department had developed over the previous weeks. Like the LAPD, the

---

[26]The Los Angeles City Fire Department was divided into sixteen battalions.

[27]In response to a medical call, the fire department would typically send a paramedic ambulance, the closest fire engine, and sometimes an additional fire resource.

[28]Timothy V. Manning, Terrance J. Manning, and Christopher S. Kawai, *Los Angeles City Fire Department Historical Overview: Los Angeles Civil Disturbance*, April 29, 1992 (Los Angeles, Calif.: October 1992), 50.

Los Angeles City Fire Department was part of Region I under the state's mutual aid plan. If the city needed additional resources to respond to a fire or medical emergency, it requested aid from the Los Angeles County fire chief, who was the regional coordinator. Unlike the police, however, who did not routinely depend on outside resources, mutual aid was part of the very fabric of firefighting and calling in additional resources from adjacent cities and the county was one of the department's first moves as the riots escalated. At 7:45, Deputy Chief Anthony asked the county to place several mutual aid strike teams on alert, and just after 8:00, he asked for five strike teams to be sent to the city and for ten more to be put on standby. Twenty minutes later, Manning established a Department Command—a centralized command structure used by the department during major events—to manage all the fires as a single incident, thus simplifying and focusing planning and support. At the same time he named Anthony operations commander.

Fighting Fires: A Struggle for Control

While Chief Manning implemented emergency plans at headquarters, one of his two firefighter sons, Battalion Commander Timothy Manning, was setting up a medical center at the 54th and Arlington command post at the request of the LAPD. At 8:00, realizing that the situation was rapidly worsening, Timothy Manning expanded the medical center into a full command post and staging area that would allow fire companies in the affected area to be matched with police escorts from the officers already gathering.

Terrance Manning, meanwhile, then commander of Battalion 13, a South Central battalion, was at the Southeast Police Station when the first call came in about a structure fire in the Florence-Normandie area, just minutes after truck driver Reginald Denny was attacked. On the way to the fire, Manning says, he quickly became aware of how bad the rioting already had become. At the Florence-Normandie intersection, a crowd temporarily blocked his fire department car, and a pickax thrown at the vehicle pierced the roof above Manning's head. Despite being pelted with rocks and bottles, Manning and his driver managed to reach firefighters already battling a blaze a few blocks from the intersection. But with only two police sergeants there to protect the firefighters, the group soon beat an awkward retreat and headed, with lights flashing, for the safety of the command post. At the same time, Manning put out the first radio message for all fire crews to wear body armor and to operate with a police escort.

Fire department dispatchers, however, were largely unable to get through to LAPD dispatchers, who were overwhelmed with phone calls and unable to request escorts. Direct communication was also a problem because the fire department's radio channels and those used by the police were not compatible. Given the difficulty of getting police escorts,

Terrance Manning says, the fire department at about 8:15 ordered all resources in the area to pull out of South Central and report to the 54th and Arlington command post. "Once we started getting guys injured," Manning says, "we pulled back there with the thought that we would immediately get them escorted and sent back."

By around 8:30, Terrance Manning says, firefighters at the post had formed tactical strike teams. Although a standard strike team consisted of five fire engines staffed by four fire-fighters each, fire department officials cut the number of engine companies to three in order to increase the number of teams that could respond, make the teams more maneuverable, and present a smaller target to rioters. Each team was to be paired with a police escort of two police cars with a minimum of three police officers per car. For a medical emergency, mean-while, the fire department prepared to send a fire engine, two ambulances, and a similar police escort. Unfortunately, no other police officers were immediately made available. Al-though, as estimated by Terrance Manning, there were twenty to thirty structure fires burn-ing unchecked by this time and more than two hundred LAPD officers awaiting direction at the command center, the first firefighting team didn't get an escort until 9:43, despite fire of-ficial complaints.

The necessity of having police alongside was driven home at 9:48 when firefighter Scott Miller became the first public safety official to be injured during the riots as he drove a fire truck toward a blaze. Miller, who was shot in the face, barely survived the attack. In fact, there were more than twelve documented attempts to kill firefighters and paramedics in just the first 3 hours of the riots.[29] Even during this dangerous period, however, some engine companies stayed in the field. "It was what they call command paralysis," Terrance Manning says. "The [police] officers in the street were embarrassed and ashamed of what happened because they felt they wanted to be involved, they wanted to do the job, but management was not prepared for this magnitude of event."

The delay in arranging police escorts, many critics felt, allowed arsonists to get the upper hand. While there were only fifteen arson fires burning in the city at 8:00 p.m.—when Deputy Chief Frankle finally ordered the LAPD mobilization—2 hours later there were at least forty-seven fires, and many were blazing unchecked.[30] Late in the night, Metro officers were finally designated as fire department escorts, but by this time, there were too many fires, and the streets had become too dangerous, for the firefighters to have much effect. Chief Manning had already instructed firefighters to use a "hit-and-run" approach, dousing fires and then moving on rather than devoting the time it would take to make sure each fire was completely extinguished.

---

[29]Ibid., 23.
[30]Cannon, *Official Negligence*, 322.

Dealing with the Press

As the situation in South Central spiraled out of control, local and national news operations flocked to the riot areas, putting reporters on the streets, sending up news helicopters to provide vivid live footage of the worsening disturbance, and besieging the LAPD and other city departments with requests for information. For the agencies involved, providing an accurate and comprehensive summary of the riots—and their responses to them—wasn't easy.

Even under the best of circumstances, Los Angeles had no real centralized news function. The mayor, as head of the Emergency Operations Organization (EOO), was the city's official emergency spokesman, but his role had less to do with dispensing information than with establishing calm.

The EOC, meanwhile, was the city's central clearinghouse for information during emergencies. However, rather than overseeing a cooperative public information effort, says the LAPD's Bayan Lewis, the EOC simply collected and distributed the reports sent in by the various dispatch centers. "There was no established procedure to do joint press releases," says Lewis. "We would have a press officer available at the command post, while the fire department was making their own press releases somewhere else, and the sheriff's was doing theirs somewhere else."

As the riots escalated, the dispatch centers failed to relay accurate and up-to-date information to the EOC, mainly because their own understanding of the evolving situation was so poor and they were too busy trying to manage circumstances in the field. "During the first 36 or 48 hours it was extremely difficult to get out information about exactly what was happening," Richard Andrews of the state OES recalls. Not only that, those reports coming in from police officers and firefighters in the field often conflicted because of the chaotic and quickly changing conditions.[31]

According to police and fire representatives, both agencies understood the importance of providing good information to the press. But in the chaos of trying to respond to the worsening crisis, neither agency reached out effectively, especially because normal operating procedures didn't appear to work. During a typical fire emergency, for example, Battalion Chief Dean Cathey (then the fire department's community liaison officer) explains, the officer who had assumed command would call the dispatch center if it was a newsworthy incident.[32] A public service officer based at the dispatch center would then contact local media

---

[31]In the wake of the riots, Bayan Lewis says city and county agencies agreed to establish a joint public information operation during future emergencies that would be staffed with a press relations team from each agency and that would hold regular half-hour briefings.

[32]Interview with Battalion Chief Dean Cathey, Los Angeles Fire Department, June 30, 2000. Unless noted, subsequent quotations from Cathey are also from this interview.

outlets within the Los Angeles area and provide them with information about the blaze. Back at the fire scene, meanwhile, the incident commander would either appoint someone to speak with the press or would contact Cathey's group and request a public information officer (PIO) to report to the scene from headquarters to assist with the media.

On the evening of April 29, however, there was no specific focal point as fires broke out over a wide area of South Central Los Angeles. Neither the PIOs in the field nor the public service officers at the dispatch center could provide a citywide overview of what was happening or of how firefighters were responding, since the dispatch center was already overwhelmed just trying to respond to calls and arrange police escorts.

Almost as soon as the rioting started, the media had begun to criticize the LAPD for its slow and apparently ineffective response to the disturbance. That criticism quickly spread to the fire department, as television and print reporters—who had free access[33] to the riot areas—noted the absence of firefighters at many of the worst arson sites.

At about 10:00 p.m., Cathey sent one PIO equipped with a cell phone to the 54th and Arlington command post and called the other PIOs back to headquarters. "I brought them in and I said, 'OK, get on the phone to each of the news outlets, television first, and state here's what's happening, and here's what we're doing, and here's what our problems are,'" Cathey says. "We were talking about specific examples of the problems that firefighters were facing, getting the message to the public that we're trying to get a handle on this and bring back the calm as much as we can." In addition, the PIOs used the press to warn people to stay home if possible and to avoid the areas where there was severe unrest. After making calls for about 2 hours and arranging for immediate appearances at local television stations of uniformed fire officials who could discuss the developing crisis, Cathey says that the tenor of the news stories abruptly changed. "By about 11:30 p.m., we turned the story around. Then it was like a wave—the outpouring of support was incredible."

For the LAPD, however, there was no such quick turnaround. According to Bayan Lewis, although the department had a commander and several officers running its press relations group, the unexpectedness of the riots and the speed at which they spread completely overwhelmed the LAPD's ability to gather and distribute information to the press.

Given the LAPD's flawed response at the onset of the disturbance, Lewis concedes, even a topnotch public relations effort couldn't have deflected much of the criticism that rained down on the force in the wake of such incidents as the beating of trucker Reginald Denny. Nevertheless, he says, had the police been able to relay more timely and effective warnings to residents through the press, some of the violence that occurred might have been averted.

---

[33]According to police and fire department policies, the press had free access to evolving incidents, even violent ones, as long as reporters did not interfere with the work of officers or firefighters.

Taking Stock

During the afternoon, as the situation in South Central worsened, Governor Pete Wilson had watched the television with mounting concern. Critics of the LAPD, including many of the same black leaders who had cautioned the police not to make overt pre-verdict preparations, were decrying the LAPD's unwillingness or inability to retake the streets of South Central and protect the area's residents. Indeed, in the first day of rioting, officers from the Central and South LAPD Bureaus together arrested only 131 people.[34] At 7:00, soon after the Reginald Denny attack, Wilson called Mayor Bradley's office to ask if the mayor wanted to request the California National Guard to help combat the riot.[35] "[The attack on Denny] was an ugly scene, and the viciousness and the violence were unnerving. . . . it scared the hell out of a lot of people," Wilson recalls. "What we wanted to do, frankly, was to have the kind of show of force that would intimidate anybody who was seeking to take advantage of the apparent default on the part of law enforcement."[36]

At that time, Bradley was still at the Operation Cool Response rally, but when his aides contacted him there, the mayor said he would give Wilson an answer after talking with police leaders.[37] Back at City Hall, Bradley conferred with Deputy Chief Frankle and two police commissioners.[38] At 8:45, Bradley called Wilson and accepted the offer, officially requesting the National Guard; at the same time he declared a city emergency.[39]

Bradley's request ignored the standard protocol of the state's mutual aid system. Under the OES, an appeal for National Guard troops should have originated with the LAPD and progressed through the mayor to the Sheriff's Department, the OES, and finally the governor. As it was, not only had the LAPD not initiated the request, neither the Sheriff's Department nor the city's EOC was even aware initially that the mayor had asked for the National Guard. "Block was mad that Gates didn't call him and ask for help," says Richard Andrews, then of OES, "and he was mad that Bradley didn't call him and ask for help, and that Bradley went straight to the governor."

---

[34]News reports featured a number of Korean American merchants who, having given up on police protection, brought out shotguns and guarded their own stores.

[35]Wilson, as governor, was commander-in-chief of the state National Guard.

[36]Interview with Governor Pete Wilson, March 29, 2000. Unless noted, subsequent quotations from Wilson are also from this interview.

[37]In fact, Deputy Chief Hunt, the head of the LAPD South Bureau, who was with the mayor at the rally, had already suggested the possibility of calling in the National Guard.

[38]Gates was still unavailable, having taken off in a helicopter after returning from the fundraiser to gather his own impressions of the riot. After more than an hour in the air, Gates tried to land at the field command post to order a more aggressive response, but the helicopter's radios wouldn't work and the pilot would not land without clearance from the post.

[39]Although Bradley was a Democrat and Wilson a Republican, the two men had developed a good working relationship during Wilson's earlier stint as mayor of San Diego.

But although this break with protocol undoubtedly irritated leaders of both the LAPD and the Sheriff's Department, Andrews says, the direct contact between the mayor and the governor was an appropriate way to get the fastest possible response. "If [Bradley and Wilson] say we're going to use National Guard troops, my understanding of how responsibility and command works is you say, 'Yes, sir, that's what we're going to do,'" Andrews says. "You don't say, 'Wait a minute, you didn't follow the right protocol here. This guy should have called this guy, and this guy should have called this guy.'" Andrews adds, "The directions that I always had from Wilson were, 'If you get a request, I don't care where it's from. You just have to confirm that it's legitimate, and you provide the assistance. I don't want to hear excuses about the niceties of protocols and procedures.'"

The 1992 Los Angeles Riots (C): Calling up the National Guard

In many respects, it was not surprising that Governor Pete Wilson offered the services of the California National Guard to help quell the riots that had engulfed South Central Los Angeles. The National Guard had played a prominent role in responding to civil disturbances during the 1960s, with more than 13,000 troops deployed during the Watts riots alone. As in other parts of the country, National Guard troops had also been mobilized to respond to anti-Vietnam protests and other student demonstrations in the 1960s and early 1970s.

But over the following 2 decades, federal and state support to fund National Guard preparedness for civil disturbance responses had tailed off as law enforcement agencies' need for military support seemed to lessen. Beginning in 1989, staff officers from the National Guard had attended a series of meetings with the state Office of Emergency Services (OES) and other law enforcement groups, in part to discuss the National Guard's role in mutual aid. Based on the meetings, some officials at National Guard headquarters concluded that the state's improved mutual aid system had largely negated the need for National Guard troops to respond to civil unrest. As stated in the OES Law Enforcement Mutual Aid Plan, dated October 1991,

Normally, military support will be provided to local jurisdictions only after a request is made by the chief executive of a city or county or sheriff of a county, and only after the disturbance has been determined to be, or to likely become, beyond the capabilities of local law enforcement forces, as supplemented by forces made available under the existing mutual aid agreements.

Under the mutual aid plan, therefore, a police department such as the Los Angeles Police Department (LAPD) would first call on the county Sheriff's Department and other local agencies before considering state or federal resources.

Based on these funding and priority changes, National Guard forces slated to receive civil disturbance training were cut from 10,000 to only 5,000, and, according to some observers, scant attention was paid to whether even that number of troops was trained. As in the city of Los Angeles, most civil emergency preparedness focused on natural disasters, and in particular, earthquakes. Moreover, other activities took priority, such as military preparedness for overseas operations (including the Gulf War in 1991) and the war on drugs. Nevertheless, notes Richard Andrews, former OES director, although National Guard officials may have believed that their future role in civil disturbances would be limited to administrative or logistical support, the National Guard mission statements still clearly stated the need to maintain readiness for a riot response.[1]

---

[1] Interview with Richard Andrews, former director, Office of Emergency Services, March 27, 2000. Unless noted, subsequent quotations from Andrews are also from this interview.

During the trial of the police officers accused of beating Rodney King, the National Guard had received signals that there could be serious trouble in Los Angeles. Still, because of the revised understanding of its role and the fact that there had been no official request from Los Angeles law enforcement agencies or OES to be on alert, the state National Guard made no special preparations during the trial.

At about 8:30 p.m. on April 29, however, Wilson's office called the adjutant general of the California National Guard, Major General Robert Thrasher, to let him know that the governor was considering calling up the National Guard. A half hour later, at Mayor Bradley's request, the governor authorized the deployment of 2,000 National Guard troops to help restore order in Los Angeles. "As the seriousness of the situation started to become evident, everybody recognized that putting the National Guard on the street would send a very strong message," says Richard Andrews. Thrasher quickly called Andrews, hoping to learn more details about the National Guard's mission, but Andrews could only promise to check with the LAPD and the Sheriff's Department for more information.[2] At 9:15, Thrasher ordered the troop mobilization. No specific time had been set for soldiers to be on the streets, but Thrasher told the governor's staff that troops would be "in their armories" in about 6 hours.

At 10:13, Richard Andrews of OES arranged the first in what would be a series of conference calls, usually including the same individuals: Governor Wilson, General Thrasher, Mayor Bradley, Sheriff Sherman Block, Police Chief Daryl Gates, and California Highway Patrol (CHP) Commissioner Maurice Hannigan. The riots, according to Gates, had spread to an area of about 45–50 square miles, and there were 400–500 police in the area. Sheriff Block also reported spreading unrest, and what he described as a "Mardi Gras"–like atmosphere in the streets in some areas of the county.[3] Nevertheless, neither Gates nor Block felt the National Guard was needed, although when pressed by the governor, they endorsed the call-up. Both officials, however, welcomed the CHP's offer of 1,500 officers, whom they planned to use for tasks such as securing the perimeters of riot-torn areas. "The Highway Patrol was a very highly professional, very disciplined organization," says Andrews, "and not a territorial threat."[4]

As it turned out, the CHP—one of whose missions is to assist local law enforcement—was well prepared to take action. According to then Chief Edward Gomez, commander of

---

[2]Under the mutual aid system, when a local government requested assistance from the National Guard, OES provided the mission assignment.

[3]Quoted in Lt. Gen. William H. Harrison, *Assessment of the Performance of the California National Guard During the Civil Disturbances in Los Angeles, April & May 1992: Report to the Honorable Pete Wilson, Governor, State of California* (Sacramento, Calif.: October 2, 1992), A-7.

[4]The Sheriff's Department earlier that evening had already asked for fifty CHP officers to help return prisoners who had escaped from an honor farm north of Los Angeles.

the CHP's Southern Division, overseeing Los Angeles County, the agency had taken the possibility of a disturbance seriously, and more than a month before the trial ended, it had drafted a contingency plan, dubbed the Red Plan, that mandated different levels of response depending on the extent of any unrest. A Level One response, for example, would commit as many as 400 of the approximately 1,000 officers in the Southern Division to a disturbance; Level Two would draw in additional officers from neighboring divisions; and Level Three would deploy officers from around the state.

Gomez initiated the Red Plan as soon as the judge in the Rodney King beating trial gave notice that the verdicts would be announced in 2 hours. Along with his top officers, Gomez watched the verdicts being read, then immediately called a tactical alert, which put officers on 12-hour shifts and alerted them to wear riot gear. "You can't get in trouble by having too many people ready and available," Gomez asserts. "You can always de-escalate and send them home if after 6 hours nothing happens." [5] Even before Gates and Block accepted the officers, the Red Plan had moved to Level Three, and the CHP was ready to support local law enforcement in large numbers as needed.

Other than accepting the CHP officers, however, Gates made almost no use of outside law enforcement agencies in the first hours of the riot. During the conference call, Sheriff Block offered Gates five hundred deputies, but—reminiscent of the Watts riots experience—Gates refused the offer, preferring not to rely on his rival and still believing that the LAPD would regain control on its own. After Gates's negative response, Block, as regional coordinator of the mutual aid plan, turned down several offers of help from other area law enforcement agencies during the tumultuous first night of rioting, assuming that Gates would not be interested. The only local police forces tapped by the LAPD were the Rapid Transit District Police and the University of California–Los Angeles Police Department, both forces with which the LAPD had had substantial interactions in the past.

Nor did the LAPD make good use of the CHP that first night. Although some officers were sent to escort firefighters, about 120 CHP officers who had been available in Los Angeles since 9 p.m. watched television at their headquarters all night because they were given nothing to do, and in the midst of the chaos, neither the sheriff's office nor the LAPD could immediately find tasks for the 1,500 officers CHP Commissioner Hannigan had offered.

Gates, meanwhile, spent much of the first night touring the streets of Los Angeles with a driver and aide, finally reporting to the city's Emergency Operations Center (EOC) at 6:00 a.m. "Daryl was a very dedicated police officer, but if he had two shortcomings, one was what many people would call arrogance, and the other was his absolute unbridled belief that the LAPD could and would handle anything," says former Los Angeles City Fire Chief

---

[5]Interview with Chief Edward Gomez, commander, California Highway Patrol Southern Division, March 28, 2000. Unless noted, subsequent quotations from Gomez are also from this interview.

Donald Manning. "He couldn't come to grips with the fact that his people couldn't and weren't handling the whole thing."[6]

A Flawed Mobilization

The National Guard deployment began with many questions unanswered. Although the conference call participants had agreed on a target time of 4:00 p.m. the next day (April 30) for getting troops on the streets, no one had declared which agency would coordinate the National Guard's involvement, decided what its missions would be, or estimated how many more troops ultimately might be called. In addition, some of the officials involved, including Sheriff Block and Police Chief Gates, felt the National Guard had been called up prematurely. After all, says Sheriff's Lieutenant Dennis Beene, a team leader at the county EOC, "there were about 20,000 police officers and deputies in this county, looking at the LAPD, the deputies, and the other 46 [Los Angeles County municipal police] agencies. Had we managed those resources properly, we would not have needed anybody from outside to deal with what we had."[7] Nevertheless, with the riot spreading, and no evidence that the LAPD had the situation under control, Mayor Bradley and Governor Wilson pushed forward on the National Guard deployment.

The initial mobilization went well. The troops chosen for deployment responded quickly, and almost the entire contingent of 2,000 soldiers had reported to about ten armories in the city area by 4:00 a.m. Once the troops reported, however, the National Guard's lack of focus on civil disturbance preparedness became evident. Commanders at the armories hastily conducted basic riot training as troops assembled. In addition, all soldiers had to read and sign a copy of the Rules of Engagement that the National Guard headquarters had hastily prepared (see Exhibit 3C-1 for a copy of the Rules of Engagement). The rules were intended to emphasize the importance of restraint, so that soldiers wouldn't leave themselves open to charges, such as those that arose after the Watts riots, of having fired on rioters without adequate cause.

But the real holdup was the fact that there was not enough ammunition or basic equipment, such as flak vests, face shields, and riot batons, for the troops to deploy. Until earlier that year, ammunition had been stored at the local armories, enough to supply the soldiers, at least initially. But, ammunition that had been at scattered sites was now consolidated at Camp Roberts, a National Guard base about 230 miles north of Los Angeles. A combination

---

[6]Interview with Fire Chief Donald Manning, March 28, 2000. Unless noted, subsequent quotations from Donald Manning are also from this interview.

[7]Interview with Lieutenant Dennis Beene, Los Angeles County Sheriff's Department and team leader at the county Emergency Operations Center, March 29, 2000. Unless noted, subsequent quotations from Beene are also from this interview.

Exhibit 3C-1   Rules of engagement

RULES OF ENGAGEMENT
(29 April–1 May 1992)

I understand that I may be deployed to perform law enforcement support missions including crowd control, traffic control, perimeter security, protection of public safety employees such as firefighters, area security or roving patrols. I understand the following rules on the use of deadly and non-deadly force:

NON-DEADLY FORCE

1.   Non-deadly force involves the use of physical contact, restraint, baton, M16/A 1/2 with bayonet or chemicals such as tear gas or MACE.

2.   Non-deadly force will always be the minimum necessary to protect yourself, a team member, or a law enforcement officer or citizen from serious bodily injury.

3.   Non-deadly force should only be used at the discretion of a superior officer or non-commissioned office, a law enforcement officer, or in emergency situations.

USE OF DEADLY FORCE

1.   Deadly force refers to the use of any type of physical force in a manner that could reasonably be expected to result in death whether or not death is the intent.

2.   The use of deadly force is authorized only where all three of the following circumstances are present:

   a. All other means have been exhausted or are not readily available.

   b. The risk of death or serious bodily harm to innocent persons is not significantly increased by its use.

   c. The purpose of its use is one or more of the following:

   (1) Self-defense to avoid death or serious bodily harm (threat of harm is not restricted to firearms, but may include assault with bricks, pipes or other heavy missiles, incendiary and explosive devices, or any other material which could cause death or serious bodily harm).

   (2) Prevention of a crime which involves substantial risk of death or serious bodily harm.

   (3) Defense of others where there is substantial risk of death or serious bodily harm.

   (4) Detention or prevention of the escape of persons against whom the use of deadly force is authorized in subparagraphs (1), (2), and (3) above.

CIVIL DISTURBANCE TRAINING

I acknowledge that I have received basic civil disturbance training prior to my actual deployment in support of law enforcement.

I HAVE READ AND UNDERSTAND THE ABOVE USE OF DEADLY FORCE.

_____
   Signed/date

Source: Reprinted in James D. Delk, *Fires & Furies: The Los Angeles Riots of 1992* (Palm Springs, Calif.: ETC Publications, 1995), 341–342.

of poor communication, inexperience, and bad judgment badly delayed the delivery of this ammunition.

Other glitches further slowed the drop-off. Because crew members were transporting tear gas grenades, they had to bring gas masks, which took extra time to locate. At Camp Roberts, they had to refuel the helicopter at a point distant from the ammunition. By the time the supplies were trucked to the aircraft, it was already 7:15, just 45 minutes before the helicopter was originally to have delivered its load to the Los Alamitos Armed Forces Reserve Center. The crew, which had no experience in loading pallets of ammunition, didn't bring rollers to help transfer the loads, nor did the helicopter winch system work properly, so crew members ultimately loaded the pallets by hand. To make matters worse, the crew learned that some of the tear gas grenades on board were out of date. By the time they had unloaded part of the ammunition, located the bad grenades, found new ones, rebanded the pallets, and reloaded the supplies, the helicopter didn't take off until 9:45 a.m., with the equipment pickup still to come.

At Camp San Luis Obispo, the setbacks continued. The equipment wouldn't fit with what was already loaded, so the crew once again had to remove some of the heavy ammunition in order to fit flak vests, riot batons, and face shields on board. Then they had to wait for the arrival of lock plates, devices required by the federal government in any civil disturbance response to keep the soldiers' M16 rifles from firing on automatic. As a result, the helicopter did not arrive at Los Alamitos until 1:50 p.m., almost 6 hours later than originally expected. Remarkably, those responsible for delivering the ammunition and equipment also had apparently made no effort to inform officials at Los Alamitos, the adjutant general's office, or the governor's office of the delay.

The Dawning of the Second Day

Had the riots subsided as daylight broke April 30, as most observers were predicting, the slower-than-expected deployment of the National Guard might not have been an issue. Although Governor Wilson had declared a state of emergency for all of Los Angeles County at 12:05 a.m. on April 30, and Mayor Bradley had declared a dusk-to-dawn curfew for the South Central area at 12:15 a.m., Daryl Gates stated in a television interview about a half hour later that not only was it unlikely that additional National Guard forces would be called but he was not even convinced that the first 2,000 were needed. And although by morning there had been 9 riot-related deaths and more than 150 injuries, the Metropolitan Division (Metro), the LAPD unit with the most crisis training and experience, had been given a 4:00 p.m. report time the second day to give officers a chance to rest before reporting back for duty and under the assumption that they wouldn't be needed until dark.[8]

---

[8]Ultimately, Metro was called back 2 hours earlier, at 2:00 p.m.

But the riots, which had already spread north and west during the night into downtown Los Angeles and Koreatown, continued unabated, particularly in South Central. Rioters, looters, and arsonists didn't follow the pattern of previous incidents of unrest and seemed to feel no desire to wait until dark. According to a later study, the uprising was fueled by an estimated 50,000 men in South Central between the ages of 16 and 34 who were out of school, jobless, and had no father at home and who were therefore free to join in the rioting with few constraints.[9] In addition, new weapons were flooding the streets. Despite Commander Bayan Lewis's earlier department advisory to guard the gun stores, looters took 1,150 firearms from one unprotected store—including more than 600 automatics or semi-automatics—and another 970 firearms from a pawn shop in the first night of the riots alone. "There was nobody to cover them," Lewis declares.[10]

The demographics of those involved in the rioting had also changed by the second day. While the first night was in part a spontaneous expression of the African American community's rage at the Rodney King verdict—manifested in the attacks of young black males on whites, Latinos, and Asians caught in the middle of the outbreak—by the second day, looting had become an end in itself, and people of all races, ages, and gender were taking part. Indeed, according to later records of those arrested during the disturbance, Latinos (in particular, recent immigrants) outnumbered blacks. Furthermore, law enforcement officials reported seeing a number of wealthy residents coming into the riot area to fill their cars with loot.

Amid the spreading disturbance, the city's seven major commercial television stations, which were providing near 24-hour live coverage of the riots, continued to play a surprisingly powerful role. As in the first hours of the unrest, television reports showing a lackluster or passive police presence emboldened potential looters. Terrance Manning, Los Angeles City Fire Department battalion commander, also recalls, "You could almost get a game plan off television, because they would gather concerns from the local officials about where it was happening and what was happening. I think that gave a lot of direction to the rioters."[11]

In addition, as bad as the rioting was, many observers felt that the media—and particularly television—were exaggerating the extent of the rioting. The constant images of burning buildings and looting gave many viewers the impression that all of South Central was going up in flames and that vast areas of the city were endangered.

---

[9]Lou Cannon, *Official Negligence: How Rodney King and the Riots Changed Los Angeles and the LAPD* (Boulder, Colo.: Westview Press, 1999), 350.

[10]Interview with Commander Bayan Lewis, Uniformed Services Group, March 27, 2000. Unless noted, subsequent comments by Lewis are also from this interview.

[11]Interview with Terrance Manning, battalion commander, Los Angeles Fire Department, March 28, 2000. Unless noted, subsequent quotations from Terrance Manning are also from this interview.

Deploying the National Guard

By mid-morning April 30, there was still confusion over the exact role of the National Guard, including wildly different expectations about when they could and should deploy. At 10:00 a.m., for example, Mayor Bradley told the City Council that National Guard troops would be on the streets by noon. Minutes later, however, a state OES liaison officer, who was unaware of the growing panic within the city, reconfirmed with the National Guard EOC the original mobilization target of 4:00 p.m. Around the same time, alarmed Sheriff's Department officials called out for a stronger law enforcement presence on the streets, and General Thrasher (who hadn't been told about the equipment and ammunition delay) phoned Sheriff Sherman Block and told him that 2,000 National Guard troops were already in their armories and waiting to deploy.[12] Shortly after 11:00, meanwhile, Governor Wilson approved a Los Angeles County request that 2,000 more National Guard troops be mobilized, bringing the total to 4,000. Finally, during a noon conference call, Wilson pressed the LAPD and the Sheriff's Department to put National Guard troops on the street as soon as possible, and Mayor Bradley called Wilson at 12:30 to complain that soldiers still hadn't been deployed.

As this was occurring, officials at Los Alamitos were still trying to sort out when to mobilize. Faced with conflicting directions and information, frustrated National Guard personnel at Los Alamitos called Thrasher at 1:15 to find out who was in charge—the LAPD or the Sheriff's Department. When Thrasher called Undersheriff Bob Edmonds at about 1:20 to clarify the chain of command, the general learned for the first time that his troops were still waiting for equipment. "Everything that could go wrong did go wrong with the National Guard deployment," says Richard Andrews of OES. "For whatever reason, there was not accurate, consistent information being provided up the chain of command within the National Guard as to what was going on. There were a lot of people, Thrasher in particular, who were blindsided at almost every turn."[13]

Meanwhile, Brig. Gen. James Delk, the National Guard's military field commander, got two platoons ready to go by 1:30 p.m., but they didn't leave Los Alamitos until 2:35, mainly because the Sheriff's Department changed their mission. "We had never done anything with the Guard, so the question was, 'What are we going to do with them?'" recalls Sheriff's

---

[12]Also at around 10:00 a.m., Chief Gates finally accepted two platoons of about 112 deputies from the Sheriff's Department and put them to work making arrests in South Central.

[13]In part because of misunderstandings caused by the conflicting accounts of the deployment issued by the governor's press office, the National Guard public affairs office, and National Guard staff at Los Alamitos, the governor's staff finally requested on May 4 that all statements and releases about Guard activities be cleared with the governor's press office. In fact, according to Richard Andrews, the problems convinced OES to keep an unusually low press profile. "There was just so much confusion about what was the chain of events from the time they got the order to deploy, and to exactly what occurred with the decisions that were being made in the releases by the National Guard press office, that we made a decision not to add another voice to the confusion," he says.

Department Lieutenant Dennis Beene, who was helping coordinate operations from the county EOC. "Our platoon commanders out there had no idea how to make use of these resources coming in. We'd never really trained together, never really talked together. What can they do? It became a problem."

The awkward and delayed deployment of the National Guard exacerbated mounting tensions over how well the mutual aid system was working. During the early afternoon, Governor Wilson and other officials began to call Thrasher, demanding to know why the National Guard troops were not yet on the streets. "There was really no excuse for their not moving faster in a time of what appeared to be genuine crisis, particularly in light of what it was that held them up," the former governor asserts. "I mean, the ammunition snafu—to me—was stupidity."[14] During a conference call shortly after 2:00, officials finally agreed that the sheriff's EOC would coordinate National Guard missions, as dictated by the mutual aid plan. The group also agreed that troops should be sent out even if they hadn't installed lock plates on their M16s.[15] The risk of misusing the guns appeared small compared to the danger posed by the growing chaos in South Central.[16]

Protecting Firefighters

During Thursday morning, April 30, as officials tried to sort out when and how they could use the National Guard, Fire Chief Donald Manning was struggling with a different problem—obtaining adequate protection for his firefighters. By 10 a.m. that morning, the mutual aid system had brought in a total of fifty-six fire strike teams, including eleven from the county, twenty-three from Region I, and twenty-two from elsewhere in the state. But although the LAPD had finally assigned a contingent of Metro officers and other police to help escort firefighters, there still weren't enough to protect all the firefighting resources needed to bring the wave of arson under control. As a result, some city firefighters and mutual aid companies had been stuck waiting until escorts became available or had gone out without proper protection.

Further compounding the problem, police had not proven to be ideal escorts. According to Terrance Manning, many officers viewed the escort duty as less important than direct engagement with rioters, and in some cases, police deserted the firefighters they were supposed to be protecting when they received a call for help from another officer. There were also

---

[14]Interview with Governor Pete Wilson, March 29, 2000. Unless noted, subsequent quotations from Wilson are also from this interview.

[15]As stated earlier, even though federal regulations clearly stated the need for lock plates in a civil disturbance, most Guard units didn't have them when they reported for duty.

[16]Guard troops without lock plates supposedly were to be given only one bullet each, at the suggestion of Governor Wilson, with more ammunition to be held by their squad leaders. In practice, however, this never happened because Guard officials believed such an approach would subject soldiers to unacceptable risk.

scheduling and jurisdictional conflicts. Police officers generally adhered strictly to their 12-hour shifts, Manning says, and would leave at the end, even if that meant abandoning firefighters in the middle of an engagement. Moreover, the police operated within rigid geographical boundaries, while the fire department, by the nature of its operations, moved freely throughout the city as needed. As a result, firefighters often lost their police escorts as they traveled from one area to another and had to continue unprotected until police in the new jurisdiction were able to respond.

At 11:00 Thursday morning, Chief Donald Manning called a meeting at fire department headquarters that included representatives from the LAPD, the Sheriff's Department, the National Guard, the Federal Bureau of Investigation, and the CHP. "I was desperate," Manning says. "I would take anything." As he went around the table, Manning recalls, all the representatives turned him down, claiming either a lack of resources or more pressing missions—until he reached CHP Commander Gomez. "When I told him I needed about 300 officers, he said, 'You got it.'" By 6:30 p.m., the CHP had deployed three hundred officers as escorts, one hundred at the 54th and Arlington command and two hundred dispersed among four of the additional seven staging areas that Deputy Chief Donald Anthony had just established throughout the city. The CHP escorts typically consisted of three cars, with eight or nine officers and a sergeant, Manning says, and the officers were not held to strict shift limitations, nor were they limited by geographical boundaries. "That was a turning point for the fire service to be supported and protected to carry out their mission," Manning says.

The Sheriff's Department and the LAPD , which had become more organized during the second day of the riots, had also found jobs for the CHP, in particular, perimeter control and providing escorts for fuel trucks, utility vehicles, county firefighters, and other city and county vehicles. By the evening of April 30, there were some 2,500 CHP officers deployed in Los Angeles County.

Chaos Continues

Meanwhile, as the first National Guard platoons finally began to deploy shortly after 2:30 p.m., April 30, Sheriff Block, CHP Commissioner Hannigan, Chief Gates, and National Guard Field Commander General James Delk met to divide up the duties of the various forces. With the CHP escorting firefighters and providing key perimeter control, the group agreed that the National Guard would be responsible for most other missions required by the Sheriff's Department and the LAPD, including securing retail stores after police had established control, manning traffic control points, and conducting area patrols. Because the Sheriff's Department was to coordinate the mutual aid response, all law enforcement organizations agreed to station representatives at the county EOC, already filled beyond capacity with some eighty city and county representatives. Together, the LAPD and Sheriff's Department began to prioritize the flood of incoming requests from utilities, departments, and agencies for protective gear and protection of key facilities.

As the situation on the street worsened, Governor Wilson announced at 4:00 p.m. that he would personally fly to Los Angeles to make sure the National Guard deployment moved forward quickly. At about the same time, Mayor Bradley extended the dusk-to-dawn curfew from South Central to the entire city, as Gates had originally wished. The curfew probably didn't carry as much weight as it might have, however, because Bradley, apparently concerned about inconveniencing the city's business community, worded the announcement in such a way that the curfew sounded voluntary.[17] Some television stations duly reported the curfew as voluntary, and it took hours for the mayor's office to clear up the confusion.

Although the sheriff was supposed to be the top law enforcement official overseeing the mutual aid response, this protocol was often ignored as the riots raged on. Mayor Bradley, furious over the National Guard's deployment delay, continued to go straight to Governor Wilson with criticisms and requests. Similarly, the LAPD often gave mission requests directly to National Guard officials rather than processing them through the county EOC. Finally, some police officers phoned individual friends in departments and agencies elsewhere in the state, asking them for help. "Our captains and staff didn't know how to do mutual aid," exclaims Bayan Lewis. "We'd never done if before." The lack of a coordinated response made it significantly harder for EOC personnel to know who was available for missions, which areas of the city and county were covered, and what new sources of aid could still be tapped.

The eagerly awaited deployment of the National Guard also got off to a patchy start. Troops typically were sent to the specific law enforcement agency that had asked for them, and a National Guard unit commander, if present, would confer with the senior police official or sheriff's deputy from that jurisdiction to decide what the soldiers should do. According to General Delk, he and his officers had decided the troops would have the most impact if deployed in small groups rather than platoon-size units—a risky but conscious strategy. "What we first did was had a show of force," Delk explains, "and then we left soldiers behind two by two."[18] The troops were not only expected to help law enforcement officials hold on to the gains they had made; they were meant to be a visible symbol of the return of law and order to the streets of Los Angeles.[19]

---

[17]William H. Webster and Hubert Williams, *The City in Crisis: A Report by the Special Advisor to the Board of Police Commissioners on the Civil Disorder in Los Angeles* (Los Angeles, Calif.: October 21, 1992), Vol. 1, 129.

[18]Interview with Brig. Gen. James Delk, National Guard, April 5, 2000. Unless noted, subsequent quotations from Delk are also from this interview. While stationed in pairs, troops typically were in sight of other soldiers and had access to a radio, a cell phone, or a pay phone.

[19]William W. Mendel, "Combat in Cities: The LA Riots and Operation Rio," Foreign Military Studies Office, Fort Leavenworth, Kans., July 1996.

Due to the piecemeal fashion in which soldiers were deployed, however, the 40th Infantry Division didn't always know where all its troops were and had no easy way to contact them. In addition, although the mayor and governor had faulted the National Guard for its slow mobilization, many of those soldiers, after finally being equipped, sat idle because the Sheriff's Department and the LAPD didn't know where to put them. "We never had less than a battalion standing around," recalls Delk. "Never less, normally more." [20]

Also troubling, some law enforcement officials say, was the fact that a few newscasters had not only reported that the National Guard initially lacked ammunition but mistakenly announced that soldiers on the street were still unarmed. As a result of the misinformation, Delk says, looters and gang members were often brazen and aggressive, taunting the soldiers with their presumed inability to fire back.

---

[20]A Guard battalion can range from about 350 troops to more than 1,000.

The 1992 Los Angeles Riots (D): Bringing the Riots to an End

On the first afternoon of the National Guard deployment in Los Angeles, the number of troops on patrol was still so small that their effectiveness was largely untested. At 4:30 on April 30, one day after the riots had begun, Warren Christopher, who had headed up the earlier assessment of the Los Angeles Police Department (LAPD) and who viewed the slow National Guard deployment with real concern, asked Mayor Tom Bradley's staff whether the mayor was considering requesting federal troops. In fact, both Mayor Bradley and Governor Pete Wilson were alarmed by the fact that the National Guard had been unable to move in swiftly to quash the disturbance and feared that if the riots were not stopped by the weekend, they would likely spread and intensify.

As it was, the impact had already been profound. By mid-day, authorities had reported at least twenty deaths in the disturbance and more than five hundred people injured; and hundreds of fires still burned. The Southern California Rapid Transit District had cancelled all bus service, schools in Los Angeles and Compton had closed, and many businesses had sent workers home Thursday for an extended weekend, even in areas away from the rioting. Both because of heavy smoke and the possibility of gunfire striking an aircraft, Los Angeles International Airport had begun redirecting arriving and departing flights over the Pacific Ocean, reducing activity to less than a quarter the normal rate and creating gridlock up and down the West Coast.

In addition, with the riots still spreading, the feeling had grown throughout Los Angeles that no area was safe and that even wealthy communities previously untouched by urban unrest faced the possibility of violence and destruction. According to former Governor Wilson, his office was being inundated by calls from politicians and business people. "There was a concern that there could be a highly lawless element who, encouraged by the initial default, would just take full advantage of it," says Wilson, "and there were a number of people within the community who were panicking." [1]

Bradley took Warren Christopher's suggestion seriously. That evening, he authorized a request for federal troops, asking Christopher to contact federal authorities and to initiate the process of procuring federal forces. Much to Bradley's horror, as of 8 p.m., there were still only 1,000 National Guard troops deployed. At another meeting of top officials a few hours later, Bradley insisted that he needed more National Guard forces and that he would call in federal troops the following morning if there still weren't enough soldiers on the streets. Just

---

[1] Interview with Governor Pete Wilson, March 29, 2000. Unless noted, subsequent quotations from Wilson are also from this interview.

before midnight, meanwhile, Police Chief Daryl Gates and Sheriff Sherman Block requested another 2,000 National Guard troops. Clearly, however, there was still a critical disconnect between the need on the streets and the ability of the Sheriff's Department and the LAPD to put troops to work. At Los Alamitos, National Guard officials questioned the need to call up more troops—more than 4,000 were already present or would be reporting soon, and many units still had no missions and were waiting in armories with nothing to do.

By midnight, the riots' toll had mounted. According to official estimates, there had been 31 riot-related deaths in all and more than 1,000 injuries. The three hospitals closest to the rioting—Martin Luther King Jr. General Hospital, Daniel Freeman Memorial Hospital, and the St. Francis Medical Center—had been inundated with patients, and the county Emergency Operations Center (EOC) had directed ambulances to go to less crowded hospitals nearby.[2] Meanwhile, the record number of emergency 911 calls on Thursday—62,749, up from 35,558 the previous day—had overwhelmed the ability of dispatchers to handle them.[3] Although fire personnel were feeling more secure with their California Highway Patrol (CHP) escorts, Thursday evening had been significantly worse than the first night of the riots. At 11 p.m., a total of 950 firefighters and paramedics were on the streets, including firefighters from forty-eight different mutual aid agencies, and during the 24-hour period of April 30, firefighters received reports of almost 3,250 structure fires, compared to 32 calls on an average day.[4]

Shortly after 1 a.m., Governor Wilson put in a formal request to President George H. W. Bush for federal troops, and by 3:30 a.m., 3,500 troops were on their way to Los Angeles for possible deployment.[5] In addition, after discussing the issue with the chairman of the Joint Chiefs of Staff, Gen. Colin Powell, Wilson decided that if federal troops deployed, he would federalize the National Guard, which would remove the Guard from state control and put them instead under a federal chain of command. "If there were going to be federal troops involved," Wilson says, "it simply made sense from the standpoint of command and control that there be a single command." But Richard Andrews, formerly of the Office of Emergency Services (OES), says it was more than that. "Wilson was so fed up with the information that he was getting, and the information that he wasn't getting, and the mixed signals, that he had basically lost confidence in the command structure of the Guard."[6]

---

[2]As an emergency room filled up, it notified the county, which then alerted paramedics to divert to the next closest hospital. None of the hospitals, however, turned away the many patients who came on their own.

[3]William H. Webster and Hubert Williams, *The City in Crisis: A Report by the Special Advisor to the Board of Police Commissioners on the Civil Disorder in Los Angeles* (Los Angeles, Calif.: October 21, 1992), Vol. 1, 110. The normal volume was 6,500 calls for the LAPD and 900 for the fire department.

[4]Although still sobering, the number of structures actually damaged or destroyed by fire during the riots was fewer than 1,150. Timothy V. Manning, Terrance J. Manning, and Christopher S. Kawai, *Los Angeles City Fire Department Historical Overview: Los Angeles Civil Disturbance, April 29, 1992* (Los Angeles, Calif.: October 1992), 8, 42, 144.

[5]A decision about whether to actually use the troops was not made until later that day.

[6]Interview with Richard Andrews, former director, Office of Emergency Services, March 27, 2000. Unless noted, subsequent quotations from Andrews are also from this interview.

Putting the National Guard to Work

Despite the devastation of the previous night, by Friday morning, May 1, many emergency personnel in Los Angeles began to feel a sense of hope. Due in part to the curfew and the gradually increasing presence of National Guard troops and law enforcement officers on the street, both looting and new incidents of arson had fallen off sharply after midnight. According to Battalion Commander Terrance Manning, after a 36-hour period that had demanded the largest commitment of resources in the history of the fire department, firefighters had begun to consider the arson situation largely under control.[7] Many within the LAPD also felt the worst was over. "We had half the department out that second night, and we had what I felt was good blanket coverage," recalls Bayan Lewis. "We were making arrests, we were not allowing ourselves to be driven by the news media—which happened the first night—and people realized very quickly that if they were out on the street, they went to jail."[8]

The National Guard roll-out hadn't made great strides overnight, however. As of 6:00 a.m., there were still only 1,555 National Guard soldiers on the street, with another 2,743 waiting for missions and more arriving in the armories. But by early afternoon, the LAPD and the Sheriff's Department finally began to deploy the National Guard in large numbers. The LAPD, in particular, requested thousands of additional troops, staging many as an instantly available reserve force at the Sports Arena–Coliseum complex toward the north edge of South Central by the University of Southern California. By 2:47 p.m., there were more than 3,000 National Guard troops performing missions, with 2,300 available and waiting. Three hours later, another 1,385 were on their way to specific missions.[9]

The sight of the uniformed soldiers, who finally began to appear in force on the third day of the riots, had a significant impact, LAPD officers say. Gang members and looters generally took the presence of troops more seriously than that of regular law enforcement officers, despite questions over whether all soldiers had ammunition. "We needed that psychological, mental impact that the army is in the streets, and government is back in control," Bayan Lewis says. "The Guard clearly gave us that."

In addition, Lewis and other officers say, National Guard soldiers distinguished themselves by being highly responsive to the needs of the police and the Sheriff's Department,

---

[7]Interview with Terrance Manning, battalion commander, Los Angeles Fire Department, March 28, 2000. Unless noted, subsequent quotations from Terrance Manning are also from this interview. During these initial 36 hours, the dispatch center had created 6,529 emergency incidents, including fires and related violence, and 862 structures had been burned within the city.

[8]Interview with Commander Bayan Lewis, Uniformed Services Group, March 27, 2000. Unless noted, subsequent comments by Lewis are also from this interview.

[9]A full brigade of National Guard troops from northern California, ordered to head south around midnight the previous night, was also on its way, despite assertions by Maj. Gen. Daniel Hernandez, commander of the 40th Infantry Division, that by the time they arrived they would not be needed.

taking on almost all tasks asked of them. Typical National Guard missions included managing traffic control points; patrolling shopping centers to prevent looting; riding along in police cars to provide extra law enforcement power; guarding emergency work crews; and protecting sensitive sites, such as utility buildings and fire departments.

Even as the situation on the streets began to improve, however, the planned mobilization of federal troops moved forward. "We are going to see to it that the people of this city are protected," Governor Wilson declared at a 1:00 p.m. press conference. At 6:00 p.m., President George Bush announced on television that the decision had been made to deploy federal troops into the streets of Los Angeles and that the National Guard would be federalized. In addition, the government had begun to send in more than 1,700 federal agents with special riot training from such agencies as the Federal Bureau of Investigation, the United States Border Patrol, and the Federal Marshals office. Governor Wilson recounts, "The further word that federal troops were coming indicated that, however much people had been free to raise hell and set things afire on the first night, that time was over."

Like the earlier delays in the LAPD and National Guard responses, however, federal troops did not appear on the streets of Los Angeles as quickly as either Mayor Bradley or Governor Wilson had expected. "There was a reluctance on the part of the military to come in," Wilson says. "They don't like the idea of being called in to be a substitute for the police department in a domestic setting."

The Pentagon had appointed Maj. Gen. Marvin Covault, commander of the U.S. Army's 7th Infantry Division at Fort Ord, California, to be Joint Task Force commander of the 2,023 U.S. Army and 1,508 U.S. Marine Corps troops assembling at staging areas south of Los Angeles during the day.[10] In a conversation with Wilson late afternoon Friday, General Covault informed the governor that federal forces wouldn't be ready to deploy until the following day, after all the soldiers had arrived and had had a chance to train. There was no need for federal troops to rush in without adequate preparation, Covault told Wilson, particularly because the crisis was no longer as acute and there were still National Guard troops who had not been given specific missions.[11]

At 10 p.m., General Covault met with Gates and Block to discuss how federal troops would be deployed. The police chief and the sheriff were already dubious about the federal deployment, and the discussion with Covault only worsened their fears. Gates and Block

---

[10]The army troops were members of the 7th Infantry Division at Fort Ord and were designed to respond quickly to urban warfare situations, while the marines were a battalion from the 1st Marine Expeditionary Force, based at Camp Pendleton, California.

[11]James D. Delk, *Fires & Furies: The Los Angeles Riots of 1992* (Palm Springs, Calif.: ETC Publications, 1995), 116. Although the LAPD had requested all available National Guard troops by the time it got dark, many were simply posted at central locations such as the Hollywood Bowl and Dodger Stadium, and some units sent to the Coliseum waited more than 24 hours before receiving a mission.

had hoped to use federal troops much as they had used the National Guard, not only post-ing them in volatile areas but also assigning them to specific law enforcement missions. Covault, however, had apparently concluded that the Guard had already restored law and order, and that federal troops (and the federalized National Guard) should be used only to maintain control and should not perform the sort of routine law enforcement duties that Guard troops had previously undertaken.

According to some observers, Covault's decision to limit the role of the troops was based on a mistaken application of the federal Posse Comitatus Act, legislation dating from the end of Reconstruction that was designed to keep military forces out of domestic police ac-tivities and that prohibited soldiers from performing law enforcement duties. The act did not apply, however, when a president called in troops to respond to a civil disturbance un-der federal statute, such as had occurred in Los Angeles. Others, however, insisted that Co-vault was fully aware he was not restricted by Posse Comitatus but had decided that keeping the mission of troops narrow was both in line with Bush's executive order and the appro-priate use of federal forces. "It was not the military's mission to solve Los Angeles's crime problem, nor were we trained to do so," Covault later said in response to criticisms of the federal troop role.[12] Adds Brig. Gen. Edward Buckley, then a colonel and the commander of the 2nd Brigade of the 7th Infantry Division, "We weren't going to try to do police work. We were there to provide stability, to provide a force presence to essentially take back control of the crisis."[13] In any event, Gates and Block viewed the upcoming change in the National Guard's role with disappointment and alarm.

An Uneasy Collaboration

Emergency personnel pointed to Friday night as the turning point in the riots, but the third day and night of the disturbance were still violent and destructive. By Saturday morning, May 2, there had been twelve more deaths and 1,172 more structural fires. Nevertheless, the tide had begun to turn. Things were finally running smoothly at the city's EOC, according to Shirley Mattingly, coordinator of the city's Emergency Operations Organization (EOO), and members of both the Emergency Operations Board and the Emergency Management Committee were meeting to coordinate agency responses.[14] Emergency 911 calls on Friday had dropped to below the level of the first day of the riots, and by 11 a.m. Saturday, there were more than 6,000 National Guard troops engaged, more than 1,000 waiting for deploy-

---

[12]Quoted in Ibid., 320.

[13]Interview with Brig. Gen. Edward Buckley, in 1992 a colonel and the commander of the 2nd Brigade, 7th In-fantry Division, April 5, 2000. Unless noted, subsequent comments by Buckley are also from this interview.

[14]Interview with Shirley Mattingly, director of emergency management, April 7, 2000. Unless noted, subse-quent comments by Mattingly are also from this interview.

ment, and another 1,856 getting ready to deploy. With troops and Humvees on the streets and helicopters overhead, most law enforcement officials no longer felt South Central was out of control. While some buildings were still smoldering, volunteers in parts of the community had begun to rally to clean up the residue of rioting and looting. A few businesses in riot-torn areas even began to re-open.

Against this backdrop, the first federal troops, the marine battalion, finally deployed Saturday afternoon to the Compton and Long Beach areas, and soon after, the contingent of 2,500 army troops was stationed around Watts and nearby Huntington Park. According to Brig. Gen. Edward Buckley, the National Guard had been effective, but the federal soldiers still had work to do. "The crisis wasn't over. The problem was we were still having incidents occur, and I think Governor Wilson wanted to end this as quickly as possible." But according to many observers, particularly within the LAPD and the Sheriff's Department, the more structured command and control inherent in a federal military response—in particular, the rules governing mission tasking and troop strength—eliminated most of the flexibility and responsiveness that had characterized the initial National Guard response and immediately reduced the usefulness of military troops to local law enforcement. As Sheriff's Lieutenant Sid Heal complains, "Just when we were getting to where we thought the Guard was really being effective, they federalized them." [15]

When the National Guard was under state control, a Guard officer stationed at the county EOC had approved virtually all the requests that local law enforcement officials submitted, and Guard troops had been able to move fluidly from one task to another. But the federal mission approval process was less direct and flexible. First, Joint Task Force representatives based at the county EOC had to prioritize incoming requests from the LAPD and the rest of the county. Once done, they submitted the requests to the task force headquarters at Los Alamitos for review by General Covault, the operations officer, and the senior civilian representative of the attorney general representing the U.S. Department of Justice. [16] The new review process was not only far more time-consuming, often taking 6–8 hours, but also resulted in only about 20 percent of the requests' being approved. With the riots largely under control, many remaining tasks—such as police ride-alongs, traffic control points, and area patrols—could easily be classified as law enforcement–related, and they were therefore judged inappropriate for federal troops and the federalized National Guard.

In addition, rather than sending out small squads of soldiers on demand, an approach that National Guard Field Commander Delk had acknowledged as being risky but effective,

---

[15]Interview with Lieutenant Sid Heal, Los Angeles County Sheriff's Department, March 29, 2000. Unless noted, subsequent quotations from Heal are also from this interview.

[16]When the military was involved in a domestic civil disturbance, the lead agency was typically the Department of Justice.

the Joint Task Force directed troops to deploy in platoon strength—or in groups of about forty soldiers—under the command of a commissioned officer, as their training had prepared them to do. According to General Buckley, those forty soldiers might disperse over an area of a couple of blocks, but they would still be close enough to respond to each other if a larger force was needed. Although General Covault didn't insist that all National Guard missions immediately comply with that order, new missions were expected to follow the new protocol. While many local law enforcement officers saw the order as unnecessarily restrictive, most military personnel believed it was essential for the safety of soldiers and citizens alike that the troops report as a unit.

One additional change, although less significant from the standpoint of the police, was particularly frustrating for National Guard officers and troops, according to Delk.[17] Instead of allowing troops latitude in deciding whether to have ammunition in their guns and at what degree of readiness to keep their weapons, the Joint Task Force issued a new arming order prohibiting troops from having ammunition in their weapons without special approval from headquarters.[18] Although Joint Task Force officials told Delk that the order was intended as a guideline and need not be applied to all situations, that distinction was never made official. As a result, some units felt compelled to follow the order, other units ignored it, and still others began sending out only those soldiers who volunteered for duty because officers believed the order subjected soldiers to unnecessary and unacceptable risk.

Finally, local law enforcement officials were having trouble accommodating the large and varied contingent of federal officers, numbering more than 1,700, that had been sent in as part of the federal response, many without vehicles. Police officers and sheriff's deputies who had been riding four to a car found themselves having to eject their own experienced personnel in order to include some of these federal officers.

Even though the local, state, and federal collaboration was not always smooth, the assembled law enforcement presence was impressive. By Sunday, a force of 13,000 was deployed in and around Los Angeles, including some 7,000 National Guard troops; the 3,500 federal troops; and an amalgam of officers from local, state, and federal agencies. "It's better to be too strong and to reduce the strength than to create a vacuum in which violence can take place and escalate," says Wilson. That night, there were only a few new fatalities, and the accumulated efforts of some 2,000 firefighters drawn in through the fire department's mutual aid system had finally extinguished most of the fires that had been burning in Los Angeles since the night of April 29.

---

[17]Interview with Brig. Gen. James Delk, National Guard, April 5, 2000. Unless noted, subsequent comments by Delk are also from this interview.

[18]The order again raised speculation about National Guard troops being sent out without ammunition.

The Effort to Disengage

The Los Angeles riots were considered officially over when Mayor Bradley lifted the curfew Monday evening (May 4), 5 days after the violence had begun. The following day, most federal agents were released, but civilian officials argued against letting go of the federal and National Guard troops. Bradley, in particular, wanted to make sure that Los Angeles had returned to normal before the soldiers departed and had been visiting churches, civic groups, and other organizations, both to impart a sense of calm and to try to gauge the mood in South Central and other parts of the city. "This was a very traumatic event for the city, for Bradley, for everybody," says former OES Director Richard Andrews. "They didn't want to say it's all over and send these guys home, and bam, the whole thing erupts again." Even Daryl Gates was arguing to keep the military presence in place, particularly at night, in order to maintain control and provide additional backup so that officers could rest. In addition, there were widespread rumors that gangs were going to target police officers once the soldiers had departed.

General Covault, however, believed federal and National Guard troops should leave as soon as possible. Although the rioting had stopped, gang and criminal activity in South Central and other areas of Los Angeles was still rampant, and National Guard and federal troops continued to find themselves in explosive situations. On Sunday night, for example, police and marines were responding to a disturbance in Compton, which turned out to be a domestic dispute, when two shotgun rounds were fired through the door. One of the police officers shouted, "Cover me," meaning that the marines should have their weapons ready to respond if necessary. But the marines, understanding "cover me" to mean providing cover by using firepower, shot off what was later estimated to have been more than two hundred rounds. Remarkably, neither the man inside who fired the original shots nor the woman and children who turned out to be in the apartment were hit by the bullets.[19]

In recognition of the problems that could result from using soldiers in nonriot incidents, the Joint Task Force issued a new Operations Order at 7:00 Monday morning, declaring that troops would no longer patrol the streets during the day and that the role of military forces was to be "one of less visible backup and reinforcement capabilities." By Tuesday, Covault believed it was time for federal forces to go. "At this point," Covault wrote in a report to Fort Ord, "the military is providing 10,000 targets for the type of activity going on in the streets (i.e.[,] pure lawlessness versus civil disturbance). The potential downside to continue in the law enforcement mode is enormous (not trained and ready to do so)."[20] Over the next few days, Covault began canceling military missions—often without consulting with local law

---

[19]Delk, *Fires & Furies,* 221.
[20]Quoted in ibid., 235.

enforcement agencies—disengaging federal troops and letting the National Guard take their place.

On Saturday, May 9, federal troops finally began to depart, and the National Guard reverted to state status.[21] With defederalization, the National Guard once again accepted a broader range of assignments, including controlling traffic and accompanying police officers and deputies on patrols. Just 5 days later, however, the National Guard also began to disengage, although, Delk says, the transition wasn't easy. "Nobody wanted to let us go," he notes. On Wednesday, May 27, the last soldiers headed home.

The Aftermath

The riots left Los Angeles in disarray. An area of 105 square miles within the city had been affected, and South Central and other areas of the city and county had been devastated, with some 1,148 structures damaged or destroyed. Even before federal troops left the area, Mayor Bradley had created a nonprofit task force, dubbed Rebuild L.A., whose mission was to reconstruct the damaged inner city of Los Angeles.

As the city launched into the reconstruction effort, it soon became clear that the riots had altered not just the physical landscape of the city but the political landscape as well. On May 11, the Los Angeles Board of Police Commissioners initiated an investigation of the flawed LAPD response, and Governor Wilson ordered an informal report assessing the performance of the state National Guard. The following month, Los Angeles voters passed Amendment F, which Police Chief Gates had strongly opposed.[22] Under the amendment, future police chiefs could serve only two 5-year terms, as earlier recommended by the Christopher Commission, and officers who broke rules, such as those prohibiting excessive force, could be more easily disciplined. On June 26, Gates finally stepped down, making way for his successor, former Philadelphia Police Commissioner Willie L. Williams. General Thrasher, adjutant general of the National Guard, left in what Wilson describes as a "mutual decision." And in September, Mayor Bradley announced he would not seek a sixth term in 1993, a decision that some observers linked to the fallout from the riots.

In the aftermath of the disturbance, the city's EOO and the region's emergency response organizations—from the LAPD to the Sheriff's Department to the National Guard—also

---

[21]In fact, Covault and his troops began to leave before an official announcement had been made. Richard Andrews, alerted to the soldiers' imminent departure, quickly scheduled a press conference at which Governor Wilson could thank the federal forces for their role and bid them farewell. "We didn't want the impression that these guys were totally independent agents," Andrews recalls.

[22]Defeating the amendment was the focus of the fund-raiser that Gates had attended as the riots were first breaking out.

began to retool their civil disturbance training and preparedness and vowed not to be caught unprepared again. But despite such good intentions, keeping law enforcement and other emergency personnel properly prepared for an event as unexpected, unpredictable, and unlikely as a riot proved to be a tremendous challenge, warns Bayan Lewis, especially because the tendency of emergency planners was to focus on the last emergency they had experienced. When he thinks about riot preparedness, Lewis says, he imagines himself about 20 years in the future, sitting on the porch of a Nevada rest home. "Somebody will open the *Los Angeles Times* for me," he says, "and it will say, 'Major Riot 27 Years Later: LAPD Unprepared.'"

Key Players in the 1992 Los Angeles Riots

Los Angeles Police Department

Daryl Gates, chief of police

Robert Vernon, assistant chief and
director, Office of Operations

Ronald Frankle, deputy chief and
commanding officer, Headquarters
Bureau

Matthew Hunt, deputy chief and
commander, South Bureau

Michael Hillmann, lieutenant and interim
commander, Metropolitan Division

Paul Jefferson, captain and commander,
77th Street Division

Bayan Lewis, commander, Uniformed
Services Group

Michael Moulin, lieutenant and ranking
officer during the Florence-Normandie
retreat

Officers prosecuted in *People of California v. Powell*

Theodore Briseno

Stacey Koon

Laurence Powell

Timothy Wind

Los Angeles County Sheriff's Department

Sherman Block, sheriff

Dennis Beene, lieutenant and team leader
at the county Emergency Operations
Center

Bob Edmonds, undersheriff

Sid Heal, lieutenant

Los Angeles Fire Department

Donald Manning, fire chief

Donald Anthony, deputy chief and
commander, Bureau of Fire
Suppression and Rescue

Dean Cathey, battalion chief and
community liaison officer

Terrance Manning, battalion commander

Timothy Manning, battalion commander

City of Los Angeles Officials

Tom Bradley, mayor

Warren Christopher, chairman of the
Independent Commission on the Los
Angeles Police Department (also
referred to as the Christopher
Commission)

Philip Depoian, special councilor to
Mayor Bradley and police department
liaison

Shirley Mattingly, director of emergency
management and coordinator,
Emergency Operations Organization
(EOO)

State of California Officials

Pete Wilson, governor

Richard Andrews, director, Office of
Emergency Services (OES)

Stanley Weisberg, presiding judge, *People
of California v. Powell*

California Highway Patrol

Maurice Hannigan, commissioner

Edward Gomez, chief and commander, California Highway Patrol Southern Division

California National Guard

Maj. Gen. Robert Thrasher, adjutant general of the California National Guard

Brig. Gen. James Delk, National Guard military field commander for the riots

U.S. Army

Maj. Gen. Marvin Covault, commander of the 7th Infantry Division and commander of the Joint Task Force

Col. Edward Buckley, commander of the 2nd Brigade, 7th Infantry Division

Federal Officials

George H. W. Bush, president

Gen. Colin Powell, chairman of the Joint Chiefs of Staff

Others

Rodney King, driver whose beating and arrest precipitated the 1992 riots

Reginald Denny, truck driver beaten in South Central during the riots

Soon Ja Du, Korean shopkeeper convicted of voluntary manslaughter in the death of Latasha Harlins, a 15-year-old African American customer

George Holliday, witness to the beating and arrest of Rodney King

The 1992 Los Angeles Riots

Chronology of Events

1991

Sunday, March 3

Rodney King, a speeding motorist, is pursued through northern Los Angeles by officers from the Los Angeles Police Department (LAPD), the California Highway Patrol (CHP), and the Los Angeles Unified School District. After being brought to a stop, King is beaten and arrested.

Monday, March 4

A homemade video showing LAPD officers beating King is broadcast nationwide, spurring charges of racism and police brutality.

Thursday, March 7

LAPD Police Chief Daryl Gates announces that the officers involved in King's beating will be prosecuted.

Thursday, March 14

A grand jury indicts Laurence Powell, Stacey Koon, Theodore Briseno, and Timothy Wind, the four police officers involved in the Rodney King beating.

Saturday, March 16

Soon Ja Du, a Korean shopkeeper, shoots and kills a 15-year-old African American girl, Latasha Harlins, after an altercation over a container of orange juice.

Monday, April 1

Mayor Bradley appoints the Independent Commission on the Los Angeles Police Department (dubbed the Christopher Commission) to investigate LAPD policies and the leadership of Chief Gates.

Tuesday, July 9

The Christopher Commission releases a report calling for LAPD reforms and recommending the resignation of Chief Gates. Gates refuses to step down but begins implementing many of the other recommendations issued in the report.

Friday, November 15

A jury finds Soon Ja Du guilty of manslaughter. Du receives a suspended sentence.

Tuesday, November 26

Stanley Weisberg, the judge presiding over the trial of the four officers accused of beating Rodney King (*People of California v. Powell*), announces that the trial will be held in the mostly white community of Simi Valley, Ventura County.

1992

Monday, March 2, 1992

The jury for *People of California v. Powell* is seated.

Early April

A few LAPD officers make efforts to prepare for a possible civil disturbance in response to the upcoming verdicts in the Rodney King trial. In general, however, the department keeps a low profile.

Wednesday, April 29

1:00 p.m.: Judge Weisberg announces that the jury's verdicts will be read in 2 hours, giving police and other emergency agencies a window to prepare for possible unrest.

3:15 p.m.: The verdicts in *People of California v. Powell* are announced. The jury acquits three officers of all charges and is deadlocked on one charge against the fourth officer. The verdicts spark immediate unrest and demonstrations, but LAPD leadership takes few immediate response measures.

4:15 p.m.: Several young African American men steal beer from a Korean American store in South Central Los Angeles, attack the store owner's son, and break a door, marking the start of the Los Angeles riots.

4:45 p.m.: The Emergency Operations Board begins to assemble at LA's Emergency Operations Center (EOC) to coordinate the city's response.

5:15 p.m.: Mayor Tom Bradley addresses the city, declaring that "we will not tolerate the savage beating of our citizens by a few renegade cops." Critics charge that the Mayor's words inflame the rioting.

5:23 p.m.: Police officers arrest a young African American male in South Central Los Angels after witnessing him smash the windshield of a car with a baseball bat. A gathering crowd chants, "Rodney King, Rodney King, Rodney King."

5:38 p.m.: Chief Gates declares that his officers are prepared to deal with any disturbances. But in the LAPD's South Central 77th Street District, the emergency is quickly intensifying. There, a group of policemen are cornered by an angry crowd near the intersection of Florence and Normandie.

5:43 p.m.: LAPD Lieutenant Michael Moulin, watch commander at the 77th Street Station, orders the retreat of police officers from Florence and Normandie.

6:00 p.m.: Lieutenant Moulin begins setting up a staging area at 54th and Arlington Streets, about 2 miles from the rioting.

6:20 p.m.: Lieutenant Moulin orders a halt to all police rescue efforts in the Florence-Normandie area. Looting and rioting go on unchecked.

6:30 p.m.: Chief Gates leaves police headquarters for a fund-raiser outside of Los Angeles.

6:40 p.m.: Rioters storm LAPD headquarters. An hour later, after police finally push them back, the demonstrators proceed to damage other buildings in the area.

6:46 p.m.: Television stations broadcast live a brutal attack on trucker Reginald Denny at the Florence and Normandie intersection.

7:00 p.m.: LAPD Commander Bayan Lewis designates the 54th and Arlington Streets staging area as an LAPD command post.

Fire Chief Donald Manning returns to Los Angeles Fire Department headquarters and recalls his staff.

Governor Pete Wilson offers Mayor Bradley the California National Guard to help quell the rioting.

7:30 p.m.: Fires begin to break out in South Central riot areas.

8:00 p.m.: LAPD Deputy Chief Ronald Frankle orders the mobilization of the LAPD, lengthening officer shifts, calling back off-duty police, and canceling leave.

Deputy Fire Chief Donald Anthony places his first request for mutual aid strike teams.

Battalion Commander Timothy Manning sets up a Los Angeles Fire Department command post at the LAPD's 54th and Arlington Streets site.

8:15 p.m.: An 18-year-old dies after being shot by rioters, becoming the first fatality of the riots.

The fire department orders firefighters to withdraw from South Central and report to the 54th and Arlington Streets command post.

8:20 p.m.: Fire Chief Manning establishes a Department Command to manage all fires as a single incident. He makes Deputy Fire Chief Anthony the operations commander.

8:30 p.m.: Firefighters at the 54th and Arlington Streets command post form strike teams and await police escorts.

8:45 p.m.: Mayor Bradley accepts Governor Wilson's offer and requests the National Guard. He also declares a city emergency.

9:00 p.m.: Deputy Chief Matthew Hunt, head of the LAPD's South Bureau, arrives at the command post.

Governor Wilson authorizes the deployment of 2,000 California National Guard troops.

9:15 p.m.: Maj. Gen. Robert Thrasher, adjutant general of the California National Guard, orders the mobilization of National Guard troops.

9:43 p.m.: Fire department strike teams finally start to be paired with police escorts.

10:00 p.m.: Dozens of fires burn across Los Angeles.

Chief Gates arrives at the LAPD's command post and proceeds to lambaste Deputy Hunt for the failed police response.

10:13 p.m.: During a conference call of top officials, Chief Gates and Los Angeles County Sheriff Sherman Block both doubt the need for National Guard troops but welcome the assistance of the CHP. Gates turns down Block's offer of five hundred sheriff's deputies, however.

Thursday, April 30

12:05 a.m.: Governor Wilson declares a state of emergency for Los Angeles County.

12:15 a.m.: Mayor Bradley declares a dusk-to-dawn curfew for South Central Los Angeles.

4:00 a.m.: Most of the 2,000 National Guard troops called up by the governor have reported to Los Angeles armories, where they await supplies and ammunition.

6:00 a.m.: Police Chief Gates arrives at the city's EOC after a night spent viewing the riot areas.

10:00 a.m.: Mayor Bradley informs the City Council that National Guard troops will be on the streets within 2 hours. But a state Office of Emergency Services liaison officer reconfirms with the National Guard EOC the deployment target of 4:00 p.m.

General Thrasher of the National Guard, unaware that troops are still waiting for equipment and ammunition, tells Sheriff Block that troops are ready to deploy.

11:00 a.m.: Governor Wilson approves the mobilization of 2,000 additional National Guard troops.

12:00 p.m.: In a conference call, Governor Wilson urges Chief Gates and Sheriff Block to deploy the National Guard troops.

12:30 p.m.: Mayor Bradley phones Governor Wilson to complain about the delayed deployment of National Guard troops.

1:20 p.m.: General Thrasher learns from the Sheriff's Department that the National Guard troops are still waiting for supplies they need to deploy.

1:30 p.m.: Brig. Gen. James Delk, the National Guard's military field commander, determines that two Guard platoons are now ready to deploy.

1:50 p.m.: A helicopter carrying ammunition and supplies for National Guard troops lands at the Los Alamitos Armed Forces Reserve Center, the designated staging area, about 6 hours later than had been expected.

2:35 p.m.: The two waiting National Guard platoons finally deploy.

Law enforcement officials agree that the National Guard will be responsible for most missions required by the Sheriff's Department and LAPD, other than escort duty and perimeter control, which are being handled primarily by the CHP.

4:00 p.m.: Mayor Bradley extends the dusk-to-dawn curfew to all of Los Angeles as the riots continue.

Governor Wilson announces the he is flying to Los Angeles to ensure the speedy deployment of National Guard troops.

4:30 p.m.: Warren Christopher suggests to the mayor's office the possibility of calling in federal troops. A few hours later, Mayor Bradley asks Christopher to initiate a request for federal troops.

Friday, May 1
12:00 a.m.: The LAPD and the Sheriff's Department ask for an additional 2,000 National Guard troops.

1 a.m.: Governor Wilson submits a formal request to President George H. W. Bush for federal troops.

Early morning: After 36 hours, the Los Angeles Fire Department determines that the fires are under control.

2:47 p.m.: More than 3,000 National Guard troops are on the streets performing missions.

6:00 p.m.: President Bush announces the planned deployment of federal troops and the federalization of the National Guard.

Saturday, May 2
11:00 a.m.: More than 6,000 National Guard troops are on the streets.

Afternoon: Federal troops deploy to Compton, Long Beach, Watts, and Huntington Park.

Sunday, May 3
Morning: A combined force of more than 13,000 National Guard troops; federal soldiers; and local, state, and federal law enforcement officers is deployed in and around Los Angeles.

Monday, May 4

7:00 a.m.: Joint Task Force Commander Maj. Gen. Marvin Covault ends the day patrols, relegating federal troops to a less visible backup role.

Evening: Mayor Bradley lifts the dusk-to-dawn curfew, signaling the official end of the riots.

Tuesday, May 5 to Friday, May 8

General Covault continues the disengagement of federal troops.

Saturday, May 9

Federal troops depart and the federalization of the National Guard ends.

Wednesday, May 13

The first National Guard troops begin to disengage.

Wednesday, May 27

The last National Guard troops depart Los Angeles.

4   The Baltimore Tunnel Fire of 2001 (A): The Crisis Unfolds

Esther Scott

In any city, government may have to respond with great speed to a large-scale physical emergency that strikes with little or no warning. The safety of citizens, preservation of property, and even the chance to keep a disaster from mushrooming in scale depend on how rapidly and effectively a city can mobilize, deploy its emergency workers, and execute emergency plans.

When a disaster is particularly large, however, even the best efforts of a given jurisdiction may be insufficient to cope. In this case study in Baltimore, what starts as a fire, primarily involving fire department responders, becomes a far more complicated situation that requires the coordinated action of workers from a number of different departments, professions, and levels of government. These responders have to be integrated with the city's own capacity, and the full set of emergency workers needs to operate in functional harmony, notwithstanding the pressures and dangers of the situation and the fact that many may never have met or worked together before.

In July 2001, a CSX freight train derailed inside a privately owned and operated railroad tunnel underneath the downtown area of Baltimore, Maryland. Unable to address the situation as smoke rapidly filled the tunnel—or even to determine exactly what had happened—engineers on the train were fortunately able to make their way out.

Responding firefighting units described thick smoke coming from the tunnel's south end and, after an exploratory foray into the tunnel, intense heat; but they could not determine the extent, nature, or prognosis of the fire. As more information was assembled about the contents of the train, which included some cars transporting potentially dangerous chemicals, it quickly became apparent that a number of different agencies would have to be involved in designing and carrying out the response to the situation. These ranged from the firefighters who would fight the fire, to police officers who would control the scene, to state and local environmental officials who would assess the environmental implications and consequences of different approaches, and to local public works officials whose infrastructure (water pipes, supports for surface transportation, and so on) stood over and around the fire.

Subcase A describes the genesis of the fire, the initial response, efforts to determine the nature and extent of the emergency, and the dilemma of deciding whether to evacuate people from the areas above the tunnel. In Subcase B, the city copes with the disruption caused by the ongoing blaze, including some additional—but quite different—problems that develop from the fire situation. Subcase C describes how the responders struggle with

This is an abridged version of a case written by Esther Scott for Herman B. "Dutch" Leonard, George F. Baker Jr. Professor of Public Management, and Arnold M. Howitt, executive director of the Taubman Center for State and Local Government, for use at the John F. Kennedy School of Government, Harvard University. Funding for the case was provided by the Robert Wood Johnson Foundation. Kennedy School of Government Case Program, C16-04-1767.0, C16-04-1768.0, and C16-04-1769.0. Copyright © 2004, 2007 by the President and Fellows of Harvard College.

the complexities of their joint efforts over a number of days as the fire is contained and extinguished.

The Baltimore tunnel fire situation illustrates the challenges—but also the potential value—of having mechanisms that allow us suddenly but effectively to coordinate the work of multiple agencies. This is especially difficult when the agencies are in different authority structures, as when someone from a state environmental agency must interact with a local fire official. As you read about this situation, think about how the incident management system allowed these agencies rapidly to come together and work on the significant challenges they faced in the midst of great uncertainty about the actual conditions.

Discussion Questions

- How well do you think the city (and supporting forces from elsewhere) did in responding to the CSX tunnel fire? What strengths and weaknesses of preparedness were evident in this crisis?
- Suppose that the fire had been even more threatening. Would Baltimore have been able to handle the situation if (a) the engineers had been trapped in the tunnel? (b) a mass evacuation had been necessary? (c) a toxic plume had floated over the downtown area as a result of combustion of dangerous chemicals?
- How would you advise Mayor O'Malley about how to improve preparedness in light of the tunnel fire?

In the late afternoon of a hot day in July 2001, the Baltimore City Fire Department began receiving calls about smoke coming from a train tunnel that ran under Howard Street, a major downtown thoroughfare. This was hardly a novel event; the fire department was frequently summoned to the north end of the tunnel by people who had mistaken diesel fumes from freight trains passing through for smoke from a fire. But it quickly became clear that this was not a routine false alarm. A freight train belonging to CSX Corporation had derailed and caught fire in the tunnel. More worrisome still, there were several different hazardous chemicals on board the train. Fire officials knew that, under conditions like these, hazardous chemicals could present grave threats to the public health. Some could, for instance, explode when heated by fire, and others could release clouds of toxic vapor. What perils the particular "witches' brew" of chemicals on the derailed train might pose was uncertain, but the plumes of thick black smoke belching from either end of the tunnel and drifting over the city were not a reassuring sight.

It was with a sense of some urgency, then, that emergency responders converged on the scene soon after the first alarms sounded and city officials huddled to consider how best to support their efforts to manage a situation that had no parallels in their collective experience—a fire deep under the heart of the city that no one could see or even approach and that could potentially unleash a catastrophic chemical reaction affecting thousands of people in the area. It was, one city official reflects, "everyone's worst nightmare." The nightmare intensified a couple of hours later when a major water main situated directly over the tunnel ruptured, sending hundreds of thousands of gallons of water cascading into an intersection on Howard Street, flooding nearby buildings and threatening the structural integrity of the road. The challenges posed by this multidimensional crisis involved over a dozen city, state, and federal agencies, as well as several private companies and contractors, and severely tested their capacity to work together over a period of days, often under chaotic conditions.

Background: The Howard Street Tunnel

Completed in 1896, the Howard Street Tunnel was owned and operated by the CSX Corporation; at 1.7 miles long, it was believed to be the longest underground freight conduit on the Atlantic seaboard. At its deepest, it lay 60 feet below the street surface, at its shallowest 3 feet.[1]

The tunnel ran beneath the heart of the city's busy downtown. At its north end was the Mt. Royal Station, a stop on the state-run light rail system, as well as an art school, a concert hall, and an opera house; about 500 feet away stood Sutton Place, a high-rise apartment building that housed several hundred people. At its south end was Camden Yards, home to Oriole Park, the Baltimore Orioles's baseball stadium, and nearby was the city's Inner Harbor which, with its aquarium, restaurants, and shops, was a popular tourist destination. In between were a Holiday Inn, state office buildings, and a host of businesses small and large. There were, as well, three hospitals, a market, a museum, a convention center, a courthouse, and more, all within 1,000–2,000 feet of the tunnel.[2]

Howard Street was, moreover, an important north-south route, intersecting with many of the city's east-west roads. Interstate 395, which connected I-95 (the major north-south highway in the eastern United States) to downtown Baltimore, terminated at the south end of Howard Street, right over the tunnel; other key routes—for example, the entry to the Baltimore-Washington Parkway and the connector to Baltimore-Washington International Airport—ran nearby. Light rail trains ran directly over the Howard Street Tunnel, and the

---

[1] "Effects of Catastrophic Events on Transportation System Management and Operations: Howard Street Tunnel Fire, Baltimore City, Maryland, July 18, 2001; Findings," prepared by Science Applications International Corporation (SAIC) for the U.S. Department of Transportation, July 2002 (hereafter, SAIC report), 11–12.

[2] Ibid., 10.

subway system passed beneath it; the commuter rail system's Camden Line operated over CSX track and terminated at the Camden Yards Station.[3] (See Exhibit 4A-1.)

Passenger service through the tunnel had ended in 1961, but the passage remained a key artery in the nation's freight system, the only through-route on the northeast corridor linking North and South.[4] In 2001, after years of steadily growing freight traffic, an average of twenty-eight to thirty-two trains chugged through the tunnel each day, but except for residents and business owners in the area, who heard the trains rumbling underground, most Baltimoreans were unaware of the tunnel that ran under one of the city's main downtown streets.[5] This included the city's mayor, Martin O'Malley, who had served 8 years on the Baltimore City Council before winning the mayoral campaign in November 1999. "I didn't even know," he says, "we had a tunnel down there."[6] It was, one railroad historian told the *Baltimore Sun,* "basically an invisible line. Until smoke starts pouring out of it."[7]

The possibility that the "invisible line" could turn into an inferno had occurred to some. Back in 1985, the *Baltimore Sun* reported, an unnamed federal transportation safety official had observed that if there were an explosion in the tunnel, "fire could shoot out both ends like a bazooka."[8] But little had been done at the federal, state, or local level to prepare for such an eventuality. The city's 440-page emergency plan, drafted in 1987 in compliance with federal law, included no provisions for a hazardous chemical accident in the tunnel; nor did it, for that matter, make any reference to the existence of the tunnel.[9] As part of its ongoing training program, the fire department did run tunnel drills, but these took place in the Amtrak and subway tunnels and were meant as exercises for a passenger train accident, not one involving a freight train hauling dangerous chemicals.[10] "To be honest," one fire department spokesman later remarked, "if someone had suggested a scenario such as this, with train derailments, chemical fires and burst water mains, we would have said, no, that's too far-fetched."[11]

---

[3]Ibid, 11, 7.

[4]Ibid., 11; Alexander D. Mitchell IV, "Fire in the Hole," *Railfan & Railroad,* November 2001, 44.

[5]Mitchell, "Fire in the Hole," 44.

[6]Interview with Martin O'Malley, mayor of Baltimore, 2004. Unless noted, subsequent quotations from O'Malley are also from this interview.

[7]Scott Calvert, "'Hidden Historical Asset of Baltimore' Was Born Of Necessity," *Baltimore Sun,* July 19, 2001, 9A.

[8]Ibid.

[9]Heather Dewar, Marcia Myers, and Kimberly Wilson, "Accident Plan Leaves City Unprepared," *Baltimore Sun,* July 26, 2001, 1A.

[10]Hilary Styron, "CSX Tunnel Fire, Baltimore, MD," report for the U.S. Fire Administration (USFA), Federal Emergency Management Agency, n.d., 15.

[11]Quoted in "Inadequate Disaster Plan Left US Tunnel Ablaze for Five Days," *Construction Plus,* July 26, 2001. Available at www.nce.co.uk/news/2001/07/inadequate_disaster_plans_left_us_tunnel_ablaze_for_five_days.html.

Exhibit 4A-1   Howard Street Tunnel area

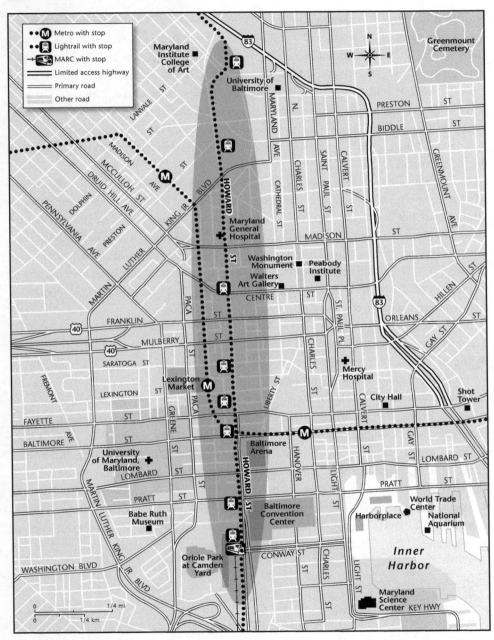

Crisis in the Tunnel

Shortly after 3:00 p.m. on Wednesday, July 18, 2001, a CSX freight train bound for Newark, New Jersey, entered the south end of the Howard Street Tunnel. It was hauling sixty cars, twenty-nine of them empty and the rest carrying a mixed cargo that included paper products, plywood, soy oil, and several tank cars of chemicals. Just a few minutes later, at about 3:07, the train with its two-man crew lurched to an unexpected and abrupt halt. The crew was unable to reach the CSX dispatcher in Jacksonville, Florida, by radio to alert him to the situation and, worried about what they assumed were choking diesel exhaust fumes, uncoupled the train's three locomotives from the freight cars and drove them out of the north end of the tunnel.

Once clear of the tunnel, at about 3:25, the crew members were able to radio the dispatcher for permission to reenter the tunnel with the locomotives as soon as the fumes cleared up.[12] But "many minutes later," in the words of one account, "they realized that the smoke was not dissipating at all. It was increasing."[13] The smoke, it now dawned on them, was the result of a fire, not diesel fumes, most likely due to a derailment; when they reviewed the waybill, or bill of lading, they realized further that there were hazardous materials in the tunnel, either already burning or in danger of igniting. They radioed the CSX dispatcher again to relay the disturbing news.

The Fire Department Responds

By the time the Baltimore City Fire Department was notified by the CSX dispatcher—at 4:15 p.m., according to fire department records[14]—it had already been receiving reports from the public about smoke coming out of a manhole at the intersection of Howard and Lombard Streets, recalls Chief Donald Heinbuch, who was at the time acting assistant chief of operations. The engine company that was dispatched to the manhole observed "a huge plume of smoke" from the south end of the tunnel, about four blocks away, and headed there, thinking, Heinbuch says, that it had a brushfire on its hands. At the same time, calls began coming in about black smoke pouring out of the tunnel's north end as well. On the face of it, these calls were not unusual. Firefighters, Heinbuch explains, were "used to responding to the north end of the tunnel specifically, because a lot of times a train will go through there, [and] will emit smoke," which was often taken by passersby as a sign of fire.

---

[12]There are several different chronologies of the events surrounding the derailment, none of which entirely agrees with the others; the times given here are a composite.

[13]Mitchell, "Fire in the Hole," 43.

[14]The timing of CSX's call was a matter of dispute. CSX asserted that it notified the fire department at 3:35 p.m., according to one account; but fire officials said that their records showed that they were not contacted by CSX until 4:15—over an hour after the derailment. The U.S. Fire Administration report indicated that CSX had called Baltimore's 911 Center to report the accident at 4:04 p.m.

"So it's like a routine call." In this case, however, the reports from the public were supplemented by an ominous communication from CSX that "they had a derailment and a hazmat [hazardous materials] situation. . . . So we were getting a lot of information very quickly at that point."[15]

The first firefighters to respond to the north end of the tunnel, where the train crew was waiting for them, were shown the waybill, which indicated that eight of the train's cars carried hazardous chemicals: two tanker cars of hydrochloric acid; two of fluorosilicic acid; and one each of tripropylene, glacial acetic acid, ethyl hexyl phthalate, and propylene glycol. Some of these were combustible; others were highly corrosive and could cause breathing problems or severe skin burns. In the first moments of the fire, no one was quite sure what these chemicals would do, either alone or in combination, or how many of the tank cars were on fire—or even where they were located in the tunnel. But, Heinbuch recalls, "I think we all knew that there was a potential for something really serious with the hazmat component."

One worrisome possibility was an explosion triggered by chemicals heated to the boiling point—known as a boiling liquid expanding vapor explosion (BLEVE, pronounced "blevvy"). Heinbuch knew that a BLEVE had the potential to cause enormous devastation. "It has wiped out small towns," he says. "A train BLEVEs—the town's gone." Fire officials were not familiar with the chemicals on the derailed CSX train and could not predict how they would react to the intense heat of the fire—later estimated to be as high as 1,500 degrees Fahrenheit—or what would happen if they did explode. Should a BLEVE occur "in a big tank in that tunnel . . . ," Heinbuch muses, "I couldn't tell what that was going to do to the tunnel."

An explosion was not the only concern, however. Chief Terry Ryer, then head of the fire department's 6th Battalion hazmat unit, which arrived at the scene on the heels of the first engine companies to respond, recalls wondering what was in the black smoke boiling out of both ends of the tunnel. His "immediate concern from a hazardous materials standpoint," he says, was "did [the fire] involve any of the acids and corrosives that could have released a vapor cloud?"[16] To complicate matters, notes Fire Department Chief William Goodwin, who at the time was the department's director of training, "what we were dealing with here was [a] type of incident that you could not see; it was a mile inside [the tunnel], under the ground"[17]; it was, as Mayor O'Malley later described it, like a fire "in a long brick oven."

---

[15]Interview with Donald Heinbuch, acting assistant chief of operations, Baltimore City Fire Department, 2004. Unless noted, subsequent quotations from Heinbuch are also from this interview.

[16]Interview with Chief Terry Ryer, head of 6th Battalion hazmat unit, Baltimore City Fire Department, 2004. Unless noted, subsequent quotations from Ryer are also from this interview.

[17]Interview with Chief William Goodwin, director of training, Baltimore City Fire Department, 2004. Unless noted, subsequent quotations from Goodwin are also from this interview.

Not being able to tell what exactly was burning or even to see what the fire looked like left officials in the dark and guessing. In the first half hour or so, Ryer remembers, there were mainly "unknowns." Firefighters could react only to the visible evidence—"the volume of the smoke, the color of the smoke, the intensity of the smoke." Those at the scene felt uneasy with the unfamiliarity of the situation and their own helplessness in it. "We usually deal with dwelling fires," one firefighter told a reporter, "and I'd much rather be doing that. With chemicals, you don't know what you're dealing with, and by the time you do, it's too late." [18]

To make matters worse, the fire could hardly have come at a more inopportune time. The downtown roads were about to be clogged with commuters heading home for the day and with baseball fans streaming toward Camden Yards to see the Baltimore Orioles play the second game of a day-night doubleheader with the Texas Rangers. As firefighters rushed to the scene, they could see plumes of black smoke ominously drifting over in the direction of Oriole Park, where an estimated 2,500–5,000 fans (along with some 2,000 employees) were milling around after the first game of the doubleheader, which was just ending.[19] No one in the city had ever witnessed anything quite like this. In his 3-plus decades with the Baltimore City Fire Department, says Carl McDonald, who was then acting department chief (he retired in February 2002), "this had the most potential to be the most devastating event" in his experience.[20]

Taking Command

At the time of the fire, according to Goodwin, the city's emergency response plan did not spell out procedures for determining who took command of an incident; however, it did stipulate that the agency having jurisdiction—usually, the first responder—would take the lead. In this case, it was the fire department. It was a responsibility that its members felt well-prepared to take on. "Our training with the incident command procedure," McDonald explains, "goes all the way down to the company level . . . so that you know what you're supposed to do to start building the incident command." A departmental manual spelled out the succession of incident commanders, starting with the senior officer of the first unit on the scene and, depending on the severity of the incident, extending all the way up to the department chief himself. In the case of the tunnel fire, the incident command quickly moved up the hierarchy to Chief Heinbuch, who took charge soon after the first units

---

[18]Quoted in Stephen Kiehl and Erika Niedowski, "Battling the Unknown Dangers," *Baltimore Sun,* July 19, 2001, 1A.

[19]John Rivera and Kimberly Wilson, "Baseball Fans and Commuters Held Hostage by Road Closings," *Baltimore Sun,* July 19, 2001, 10A.

[20]Interview with Carl McDonald, acting department chief, Baltimore City Fire Department, 2004. Unless noted, subsequent quotations from McDonald are also from this interview.

responded. Heinbuch set up a command post near the north end of the tunnel; later that evening, he moved it to the south end. When McDonald arrived at the scene at around 5:00 p.m.—roughly 45 minutes after the initial alarm had sounded—he decided to leave the tactical command in Heinbuch's hands and to assume the role of "overall commander," whose job, he explains, "was to direct and coordinate all the responding agencies that were coming to assist us."

Firefighters who had been trained to handle hazardous materials accidents also felt well-prepared, even though they had not been drilled specifically for a fire involving chemicals in a train tunnel. "We had a fire and a chemical leak in a confined space," says Chief Ronald Addison, who was then the fire department's hazmat coordinator. "We trained to do all three of those things."[21] They had, moreover, worked extensively with members of the Maryland Department of the Environment (MDE), the state agency responsible for managing environmental emergencies, such as chemical "releases." "We work with . . . the Baltimore City Fire Department quite a bit in developing response plans," says Alan Williams, program manager for MDE's emergency response program. "We exercise together; we train together. . . . When the city hazmat team . . . runs into an environmental problem, they invariably call us and ask us to run with them."[22] The years of joint training and incident response had built a strong mutual trust between the two departments. "I consider the Maryland Department of the Environment just like another fire company," Heinbuch observes, "because I can rely on them. They always come [through]." McDonald agrees: "I had a good working relationship with [MDE] from when I was the hazmat commander. They basically knew what I needed before I had to tell them."

Even before the fire department notified MDE, officials from the state environmental agency were already on their way to the fire scene. They routinely monitored fire department scanners, Williams explains, "and heard the [first] units being dispatched. . . . Based on that information [about a possible hazmat situation], we started responding." Similarly, the fire department's own hazmat team responded preemptively to the developing crisis in the Howard Street Tunnel. Terry Ryer, of the 6th Battalion's hazmat unit, was on his way to a meeting downtown when he heard reports of a possible hazmat incident; he immediately radioed to ask the fire official who was summoning other units to the scene to "put me on the box" (that is, include the hazmat unit on the alarm). As a result, MDE and fire department hazmat personnel were on the scene within minutes of the first alarms. "Everybody jumped on this call," Heinbuch says. "Some people jumped on it ahead of their notification; so in terms of response time, it was almost negative."

---

[21]Interview with Ronald Addison, chief and hazmat coordinator, Baltimore City Fire Department, 2004. Unless noted, subsequent quotations from Addison are also from this interview.

[22]Interview with Alan Williams, program manager, Emergency Response Program, Maryland Department of the Environment, 2004. Unless noted, subsequent quotations from Williams are also from this interview.

First Steps

In some respects, Heinbuch reflects, the initial response to the tunnel fire rolled out as smoothly as a training exercise, "because everything we were supposed to know about dealing with a situation was being carried out, just like a normal fire. Our engine companies were dropping hose. Our people were geared up. They had their masks on; they were ready to go. The hazmat component was added in there." But this was no ordinary fire—the tunnel blaze proved to be a formidable adversary, stymieing efforts to control it or even reach it. Roughly 150 firefighters—including some from Baltimore County—assembled at the north end of the tunnel along with about forty pieces of equipment, but in the first hours of the fire, there was little they could do. Early attempts to enter the tunnel proved fruitless as firefighters, wearing standard turnout gear, were beaten back by the intense heat and what some worried might be skin burns from the chemicals on the train. Those who advanced a small way into the tunnel reported seeing tanker cars glowing from the heat of the fire but little else. "It's just like walking into an oven," one firefighter told reporters. "The smoke is so thick you can't even see your hand in front of your face." [23]

The firefighters' inability to approach the fire was a serious handicap as officials tried to evaluate the situation and formulate a plan of attack. "The only way to really build a confident decision-making process," says William Goodwin, who succeeded McDonald as fire department chief in 2002, "was to actually have somebody go in there and physically get close to the actual incident and assess it, relay the information, continue to build the decision-making model." In the absence of firsthand observation, officials fell back on the data available to them from other sources. They had the waybill, which told them the contents of each car as well as its location on the train, although, according to Goodwin, the sequence of cars as recorded in the waybill "turned out to be . . . not necessarily accurate." [24] It would be hours before officials determined exactly which cars were burning and which were in close proximity to burning cars—and therefore in danger of igniting.

But other important information could be quickly gleaned from the data, with the help of expert opinion provided by two chemists summoned to the scene by MDE officials. The chemists worked for firms that were members of the South Baltimore Industrial Mutual Aid Plan (SBIMAP), a consortium of private companies that manufactured, transported, or stored chemicals and public environmental and emergency agencies, which was established in 1982 to deal with just the sort of chemical emergency now facing the city of Baltimore. Soon after their arrival—at 4:35 p.m., according to one report—they were able to offer some reassurance on one point; a catastrophic explosion, they told Heinbuch, was unlikely. "We

---

[23] Quoted in David Michael Ettlin, "Burning Cars in Rail Tunnel Resist Control," *Baltimore Sun*, July 20, 2001, 1A.

[24] According to Mayor O'Malley's office, two of the rail cars—one containing tripropylene and one containing paper—were not in the order indicated on the waybill.

weren't looking at propane; we weren't looking at butane," Heinbuch recalls being told. "We weren't looking at materials that, had they been involved, would have BLEVEd, would have [led to] a catastrophic situation. I think I went back two or three times and asked about that BLEVE, because I was so gun-shy." The waybill indicated the presence of only one highly flammable chemical—tripropylene—that officials suspected had caught fire during the derailment. But other dangers still lurked. Some of the chemicals on the train—particularly the fluorosilicic acid—could release vapors from the heat that could be toxic for firefighters and emergency workers at the scene and possibly for the surrounding population. "Acids are very soluble in water," a pulmonary expert told the *Baltimore Sun*, "so when you breathe them in, it's as if you're pouring the acid right into your body." [25]

Shortly before 5:00 p.m., MDE and fire department hazmat officials began testing the air near the tunnel and in nearby Camden Yards for the presence of toxic substances. Data from the air monitoring was not long in coming, but a number of crucial decisions had to be made before the definitive results were in: what to do about the people living, working, or visiting in the immediate vicinity of the fire; and what to do about the roads and transit systems that criss-crossed the smoldering tunnel. These decisions were the responsibility of the incident commander, Chief Heinbuch, but he needed the cooperation and support of numerous city agencies and officials, who were themselves scrambling to organize in response to the crisis.

The City Responds

The tunnel fire occurred about a year and a half into the first term of Martin O'Malley, one of the youngest big-city mayors in the United States at the time he took office in December 1999, and presented him with the first major emergency of his administration. O'Malley had been attending a political event on Maryland's Eastern Shore, on July 18; in the car on the way back to Baltimore, a drive of more than 2 hours, he got a call from Michael Enright, his first deputy mayor. "[Enright] said," O'Malley recalls, "'We've had a bit of a train wreck here in the city.'" The mayor took this to be a metaphorical reference to other headaches facing his administration, "but Enright said, 'No, I'm serious—a real train wreck, . . . and there's smoke and it's coming out of Camden Yards, and there's a doubleheader and a bunch of people there. You might want to turn on WBAL [the local news radio station] and listen.'" For most of the long trip back, O'Malley had to content himself with WBAL broadcasts and fitful contact by phone while agency officials in Baltimore gathered to advise and assist Chief Heinbuch at the fire scene.

---

[25] Quoted in David Michael Ettlin and Del Quentin Wilber, "Train Fire, Toxic Cargo Shut City," *Baltimore Sun,* July 19, 2001, 1A.

At the time of the tunnel fire, Baltimore did not have an established crisis management team of agency heads and other officials that would be expected to convene when a major crisis occurred. "Relevant department heads," according to O'Malley, essentially knew to assemble, even in the absence of the city's political leader. "There are a lot of things that happen in this organism, this body called city government . . . ," he observes, "that happen regardless of whether or not the temporary generalist employed at the top is aware that they're happening."

The city did have an Office of Emergency Management, which was then lodged in the Department of Public Works (DPW), but it was not a major force in the city. A relic of the civil defense era, the office had shrunk from a staff of twenty in its heyday in the 1950s to only three by 2001, including its director, Richard McKoy. The emergency management unit was responsible, McKoy explains, for "the coordination of resources and/or agency responses to emergencies," for creating the city's emergency plans, and for the "activation of the emergency operations center" (EOC) in the event of a crisis. Although the city did have an EOC, according to McKoy, it was "sparingly used," more for "simulations" than for "real-life emergencies."[26] Its existence, moreover, did not appear to be common knowledge. "Nobody knew where the emergency operations center was," says the fire department's Ronald Addison.[27]

In theory, McKoy explains, the EOC would have liaisons from each of the city's agencies on hand during an emergency, who would be "receiving feedback from the incident commander" about what assistance and support were needed in the field. But lacking the resources to staff such a "secure facility," McKoy became, in essence, a mobile EOC, traveling to the site of emergencies when they arose and carrying out his coordinating duties from there. "So the things that would occur in an emergency operations center," he says, "I primarily carried with me in my vehicle. . . ." Accordingly, when McKoy learned of the fire under Howard Street, he headed directly for the incident command post at the north end of the tunnel.

In the Comstat Room

Meanwhile, it was not clear where the rest of the city's leadership should assemble. In terms of "where the city comes together to do emergency management or make decisions," Heinbuch observes, "they didn't know where to go." Heinbuch himself had assumed that "everyone [w]ould have gone to the snow room [a facility equipped with cameras and monitors that was used to manage snow-removal operations] because that's what we had been doing

---

[26]Interview with Richard McKoy, director, Office of Emergency Management, Department of Public Works, City of Baltimore, 2004. Unless noted, subsequent quotations from McKoy are also from this interview.

[27]The fire department's command structure, McDonald maintains, did in fact know where the EOC was, but in any event, "it wasn't functional."

[in the past]." Instead, administration officials gathered at the Comstat room in police head-quarters, which was outfitted with phones, videocameras and monitors, and computer hook-ups. The Comstat room, which police used to analyze crime data and manage weekly redeployments, was, says Goodwin, "probably one of the most sophisticated telecommunications rooms in the city at the time"; and was in addition, McKoy notes, convenient to city hall. Among those in attendance on the afternoon of July 18 were George Winfield, director of the DPW; Michael Rice, head of the city's transportation bureau, which was at that time part of DPW;[28] then Police Commissioner Edward Norris and several aides; Peter Beilenson, commissioner of public health; and William Goodwin, the fire department's director of training.

The assembled city officials viewed their role as one of support for the incident command. Whatever decisions were made, says J. Charles Gutberlet, who was then a police district commander, was "their call. We, as a police department, [were] supportive to them."[29] Members of DPW took a similar stance. "One of the things we in public works and transportation pride ourselves on," Jerry Young, chief of training and safety in the DPW, notes, "is that we are resources for the first responders. We don't take the lead; we go to the incident commander and say, 'What do you need from us?'"[30]

Perhaps the most pressing question facing Heinbuch at the fire site and city officials in the Comstat room was whether it was advisable to evacuate residents and visitors from the area around the tunnel. This would be a "very hard decision," says Young, "because there was a high-rise [apartment building] right there at Howard Street, that was in the plume area," as well as the Holiday Inn situated only about 30 feet from the tunnel and the baseball park adjacent to its southern end. There were also the question of how to inform the public of what precautions or actions—if any—should be taken in regard to the fire and the issue of what to do about managing the heavy flow of traffic into and out of the Howard Street area. For all these decisions, there was little time to weigh the options carefully. "The smoke was billowing," McKoy recalls. "It was not a slow-moving situation."

---

[28]The transportation bureau, which was responsible for traffic management and enforcement of parking regulations, was made an autonomous organization—the Office of Transportation—in October 2002.

[29]Interview with J. Charles Gutberlet, central district commander, Police Department, City of Baltimore, 2004. Unless noted, subsequent quotations from Gutberlet are also from this interview.

[30]Interview with Jerry Young, chief of training and safety, Department of Public Works, City of Baltimore, 2004. Unless noted, subsequent quotations from Young are also from this interview.

The Baltimore Tunnel Fire of 2001 (B):
Responding to the Fire, Bracing for a Flood

After conferring with emergency personnel on the scene, Chief Donald Heinbuch, the incident commander for the Howard Street Tunnel fire, decided against ordering a wholesale evacuation of the area around the blaze. He and other fire officials viewed evacuation as a last resort, fearing that a mass exodus could lead to panic and clogged streets at a time when it was important to keep the roads clear for emergency vehicles; it could also, notes then Fire Department Chief Carl McDonald, potentially do more harm than good by exposing people to toxic vapors as they left their shelter to flee the fire. "Evacuation," says Alan Williams, Maryland Department of the Environment (MDE), "is not a benign alternative."[1]

Making the Call

Accordingly, it was decided that residents and others in the area would be advised to "shelter in place," that is, to remain indoors with windows closed and air conditioners and window fans turned off. The only exception was the ballpark at Camden Yards, where several thousand fans—with many more expected—were out in the open, vulnerable to the black smoke that was wafting their way. At about 5:00 p.m., Heinbuch gave the order to evacuate all fans, ballplayers, and staff from the stadium; later, the ballgame scheduled for that evening was cancelled. "No one disputed it," says Terry Ryer of the Baltimore City Fire Department, "because of the volume of the smoke."[2]

Still, despite the decision to shelter in place, the police, who would be responsible for directing an evacuation, were taking no chances. They arranged with the state Mass Transit Administration (MTA) to have buses on standby in the event an evacuation ultimately proved necessary. According to J. Charles Gutberlet, who was then commander of the central district (which included the tunnel area), city police summoned a representative of the MTA's police department to the meeting in the Comstat room to discuss the situation. "He made the call to his counterparts with mass transit," Gutberlet recalls, "and said, 'Look, they've got a situation downtown. The worst-case scenario is there could be mass evacuations. They're going to need our coaches to evacuate. Don't let anybody go home. Keep the buses running; keep them fueled up.'"

---

[1]Interview with Alan Williams, program manager, Emergency Response Program, Maryland Department of the Environment, 2004. Unless noted, subsequent quotations from Williams are also from this interview.

[2]Interview with Terry Ryer, head of 6th Battalion hazmat unit, Baltimore City Fire Department, 2004. Unless noted, subsequent quotations from Ryer are also from this interview.

Sounding the Sirens

Once the decision about evacuation was resolved, there remained the question of how to inform people in the area of what they should do. At Heinbuch's request, the police department dispatched officers to the high-rise apartment building, where he had spotted residents out on their balconies watching the dramatic developments at the tunnel below and, in the process, explains Heinbuch, "subjecting themselves to the smoke." The officers, supplemented by some firefighting units, were asked to "go into the building and walk the hallways, and tell people to go back to [their] apartments, stay off the balconies, shelter in place." [3] Soon after, Heinbuch recalls, he was approached by Richard McKoy, director of the city's Office of Emergency Management, and Hector Torres, a fire department public information officer, "who wanted to go with the sirens and a public information announcement." McKoy and Torres were recommending that the fire department activate the city's air raid sirens to alert the public to the need to shelter in place. "The whole idea of an alerting siren," McKoy explains, "is to get the attention of the public . . . to tell them what we wanted them to do as a result of the smoke." This would be something of a novel approach—the sirens had not been sounded citywide, other than in weekly tests on Mondays at 1:00 p.m., since they were first installed in 1952. Ideally, this was a decision that would be made "in conjunction with the mayor's office," says McKoy. But "the mayor wasn't at the scene, and you had to make a determination at the scene. The smoke was not waiting for anybody." [4]

Heinbuch gave McKoy and Torres the green light to sound the sirens and prepare a public announcement that would run on local TV and radio stations advising the public on what actions to take. But when the sirens began to wail at 5:45 p.m., citizens seemed largely perplexed about what they were supposed to do in response. "People have forgotten . . . ," McKoy later told the *Baltimore Sun*, "what the siren's purpose was." Many called City Hall to find out what was going on. "So our City Hall telephone lines were inundated for a while there," McKoy acknowledged. "So that created somewhat of a problem for us." [5] Those who did turn on their TVs and radios were not immediately enlightened because it took awhile for Hector Torres to telephone local stations with the details of the shelter advisory. Mayor Martin O'Malley, still in his car, was listening to WBAL when he heard "the air raid siren in the backgound" but no explanation of the cause or instructions on what to do. "WBAL was in the dark for about 15–20 minutes as to why the sirens were going off," he recalls, "which was pretty disconcerting." [6]

---

[3]Interview with Donald Heinbuch, acting assistant chief of operations, Baltimore City Fire Department, 2004. Unless noted, subsequent quotations from Heinbuch are also from this interview.

[4]Interview with Richard McKoy, director, Office of Emergency Management, Department of Public Works, City of Baltimore, 2004. Unless noted, subsequent quotations from McKoy are also from this interview.

[5]Quoted in Carl Schoettler, "Duck and Cover? No, Find the Remote," *Baltimore Sun*, July 20, 2001, 1E.

[6]Interview with Martin O'Malley, mayor of Baltimore, 2004. Unless noted, subsequent quotations from O'Malley are also from this interview.

Traffic Control

The general public was confused by the city's purpose in sounding its air raid sirens, but the commuting public was sorely tried by the city's traffic control efforts in support of Heinbuch and his crew—specifically, keeping traffic away from the "hot zone" near the tunnel and clearing key roads to allow emergency vehicles access to the fire site. Heinbuch had left the particulars of traffic flow for others to work out. While he and his team of firefighters battled the tunnel blaze, police and DPW officials in the Comstat room grappled with the best way to meet the fire department's needs.

There was some difference of opinion, Chief Gutberlet recalls, about which approach to take. "There was a discussion as to what area we wanted to keep people out of," he says. "The non-police personnel [from the Department of Public Works (DPW), health, and fire] wanted a very small area. . . . Their main concern was the area that was impacted [by the fire]." The police, on the other hand, argued for a more expansive shut-down. "We knew from a tactical standpoint that you have to take a large area . . . ," Gutberlet explains. "If you don't need it, you can always get smaller. But if you start off too small and your inner perimeter is too small, it's tough to take it back." The police prevailed. "We asked the fire department," Gutberlet continues, "worst-case scenario, what do you need? And they told us, Howard Street, two blocks in each direction. So we took down five blocks, right up the middle of the city and shut it down." [7] (See Exhibit 4B-1.) This "effectively erected a 'Berlin Wall' style barrier," in the words of one account, "through the heart of the city just as the rush hour began." [8] Equally strong measures were taken to prevent more traffic from entering the city. "There was a quick decision made as to what key points did we want to shut traffic off," Gutberlet remembers. Within 5 minutes, he says, with the aid of state police and Baltimore County officials, entrances to the city from Interstates 83 and 395, as well as Route 40, were closed down.

The road closings, particularly around Howard Street, led to gridlock, as rush hour drivers trapped in the downtown area sought alternative ways out of the city. "Block after block of frustrated commuters sat and fumed in bumper to bumper traffic," reported the *Baltimore Sun*, while others waited, sometimes for hours, for buses that had been diverted from their regular routes. [9] By 8:00 p.m., however, according to one report, the city had been cleared of the worst of its traffic jams. [10] Looking back, Chief McDonald had no quarrel with

---

[7]Interview with J. Charles Gutberlet, central district commander, Police Department, City of Baltimore, 2004. Unless noted, subsequent quotations from Gutberlet are also from this interview.

[8]Alexander D. Mitchell IV, "Fire in the Hole," *Railfan & Railroad*, November 2001, 45.

[9]John Rivera and Kimberly Wilson, "Baseball Fans and Commuters Held Hostage by Road Closings," *Baltimore Sun*, July 19, 2001, 10A.

[10]"Effects of Catastrophic Events on Transportation System Management and Operations: Howard Street Tunnel Fire, Baltimore City, Maryland, July 18, 2001; Findings," prepared by Science Applications International Corporation (SAIC) for the US Department of Transportation, July 2002, p. 19. According to SAIC, the interstates were ordered closed at 4:30 p.m. Other reports put the time later.

Exhibit 4B-1   Train derailment traffic advisory—road closures

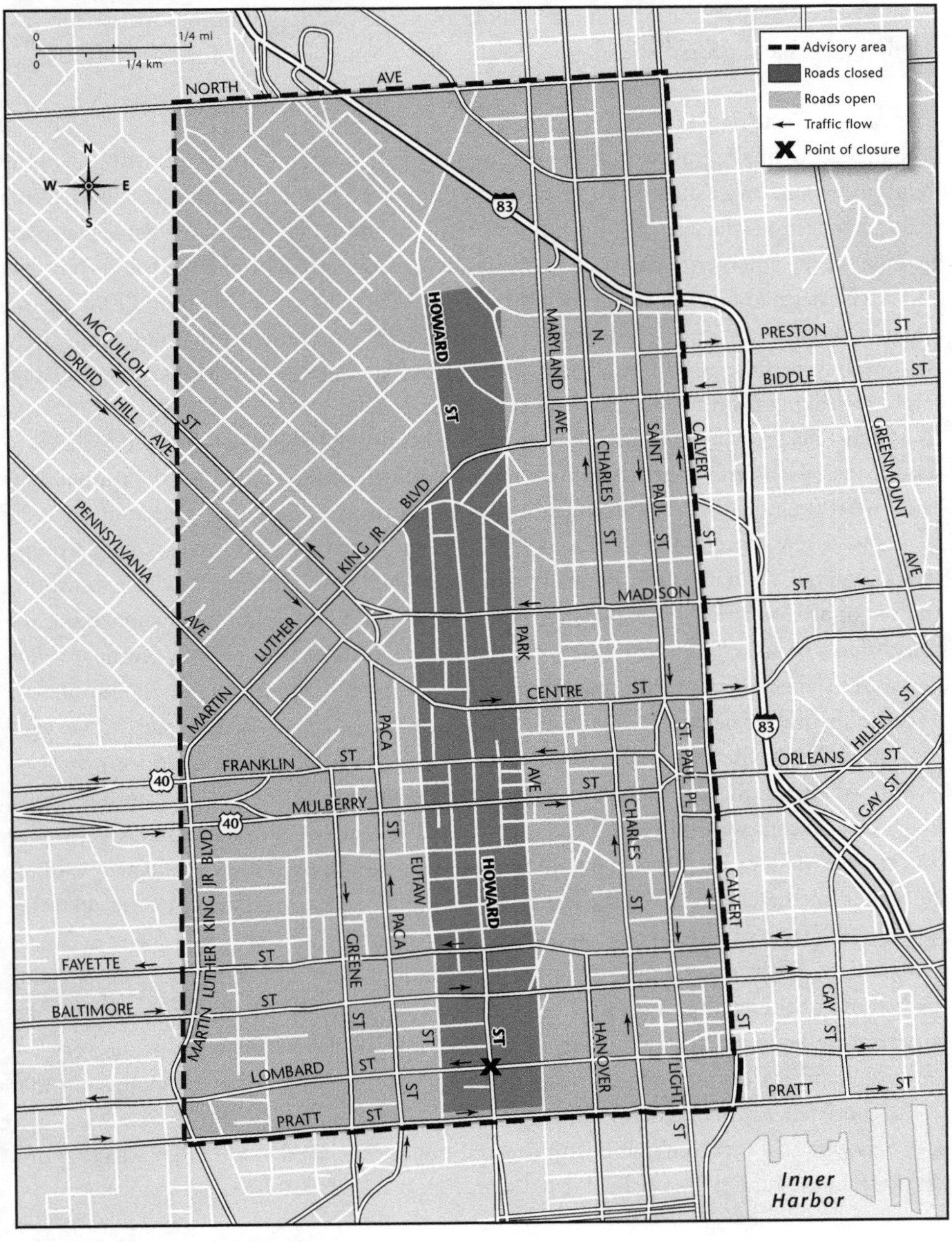

Source: Baltimore City Police Department

the police department's decisions on road closings. "I thought that what we shut down was necessary for safety operations," he says, "both from the standpoint of the citizens and [of] the firefighters and people working on that incident."[11]

The Mayor Returns

O'Malley's car finally pulled into the city around 6:00 p.m., only after resorting to "blue lights and siren," as he puts it, "to get through gridlocked traffic from the closing of all the major arteries into the city." By this time, many of the immediate decisions related to management of the emergency had been made: roads and streets had been closed, and warnings and advisories had been issued. Officials from the MDE had alerted the U.S. Coast Guard, which had closed the Inner Harbor to boat traffic at 5:00 and sent its Atlantic strike team to Baltimore to test the runoff into the harbor for the presence of hazardous chemicals that might be leaking from the derailed tanker cars.

Meanwhile, the MDE had also asked the U.S. Environmental Protection Agency (EPA) to send some of its staff to the site to help monitor the air in the vicinity of the tunnel. Precisely what time the first data from the air tests became available is not clear, but the early results were reassuring—the smoke from the fire indicated the presence of only carbonaceous material. "What you've basically got," Alan Williams explains, "is a big campfire. You've got plywood, you've got paper, and it's smoky and it smells, but we are not seeing any constituents of any chemicals in the smoke." Although this did not entirely eliminate worries about the chemicals in the still-unchecked blaze, it did appear to ease the immediate threat to the public health. "Within an hour [of the first alarms]," McKoy recalls, "we were comfortable that what was in the smoke was not going to be of any major concern."

Still, when the mayor arrived in Baltimore and headed to the police Comstat room, where city officials were still gathered, he took up the question of evacuation. "My primary concern," O'Malley says, "was, in the interest of safety, do we need to evacuate people off of the area immediately on top of the length of the tunnel." His own inclination, he acknowledges, was "that it's better to overreact than under-react if you don't know." The police, as O'Malley recalls the discussion, also favored evacuation: "they just wanted to get everybody the hell out of there," but in the end he let himself be guided by the fire chief. The fire department, he explains, "was telling me, we're doing [air] readings constantly—like every five minutes—and it's not at a toxic level. They were telling me that there was nothing that would cause [them] to evacuate people."

It was while he was conferring with fire and police officials that O'Malley was told of a new kink in the tunnel fire crisis. "We got word," he recalls, "that the rapids had started."

---

[11]Interview with Carl McDonald, acting department chief, Baltimore City Fire Department, 2004. Unless noted, subsequent quotations from McDonald are also from this interview.

A Break in the Main

The "rapids" that O'Malley was referring to were the hundreds of gallons of water that began gushing into the intersection of Howard and Lombard Streets at about 6:15 p.m. on July 18, roughly 2 hours after the first fire alarms had sounded. The water came from a ruptured 40-inch main that lay directly over the tunnel; by the time DPW Director George Winfield arrived at the scene, parts of the intersection lay under 2 feet of water, with much more in some spots. To add to the beleaguered downtown's woes, the break flooded nearby buildings and knocked out electricity to almost 1,200 residences and businesses. As he catalogued the by now considerable challenges facing the city, fire department spokesman Hector Torres told a CNN reporter, with some understatement, "There's just a multitude of sins here."[12]

But the water main rupture turned out to have a silver lining. Almost as soon as the water began pouring out of the broken pipe, the smoke from the tunnel fire changed dramatically, from black to white. Fire officials at the tunnel's end, still unaware of the break, noted the change but were initially unsure how to interpret it. Normally, says Chief Ronald Addison of the city fire department, they would assume that "we've got water" on the blaze;[13] but because firefighters had not yet been able to get close enough to the blaze to train their hoses on it, they worried that, instead, it meant, as Terry Ryer puts it, "we had a chemical reaction due to a vapor release." Shortly thereafter, however, Heinbuch was told that water—from the ruptured pipe, not firefighters' hoses—was in fact the cause of the change in color and, even better news, that the most recent air tests indicated that the contents of the smoke were 95 percent steam and the rest "ordinary products of combustion."[14] So, Heinbuch says, after the water main break, "the way I characterized [the tunnel blaze] was a big dumpster fire."

The salutary effect of the water main break prompted fire officials to make an unusual request of DPW officials—that they not try to stanch the flow of water from the ruptured pipe. "They wanted us not to turn the water off," Winfield remembers, "because they thought it would help douse the fire."[15] This required the DPW to go against the grain of long-established practice. "Used to simply shutting things off as soon as possible," as the *Baltimore Sun* put it,[16] the department was being asked, in essence, to stand by and do

---

[12]Interview by Daryn Kagan, "Baltimore Tunnel Fire: Baltimore Fire Chief Discusses Situation," *CNN Live This Morning*, with Hector Torres, July 19, 2001.

[13]Interview with Ronald Addison, chief and hazmat coordinator, Baltimore City Fire Department, 2004. Unless noted, subsequent quotations from Addison are also from this interview.

[14]Hilary Styron, "CSX Tunnel Fire, Baltimore, MD," report for the U.S. Fire Administration (USFA), Federal Emergency Management Agency, n.d., 12.

[15]Interview with Director George Winfield, Department of Public Works, City of Baltimore, 2004. Unless noted, subsequent quotations from Winfield are also from this interview.

[16]Dan Fesperman, "With a Rumble, Chaos," *Baltimore Sun*, July 21, 2001, 1A.

nothing—a tough assignment for an agency that was, as Winfield points out, "responsible for the water system for the metropolitan area," and therefore "always concerned about being able to address whatever the issue is as rapidly as possible." At issue in this case was a massive leak that, on the one hand, could threaten "the entire [water delivery] system [serving] 1.8 million people," Winfield notes, by cutting water pressure to worrisomely low levels but, on the other, might help tame a dangerous blaze that had so far foiled the fire department's efforts to attack it.

The Baltimore Tunnel Fire of 2001 (C):
Struggling to Bring the Crisis to an End

Department of Public Works (DPW) Director George Winfield acceded to the Baltimore City Fire Department's request and allowed water from a broken main to continue gushing out unabated. For at least 2 hours—up to 4 hours, according to some accounts—water poured into the intersection of Howard and Lombard and southward down Howard Street, where some of it flowed into the tunnel. But this was a costly action for the DPW; some 60 million gallons of water were lost over this period, and the Druid Hill Reservoir, as the *Baltimore Sun* reported, dropped 3 feet in the space of about 4 hours. After a time, the torrent of water began taking its toll on the street itself, carving "earthquake-like fissures into the pavement," in the words of one account.[1] Concerned that "we were losing the entire [water delivery] system," Winfield says, and mindful of "feedback from property owners and from the field people that we were losing the street," the DPW "passed that information on to the fire department that we had to shut the water off."[2]

Meanwhile, firefighters made some progress in their arduous efforts to inch their way into the tunnel and get closer to the fire. After two failed attempts, a new team, led by William Goodwin, the fire department's director of training, and equipped with supplemental oxygen supplies, made a third try at penetrating the smoke-filled tunnel. They drove into the tunnel in reverse—so they would be pointed the right way out in case they needed to make an "expedient escape," as Goodwin puts it—in a CSX truck equipped with railway wheels. It was a slow and perilous trip, but the crew, says Goodwin, "did make physical contact with the train,"[3] providing the first hard data on its location in the tunnel.

Even with immediate concerns for public safety somewhat alleviated and some headway made in approaching the blaze, it was becoming increasingly clear that the city was in for a long haul—that it would be days, not hours, before the dozens of freight cars could be pulled out of the tunnel and the fire suppressed, and days, too, before the 6-by 8-foot break in the water main, which inconveniently rested just 9 inches atop the tunnel, could be repaired.

---

[1]Scott Calvert and Michael Scarcella, "Rail Accident Linked to Water Main Break," *Baltimore Sun*, July 20, 2001, 11A.

[2]Interview with George Winfield, director, Department of Public Works, City of Baltimore, 2004. Unless noted, subsequent quotations from Winfield are also from this interview. Even after the DPW turned off the water supply leading to the ruptured main, however, some water continued to flow into the intersection due to a broken valve.

[3]Interview with Chief William Goodwin, director of training, Baltimore City Fire Department, 2004. Unless noted, subsequent quotations from Goodwin are also from this interview.

The repercussions of a protracted incident would be felt near and far. As a result of the ongoing fire and then the flooding, traffic, including light rail service, continued to be barred from Howard Street and environs, which created hardships for local businesses, not to mention the Baltimore Orioles, who were in the midst of a home stand.[4] The same was true for CSX. The Howard Street Tunnel was a "chokepoint," as one CBS correspondent put it[5]—the railroad line's only throughway linking the South to the Northeast. Until the fire could be doused and the tunnel reopened, CSX had to reroute rail traffic over lines as far away as Pittsburgh and Cleveland to keep its freight moving. What's more, the tunnel was not just a conduit for rail freight—fiber-optic cable for voice and data ran through it, and when it was damaged by the fire, Internet service was slowed in places as far away as Seattle, Los Angeles, and even Africa.

Meanwhile, "the domino effect of events," in the words of one account, "combined with the sheer spectacle of a fire under the downtown of a major city, created a media frenzy garnering national and international exposure."[6] With TV cameras trained on them and reporters pressing for information on their progress, city officials, joined by representatives of a number of state and federal agencies, struggled to coordinate and control the many activities taking place at the increasingly crowded fire site. Most of those present had never experienced a crisis of this complexity and duration. "With usual incidents," Goodwin observes, "things begin to go in the decision model, or at least in the right direction, within a relatively short period of time. This was not the case with this situation, as we found out."

The Long Haul

The first signs that things were not quickly moving in the right direction, in Goodwin's view, were evident in the efforts of the group assembled in the Comstat room, where he had been directed to go by Chief Heinbuch. "They were making an attempt at a unified command," he says, but what he found instead was, he judged, "a real inefficient operation." Despite its advanced telecommunications equipment, the room was not, he concluded, well suited for emergency management. "It was not really set up to go external," he explains, "to provide in and out feeds to the rest of the city. . . . The police building, being a secure location, [had] no access to the news media. . . ." The fire department's radios, moreover, "did not always work" in the Comstat room, Heinbuch notes,[7] so fire officials in the room had to communicate with

---

[4]The major roads and highways into the city were, however, reopened the following morning, July 19; the Inner Harbor also reopened early that morning.

[5]Eric Engberg, "Nation's Rail Lines in Need of Solutions to Overuse," *CBS Evening News,* July 21, 2001.

[6]Alexander D. Mitchell IV, "Fire in the Hole," *Railfan & Railroad,* November 2001, 45.

[7]Interview with Donald Heinbuch, acting assistant chief of operations, Baltimore City Fire Department, 2004. Unless noted, subsequent quotations from Heinbuch are also from this interview.

the field by phone. "The fire department [was] the lead command organization," Goodwin observes tartly, "[but] we were in the police building, and I didn't even have a seat at the table or a telephone. I was operating off my portable radio in the hall." Frustrated that the Comstat gathering "was not satisfying the unified command that was necessary," he continues, "I recommended abandoning the position, and was finally given the authority to do so."

Goodwin defined unified command as "the assembling of everybody that happens to be stakeholders in the operation, so that they're all in one location should a need arise to make a decision—not the incident command decision, not the tactical decision, [but] the overall decision and how it would affect all the individuals involved." There was widespread agreement that, in this pre–September 11 era, the city was ill-equipped to run a unified command. For one thing, Goodwin points out, it did not have a functioning emergency operations center, "so Comstat was sort of quasi-the-next-best-thing, but did not really have the mechanics" to facilitate the decisions of the command. For another, city officials had little practice in operating a unified command. "We had some rudimentary training," says former Fire Department Chief Carl McDonald, "but not the in-depth training that should have gone on, so that everybody knows this is a fire emergency situation, that the fire department is in command and everybody else is support." There had been "some tabletop exercises," he continues, but "no formalized training between the different agencies. Everybody had the idea of what was supposed to go on, but it had never actually been walked through."[8]

Moreover, Goodwin notes, city officials were "not really used to [managing] a protracted incident over many days. A few hours—that we're used to, but a thing that shuts down a good portion of your city for days is something that, luckily, most urban areas deal with in the theoretical aspect, but don't really deal with maybe during somebody's whole career." McDonald agrees: "In my 37 years [with the fire department], we never had an incident of that magnitude that required that much coordination between other agencies."

Going to the Site
When Mayor Martin O'Malley arrived at the Comstat room, he soon reached essentially the same conclusion that Goodwin had—that it was not the ideal place for managing the crisis.[9] "Communication was strained," he recalls, and he decided it would be "a hell of a lot easier to stay on top of what was going on" if he were closer to the action. "I think it probably violates textbook," he acknowledges, "[but] we quickly moved our command center to the actual fire grounds."[10]

---

[8]Interview with Carl McDonald, acting department chief, Baltimore City Fire Department, 2004. Unless noted, subsequent quotations from McDonald are also from this interview.

[9]Goodwin had left the Comstat room before Mayor O'Malley arrived.

[10]Interview with Martin O'Malley, mayor of Baltimore, 2004. Unless noted, subsequent quotations from O'Malley are also from this interview.

By nightfall of July 18, the fire site was filling up with agency officials and workers who had gathered to help with different facets of the crisis. These included members of the city's fire, police, public health, and public works departments; the state's departments of transportation, the environment, and emergency management; the U.S. Coast Guard; the U.S. Environmental Protection Agency (EPA); the National Transportation Safety Board, which came to investigate the derailment the following day; and several different private contractors hired by CSX who specialized in chemical accidents and derailments. At first, recalls Deputy Mayor Michael Enright, the scene was "confusing," as he tried to "figure out where the mayor is supposed to go."[11] The fire department, having initially set up a command post at the north end of the tunnel, moved it to the south end, in the parking lot at Camden Yards, later that night, but it also maintained secondary posts at the north end and at the manhole at Howard and Lombard Streets. DPW officials set up their own command trailer at the intersection of Howard and Lombard, where the water main break had occurred. Other agencies established posts at Camden Yards as well. The police, for example, brought their own van (a Winnebago) to the site, and state transportation officials installed a bus, which the Maryland Department of the Environment (MDE) used as its post as well. "We had the police here and we had the fire department here and we had us here," the MDE's Alan Williams recalls. "Everybody was setting up their little kingdom in different places."[12] It was, as Goodwin puts it, "a campground of individuals." Eventually, the mayor settled into the police Winnebago—"where I hung out," he says, "and where my people and press people hung out"—thereby not crowding the fire department's command post, but remaining "always within earshot."

Although moving to the fire scene essentially brought the city together on one site, it did not immediately lead to an improvement in communications or decision making among those working to solve the many challenges posed by the fire and the water main break. On the contrary, says Goodwin, the situation got "more and more convoluted as additional agencies became involved." The participation of so many different organizations meant transitioning from an incident command, with which, as Terry Ryer observes, the fire department was "historically and traditionally" familiar,[13] to the much less familiar operation of a unified command. "For instance," Heinbuch explains, "early on, CSX Railroad were just players, . . . but as things went on, they became decision makers, too, as did public works. So when we were going to do something, everybody had to have a buy-in." The problem,

---

[11]Interview with Michael Enright, first deputy mayor of Baltimore, 2004. Unless noted, subsequent quotations from Enright are also from this interview.

[12]Interview with Alan Williams, program manager, Emergency Response Program, Maryland Department of the Environment, 2004. Unless noted, subsequent quotations from Williams are also from this interview.

[13]Interview with Terry Ryer, head of 6th Battalion hazmat unit, Baltimore City Fire Department, 2004. Unless noted, subsequent quotations from Ryer are also from this interview.

however, was that the people who could provide the buy-in were, in the first hours of the fire, often not on hand when needed. Heinbuch faulted himself in part for this. "As incident commander," he acknowledges, "I should have made that liaison [with other agencies] more solid, but I [was reactive] more than being proactive." Goodwin agrees, "There was no glue, no cohesiveness [among the agencies and organizations gathered at the fire grounds]. . . . And I have to say that's our responsibility as incident command; we didn't [have that] fully in place." In addition, and perhaps more seriously, it was not always clear to some of those involved who, formally, was in command of the increasingly complex situation at the Howard Street Tunnel.

Friction

The difficulties of managing communications in an incident with multiples sites and multiple problems and sometimes clashing priorities became perhaps most starkly apparent when the DPW decided to commence work on the ruptured water pipe. DPW officials, according to Winfield, were doing "our own independent things" at the site, focusing on the issue of most immediate concern to them—the repair of a major water main break—and did not forewarn Heinbuch of their plans. Unlike the fire department, which had "always worked in an incident command situation," the DPW "had never" done so, Winfield maintains. At the time, moreover, "I would say there was no formal procedure whereby DPW would have recognized the fire department as being the lead agency for this incident." On the morning of July 19, DPW crews began excavations at the intersection of Howard and Lombard in an effort, Winfield explains, "to locate where exactly the break occurred." As it happened, there were firefighters in the tunnel at the same time that the DPW began digging over it. When water suddenly began pouring into the tunnel from a broken valve, the firefighters were hastily evacuated and the DPW was told to cease its operations. Fire officials were upset that their men had been put at risk by DPW's actions; "it could have killed some of them," Heinbuch maintains. "We worried long and hard," McDonald notes, "about putting guys down in that tunnel in the first place."

Meanwhile, fire officials were also having problems with CSX that were slowing their efforts to reach the derailed cars in the tunnel. Under Federal Railroad Administration guidelines, Goodwin explains, CSX workers on the scene had to obtain approval from company officials based in Jacksonville, Florida, each time they or city firefighters entered the tunnel. This process proved cumbersome and time-consuming and, to Goodwin and others in the fire department, deeply frustrating. "I was, along with a few others, really intense," he maintains, "about a unified command structure being set up so that when we needed a CSX asset, somebody didn't have to look for the CSX man with the radio [to contact Jacksonville]. There needed to be somebody next to our decision maker [who] could effect things immediately." The need for this was driven home after a harrowing incident in which CSX workers left Goodwin and other firefighters deep inside the tunnel, intending to return shortly with their vehicle to pick them up. But obtaining permission from CSX to reenter the tunnel took longer than anticipated and, with their oxygen supplies running dangerously low, firefighters were forced to walk three-quarters of a mile to make their own way out of the tunnel. Soon after that, Goodwin recalls, during a "debriefing of the last chain of events" with a group of city officials that included O'Malley and McDonald, "I extremely reiterated the need for a unified command to stop this."

The Mayor Steps In

Looking back, Carl McDonald was philosophical about the disorder that characterized the first hectic hours of the tunnel fire and accompanying water main break. "Anytime you have an incident of that magnitude," he reflects, "there's going to be some disconnect, especially when agencies that had not traditionally worked together in a coordinated effort are thrown together and there's been no training or practice. . . . There's always some confusion [and] disconnect, until the lines of authority are clearly defined." The one who ultimately did the defining, by most accounts, was Mayor O'Malley.

O'Malley accomplished this in ways that were both particular and general. In response to the incident with the DPW, for example, "the mayor got involved," Winfield recalls, "and said we need somebody from DPW down at the incident command center with the fire department so that we all know what each other is doing. And that's what happened. We got pulled into that environment because we needed to coordinate our work efforts." The mayor and his staff also let DPW officials know that they were expected to yield to the authority of the fire chief. "We stressed to them," Enright says, "[that] you're working for him now, and you don't make any decisions operationally on your end that he doesn't approve."

Similarly, after hearing of persistent problems with CSX—and, in particular, the stranding of the firefighters in the tunnel—O'Malley personally phoned the CEO of the company, John Snow.[14] Later, the mayor recalled "berating the CEO of CSX" in the course of their conversation for leaving "our firefighters in a tunnel hundreds of feet from safety." And he also impressed on Snow the need for improved coordination and communication with CSX. Snow was "very understanding," says Enright. He immediately appointed "somebody with authority," as McDonald puts it, to stay at the fire scene and expedite the company's response to the fire department's requests for assistance. O'Malley "went right to the top guy," McDonald notes, "and said, 'Look, this is what I need.' . . . That's when we started getting absolute cooperation from CSX."

The mayor did more than mediate specific problems that arose at the fire scene; at a meeting sometime on Thursday, July 19, he "made it clear to everybody . . . ," says

---

[14]In January 2003, Snow was appointed secretary of the Treasury by President George W. Bush.

McDonald, "who was in command of this incident until it was resolved," that is, McDonald himself. As chief executive, McDonald notes, O'Malley had the option of assuming command of the emergency himself; instead, however, "he left it in my hands." As O'Malley recalls it, once the "evacuation crisis" had been settled, the focus "shifted from being primarily a police 'get-people-out-of-harm's-way' function" to one in which "the fire department was then the lead [agency]." His own role, he decided, would be "to become the best deputy the fire chief ever had, and [to] force these other agencies to cooperate."

One way that the mayor did this was by making sure that every agency and organization involved in the incident appointed liaisons, "whose job it was," explains O'Malley, "to sit by the fire chief's command post," essentially at his beck and call. Their presence would help prevent agencies from working at cross-purposes and ease the burden on the fire department of tracking down officials whose cooperation or assistance it needed. "Whenever Chief Heinbuch and I were interfacing," McDonald explains, "we would bring [the liaisons] in so that they could [hear] firsthand what was going on, what our plan was, what we would need from their agency or whether we needed their agency or not." The liaisons at the command post went a long way toward opening lines of communication among the disparate encampments at the fire site. Still, even more important, McDonald believed, was the new-found clarity about the command structure. "I would say," he reflects, "that it really began operating a lot smoother when the mayor made it clear to everybody who was in command of the incident. That was the defining factor."

As he looked back, Goodwin believed that the passage of time also helped build trust and, consequently, teamwork among the groups working on the incident. After about 12 hours on the scene, he points out, they began to feel comfortable working together. Whatever the precise combination of causes, most of those present agreed that by the second day of the blaze, things were running much more efficiently at the site. "By that day," Goodwin recalls, "we set the entire incident up in a textbook command structure. We had the incident command properly identified, with individuals from unified command at or in proximity to that location." Moreover, he continues, "we really not only built the unified command as it should be, but we built a reliance and a trust in each other that continued day after day, for six days."

Progress

By the end of Thursday, July 19, the second day of the incident, the city was able to report real progress in its battle to subdue the tunnel blaze. Still unable to reach it from either end of the tunnel, firefighters had changed tactics and attacked the fire through the manhole at Howard and Lombard Streets, which provided access to the tunnel. In addition, contract workers had begun pumping 20,000 gallons of hydrochloric acid out of a leaking tanker car through the manhole. These and other efforts paid off—crews were finally able to start hauling cars from the tunnel and, by late Friday, July 20, a total of twenty-two had been removed. There were still thirty-eight cars left, some of them burning, but, as McDonald told reporters, "We see light at the end of the tunnel."[15]

Despite the progress, however, citizens were beginning to chafe at the inconvenience and cost of the ongoing incident. After a couple of days, Goodwin observes, "it was not as intense [a threat] to the private citizen and to the business person as it was a disruption, so that they started to feel more the disruption than the fear of anything else happening." O'Malley agrees: "Merchants were disgruntled" over street closures, and the Baltimore Orioles were unhappy when O'Malley called them, on July 19 and again on July 20, to tell them that the games scheduled for those two days would have to be cancelled. This was expensive for the team, which put its losses for the three cancelled games at between $3.5 and $4 million, and initially Orioles officials let the city know their displeasure. "The Orioles management were insisting that they were going to play [that] night," O'Malley recalls, "and on the radio I said, 'Well, they're welcome to play, but they can't do it here.'" After that testy start, however, communications between the city and Orioles's management improved, and the ball club opened its parking lot and facilities to firefighters while they battled the blaze. When the Orioles were finally permitted to play, on Saturday, July 21, it happened to be, coincidentally, Firefighter Appreciation Day at the ballpark, an event scheduled months earlier.

The Orioles and local merchants were not the only ones eager to see the tunnel fire extinguished and traffic restored to normal. CSX had been scrambling for days to reroute the thirty-plus trains that usually plied the north-south rails each day. The company "applied a great deal of pressure to the fire department," says Jerry Young of the DPW, "to get the tunnel back in service."[16] But the mayor supported fire officials' careful approach to the blaze. "I try never to get in the way of operational decisions," he says. "I would never say [for example], 'Come on, Carl, can't we pull that one out sooner?' . . . What I tried not to do was apply time pressures on them. . . . My primary concern was to err on the side of, just do it methodically, get it done." Those on the scene appreciated O'Malley's tact and his backing. "One of the things that went well with this [incident]," says Alan Williams of MDE, "was strong mayoral support. [O'Malley] was giving support to the responders, and I can't stress the importance of that enough."

---

[15]John Bierner, "Firefighters Extinguish Two Burning Train Cars, Remove 16 More," Associated Press, July 20, 2001.

[16]Interview with Jerry Young, chief of training and safety, Department of Public Works, City of Baltimore, 2004. Unless noted, subsequent quotations from Young are also from this interview.

Endgame

On Saturday night, July 21, emergency crews hauled three boxcars filled with burning paper out of the Howard Street Tunnel; it took nearly a day, according to one account, to put out the fires in the three cars.[17] Events moved quickly after that. On Monday, July 23, the last of the freight cars were removed; the following day, after an inspection uncovered no structural damage, CSX resumed partial freight service through the tunnel. Meanwhile, also on July 23, the DPW was finally able to repair the broken valve that had allowed water to continue leaking into the intersection of Howard and Lombard and to begin repairs on the ruptured water main. It had been a trying time for the DPW, which had had to cool its heels while the fire department had battled the blaze. "The first couple of days," Winfield says, "we were kind of delayed from doing what we thought we should have been doing"; but, he adds, once "we had this coordinated effort" with the fire department, so that each knew when the other was working in or on the tunnel, "we were able to move forward with the repair." The DPW completed repairs on the water main itself on July 29, but the intersection of Howard and Lombard remained closed to traffic and to light rail service until early September, while the DPW replaced pipe adjacent to the repaired main.

Looking back on the incident as it wound down, most observers applauded the way the city had managed the crisis. The city had had "a close call," the *Baltimore Sun* editorialized, and was indebted to its "courageous firefighters," as well as to "the police, hazardous materials experts and public works workers who toiled on no notice through the night to cope with fire, train mishap, water main break and power outage." Aside from the siren alert, which proved more mystifying than enlightening, the city and other authorities had been "right to err on the side of caution," the *Sun* continued, "in closing roads, waterways, baseball, business and normal life until public safety was secured." The situation would have been considerably worse, the paper noted, if the chemicals had caught fire or released toxic fumes into the atmosphere—or if, as others later pointed out, it had been carrying radioactive waste. In the end, the tunnel fire was, as one citizen pointed out, "almost a worst-case scenario."[18]

The last clean-up work related to the fire—repairs on the road surfaces in the tunnel area—was completed on September 10, 2001.

---

[17]Mitchell, "Fire in the Hole," 47.

[18]Michael James, "'It's a Little Bit of Hell'; 22 Smoldering Cars Pulled Out," *Baltimore Sun,* July 21, 2001, 1A.

Key Actors in the Baltimore Tunnel Fire

City of Baltimore Officials
Mayor's Office
Martin O'Malley, mayor of Baltimore
Michael Enright, first deputy mayor of
　Baltimore

Fire Department
Donald Heinbuch, acting assistant chief of
　operations, Baltimore City Fire
　Department, and incident commander,
　Howard Street Tunnel Fire
Carl McDonald, acting department chief,
　Baltimore City Fire Department
William Goodwin, chief and director of
　training, Baltimore City Fire
　Department
Ronald Addison, chief and hazmat
　coordinator, Baltimore City Fire
　Department
Terry Ryer, chief and head of 6th Battalion
　hazmat unit, Baltimore City Fire
　Department
Hector Torres, public information officer,
　Baltimore City Fire Department

Department of Public Works
George Winfield, director, Department of
　Public Works, City of Baltimore
Richard McKoy, director, Office of
　Emergency Management, Department
　of Public Works, City of Baltimore

Michael Rice, head, Transportation
　Bureau, Department of Public Works,
　City of Baltimore
Jerry Young, chief of training and safety,
　Department of Public Works, City of
　Baltimore

Police Department
Edward Norris, police commissioner, City
　of Baltimore
J. Charles Gutberlet, central district
　commander, Police Department, City
　of Baltimore

Other
Peter Beilenson, commissioner of health,
　City of Baltimore

State of Maryland Officials
Alan Williams, program manager,
　Emergency Response Program,
　Maryland Department of the
　Environment

Other
John Snow, chief executive officer, CSX
　Corporation

Baltimore Tunnel Fire, July 2001

Chronology of Events

Wednesday, July 18

3:00 p.m.: A CSX Corp. freight train bound for Newark, New Jersey, enters the south end of Baltimore's Howard Street Tunnel, laden with paper products, plywood, soy oil, and several tanks of chemicals.

3:07 p.m.: The train comes to an abrupt halt. The train's two-man crew attempts to contact the CSX dispatcher in Jacksonville, Florida, to report the situation but does not get through. Worried about what appears to be choking diesel exhaust fumes, the crew uncouples the train's three locomotives and drives them out of the north end of the tunnel.

3:25 p.m.: The crew realizes that the smoke is increasing in volume, most likely the result of fire. They again radio the dispatcher, noting that the chemicals on board are in danger of igniting.

The Baltimore City Fire Department begins receiving calls from the public reporting smoke coming out of a manhole at the intersection of Howard and Lombard Streets. Dispatched firefighters observe a large plume of smoke billowing out of the south end of the tunnel, four blocks away.

The train crew meets firefighters and informs them that the train is carrying a mix of chemicals, some of which are combustible and others that can cause serious respiratory or burn injuries.

The 6th Battalion's hazmat unit is dispatched to the scene. Officials of the Maryland Department of the Environment (MDE) start mobilizing after learning (via fire department scanners) of the incident.

Over the course of the next few hours, about 150 fire fighters struggle to fight the powerful fires. With the situation continuing to escalate, Acting Assistant Chief of Operations Donald Heinbuch assumes command of the incident.

Mayor Martin O'Malley is informed of the fires while driving back from an event on Maryland's Eastern Shore. Senior city officials begin to gather in the police department's Comstat room, a data analysis center well-equipped with telecommunications equipment.

4:35 p.m.: Two private chemists reassure responders that a catastrophic explosion is unlikely, although concerns remain regarding the release of toxic vapors.

Shortly before 5:00 p.m.: Hazmat officials begin testing the air near the tunnel and in nearby Camden Yards for toxic substances. Definitive results, however, are not immediately available.

5:00 p.m.: Acting Baltimore City Fire Department Chief Carl McDonald arrives at the scene but leaves tactical command in Heinbuch's hands while designating himself overall commander, taking on the responsibility of coordinating the many agencies active in the response.

After discussing evacuation options, authorities advise residents of the affected area to shelter in place. The city decides, however, to evacuate the Baltimore Orioles's ballpark, which sits directly in the path of the smoke plume.

Baltimore police block off a five-block area around Howard Street. They also cut off the main access points into the city.

Contacted by MDE, the U.S. Coast Guard closes the Inner Harbor to boat traffic and sends in a strike team to test the harbor for the presence of chemicals that may be leaking from the CSX freight cars.

5:45 p.m.: The city's air raid sirens are activated, but because the public has little experience with the system and because of a delay in informing TV and radio stations of the shelter in place advisory, they leave residents confused.

6:00 p.m.: Mayor O'Malley arrives in Baltimore and heads to the police department's Comstat room. After revisiting the issue of evacuation, he is convinced by the fire chief (and by the U.S. Environmental Protection Agency, EPA, data indicating that chemicals are not being released into the air) to continue the policy of shelter in place.

6:15 p.m.: Hundreds of gallons of water pour from a ruptured main, complicating the response effort. But it begins to douse the fire in the tunnel below, so fire officials ask the Department of Public Works (DPW) to allow the leak to continue, despite potentially compromising the region's water supply.

Firefighters are finally able to enter the tunnel and gain some situational awareness.

8:00 p.m.: Gridlock is cleared.

Late evening: Problems with interagency communications and decision-making develop.

Thursday, July 19

Without informing the fire department, DPW crews begin excavating at the Howard and Lombard intersection, hoping to identify the location of the water main break. The excavation puts the firefighters then in the tunnel at risk; they rush out when water begins to pour in. Mayor O'Malley subsequently makes clear that all agencies are to coordinate their work under the command of Fire Chief McDonald.

Progress is made in bringing the tunnel fires under control.

Friday, July 20

Chief McDonald tells reporters that with twenty-two of the sixty freight cars now above ground, "We see light at the end of the tunnel."

Saturday, July 21

Emergency crews haul three cars filled with burning paper out of the tunnel. It takes almost a day to extinguish the fires in these cars.

Monday, July 23

The last of the freight cars are removed from the tunnel.

The DPW begins work on the ruptured water main.

Tuesday, July 24

After an inspection reveals no structural damage, CSX resumes partial freight service through the tunnel.

Sunday, July 29

The DPW finishes the repairs of the ruptured water main.

5 The 9/11 Pentagon Emergency (A): Command Performance—County Firefighters Take Charge

Pamela Varley

Crises bring together groups of responders who may never have worked together before. They may come from different types of agencies, represent different professions, come from different jurisdictions or levels of government (local, state, and federal), even from different countries. Yet in a moment of grave risk and danger, they must function with skill and in coordination with one another—protecting lives and property effectively while making sure they do not interfere with or endanger one another.

As described in the introduction to Part II, an organizational template for managing this problem in severe emergencies—called the Incident Management System (IMS) or Incident Command System (ICS)—has been developed in the United States in the past 35 years. Congress recognized its promise when the Homeland Security Act of 2002 mandated the adoption of a National Incident Management System (NIMS) as the operating method for emergency responders at all levels of government in the United States. Yet IMS remains controversial among some groups of responders, who question its effectiveness or appropriateness for their professional disciplines.

The terrorist attack on the Pentagon on September 11, 2001, provides some evidence about the utility of ICS and the potential of the NIMS system. When a hijacked, fuel-laden Boeing 757-200 jetliner slammed into the west side of the Pentagon at 9:38 a.m., its momentum and the massive explosion caused by the crash left a gaping hole in the building, sparked an intense fire, and significantly destabilized the remaining structure. In addition to the hijackers, 125 people at the Pentagon and 59 passengers and crew members on the plane died in the attack.

Subcase A describes how leaders of the Arlington County Fire Department, first to arrive on the scene, used ICS to organize the emergency response, which swiftly began to "scale up" as more and more emergency workers arrived on the scene. From the outset, responders to the situation came from a multiplicity of agencies, including military and civilian personnel from the Department of Defense, firefighters from the Arlington County Fire Department and other nearby fire departments, law enforcement officials from the Federal Bureau of Investigation (FBI), and many others. Members of the public also arrived on the scene to offer assistance.

Given the scale of the disaster and the variety of responding organizations, the response leaders quickly established a Unified Command structure to coordinate the cooperating agencies, a shift that is described in Subcase B. This eventually included representatives of key operational units and agencies with roles in supplying resources to the site. Effective

This is an abridged version of a case written by Pamela Varley for Arnold M. Howitt, executive director, Taubman Center for State and Local Government, for use at the Executive Session on Domestic Preparedness, John F. Kennedy School of Government, Harvard University. Funding was provided by the Office of Justice Programs, U.S. Department of Justice. C16-03-1712.0. Copyright © 2003, 2007 by the President and Fellows of Harvard College.

coordination early in the response saved lives when all rescuers, from multiple different agencies, were simultaneously ordered to evacuate from part of the burning building that was about to collapse. Operations for rescue, stabilization, and crime-scene investigation were carried out at the site over a period of several weeks, with the main role of the Unified Command group correspondingly shifting from fire and rescue to law enforcement.

As you read through the description of the events of that terrible day and the days that followed, think about the challenges of organizing responders and investigators (not to mention reporters, politicians, and senior Department of Defense officials) and maintaining an effective, coordinated response.

Discussion Questions

- What coordination and jurisdictional problems did the emergency response to the Pentagon attack encounter?
- To what extent and in what ways was ICS, including the Unified Command structure, an effective way of coping with these problems? Were there shortcomings in ICS that this situation revealed?
- What prerequisite preparations were necessary for the positive results to occur?
- What opportunities do you see for further improvements in the design and operation of IMS-organized emergency responses?

At the end of the morning rush hour on September 11, 2001, a group of Arlington County firefighters were deep in conversation about the events unfolding at the World Trade Center in New York City when they noticed a plane in their own air space behaving oddly. It descended quickly, banked right, then plunged sharply toward the ground, and disappeared behind the horizon. An instant later came a crash and a dark plume of smoke.

The details of the incident emerged over a period of hours and days. At 8:10 a.m., American Airlines Flight #77 had departed Washington Dulles International Airport bound for Los Angeles. During the next 88 minutes, five terrorists hijacked the Boeing 757, flew it back into Washington, D.C., aimed it at the southwest side of the Pentagon, and accelerated. The plane, carrying almost 11,000 gallons of jet fuel, slammed into the building, igniting a fire the size of a modern shopping mall and precipitating a five-story structural collapse in the area of impact. It required a 10-day effort to put out the fire and complete the search and rescue operation.

The emergency response to the attack proved complicated, combining all the difficulties of a plane crash, fire, and building collapse in a single location. Firefighters first battled a persistent, hot-burning fire and then—with the help of search and rescue experts, structural engineers, and shoring and stabilizing teams—hunted for survivors in a dangerously unstable structure.

Like any major emergency, the response was further complicated by the number of agencies and jurisdictions involved. In addition to the numerous fire departments that sent resources to the Pentagon, this included thirty local, state, and federal law enforcement agencies; four Federal Emergency Management Agency (FEMA) urban search and rescue teams; twenty health, safety, and environmental groups; and an assortment of other government agencies, voluntary organizations, and businesses bringing supplies and expertise to the response effort.

The response also took place in the context of a national security crisis—a bold attack on the headquarters of the U.S. military establishment, following on the heels of the crash of the two other hijacked jetliners into the World Trade Center. That meant that the fire and rescue response at the Pentagon was not the only undertaking of the next 10 days. The Department of Defense was still there in force, working to increase domestic military security, to gather military intelligence, and to protect sensitive information that had been made vulnerable in the attack. The Federal Bureau of Investigation (FBI) was there, too, preserving the crime scene, collecting evidence for its criminal investigation of the attack, preventing secondary attacks, and creating an off-site Joint Operations Center (JOC)—a meeting ground for federal, state, and local agencies with a role in either responding to the Pentagon attack or fending off future terrorist attacks. The Pentagon also drew hundreds of visits from political leaders and government officials—including the president, cabinet officials, senators, members of Congress, and governors—who came to see firsthand what had happened and express their sorrow and outrage. And a large contingent of national and international journalists needed regular updates about the attack, the casualties, and the response effort.

The person named to preside over the emergency response—and by extension the entire Pentagon site—was neither a high political official nor a four-star general but, remarkably, the assistant chief of the modest-size fire department in Arlington County, Virginia.[1] In fact, on the evening of September 11, the Pentagon's liaison to the Arlington County Fire Department (ACFD) underscored the ACFD's authority by introducing the assistant fire chief to Defense Secretary Donald Rumsfeld (famous for his take-charge persona) as "the man who owns this ground."[2] Under the Tenth Amendment to the U.S. Constitution, the authority to respond to emergencies is largely reserved to the states, and most states have del-

---

[1] At 26 square miles, Arlington County has the smallest land area of any county in the United States. Its population was 194,000.

[2] "Observing and Documenting the Inter-Organizational Response to the September 11th Attack on the Pentagon," George Washington University Institute for Crisis, Disaster, and Risk Management, Washington, D.C., July 15, 2002. Available at www.gwu.edu/~icdrm/publications/nsf911/response.html.

egated this authority, in whole or in part, to local jurisdictions. A local government typically responds first to emergencies within its jurisdiction, seeking help from neighboring communities if necessary. In major disasters or situations requiring specialized capabilities, the state government may provide help. Under the 1974 Stafford Disaster Relief and Emergency Assistance Act, the governor of a state, in turn, can ask for federal help. Because the Pentagon is located in Arlington County, Virginia, the initiative for responding to the Pentagon attack thus belonged to the ACFD.[3]

Arlington is a small county, and its fire department fielded only sixty-seven to seventy-one firefighters and paramedics per shift. But the ACFD was not an unsophisticated organization. It was one of the three fire departments rated highest in the state of Virginia by the Insurance Services Organization. It had cultivated good relationships and a tight-knit mutual aid system with its neighboring northern Virginia jurisdictions, and it had played a leadership role in regional efforts to plan for terrorist attacks.

For many years, the ACFD had managed every emergency incident in the county using the Incident Command System (ICS), a flexible, scalable, organizational template for coordinating different fire departments and other government agencies at the scene of a major disaster. This gave the department a potent tool to address the organizational complexity of the Pentagon emergency. To use ICS most effectively, however, the organizations participating in a given response effort had to be familiar with ICS and willing to submit to its rules. Although this was true of some responders at the Pentagon, it was certainly not true of all.

The ACFD, moreover, had to decide what to do when the professional mandates of the Department of Defense (DOD), FBI, and U.S. Environmental Protection Agency (EPA) collided with those of its own firefighting and rescue effort. Despite their years of practice and preparation, Arlington County fire officials faced a string of predicaments in the course of the Pentagon emergency that they had never foreseen—situations that demanded judgments and capacities, as ACFD Chief Edward Plaugher puts it, that "they don't teach you in fire chief school."[4]

September 11, 9:38 a.m.

On the morning of September 11, the assistant chief for operations in the ACFD, James Schwartz (an 18-year veteran of the department), was in the ACFD headquarters office,

---

[3]The Stafford Act also states that the federal government can assume primary jurisdiction over an emergency in certain circumstances: (1) in the event of an insurrection or foreign attack and (2) when the emergency takes place on federal property. Thus, under one or both of these provisos, the federal government could, in theory, have taken command of the Pentagon emergency. But in reality, the federal government did not have the capacity to mobilize several hundred firefighters in the first minutes and hours of the response, as the local fire department did, so this idea never received serious consideration.

[4]Interview with Fire Chief Edward P. Plaugher, Arlington County Fire Department, 2003. Unless noted, subsequent quotations from Plaugher are also from this interview.

watching the latest reports about the World Trade Center emergency. Although many Americans reeled in disbelief at the mounting evidence of a well-planned, deadly attack on U.S. soil, Schwartz and his colleagues had long been expecting a terrorist assault of some kind. When the first confused reports began to emerge from New York City, ACFD commanders quickly moved past shock and began to discuss the possibility of further attacks in the Washington, D.C., area. This fear was soon realized when a radio dispatch announced a plane crash at the Pentagon. It was 9:38 a.m. Schwartz raced to the Pentagon, arriving 5 minutes later to a scene of pandemonium.

The State of Affairs at the Pentagon

Built in 1941, the massive Pentagon structure provided office space for 23,000 military and civilian personnel. Although only 77 feet tall—five stories plus a mezzanine—it covered 29 acres, encircled a 5-acre courtyard, contained 17.5 miles of corridors, and was surrounded by 67 acres of parking. The interior of the building was designed as a set of five concentric rings with ten spokelike corridors radiating out from the central courtyard. (See Exhibit 5A-1 for a diagram of the building.) In essence, the Pentagon was a fortress, stoutly constructed of steel and reinforced concrete. Its squat design and sturdy exterior undoubtedly lessened the scope of the damage from the September 11 crash, but the destruction was still "immediate and catastrophic." According to a report commissioned by Arlington County:

The 270,000 pounds of metal and jet fuel hurtling into the solid mass of the Pentagon [were] the equivalent in weight of a diesel train locomotive, except it [was] traveling at more than 400 miles per hour. More than 600,000 airframe bolts and rivets and 60 miles of wire were instantly transformed into white-hot shrapnel. The resulting impact, penetration and burning fuel had catastrophic effects to the five floors and three rings in and around Pentagon Corridors 4 and 5.[5]

Fortuitously, the Pentagon had been undergoing renovation at the time of the crash. Work had just been completed in the area of impact, and only 850 employees had returned to that part of the building.

Schwartz knew none of this as he pulled up to the Pentagon. He saw a great gash in the southwest side of the building and smoke rising up from inside. There was no sign of the plane; how far it had penetrated the building, he could not see. Thousands of people were fleeing—ambulatory people suffering from smoke inhalation and burns were hitching rides with colleagues and flagging down ambulances, and hundreds of Pentagon workers were frantically trying to help others escape or get medical treatment.

By the time Schwartz arrived, Arlington County police were securing the entrances to the site and managing traffic on the surrounding roads to clear the way for emergency vehicles.

---

[5]"Introduction," in *Arlington County After-Action Report on the Response to the September 11 Terrorist Attack on the Pentagon*, Titan Systems Corporation, July 2002, 9.

Exhibit 5A-1   Initial triage and treatment sites at the Pentagon

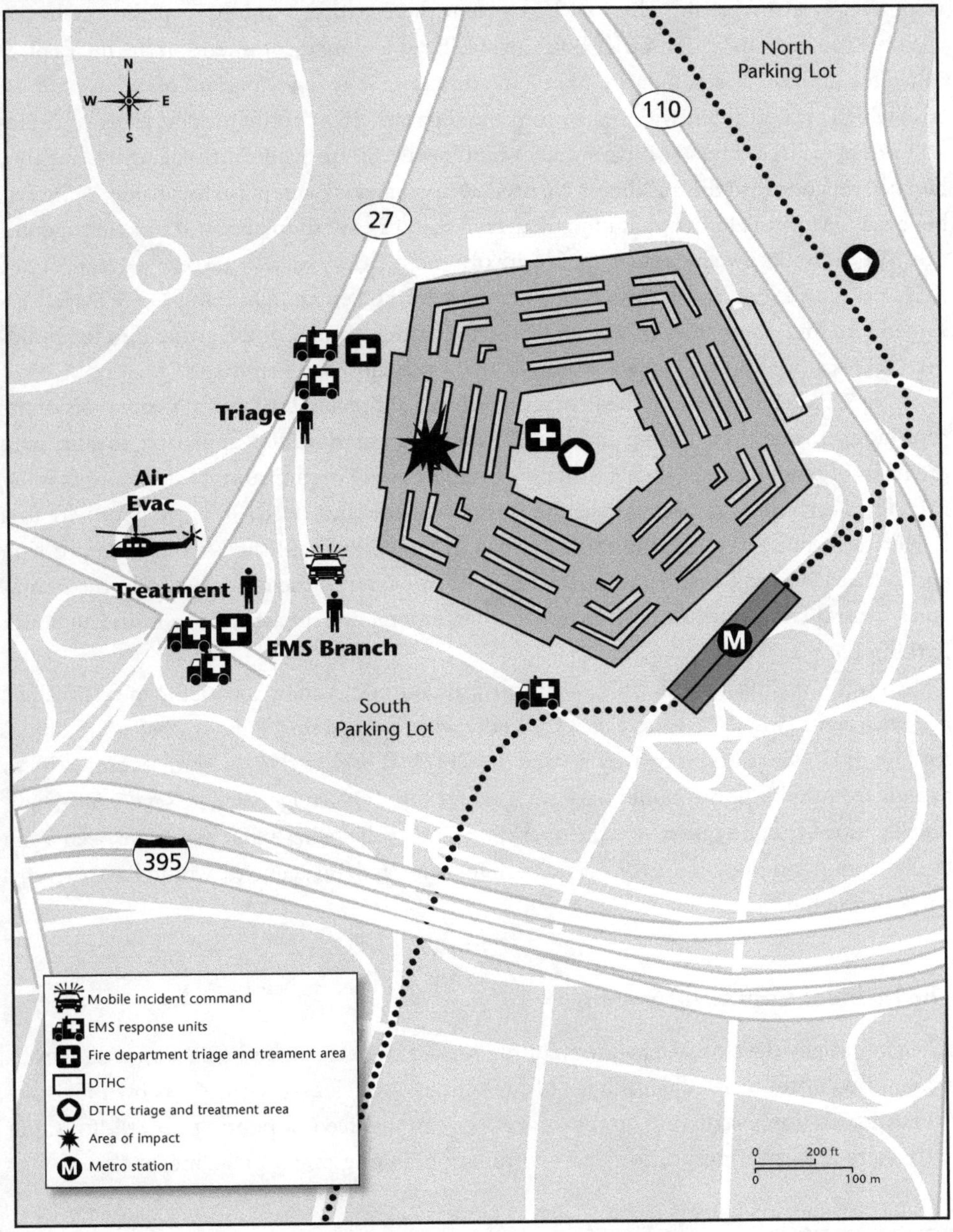

Source: "Section Annex A: Fire Department and Operations," in *Arlington County After-Action Report on the Response to the September 11 Terrorist Attack on the Pentagon,* Titan Systems Corporation, July 2002, 34.

Note: EMS, emergency medical service; DTHC, DiLorenzo TRICARE Health Clinic.

The Pentagon's internal police service was evacuating the building. Several ACFD fire trucks were already at the scene. The first had gotten there within 2 minutes of the crash, and within 4 minutes, Battalion Chief Bob Cornwell had assumed command of the incident, as called for under ICS, setting up a makeshift command post in the back of his Chevy Suburban, which was outfitted with maps, command charts, and a more modest array of radios and phones. Firefighters and paramedics had hastily set up medical triage areas, but they had not yet gone into the building. "We needed to get an assessment on the inside," Schwartz believed. "We didn't know what kind of aircraft this was. We didn't know the extent of damage. We didn't know the extent of fire involvement." Cornwell, a 35-year veteran of the ACFD, was an expert in the layout and structure of the Pentagon building, so Schwartz assigned him four companies (twelve to fifteen firefighters) and sent the group into the building. "It was at that point," Schwartz notes, "that I actually took command."[6]

In the chaotic first hour at the Pentagon, Schwartz directed the tactical maneuvers of the responders inside the building and out. This was the standard ICS approach, to start with the most urgent tasks and then gradually develop a larger organizational structure as more fire crews arrived at the scene and the immediate life-and-death struggle gave way to a longer-term campaign. During this early phase, Schwartz established two fire suppression and rescue divisions: one based at the point of impact and the other based in the Pentagon's central courtyard. He also established an emergency medical division in the South Parking Lot.

ICS was not a magic bullet, Schwartz cautions, but it did allow the ACFD to establish its presence right away. "We were clear: We know what we're doing. This is what we're doing. And we did it." Schwartz is convinced that if ACFD had hesitated or faltered, its authority to preside over the response would have counted for little. Other agencies, he says, would have quickly moved in and taken over the operation: "I do fully believe that had there been a gap in that command presence, FEMA, and perhaps other federal agencies, would have driven a truck through it."

The Incident Command System

ICS was initially developed by a group of fire service leaders in California after a disastrous string of wildfires in 1970. Hundreds of firefighting agencies—each with its own jurisdiction, organizational structure, and protocols—were involved in fighting the wildfires, but there were little communication and coordination among them. "This meant that as fires

---

[6]Interview with Assistant Fire Chief James H. Schwartz, Operations Division, Arlington County Fire Department, and incident commander for the Pentagon 9/11 response, 2003. Unless noted, subsequent quotations from Schwartz are also from this interview.

burned across and out of one jurisdiction to another, individual jurisdictions were often 'flying blind' and forced to improvise management response with no clear organization of authority between departments, no predetermined rules for collective decision-making, and no coordination of even the most basic communications," wrote Dana Cole, assistant chief of the California Department of Forestry and Fire Protection in a February 2000 report.[7]

In the aftermath of the 1970 fire season, representatives of seven California firefighting agencies joined forces to develop a template that would allow the emergency responders at an incident scene to quickly create an ad hoc organization for managing the emergency response and coordinating the assistance offered by neighboring departments or jurisdictions. By 1982, their ICS had evolved to address a broader array of disaster scenarios and had been adopted as the centerpiece of the National Incident Management System (NIMS), the federal plan for improving coordination among agencies in a broad range of large-scale emergencies. By 2000, ICS had become "the world's leading management system for the command, control and coordination of emergency scenes," according to Cole.[8]

Fundamentals of the Incident Command System

The Incident Command organization is governed by three central principles:

1. There is to be a clear *chain of command* linking every member of the emergency response to the incident commander or Unified Command team.
2. There is to be *unity of command*—one and only one supervisor per employee.
3. There is to be a standardized *span-of-control*—a range of three to seven people that any one supervisor could directly oversee.

It is crucial that either a single person or a small cohesive group be in charge of the emergency response. In either case, the job of the commander/s is to set objectives and priorities for the response effort; approve the Incident Action Plan, which delineates the goals of the response effort shift by shift; and oversee the work of the operations chief, who manages all tactical aspects of the response.

A single incident commander is to manage an emergency when the question of jurisdiction is clear-cut. If a major fire occurs entirely within the boundaries of City A, for example, it is the responsibility of the City A Fire Department to put it out. The City A Fire Department may ask the fire departments from Cities B and C for assistance, but the City A fire chief remains in charge and serves as incident commander or assigns someone to the position.

---

[7]Dana Cole, "The Incident Command System: A 25-Year Evaluation by California Practitioners," submitted to the National Fire Academy as part of the Executive Fire Officer Program, February 2000, Emmitsburg, MD, 209.
[8]Ibid., 203.

A Unified Command is established when the question of jurisdiction is more compli-cated. For instance, if a major fire straddles the border between Cities A and B, the fire chiefs from both A and B (or their designees) are to manage the emergency response together. Or, if a riot and fire occur simultaneously in the downtown section of City A, the City A fire and police chiefs jointly manage the response. Or, as in the case of the Pentagon attack, if state or federal agencies are legally mandated to perform certain functions at the same time that the emergency response is taking place, then senior representatives from those agencies and the leaders of the local emergency response organizations form a Unified Command.

In addition to the command structure, ICS features a preestablished organizational tem-plate that has the advantage of being simple, consistent, and flexible. Pieces of the ICS struc-ture can be expanded, contracted, or eliminated to adapt to emergencies of varying sizes and types. (See Exhibit 5A-2 for the basic ICS structure.) At the top of the pyramid is either the

Exhibit 5A-2   Basic Incident Command System structure

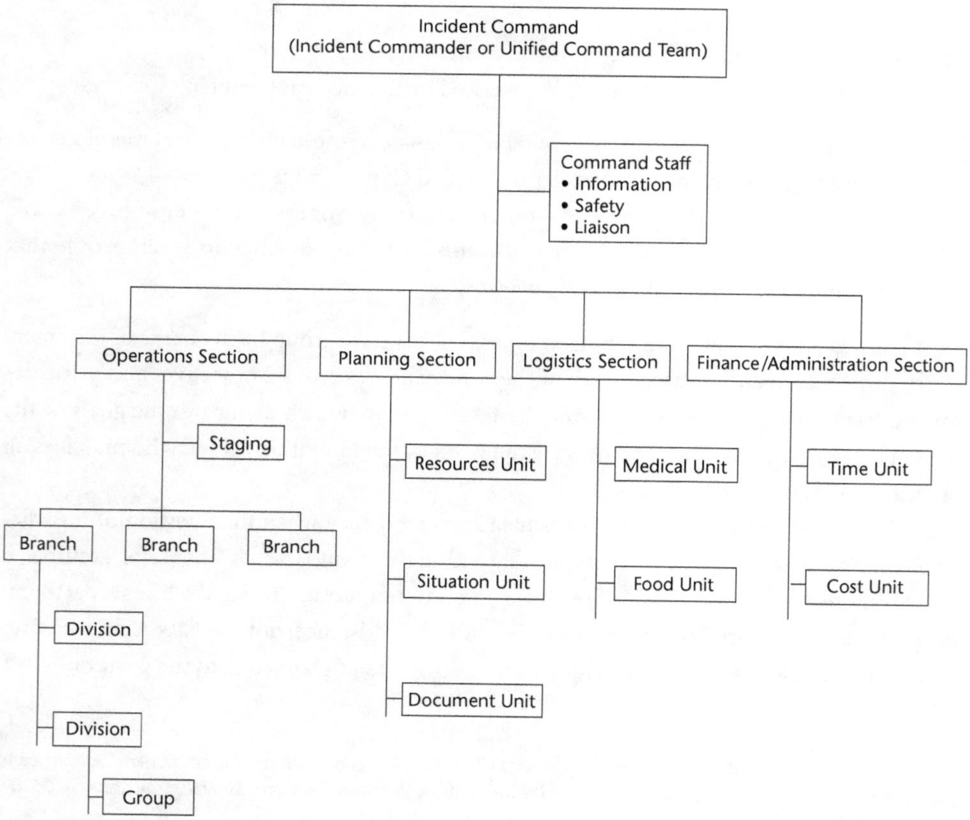

incident commander or the Unified Command team, served by a command staff that includes an information officer (to dispense information to other agencies and sometimes to the media), a safety officer (to look out for the safety of response personnel), and a liaison officer (to serve as the point of contact for other emergency workers at the scene).

Below the command group are up to four sections that could be subdivided into assorted branches, divisions, groups, and units, depending on the demands and complexity of the incident:

- The Operations Section manages all tactical activities.
- The Planning Section gathers and evaluates current and forecasted information so that the command group can create and update the Incident Action Plan.
- The Logistics Section provides ongoing support for the responders, procuring supplies; arranging for facilities, transportation, equipment maintenance and fuel; and providing food, counseling, rest/sleeping arrangements, medical care, and so on.
- The Finance/Administration Section keeps track of the money and time spent on the emergency response by any agency that does not have the in-house capacity to track such information.

ICS also calls for establishing temporary incident facilities: a single recognizable Incident Command Post; incident bases, where support services such as food provision and sleeping areas are located; camps, where resources are stored; and staging areas, where responders and equipment are temporarily located just before deployment.

Communications systems are to be integrated. Recognizing that the specialized terminology of one profession might not be familiar to members of another, responders are to communicate in simple text messages rather than codes, which might not be understood across departments. In addition, ICS establishes a consistent set of terms for major functions and functional units, resources, and facilities, so that anyone familiar with the system can immediately understand the lay of the land and communicate to others clearly and quickly.

A critically important aspect of ICS is that all the emergency responders and organizations at the scene share a knowledge of and commitment to ICS. In this way, all responders are integrated into a single system. No matter what their jurisdiction, arriving firefighters, for instance, are expected to know that instead of heading directly to the fire or crash site, they must report to a staging area. There, they are to wait until needed and, when deployed, report to one of the commanders in the Operations Section. Support organizations—the Red Cross and Salvation Army, for example—are not expected to understand the system in as much detail as the emergency responders; but they are expected to understand the basics, that is, that they will be assigned to work under the management of a commander in the ICS Logistics Section.

Chief Plaugher Speeds to the Pentagon

Arlington Fire Chief Edward Plaugher was in Fairfax, Virginia—20 miles away from the Pentagon—when he heard a vague report that planes had crashed into the World Trade Center and that "something had happened at the Pentagon." At that, he jumped into his Ford Crown Victoria and raced back to Arlington, arriving shortly after 10:00 a.m.

As Schwartz saw him approach, the assistant chief took off his blue Incident Command vest and offered it to the chief. Plaugher waved him off. "I told him, 'No, you keep it. I can be of much better help to you doing some other things,'" he recalls. Plaugher's decision to forgo the role of incident commander at the Pentagon response won praise and respect from analysts later, both because of the chief's willingness to set his own ego aside and because he had the imagination to foresee that he would be needed in another role. To Plaugher, however, the decision was an obvious one. "One of the keys to any incident is to let people do the role they do everyday—because as soon as you step away from that, you end up with people not knowing what's expected of them, and your chance of having huge catastrophic failures increases dramatically," he explains. In fact, in contrast to Schwartz, it had been years since he had functioned as an incident commander. "I've got a Chief of Operations who works with these battalion chiefs everyday. He knows their strengths and weaknesses. He gets the maximum utilization out of them all the time. Why would I want to interfere with that? As far as I'm concerned, it would have been a colossal mistake." [9]

Instead, Plaugher met with Schwartz for a few minutes to discuss where things stood:

I asked the same kind of questions that I ask, basically, every day. The number one thing in this business is rescue—saving lives—[so I asked,] "How are we doing with our triage and transport? Are we able to keep up, or are we having more victims than we have the ability to deal with?" He [Schwartz] said, "We're doing fine. We're keeping up with the flow. Every victim we have is either being med-evac'd[10] or transported immediately." The next question I asked is, "Okay, tell me the extent of damage in the Pentagon, so we can get our arms around this incident." And he said, "I don't know." So I said, "Okay, I'll find out for you."

The sheer size of the Pentagon made it hard to get a comprehensive picture of the damage. So Plaugher "commandeered" a med-evac helicopter "to have a global look-

---

[9]The Arlington County Police Department also used ICS to manage its own support operations, according to former Arlington Police Chief Ed Flynn. Like Plaugher, Flynn declined to serve as incident commander, delegating that job to his deputy chief. "I really think the senior commander has got to preserve some space between him- or herself and the demands of the specific incident. You've got to be in a position to concentrate on the biggest possible picture. You've got to be able to move around and see for yourself. And," he adds, "you've got to be in a position to relieve the incident commander when they're tired or stressed or just burned out." Interview with Chief Edward Flynn, Arlington County Police Department, 2003. Unless noted, subsequent quotations from Flynn are also from this interview.

[10]To be *med-evac'd* is to be transported to the hospital by helicopter.

down view" of the incident. For the first time, it was possible to see how deeply the plane had penetrated the interior of the Pentagon—it had broken through three of the building's five concentric rings. He could also see that the fire inside was huge and intense. Coupled with the knowledge that the Pentagon was constructed of reinforced concrete, which holds heat in a fire, this was bad news. "It seemed like we were in for a long firefight," he says.

Another Hijacked Plane Heading toward Washington, D.C.

By the time Plaugher had completed his aerial assessment, there was a new emergency on the ground. At 10:14 a.m., Schwartz had received FBI intelligence that another hijacked plane—United Airlines Flight #93—was 20 miles away and heading toward Washington, D.C. This news came in the context of tremendous anxiety about the scope and sophistication of the terrorist attack. There were stories of an explosion at the White House, a car bomb at the State Department, an attack on Camp David, and a plane crash into the Sears Tower in Chicago. No one knew fact from fiction.

Given the fact that the terrorists had struck the World Trade Center twice, Schwartz thought they could be planning a second strike on the Pentagon as well, perhaps with the specific intention of killing emergency responders and crippling the emergency response. At this point, 45 minutes into the rescue and firefighting effort, the hope of saving more lives hinged on putting out the fire as quickly as possible. Schwartz knew that evacuating rescue personnel from the building at such a juncture would be a controversial decision. But if there were a secondary attack, it would be devastating. At 10:15, therefore, he called for a full evacuation of the site. All seriously injured people were to be immediately evacuated from the scene, while responders and people with less serious injuries were to relocated to a highway overpass nearby.

At 10:37 a.m., the United Airlines jetliner crashed into a field near Shanksville, Pennsylvania, after passengers tried to overpower the hijackers. No one has ever learned where the hijackers had intended to take the plane. And no one ever knew whether any victims of the Pentagon attack were lost during the 20-minute evacuation. Schwartz says that, after the fact, some people (including journalists) questioned his decision. Schwartz explains, "Had New York not happened, the notion of another airplane hitting the building—the notion of the airplane as a weapon—wouldn't have been within my scope of reference." He continues, "I guess we could have held our ground out there, and we probably would have been patted on the back because that airplane crashed in Pennsylvania and never was a threat here, but in the environment that we were dealing with on that morning, we had no way of knowing that. I'd make that decision to withdraw those resources again, given that same information."

Culture Clash: The Pentagon Soldiers and the Firefighters

When Schwartz sounded the all clear at the end of the evacuation, he also took the first step in developing his Incident Command organization. He created an Operations Section and named one of his battalion chiefs, Randy Gray, its chief. He and Gray established the new Operations Section adjacent to the Pentagon crash site, but decided to keep the Incident Command Post under the highway overpass, in case another evacuation became necessary.

Having delegated the tactical responsibilities for the response, Schwartz tried to turn his attention to longer-range strategic planning. Almost immediately, however, Gray and the fire crews working at the crash site called on Schwartz for advice on handling a tricky problem—hundreds of Pentagon soldiers were running in and out of the burning, unstable structure in search of colleagues, ignoring orders from fire chiefs and commanders to stay clear of the building.

In fact, the Pentagon's ad hoc rescue effort had been underway since the crash. Schwartz estimates that when he first arrived at the scene, between 500 and 1,000 Pentagon workers were searching the building, rescuing wounded, disoriented, and unconscious coworkers. These efforts were extremely risky to the rescuers but also crucial in saving lives at the Pentagon. It eventually became clear that the only people to survive the attack had gotten out in the first few minutes, either on their own steam or with help from colleagues. In all, 189 people died in the Pentagon attack, including the five hijackers and fifty-nine others on the plane. Another 106 escaped with moderate to severe injuries (although one of these died later at a hospital).

Initially, firefighters had been too busy with their own rescue efforts to focus on the Pentagon soldiers. When they returned to the crash site after the evacuation, however, the ACFD began its full-scale firefight and could no longer countenance the independent efforts of the military men. First, the soldiers did not have the training to operate in a burning building, nor did they have protective suits or breathing apparatus. Second, their forays into the building were uncoordinated. No one was keeping track of who was in the building or where in the building they were headed. No one was making command-level decisions about how to maximize safety or rationalize the rescue efforts. According to Schwartz,

[There was] chaos on the west lawn. . . . If these guys out [there], with their hearts in the right place, are trying to do something they're not trained or equipped to do, they run the risk of causing me to have to re-double my efforts in terms of my resources, to get them out of harm's way, to get them out of situations they may have put themselves in, to care for them if they are injured. And I've already got enough to deal with.

The ACFD commanders, for their part, were not prepared to handle a flat disregard of their orders. "We're used to bystanders," notes Schwartz, and in most cases, civilian bystanders obediently stepped aside when told to do so. So, the firefighters at the Pentagon were at sea. Should they physically restrain the soldiers?

When he saw the scope of the problem, Schwartz decided that yes, they needed to get physical. He ordered the ACFD to send a group of firefighters to stand in front of the building and prohibit anyone from entering. Most of the Pentagon workers backed down at this point, but a few did not. Two tussles ensued. In one case, a three-star general was knocked off his feet when he tried to push his way past the firefighters into the building. In another, Ted Anderson, an army lieutenant colonel who had already participated in several harrowing rescues, had to be wrestled to the ground to prevent his return to the building.[11] Three generals then appeared, and Anderson—quite distraught—told them what was happening. The highest ranking of the three approached Schwartz. "[He said,] 'Look, I will take full responsibility. We're going to mount a rescue effort. We've got two guys here that have already been inside. They will lead our rescue effort, but we need to make an attempt to go in and get our people out.' " Schwartz overruled him, and the general finally gave in.

Later, people on both sides agreed that different training and different organizational cultures in the military and the fire service led the soldiers and the firefighters to see the incident very differently. To the ACFD, the goal was to save as many lives as possible, but not at the expense of the lives of the rescuers. The soldiers operated by a different code. As Anderson later explained to a *Newsweek* reporter, "The code states that if my brother, my comrade, is injured and is on the battlefield, you never leave him there. If I have to give my life, I will give my life, but I cannot leave my buddy behind. Never. Period. End of sentence."[12]

Although incensed at the time, Anderson later came to believe Schwartz had made the right decision: "I am now certain that they saved my life. . . . I have talked to firemen who later went into that area and there was no way out. That last burned guy we brought out was the last person to come out of the building alive on the exterior side of the Pentagon."[13]

Building the Incident Command Organization

During the first few hours at the Pentagon, Schwartz and the other ACFD commanders found themselves in conflict with the DOD leadership over another issue—the DOD's insistence on keeping a significant part of the Pentagon operational even though the building was on fire. A little later, Schwartz also became frustrated with the FBI when, consumed with its own multiple responsibilities, the agency removed its liaison to the Incident Command

---

[11]Mitchell Fink and Lois Mathias, *Never Forget: An Oral History of September 11, 2001* (New York: Harper-Collins, 2002), 145–151.

[12]*Newsweek* Web exclusive, September 28, 2001, available at www.newsweek.com/id/75861/page/2.

[13]Unless otherwise noted, all quotations from Anderson are drawn from Fink and Mathias, *Never Forget,* 145–151.

Post, cutting Schwartz off from a valuable source of intelligence information. Schwartz knew that the emergency response should be managed by a Unified Command team that included their top administrators at the scene. He could see that Unified Command was the only way to ensure that the DOD, FBI, and ACFD actively supported one another's operations and directly addressed any conflicts among themselves.

In the first few hours after the crash, however, the pace of events was too frenetic to allow for a deliberative group process. Hundreds of fire rigs from across the metro area came streaming into the site, along with thousands of firefighters; paramedics; fire and rescue teams; engineers; health and safety inspectors; and representatives from more than one hundred federal, state, and local government agencies, voluntary organizations, and businesses.

Through the first 8 hours, therefore, Schwartz remained in charge as incident commander and slowly built up the emergency response organization. His first step in this process had been to establish the Operations Section after the evacuation. Then, at about 1:00 p.m., Schwartz gave John White, the ACFD assistant chief for technical services, the task of organizing the Logistics Section. This was a challenging assignment. The job of the Logistics Section was to provide all the equipment and support necessary to sustain a large-scale 10-day operation; for example, a later tally showed that in the course of the response effort 187,941 meals were supplied, 100 portable toilets were serviced twice daily, 12 tractor trailer loads of construction materials were brought in for shoring operations, and thousands of gallons of diesel and gasoline were supplied, among other items.

ACFD's size put it at a disadvantage in this area because the department did not have a day-to-day logistics function, as many larger departments did, nor did it have a centralized supply and storage system with a stockpile of supplies to be used in longer-term emergencies. But White knew that the Fairfax County Fire Department had a seasoned logistics officer and team. He lost no time in asking for their help. The next day, the Fairfax logistics officer arrived with his entire team and worked side by side with the ACFD personnel, teaching them how to organize, staff up, and manage a campaign-style Logistics Section for the duration of the incident response.

Analysts later observed that one of the hallmarks of the ACFD's Incident Command organization was its unorthodox policy of inviting fire service commanders from other Virginia communities to play critical leadership roles. For example, in the late morning, Schwartz named Loudon County Fire Chief Jack Brown chief of the Incident Command Planning Section.

As the incident developed, however, Schwartz realized that he needed Brown in yet another capacity—as a special liaison to the team of planners and advisers in an Incident Support Team (IST) that FEMA, at Schwartz's request, had deployed along with four 62-member urban search and rescue (USAR) teams. The IST was not working out of the

Incident Command Post, however, and Schwartz wanted to prevent any breakdown of communication between him and the team. Schwartz believed that Brown (who had once served on the Fairfax USAR team and was familiar with USAR operations) was the best person to serve as a bridge between him and the IST. Schwartz then appointed Tom Owens, the chief of the Fairfax City Fire Department, to replace Brown as chief of the Planning Section. A George Washington University study later praised Schwartz and Plaugher for their expansive and open approach and for using the "best available asset for the task" as their guide rather than the more parochial—and more typical—"ours first" approach.[14]

---

[14]"Observing and Documenting the Inter-Organizational Response." Within the ACFD ranks, however, some were angry that the chiefs had given away plum planning and advisory roles to outsiders.

The 9/11 Pentagon Emergency (B):
The Shift to Unified Command

By early afternoon on September 11, Arlington County Assistant Fire Chief Jim Schwartz could see that the pace of decision making at the Incident Command level was slowing. By the end of the day, he decided, it would be possible to shift the management of the incident from a single incident commander to a Unified Command team. Schwartz himself would be first among equals on the team, however—the lead member of the team with the power to make decisions if the rest of the group could not agree. It was also up to Schwartz to decide which organizations to include.

The most important of these, given the danger of working at cross-purposes, were the Department of Defense (DOD) and Federal Bureau of Investigation (FBI). The obvious person to represent the DOD was Gen. James Jackson, the commanding general of the Military District of Washington and the DOD's liaison to the Pentagon emergency response. The liaison for the FBI's Washington Field Office to local fire departments, Christopher Combs, had arrived at the scene minutes after the crash and was Schwartz's choice to represent the FBI.

In addition, Schwartz wanted to include Arlington County Police Chief Ed Flynn. The police controlled traffic on the surrounding roadways; posted snipers on building tops in the area to protect the crews on-site; guarded all entrances to the Pentagon site; and, in some cases, provided escorts for visitors and suppliers to make sure they reached the appropriate destination within the Pentagon site. In the context of Arlington County government, the police department's role in the response was secondary to the fire department's, but its operations fell outside the scope of the fire department's Incident Command organization.

Schwartz also decided to include in Unified Command the director of the Federal Emergency Management Agency (FEMA) Urban Search and Rescue (USAR) Incident Support Team (IST) and a representative of FEMA's headquarters office in Washington. In truth, the idea of including these FEMA administrators on the team was anathema in orthodox Incident Command System (ICS). The ICS holds that only agencies with a responsibility to manage an activity at the emergency site—independent of the Incident Command organization—should be included. It had long been resolved that the expertise and resources of FEMA were to assist, not displace, the local emergency response. Thus, the USAR teams were supposed to operate under the management of the local operations chief. Likewise, if a high-level FEMA official came to the scene, his or her role was to offer advice to the incident commander, not to shoulder in and take over. To local emergency response agencies, this was a sensitive point. In the past, local officials had complained that—despite this

250

policy—FEMA officials sometimes had, in fact, rolled into town and muscled them aside. Thus, most local officials would have been loathe to turn around and invite these federal administrators to share formally in the management of the incident.

Schwartz, however, thought the presence of the two FEMA administrators would be very useful. The FEMA IST had significant expertise in search and rescue, which would become the sole focus of the 10-day emergency response once the fire was extinguished. In addition, the IST was itself set up as a small, but full-blown, Incident Command organization and could not be easily incorporated into the local Incident Command organization. FEMA had argued that the IST director should simply serve as an adviser to the incident commander. That arrangement was vague, however, and Schwartz believed it would be more efficient to hear the IST director's advice at regular intervals in the context of the Unified Command team and its strategic planning for the response.

The inclusion of an official from FEMA headquarters would be useful in a different way, Schwartz believed. Because the Pentagon attack took place at the edge of the nation's capital, a representative from FEMA headquarters had appeared at the scene almost immediately. Typically, when an incident commander needed federal approval to bring equipment or expertise to an emergency event, he or she asked the local government to ask the state government to ask FEMA to authorize it. The process often took 8–12 hours. But with a representative of FEMA headquarters on hand, Schwartz found he was able to secure things in "8 to 12 *minutes!*" In fact, ACFD's request for the four USAR teams had received immediate approval. "One of the truly remarkable things about the response to the Pentagon was the fact that the bureaucracies didn't get in the way," Schwartz adds. "FEMA didn't say, 'Oh, no no no, don't ask us—go [through channels] to your state.' The state didn't say, 'Don't you dare go to FEMA—ask us first.'"[1]

The FEMA headquarters representative was able to help in another way as well, Schwartz adds. "They had a lot of experience with large-scale incidents," he says. "I'll give you a great example. I never would have thought about how we would meet the nutritional needs of responders on a campaign-style incident. Food—yes. Nutrition—no." Schwartz was accustomed to incidents that lasted a few hours, not a week and a half. Even if the incident lasted as long as 24 hours, he says, "You can get through 24 hours on Power Bars and orange juice. But when you're going to be there for an extended period of time, you really do need to be thinking about how you are going to sustain your people on a nutritional level."

Both in terms of lining up resources and getting useful advice, therefore, Schwartz found that his job was easier when the FEMA official was close at hand. Even if it was unorthodox

---

[1] Interview with Assistant Fire Chief James H. Schwartz, Operations Division, Arlington County Fire Department, and incident commander for the Pentagon 9/11 response, 2003. Unless noted, subsequent quotations from Schwartz are also from this interview.

to ask an official from FEMA headquarters to join the Unified Command team, Schwartz thought it made sense in this situation.

Implementing Unified Command

The All-Agency 6:00 p.m. Meeting

The next issue was how to make the shift to Unified Command actually happen. In theory, this was a simple matter. The authors of ICS had assumed that any agency to be included on the Unified Command team would already be keeping in close touch with the incident commander, or—better yet—would have stationed an agency liaison at the Incident Command Post. But at the Pentagon, this was not true. The agencies were not hostile to the Incident Command effort, but they were preoccupied with concerns of their own and rarely, if ever, checked in with the incident commander. Given this state of affairs, Schwartz conceived the idea of holding a special meeting, in order to corral all the agency representatives and explain his thinking. This approach "should not be the norm," he emphasized. "We should not have to go out and gather up the people to be a part of Unified Command. The mechanism should be there to make it automatic. I had to conduct that meeting because I had to *find* the people."

What's more, Schwartz realized that the vast majority of the emergency workers at the Pentagon were oblivious to ICS and thus were not taking steps to integrate themselves. Schwartz decided to hold a site-wide meeting at 6:00 p.m., gathering more than one hundred people. He made a brief presentation.

I said, "We have been doing a great job for the first 8 hours of this incident. We are going to be here 8 more days. And we cannot continue to operate under the kind of management structure we have—and here's what we're going to do." . . . I spent about 10 minutes explaining what our Incident Command System was, who I was, why I had the authority to do this—why this was essentially our incident. And then I explained to them what Unified Command was, and that that was the system that we were going to go to, and then I identified the players that I wanted as a part of the Unified Command team.

Representatives of the agencies he identified all agreed to participate in the team, though both General Jackson from DOD and Chief Flynn from the Arlington County Police Department sent designees instead of coming themselves.

Modus Operandi

Under the usual ICS arrangement, the Unified Command team was expected to remain at the Incident Command Post round-the-clock. Schwartz knew this idea would meet resistance from the participants, and he, too, thought it unnecessarily burdensome. So, instead, he announced that he would convene Unified Command team meetings every 4 hours, at which time each agency representative would give a brief update, and then the group would discuss decisions that they needed to make jointly.

This proved effective in two respects, Schwartz says. First, it allowed each team member to spend most of his time with the rest of his own agency operation on-site. If Schwartz needed to reach a team member between meetings, "we had communications, we had cell phones, we had radios, we had staff aides that were shadowing each of these principal people around. Communications wasn't a problem." Second, the periodic meetings established de facto deadlines for producing requested information or resolving issues. Schwartz says that he heard back after the fact from one team member that the knowledge of an upcoming meeting made the team feel "somewhat under the gun" to deliver.

Wrecking Ball

One example of the Unified Command team in action came up on the evening of September 11. The rescue teams needed to begin searching for survivors in the collapsed part of the building. Although the hope of finding anyone alive was not great, the best chance was in this area, where someone might have been trapped in an air pocket beneath the debris. This area also posed the greatest risk for responders, however, because an unstable debris pile might turn into a landslide. One expert at the scene thought the only thing to do to ensure the safety of the responders was to bring in a wrecking ball to take down a particularly unstable part of the building. "Well," says Schwartz, "I immediately recognized that if we brought in a wrecking ball and started swinging it against the building—what kind of signal was that going to send to anybody who had hopes there were live victims in there? This was only 12 hours in." Still, Schwartz had to do something about the collapsed area, and he could not subject responders to a landslide risk, "so I had to go tell the FBI and the DOD that this was the way it was looking—and they were as horrified as I had been."

In the end, a member of the FEMA IST saved the day. He knew about a rare excavator that could dismantle a precarious pile of rubble delicately. The IST managed to track one down at a demolition site nearby in Baltimore. That machine "changed things completely," says Schwartz. Without endangering the search and rescue personnel, "we could continue to send some messages of hope."

Chief Plaugher's Role

While Schwartz was embroiled in troubleshooting and developing a workable system for managing all the various players at the Pentagon, ACFD Chief Ed Plaugher played several roles. To Schwartz, he served as a senior adviser; to other government agencies, he represented the ultimate ACFD authority. But the biggest role Plaugher was to play was that of the public face of the emergency response effort. In this, he points out, he was doing what he always did as chief—tending to external relations on behalf of his fire department. But in the case of the Pentagon emergency, the nature of this task was not the usual.

Toward the end of the day on September 11, Plaugher discovered that something important had slipped through the cracks—supplying the media with information about the Pentagon attack and the progress of firefighting and search and rescue operations. Under the 1997 Terrorism Annex to the Federal Response Plan,[2] the FBI was supposed to establish a Joint Information Center (JIC) as an adjunct to its Joint Operations Center (JOC). The JIC was to provide a way for government agencies to give a coordinated and consistent account of the terrorism incident and government's response to it. Belatedly, Plaugher learned that the FBI—concerned about respecting the turf of the DOD press office and stretched thin by the simultaneous demands of the September 11 terrorist attacks—had decided not to create a JIC for the Pentagon incident. However, the DOD press office was focused on the big picture. "Their perspective is not about a hole in the side of their building. Their perspective is about that whole other thing—a nation that was under pretty serious attack," says Plaugher.[3]

Faced with an information void about emergency response, the press relied on unofficial bits and pieces of information, some speculative and some flatly inaccurate. "If we don't fill the information gap, it's going to be filled in [by someone else] and oftentimes we know it's not very positive," Plaugher explains. What's more, Plaugher believed it was important to convey to the public that however appalling the attack on the Pentagon, the situation was now well in-hand. Thus, he arranged with the DOD's General Jackson to conduct a joint news conference with him at 11:00 p.m. on September 11. As Plaugher puts it:

People needed to know what was going on, and they needed to have their comfort level raised. . . . I mean, let's face it. The American public was glued at the TV set and they were not getting any information whatsoever out of New York. They needed to hear that things were on the way to recovery. . . . They needed to see a representative. They needed to feel that the person in charge was there and accessible and answering questions.

After that initial press conference, Arlington County's assistant county manager for public affairs took over the press function, although Plaugher continued to make brief appearances to provide major updates. Plaugher also became the host dignitary who escorted most of the visiting VIPs around the Pentagon site. Well over one hundred people—including the president, vice president, cabinet officials, members of Congress, and state and county luminaries—made a pilgrimage to the Pentagon site in the course of the emergency response.

---

[2]The Federal Response Plan detailed how federal assistance was to be provided to states in a presidentially declared disaster. The Terrorism Annex described additional federal assistance if the disaster was caused by a terrorist attack.

[3]Interview with Fire Chief Edward P. Plaugher, Arlington County Fire Department, 2003. Unless noted, subsequent quotations from Plaugher are also from this interview.

Mixing It Up with the Feds

By the end of the second day of the Pentagon response, the various agencies at the site settled into relationships that analysts later characterized as unusually effective and collegial by comparison to those in other large response efforts. During the first 2 days, however, the ACFD found its mission and protocols in conflict with those of three federal agencies—the DOD, FBI, and U.S. Environmental Protection Agency (EPA). In each case, the ACFD leadership tried to find its way to a compromise that all agencies could live with—with varied results.

The Arlington County Fire Department and the U.S. Department of Defense

Keeping the National Military Command Center Open

Perhaps no relationship was as delicate as the one between the ACFD and the DOD. The DOD, suddenly on high alert to cope with an attack on U.S. soil, was glad to have the local fire department rush in with all its reinforcements to put out the Pentagon fire and rescue Pentagon workers. But during the first day especially, the DOD leadership was quite resistant to being told what it could and could not do in its own building.

When American Airlines Flight #77 crashed into the Pentagon, almost everyone in the building was evacuated; but Secretary of Defense Donald Rumsfeld ordered the staff in the most secure area inside the building—the National Military Command Center (NMCC)—to remain in place. The NMCC was the highly sensitive communications intermediary between the joint chiefs of staff; the National Command Authority (which made decisions about deploying nuclear weapons); and critical worldwide information sources, weapons systems, missile warning systems, and so on.

The center, where some three hundred people worked, had not suffered any direct damage in the blast, but it was uncomfortably close to the fire. To the ACFD, it was unsafe and imprudent to keep the NMCC up and running, with the fire out of control and spreading. When ACFD Chief Plaugher discovered that the center had not evacuated, he met with a high-level DOD representative to discuss the matter. "I said, 'Your building is on fire,'" recalls Plaugher. "I told them to leave the National Command center, and they said, 'No, we're not leaving.'" Plaugher tried to persuade them with several arguments. For example, he explained the dangers of carbon monoxide poisoning, noting that "the first thing carbon monoxide does is to make you do wacky things." Surely, he suggested, it was not a good idea to take the risk that the NMCC staff, in their sensitive position, might be working in an unreliable state of mind? The DOD leadership remained adamant, however, and Plaugher realized that he was not going to win this argument. "I'm doing this negotiation with a guy who's wearing a .45 on his arm, and he's got F-15's flying overhead. What am I supposed to do?" he laughs. "And," he adds, "I fully acquiesced to the need, the critical need, of the National Command Center during that time."

So, in the end, the ACFD and the DOD crafted a compromise of sorts. The ACFD gave the command center twenty-five sets of breathing apparatus and a monitor to keep tabs on the carbon monoxide levels. But beyond that, Plaugher said, the command center staff would have to take responsibility for its own safety. "I've got 400,000 square feet of building actively on fire," he says. "I can't now also worry about these people from the National Command Center." That recollection notwithstanding, the ACFD may have taken a softer stance over the next few hours. When informed that smoke was seeping into the center, the ACFD did send two companies of firefighters into the building with hoses. Luckily, the fire was not as close to the center as feared. The problem was that the NMCC's ventilation system was pulling in smoke and hot air from the direction of the fire, and to the relief of all concerned, NMCC personnel were able to reconfigure the ventilation system to bring cooler air in and keep the smoke out.[4]

A Symbolic Return on September 12

A second point of contention with the DOD occurred on the afternoon of September 11, when Rumsfeld announced his intention to open the Pentagon for business the next day, September 12, even though the search and rescue effort was in full swing, an unknown number of dead bodies was still inside the building, and the roof was still on fire. As the *Washington Post* reported, "For the nation's military establishment, it was a deliberate, even defiant statement that Tuesday's terror attack had not brought the Pentagon to its knees."[5]

Plaugher readily grasped the symbolic importance of the gesture, but nonetheless tried to persuade the secretary of defense against it. From a fire safety perspective, it was not considered wise to have the utilities turned back on in parts of the building while the roof was on fire and a large volume of water was being sprayed there. In addition, the crash and fire were emitting potentially dangerous toxins into the building's air supply. Finally, to have thousands of workers coming and going from the Pentagon complicated the task of controlling and securing the site, and threatened to impede the emergency response.

Once again, Plaugher realized this was not an argument the ACFD was going to win. But the DOD did agree to air-quality monitoring, barriers between the occupied and unoccupied sections of the complex, and a system for moving workers in and out of the Pentagon without interfering with the emergency response or compromising site security. The responsibility for implementing a compromise acceptable to ACFD fell to John Jester, the director of the Pentagon's internal police force, the Defense Protective Service. Jester and Plaugher knew one another well and their agencies had exercised together in the past, a factor that the chief considers important to the amicable resolution of the issue. "What made the whole thing do-able was the fact that we knew each other, we had trust and confidence in each other," Plaugher says.

---

[4]Drawn from Mitchell Fink and Lois Mathias, *Never Forget: An Oral History of September 11, 2001* (New York: HarperCollins, 2002), 145–151.

[5]Steve Vogel, "Defiant Workers Return to Posts at the Pentagon," *Washington Post*, September 13, 2001, A 15.

Sensitive Materials

A third area of conflict between ACFD and DOD concerned dozens of requests, beginning the second day of the response, from people who had worked in the areas damaged in the crash to return to their damaged offices and retrieve certain items. These were sometimes matters of national security, sometimes sensitive budget documents, and sometimes personal effects.

Such requests required the ACFD to figure out whether the office could be reached safely, given the building's structural instability in and around the crash site. It also required escort arrangements. And—because the Pentagon was also a crime scene—an FBI representative had to be part of the escort team to ensure that no evidence was compromised. Schwartz wanted the practice limited to the most urgent cases. At the same time, he readily acknowledged that neither the ACFD nor the FBI could judge the urgency or merits of the requests.

A compromise solution was developed by the Unified Command team working with the FBI's JOC. The JOC would create a special team to evaluate each request, and one member of this team—an ACFD liaison—would provide information about the safety of retrieving items from the office in question. If the office was deemed safe, the rest of the team would decide whether the request was persuasive enough to merit action. If the request was approved, the Incident Command staff would schedule the visit for the next work shift.

On Balance, a Show of Military Restraint

Notwithstanding these conflicts, analysts writing after the fact noted that the DOD could easily have been more high-handed in its dealings with the ACFD and praised the restraint shown by the military leadership. The study by George Washington University gave high points to General Jackson, in particular. When Schwartz addressed the agencies at the Pentagon at his 6:00 p.m. meeting on September 11, Jackson made a point of telling him he would support him fully. True to his word, Jackson made between five hundred and seven hundred soldiers available each day to the incident commander, in addition to specialized equipment. He also kept military leaders apprised of the status of the fire and rescue work, conveying between the lines that the ACFD had the situation well in hand.

The Arlington County Fire Department and the Federal Bureau of Investigation: Who's at the Hub of the Wheel?

The relationship between the ACFD and the FBI on September 11 began extremely well. Moments after Schwartz arrived at the Pentagon, Special Agent Christopher Combs, liaison to metro-area fire departments for the FBI's National Capital Response Squad, also arrived. A former New York firefighter, Combs had proposed and developed the FBI's fire department liaison program himself. Through this program, he and Schwartz had worked together and had established a relationship of trust and respect well before the Pentagon was attacked.

Combs stayed at the Incident Command Post for the first 3 hours of the emergency response, providing Schwartz with detailed, timely intelligence information. For example, when United Airlines Flight #93 was hijacked and was heading toward Washington D.C., "Chris was standing next to me giving me a countdown," Schwartz recalls. "He was telling me how much time we had, based on their calculations." When the FBI Evidence Recovery Team arrived at the Pentagon minutes after the crash, Schwartz assigned an ACFD fire-fighter to serve as their liaison, keeping the team informed about the status of the firefight-ing effort and also providing the group with useful site information. This kind of mutual cooperation might have been considered positive but unremarkable were it not for the fact that, by reputation, relationships between the FBI and local public safety agencies tended to be hostile and competitive. Schwartz and Combs were united, however, in believing that such dynamics were unnecessary and counterproductive.

At about 1:00 p.m., however, the FBI's on-site commander assigned Combs to serve as his own adviser, and the two proceeded to relocate the FBI's command center to the nearby Virginia State Police Barracks, where they had more room. But the FBI did not assign any-one to replace Combs at the Incident Command Post. On a day of unprecedented terrorist attacks, with rumors flying wild, Schwartz was unhappy to lose his ready access to reliable intelligence information.

The consequences of losing the FBI presence were apparent almost immediately. At 2:00 p.m., Schwartz received word from the control tower at Ronald Reagan Washington Na-tional Airport that an "unidentified aircraft" was headed their way. Schwartz thought he had understood that all air traffic had been grounded, but the airport control tower was cer-tainly a reputable source. With no idea how far away the plane was, Schwartz ordered all responders to evacuate the site immediately, decamping once again to the safety of the high-way underpass. But deciding to evacuate firefighters from the Pentagon building was costly in terms of their energy and morale. During the evacuation, the fire inside the Pentagon spread back into areas where it had just been extinguished, so that when the firefighters re-turned to the building, they had lost ground. And the evacuation order required the fire-fighters to run several hundred yards to the highway underpass wearing hot and bulky fire protection gear, which was exhausting. Shortly thereafter, Schwartz learned that the plane was, in fact, friendly, and was shepherding Attorney General John Ashcroft to the site. Schwartz was extremely frustrated by this episode, but he hoped the communication prob-lem would be remedied when he established his Unified Command team (which would in-clude Combs as the FBI representative).[6]

---

[6]The next day at 10:00 a.m., the scenario repeated itself, however. The control tower reported another uniden-tified aircraft heading toward Washington, D.C., and, once again, Schwartz felt he had to call for an evacuation. This time, the friendly plane was bringing FEMA Director Joseph Allbaugh to the site.

The FBI, meanwhile, was quite focused on setting up its JOC. The JOC had been conceived as part of the 1997 Terrorism Incident Annex to the Federal Response Plan. It had been activated for planned events but never for an emergency situation. The mission of the JOC was to coordinate high-level representatives of selected federal, state, and local agencies with a role in responding to actual or threatened terrorist acts. But even though he had sat in on FBI briefings about the JOC about a year previous, it had never been clear to Schwartz exactly how the JOC would operate or how it would interact with local ICS. Schwartz believed ICS and the JOC should operate independently but maintain good communication by exchanging high-level liaisons. Thus, in his view, an FBI liaison would be stationed at the Incident Command Post, and an ACFD liaison would participate in the JOC.

As the JOC began to take shape, however, it became clear that the FBI had a different idea in mind. To the FBI, the JOC was to be the center of gravity for all government response to the Pentagon attack and to the threat of subsequent attacks in the Washington area. What's more, the FBI wanted Schwartz to participate on the JOC Command Team. The JOC Command Team would not play any oversight role with respect to the local emergency response, but Schwartz's membership on the team would necessitate the relocation of his Incident Command Post to the JOC facility, located 2 miles from the Pentagon at Ft. Myer.

The FBI expectations placed Schwartz in an awkward position. He wanted to be cooperative with the FBI, and he had to admit that, in theory, the Incident Command Post did not have to be located at the incident site. After all, its responsibilities were at the strategic planning level, not the tactical level. "For the sake of the relationship and keeping things well-oiled, I agreed to it," he says. But after just a few hours, Schwartz realized that the arrangement was not working.

First, the location did prove problematic after all. Several members of the Unified Command team indicated to Schwartz that they could not afford the time to travel to Ft. Myer for meetings every 4 hours. What's more, as incident commander, Schwartz had a host of pressing responsibilities, yet was expected to attend JOC Command Team meetings that neither helped him to fulfill these responsibilities nor benefited from his expertise. For example, the JOC team met on the morning of September 12 to listen to a concern of the medical examiner from the state of Virginia. Under law, her department had responsibility for examining the remains of the dead in the Pentagon; in this case, the FBI wanted to conduct those investigations itself. The Virginia medical examiner did not object, but insisted that the federal attorney general send a letter to that effect to the Virginia state attorney general. "Perfectly reasonable conversation. Perfectly understandable need to have that conversation," says Schwartz. "Other than telling me what the decision is, I had *no* reason to be at that meeting. That's not what my role should be."

After 24 hours, Schwartz had had enough. He decided to leave the JOC and reestablish his Incident Command Post at its previous location, adjacent to the Pentagon. "What I said to them was, 'This isn't working. I'm taking the Unified Command team out of here, and I want the FBI representative to come with me down to the [Pentagon],'" he says. "They gave me about five minutes of argument," but then agreed to let Schwartz go and to send Combs with him. Schwartz, in turn, assigned Assistant Chief White to represent the ACFD and the Incident Command organization at the JOC.[7]

At the Pentagon site, he adds, the FBI and the ACFD were able to carve out a very cooperative arrangement. By the afternoon of September 12, the fire at the Pentagon had been extinguished, and the firefighters, search and rescue teams, and FBI evidence teams were working together inside the Pentagon. They adopted some cooperative measures that the FBI had developed when working with FEMA USAR teams after the 1998 terrorist bombing of U.S. embassies in Kenya and Tanzania. As Schwartz says:

Very early on, we got the system established where, if a firefighter or rescue technician saw evidence—and that was mostly human remains—they took a yellow flag and they stuck it down in that area. . . . At a certain point, when the incident became more manageable, we'd bring the evidence technicians in [when we found evidence]. They would do their work, they'd give the all clear, and the rescue technicians would go back to work. It was very coordinated. It came from an understanding of what their needs were, and how our needs could take a break, or stand to the sidelines for a few minutes—because again, the situation was more stable.

Analysts later praised ACFD for its flexibility because, by rights, it could have insisted that the FBI Evidence Recovery Team stay out of the Pentagon building altogether until the search and rescue phase of the operation was complete.

The Arlington County Fire Department and the Environmental Protection Agency: Who Decides What's Safe?

An aircraft explosion, fire, and structural collapse in a 60-year-old, recently renovated building was bound to release dangerous contaminants into the air, water, and debris in and around the building. Immediately after the crash, the regional office of the EPA began 24-hour operations at the Pentagon, sending a team of coordinators and inspectors to conduct numerous tests and set standards for the safety of firefighters and search teams, Pentagon employees working in undamaged sections of the building, and nearby residents.

The EPA was not the only agency at the Pentagon with this responsibility. More than twenty environmental, hazardous material, and health and safety agencies—federal, state, and county—appeared at the Pentagon to address safety concerns of one type or another.

---

[7]Schwartz notes that, in the aftermath of the Pentagon incident, the FBI redefined the JOC's role to cover "crime specific" aspects of the incident, coordinating with the Incident Command or Unified Command of the emergency response as necessary and useful to both operations.

Among them, there was a great deal of overlap—and inconsistency—in their assessments of contamination and health risk. For Schwartz and his safety officer, Captain Robert Swarthout, this swiftly became a management headache, and in an effort to better coordinate the environmental work, Swarthout began to bring the groups together. Schwartz, in turn, decided to turn the fledgling environmental safety group into a new ICS section led by Swarthout. The task of the section was to develop a single comprehensive safety plan for the Pentagon site for the duration of the emergency response. This plan was ultimately integrated into the Incident Action Plan and approved by the Unified Command team.

To cope with conflicting appraisals of the contamination, Schwartz asked the EPA to analyze the data and make a single report with recommendations. For emergency responders inside the Pentagon, the EPA concluded that it was necessary to wear respirators and protective Tyvek suits at all times. Part of this assessment struck Schwartz as unnecessarily strict. Although he had no problem with responders having to use respirators, he balked at the requirement that all responders wear Tyvek suits all the time. "It was September—it was warm. That was like zipping people up in baggies. It was going to significantly reduce the ability of the responders and rescue technicians to work for extended periods of time," he says. "Their answer was, shorten the work periods." But to Schwartz, this was not reasonable. He said to them, "We are still hoping to find live victims in here. It's a life safety situation—it's a rescue situation—and we don't operate the same way you do when you're at an EPA waste cleanup site."

The EPA argued back that the issue was not only the immediate protection of the responders, although that was part of it. If they did not wear Tyvek suits that they could remove at shift's end and leave at the site, they might end up carrying contaminants out of the site to their homes, cars, and other areas. Schwartz countered that the ACFD's decontamination procedure already provided adequate safeguards against exporting contaminants. At the end of each shift, every emergency worker headed for a decontamination tent, dumped his or her clothes in a laundry pile, took a shower on site, and dressed in clean clothes brought from home. A commercial laundry washed the contaminated clothes after each shift. The EPA was never entirely sanguine about this, but Schwartz's decision stuck.

Worries about Site Security

In addition to tricky relationships with federal agencies, Schwartz and Plaugher had to contend with concerns over the security of the Pentagon site. By mid-afternoon on September 11, about 3,000 people were on the Pentagon grounds. Most were affiliated with government agencies or charitable organizations. But some were volunteer-hopefuls, souvenir-hunters, and "weird people who just like to be around critical incidents," says Arlington

County Police Chief Ed Flynn.[8] Arlington County police guarded all the vehicular entrances to the Pentagon site, but they wanted to facilitate (not obstruct) the emergency response. Especially in the early hours of the emergency, the police tried to keep order, prevent traffic jams, and wave the responders into the site as quickly as possible.

In the process, some people who entered the site did not belong there. "The first day or two, there was really no way to limit access to the grounds because there was no way of identifying who belonged and who didn't," Flynn says. For example, not only were uniformed firefighters entering the site, but so were plainclothes construction workers, who had been renovating the Pentagon "and were in the position of providing important rescue equipment or operating heavy machinery and things of that nature." In addition, people flashed all kinds of identification cards, and the police had no way to assess their legitimacy, Flynn adds. "We tried to be on our guard, but it was a rough cut, no doubt about that."

On the one hand, these decisions made sense to Schwartz; no one wanted to see an emergency response bog down in bureaucratic red tape when lives were hanging in the balance. But the situation also made him exceedingly uncomfortable. After all, at the heart of this incident was a terrorist attack. "If you were a bad guy and wanted to get in, it wouldn't be too hard to come up with a uniform that looks semi-official and walk right through," says Schwartz. Once they were in the throes of an emergency, however, it was not possible to devise a quick workable identification system—that was something that emergency planners had to develop in advance.[9]

So Schwartz faced the unenviable job of trying to improve site security despite the lack of a well-designed identification system and despite the fact that scores of people who did not belong on the Pentagon grounds had already entered. Still, he reasoned, people did not come to the Pentagon site and remain there for days on end; they came and went. To create some kind of check-in procedure, therefore—even 24 hours after the plane crash—was still worth doing. Schwartz began to discuss the idea of creating a badge for site entrance with the ACPD and the FBI. In the police command van, someone discovered a cache of wrist bands, which they began using as a "very first rough credential to get on the site." But the Secret Service later arrived with a better solution—a machine that could make ID cards on the spot—and on the second day of the response, the badging operation began in earnest.

---

[8] Interview with Chief Edward Flynn, Arlington County Police Department, 2003. Unless noted, subsequent quotations from Flynn are also from this interview.

[9] For example, the communities in the northern Virginia mutual aid area—Arlington, Alexandria, Fairfax, Ft. Belvoir, and the airports—had joined together in a single, seamless identification program. "We have a very robust and well-managed accountability system," Schwartz says. "You go to an incident in any of those jurisdictions, and I can hand you my tag, and you can hand me your tag, and it all works, because it's the same system, the same procedure." But that particular system was of no use at the Pentagon, Schwartz adds, because it was "bounded by the organizations that we deal with on a regular basis."

Under this system, managed by the FBI, each applicant was required to produce identification and to explain why he or she wanted to enter the site. The FBI also kept a list of all the people who had received a badge, along with their affiliation.

Once the system was up and running, Schwartz gave the matter little thought until his aide came into the Incident Command Post and said, "You've got to see the line at the ID tent!" Schwartz's reply was "What are you talking about? He said, 'It snakes all through the parking lot. It's unbelievable.' And I said, 'Who's in it?' And he said, 'I have no idea.'" Schwartz left the Command Post and headed over to the badging area. "I started walking the line and saying, 'Who are you and why are you here?'" If they did not have a good answer, in Schwartz's view, he thanked them for their support and sent them home.

One of my key indicators was, did you come here with an organization or did you come here on your own? A lot of them came on their own. We had volunteer firefighters from 20 miles away who'd say, on the 12th, "What the heck—let's get in the car and drive up there and see what we can do." Honorable—I love their motives. But I didn't want to take on that additional responsibility.

Notwithstanding Schwartz's brief effort to thin out the ranks of people in line, the FBI did not weed out many applicants. Schwartz recalls that later in the day, "The FBI came to me and they said, 'we have good news and we have bad news. The good news is everybody's badged. The bad news is we have issued *8,000 badges*.'" Schwartz laughs. "So we didn't accomplish anything in terms of the security we were trying to achieve."

In the long run, he argues, a more rigorous and sophisticated system was needed. ("We used driver's licenses for identification in order to get a badge. Well, the terrorists *had* those!") In the short term, Schwartz worked with the FBI to revise the badging operation at the Pentagon as best they could. First, a group of firefighters culled through the list of people with badges "and got rid of a bunch of people we didn't think needed to be there," he says. The problem, of course, was that by this time these nonessential people already had been issued badges. But Schwartz and the FBI agreed to create another badge in a different color (red) that would allow entry into a newly designated inner perimeter. Although the red badges did reduce the number of people in the critical areas of the site, they also proved generally unpopular, according to the *Arlington County After-Action Report,* because the system was cumbersome and time-consuming.

Freelancers and Cowboys

Also in the early afternoon of September 11, Schwartz began to tackle yet another problem. There were, by this point, several hundred fire rigs at the Pentagon and close to 2,000 firefighters. Schwartz knew how many firefighters had come from Arlington County and from Arlington's northern Virginia mutual aid partners, but hundreds of additional engines, ladder trucks, rescue units, and ambulances from across the broader metropolitan area had also converged on the scene.

To exercise effective command, Schwartz had to find out who was out there. For one thing, he had to try to bring those resources into ICS, that is, under the management control of his operations chief. For another, he had to learn which resources were already at the Pentagon before he could make intelligent requests for additional resources. Thus, about 2 hours after the crash, Schwartz decided to take inventory. As they had been all morning, radio communications were unreliable because the radio waves were overwhelmed with traffic, so Schwartz asked one of his captains to send two firefighters out to jog around the Pentagon site and write down who was there and with what equipment.

In an ideal world, an incident commander should not have had to do this. In theory, the incident commander tells the emergency dispatcher what complement of firefighters and equipment he or she needs, and the dispatcher calls in the closest available units. If a fire crew hears of a nearby emergency, it can "self-dispatch" in the interests of a timely arrival, but en route it is supposed to check in with the dispatcher from the host jurisdiction and then respect the dispatcher's order to proceed to the scene, wait at a staging area, or return home. When a crew did arrive at the scene, it was supposed to report to the Incident Command liaison or to an operations staging area for further instructions

"Now, I will grant you, on an incident as large as the Pentagon, people are not really paying attention to that. They're not checking in, in the early stages," says Schwartz. And, in the first hour or so after the crash, that made sense, he adds. ACFD did benefit from the overwhelming response from fire departments across the region. "It's a very big scene, our resources were outstripped for the scale of the incident, so it's not the first thing everybody's thinking about. It's a rule that gets in the way of practical application—of doing something to help people."

Nonetheless, some departments were scrupulous about following the Incident Command protocols from the beginning. Minutes after the crash, Arlington County's emergency dispatchers had asked Fairfax County and Alexandria to each deploy "one alarm"—a complement of four engines, two ladder trucks, one rescue unit, four emergency medical service (EMS) units, and a command officer—and hold it at a prescribed staging area, awaiting further instructions. They both did exactly as asked. What's more, most of the firefighting crews that had self-dispatched to the Pentagon did check in with the Incident Command Post at some point over the course of the first day. And when Attorney General Ashcroft's plane was reported to Schwartz as an unidentified plane, forcing a precautionary evacuation, Schwartz and his commanders took this opportunity to collar the fire crews and bring them into ICS.

Plaugher, Schwartz, and two after-the-fact analyses of the event all reported that one fire department consistently flouted Arlington County's Incident Command, however—the

Washington, D.C., Fire Department (although both Plaugher and Schwartz were quick to say that the problems were with the D.C. leadership, not with the rank and file firefighters, for whom they had warm praise). At the same time that Arlington County's emergency dispatcher asked the Fairfax County and Alexandria fire departments to bring one alarm apiece to a staging area and wait there, he made the same request of the Washington, D.C., Fire Department. The D.C. fire department dispatched three alarms, which all proceeded directly to the scene. "They didn't even miss a gear—they came right over the bridge," recounts Plaugher. What's more, in order to make sure that Washington, D.C., itself was still adequately protected, D.C. activated its own mutual aid agreement, unbeknown to Arlington County, and brought some Maryland trucks and firefighters as part of its third alarm to the Pentagon. Schwartz recalls doing a double take as he walked through the Pentagon's South Parking Lot on the evening of September 11: "I remember this so vividly. Here comes a [fire] truck from *Greenville, Maryland*. And I remember looking at it and saying, to no one in particular, 'Greenville? How did they get here?' And a chief from D.C. said, 'Oh, they were part of our third alarm.' And I looked over at him and I said, '*What* third alarm? We never called for a *second* alarm from you!'"

What's more, even after the initial chaotic phase of the response was over, most of the command-level officers from D.C. never worked in concert with the Operations Section. In fact, in a later article for *Firehouse Magazine*, Washington, D.C., Deputy Chief Michael Smith wrote that the D.C. fire department had established its own command post at the Pentagon site.[10] Schwartz (who had not known about D.C.'s rival command post until he read the article) says that, as a practical matter, the parallel command operation did not undermine Arlington's command because, for the most part, individual D.C. firefighters and tactical units "cooperated with our division leaders and our branch directors in a very cohesive, coordinated fashion."

Plaugher concurs but is nonetheless angry because he believes the action demonstrated a "total lack of respect for our command and control. . . . They think they've got to come over and put our fire out because they're the fire dogs of the region." This view was only bolstered when D.C.'s Smith, in a later *Firehouse Magazine* column, remarked, "Much has been written about Arlington's 40 firefighters accomplishing feats of inhuman strength and skill at the Pentagon. I'm just glad the 200 D.C. fire department firefighters, paramedics and chiefs were able to assist."[11]

One consulting firm later recommended that, in the future, any fire department at a major incident that did not participate in ICS be ordered to leave the site. Plaugher agrees with

---

[10]"DC Crews Dispatched to the Pentagon," *Firehouse Magazine*, November 2002.
[11]"Terrorism & the First Responder," *Firehouse Magazine*, December 2002.

this idea in theory, but believes it would have been unrealistic at the Pentagon. Given the skepticism with which the Washington, D.C., Fire Department and its suburban counterparts had traditionally viewed one another, such a move would have been politically inflammatory and might have created bad feeling for years to come. "I've got 400,000 square feet of a building that's on fire, and I'm going to order firefighters away?" he asks. "How could I do that?"

Repercussions

Within the fire service profession, firefighters that self-dispatched and otherwise worked outside ICS were known as freelancers and cowboys, and were a much-discussed problem. At the Pentagon, the freelancers and cowboys created safety problems and a legacy of bitter feelings for many months afterward. For example, some freelance units were quite poorly managed, and because the damaged area of the Pentagon was large, hot, and confusing, some of these firefighters became lost and separated from their crews. Thus, explains Plaugher,

We had units encountering other units, "Where did you come from? How did you get in here?" We had [lone] firefighters roaming around inside this oven that was baking. It was like, "Well, where's your crew?" They didn't have a clue where their crew was. They didn't have a clue where anything was. You can't run an emergency operation like that. They then jeopardized the sanctity of the entire system. Because if they'd gone down because they ran out of air, because they got themselves into trouble, we would have had to take resources and put them in harm's way to get them.

In addition, had there been a second attack on the Pentagon or another building collapse, Schwartz and his Operations Section would not have known how many firefighters were inside or where they were, thus reducing the chance of a successful rescue.

Rewards to the Rogues

Nor was safety the only issue. By self-dispatching to the scene, freelance rigs effectively displaced other crews that, arguably, had a greater claim to be there, for example, Arlington County's off-duty firefighters. As Schwartz explains,

Look, everybody wants to go to the dance. These are not people that live their lives sitting on their hands. We understand both the moral and the practical imperative, and the desire. Everybody wants to go do good. But the reality is, we had far more resources at the Pentagon than we needed to handle that incident.

I had a whole cadre of my off-duty folks who came in to fire stations all across the county and watched this incident on television, champing at the bit to get down there: "Damn it, this is where I work! . . . That's my fire, that's my incident. How come I don't get to go?" And the simple answer was, I wouldn't let them come because I didn't need more than was [already] out there.

ACFD had to cope with the ramifications of this situation for many months to come, he adds. In the aftermath of the Pentagon emergency, Schwartz says, there were two groups of people in the Arlington County Fire Department suffering from stress: those who had gone to the Pentagon during the first 2 days and witnessed a scene of horrific carnage and those who had not gone to the Pentagon until after the firefight was over. The reaction from Arlington County's disciplined northern Virginia colleagues was similar. As requested, they were standing by, waiting to be called to the scene, while hundreds of other firefighters drove right in. Says Plaugher, "I left my mutual aid partners that I work with every day waiting in the wings, which is not a good thing. It has really made relationships difficult. What the individual firefighters said was, 'Well, we should have just freelanced and did what D.C. did, and we could have gone to the biggest fire in the history of the region. So we got punished because we were disciplined.'"

Sense and Sensibility

The conflict between the gung-ho determination of firefighters to be part of the Pentagon response and the more considered rules of ICS came up in another context as well—firefighters who refused to go home after their 12-hour shift was up. Buses were provided to take them back to their own cars, but "the number of them that got in their personal cars and then drove back up 395 into South Parking at the Pentagon and went back to work for another 12 hours was—I can't even calculate how many there were. They just weren't going to give up," says Schwartz.

The assistant chief notes that he himself did not take a real break and go home—even though he lived near the Pentagon—for 2.5 days. "It was lunacy, in retrospect," he says. "I would probably advocate establishing a mechanism to relieve an Incident Commander, on this kind of an incident, probably after the first four or six hours, and send them home, and not let them come back until the following day. Because it is so intense—there is so much decision making going on." At the same time, when asked how he would have reacted if someone had tried to send him home after 4 or 6 hours, he concedes, "I probably would have chased them away." The stakes of being there, or not being there, were particularly high in the case of the Pentagon, Schwartz explains. "There'll always be another house fire, there'll always be another apartment fire, but this was the event of a lifetime. At least," he adds, "we're hoping it was the event of a lifetime."

The Keys to Success

In the end, the emergency response at the Pentagon and the role of the ACFD in managing that response were both judged a success. Not perfect, but compared to other large-scale, multiagency incidents, considerably better than average. As the assessment commissioned by Arlington County concluded,

It is clear that, at the time of the Pentagon attack, the state of preparedness of the ACFD was very high. There were no fatalities or serious injuries among the responders. The fire was contained and controlled relatively quickly. The collapse potential was recognized early and precautions were taken. Individuals from different organizations were able to work together effectively as ad hoc team members. . . .[12]

To Schwartz, Plaugher, and Police Chief Flynn, the emergency response went as well as it did primarily because of three things: (1) the familiarity of the ACFD and its northern Virginia mutual aid partners with ICS, the result of years of practicing the ICS approach at every emergency incident; (2) the limited number of local jurisdictions in the Washington, D.C., area; and (3) the trust that grew from the preestablished relationships between the ACFD and other agencies, federal, state, and local.

Practice, Practice, Practice

As Schwartz explains, "As long as we've been doing Incident Command, we've done it with the recognition that if we didn't do it every day on everything we go to, we would never do it for the *big one*. Or we'd never do it *well* for the big one." One of the reasons the ICS approach requires practice, he continues, is that it takes fire service commanders up and down the chain of command some time to operate at the appropriate level. "We all love to crawl down smoky holes," says Schwartz. That is where firefighters began their training and careers. "It's where we're comfortable." But ICS requires section leaders and, especially, the incident commander to operate at a more strategic level, and that takes getting used to. "If I [as incident commander] get down there and figure out where those hose lines ought to go, and how long they ought to be, and how big they ought to be, and how many people ought to be on them, I'm missing something else up here at the strategy level," Schwartz says.

In addition, experience with ICS gives a commander the confidence to use the system in a flexible way, Schwartz says. In fact, Schwartz did a number of unorthodox things in the course of developing the Incident Command organization: he appointed people from other fire departments to leadership positions, he appointed two FEMA administrators to the Unified Command team, he allowed the team to disperse between meetings, he created a new section to address health and safety concerns, and he was willing to try moving the Incident Command Post to the FBI's JOC site and was not afraid to call the experiment a failure after 24 hours and take the Incident Command Post back to the incident site. "One of

---

[12] *Arlington County After-Action Report on the Response to the September 11 Terrorist Attack on the Pentagon*, Titan Systems Corporation, July 2002, A73–A74.

the interesting things about an experience like this is that there is so much you *can't* prepare for," says Schwartz. "To be able to manage an incident like this—to be in the position of an Incident Commander—you have to be experienced," but, he adds, part of the reason the experience is so important is so the incident commander has the confidence to depart from the boilerplate organization chart.

A Small Number of Large Jurisdictions

Flynn notes that unlike many large cities across the country, emergency services outside Washington, D.C., are provided by a few large, relatively well-financed counties and not by dozens of small cities and towns. "If you draw a circle with a radius of 15 miles outside of Washington, D.C., you're going to encompass about six or eight significant jurisdictions. County government is strong in Maryland and Northern Virginia. But if you drew that same circle around Boston, you'd have 75 cities!" he says. That, of course, means the difference between coordinating among eight fire chiefs and seventy-five in a regional emergency. "Having an Incident Command template was a wonderful help, but it would be harder to replicate in Boston, or suburban New York City, or suburban Philadelphia, or suburban Chicago. All those communities have such a premium on town government. You would be trying to coordinate, in some cases, hundreds of agencies."

Relationships and Trust

Schwartz, Plaugher, and Flynn agree that there were many points during the Pentagon emergency response where things went especially well due to previously established relationships across agency lines. Such relationships gave commanders in all agencies the comfort of knowing about one another's strengths and weaknesses, and, in cases where respect and friendship had blossomed, a secure foundation of trust. As Flynn puts it:

I mean, let's face it. You are *exposed* in these situations. You're not going to make the perfect decision every single time. So you need colleagues who will say, "I'm willing to do that, but if we do that, this will happen,"—as opposed to just doing it and then saying, "I told you so," to a reporter someday. You need to know and trust each other so you can talk to each other frankly in a crisis without worrying about having to repair relations later.

Over a number of years, the ACFD had sought out opportunities to forge such relationships with other fire departments and other emergency response agencies. The department had trained and exercised with many other organizations.

In addition, Plaugher had involved the department in terrorism preparedness work back in 1996, in the aftermath of the March 1995 sarin nerve agent attack in a Tokyo subway that killed twelve and injured hundreds. With the U.S. Public Health Service and a host of other agencies, Plaugher and the ACFD worked on developing the nation's first locally based terrorism response team, focused on chemical and biological attacks. Although he had no notion of it at the time, he now believes the planning work was probably more important for the relationships it forged than for the plan itself:

What we set out to build is not what we built. We were building a network, we were building a system, we were building friendships. When the plane flew into the side of the Pentagon—it was not chemical, it was not biological—it wasn't any of those things we had prepared for. It ended up being a building collapse and a building fire. But what *managed* the Pentagon was those relationships—was a system we didn't even know we were growing.

Key Actors in the 9/11 Pentagon Emergency

Arlington County, Virginia, Officials

James H. Schwartz, assistant fire chief, Operations Division, Arlington County Fire Department, and incident commander for the Pentagon 9/11 response

Edward P. Plaugher, fire chief, Arlington County Fire Department (ACFD)

Edward Flynn, chief, Arlington County Police Department (ACPD)

Bob Cornwell, battalion chief, Arlington County Fire Department

Randy Gray, battalion chief, Arlington County Fire Department, and chief of the Operations Section, Pentagon 9/11 Incident Command

John White, assistant fire chief, Technical Services Division, Arlington County Fire Department; chief of the Logistics Section, Pentagon 9/11 Incident Command; and liaison for Incident Command to the FBI's Joint Operations Center (JOC)

Robert Swarthout, captain and safety officer, Arlington County Fire Department

Federal Officials

Christopher Combs, special agent and liaison for the National Capital Response Squad, Federal Bureau of Investigation (FBI)

Donald H. Rumsfeld, secretary of defense

John Jester, director, Defense Protective Service, Department of Defense

Joseph M. Allbaugh, director, Federal Emergency Management Agency (FEMA)

John D. Ashcroft, attorney general

U.S. Military

Gen. James T. Jackson, commanding general, Military District of Washington, and Department of Defense liaison for the 9/11 Pentagon fires

Lt. Col. Ted Anderson, U.S. Army

Other Officials

Jack Brown, fire chief, Loudon County Fire Department; original chief of the Planning Section, Pentagon 9/11 Incident Command; and later special liaison for Incident Command to FEMA's Incident Support Team

Tom Owens, chief, Fairfax City Fire Department, and chief of the Planning Section, Pentagon 9/11 Incident Command (following Brown's reassignment)

Michael Smith, deputy chief, District of Columbia Fire Department

Pentagon Fires, September 11, 2001

Chronology of Events

Tuesday, September 11

8:10 a.m.: American Airlines Flight #77, departing Washington, D.C., Dulles International Airport for Los Angeles, is hijacked by terrorists and redirected back toward Washington.

9:38 a.m.: Radio dispatch announces a plane crash at the Pentagon. Jim Schwartz, assistant chief for Operations, Arlington County Fire Department (ACFD), races to the Pentagon and assumes command of the emerging response to the fire there.

10:00 a.m.: ACFD Chief Edward Plaugher arrives at the Pentagon. Schwartz offers to turn command over to him, but Plaugher declines, noting that Schwartz has more recent incident command experience.

10:14 a.m.: Schwartz receives Federal Bureau of Investigation (FBI) intelligence that United Airlines Flight #93 has also been hijacked and is headed toward Washington, D.C.

10:15 a.m.: Worried that the Pentagon might be the target of a second plane attack (as the World Trade Center had been earlier in the morning), Schwartz calls for a full evacuation of the area.

10:37 a.m.: United Airlines Flight #93 crashes near Shanksville, Pennsylvania, after passengers attempt to overpower the hijackers. After learning of the crash, Schwartz orders the resumption of response activities.

Thousands of firefighters and other emergency responders continue to arrive on scene. More than one hundred federal, state, and local agencies, as well as businesses and nonprofits, are represented. Despite recognizing the eventual need for setting up a unified command to coordinate these agencies, Schwartz retains command over the next 8 hours, due in large part to the frenetic pace of the early response.

1:00 p.m.: Christopher Combs, Schwartz's FBI liaison, is removed from Incident Command and is tasked to serve as advisor to the FBI's on-site commander. He is not replaced, frustrating Schwartz, who had come to value Combs's access to critical and time-sensitive intelligence.

2:00 p.m.: The control tower at Ronald Reagan Washington National Airport informs Schwartz that an "unidentified aircraft" is headed toward the Pentagon. Schwartz orders yet another evacuation—which he calls off after learning that the plane is carrying U.S. Attorney General John Ashcroft.

Early-to-mid afternoon: Schwartz begins taking inventory of the vast amount of resources brought by different response organizations. Over the course of the day, Schwartz and his team work to integrate these resources and their respective agencies into the Incident Command structure taking shape at the Pentagon.

Secretary of Defense Donald Rumsfeld announces that the Pentagon will open for business the next day. Although ACFD officials fail in their attempts to persuade the Secretary to delay the opening, they manage to convince the Department of Defense to implement a mix of safety precautions.

6:00 p.m.: Schwartz gathers over one hundred representatives from the different organizations present at the disaster site to announce his decision to shift to Unified Command. Among others, the Unified Command team comes to include representatives from the military, the FBI, Federal Emergency Management Agency (FEMA), and the Arlington County Police Department, some of the agencies most involved in the response effort. Coordination with the FBI, however, is complicated by its decision to separately set up a Joint Operations Center (JOC), with the goal of coordinating the entire government response to the Pentagon attack.

11:00 p.m.: ACFD Chief Plaugher organizes a news conference with General James Jackson, the commanding general of the Military District of Washington, assuring the public that the response is under control.

Wednesday, September 12

Pentagon personnel repeatedly request permission to return to their damaged offices to retrieve items left behind.

10:00 a.m.: The control tower at Ronald Reagan Washington National Airport reports another unidentified aircraft heading toward Washington. Once again, Schwartz orders an evacuation of the site.

Afternoon: The Pentagon fires are extinguished. However, search and rescue and evidence recovery efforts continue for over a week.

Part III   Adapting to Novelty

In the introduction to Part I, we distinguished between routine and crisis emergencies along a spectrum of emergency situations. We categorize some situations as *routine emergencies*, not because they are "easy" but because the predictability of the general type of situation permits agencies to prepare in advance and take advantage of lessons from prior experience—even when circumstances are quite severe. By contrast, *crisis emergencies* are distinguished by significant elements of *novelty*. These novel features may result from threats never before encountered; from a more familiar event occurring at an unprecedented scale, outstripping available resources; or from a confluence of forces, which, although not new, in combination pose unique challenges. Crucially, novel circumstances may make routine response seriously inadequate or invalidate it entirely, making it counterproductive.

That does not change the fact that the capacity to treat a wide range of contingencies, including quite threatening ones, as routine constitutes an enormous source of strength for emergency response personnel and organizations. Responders are *ready* in multiple dimensions of the term. In moments when delay may literally make a difference of life or death, they don't need to size up the situation for an extended period, plan their response from scratch, assemble people and resources, and divide up roles and responsibilities. They can act swiftly, surely, confidently, and reliably.

But crises serve up challenges that, by our definition, go beyond those for which responders are ready. In Part II, we explored the potential of the Incident Management System (IMS) to enhance responders' capacity to handle major emergencies, even when they exhibited significant elements of novelty. Through the structuring of response that IMS enables, even an unprecedented occurrence like the 9/11 attack on the Pentagon can be treated, at least in part, as a routine emergency. In this part, we delve more deeply into the way in which novelty affects crisis response. We present four case studies that depict different novel challenges to emergency responders, both to give readers a greater appreciation of the way in which the unexpected can invalidate routines and to pose clearly the problem of recognizing and acting on novelty.

Before doing so, however, we examine the differences between routine and crisis emergencies in greater depth.

Routine Emergencies:
Honing Judgment and Skills for Effective Performance

Many forms of emergency happen with regularity. House fires and multivehicle traffic accidents occur in major cities nearly every day. Even though plane crashes, major wildland fires, and floods that drive hundreds or thousands from their homes occur less frequently in any particular jurisdiction, their possibility is often enough to prompt serious efforts to train, organize, and mobilize response units to deal effectively with them.

Emergency situations that occur with relatively high frequency—and which, as a consequence, are predictable, at least in general terms—can be considered routine emergencies. Calling them "routine" does not mean that they are unimportant or easy to handle or that their consequences are minor; their impact can be extremely severe indeed. The term *routine emergency* simply means that because similar situations have been seen repeatedly in the past, responders should have developed well-designed organizations and processes through which they can respond effectively and efficiently. Of course, no two emergencies— even routine emergencies of the same type, such as house fires—are precisely alike. But because responders have seen many house fires before and can anticipate that they will see more in the future with some regularity, they can learn general lessons; build expert organizations; and provide training, equipment, capacities, and leadership that will allow them to provide relatively quick, sure, and effective responses when such emergencies arise again.

Organizations that respond to routine emergencies develop mutually reinforcing practices that enable them to perform well. They work out *scripts* or *templates*—guides, checklists, and norms that dictate the set of things that need to be done, their order, the way they are organized, and so on. Exercising these scripts hones the organization's capabilities for performance. Repeated actual experience develops the managerial and leadership abilities of those directing the responses and allows the organization to determine which equipment and staffing are required to meet these recurrent challenges efficiently. Rules, procedures, and norms are further developed, inculcated, and practiced so that people in the organization operate more or less instinctively within the domain of routine situations. An organizational culture develops that attracts people who are able to operate successfully within the established norms. Because scripts and templates exist, the principal problem in a given routine emergency is not designing the response—that has already been done in the development of the script—but in executing it effectively. An authority-driven command and control hierarchy is a good organizational form for producing the efficient execution of known and practiced routine actions, and nearly all emergency response agencies adopt orderly command and control organizations for dealing with routine emergencies.

Given this experience and capacity, operational managers responding to a routine emergency face a sequence of significant but familiar challenges. First, they need to recognize and categorize the form of routine situation they are facing and develop a sufficiently detailed understanding of the particular circumstances of this specific event to be able to proceed effectively. The general routine that fits emergencies of a particular type must be adapted at the margin to the individual circumstances of this specific event. Because the general characteristics and many specific elements of the situation are familiar, response leaders have a clear idea of what they need to know before they proceed. Part of their script is a set of instructions about which key variables have to be assessed before the general operational plan can be customized and executed. Facing an ordinary house fire, firefighters will determine where the fire is located, whether people are thought to be inside the building, whether there are volatile fuels present (paint, kerosene, natural gas, or propane tanks), and so on. When they arrive, they don't know these facts, but they do know which facts they need to determine before they can safely proceed. In routine emergencies, managers are facing "known unknowns."[1] The fact that they have a well-defined list of data to collect, which allows them to make a reasonably comprehensive assessment, is part of what makes the situation routine.

Second, having developed an understanding of the situation, they must identify the associated script and customize it for the specific, detailed characteristics of the situation they are facing. Decision making in the design phase of routine response usually does not require large amounts of conscious thought or analysis. This form of decision making has been referred to as *recognition-primed*, that is, driven by the recognition of the situation as a pattern, which primes the response that has become ingrained by training and practice.[2] Experienced operational commanders, once they have a firm grasp of the particular situation, typically formulate an action plan based on the general action template for such events, modestly adapted to or customized for the particular characteristics of the specific event.

Third, operational leaders must organize and deploy the people and equipment needed to execute the action plan they have framed. Again, this generally does not require lengthy reflection or analysis; it too tends to be triggered by *pattern recognition,* the near-automatic awareness enabled by training and accumulated experience. In this phase, both the process of ordering and directing the components of the response by operational commanders and

---

[1]Former U.S. Defense Secretary Donald Rumsfeld has been ridiculed, in our view unjustly, for framing the distinctions between "known knowns" (variables whose significance and numerical or qualitative values have been determined), "known unknowns" (variables whose significance is recognized even though no specific quantitative or qualitative values have yet been established), and "unknown unknowns" (potentially important factors that have neither been identified nor measured in any way). In a fast-developing emergency, there may well be factors that could significantly affect outcomes but whose existence and importance have not yet been taken into account as part of situational awareness.

[2]Gary Klein, *Sources of Power: How People Make Decisions* (Cambridge, Mass.: MIT Press, 1999).

the more detailed tactical decisions made by those actually executing the response can be done largely on the basis of the scripts and ingrained muscle-memory actions. For example, firefighters don't have to give a lot of thought to how to position a ladder so that it can be climbed safely; they have trained and practiced enough that it is second nature, and they can do it almost automatically. As we have seen in Part II, moreover, IMS provides an organizational and operational template that can enable groups of emergency workers—including the very large numbers who respond to major events like forest fires—to routinize the integration of their varying functional capabilities in dealing with an emergency.

Crisis Emergencies: Confronting Novelty

But what happens when situations are *not* routine? What if an emergency has significant elements of novelty, has features that appear in unusual combinations or presents at a materially different scale than has been contemplated or prepared for? The presence of significant novelty as the defining feature of crisis emergencies creates an array of distinctive challenges, requiring significantly different approaches, techniques, and processes by those engaged in them.

Novelty comes in many forms and from many different sources. Which elements make an event sufficiently novel that it calls for significantly different response strategies? One example is a crisis that flows from an unusual, rare, and unpredicted event, such as the tsunami that hit South Asia in December 2004. Similar events had occurred before (one of roughly similar size 150 years before and several smaller ones since then), but in most of the affected communities they had been largely lost from human consciousness and attention.[3] Another example flows from a combination of two or more events that interact in ways that invalidate the routine response to either one, as we have seen when Hurricane Katrina first caused widespread wind and rain damage (over an area roughly the size of the United Kingdom, about 90,000 square miles) and then breached the levee system in New Orleans, leaving 140 square miles of the city under 2–15 feet of water.[4] The attempts to cope with the significant flood were confounded by the fact that it was inside a vast area with damaged infrastructure, communications, and transportation. A third possibility is that a situation may be novel simply by virtue of its scale. If we have done our preparations well, we have prepared for disasters of a scale that are reasonably probable, and perhaps a little

---

[3]But not in all. In the Andaman Islands, off the coast of India, native inhabitants immediately turned and ran for high ground when the waters at the shoreline suddenly withdrew—and as a consequence virtually no lives were lost when the tsunami waves came ashore moments later. This essential survival knowledge had been successfully encoded into the community's culture through stories and songs that told people what to do when the waters receded.

[4]See Case 1, "Hurricane Katrina."

beyond; but if a disaster occurs that is of significantly greater scale than we have planned for, we may not be able to address it adequately using our prepared routine response.

Of course, all emergencies involve uncertainty and some degree of novelty; no two emergency situations are ever exactly alike, and all involve elements of unpredictability and surprise. Consequently, even in routine emergencies the responders need to be adaptive, customizing their response to the specific details of the circumstances, and they need to be on the lookout for *pattern breaks* or other departures from the strictly routine occurrences within the event. But, as we have seen in Part II, when an emergency organization has seen many examples of a particular emergency, and has trained and practiced and organized itself to cope with them, most of the variations it encounters will be minor and relatively easy to adapt to. Indeed, the ability to observe these variations—to maintain *situational awareness* of the specific circumstances and how they may depart in minor ways from the strictly routine scenario—is a hallmark of an effective response to a routine emergency.

The presence of significant novelty, however, calls for more than just minor variations in or customization of the routine response. In routine situations, there is a template or script that lays out the basic elements of the response in sufficient detail to provide a clear and useful roadmap for action. The presence of significant novelty, at the very least, calls into question whether the existing template or script will work (or whether it is the best approach), and it may completely invalidate the planned approaches, demanding new, unplanned, and unrehearsed actions.

The challenges of responding to novel situations as successfully as is reasonably possible are thus very different from those faced in routine situations. In routine circumstances, we need to recognize the challenge, recall the associated script, and execute according to prearranged plans, with some modest variations around the edges to accommodate the minor differences between the specific situation at hand and its archetypal routine form. By contrast, in novel circumstances there is no comprehensive script or template to work from. The essence of response to a true crisis is that leaders, often under extreme pressure because of the high stakes and compressed time, must formulate a new approach and then execute responses or combinations of responses that at best are unpracticed and at worst may require the violation of rules, procedures, and norms established to deal with routine situations. Leaders are, in short, *improvising*—they are innovating and inventing under extreme time pressure and with lives and property at high risk.

There are several key challenges involved in the process of improvising under pressure that crisis leaders must be able to address. First, response leaders must recognize that the situation is not routine and that improvisation is required. Often, this is much more difficult than it sounds. Especially in the midst of high-stress events, people frequently see the more familiar elements long before they spot the ways in which the situation differs from what they have seen before. Trained responders tend to see the elements of the situation that they have been trained to deal with and sometimes miss the features that make the situation dangerously different.

Second, they need to develop an understanding of the situation so that they can address it. But situational awareness, in this sense, may be highly problematic. The key elements may not be obvious. In a routine situation, we generally know what we need to find out before we can begin to act. For example, in the typical wildland fire, firefighters need to find out the current and forecasted weather; the terrain; the kind of wood, brush, or grass (fuel type) in which the fire is burning; and the density and dryness of the fuels before they can formulate a plan to attack the fire. They have a list of these key items, and they collect data and fill in the blanks on that list before they proceed. Indeed, part of their routine script is precisely to collect the requisite data, make an assessment, and customize their response. At the beginning of their work, they don't yet have the data, but they at least *know* what data they need to get. They face, in the words of Secretary Rumsfeld, "known unknowns." By contrast, in a true crisis, the presence of novelty implies that there is no script or template, which means that leaders may *not be aware of* what they don't know—they aren't even sure what data they need in order to have a good understanding of the situation that they are facing. They are confronting what Rumsfeld has called "unknown unknowns."

Third, once the situation has been sufficiently understood (that is, situational awareness has been established), they need to design a set and sequence of actions that can address the situation as well as is reasonably possible within existing constraints of capabilities, skills, available personnel, equipment, and political support. Because the situation involves novel elements, the responses may need to be novel as well; that is, they may have to be invented or improvised, on the spot, under the stress of a compressed time frame and looming consequences.

Finally, given the "best available in the circumstances" design for action, they need to direct the execution of the newly developed strategy and tactics. Most of the capabilities available will be those designed for routine circumstances. Often, an effective true crisis response involves the utilization of these same (routine) capabilities but in potentially novel combinations or forms. Sometimes, this involves violating established norms and procedures that were developed to make the scripted actions safe and effective in routine circumstances—and this is often resisted by the operational managers, who feel unsafe pushing the routines they have practiced outside the boundaries in which they normally operate.

The four cases that follow illustrate several different sources of novelty and implications of dealing with novelty in emergency situations:

- When Hurricane Floyd threatened the east coast of Florida, human behavior—specifically, the reaction of the public to news coverage—created a significantly novel set of circumstances that largely confounded emergency management officials handling the situation.

- When letters containing anthrax were mailed through the U.S. postal system in October 2001 (in the immediate aftermath of 9/11), the postal service and a number of other agencies were suddenly confronted by a multidimensional, multijurisdictional, complex, and confusing event that demanded swift and coordinated action across a group of agencies and organizations that had little prior acquaintance with one another and that operated in a wide variety of locations.
- When a series of major wildland fires broke out in southern California in October 2003, particularly in the area around San Diego, the large scale of the response and the intensity of the political issues raised by the fires combined to create a novel mix of challenges for response leaders.
- When Hurricane Katrina wreaked havoc in New Orleans and more widely on the Gulf coast in 2005, Wal-Mart emergency managers and corporate executives sought to use the company's considerable resources to support public relief efforts; but the company found numerous obstacles to useful engagement and the fulfillment of its potential to help threatened individuals and communities.

As you read these cases, think about how novelty arises and how leaders can assess whether it is sufficiently significant to call for a different form of response or organization to cope with it. What kinds of leadership and what forms of organizational structure and decision making seem to be most effective in the face of unprecedented events?

6　The Hurricane Floyd Evacuation in Florida (A): Safe but Annoyed

Howard Husock

As Hurricane Floyd bore down on the east coast of Florida in fall 1999, emergency management officials at the state level and in counties up the coast sprang into action. Accustomed to hurricane threats, they had extensively prepared in advance for the possibility of serious storms. With Floyd approaching, a variety of contingency plans designed to protect people and property were swiftly adjusted and implemented for the forecasted conditions, including plans for the evacuation of residents, tourists, and other visitors who might be in endangered areas.

News coverage put Floridians on edge, as did vivid memories of Hurricane Andrew, which only a few years earlier had wreaked savage and costly violence on residential areas south of Miami. The news media, particularly television, gave the storm massive coverage. Reporters mixed information about the storm, precautions that citizens should take, and protective measures with concerned commentary on the looming menace. Specific advice from emergency officials either failed to reach some of its intended audience or was ignored. The approaching storm seemed gigantic; and its expected track could produce high risk to people and property subject to wind and water danger.

When county governments up the coast began to give evacuation orders, people responded. But not only did those whom emergency managers regarded as at risk get on the road, many thousands of others who were not obviously endangered decided to evacuate as well. As traffic moved up the coast, the roads became clogged with traffic and travel speeds declined, often to a crawl. Actual clearance time (the period during which evacuees were on the road before reaching shelter) was much higher than emergency managers had anticipated. Shadow evacuation (by people who had not been advised to leave but who nonetheless departed for seemingly safer places) was one major cause of the congestion. Had Floyd hit with the ferocity that had been forecast, many evacuees might have been exposed to great danger from high winds and water while stuck in traffic on Florida highways.

Fortunately, Hurricane Floyd skirted the coast, so the traffic tie-ups produced frustration but little danger. In the aftermath, Florida's officials were left to ponder exactly what had gone wrong and what they needed to do to avoid such problems in future hurricane evacuations.

This is an abridged version of a case written by Howard Husock for Arnold M. Howitt, executive director, Taubman Center for State and Local Government, for use at the Executive Session on Domestic Preparedness, John F. Kennedy School of Government, Harvard University. Funding was provided by the U.S. Department of Transportation through the New England University Transportation Center. Kennedy School of Government Case Program, C16-02-1652.0. Copyright © 2002, 2007 by the President and Fellows of Harvard College.

Discussion Questions

- Could the Florida emergency management system have better handled the Hurricane Floyd evacuation? If so, how?
- How can officials trying to communicate with the public cope with parallel reporting from the news media, which may be presenting conflicting information?
- Can emergency managers cope with the following dilemma? In the absence of crisis, the public isn't motivated to listen to information about emergency precautions or procedures. In the midst of crisis, the window of opportunity to provide this information effectively is very narrow.
- Can crisis managers plan for unanticipated public response, including unexpected action, inaction, or panic?

On Monday, September 13, 1999, a hurricane as large as any in the state's history approached the Florida peninsula. As Hurricane Floyd threatened to make landfall, officials at the state's Division of Emergency Management believed they had devised a practical, if extensive, plan for a large-scale evacuation of areas at risk for severe damage from the storm. Because the hurricane seemed likely to affect different parts of the state at different times and in different ways, officials envisioned a massive but staged evacuation. Limited evacuation from the southeastern part of the state would be followed by more extensive evacuation in the central and northern parts of Florida's east coast. Along with early warning, this would, it was thought, allow enough time to achieve the emergency planners' crucial goal—to ensure efficient "clearance, or the complete movement of all those in harm's way from their homes, off the highways and into sheltered locations, before the storm hit." Protection could take the form of public shelters, hotels, motels, or the homes of friends and relatives outside the impacted area.

Four days later, 2.5 million Floridians had evacuated and then returned home. They were part of a four-state (Florida, Georgia, and North and South Carolina) evacuation that, in terms of the number of people involved, was the largest in U.S. history. As it turned out, there had been no storm-related casualties in Florida. Hurricane Floyd had bypassed the state completely, its 140-mile-per-hour winds skirting the peninsula just off the coastline. Yet, far from being hailed as a prudent step that had turned out for the best, the Hurricane Floyd evacuation provoked sharp public outcry. Mammoth traffic jams had left motorists stuck, in many instances, bumper-to-bumper on interstate highways for 10 hours or more, while they were trying to complete drives to safety that they expected would last 2–3 hours.

As ABC News put it, many evacuees were "safe but annoyed." Many expressed doubt that the evacuation was really necessary, or that it was handled well. "After five hurricanes in three years," complained one representative radio talk show caller, "you think they'd have a clue about getting people out of danger." Such pique stemmed from the fact that, in general, clearance times had proven to be far higher than officials had anticipated. Officials, however, were less concerned about public annoyance than the possibility that the traffic jams could have proven deadly; they were cognizant of the fact that had Hurricane Floyd tracked inland, thousands of Florida residents might have been exposed to its impact with nothing more than the flimsy protection of their cars as they crawled along the interstates.

Even before the evacuation was over, some local elected officials had begun to respond to the public outcry by calling for more efficient evacuation procedures, in particular, the *reverse-laning* of interstate highways (that is, the use of lanes on both sides of the road for evacuating traffic in the same direction). At the same time, emergency management officials were well aware of the fact that although they had issued orders expected to lead 1.5 million people to evacuate their homes, at least a million more than this had done so. Officials were left to figure out both what had caused an evacuation far more extensive than the one they had anticipated and how they should respond to calls for change.

Emergency Management in Florida

In part because of the regular threat of hurricanes and their impact on a state surrounded on three sides by water, Florida had a well-developed emergency management system. This system was largely decentralized. Each of the state's sixty-seven counties had its own director of emergency management. Mayors and the chairs of county commissions exercised authority delegated from the governor to issue evacuation orders for their jurisdictions. As a practical matter, the key decisions about how to respond to disasters were made by local directors of emergency management. Says one director, "It's a rare elected leader that would go against that recommendation." But local officials worked closely with officials in Tallahassee, the state capital. No evacuation could be ordered anywhere in the state without an executive order, issued by the governor, formally declaring the existence of a state of emergency. Absent such an order, no county could begin its disaster response—whether that response was to order an evacuation, to open public shelters, or to order the closing of schools or businesses.

The big picture planning for disasters was the responsibility of the state Division of Emergency Management in the Department of Community Affairs. The division was set up to prepare and to coordinate the response to a wide range of potential disasters. Its work was divided among three major divisions: the Office of Policy and Planning, the Bureau of Recovery and Mitigation, and the Bureau of Preparedness and Response. Each can be seen as corresponding to a different stage of a potential disaster.

The Office of Policy and Planning had the big-picture "before the disaster" responsibilities, envisioning what sorts of potential natural or human-made disasters Florida faced and then developing general plans for coping with those threats. If planners determined, for instance, that the best response to severe weather was a marked increase in the number of public shelters in the state, the office would include proposals for the funding of such shelters in a plan it would develop and submit to the governor's office. If such funds were ultimately included in the state budget, counties would apply for grants for the actual construction or improvement of public shelters. The Office of Policy and Planning also distributed information designed to help households decide whether to evacuate in the event of a major storm and which sorts of provisions to stock to remain safely at home rather than evacuate. This literature urged Floridians to develop family preparedness plans, which not only would provide a supply of drinking water and nonperishable foods but also encouraged efforts to storm-proof existing homes and the purchasing of new homes built to withstand high winds.

The Bureau of Recovery and Mitigation was the "after the disaster" portion of the state response, the vehicle through which postdisaster relief funds were to be channeled to counties and individuals. It was also responsible for developing new approaches to reducing the impact of future disasters. Inevitably, some of its activities in response to the previous storm began to take the form of a "before the disaster" response to the next storm. For instance, the bureau offered technical training for county building officials on how to evaluate and improve structures that might be pressed into service as public emergency shelters so that they could withstand high winds or water.

But it was the Bureau of Preparedness and Response that stood most clearly on the front lines of the state's reaction to an imminent disaster, through the coordination of response to emergencies as they arose. From its base operations in the state's Emergency Command Center (ECC) in Tallahassee, the bureau alerted county emergency management directors that a formal state of emergency was imminent and initiated statewide (and even interstate) conference calls in which dozens of county officials discussed the nature of the appropriate response. It also directed other state agencies to take actions to support the plans implemented by county officials. Here lay the heart of response to an actual emergency, particularly the approach to evacuation.

In order to provide advice to local officials, the bureau had studied a wide range of hurricane scenarios. Specifically, it had estimated how many households would be affected by storms of various magnitudes, ranging from the weakest storm (a Category 1 on the Saffir-

Simpson hurricane rating scale) to the strongest (a Category 5). The estimates considered potential damage from severe flooding and water damage, known as storm surge and largely confined to the immediate coastal areas, as well as wind damage, which could reach far inland. Based on the strength and potential impact of various types of storms, the bureau estimated how many people would have to be ordered to evacuate. Those estimates were tempered by the knowledge that, historically, some number of Floridians chose not to evacuate, despite orders that they do so. Recognizing this, the bureau had prepared statistical samples based on surveys, to determine what percentage of those asked to evacuate would actually do so. The combination of estimating the impact of a storm and estimating compliance levels with evacuation orders led state officials to their estimates of *clearance time,* the time it would take for evacuation traffic to clear and residents to reach safety, and thus how much in advance of a storm's potential impact an evacuation would have to start.

More broadly, the bureau divided the response to major disasters such as hurricanes into four parts: decision making (whether to declare an emergency and whether to order an evacuation), traffic management, sheltering, and emergency public information. It fell to the county emergency management officials, each of whom had his own staff and emergency command center, to make the call about when and to what extent an evacuation should be called for and to make sure the right information got to the public as a hurricane approached.

Floyd Approaches

Hurricanes have, historically, posed a threat to Florida. Between 1884 and 1999, the state was struck by an estimated 150 hurricanes, as well as 260 tropical storms. Hurricanes that strike Florida bring with them not only winds as high as 150 miles per hour but extremely high storm surges of ocean water. Such surges can inundate low-lying areas, which have, in recent years, been heavily built up with resorts, marinas, and new homes. The fact that so many Florida residents (7 million of 11.5 million) live so close to either the state's east or west coast, combined with the fact that the Florida peninsula is narrow, means that there are a limited number of sheltered inland locations in the state. Thus, the National Hurricane Center (in Miami) concluded that Florida was the state in the United States most vulnerable to hurricanes.

The perception of a hurricane threat in Florida in the 1990s was profoundly reinforced by Hurricane Andrew, a Category 4 storm that struck south Florida in 1992. Andrew was a disaster of major proportions, leaving in its wake 26 dead, 160,000 homeless, and some $25 billion in property damage. Although Andrew spared the central and northern parts of the state, it affected attitudes toward hurricanes statewide. Andrew had, in fact, prompted much of the high-level storm preparation that was in place with the approach of Floyd.

Soon after it was being tracked as a tropical storm, at the start of the second week of September 1999, Floyd was being judged as larger and potentially more dangerous than even Andrew. By Monday morning, September 13, readers of the *Miami Herald* awoke to read:

Forecasters were poised to post hurricane watches in Florida before dawn today as Hurricane Floyd developed the same catastrophic power as Hurricane Andrew—but grew much larger and prowled ever closer to the state. Floyd expanded to monstrous proportions Sunday night—a Category 4 storm—virtually as big in area as the entire state of Florida, with winds of 145 miles per hour. With nothing to inhibit it, Floyd could become that rare, top-of-the-scale Category 5 hurricane tonight, with winds exceeding 155 mph.[1]

A decision was "near on possible evacuations," the *Herald* reported.[2] There was little doubt, however, that evacuations were in the offing when Governor Jeb Bush, as he issued an executive order declaring a state of emergency on Monday, September 13, observed publicly, "It's scary. It's very scary. Andrew hit Miami in the middle of the night and it was haunting. This is as strong and three times bigger."[3]

State Planning

The decision-making process on the specific form of evacuation to recommend was centered in Tallahassee, at the Division of Emergency Management's Bureau of Preparedness and Response. There, recalls the division's Deputy Director Robert Collins, state officials were applying all the techniques at their disposal to align recommendations about evacuation with their best estimate of the storm's size, track, and intensity.

Fundamental to the state's effort was its use of the Hurricane Evacuation (HRVAC) computer imaging program, which drew on the information provided by the National Hurricane Information Center in Miami. Says Collins: "The program . . . allows you, for instance, to look at the 72-hour forecast track, to look at the actual location of where the storm is for a specific advisory, and every previous advisory. So you can look at the entire course of the storm up to the advisory that you're using the program for."[4] Based on forecasted storm tracks, the bureau could turn to its statistical models and decide whether and when to suggest to county officials that evacuations should begin and who should be told to evacuate. "With a 72-hour forecast period," observes Collins, "we can do things like factor in clearance

---

[1] *Miami Herald,* September 13, 1999.

[2] Ibid.

[3] Tracy Fields, Associated Press, *Portland Press Herald* (Maine). "'Very Scary' Floyd Closes In; One Million People Are Ordered to Evacuate as the Hurricane Heads toward Florida's Coast with Winds Reaching 155 mph," September 14, 1999, 1A.

[4] Interview with Robert Collins, deputy director, Division of Emergency Management, Florida Department of Community Affairs, 2002. Unless noted, subsequent quotations from Collins are also from this interview.

times, how long we'll need to get people on and off the roads and when they'd have to leave their houses." And, he adds, state emergency management officials can estimate when they have to order other officials to do their part to make evacuation possible, such as halting construction projects and toll collection on major highways or deploying law enforcement personnel (for example, the Florida Highway Patrol) to help direct traffic and deal with accidents and breakdowns, with their potential for creating significant delays.

By the morning of Monday, September 13, 1999, the Division of Emergency Management was moving rapidly toward recommending evacuations. State officials organized conference calls with representatives from fifty-seven of Florida's sixty-seven counties—many more than those at risk from Floyd's direct impact. They felt it crucial to advise not just the officials who might have to order evacuations but also emergency officials from the potential "host" counties, areas in the central and western part of the state and in the adjoining southeastern states to which evacuees would head for shelter. The calls also served as a forum for hammering out the specifics of the evacuation plan. Officials did not regard the response to Floyd as a straightforward call. As Bob Collins observes, "There's a conundrum we face every time we discuss evacuation. If we make a decision that's very catholic, we stand a chance of putting more people on the roads than the roads can process, and we leave them stranded out on that roadway. But, if we're very conservative, we run the risk of leaving people in areas that might be impacted by storm surge." In the case of Floyd, the stakes in the evacuation planning were raised by the sheer size of the storm. If officials based their planning on a storm track that portended limited impact and evacuation orders were relatively limited, thousands could have been at risk if the storm actually followed a different track.

Central to the evacuation planning was the officials' belief, based on 72-hour forecasting capacity, that the storm would not strike Florida directly. Instead, they expected that it would track northeast, avoiding landfall but coming as close as 25 miles off the state's east coast. Such a track still posed grave peril for coastal areas. Storm surge could affect those on the immediate coast, while high winds threatened structures not able to withstand them, including tens of thousands of mobile homes. Thus, the fact that the storm might not come ashore did not mean there was no need for evacuations. It did, however, mean those evacuations could be at least somewhat limited. Even though Floyd was, by Monday, September 13, classified as a Category 4 storm, its track was expected to mean that southeast Florida would experience it as only a Category 1 storm, thus requiring minimal evacuation.

Emergency officials expected, however, that Floyd would have a more powerful effect on the central and northeast Florida coastal areas—that winds would be higher there and the potential for storm surge greater. They also believed that because the first stage of evacuation, if it began on Monday, September 13, in south Florida, would not put that many cars on the road, there would still be enough capacity on the highways to accommodate the second wave of evacuees and enough room at motels and shelters for them at the end of their journey. The one wild card was the possibility that the storm could follow a more inland track. Should it do so, the risks were great. Even standard homes built on foundations and in full compliance with housing codes might not be able to withstand winds of more than 125 miles per hour.

Such threats notwithstanding, by the end of the fifty-county conference call on September 13, a *staged evacuation strategy* had taken shape: an evacuation to a Category 1 level for coastal counties in the southern quarter of the state, and evacuation to a Category 4 level, including structures within 20 miles of the coast and mobile homes farther inland, for the northern three-quarters of the Florida east coast, roughly from Indian River to the Georgia border (see Exhibit 6A-1). It was expected that the evacuation orders would mean that 1.3 million people would leave their homes and head north and/or west. This mass exodus would begin on Monday in the southeast, in counties including Dade County (metro Miami), and 50 miles farther north, in Palm Beach County.

Southeast Florida: Palm Beach County

Located 60 miles north of Miami, Palm Beach County's 47 miles of beaches and luxury high-rise beachfront apartment buildings, looked to be at risk from Hurricane Floyd. However, the danger to this sprawling county was thought to be limited to the coastline; this was a locale in which the storm would be effectively a Category 1 event. Thus, recalls County Director of Emergency Management William O'Brien, officials believed evacuation should be limited and that, for the most part, it would mean relatively short drives for the people affected. "We needed people to get off the beaches and drive west of Interstate 95," says O'Brien, referring to the north-south highway that runs through the county only a few miles inland from the coast. Explains O'Brien, "The National Hurricane Center was very confident the storm was going to turn. We ordered a Category 1 evacuation just to get people off the beach. There was no question in their minds it was going to turn." [5]

He had reason to hope, too, that those at risk would know who they were. Like other Florida coastal counties, Palm Beach had sought to educate members of the public about whether they lived in a storm surge area—which would have to evacuate, even for a Category 1 hurricane. According to O'Brien, "We distribute brochures which have evacuation zones clearly identified. People should be aware of whether they're in an evacuation zone or not." The county had sought to reach every household, distributing the evacuation zone brochures with utility bills, for instance. Through extensive public speaking, O'Brien had

---

[5]Interview with William O'Brien, director of emergency management, Palm Beach County, 2002. Unless noted, subsequent quotations from O'Brien are also from this interview.

Exhibit 6A-1   Florida roadways

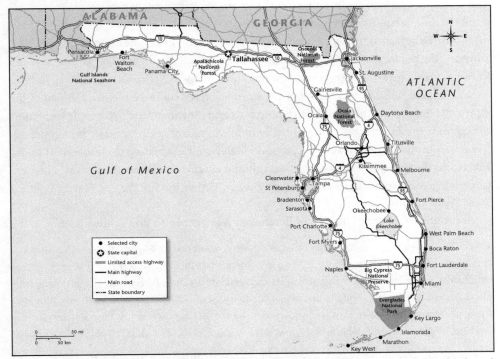

Source: U.S. Department of Transportation, Federal Highway Administration, www.fhwa.dot.gov/planning/nhs/maps/
fl/fl_floridaeast.pdf

also encouraged Palm Beach residents not to think of evacuation as a first option. Instead, he had urged that they take steps to reinforce their homes as the best means of protection from most storms. At the same time, he had reason to believe that this education attempt had not penetrated all that deeply, at least in part because of the large number of newcomers arriving regularly in Palm Beach County. "We have an awful lot of new folks moving in. We're always trying to keep up public education to reach those folks. But it's hard; you find yourself thinking after several talks and the same speech that maybe you've reached everybody. But you know you haven't."

If the evacuation went as planned—that is, if only those at risk in a Category 1 storm evacuated—the event for Palm Beach County should have been a relatively small one. As O'Brien explains, "As far as numbers, we were looking at something in the mid to low thousands." With the storm scheduled to begin to affect Palm Beach during the daytime on Tuesday, September 14, evacuation was officially ordered at 7 p.m. the day before. According to the official county press release, the evacuation was "ordered effective for residents of barrier islands, mobile homes and those areas subject to severe flooding." Officials believed that even that description of who was in danger was likely an overstatement, in part because of the difficulty in describing the exact locations of those at risk.

If officials regarded the Palm Beach County evacuation as a minor one, it was not portrayed to the public that way, largely because of the size of the storm. "The media," says Bill O'Brien, "made sure that everybody knew that this storm was Andrew's big brother." Indeed, the emphasis in television coverage of the storm centered on three themes: the size of the storm, the question of the direction it would take, and the extent to which people were complying with the evacuation order issued late on the morning of Monday, September 13. There was more discussion about what to do with pets if evacuating to a motel that might not accept them than there was about who should evacuate and who should not. The clear underlying concern centered on the question of whether the full fury of Floyd might hit Palm Beach County.

According to the state Division of Emergency Management's Bob Collins,

Especially in those large media markets like, say, down in southeastern Florida, they're all competing, they're all scrapping for that scoop. . . . And so unfortunately there is a large sort of tendency for sensationalism in the way that the meteorologists and certainly the news is reporting the hurricane situation. And so here we are, trying to say, well, if you live west of U.S. [Highway] 1, really you shouldn't evacuate. Meanwhile, you've got some wild-eyed meteorologist out there saying basically this storm is Andrew's bigger brother. You know, who do you think is actually going to hold sway in people's mind?

One south Florida meteorologist, Steve Lyons of WPBF-TV, West Palm Beach's Fox network affiliate, disagrees, saying that it was the sheer size of the storm, coupled with the inherent uncertainty of predictions, that led to widespread concern, not media hype.

You're always conscious of your responsibility to inform, not alarm. But I'll be honest. When you looked at that satellite photograph of Floyd and compared its size to the size of the entire state of Florida, it scared the pants off you. It wouldn't have taken much for it to take a dodge to the west and we'd have been up to our ankles in all sorts of problems. If Floyd had hit where Andrew hit, we'd still be picking up the pieces. And so you had people evacuating who would never ordinarily evacuate. People weren't listening to the emergency operations folks. They were looking at the image of the storm and making the decision to get out of Dodge.[6]

In fact, it was difficult to tell from the television coverage that officials had ordered only a limited evacuation. On WPBF, there were only passing references to the need for residents to determine whether they were in a storm surge area or not; news anchors mentioned that

---

[6]Interview with Steve Lyons, WPBF-TV, 2002. Unless noted, subsequent quotations from Lyons are also from this interview.

residents who wanted to be sure could consult the maps posted at branches of the local Publix supermarket chain. Nor was it made clear that although Floyd was a Category 4 storm, Palm Beach County was under a Category 1 evacuation order. WPFB did not address the question of who should evacuate but, rather, where it was best to go, noting that there was limited public shelter space and that shelters should be considered a last resort after seeking safe harbor with friends or family or at motels.

There was, in fact, cause to stress the limits of designated public shelters. A recent American Red Cross report had found that many Florida public buildings designated as hurricane shelters were not up to the required high-wind standards. But rather than acting as a deterrent for those considering whether to evacuate, the limited shelter space appeared to reinforce plans by evacuating residents to leave the county altogether, heading north and west.

So it was that the evacuation from Palm Beach County turned out not to be a minor event at all. In fact, a federal study[7] of the Floyd evacuation later found that significant percentages of households that were not supposed to be affected by the evacuation order—including, for instance, 23 percent of households in nonsurge zones near the coast and 22 percent in noncoastal areas—nonetheless evacuated. In the emergency management business, this nonmandated level of departure is known as a *shadow evacuation.*

The evacuation-related congestion was made worse by the routes followed by drivers. Most chose to take main routes, such as Interstate 95 and the Florida Turnpike (another north-south limited-access highway; see Exhibit 6A-1) rather than less congested secondary roads. Although the state effectively implemented its plan to halt construction work and stop toll collection, huge traffic jams nevertheless ensued. Clearance time for Palm Beach County evacuation traffic had been estimated at 22.5 hours but actually lasted 30 hours (see Exhibit 6A-2 for a summary of the transportation issues in selected counties). Significant percentages of drivers took 5–10 hours to reach their destinations. As Bob Collins says, "When we issued the evacuation order for southeastern Florida, we were expecting that most of those folks would pretty much stay in their own counties, that for the most part they wouldn't get in the car and drive all the way over to the other end of the state or way up north. But they did."

By late Monday and early Tuesday, evacuees from areas further north were hitting the road and beginning their own search for shelter. Those evacuating areas such as Brevard County, in the central portion of Florida's east coast, encountered the mounting wave of evacuees coming from the southeast.

---

[7]U.S. Army Corps of Engineers, *Hurricane Floyd Assessment: Review of Hurricane Evacuation Studies Utilization and Information Dissemination,* National Oceanic and Atmospheric Administration and Federal Emergency Management Agency, May 2000.

Exhibit 6A-2   Hurricane Floyd evacuation assessment: Transportation/clearance time data summary (for selected counties)

Location	Evacuation roadway network accurate?	Clearance time experienced (hours)	Study calculated time (hours)	Traffic control actions	Problems encountered
Duval County	Yes	10 (traffic loading); longer duration and commutes	17.5	Traffic control points	Congestion/traffic jams
				Barricades	Inadequate signage
				Roving/staged vehicle assistance	
				Coordinated traffic lights	
				Redirecting traffic	
Brevard County	Yes	24	20.5	Traffic control points	Congestion/traffic jams
				Barricades	Inadequate traffic control
				Locking down drawbridges	
				AM radio messages	Uncoordinated traffic lights
				Message signs	
Palm Beach County	Yes	30	22.5	Barricades	None reported
				Locking down drawbridges	

Source: U.S. Army Corps of Engineers, *Hurricane Floyd Assessment: Review of Hurricane Evacuation Studies Utilization and Information Dissemination,* National Oceanic and Atmospheric Administration and Federal Emergency Management Agency, May 2000.

Central Florida: Brevard County

Hurricane Floyd looked, on September 13, like a more important event for the central Florida coastline than for the areas farther south. Not only was Floyd expected to bring Category 4 winds to Brevard County, centered around the city of Melbourne, but much of the county's population clearly lived in high-risk areas. Of a population of just under 400,000, no fewer than 185,000 lived on its barrier islands, connected to the mainland by a series of seven causeways. That population was at risk both because of storm surge on the islands and the possibility that the bridges could be inundated and access to mainland escape routes cut off. In addition, large colonies of mobile home parks, although lying inland along the Indian River, were under a mandatory evacuation order in the event of a storm of Floyd's magnitude.

The risk to Brevard was such that by Sunday, September 12, County Director of Emergency Management Robert Lay was already leaning strongly toward an early evacuation order. He knew that the evacuation of identified special needs residents, including the handicapped and elderly, could take up to 30 hours and would involve several thousand people. (Special needs evacuation planning had been instituted statewide in the aftermath of Hurricane Andrew.) And he knew that an early warning might reinforce the seriousness of the storm in an area that had been spared the impact of Hurricane Andrew and had not, in recent years, been affected by any storm more powerful than a Category 1 hurricane. With Floyd bearing down on the county, officials decided to issue a mandatory evacuation order for four barrier islands and manufactured home parks, effective at 4:00 p.m. Monday, September 13. In order to get information out as early as possible, Director Lay briefed the press that day, just after 11 a.m.[8]

Brevard's decision interacted with what was happening further south. Lay was acting on the belief that an early announcement would give people who wanted to get a head start the chance to do so and would help spread out the traffic. Thus, Lay was, in effect, ordering an evacuation at roughly the same time as that of Palm Beach County, although the closer proximity of the storm to the more southerly areas meant that many households there had begun their evacuation earlier, during the morning of September 13.

Brevard County residents responded with the utmost seriousness. Traffic began to fill the roads well before the 4:00 p.m. deadline for mandatory evacuation. Some evacuees took more than one car; others took larger vehicles, stocked with possessions. An account in a Tampa newspaper told the story of Steve Carver of Brevard's Satellite Beach who "packed a 22-foot rental truck with half his household goods. 'I couldn't get it all, but better something than nothing.'"[9]

Lay believes the resulting levels of evacuation were, in contrast to those of Palm Beach County, appropriate—about 140,000 of the county's 400,000 residents left their homes. No one could be sure, says Lay, that even standard homes could withstand winds of 140 miles per hour. An important complication in Brevard County, however, involved its system of public sheltering. Despite the size of the evacuation, a smaller-than-anticipated number of Brevard residents chose to use area shelters. Some 84 percent of those who evacuated, in fact, left the county entirely, while only 7,000 of an expected 8,500 residents used county shelters. This may have been the result of warnings by county officials that shelters should be viewed as a refuge of last resort. Officials were concerned that if the general population sought protection in the shelters, those with no other options might have no place to go.

[8]Interview with Robert Lay, director of emergency management, Brevard County, 2002. Unless noted, subsequent quotations from Lay are also from this interview.

[9]John Reinan, Peter Howard, Ken Koehn, and Karen Haymon-Long, "Fleeing Floyd: The Hurricane Spawns a Record-Setting Evacuation That Jams Highways and Hotels from Tampa to Tallahassee," *Tampa Tribune*, September 15, 1999, 1.

Low use of the shelters was, however, also a result of the fact that the county could not open all its shelter locations. The county employees and volunteers who had been expected to provide staffing chose, in many cases, to evacuate themselves. Says Bob Lay, "It turns out that you cannot expect families to split up, for one to stay and work while the rest of the family takes off somewhere."

Traffic Impacts

The effect of there being large numbers of evacuees, along with their overwhelming preference to leave the county heading north and west, set the stage for complications, including long traffic delays. While 70 percent of those evacuating expected they'd be able to reach their destinations in less than 2 hours, fewer than half were able to do so; residents of some surge zones took as long as 15–20 hours to reach their destinations. Although the actual numbers of cars on the road for that long was relatively small, such delays meant that hundreds were on the roads at a time when the brunt of the storm could possibly have hit. The traffic jams were caused both by the sheer number of evacuees from Brevard and other central Florida counties and by what was, in effect, their collision with the first wave of evacuees coming up from the south along Interstate 95 and the Florida Turnpike.

Bob Lay recalls wishing that he could have communicated with drivers to tell them to take alternate, secondary routes. But he could not do so. Says Lay, "We could talk to people over TV and we could talk to them over the radio but the minute they got in their car then we'd effectively lost them. Unless they were tuned to the right station at the right time, then they're not going to get the right information." Lay was aware of the potential of so-called variable messaging technology (electronic signs whose messages could be quickly updated to divert drivers to alternate routes), but the county lacked enough signs for them to play a major role.

Had Floyd moved inland, the results of such traffic snafus could have been devastating. The actual overall clearance time for the county was 24 hours—some 4 hours more than the county projected (see Exhibit 6A-2). The number of drivers potentially in peril was relatively limited, says Bob Lay, only because the county had ordered its evacuation relatively early. "I'll be honest with you; had we waited until Tuesday morning to order that evacuation, we would have waited until too late. We would have put people on the road and they would not have been able to get out where they needed to go and would have been on the road at a time of potentially high winds." Residents who delayed faced the longest time on the road.

All this had occurred even before the last, most northern stage of the planned evacuation had even gotten started. Bob Collins of Florida's Division of Emergency Management recalls that by the time evacuation from Florida's most northern major coastal city, Jacksonville, was set to start, virtually all the hotel rooms in the central and western parts of the state were already filled.

North Florida: Jacksonville

Like their counterparts in southeast Florida, emergency management officials in and around Jacksonville would have liked to limit the Hurricane Floyd evacuation, focusing on those homes in coastal storm surge areas. Moreover, when it became clear late Tuesday night that Floyd might not be the punishing storm some feared—that the track forecast by the National Hurricane Center was correct (Category 4, likely to move parallel with the coast)—the case for a limited evacuation became stronger. If Floyd hit Jacksonville at all, it would be the immediate coast that would be most affected.

As in southeastern Florida, however, limiting the evacuation proved to be easier said than done. Public concern about the track of the monster storm continued to run high. President Bill Clinton had, by Wednesday morning, September 15, gone so far as to issue a preemptive disaster declaration for the state of Florida. The *Florida Times-Union*, published in Jacksonville, described Floyd as "the strongest storm to threaten Jacksonville in the 20th century." [10] The city's mayor, John Delaney, was quoted as saying, "This could very well be a storm that could flatten hundreds of homes out at the beach." [11]

Chip Patterson, director of emergency management for Duval County, the major northeastern Florida county (population, 778,000), faced a special problem. The fact that the St. Johns River met the Atlantic at Jacksonville complicated the contours of the storm surge zone. The hurricane, observed the *Florida Times-Union*, "could push ocean water into the St. Johns, causing the river to back up and flood." [12] The county, says Patterson, had tried to conduct extensive "preparedness-type education," including newspaper inserts designed to help residents learn whether they lived in an area at risk of storm surge. But, he says, "most people tune these things out, until the local media starts pumping the latest storm." [13]

Communication Issues

The time when a storm is imminent, says Patterson, is not the easiest for communicating detailed information. "By the time the storm is coming, we've missed our window of opportunity," he says. "Now we're communicating in 15-second sound bites. And you can't communicate detailed information about storm surge zones under those circumstances. I think it's reasonable to say that we did not have ways to dampen the shadow evacuation." In other words, almost inevitably, an announcement instructing those at risk of storm surge to evacuate would lead to a larger evacuation than necessary.

---

[10]Jessie-Lynne Kerrr and Steve Patterson, "Floyd Should Pass Just off the Coast," *Florida Times-Union*, September 15, 1999, A-1.

[11]Quoted in ibid.

[12]Ibid.

[13]Interview with Chip Patterson, director of emergency management, Duval County, 2002. Unless noted, subsequent quotations from Patterson are also from this interview.

Like other county emergency management directors, moreover, Patterson also saw Floyd's high winds as a factor that could lead those not at risk from water to decide to leave as well. Nor did he feel secure in telling them not to do so.

The capacity to issue a dampening message, to discourage evacuation, has everything to do with how you've been doing with mitigation and preparation. If I had felt confident that homeowners had been taking wind seriously and really had gone in and retrofitted their homes to withstand it, then I would have felt we had some immunity from the storm as a county. But we hadn't pushed retrofitting as energetically as we should have. So, although I did feel confident telling individuals that I knew—and whose homes I was familiar with—that they didn't have to leave, as far as making a public announcement, that was different. At the same time, we knew people could be at risk out on the highway.

That risk stemmed in part from the fact that, like their counterparts elsewhere, northeast Florida residents chose to drive not only away from the coast but also out of the county and out of the state, at times without any final destination in mind. Bob Collins of the state Division of Emergency Management was struck by the number of families from inland areas who had no evident reason to evacuate but who nonetheless did so.

Notwithstanding such shadow evacuation, the northeast Florida clearance time was actually 7.5 hours less than officials had projected (see Exhibit 6A-2). For state and county officials, this was something of a triumph, reflecting not only early departures by some households but adept deployment of a wide range of services provided by state agencies. Tow trucks were deployed to prevent lanes from being blocked by breakdowns. Tanker trucks filled with gasoline were deployed to prevent cars from running out of fuel, despite the long waits in slow traffic. Extra portable restrooms were put out at rest stops. But, from the point of view of the evacuating households, it still took far longer than normal to reach such destinations as Tallahassee, where evacuees found no motel rooms were available.

More, says Chip Patterson, might have been able to take advantage of available space in public shelters. But the heavy traffic had had another side effect, he says—the county was not able to open all its shelters. Unlike in central Florida, this was not the result of emergency personnel choosing to evacuate rather than showing up for work. Rather, it was, says Patterson, the result of a plan to open shelters on an "as needed basis"; that is, as one filled up, another would be opened. "This usually makes wonderful sense," he observes. "But it did not serve us well during the Hurricane Floyd evacuation." The problem was that once it became clear that more shelters, particularly in the western part of the county, were needed, gridlock prevented emergency personnel from reaching the shelters in order to operate them.

Perhaps because it became clear soon after the Jacksonville area evacuated that Floyd would not make landfall in Florida after all, public annoyance surfaced most notably there. Mary Ann Vitkauskas, who traveled with her family to rural Georgia, where they spent the night parked on farmland, told the Associated Press that any future evacuation "is going to have to be real mandatory for us to do what we did again." [14] Observes Chip Patterson, tartly, "There are a lot of people for whom any inconvenience is deemed to be intolerable."

Local elected officials defended the evacuation. "I don't think anyone that lives at the beach questions the decision," said Jacksonville Mayor John Delaney. "There was no way you could have taken the chance of that thing not turning and (then) tried to move those people." [15] Many other local officials struck a similar defensive tone about the evacuation.

Aftermath

Hurricane Floyd caused only minor property damage and no fatalities as it skirted the state of Florida. Nonetheless, as hundreds of thousands of households filtered back to their homes, there was a widespread sense that the evacuation, if not a fiasco, could have been handled far more efficiently. Editorial writers throughout the United States took notice of the fact that the Floyd evacuation routes had been, as the *Columbus (Ohio) Dispatch* had put it, "reduced to parking lots." Opined the *Dispatch,* "Fortunately the scene was not one of desperation. But many are asking, what if the threat had prompted the hysteria of an imminent Cold War attack? Would the highway system have been worse than just jammed? Might it not have become a death trap?" [16]

On September 18, Florida Governor Jeb Bush ordered a special study of evacuation policies. A central part of the study was to be the examination of *reverse-laning,* which would turn selected interstate highways into one-way roads, headed in the direction of the evacuation wave. It was a step that, on the surface, promised to be an easy way to increase highway capacity in an emergency, ostensibly doubling road capacity, temporarily, in a state in which road construction had not kept up with the growth in the auto or total population. The idea was buttressed, in Floyd's wake, by the decision of South Carolina Governor Jim Hodges to reverse-lane Interstate 26 for evacuees returning to Charleston. The return appeared to go more smoothly than the evacuation, Charlestown's Mayor Joseph Riley observed.[17] In addition, federal officials expressed the view that reverse-laning could be selectively employed to good effect.

Even though there was public clamor for such a policy, Florida emergency management officials were not quick to jump on the bandwagon. Major Kevin Guidry, in charge of evacuation issues for the Florida Highway Patrol, told the *St. Petersburg Times,* in effect, that in

---

[14]Quoted in Amanda Riddle, "Coast Better Prepared for Hurricane," Associated Press Online, May 27, 2000.

[15]Quoted in Bill Kaczor, "Traffic jammed, shelters filled, but Bush says everyone got out on time," Associated Press State and Local Wire, September 16, 1999.

[16]"Floyd's Jammed Evacuation Routes Reduced to Parking Lots," *Columbus Dispatch,* September 24, 1999, 12A.

[17]Arlie Porter, "Officials Debate Traffic Headaches," *Post and Courier,* September 17, 1999, A-5.

an evacuation traffic jams were inevitable. "There's just not enough road to handle that flow. From our standpoint, if the traffic keeps moving, that's about the best that people could expect." Guidry noted that to enforce reverse-laning the state would need "enormous staffing and a lot of equipment. You have to have people at all the entrance ramps and you have to have backups to relieve those people." Barriers alone would not prevent drivers from using closed entrance ramps, said Guidry. "I've seen people drive around wooden and concrete barriers. Cones certainly won't stop them." He noted, too, that at some point the one-way designation must end. "What happens then? You are sending a whole lot of people from populated areas where there is law enforcement to unpopulated areas where there is almost no law enforcement." [18] State emergency officials stressed, too, the need for evacuees to consider using secondary routes instead of main highways and to be made aware, perhaps through electronic messaging signs or through faxes sent to gas stations and restaurants, of places they could go—shelters or motels—so that traffic would gradually decrease as cars peeled off to destinations along the way.

But in the aftermath of Hurricane Floyd, most officials emphasized their hope that somehow the magnitude of future evacuations could be decreased. Said Steve Seibert, Secretary of the Florida Department of Community Affairs, "If you live in an area not subject to storm surge, keep your family safe at home." [19] Hurricane Floyd had left in its wake little damage but, nonetheless, a new challenge for emergency management officials—devising ways to convince residents not to evacuate unnecessarily. "We've done a good job at telling people the sky is falling," says Bob Collins of the state's Division of Emergency Management. "We have to do a little better on the subtleties."

---

[18]Quoted in David Ballingrud, "Officials Try to Plan Next Mass Evacuation," *St. Petersburg Times*, October 3, 1999, 1B.
[19]Quoted in Ibid.

The Hurricane Floyd Evacuation in Florida (B): Epilogue

In February 2000, the Governor's *Hurricane Evacuation Task Force Report* was issued. It included twenty-two recommendations and focused in particular on reverse-laning. The task force concluded, however, that the safety and logistical problems posed by reverse-laning dictated that it "must only be used as a last resort when conditions are dire." [1] The use of paved highway shoulders as a third lane of traffic was deemed to be more widely practical. And although seven specific highways were identified for potential reverse-laning, "there are many less drastic steps which can be taken." The task force observed that "the state must focus more attention on finding alternatives to evacuation as one of our primary means of providing protective actions to its citizens." [2] The report emphasized the need for efforts to encourage residents to retrofit their homes to become hurricane-proof and the need for emergency management officials to encourage the use of neighborhood shelters to "leave room on critical evacuation routes for those who truly need to leave and seek safety." The task force went so far as to call for the possible use of "military assets" as shelters to augment the state's limited shelter capacity. [3]

The report led to the designation of the state's network of public radio stations as the place to which drivers could reliably turn for information about traffic congestion and alternative routes during a large-scale evacuation. It led, as well, to the expanded use of electronic variable message signage. The task force did not, however, offer a simple answer to the problem of shadow evacuation. Rather, it placed its faith in the potential for better dissemination of public information and, particularly, the use of the Internet to "improve the amount and availability of emergency information." [4]

---

[1] Walter Revell et al., *Governor's Hurricane Evacuation Task Force Report: Executive Summary,* available at www.floridadisaster.org/documents/HurricaneTaskForceReport.pdf.

[2] Ibid.

[3] Ibid., App. III.

[4] Ibid.

Key Actors in the Hurricane Floyd Evacuation in Florida

State of Florida

Robert (Bob) Collins, deputy director, Division of Emergency Management, Florida Department of Community Affairs

Steve Seibert, secretary, Florida Department of Community Affairs

Kevin Guidry, major, Florida Highway Patrol

Jeb Bush, governor

Brevard County

Robert (Bob) Lay, director of emergency management

Duval County

Chip Patterson, director of emergency management

Palm Beach County

William (Bill) O'Brien, director of emergency management

City of Jacksonville, Florida

John Delaney, mayor

Others

Jim Hodges, governor of South Carolina

Joseph Riley, mayor, Charleston, South Carolina

Hurricane Floyd Evacuation in Florida, 1999

Chronology of Events

Sunday, September 12

Hurricane Floyd strengthens into a massive Category 4 storm, threatening to become one of the most destructive hurricanes in Florida's history.

Monday, September 13

Governor Jeb Bush declares a state of emergency.

The state's Division of Emergency Management discusses evacuation plans with county officials. They decide on a staged process: southeastern coastal communities will evacuate first, at a Category 1 level; the evacuation of more vulnerable communities farther to the north will follow at a Category 4 level.

An evacuation order for Palm Beach County is issued late in the morning. What is supposed to be a limited evacuation turns into a mass exodus, triggering congestion along roadways. Clearance of Palm Beach County evacuation traffic lasts up to 30 hours.

11:00 a.m.: Worried that Floyd could hit the central coast at Category 4 strength, Brevard County Emergency Management Director Robert Lay holds a press conference, giving early notice of the county's evacuation plans.

Early afternoon: Brevard County residents, not waiting for the official start of the evacuation, flock to the roads. Many evacuate the county entirely, bypassing area shelters.

Evacuation traffic from Brevard County collides with that from Palm Beach and points south, triggering traffic jams. Drives last up to 20 hours.

4:00 p.m.: A mandatory evacuation of barrier islands and mobile home parks in Brevard County officially goes into effect.

Tuesday, September 14

Counties along Florida's central and north Atlantic coast issue evacuation orders.

The hurricane threat diminishes during the night as forecasters predict that the storm will not make landfall. But residents of the Jacksonville area, where the worst of the storm had been expected, begin evacuating in large numbers.

Even though the clearance time for northeast Florida is less than projected, drives last far longer than usual. Evacuees have a difficult time finding shelter even in places far inland.

Wednesday, September 15, to Saturday, September 18

Wednesday morning: President Clinton issues a preemptive disaster declaration for the state of Florida.

Floyd ultimately skirts the state, causing minor property damage. Residents return to their homes.

In South Carolina, Governor Jim Hodges decides to reverse-lane traffic for evacuees returning to the city of Charleston. Their return trip proceeds far more smoothly than the evacuations earlier in the week, prompting calls for more extensive reverse-laning in the future.

Amid mounting criticism of the Hurricane Floyd evacuation, Governor Bush orders a review of evacuation policies. A central focus of the study is the viability of reverse-laning.

7 The 2003 San Diego Firestorm (A): When Imperatives Collide

Kirsten Lundberg

In October 2003, southern California was threatened by wide areas of extremely high fire danger. Much of the rural landscape in this area is dominated by highly flammable grasses, brush, and pine trees in a fire-adapted ecosystem, in which fire is a recurrent and indeed inevitable event. Several years of drought and a long, hot, dry summer had made even live growth nearly as dry as tinder. In the years since the last major fires in much of the area, fuels in forests, brushy areas, and grasslands had built up to the point where any significant fire would become extremely intense. In addition, infestations of insects had left many dead and dried-out trees standing, adding to the potentially explosive conditions. All it would take was an ignition source—a careless camper letting a campfire expand, a lit cigarette dropped in the wrong place, a lightning strike—combined with a wind event (a weather condition leading to steady, high winds for a period of hours or days), and a major conflagration might ensue. Because ignition sources are more or less continuous and wind events common at that time of year in southern California, this combination was all but inevitable.

In the face of the extremely high fire danger, state, local, and federal fire agencies cooperated to pre-position additional firefighting resources in the area to make it possible to respond quickly in the event that significant fires began. Equipment and firefighting teams, together with overhead teams, teams of supervisors to plan, direct, and oversee the activities of operational units, were moved into areas where fires were anticipated.

Over a 2-week period, hundreds of fires started in the affected areas. Fortunately, most either self-extinguished or were put out while they were small and relatively easy to contain. About fifteen of them, however, became major fires that endangered significant numbers of people and large amounts of property. Eventually, these fires resulted in billions of dollars of losses, and, tragically, more than twenty deaths.

Because of the intensity of the fires and the large numbers of people potentially affected, these fires were political as well as emergency response events. Elected officials responded to the concerns and fears of their constituents, seeking additional help in the form of firefighting teams and equipment to protect their communities.

In reading about these events and the response, think about the organizational structure through which the response was coordinated. Pay particular attention to the interaction between the operational command process in a classic IMS framework and the politicians who became involved. Reflect on the causes, consequences, and potential solutions to the conflict that emerged.

This is an abridged version of a case written by Kirsten Lundberg for Professor Herman B. "Dutch" Leonard, George F. Baker Jr. Professor of Public Management, and Arnold M. Howitt, executive director of the Taubman Center for State and Local Government of the Kennedy School of Government, for the National Preparedness Leadership Institute. Funding for the case was provided by the US Centers for Disease Control and Prevention through the National Preparedness Leadership Initiative. Kennedy School of Government Case Program, C16-05-1814.0 and C16-05-1814.1. Copyright © 2005, 2007 by the President and Fellows of Harvard College.

305

Discussion Questions

- What were the main issues related to fighting the southern California fires once they had started? Which of these issues were technical, and which were political?
- How effectively did the Incident Management System handle this complicated complex of events? Do you see any shortcomings in how it operated in this situation?
- How productive were the interactions between political leaders and operational officials involved in fighting the fires? What do you think could be done to ensure that such interactions are as productive as possible in the future?

When it came to fighting wildfires, few states had as good a record of interagency collaboration as California. Since the 1960s, what had been an inefficient and ad hoc approach to firefighting had evolved into an *Incident Command System* (ICS) that became the model for the nation. California's elected officials were proud of the state's firefighting professionals, who, together with federal colleagues, developed strategy and allocated resources during wildfires.

On rare occasions, however, the magnitude of a fire outstripped the ability of fire officials to deal with it. Such an occasion arose in southern California in October 2003, when multiple major fires ignited over a period of a few days. By early evening on Saturday, October 25, there were seven serious fires already burning when a lost amateur hunter in the Cleveland National Forest in San Diego County put up a flare for help, thus igniting what became the largest fire in California state history. By morning, the fire, designated the Cedar Fire, had spread beyond all expectation, consuming at its height 12,000 acres per hour.[1] It eventually destroyed over 273,000 acres, consumed some 2,200 homes, and killed 14 people.

Federal, state, and local fire officials in San Diego County faced a shortage of crews and equipment because many had been sent to battle the earlier fires further north. As they scrambled to deploy what forces were left, a call came in from a local member of Congress, Representative Duncan Hunter (R-Calif.), whose house was in the danger area. Hunter, who was chair of the U.S. House of Representatives Armed Services Committee, had obtained permission from the chairman of the Joint Chiefs of Staff to send special military firefighting C-130 aircraft to fight the Cedar Fire. Who, asked Hunter, had the authority to accept the planes?

But fire officials, for safety and logistical reasons, neither wanted nor felt they could use the planes, and they told Hunter so. So Hunter took his request up the chain of command. Until well past midnight, he and California Assemblyman Jay LaSuer (R-La Mesa) telephoned anyone they could think of who could help get the planes to southern California.

---

[1] U.S. Forest Service and California Department of Forestry and Fire Protection, *California Fire Siege 2003: The Story* (hereafter, *The Story*), 72.

As the firestorm raged, the parallel political storm between the operational fire officials and politicians escalated. At issue were the responsibility and authority of the operations people to fight the fires effectively but safely according to battle-tested procedures versus the responsibility and authority of the elected officials to override established procedure in a crisis to protect the public. The Cedar Fire also called into question how prepared San Diego County was for a large-scale fire and whether preparedness levels played a role in the scale and speed of the fire devastation.

Southern California Fire History

The Cedar Fire was far from the first destructive fire to hit southern California. In 1961, fire swept through the upscale Bel Air section of Los Angeles, destroying 484 homes. In September 1970, the Laguna Fire burned 175,425 acres of San Diego County, destroyed 382 homes, and killed 8 people. Major wildfires in 1980 destroyed over three hundred houses in San Bernardino County. The 1993 fire season was marked by the Laguna Beach Fire, which destroyed four hundred houses; other fires that season killed four people and burned another 1,200 structures. Fires in 1994 killed fourteen California firefighters.

Each of the monster fires resulted in new legislation and calls for ever greater preparation and coordination. The 1961 fire led to calls for limits on building in the wildlands as well as better, more fireproof structures. In 1971, federal and state funding created Firefighting Resources of Southern California Organized for Potential Emergencies (FIRESCOPE), an integrated system for fighting fires.[2]

After the 1993 Laguna Beach Fire and other fires, state fire officials developed the voluntary California Fire Plan to reduce costs and losses from wildfires, and interested communities created Fire Safe Councils to plan for local responses to fires. The U.S. Forest Service (USFS) trained local fire service personnel in the best tactics for wildland urban interface (WUI) fires, fires in which houses backed up to open space. The sobering firefighter fatalities in 1994 led to a reexamination and respecification of priorities: first was protection of human life; second was protection of natural and cultural resources and property. In 2001, a California Wildfire Coordinating Group identified communities at risk from wildfires.

Who's in Charge: Feds, State, and Local

Two agencies in particular held responsibility for fighting fires in California: the USFS at the federal level and the California Department of Forestry and Fire Protection (CDF) at the state level. A U.S. Department of Agriculture agency, USFS managed some 193 million acres of public lands and took responsibility for any fire that started within a national forest. In

---

[2]FIRESCOPE put in place a statewide Incident Command System (ICS), a Multi-Agency Coordination System (MAC), a system for information management, technological support for firefighters, and a common communications system.

southern California, the USFS Pacific Southwest Division, known as Region 5, oversaw 20 million acres. A regional forester, Jack Blackwell, administered Region 5 with an annual budget in 2003 of $500 million and more than 5,000 permanent and 2,800 seasonal employees. Ray Quintanar was his director for fire and aviation management.

CDF, meanwhile, was charged with managing and protecting 31 million acres of privately owned California wildlands. It took command responsibility for any fire that started on land that it managed. CDF employed 3,800 people full time and added another 1,400 during fire season. Its director, Andrea Tuttle, was appointed by the governor. Her chief deputy director, Ray Snodgrass, was a career CDF official who had moved into the deputy position in June 2003. CDF divided the state into twenty-one units, each with its own chief. The unit chief for San Diego was Chuck Maner.

Who Owned What

Each agency deployed firefighting equipment, but ownership structures varied. USFS Region 5, for example, owned and maintained some 175 engines, of which about 150 were staffed and ready to deploy at any given moment. USFS did not, however, own firefighting aircraft. Instead, it leased them from private contractors. USFS also had contracts nationwide with some thirty-three commercial air tankers outfitted to drop retardant or water on fires. In addition, it contracted for about twenty-nine helicopters stationed in California.

For its part, CDF owned approximately 330 fire engines, complemented by another 750 engines owned by local communities but maintained by CDF. It also owned twenty-three air tankers and eleven helicopters.[3] The governor of California could also, through the Office of Emergency Services (OES), order up eight California National Guard–owned Blackhawk helicopters outfitted to fight fires. Aircraft were considered most effective in the initial attack at the start of a fire, when well-targeted dumps could stop a fire in its tracks or slow its growth dramatically. Planes and helicopters most commonly operated as backup for ground crews, giving them the breathing space they needed to fight the fire with ground tactics. Different kinds of aircraft brought different advantages. Fixed-wing air tankers carried fire retardant or water, which could be dropped in advance of a fire or directly on the flames and could travel long distances quickly. Each cost a daily fee of some $2,000–3,000 to be on call, plus an hourly rate of several hundred dollars if used. Helicopters, meanwhile, were more agile than fixed-wing planes. Some were equipped with water or retardant tanks; others carried Bambi buckets slung from the undercarriage. But they were also expensive to fly—some $7,000 per hour.

---

[3]It also owned thirteen so-called air-tactical planes, aircraft that oversaw a complex air operation or that led firefighting aircraft into difficult terrain. For statistics on CDF, see www.fire.ca.gov/communications/downloads/fact_sheets/Glance.pdf.

In deciding which aircraft to use, fire managers had to consider wind conditions, visibility, and how congested the air space might be; sometimes using no aircraft was the best choice. Larry Hamilton, director of Fire and Aviation for the Bureau of Land Management (BLM) at the U.S. Department of the Interior, adds that the public often thinks that aircraft are more effective in fighting fires than is actually the case. He comments, "A lot of people think you go in there and you put the fire out with an air tanker. But that doesn't happen. You use it as a tool to impede the progress of the fire, so that firefighters can get a line in."[4]

Incident Responsibility

To manage a fire, California depended first and foremost on its ICS. Under ICS, the incident commander had on-the-ground operational responsibility, making the minute-by-minute decisions on how to fight the fire: how many engines to send, how many personnel to send, whether to use aircraft, and so forth. The agency on whose land the fire started held primary responsibility for the fire.

As soon as a fire grew large enough to cross into another jurisdiction, each affected agency appointed its own incident commander. This was called Unified Command. As a fire became more complex, however, it could outstrip the ability of one or two individuals to manage. Under ICS, both CDF and USFS had created standing incident command teams—preexisting groups whose members had complementary expertise and were trained to work together. These forty-person teams could be sent to larger fires as a single unit. Two incident commanders, one from each agency, took operational charge. If several fires burned simultaneously in the same area, an area command team would take over. Area command teams could be state or federal. CDF maintained ten incident command teams; USFS within California fielded five Type 1 (highest expertise) and six Type 2 (significant expertise) teams. In addition, USFS could call on another twelve Type 1 national incident command teams from across the country.

There were two aspects to fighting fires, however. While ICS took care of operational collaboration, other mechanisms controlled the allocation of resources across the federal, state, and local levels.

Coordination: National and State

At the national level, coordination took place at the National Interagency Fire Center (NIFC) in Boise, Idaho. The NIFC brought together representatives from USFS, the Bureau of Indian Affairs, BLM (the host agency for the center), the Department of Fish and Wildlife, the National Park Service, the National Association of State Foresters, the National

---

[4]Telephone interview with Larry Hamilton, Bureau of Land Management, July 13, 2005. Unless noted, subsequent quotations from Hamilton are also from this interview.

Weather Service, and the Office of Aircraft Services. The Federal Emergency Management Agency (FEMA) also had a representative, and a full-time military advisor monitored for the need for military involvement.

Once a fire became severe enough to overwhelm state capabilities and require a national response, NIFC convened a Multi-Agency Coordination System (MAC) group of firefighting agency directors to take charge. The MAC group set national priorities for where to send equipment, supplies, and personnel, which in a multifire season could be in short supply.

Among other resources, NIFC controlled the disposition of military assets, including over two hundred helicopters, about forty fixed-wing aircraft (heavy air tankers), and some eight battalions (each five hundred strong) of soldiers or marines. They also controlled the use of eight Modular Airborne Firefighting System (MAFFS) planes, which were C-130 aircraft converted to fight fires. Each plane could carry 2,700 gallons of fire retardant. The MAFFS planes belonged to the National Guard or the Air Force. Two were stationed permanently in California, and the governor of California had independent authority to mobilize them for use in-state. Otherwise, only the USFS could channel requests for MAFFS planes to NIFC.

MAFFS planes were, by common consensus, a blunt instrument. Once a MAFFS cargo bay opened, it had to dump its entire load; partial or targeted dumping was technically impossible. So MAFFS planes were useful in covering the wide flank of a fire along a mountain ridge, but they were less useful in constricted valleys or canyons, where agility was paramount. They were also expensive to deploy. A single flight could cost upward of $20,000 in retardant, fuel, maintenance, and personnel costs.

Under a provision of the Economy Act of 1932 (31 USC 1535), NIFC could release MAFFS planes to a fire *only* after the available supply of contract civilian aircraft had been exhausted. The act, passed in the depths of the Depression, was intended to protect private-sector jobs, but by 2003 many lawmakers considered it outdated and counterproductive. In March of that year, six representatives sponsored a bill that would have removed the restriction on the use of military aircraft to fight fires.[5] The bill passed the House as an amendment to the 2004 Defense Authorization Bill, but by October 2003 it had gone no further.

State Coordination

At the state level, in California, a Master Mutual Aid Agreement provided for fire departments to dispatch equipment and personnel as possible to beleaguered colleagues statewide. But if the plan was overwhelmed and a state of emergency declared, the OES took charge of allocating additional resources.

---

[5]House of Representatives Bill 1061: Wildfire Response Enhancement Act. This would have allowed the secretaries of agriculture or the interior to conclude agreements with any federal agency for goods and services directly related to improving or using wildfire fighting capability. See http://govtrack.us/congress/bill.xpd?bill=h108-1061&page-c.

Mirroring the MAC group at NIFC, California maintained geographical area coordinating centers (GACCs), which prioritized incidents and allocated resources in the event of multiple fires statewide. The criteria for determining priority were lives at risk, structures at risk, high potential for damage, and complexity of the fire. In southern California, a GACC (commonly known as South Ops) had been established at Riverside, southeast of Los Angeles.[6] During a fire large enough to require the activation of South Ops, a multiagency management team (which we will call here the state MAC) with representatives from CDF, OES, USFS, and others gathered at South Ops. The state MAC combined facilities, equipment, personnel, procedures, and communications into a common pool, out of which it distributed resources and support to the firefighting effort.

During large multifires, on-the-scene incident commanders conferred constantly with South Ops, which ensured all needs were weighed appropriately. For then OES Director Dallas Jones, the state MAC was a considerable improvement on the situation 40 years earlier when resources were allocated based on political power plays. He explains, "What happens when you get the political structure involved is they want to take care of their turf. So it becomes a power struggle of who gets the resource, based on political whim or who can yell the loudest or who's the best connected. [The state MAC] center exists to make sure those kind of forces are resisted, and that prioritization is based on need."[7] With these coordination systems in place, fire officials felt confident they could stay on top of even the largest fires.

Conditions in 2003

Southern California had experienced plenty of fires in the late twentieth century, but the vast majority were confined to wildland areas. By 2003, however, fire officials began to worry seriously about the confluence of several factors that could affect vulnerability to fire. First, there had been 4 years of drought, leading to unusually dry brush and vegetation.[8] Second, an infestation of bark beetles had killed off an estimated 1 million trees across thousands of acres, creating potential fuel for a wildfire. Finally, there had been an explosion of housing construction in what had been wildlands, which translated into a correspondingly greater threat to human life and habitation.

Both state and federal fire officials recognized the magnitude of the threat that dead trees posed in 2003. USFS devoted $14 million to tree removal in southern California, and FEMA contributed another $3.2 million. USFS directed an additional $15 million in fire severity

---

[6]The official name was Southern California Geographic Area Coordination Center.

[7]Telephone interview with Dallas Jones, Office of Emergency Services, July 20, 2005. Unless noted, subsequent quotations from Jones are also from this interview.

[8]Megan Garvey, "Night of Fire," *Los Angeles Times,* December 28, 2003, A1.

funding to California as the season progressed. Statewide, USFS spent these monies on maximum staffing levels for 123 engines in northern California, four contract heavy helicopters, 20 fire crews, and 15 fire prevention patrol units and sent the San Bernardino National Forest a plane with fire crews plus ten extra fire engines and two bulldozers.[9]

On March 7, 2003, California Governor Gray Davis declared a state emergency and directed state agencies to prepare safety and evacuation plans, reinforce firefighting resources, assist landowners with tree removal, and expedite dead tree clearance. Electric utilities were ordered to trim trees near power lines. On April 16, 2003, he requested $430 million in emergency funds from USFS and FEMA to remove unhealthy trees on 415,000 acres of forest in San Diego, Riverside, and San Bernardino counties. "This situation is of such severity and magnitude that effective response is beyond the capabilities of the state," he wrote in a letter to President George W. Bush.[10] Eight days later, a bipartisan group of California legislators sent a second letter supporting Davis's request. But the request went unanswered until October.

On June 20, Davis allocated CDF additional funds to address the extreme fire danger. The money paid for more staff on fifty-three existing fire engines, new staff for an additional ten engine companies in the southern region, an additional helicopter with crew for the CDF San Diego unit, and a fourth firefighter on forty-one CDF-funded fire engines within Los Angeles, Orange, and Ventura counties.[11]

Finding money for fire prevention and fire fighting was not easy, however. After USFS and other federal agencies spent $1.4 billion on wildfires in 2002, NIFC declared cost-containment to be a goal for the 2003 national fire season. NIFC specifically called for more "prudent" use of air tankers in large fires because they could eat up as much as one-third of the federal firefighting budget.

USFS did not, as fire season approached, close any national forests in the southern part of the state. October was deer-hunting season, and hunters had reacted with anger to the closure of three forests the previous year. Fire agencies, instead, took other precautions. By October 2003, CDF and USFS, in response to weather predictions, had moved considerable resources from northern to southern California. But just how prepared a particular city or county might be for a large wildland fire differed considerably from community to community.

Preparedness in San Bernardino, Riverside, and Los Angeles Counties

San Bernardino and Riverside counties included extensive mountainous regions that had been hit particularly hard by the bark beetle infestation. Many of these mountain fastnesses

---

[9] *The Story,* 11.

[10] Robert Salladay and Zachary Coile, "State: Bush Ignored Fire Plea," *San Francisco Chronicle,* October 31, 2003, A1.

[11] *The Story,* 11.

were populated. Some 45,000 people, for example, lived in the popular resorts lining Lake Arrowhead in San Bernardino County. Public safety officials and political leaders were worried about the rapidly escalating threat of fire, and in 2002, each county established its own mountain area safety taskforce (MAST) to address the specific issues of public safety and forest health. Over the next year, both groups made progress on a number of fronts. They established fuel-treatment priorities, developed evacuation plans, drafted community protection plans, and began a large-scale public education campaign.

San Bernardino Forest Supervisor Gene Zimmerman comments, "No one agency had the lead. This was truly a shared responsibility. It's not the federal government pushing regulations, it's not state government. It has to come from the people within the communities, supported by the agencies. It's the corporate and political will to make a difference and do something." [12]

Each agency took action as needed—and as it could afford to. In early 2003, for example, USFS cleared dead trees from several evacuation routes, such as Highway 18 just south of the community of Lake Arrowhead. The U.S. Department of Agriculture in early August 2003 designated additional funds for the San Bernardino National Forest, and more miles of dead trees were removed along evacuation routes. Also in early 2003, MAST participants agreed on a Joint Information Center (JIC) plan that allowed for the coordinated release of information in a crisis.

OES ran tabletop exercises in late June and mid-August 2003 with some thirty participating agencies to test out fire scenarios in the MAST communities. Another preparedness exercise in early August included officials from CDF and USFS. Zimmerman also worked hard to establish cordial working relationships with agency and political leaders. He had good relations with the CDF chiefs in both San Bernardino and Riverside. He also spoke regularly with Representative Jerry Lewis (R-Calif.), who represented most of San Bernardino County and part of Riverside County.

Meanwhile, Los Angeles County had taken its own measures. The county had the best-funded fire department in the United States, financed through a special voter-approved tax assessment. The department fielded a large ground force and owned some 280 fire engines as well as several helicopters. It leased larger aircraft during the fire season. The county ranked second in the state, after Orange County, in the dollars it spent on fire preparedness.

As long ago as 1993, Los Angeles County supervisors had created a wildfire safety panel. The panel, meeting over a period of months, came up with some forty recommendations, all of which were adopted. "They changed the way new construction and replacement construction occurs in high fire-prone areas," says Los Angeles County Fire Chief Michael

---

[12]Interview with Gene Zimmerman, U.S. Forest Service, Riverside, Calif., July 26, 2005. Unless noted, subsequent quotations from Zimmerman are also from this interview.

Freeman.[13] Among other regulations, homeowners were required by county ordinance to clear brush within 100 feet of structures and within 200 feet if the vegetation was deemed high hazard.

Without preventive measures, says Jerry Williams, USFS national director for fire and aviation management, "you're saying, 'We don't care how bad the fuel is. We don't care what the homes are built of. We're going to rely on our fire department to deal with fires.' And I'm contending that's not enough." When Los Angeles County "started looking at the reality of just what their fire department could do under the most adverse weather conditions imaginable, that's when they started getting serious about prevention," Williams adds.[14]

San Diego County, by contrast, had done little.

Preparedness in San Diego County

For decades, San Diego County had been spared any major conflagration. There had been repeated fires, but they had largely burned wildlands rather than settled communities. "San Diego has been the luckiest place in the world," says San Diego City Fire Chief Jeff Bowman. "I don't know how they've escaped."[15]

Perhaps as a result of its fortunate fire history, San Diego County—spread over 2.7 million acres with some 2.9 million residents—had no county fire department and had a history of voting down bond proposals to finance enhanced fire services. Elected officials repeatedly rejected proposals for a centralized force. The closest San Diego County came to centralized authority figures were Cleveland National Forest Supervisor Ann Fege (whose expertise was in wilderness management) and CDF Unit Chief Maner.

Because of the lack of a central agency, there was no coordinated approach to fire, either its prevention or how to fight it. Instead, sixty-four separate entities were responsible for fighting fire in San Diego County, including four state and federal agencies, eighteen municipal fire departments, fourteen fire protection districts, seven volunteer fire companies, six county service areas, five water districts, and nine Indian reservation fire departments.[16] Altogether, they owned 361 fire engines. "What you have here is a mishmash of some 60 plus fire agencies, all of whom have responsibility and most of whom have no funding. . . . It's terribly ineffective from a firefighting standpoint," says Chief Bowman.

---

[13]Interview with Chief Michael Freeman, Los Angeles County Fire Department, East Los Angeles, Calif., July 26, 2005. Unless noted, subsequent quotations from Freeman are also from this interview.

[14]Telephone interview with Jerry Williams, U.S. Forest Service, July 25, 2005 and interview in San Diego, Calif. Unless noted, subsequent quotations from Williams are also from these interviews.

[15]Interview with Chief Jeff Bowman, San Diego Fire Department, San Diego, Calif., July 28, 2005. Unless noted, subsequent quotations from Bowman are also from this interview.

[16]Gerry Braun, "End in Sight," *San Diego Union-Tribune*, November 2, 2003, A1.

For its part, the city of San Diego had one of the smallest ratios of firefighters to residents of any city in America. Overall, some 875 firefighters were responsible for 330 square miles and a population of 1.3 million. By comparison, San Francisco, with 55 square miles and a population of 885,000, had 1,600 firefighters.

Residential Development

Moreover, San Diego County had experienced exploding development on what wildland management officials called the *urban interface*, where a community of homes abuts natural vegetation. Even more dangerous were areas called *urban intermix*, areas where houses were built with wildland vegetation on all four sides. Whereas a fire at an urban interface community could be fought with one fire engine for several houses, a fire at an urban intermix house required one fire engine per house.

As the houses went up, few rules governed their construction. Wood-shake shingle roofs, for example, were still allowed on new homes in San Diego County despite widespread consensus that they were flammable and a hazard. Moreover, developers had little difficulty getting approval from the Board of Supervisors to build in fire-prone canyons and on ridges in areas surrounded by chaparral and other dry vegetation. "We just continued to cover the landscape with combustible homes in the most flammable environment in the world," opines Richard Hawkins, Cleveland National Forest chief for fire and aviation management.[17]

Even when regulations existed, they were poorly enforced. A 2002 San Diego County fire code called for clearing brush and vegetation 100 feet around any structure. There was no mechanism, however, for enforcing the regulation. "The hardest part," says CDF Unit Chief Maner, "is enforcement. You can write codes all you want, but if you don't have the bodies or the people or the money to do the enforcement side, nobody's going to pay attention to it."[18]

Forest Area Safety Taskforce

One effort did hold promise for prevention. In early 2003, CDF and USFS helped convene a group called the Forest Area Safety Taskforce (FAST) to address fire policy in the eastern, more rural half of the county. FAST brought together all the agencies with responsibility for wildlands. That included USFS, CDF, community volunteer fire departments, state parks, and several county agencies such as land use, parks, the California Highway Patrol, and the sheriff's department. The California transportation agency, CalTrans, was also a member. The group prepared and practiced an evacuation plan for Palomar Mountain, an area of

---

[17]Interview with Richard Hawkins, U.S. Forest Service, Rancho Bernardo, Calif., July 27, 2005. Unless noted, subsequent quotations from Hawkins are also from this interview.

[18]Interview with Chief Chuck Maner, California Department of Forestry and Fire Protection, El Cajon, Calif., July 27, 2005. Unless noted, subsequent quotations from Maner are also from this interview.

wooden houses in a dying forest. It also was looking at a plan to remove dead trees near homes and along evacuation routes.

Organizing FAST was not easy. "Down here," says Maner, "it was me and the Forest Supervisor saying 'Look, we're got to do something about this.' For a year or more, we could get county employees to come to meetings, but not the management people, not the policy-makers." San Diego and FAST lagged at least a year behind San Bernardino and MAST in implementing preventive measures, in part because the bark beetle problem in San Bernardino was more urgent and the number of people living in threatened communities was greater. "They moved quicker and faster, and they got more political support for their needs sooner," says Hawkins.

The FAST conversations revealed that most communities in San Diego County had no evacuation plan. Evacuations were the responsibility of the county sheriff's department, but fire fighters played a key role. As Hawkins explains, "It's up to us to paint those law enforcement officers a picture of just how big is the need, and how fast do we need to do it. Because they're not experts in fighting fires, so if they don't get help from us, then they can't do their part of the job right either."

Military Presence

What did distinguish San Diego County was one of the largest military hubs in the country, from Camp Pendleton Marine Corps Base to Miramar Marine Corps Air Station to North Island Naval Air Station. These bases had not only considerable manpower but fire departments and aerial resources as well. Camp Pendleton had CH-46 helicopters, while Miramar had CH-53 helicopters. North Island's H-3 helicopters were even outfitted with firefighting buckets.[19] Neither the troops nor the helicopters, however, had trained together with USFS, CDF, or local fire departments.

The use of military forces to fight fires was considered a last resort. As retired USFS senior official Michael Edrington puts it, "It's very expensive and it's very time-consuming. They're not a quick response force."[20] Typically, the military were called in for huge timber conflagrations that had been burning for a week or more in states such as Montana and Idaho. Even then, they were deployed selectively.

In San Diego County, there had been discussions about joint training for years. CDF was the contact agency for interaction with the military. For safety reasons, CDF insisted that any military firefighting forces undergo certain minimal training. In addition, military equipment such as helicopters had to have communications systems compatible with those

---

[19]Sue Husari (review team leader), *The 2003 San Diego County Fire Siege Fire Safety Review,* U.S. Department of the Interior, National Park Service, March 2, 2004, 33.

[20]Telephone interview with Michael Edrington, U.S. Forest Service, July 18, 2005. Unless noted, subsequent quotations from Edrington are also from this interview.

used by CDF and USFS. But no agreement existed for the kind of ongoing training that would allow the military to help with firefighting in any systematic way.

There was an exception to the rules, however. Under the Robert T. Stafford Disaster Relief and Emergency Act, an individual base commander had the authority to assist in local emergencies. But the base forces would still need minimal training to allow them to work with—rather than at cross purposes to—civilian fire fighters. By October 2003, no such training had taken place.

Fire Siege Starts

The fires started gradually. The first one, dubbed Roblar 2, ignited at 12:01 p.m. on Tuesday, October 21, on the grounds of the vast Camp Pendleton Marine Corps training base in northern San Diego County. The fire quickly outstripped the capabilities of the small base fire department, so Pendleton requested help from surrounding communities. The Grand Prix Fire started 2 hours later, in San Bernardino County, followed by the Pass Fire in Riverside County, both north of San Diego.

On Thursday, October 23, the Piru Fire flashed in Ventura County at 1:30 p.m.; the Verdale Fire ignited the next day in Los Angeles County at 4:11 p.m. By midnight Friday, five fires had burned some 21,370 acres. Fighting them were 4,770 fire personnel, 409 engines, 32 helicopters, nearly 50 air tankers, 40 bulldozers, and some 500 supervisors.[21] CDF cancelled vacations and days off for all personnel. It reactivated five of ten air tankers that had gone off contract for the rest of the fire season.

Then on Saturday at 9:17 a.m., the Old Fire began in the San Bernardino National Forest. Before long, it threatened the mountain communities of Crestline, Lake Arrowhead, Running Springs, and San Bernardino. At 2:15 p.m. that afternoon, the Simi Fire started in Ventura County.

From the start, Governor Gray Davis was closely involved in the management of the fires, despite the fact that he had just lost a recall vote and would be replaced by Arnold Schwarzenegger that November. Before Saturday, October 25, was over, the governor had proclaimed a state of emergency in San Bernardino and Ventura counties. That same evening, he authorized CDF to activate the two MAFFS planes maintained by the California National Guard. The two planes flew to Point Mugu Naval Air Station in Ventura County and awaited instructions.

Meanwhile, San Diego County responded handsomely under the state's Master Mutual Aid Agreement. By the evening of October 25, the county had dispatched about seventy— or one-fifth—of its engines to help fight the fires in San Bernardino County and at Camp Pendleton. As a precaution, San Diego County fire officials decided late Saturday against lending out any more equipment or personnel.

---

[21] *The Story,* 18.

The 2003 San Diego Firestorm (B): Fighting the Cedar Fire

The Cedar Fire began on Saturday, October 25, in the Cleveland National Forest near Cedar Creek, some 25 miles east of the city of San Diego. After wandering lost in the forest for 7 hours, a first-time hunter, Sergio Martinez, had set off a flare, which started a small fire.

By the time a helicopter finally found Martinez (at 5:50 p.m.), the fire had already been reported. The first person to call it in, at 5:37 p.m., was a veteran CDF employee.[1] The call was fielded by the Monte Vista Emergency Communications Center (a dispatch office) in El Cajon to the east of San Diego City. The center was state-owned but staffed by both California Department of Forestry and Fire Protection (CDF) and U.S. Forest Service (USFS) personnel. Because the fire originated in a national forest, it was considered a USFS fire and a USFS dispatcher handled the response. Until such time as a fire was deemed an incident and assigned an incident commander, the dispatcher on duty was the person in charge. Within 2 minutes, at 5:39 p.m., the Monte Vista dispatcher sent forces: nine USFS engines from the Cleveland National Forest and five engines from CDF, carrying a total of some 320 firefighters.

The first ground forces arrived on the scene by 6:10, and USFS Division Chief Carlton Joseph became incident commander. The ground crews discovered, however, that the fire's location had been misidentified; it was some 10 miles away. When it was finally pinpointed, the fire proved to be inaccessible, in a canyon over a mile from the nearest usable road. Moreover, there were predictions of Santa Ana winds, powerful hot gusts that sweep down off the mountains toward the sea. USFS Cleveland National Forest Fire Chief Richard Hawkins says, "Because of the prediction for Santa Ana winds, the route we would have sent the ground forces in on would have been compromised by the fire, and therefore the ground forces would have been killed."[2] Joseph therefore decided to wait for daybreak when he could return with bulldozers, aircraft, and more than 1,400 firefighters.

Aircraft Attack?

The Monte Vista dispatcher also tried to send airplanes against the fire. There were two fixed-wing aircraft, capable of dropping 1,200 gallons of flame retardant, based at Ramona Air Attack Base some 10 miles west of Cedar Creek. Both planes belonged to CDF. At

---

[1] Megan Garvey, "Night of Fire," *Los Angeles Times*, December 28, 2003, A1. The CDF employee was Ron Serabia.

[2] Interview with Richard Hawkins, U.S. Forest Service, Rancho Bernardo, Calif., July 27, 2005. Unless noted, subsequent quotations from Hawkins are also from this interview.

5:42 p.m., the dispatcher radioed for the planes to launch an initial attack on the fire. But the cut-off time for planes to fly was 5:36 p.m., set for safety reasons at half an hour before sundown.[3] The pilots had already left for home. Since the 1994 fire season that cost thirty-four firefighters' lives, including some flying aircraft too late under dangerous conditions, both CDF and USFS had considered the cut-off time sacrosanct; its purpose was to save lives. CDF San Diego Unit Chief Chuck Maner explains, "The reason we have these rules is there's a lot of dead pilots who flew into canyons and couldn't fly out because they couldn't see in the shadows or the smoke."[4]

For San Diego County, there was no night-flying option. Unlike Los Angeles County, which maintained its own fleet of aircraft, San Diego County relied on CDF and USFS aircraft, whose pilots worked statewide or nationwide and were often flying in unfamiliar territory. They did not, as a matter of pilot safety, fly at night.

There was discussion later as to whether the airplanes could have extinguished the fire, which at that point was estimated at between 5 and 20 acres. CDF and USFS believe that it could not. "Up until midnight, it was still a small fire," says CDF Unit Chief Maner. "It wasn't the kind of fire we would have taken risks on." USFS Cleveland National Forest Fire Chief Hawkins notes that because firemen at that stage could not get close enough to fight the fire on the ground, the aircraft would have been of limited use. "We've never put out a fire that didn't have ground forces present," he says. "It would simply have rekindled later."

Helicopter Attack?

Separately, the sheriff's helicopter that had rescued the hunter had radioed at 5:41 p.m. for a second sheriff's helicopter to carry water to the fire. The second helicopter, equipped with a 100-gallon Bambi bucket, took off. The sheriff's copter, with two pilots on board, was some 20 minutes away from the fire when the USFS dispatcher at Monte Vista ordered it to return to base. By the time the helicopter reached the fire, it would have been nearly 30 minutes past the cut-off time and too dark to operate safely.

The two sheriff's pilots themselves later told the press they felt they could have put out the fire. But Hawkins believes they are mistaken. "One of the two pilots had never even used a bucket before, and the other had had one training assignment," he points out. "They could never have made any kind of significant progress on a fire that size with little tiny water buckets." Meanwhile, the fire was growing.

---

[3]USFS and CDF had different policies. The CDF cut-off times applied to air tankers and helicopters equally. The USFS cut-off policy referred only to air tankers. In practice, USFS allowed helicopters to fly somewhat later. Sue Husari (review team leader), *The 2003 San Diego County Fire Siege Fire Safety Review*, U.S. Department of the Interior, National Park Service, March 2, 2004, 32.

[4]Interview with Chief Chuck Maner, California Department of Forestry and Fire Protection, El Cajon, Calif., July 27, 2005. Unless noted, subsequent quotations from Maner are also from this interview.

Overnight Maelstrom

USFS took initial command of the fire because it had started on federal land. But before midnight, the predicted rising Santa Ana winds blew the fire into an area of state responsibility. As a result, at 11:56 p.m. CDF and USFS entered into a Unified Command. Joseph remained incident commander for USFS; Randy Lyle took charge for CDF.[5] By then, the fire covered 5,300 acres, with flames as high as 75–100 feet. It loomed over the suburban community of Ramona Country Estates with 10,000 residents. By midnight Saturday, USFS and CDF had sent eighteen crews, twenty-seven fire engines, and three bulldozers to contain the fire.[6]

The sheriff's department, meanwhile, had set up a command post at Country Estates. At 10:44 p.m., the sheriff's deputies ordered evacuations for Ramona.[7] According to protocol, the CDF and USFS incident commanders were to tell sheriff's deputies which neighborhoods to evacuate. But in the pandemonium of the night, evacuees were pouring out as best they could—creating a massive traffic jam. The first homes burned at 12:35 a.m. It was already clear that equipment and crews were in short supply. Instead of the typical ratio of one fire engine to two houses, CDF had one engine for every twenty houses threatened.

The situation was chaotic. Communications failed, with state and federal fire officials broadcasting on two radio channels, older fire rigs on a third, and sheriff's deputies on a fourth.[8] By 3:00 a.m., 62,000 acres were burning. Meanwhile, the fire moved on to threaten the casino on the Barona Indian Reservation. Firefighters arrived just in time to keep 2,000 gamblers and 500 employees inside the casino, where they waited out the firestorm.

The residents of Wildcat Canyon's Strange Way and the Featherstone Canyon neighborhoods were not so lucky. They relied for protection on the Rural Fire Protection District, with fourteen fulltime firefighters and ninety-seven volunteers to service 720 square miles. Only a handful of firefighters made it to Wildcat. Once there, they couldn't use the overcrowded radio channels, which could carry only four conversations at once. In Featherstone Canyon, meanwhile, fire blocked the way out. Thirteen people died Saturday night to Sunday trying to flee isolated communities. As California Assemblyman Jay LaSuer (R-La Mesa) later wrote, "People died in their garages attempting to get in their automobiles while attempting to flee the fire. Others died in their driveways, and still others were trapped on roads they thought would take them to safety."[9]

---

[5]Jeff Bowman, *Cedar Fire 2003 After Action Report,* City of San Diego Fire-Rescue Department, June 2004, 77.

[6]U.S. Forest Service and California Department of Forestry and Fire Protection, *California Fire Siege 2003: The Story* (hereafter, *The Story*), 20.

[7]Bowman, *Cedar Fire 2003 After Action Report,* 76.

[8]Garvey, "Night of Fire."

[9]Letter from Jay LaSuer to Chairman William Campbell, *Governor's Blue Ribbon Fire Commission Report,* February 26, 2004. Blue Ribbon Commission, App. G, 7.

Sunday, October 26

By the early hours of Sunday morning, the Cedar Fire was spreading at the rate of 12,000 acres an hour, a rate of spread firefighters had never seen before. "Despite our expertise," concedes USFS Fire Chief Hawkins, "we did not foresee how fast this fire would spread. . . . It was the drought and all the vegetation dying that generated a situation where the fire behaved differently than anything we'd seen in the past." CDF and USFS helicopters and air tankers launched at dawn (6 a.m.) to combat the fire. "We were using them where we could use them. . . . It did a lot of good where they were," recalls CDF Unit Chief Maner. "It bought us some time. . . . But what a lot of people don't realize is if you're ahead of the fire and the wind is blowing your way, the smoke layer is over you. Air tankers can't go in because they can't see. They can't fly."

At 5:00 a.m., the fire overran the town of Poway; there were only fifteen firefighters and four engines available to protect 49,000 residents. Other community engines were at Camp Pendleton, at Rancho Cucamonga in San Bernardino County, and at Ramona Country Estates. The fire chief evacuated more than two hundred homes.

The Cedar Fire entered San Diego City a mile from the neighborhood of Scripps Ranch between 7:00 and 7:30 a.m.[10] Scripps Ranch residents had no warning that the fire was so close. The San Diego OES office failed to activate the emergency broadcast system and the city's Emergency Operations Center (EOC) opened only at 9:10 a.m.[11] Sheriff's helicopters broadcast evacuation orders over rooftops only 20 minutes before the first houses burned. Some thirty houses were alight by 8:30 a.m.

On paper, the city had 875 firefighters and officers, 57 engines, and 11 brush units. But eleven engines and forty-four firefighters had gone to fight the Old and Grand Prix fires in San Bernardino County. Another ten engines and forty firefighters were tied down in Country Estates. The city's lease on its only firefighting helicopter had expired October 21. CDF had taken over the copter and sent it to fight the Old Fire in San Bernardino. The city dispatched what it could to Scripps Ranch—25 engines and 112 firefighters. A mutual aid plea to other fire districts went unanswered. The San Diego Fire Department (SDFD) called for all off-duty firefighters. They responded in the hundreds, but there were no engines available. Nonetheless, there were successes. The city evacuated 10,000 residents with no deaths or injuries. Also, the mayor and city manager negotiated the return of Copter 1, and it was back in the city by Monday, October 27 at 11:00 a.m.

Command Transition

Meanwhile, the severity of the fire had triggered a change in command. At 7:00 a.m. Sunday, Cleveland National Forest Fire and Aviation Management Chief Rich Hawkins replaced

---

[10]Bowman, *Cedar Fire 2003 After Action Report*, 2.
[11]Ibid.

Joseph as USFS incident commander, joining Lyle from CDF. That evening at 6:00 p.m., CDF sent a state incident command team—a pre-formed team with designated responsibilities—to relieve Lyle.[12] John Hawkins was the CDF team leader. As the fire expanded, additional incident commanders were assigned from the cities of Poway, Lakeside, and San Diego. But the command system, recalls Rich Hawkins, "didn't work well that day because we never did get all five people in one place. . . . It was very difficult because the fire was spreading so rapidly."

As Sunday progressed, the firefighting effort was overwhelmed and logistics were in disarray. Many units received no food, fuel, or supplies. Communications among firefighters, commanders, and law enforcement were unreliable and inconsistent. Some firefighters did not report to the Incident Command Post because they did not know where it was, but proceeded directly to the fire, which meant that their actions were uncoordinated and, in some cases, their whereabouts were unknown.[13]

Around noon Sunday, all aircraft were grounded after the supervisor of the Air Tactical Group (a member of the Incident Command team) flew the western edge of the fire and reported that conditions were too windy and smoky for air drops.[14] The two California-based MAFFS were also affected. Conditions did not allow them to fly over the Cedar Fire on Sunday.

Throughout Sunday, the Cedar Fire grew. At 10:00 a.m., 116,000 acres were burning.[15] By 7:00 p.m. Sunday, the fire reached 128,000 acres; by midnight, it covered 153,000 acres.[16] Altogether on Sunday, firefighting authorities deployed 30 crews, 170 fire engines, 3 helicopters, and 1 bulldozer on the Cedar Fire.[17] Adding to the burden, two more fires broke out in San Diego County on Sunday. The Paradise Fire ignited at 1:30 a.m. Sunday near the community of Valley Center, and the Otay Fire ignited at 7:18 a.m. near the San Diego City area known as Otay. On Sunday, Governor Davis extended the state of emergency to San Diego and Los Angeles counties.

The earlier fires further north continued to wreak havoc as well. Together with the Cedar Fire, they forced the Federal Aviation Authority (FAA) to evacuate the Regional Terminal Radar Approach Control Facility at Miramar. Some airports closed due to smoke; delays plagued air travel nationwide. On Sunday, San Diego Gas & Electric Co. shut down a major transmission line to 11,000 customers near the city; by Monday, thousands more were without power. The railroads were affected, too. Amtrak passenger service and rail freight were

[12]The CDF team officially took command the next morning.

[13]Husari, *2003 San Diego County Fire Siege,* 19.

[14]Bowman, *Cedar Fire 2003 After Action Report,* 84. See also William Finn Bennett, "Wind-Driven Smoke Grounds Tanker Planes," NC Times.com, October 26, 2003, available at www.nctimes.com/articles/2003/10/27/news/top_stories/10_26_0318_47_19.prt.

[15]Bowman, *Cedar Fire 2003 After Action Report,* 83.

[16]Ibid., 84.

[17]*The Story,* 24.

disrupted due to fire; Union Pacific parked thirty trains; and Burlington Northern Santa Fe delayed eighty-two trains when fires closed rail lines.[18] Interstate highways 15, 215, and 210 were closed, affecting interstate commerce.

For the first time since 1993, California asked for assistance from other states. By Sunday evening, South Ops had made 2,800 separate requests of NIFC for people and equipment; six states had responded.[19] San Bernardino County Supervisor Dennis Hansberger told the press that "everybody was deployed. Nobody was sitting around waiting. It's just that there were not enough resources."[20] Some San Diego political leaders, having observed precisely that, had been trying to do something about the resource problem all day Sunday.

Send in the Modular Airborne Firefighting System!

On Sunday, October 26, Jay LaSuer (R-La Mesa), member of the California Assembly, awoke at 5:00 a.m. with the feeling that something was very wrong. LaSuer represented 424,000 people in District 77, which covered the eastern half of the county, including the cities of El Cajon, La Mesa, and Santee. LaSuer had first been elected to the California Assembly in 2000. Before that, he had spent 6 years working in a police department and another 25 years working in the sheriff's department.

When LaSuer saw the sky that morning, he knew what it was: "I thought, 'Oh God, the world's on fire.'"[21] His first call was to Wendell Cutting, the in-district chief of staff for Representative Duncan Hunter (R-Calif.). Hunter's district included LaSuer's. It also included most of the communities affected by the Cedar Fire. LaSuer asked Cutting what kind of resources the federal government had available to send to fight the fire. Cutting responded that most likely San Diego could get access to either the six federal C-130s (MAFFS) or military helicopters based in the county.

Together, the two men called Representative Hunter in Washington to brief him on the Cedar Fire and to consult with him about available options. Hunter confirmed that, in his capacity as chair of the House of Representatives Armed Services Committee, he might be able to secure the services of the MAFFS planes. He promised to try.

Hunter, as committee chair, had a personal relationship with the chairman of the Joint Chiefs of Staff (JCS), Richard B. Myers. Hunter called General Myers at home to ask him for authority to release the MAFFS planes to California. The JCS chair said Hunter could have "anything you want."[22] Specifically, Myers said he would be happy—upon a formal request

---

[18]Ibid., 26.

[19]Jill Leovy and Julie Cart, "Stretched Thin, State Seeks Help," *Los Angeles Times,* October 27, 2003, A18.

[20]Ibid.

[21]Interview with Jay LaSuer, member of the California Assembly (R-La Mesa), La Mesa, Calif., July 25, 2005. Unless noted, subsequent quotations from LaSuer are also from this interview.

[22]Leovy and Cart, "Stretched Thin, State Seeks Help."

from fire officials in California—to release the two MAFFS planes based in Colorado Springs. He told Hunter to feel free to give his home number to the appropriate California fire official.

Delighted, Hunter passed the news to Cutting and LaSuer in San Diego and asked them to find out who could order up the planes. So Cutting and LaSuer placed a call first to the OES. OES directed their call to CDF, where the elected officials were connected to Ray Snodgrass, the agency's chief deputy director. Snodgrass, says LaSuer, informed him that no aircraft were flying in San Diego County.[23] He also said he could not make any decision about the MAFFS planes "until he could get the committee together." LaSuer, who was watching television news helicopters flying in the area, was dubious about Snodgrass's first statement; as for the second, he told the CDF official he would have Representative Hunter call him directly.

When Hunter reached Snodgrass, the CDF official explained that, under the 1932 Economy Act, the state could not request MAFFS planes until all supplies of civilian aircraft had been exhausted. Snodgrass, says then CDF Deputy Director for Fire Operations James Wright, "was trying to route it through the proper channels instead of a phone call. . . . It's our job to bring calm to chaos, not add chaos to chaos. And you do that through policies, procedures, and protocols."[24] But Hunter, says LaSuer, argued to Snodgrass that under the Stafford Act (Section 5170c, Hazard Mitigation), the governor of a state could request that the president direct the secretary of defense to mobilize military assets for an emergency.[25] Hunter even faxed Snodgrass a copy of the law. He also gave Snodgrass Myers's home number and told him to call, but Snodgrass never did.

By mid-afternoon on Sunday, Hunter learned that his own house—in the community of Peutz Valley near Alpine—had burned to the ground. Hoping to reach a fire official who would understand the nature of the help he was offering and make it happen, Hunter decided to take his request higher up the chain of command. His next call was to USFS Regional Forester for the Pacific Southwest Jack Blackwell, who handed the phone to Ray Quintanar, the fire and aviation management chief. Representative Hunter, according to Quintanar, said, "I want you to take this guy's phone number. Here's Myers's phone number, and I want you to tell him to move all available MAFFS units." Quintanar told Hunter that "my chain of authority has ended, we can't do that" because there were still commercial air tankers available and, in any event, no aircraft were flying due to smoke.[26]

---

[23]Snodgrass has since retired.

[24]Telephone interview with James Wright, California Department of Forestry and Fire Protection, July 18, 2005. Unless noted, subsequent quotations from Wright are also from this interview.

[25]The law says: "During the immediate aftermath of an incident which may ultimately qualify for assistance under this title . . . the Governor of the State in which such incident occurred may request the President to direct the Secretary of Defense to utilize the resources of the Department of Defense for the purpose of performing on public and private lands any emergency work which is made necessary by such incident and which is essential for the preservation of life and property." See www.fema.gov/pdf/about/stafford_act.pdf.

[26]Interview with Ray Quintanar, U.S. Forest Service, Riverside, Calif., July 26, 2005. Unless noted, subsequent quotations from Quintanar are also from this interview.

But Quintanar recognized that Hunter was angry. So he called Jerry Williams, the USFS national director for fire and aviation management based in Washington, D.C., to report his conversation with the member of Congress. Williams, in turn, contacted the head of USFS, Dale Bosworth, who authorized Region 5 to order up an additional MAFFS C-130 tanker. Meanwhile, at 5:00 p.m. CDF Fire Operations Director Wright contacted Quintanar separately to ask that Quintanar formally request from NIFC additional federal firefighting resources, including engines, crews, and MAFFS planes.[27] Quintanar filed the request for one additional MAFFS plane late Sunday and then called Hunter back to let him know he had ordered the plane.

For good measure, Quintanar later ordered his deputy, George Motschall, to order up every air tanker he could. Motschall objected that nothing was flying. "I said just order the damn things," recalls Quintanar. His reason, as he later told a reporter, was politics: "We have to deal with a lot of political crap. That is part of the job."[28]

Meanwhile, Hunter's District Chief of Staff Cutting was contacting other local officials. One was City Councilman Jim Madaffer, who had a good working relationship with Hunter's office.[29] On learning of the Cedar Fire, Madaffer had rushed to the SDFD operations dispatch facility, located near the airport in the heart of the city. At about 4:00 p.m. on Sunday, Cutting reached Madaffer's chief of staff, Aimee Faucett. Cutting told Faucett that MAFFS planes were available but that no one at CDF would accept them. Madaffer turned for an explanation to two men in the dispatch center with him: the mayor and San Diego Fire Chief Bowman. "I said listen, I don't understand this," recalls Madaffer. "How on earth can we be getting calls like this? Why don't we take advantage of this offer?"[30]

Bowman explained how the procedures worked—that it was not CDF but USFS that had the authority to order up MAFFS planes and that USFS could put in a request to Boise only after all contract civilian resources were gone. But to Madaffer that did not compute: "I remember how angry I was at Bowman's response—and I respect Bowman highly. . . . I'm there as the elected person representing the people, and people like me are saying what the heck are you talking about you can't use these? To the average person, it's kind of mind-boggling that they couldn't use the resources."

LaSuer and Cutting also tried to call Governor Davis on Sunday, October 26, but the governor did not return their calls. "We were getting such a runaround," says LaSuer. "I mean, it's like we want to give you firefighting equipment in the middle of the worst fire to hit the state, and you're telling me no? We'll give you pilots that can drop thousands of gallons of

[27]*Governor's Blue Ribbon Fire Commission Report,* D4 (Timeline).

[28]Quoted in Stuart Leavenworth, "Earlier Fiascos Spawned Fire Control Center," *Sacramento Bee,* November 1, 2003, A24.

[29]Madaffer represented San Diego City Council District 7.

[30]Telephone interview with Jim Madaffer, San Diego city council, August 1, 2005. Unless noted, subsequent quotations from Madaffer are also from this interview.

retardant on the fire, and you're going to say no? And pilots that have the equipment to fly right through the smoke? That just didn't make sense."

Military Helicopter Option?

LaSuer had another idea that he also put forward—that fire officials request military helicopters from Miramar Marine Corps Air Station or from Camp Pendleton. But the answer remained the same: no. For one thing, no aircraft were flying. For another, using military assets of any sort was an option of last resort, and the fire agencies still had plenty of helicopters in reserve. In addition, argued CDF and USFS fire officials, the military pilots were not trained to fight fires. "You can go over to Pendleton," says Region 5 Fire Chief Quintanar, "and they have a slew of helicopters setting out on that tarmac. But they're not all available for firefighting. Those are combat helicopters."

Moreover, the military communications equipment was incompatible with CDF and USFS radios. As Quintanar puts it, "We're not going to put up aircraft that don't have our frequencies and don't understand our air safety protocols. . . . We normally require our helicopter pilots to have 1,500 hours of flying, including about 500 hours of mountain flying." Ralph Domanski, emergency operations coordinator for Region 5, adds that training would take about 4 days—2 in the classroom and 2 flying.[31]

For his part, USFS Incident Commander Rich Hawkins felt even a fleet of helicopters could not have helped on Sunday. "I didn't consider the use of their helicopters because no number of aircraft were going to change the situation we were dealing with on October 26," he says. "It was too windy for the helicopters to be effective. To me, this was just a bunch of politicians meddling in our affairs who did not have the expertise to effectively do so." BLM Fire Director Larry Hamilton concedes that problems arise when "the county supervisors and elected officials see the news helicopter out there flying around and want to know why the hell we're not flying."[32] The difference, he clarifies, is that news helicopters were flying around the fire, not into it.

LaSuer, for one, rejected the fire officials' arguments. "They [the military] fight fires on the military reservation all the time," he says. CDF "gave us all kinds of excuses—that they couldn't talk to them on the radio, or they didn't have the skills, or they weren't certified. All that kind of stuff, just on and on and on. . . . I've never been so frustrated in my life." To claim that the military could not communicate with CDF or USFS aircraft because they had different radio systems was, says LaSuer, "an out-and-out lie. They talk to CDF all the time."

---

[31]Interview with Ralph Domanski, emergency operations coordinator for Region 5, USFS Riverside, Calif., July 26, 2005. Unless noted, subsequent quotations from Domanski are from also this interview.

[32]Telephone interview with Larry Hamilton, Bureau of Land Management, July 13, 2005. Unless noted, subsequent quotations from Hamilton are also from this interview.

Nonetheless, LaSuer offered another suggestion—that CDF simply assign the military a particular sector so the helicopters would not interfere with one another. This did not persuade the fire authorities.

The continued resistance, LaSuer hypothesizes, made it "apparent that there were some turf problems. Your interest has got to be on saving lives and property." He adds, "The whole idea when this thing first began was not to interfere, not to get in anybody's way, but to say hey, here's some equipment we can get for you. All we want to do is help you fight the fire. But there was just absolutely no way."

North Island

Ironically, another area military facility independently came forward to offer help—but it was also rebuffed. The commander of the North Island Naval Station, located on a large island just offshore from the San Diego International Airport, wanted to offer his firefighting helicopters—already equipped with Bambi buckets carrying 1,000 gallons—to the effort. Admiral Jose Betancourt was acting under the authority granted military commanders under the Stafford Act to assist in local emergencies.[33]

On Sunday morning, the North Island commander sent three choppers with full buckets to Ramona air field. CDF officials at Ramona, however, told the crews they did not have the department's permission to fight the fire.[34] One reason, CDF spokesman David Wheeler later explained, was the "military as last resort" requirement: "Agencies use local resources, then turn to the county, then to the state level, before turning to the federal government, which is the last resort."[35] Officials also argued that CDF had to certify the Navy pilots and verify the helicopters' maintenance records before they could fly.[36]

CDF, says Unit Chief Maner, was taken aback by the North Island offer. "We didn't even know they existed," he recalls. Consequently, CDF decided it could not accept the help. "We didn't have any idea what their skill capability was," says Maner. "We didn't know if their radios would talk to our radios. So we basically said not a good idea, we're not going to use you."

So the North Island commander approached the San Diego City Fire Department instead. City Councilmember Maddaffer was at the SDFD operations center Sunday evening when the call came through to Assistant Fire Chief August Ghio. Madaffer recalls:

It was clear this commander was very agitated that he had to go to the steps that he did, but he felt it his duty as a member of the military to make his equipment available to fight a very serious fire. . . .

---

[33]After the fact, the commander learned that he did not have the right to offer the helicopters. The offer had technically to come from the admiral in charge of the aviation unit, who was based in Louisiana.

[34]James W. Crawley, "Navy Helicopters Sidelined," *San Diego Union-Tribune*, October 30, 2003, A11. See also Tony Perry and Gregg Jones, "Delay in Aerial Water Drops Is Criticized," *Los Angeles Times*, October 29, 2003, A29.

[35]Quoted in ibid.

[36]Ibid.

At this point I'm getting upset and thinking 'I don't get it.' It is an emergency. We do have houses burning to the ground. I don't understand why somebody can't just say fine. . . . Sometimes you just have to do things differently than what you expected might happen.

Representative Hunter, meanwhile, had not abandoned his efforts to bring military assets to bear on the Cedar Fire. He launched an all-fronts campaign.

Hunter Works the Phones

During Sunday, Hunter or his staff called as many officials in as many agencies as he could think of. LaSuer commented Sunday night that Hunter had "gone through the White House, the Department of Homeland Security, and the California Department of Forestry to get access to an aerial firefighting unit out of Point Mugu and these planes in Colorado Springs." But the blame had shifted slightly by Sunday evening, from CDF to Governor Davis. "All that is needed," said LaSuer, "is a telephone call from Governor Davis." [37]

Among the senior officials who Representative Hunter reached Sunday was BLM Fire and Aviation Director Hamilton at NIFC in Boise. It was one of many calls that Hamilton received that day, presumably as the result of Hunter's campaign. "I was getting phone calls from the secretary of the Interior, the chief of the Forest Service, the congressional delegation there in California, phone calls from the regional forester in California, the state director for BLM," he remembers. Hunter, recalls Hamilton, was not happy. The problem for elected officials, explains Hamilton, is that "they see all those military assets sitting there and want to know why we're not using those. . . . They just see us as being ineffectual, not responsive. Or we really don't have our act together."

Office of Emergency Services Responds

As the views of Hunter and LaSuer became public, one state official decided it was time to respond. OES Director Jones let the governor's office know that he intended to rebut some of the charges being made. "As the state coordinating officer," he says, "one of the roles I played was to try to keep the political concerns from affecting the actual fire operations." In a Sunday afternoon press conference, Jones caustically offered to supply a yellow fire jacket to any elected official who might like to fly in and help fight the fires. An angry Jones observed, "If you want somebody such as a politician telling you where they want the firefighting forces, we are regressing 40 years in the state of California. I say we will work with them, get all the resources we can get into the state, and trust them [the professional fire officers] to save as many lives and as much property as possible." [38]

---

[37]Quoted in Bennett, "Wind-Driven Smoke Grounds Tanker Planes."
[38]California Office of Emergency Services, *Fire Siege 2003* [Videotape].

From Jones's point of view, Representative Hunter was not being helpful. "Instead of calling up and saying 'Do you want more at this point?' and if so, ordering them up, he was directing, or trying to direct, the use of specific aircraft," says Jones.

Jones had trouble figuring out why Hunter persisted with his requests. The representative, says Jones, "actually knew the facts on the ordering of military aircraft. He knew what we had deployed. It wasn't a question that he was ill informed. It was more one of trying to grab headlines." USFS Incident Commander Hawkins, by contrast, was sympathetic to Hunter. "I'm sure there was a belief on his part that the military could help reduce the level of carnage," says Hawkins; but he quickly adds, "I just don't agree with him."

But from Hunter's perspective, the system simply made no sense. As he later explained, "You have a bureaucracy that feels it can't request military assets up front. The key [to fighting wildfires] is getting the military into the firefight at the front of the fire." [39] He added, "There's a lot of red tape. Everybody's doing their job. The problem is, you don't have anything that's a short, fast-reacting chain of command." [40] Furthermore, "We have a policy of what I would call gradual buildup. I think the better policy would be to front-load the system. If you want economy as well as effectiveness, you want to stop the fires when they're small fires." [41]

LaSuer is more scathing:

Nobody attempted to tell anybody what to do or how to fight a fire. All we did was to try to get them to take some equipment and try to use resources that they had available to them. They refused to do it. . . . When you get to the point that it's more important for you to protect your turf than it is to do what's right, there's a problem. . . . I don't think anybody in politics is going to get involved in anything that is an operation unless their area is in danger and they can see things aren't being done. It's not my job to tell the firefighters how to fight fires. . . . But I do know that at one level or another in a command structure there's a place where decisions are made, and if you're offered equipment and it's something you need, then you take it.

Finally, after midnight on Sunday and still dissatisfied with the response he had gotten, Representative Hunter called USFS National Fire and Aviation Director Williams in Washington, D.C. "Who the hell is in charge here?" Hunter demanded. Williams tried to explain to Hunter that incident commanders on the scene of the Cedar Fire, who were ultimately those in charge, had not made any requests for additional MAFFS planes because they judged conditions to be too poor. The extra aircraft, says Williams, "wouldn't be an asset, they'd be a liability." At the same time, he could sense that trying to explain these things over the phone in the middle of the night was "not going over too well."

---

[39]Quoted in Crawley, "Navy Helicopters Sidelined," A11.

[40]Quoted in Chris Woodyard, "Red Tape Slowed Firefighters from Getting Help, Lawmaker Says," *USA Today*, October 31, 2003, 3A.

[41]Quoted in Steve Schmidt, "Resources Fell Painfully Short," *San Diego Union-Tribune*, November 1, 2003, A1.

The 2003 San Diego Firestorm (C): Epilogue

On Monday, October 27, 2003, at 11:18 a.m., California exhausted the available supply of contract air tankers.[1] Under the 1932 Economy Act, the U.S. Forest Service (USFS) was now at liberty to order up the remaining military-owned Modular Airborne Firefighting System (MAFFS) aircraft from the National Interagency Fire Center (NIFC). Accordingly, the order went out for the rest of the MAFFS planes.

The first three (including the one that USFS Region 5 Fire and Aviation Chief Ray Quintanar had ordered on Sunday night after talking to Representative Duncan Hunter) joined the existing California-based MAFFS planes at Point Mugu Naval Air Station in Ventura County on the afternoon of Tuesday, October 28. The final three MAFFS flew in late afternoon on Wednesday, October 29.[2]

The MAFFS flew some 8 hours on Monday, about the same on Tuesday, and somewhat more on Wednesday.[3] They were of limited use due to the fire and weather conditions, however. Aircraft on the Paradise Fire had to be grounded Tuesday due to strong winds, smoke, and poor visibility. Six air tankers reported damage from flying debris.[4] On Thursday, October 30, and Friday, October 31, when all eight MAFFS planes were available, none of them flew. Damp and drizzle on both days helped firefighters make considerable progress in containing the fires, however. The MAFFS planes were released on Sunday, November 2.[5]

National and international awareness of the fire siege grew. On Monday, October 27, at Governor Davis's request, President George W. Bush declared Los Angeles, San Bernardino, Ventura, and San Diego counties to be disaster areas.[6] Dan Rather anchored his CBS nightly newscast out of San Diego on Monday. The National Football League moved the Monday Night Football game scheduled for November 3 from San Diego to Tempe, Arizona. Governor Davis accompanied Homeland Security Secretary Tom Ridge on a tour of the fire area on November 1; President Bush visited on November 4 together with Governor Davis and Governor-elect Arnold Schwarzenegger.

---

[1] *Governor's Blue Ribbon Fire Commission Report*, February 26, 2004. Blue Ribbon Commission, App. D, 4 (Timeline).

[2] Ibid., App. D, 6–7.

[3] U.S. Forest Service and California Department of Forestry and Fire Protection, *California Fire Siege 2003: The Story*, 28, 32 and 36.

[4] Ibid., 32.

[5] Ibid., 49.

[6] He later added Riverside County.

The Cedar Fire was declared 100 percent contained on Tuesday, November 4. Over 10 days, it had burned 273,246 acres, destroyed 2,232 residences, 22 commercial properties, and 566 outbuildings, and it had killed fourteen people—thirteen civilians and one fire-fighter. Taken all together, the fires of the 2003 firestorm burned 729,600 acres, 3,631 homes, 36 commercial properties, and 1,169 outbuildings. They caused 246 injuries, and 24 people died. At the height of the firestorm, 15,631 firefighters were assigned to the blazes.[7]

On November 21, Congress passed the Healthy Forests Restoration Act, which mandated the systematic removal of millions of acres of brush and small trees from the nation's forests to protect them from wildfire. President Bush signed the bill on December 3, 2003. Political fallout from the fires continued for months, however, with fire agencies, politicians, developers, environmentalists, representatives of the timber industry, and others arguing over who had made operational mistakes in fighting the fire or who had blocked effective fire prevention policies.

But as USFS Fire and Aviation Management National Director Jerry Williams sees it, the point is not to affix blame but to look for new ways to fight what he calls "megafires"—those fires that by virtue of their speed, ferocity, and location outstrip the ability of fire departments to combat them. These new approaches should, he feels, emphasize preemptive action. Instead of building ever larger fire departments, says Williams, fire-prone communities should ask themselves

what things can we do to better manage the land so that we can prevent those factors from developing that lead to this catastrophic kind of fire? . . . All the helicopters in the world aren't enough if you're not managing the land, and you're not managing the growth behaviors at the [urban-wildlands] interface. If you miss those two things, you're going to have another situation where some poor slob someplace is going to have to make the right decision under the most terrible circumstances with virtually no decision space.[8]

[7] *Governor's Blue Ribbon Fire Commission Report,* 1.

[8] Telephone interview with Jerry Williams, U.S. Forest Service, July 25, 2005, and interview in San Diego, Calif. Unless noted, subsequent quotations from Williams are also from these interviews.

Key Actors in the 2003 San Diego Firestorm

Federal Government

Duncan Hunter (R-Calif.), member of the U.S. House of Representatives and chair of the House Armed Services Committee

Gen. Richard B. Myers, chairman of the Joint Chiefs of Staff

Wendell Cutting, district chief of staff for Representative Hunter

Admiral Jose Betancourt, commander, North Island Naval Station

George W. Bush, president of the United States

U.S. Forest Service, U. S. Department of Agriculture

Jerry Williams, national director, Fire and Aviation Management, U.S. Forest Service

Dale Bosworth, chief, U.S. Forest Service

Ray Quintanar, chief, Fire and Aviation Management, Pacific Southwest Region, U.S. Forest Service

Carlton Joseph, division chief and first Cedar Fire incident commander, U.S. Forest Service

Richard (Rich) Hawkins, chief, Fire and Aviation Management, Cleveland National Forest (replaced Joseph as Cedar Fire incident commander)

Ann Fege, supervisor, Cleveland National Forest

Gene Zimmerman, supervisor, San Bernardino National Forest

U.S. Department of the Interior

Larry Hamilton, director, Fire and Aviation, Bureau of Land Management

State of California

Gray Davis, governor

Dallas Jones, director, Office of Emergency Services (OES)

Jay LaSuer (R-La Mesa), California assemblyman

California Department of Forestry and Fire Protection (CDF)

Ray Snodgrass, chief deputy director

Andrea Tuttle, director

Chuck Maner, chief, San Diego Unit

James Wright, deputy director, Fire Operations

City of San Diego

Jeff Bowman, fire chief

Jim Madaffer, city councilman

Los Angeles Country

Michael Freeman, chief, Los Angeles County Fire Department

The San Diego Firestorm, 2003

Chronology of Events

Friday, March 7, 2003

Anticipating an intense wildfire season, California Governor Gray Davis declares a state of emergency. Fire prevention and mitigation measures are implemented throughout the spring and summer months.

Tuesday, October 21

12:01 p.m.: The Roblar 2 Fire begins at the Camp Pendleton Marine Corps training base in San Diego County. The Grand Prix Fire (San Bernardino County) and the Pass Fire (Riverside County) quickly follow.

Thursday, October 23

1:30 p.m.: The Piru Fire ignites in Ventura County.

Friday, October 24

4:11 p.m.: The Verdale Fire ignites in Los Angeles County.

Late evening: 4,770 fire personnel, with the support of 409 engines, 32 helicopters, and nearly 50 air tankers, battle the fires, which now burn across some 21,370 acres.

Saturday, October 25

9:17 a.m.: The Old Fire begins in the San Bernardino National Forest. It soon threatens the communities of Crestline, Lake Arrowhead, Running Springs, and San Bernardino.

2:15 p.m.: The Simi Fire begins in Ventura County.

Late afternoon and evening: Governor Davis proclaims a state of emergency for San Bernardino and Ventura counties. He authorizes the California Department of Forestry and Fire Protection (CDF) to activate the two C-130 Modular Airborne Firefighting System (MAFFS) planes maintained by the California National Guard.

5:37 p.m.: The Monte Vista Emergency Communications Center receives a report of a fire in the Cleveland National Forest. The Cedar Fire eventually evolves into the largest fire in California history.

5:39 p.m.: The Monte Vista dispatcher sends nine U.S. Forest Service (USFS) engines and five CDF engines to the scene of the fire.

5:42 p.m.: The Monte Vista dispatcher radios for the launch of two CDF fixed-wing aircraft from the Ramona Air Attack Base. The aircraft are not activated, however, because the pilots have already returned home. (The flight cut-off time went into effect just minutes earlier.)

6:10 p.m.: Ground forces arrive on the scene of the Cedar Fire. Facing intense Santa Ana winds, the incident commander, USFS Division Chief Carlton Joseph, decides to postpone the approach until daybreak.

10:44 p.m.: With the Cedar Fire threatening the suburban community of Ramona Country Estates, sheriff's deputies begin ordering residents to evacuate.

11:56 p.m.: USFS enters into a Unified Command with CDF after the fire spreads onto state land. Joseph remains the USFS incident commander, while Randy Lyle assumes command on behalf of CDF.

Sunday, October 26

Throughout the early hours of Sunday, the Cedar Fire rages, spreading at a rate of 12,000 acres an hour. Thirteen people die trying to flee isolated communities.

12:35 a.m.: The first homes in Ramona begin burning.

1:30 a.m.: The Paradise Fire ignites near the community of Valley Center in San Diego County.

3:00 a.m.: Fire threatens the Barona Indian Reservation casino; 2,000 gamblers and 500 employees take refuge inside the casino.

5:00 a.m.: The Cedar Fire overruns the town of Poway.

In a conversation with California Assemblyman Jay LaSuer (R-La Mesa), U.S. Representative Duncan Hunter (R-Calif.) promises to try to obtain additional federal C-130 MAFFS planes. Hunter then calls Gen. Richard B. Myers, chairman of the Joint Chiefs of Staff, who agrees to supply the MAFFS planes, on the condition that California fire officials make the formal request.

LaSuer and Hunter's in-district chief of staff, Wendell Cutting, meet with resistance when they subsequently contact CDF about issuing a request for MAFFS planes.

Hunter contacts CDF personally, arguing that the Stafford Act provides California with the authority to request the MAFFS planes. Ray Snodgrass, CDF's chief deputy director, replies that the 1932 Economy Act requires the state to exhaust all civilian aircraft resources before procuring federal aircraft.

6:00 a.m.: CDF and USFS aircraft launch at dawn, but smoke and weather conditions restrict flights.

7:00–7:30 a.m.: The Cedar Fire enters San Diego City. Within an hour, thirty homes are burning.

7:18 a.m.: The Otay Fire ignites near the Otay area of San Diego City.

9:10 a.m.: San Diego opens its Emergency Operations Center (EOC) 2 hours after the Cedar Fire crosses over the city line. Despite an initially slow response, the city eventually succeeds in evacuating 10,000 residents without any deaths or injuries.

Midday: CDF authorities decline an offer of additional helicopters from Admiral Jose Betancourt, commander of North Island Naval Station.

All aircraft are grounded due to excessive wind and smoke.

Governor Davis extends the state of emergency to San Diego and Los Angeles counties.

Dallas Jones, director of California's Office of Emergency Services (OES), holds a press conference, where he seeks to counter criticism of how the state has handled requests for aid.

Learning that his home in Peutz Valley has burned to the ground, Representative Hunter lobbies a range of federal and state agencies. Hunter reaches Ray Quintanar, USFS Fire and Aviation management chief for the Pacific Southwest Region, and urges him to call General Myers at home.

Informed of Quintanar's conversation with Hunter, Dale Bosworth, head of USFS, authorizes the order of one MAFFS tanker.

5:00 p.m.: Independently of Hunter's efforts, CDF Fire Operations Director Wright contacts Quintanar to request additional federal resources. Quintanar requests an additional MAFFS plane later in the evening.

Monday, October 27

12:00 a.m.: Still frustrated, Hunter calls Jerry Williams, USFS national director for Fire and Aviation Management. Williams explains that conditions have made the deployment of additional MAFFS planes impractical.

California exhausts the available supply of contract air tankers, freeing USFS to order up the remaining military-owned MAFFS aircraft.

President George W. Bush declares Los Angeles, San Bernardino, Ventura, and San Diego counties disaster areas.

Tuesday, October 28

The first three additional MAFFS planes join the existing California-based fleet. They fly some 8 hours, but fire and weather conditions limit their use.

Wednesday, October 29

The final three MAFFS planes arrive in California.

Thursday, October 30 to Friday, October 31
No MAFFS planes fly, but damp weather helps firefighters battle the fires.

Sunday, November 2
The MAFFS planes are released.

Tuesday, November 4
The Cedar Fire is declared 100 percent contained.

8   The Anthrax Crisis and the U.S. Postal Service (A): Charting a Course in a Storm

Kirsten Lundberg

During October and November 2001, only weeks after the September 11 attacks on the World Trade Center towers and the Pentagon, the United States faced another form of terrorism—a series of deaths caused by anthrax poisoning from letters containing "military-grade" anthrax powder sent through the U.S. Postal Service (USPS). Beginning with the death of a Florida-based tabloid journalist, the attacks included anthrax-laced letters sent to New York media and congressional offices, the death of a postal worker exposed to anthrax in a mail processing center, and the seemingly random deaths of people who had not directly received anthrax letters.

As these events struck fear into the hearts of many Americans, responders had to cope with much that was novel and unexpected, while many mysteries had to be unraveled. A number of public agencies—local, state, and federal law enforcement; the Centers for Disease Control and Prevention; and others—became involved in trying to understand the implications, trying to develop protections against the attack, and trying to track the person or people responsible. There appeared to be little connection among the victims. Strenuous attempts to track down the perpetrator through reverse-engineering the postal delivery system were ultimately frustrated. In trying to provide reassurance to the public, public agencies made statements in the early stages of the event on the basis of relatively sparse evidence. Some of these statements had to be retracted and many revised, adding to the confusion and stoking public distrust of official comment.

Throughout the episode, there were conspicuous problems of coordinating information and policy across geographical areas, agencies, and jurisdictional levels. Remedies routinely made available to workers in some affected agencies—most notably congressional employees, who were mostly white—were initially not given to postal workers, who were mainly minorities. This decision was made on the theory that anthrax contained in a sealed letter would not contaminate the sites through which the letter passed—a supposition that turned out to be wrong; and the decision evoked accusations that care and concern for the victims was racially discriminatory.

In reading about these crisis events, consider the problem of trying to understand and respond to a rapidly changing situation fraught with scientific and medical uncertainties. Institutionally complex and politically charged, the crisis engaged dozens of organizations (both public and private) located in different geographical areas, in different jurisdictions,

This is an abridged version of a case written by Kirsten Lundberg for Arnold M. Howitt, executive director, Taubman Center for State and Local Government, for use at the Executive Session on Domestic Preparedness, John F. Kennedy School of Government, Harvard University. Funding was provided by the Volpe National Transportation Systems Center, U.S. Department of Transportation, with additional assistance from the Robert Wood Johnson Foundation. Kennedy School of Government Case Program, C16-03-1692.0. Copyright © 2003, 2007 by the President and Fellows of Harvard College.

and at different levels of government. Stretching across many weeks, it strained the wisdom and stamina of responders and concerned bystanders alike.

Discussion Questions

- From the perspective of USPS, why were the anthrax attacks so critical? Consider the impacts on its mission, key stakeholders, and operating capacity.
- What internal and interorganizational considerations became important as USPS dealt with anthrax cleanup tasks?
- How effective were the ad hoc management structures that USPS put in place to handle the crisis?
- Could the USPS employee relations issues that arose during the crisis, particularly the charge that black postal workers were treated differently from Capitol Hill staff, have been better handled?
- What should USPS do to prepare for future bioterror attacks?

On Sunday, October 21, 2001, a postal worker from a mail sorting facility in Washington, D.C., died of inhalation anthrax—a disease virtually unseen for a century. The next day, a second employee from the same facility died. Fear of anthrax had already infected the public—media workers in Florida and New York City had contracted the disease. In addition, Senate Majority Leader Tom Daschle (D-S.D.) had received an anthrax-laden letter and the Senate and House of Representatives buildings had been closed for anthrax tests. Originally, the anthrax attack seemed plausibly targeted at the media and politicians, but with the deaths of the mail workers, the public perception of risk mushroomed. This new threat re-ignited a sense of panic among a public already reeling from the recent September 11 terrorist hijackings.

Virtually overnight, the U.S. Postal Service (USPS) found itself at the eye of a national security and public health storm—it had become a vehicle for terrorism; anyone with a mail slot felt threatened. In the midst of this turmoil, learning as it went, USPS shifted into overdrive to accomplish three overriding tasks: reassuring and keeping the public safe; reassuring and keeping its employees safe; and delivering the mail.

September to Early October: Early Days of the Anthrax Attack

The first indication that an anthrax attack was underway came in Florida, where presumably a letter containing anthrax (it was never found) was delivered to the Boca Raton headquarters of American Media Inc. (AMI), publisher of the *Sun* tabloid. On Sunday, September 30, 2001, *Sun* photo editor Robert Stevens felt ill; the next day, AMI mailroom employee Ernesto Blanco was admitted to the hospital with heart problems, coughing, fever, and fatigue. By Friday, October 5, Stevens was dead of inhalation anthrax—the first case of inhaled anthrax in the United States since 1976.

Inhalation anthrax is, without treatment, fatal. It develops when anthrax spores settle in the lymph nodes, where they grow into toxin-producing bacteria.[1] The toxins degrade lung tissue and promote fluid buildup, eventually reducing the oxygen supply. Early symptoms resemble the flu: chills, fever, nausea, and vomiting. Once the symptoms are present, antibiotics have limited effect. All the same, inhalation anthrax is difficult to contract. However, the spores can cause a milder form of the disease through touch—cutaneous, or skin, anthrax. Either the antibiotic Ciprofloxacin or the generic doxycycline cures cutaneous anthrax and is effective against inhalation anthrax if administered early.

The U.S. Centers for Disease Control and Prevention Arrives

The Stevens case swiftly attracted the attention of the U.S. Centers for Disease Control and Prevention (CDC). Together with state health authorities and other partners, CDC monitors and prevents disease outbreaks, implements disease prevention strategies, and maintains national health statistics. At the request of Florida public health authorities, CDC dispatched on October 4 a team of epidemiologists and laboratory scientists. When AMI asked whether it should close its building, CDC said no. But the next day the team swabbed the AMI mailroom, as well as Stevens's computer keyboard, and found anthrax contamination. AMI closed its headquarters on October 7. The Federal Bureau of Investigation (FBI) took over the case as a criminal matter on October 8.

Meanwhile CDC, the U.S. Department of Health and Human Services (HHS), and the White House rushed to assure the public that Stevens's illness was a unique case (Blanco was diagnosed with anthrax later, on October 15) and not the work of evildoers. "It is an isolated case, and it is not contagious," HHS Secretary Tommy G. Thompson said October 4. "There is no terrorism."[2] On October 9, President George W. Bush told citizens that the Florida case seemed to be "a very isolated incident."[3]

U.S. Postal Service Precautions

Isolated or not, the USPS vice president of public affairs and communications wanted to take no chances. On October 8, Azeezaly Jaffer watched a 9:00 p.m. television news report associating Stevens's death with a letter. He recalls:

Three things crossed my mind. Number one, that 800,000 [USPS] employees would all of a sudden become worried about handling the mail. Number two, that it would rapidly turn into a public issue.

---

[1]Diana Jean Schemo, "Postal Employee in Washington Has Anthrax in Lungs," *New York Times,* October 22, 2001, A1.

[2]Quoted in Gina Kolata, "Florida Man Is Hospitalized with Pulmonary Anthrax," *New York Times,* October 5, 2001, A16.

[3]Quoted in Stephanie Kirchgaessner and Richard Wolffe, "Bush Acts to Calm Fears on Anthrax Outbreak," *Financial Times,* October 10, 2001, 6.

Number three, it could conceivably . . . bring this organization that moves 500 million pieces of mail a day to a screeching halt, thereby bringing the economy of the United States to a complete halt.[4]

Determined to preempt employee and public concerns, Jaffer headed straight to the office to write a newsbreak (an internal communication to employees), which let them know there was no confirmation that the anthrax had come from a letter but provided guidelines in the event they suspected anthrax. During the following week, his office sent messages to employees three to four times a day, activated a website, and launched obligatory informational talks for employees. "I made a conscious decision to have the Postal Service voice louder than everybody else's voice starting on October 8," says Jaffer. "We wanted to make sure that our employees and our workforce were getting information firsthand from us and not hearing it only on the news."

Jaffer's caution paid off quickly. Starting October 12, investigators discovered that the Florida incident was not isolated. That day, Erin O'Connor, 38, *NBC News* anchor Tom Brokaw's assistant, was diagnosed with skin anthrax. Over the following week other cutaneous cases were confirmed: ABC reported that the 7-month-old son of a producer was ill; on October 18, *CBS News* aide Claire Fletcher tested positive; and on October 19, the *New York Post* confirmed that Johanna Huden, editorial page assistant, had skin anthrax.[5]

The common culprit in all these cases seemed to be infected letters. On September 18, the FBI learned, anthrax-laced letters had been posted from Trenton, New Jersey, to *NBC News* and to the *New York Post*. An unopened letter containing anthrax was found on October 19 near Huden's work station at the *Post*, and it gave authorities their first opportunity to study which strain and quality of anthrax was causing the infections among media employees.[6] The material proved rather coarse, and although it could float in the air, the particles quickly settled back on surfaces. Encouragingly, its virulence seemed limited to those who physically touched it. "We see no public health concern," said New York City Health Commissioner Dr. Neal L. Cohen.[7]

The Daschle Letter

Such calming statements did little to soothe the public, which was already reporting hundreds of cases of suspicious white powder, stockpiling protective masks, and asking for prophylactic doses of the antibiotic Cipro. There was good cause for this anxiety—4 days earlier, on Monday, October 15, an anthrax-laden letter had arrived at the office of Senate

---

[4]Telephone interview with Azeezaly Jaffer, U.S. Postal Service, September 18, 2002. Unless noted, subsequent quotations from Jaffer are also from this interview.

[5]Eric Lipton, "Media Outlets, Governor's Office and Postal Center Feel the Brunt," *New York Times*, October 31, 2001, B6.

[6]The NBC letter had been found October 13, but so little material was left that it yielded minimal information for scientists.

[7]Quoted in Eric Lipton, "Anthrax Is Found in 2 More People," *New York Times*, October 19, 2001, A1.

Majority Leader Tom Daschle in the Hart Senate Office Building. That morning, an intern opened the heavily taped envelope, which, like the Brokaw and *Post* letters, had been sent from Trenton, New Jersey. White powder fell out with the letter, whose return address was an elementary school. The Capitol police secured the area, quarantined the staff, and conducted on-the-spot tests, which were positive for anthrax.

Later that day and the next, hundreds of Hart Building staffers—many of whom had been nowhere near Daschle's office—were administered nasal swabs to see whether they had been exposed to the released anthrax; twenty-eight tested positive, some from a floor below the Daschle suite. All who wanted it were prescribed Cipro. On Tuesday, the Hart Building closed. The House of Representatives shut down for testing on Wednesday, and on Thursday night, all House and Senate office buildings were closed.

The Capitol police sent samples taken from Daschle's office, as well as the letter itself, to the U.S. Army Medical Research Institute for Infectious Disease (USAMRIID) at Fort Detrick, Maryland. By Monday night, Fort Detrick reported that the scientists had been "somewhat surprised by the nature of it . . . that it was a fine powder, that it easily went into the air." [8] On Tuesday, Daschle confirmed that "[w]e were told it was a very strong form of anthrax, a very potent form of anthrax, which clearly was produced by someone who knew what he or she was doing." [9]

But as the week progressed, Tom Ridge, President Bush's director for Homeland Security, and other spokesmen adopted milder language. The CDC called the Daschle letter's anthrax "naturally occurring," and Fort Detrick's commander, Maj. Gen. John S. Parker, termed it "common variety." [10] Despite these reassurances, many federal agencies were on heightened alert. No one could determine the level of threat. Was this a bioterrorist attack by a sophisticated adversary or the work of a backyard chemist angry at the media and government? The Postal Service leadership could not answer these questions. For the time being, says then USPS Senior Vice President for Government Relations and Public Policy Deborah Willhite, "it seemed to be more a targeted media crisis. But it seemed like it could become ours. So we were being very cautious." [11]

Post Office Business and Public and Employee Health

Although USPS did not seem to be the target of a bioterrorist attack, it was emerging as the means of delivery for bioterror. If the public had not yet fully realized that, it soon did. In

---

[8]Steve Twomey and Justin Blum, "How the Experts Missed Anthrax," *Washington Post,* November 19, 2001, A1.

[9]Quoted in Sheryl Gay Stolberg and Judith Miller, "Officials Admit Underestimating Danger Posed to Postal Workers," *New York Times,* October 24, 2001, A1.

[10]Quoted in ibid.

[11]Interview with Deborah Willhite, U.S. Postal Service, Washington, D.C., September 9, 2002. Unless noted, subsequent quotations from Willhite are also from this interview.

fact, after the Daschle letter, Congress quarantined all mail received at the Capitol from October 12 to 17. If Congress no longer trusted its mail, how long before the general public came to distrust the post?

USPS was no stranger to crisis; it had famously weathered Unabomber Ted Kaczynski and shootings by enraged postal employees. It had a professional communications department well rehearsed in crisis management. Ironically, the Postal Service for years had practiced how to deal with anthrax hoaxes but never how to handle the real thing. The rule of thumb had been that anthrax could never be sufficiently powderized (or weaponized) to be sent through the mail, and thus, there were no USPS guidelines for managing an outbreak of anthrax.

At this point, USPS could afford no fall-off in public confidence. It was a business in trouble, and it needed every customer it could get. September 11 had caused a 7 percent drop in mail volume,[12] but Postal Service troubles went back well before then. Since the 1970 Postal Reorganization Act, USPS had been quasi-governmental—a self-supporting corporation owned by the federal government.[13] Unfortunately, that had resulted in USPS suffering most of the disadvantages of public regulation while enjoying few of the advantages of a private corporation. For instance, USPS received no taxpayer money, but at the same time was not allowed to set postal rates or wages freely.

Although USPS had run a deficit of $1.68 billion in fiscal year 2001 and projected a 2002 deficit (before anthrax) of $1.35 billion, it was, some argued, too integral to the U.S. economy ever to be allowed to fail. A $70 billion organization with 800,000 employees, it was the second-largest employer in the country. Its 38,000 retail mail outlets moved 670 million pieces of mail a day, and the wider mail industry (catalogues, direct mail, paper mills, printers, and so forth) generated an estimated $900 billion.

But the congressional decision to quarantine its mail carried a second implication for USPS beyond the threat to business. If the congressional mail was actually dangerous, what did that mean for the safety of USPS employees, who had handled that mail before it ever reached Congress?

USPS leaders had been asking since Monday whether postal workers were safe, particularly those at the Brentwood sorting center in Washington, D.C. "From the descriptions of the powder that came out, and from the reaction of the Capitol physicians in inoculating and quarantining so much of the Hart Building," says USPS Senior Vice President Willhite, "we became very concerned that the Brentwood facility and our employees had been contaminated." The same question had arisen in Florida, where on Monday anthrax spores were

---

[12]Ellen Nakashima and Andrew DeMillo, "What's in the Mail: Many Doubts," *Washington Post,* November 27, 2001, A1.

[13]The law (39 USC) defines USPS as "an independent establishment of the executive branch of the federal government."

found at a Boca Raton USPS facility that handled AMI mail.[14] For answers, USPS turned to the public health authorities.

Public Health

Each state has its own public health department, which is responsible for monitoring the provision of public and private health-care services. State public health authorities also investigate and respond to outbreaks of disease. In the event of a threat to public health, the state or local health department notifies doctors and hospitals and mobilizes care. The state authority also determines whether to involve CDC, which can operate in a community only at the invitation of the state health department (state and local health departments do not answer to any federal authority).

By mid-October, USPS was already working with public health authorities in Florida. It had been closely allied since September 11 with the New York Health Department, and it was establishing ties in New Jersey. In D.C., the question of jurisdiction was complicated because it is the nation's capital. The Washington, D.C., Department of Health (DOH) had authority over most of the city, but federal establishments were independent. USPS, however, was not a federal agency, and DOH was its public health partner.

When it learned on October 15 about the Daschle letter, DOH activated its standing biohazard response plan, which called for early CDC involvement. DOH requested that, if anthrax was confirmed, CDC dispatch a team of public affairs officers, epidemiologists, and pharmaceutical logistics officials. CDC called with confirmation at 4:00 a.m. on October 16, and its team arrived in D.C. just 3 hours later. But CDC remained in an advisory capacity. Then D.C. Chief Health Officer Dr. Ivan C. A. Walks says, "The ultimate responsibility for running things in terms of how you set things up and what you do—those remained local."[15]

"No Threat" Reassurances

After determining that the Daschle letter had, in fact, traveled through its Brentwood facility en route to the Hart Office Building, USPS officials contacted DOH and CDC to ask whether Brentwood should be tested for anthrax. But the CDC and state officials downplayed any risk to the postal workers. In Trenton, state health officials on October 14 told postal workers that anthrax testing was not "medically necessary."[16] In Washington, D.C., Walks confirms, "we were all still operating under the assumption that the only place where

---

[14]Local health authorities, however, had already put these postal workers on Cipro 3 days earlier as a precaution, and there were no reported illnesses.

[15]Telephone interview with Dr. Ivan C. A. Walks, chief health officer, Washington, D.C., December 3, 2002. Unless noted, subsequent quotations from Walks are also from this interview.

[16]Sheryl Gay Stolberg, "A Quick Response for Politicians; A Slower One for Mail Workers," *New York Times*, October 23, 2001, A1.

there was danger was for the folks in the Hart Office Building." CDC officials assured USPS that anthrax posed no threat to the 1,800 Brentwood workers, pointing out:

- Only individuals who had opened a letter or been nearby when a letter was opened had become ill.
- At least 8,000–10,000 spores were needed to infect a human with inhalation anthrax, so traces of anthrax were not a risk. Moreover, the material was heavy and sticky, and so would adhere to surfaces.
- The Daschle letter had been heavily taped, and spores could not escape through an envelope.
- No postal worker was sick.

"They said there was virtually no risk of any anthrax contamination in the facility, that without the letter being opened at Brentwood, there was no risk of any anthrax escaping, so neither the facility nor the employees needed to be tested," recalled Willhite.[17] "They didn't think [testing] was necessary because in this situation they followed the science," confirms Senior Vice President for Human Resources Suzanne Medvidovich.[18]

Week of October 15

USPS accepted the CDC reassurances. In fact, to send a public message about just how safe the mail system was, the FBI and USPS on Thursday, October 18, held a joint press conference at Brentwood announcing a reward of $1 million for information leading to the arrest and conviction of those behind the anthrax mailings. Some one hundred journalists attended.[19] With FBI Deputy Director Thomas Pickard at his side, Postmaster General John "Jack" Potter delivered a reassuring message: "[T]here is only a minute chance that anthrax spores escaped from [the Daschle letter] into this facility."[20]

Despite this public display of confidence, Potter had taken some proactive measures. On Monday, October 15, he announced the formation of a Mail Security Task Force.[21] The Task Force comprised top USPS leadership plus union representatives, and its charge was to study biological hazards in the postal system. USPS also announced that it would send postcards to 135 million U.S. homes warning about biohazards and describing how to handle suspect

---

[17]Quoted in Kathy Chen, Greg Hitt, Laurie McGinley, and Andrea Petersen, "Trial and Error: Seven Days in October Spotlight Weakness of Bioterror Response," *Wall Street Journal,* November 2, 2001, A1.

[18]Interview with Suzanne Medvidovich, U.S. Postal Service, Washington, D.C., September 10, 2002. Unless noted, subsequent quotations from Medvidovich are also from this interview.

[19]John Lancaster and Justin Blum, "District Postal Worker Seriously Ill," *Washington Post,* October 22, 2001, A1.

[20]Quoted in Chen et al., "Trial and Error," A1.

[21]Potter was in Denver addressing a major mail industry meeting, but he flew home immediately after his talk.

mail.[22] Moreover, it would provide gloves and masks as soon as possible to all employees. Potter also decided to hire a private company, at USPS expense, to test Brentwood on Thursday.

The end of the week, however, brought a series of disturbing developments. On Thursday morning, Senior Vice President Willhite and other USPS officials met with Senate Sergeant-at-Arms Al Lenhardt to discuss how to handle Senate mail. Casually, someone mentioned that investigators had found four "hot spots" in the mailroom of the Dirksen Senate Office Building, well away from the Hart Building. This was urgent (and alarming) information for Willhite, who knew the Daschle letter had passed through Dirksen on its way to Hart. She reasoned that if spores had leaked at Dirksen, they might also have leaked at Brentwood.

Following the meeting, Willhite determined to involve the CDC and the D.C. Health Department despite their assurances of no risk. She called Potter, who called HHS Secretary Thompson, and by Thursday evening CDC Director Dr. Jeffrey P. Koplan had promised Potter a team would come to test Brentwood on Friday.

Hamilton Township

Bad news also arrived from New Jersey. On Thursday, October 18, Acting Governor Donald T. DiFrancesco announced that Teresa Heller, a West Trenton letter carrier, had developed skin anthrax.[23] Heller's was the first diagnosed case of a postal worker contracting anthrax. Homeland Security Director Ridge identified West Trenton as the location of the postbox into which the Brokaw and Daschle letters had been dropped.[24]

Mail from West Trenton went to the Hamilton Township Processing Center, which handled mail for forty-six branches in the Trenton area. Postal authorities had assured workers at Hamilton Township as recently as Monday, October 15, that the facility was not contaminated, but tests done on Wednesday found thirteen of twenty-three samples tested positive for anthrax.[25] On Thursday, the day Heller was diagnosed, USPS closed Hamilton Township Center for further tests. On Friday, it closed the West Trenton post office. Also Friday, Hamilton maintenance worker Patrick O'Donnell was diagnosed with skin anthrax.

As the situation worsened, New Jersey State Acting Commissioner for Health Dr. George T. DiFerdinando decided on Friday to ignore the CDC recommendations and advised Cipro for all workers at Hamilton Township.[26] The state health authority was not prepared, however,

---

[22]Spencer S. Hsu and Ellen Nakashima, "USPS to Warn Public on Biohazards in Mail," *Washington Post*, October 16, 2001, A7.

[23]Ibid.

[24]Fred Kaplan, "FBI Eyes NJ Neighborhood," *Boston Globe*, October 20, 2001, A10. It is possible this was not the culprit mailbox because, in mid-August 2002, investigators found another mailbox in Princeton that tested positive for anthrax. Karen DeMasters, "Anthrax in Princeton Mailbox," *New York Times*, August 18, 2002, Sec. 14NJ, 5.

[25]Michael Powell and Dale Russakoff, "Anthrax Fear Billows at Postal Plants," *Washington Post*, October 23, 2001, A8.

[26]Justin Blum, "Workers Question Response; CDC Says Policy Evolving," *Washington Post*, October 23, 2001, A1.

to provide the medication and suggested that Hamilton workers see their private physicians for Cipro prescriptions. Outraged by the state's response, Hamilton Mayor Glen Gilmore obtained a supply of the antibiotic, which a local hospital distributed free to postal workers.[27] The hospital's costs were absorbed by the Postal Service.

Brentwood Tested

Meanwhile, Brentwood was tested as planned. On Thursday night, URS Corp., an industrial hygiene-testing firm with whom the Postal Service had a preexisting contract, took samples. As testing contractors roamed the plant, one worker asked, "Why are you testing the machines instead of us?"[28] Brentwood's senior plant manager, Timothy Haney, assured them that if anything was found, antibiotics would be provided. But the results took 3 days. So USPS also asked the Fairfax County Fire Department to do a quick, on-the-spot test.[29] That test proved negative, but the test's reliability was a poor 50 percent. On Friday, October 19, CDC also came in to Brentwood to test. As with URS Corp., the results took a few days.

Waiting for the Unknown

Pending the Brentwood results, it still seemed that the anthrax attack could be handled along traditional crisis management lines; although two New Jersey postal workers had skin anthrax, the patients were responding to treatment. Matters were nonetheless sufficiently grave that the new USPS Mail Security Task Force held its first meeting on Friday, October 19, to discuss biohazards and mail. Task Force members were drawn from senior management and unions alike. The group's chief concern during that meeting was to calm the public, and arrangements were made for Postmaster General Potter and Chief Postal Inspector Kenneth Weaver to appear on a number of weekend news programs and talk shows to assure citizens that there was no conclusive evidence anthrax posed any general threat.

USPS did not know, however, that on Thursday night Dr. Cecele Murphy of Inova Fairfax Hospital in Virginia had telephoned the D.C. DOH with a report of a suspected anthrax case—Brentwood worker Leroy Richmond, 56.[30] It wasn't until Saturday, October 20, that Jaffer got a phone call that realized his worst fears—D.C. health officials were going to announce that a Brentwood employee had anthrax. Willhite was also notified that the mayor wanted to hold a press conference.

Now Jaffer mobilized for a major public relations effort. No one understood yet how Richmond had become ill or whether others were likewise stricken. Jaffer would have to do

---

[27]Michael Winerip, "Hail the Mayor (Whose Name Isn't Giuliani)," *New York Times,* November 14, 2001, D1.
[28]Chen et al., "Trial and Error," A1.
[29]Twomey and Blum, "How the Experts Missed Anthrax."
[30]Richmond turned 57 in the hospital on October 22. Kirk Johnson, "By Demanding a Diagnosis, He Lives to Tell of Anthrax," *New York Times,* December 3, 2001, A1.

his best to ascertain the extent of infection. He summoned his deputy, Irene Lericos, as well as Internal Communications Manager Jon Leonard. They spent Saturday night in the office working.

At the same time, Willhite and Medvidovich headed over to meet with D.C. Mayor Anthony A. Williams and D.C. Chief Health Officer Walks. "I was pretty furious," says Willhite, that city officials were holding a press conference but postal employees were not being offered either anthrax testing or prophylactic antibiotics. But Mayor Williams informed the USPS officials that he planned to test Brentwood employees at a central D.C. location and give them antibiotics. Walks, says Willhite, stressed that "we needed to give real time information about what was happening."

The press conference was scheduled for Sunday to allow the public health commissioners from Maryland, Virginia, and D.C. to participate. By Sunday, it was also likely that Richmond's condition would be confirmed. Willhite assured the city officials that USPS would pay for antibiotics for its employees.

Meanwhile, on Saturday evening Medvidovich, USPS Safety Manager Sam Pulcrano, Manager for Environmental Management Policy Dennis Baca, Chief Operating Officer (COO) Patrick Donahoe, Willhite, and communications officials went to Brentwood to draw up a plan to close the facility if anthrax were confirmed. The group, meeting upstairs, drew on a board exactly where the mail would go if Brentwood were out of commission. Pulcrano also contacted the U.S. Environmental Protection Agency (EPA) to ask for on-scene coordinators at Brentwood and Hamilton Township. "We needed the expertise," says Pulcrano. "[*Bacillus anthracis*] is not something we would deal with, obviously, on a normal basis. But it turned out it wasn't something that most others had ever dealt with [either]."[31]

Week of October 21: Bad News and Worse

On Sunday morning, October 21, at 7:00 a.m., CDC called Dr. Walks and confirmed that Richmond had inhalation anthrax. The CDC had not expected this result; its scientists, said Walks's deputy, Larry Siegel, were "astounded, really."[32] As investigators soon learned, Richmond daily brought the Express Mail from a facility near Baltimore-Washington International Airport to Brentwood. The Daschle letter had not been sent via Express Mail, but on October 11, Richmond had volunteered to clean a Brentwood mail-sorting machine.[33]

USPS also got the news, and at 10:30 Sunday morning, Safety Manager Pulcrano called Environmental Manager Baca to tell him Brentwood was closing. Baca immediately called

---

[31]Interview with Sam Pulcrano, U.S. Postal Service, Washington, D.C., September 9, 2002. Unless noted, subsequent quotations from Pulcrano are also from this interview.

[32]Quoted in Twomey and Blum, "How the Experts Missed Anthrax," A1.

[33]Johnson, "By Demanding a Diagnosis."

John Bridges, the Brentwood environmental coordinator (and the only trained incident commander in the USPS system). Bridges and an on-scene EPA coordinator, Marcos Aquino, conducted a 6-hour assessment of Brentwood. By evening, Bridges and Baca had agreed that Bridges would manage the day-to-day cleanup operations, and Baca promised to ensure that Bridges got what he needed.

On Sunday afternoon, D.C. Mayor Williams held his planned press conference. "We're going to do everything we can and everything we have to do . . . to see that people are getting the treatment they need when they need that treatment," he said.[34] He instructed Brentwood's 1,800 employees to report to a downtown office building on Sunday or, in following days, to D.C. General Hospital for nasal swabs and a 10-day supply of Cipro. At the press conference, Willhite was by his side because, she says, "I knew there had to be a postal presence from Day One or there wouldn't be a postal presence on Day Two."

But things soon grew much worse. At 8:45 p.m. on Sunday, another Brentwood worker, Thomas L. Morris Jr., died of inhalation anthrax at a Maryland hospital. Morris had tried repeatedly to get medical attention during the days preceding his death, but no one diagnosed anthrax. USPS had not even known that Morris was sick. On Monday afternoon, a second Brentwood employee, Joseph P. Curseen, died in a Maryland hospital after arriving by ambulance that morning. The same hospital had sent him home the night before. The anthrax attacks had just become a USPS crisis of unprecedented magnitude.

Staying in Business

Until the deaths of the postal workers, it had been presumed that all anthrax patients had come into physical contact with an anthrax-tainted letter. Some seemed to have contracted skin anthrax from unopened letters, but only opened envelopes had caused inhalation anthrax. But the Brentwood employees had been nowhere near one of the letters, certainly not an opened one. The machines they worked near were automated; mail moved through them at up to 30 miles per hour. How could they have become infected? Until those deaths, anthrax had been considered a killer that could at least be seen (in quantity), touched, and, it was hoped, avoided. As an understanding of the threat matured, however, scientists and the public alike learned that anthrax could in fact be an invisible stalker, spores hanging suspended in the air to be unwittingly inhaled. But it was days before that understanding became clear. Meanwhile, USPS was faced with contaminated buildings, dying employees or healthy ones who felt betrayed, and a scared public.

The first question to answer was: Should USPS continue normal operations? As Vice President Medvidovich puts it, "Are our customers safe? Are our employees safe? What could possibly have happened here?" At CDC headquarters in Atlanta, doctors gathered on Monday, October 22, in a conference call with the FBI, USPS, the Postal Inspection Service,

---

[34]Quoted in John Lancaster and Justin Blum, "District Postal Worker Seriously Ill," *Washington Post,* October 22, 2001, A1.

the Office of Homeland Security, and local law enforcement officials.[35] Each organization was on the line for a reason. Under Presidential Decision Directive 39 (PDD-39), the FBI was the lead agency on any criminal investigation of terrorism.[36] USPS was the affected agency, and the Postal Inspection Service was its law enforcement arm. The Office of Homeland Security coordinated the federal response to terrorism. Local law enforcement officials were responsible for public safety in their communities. CDC Deputy Director for Infectious Diseases Dr. Julie L. Gerberding led the discussion. Was the postal system itself contaminated? Should it be shut down?

The final decision on USPS operations rested with the postmaster general, but the verdict from the CDC conference call was to keep the mail moving because there was no evidence of widespread contamination. "This was not just the Postal Service," says Medvidovich. "This was the country and the economy."

Whose Crisis Is This?

With that issue settled, another critical question loomed: Who should manage the anthrax cleanup? One potential approach was to initiate the Federal Response Plan (FRP), an interagency strategy for dealing with natural disasters.[37] Under the FRP, the Federal Emergency Management Agency (FEMA) was designated the interagency coordinator, with wide-ranging authority to save lives, protect property, restore damaged areas, and so forth. FEMA could provide personnel, equipment, supplies, facilities, and a variety of services, plus the funding for these. But the FRP could be activated only under two conditions: (1) if the President declared a major disaster or emergency or (2) under PDD-39, in response to terrorism.

At a meeting of USPS senior management on Wednesday, October 24, Environmental Manager Baca suggested that the government initiate the FRP. The request was conveyed to a high-level team meeting under the aegis of Homeland Security to consider the broader national security implications of the anthrax deaths. "Within hours," says Baca, the Homeland Security team responded that the FRP could not be invoked "because this was not a natural disaster."[38] In the end, says Medvidovich, it hardly mattered; "We did exactly what FEMA would have done."

---

[35]Details in this paragraph come from Eric Lipton and Kirk Johnson, "Tracking Bioterror's Tangled Course," *New York Times,* December 26, 2001, A1.

[36]The FBI took precedence over the Postal Inspection Service (the USPS criminal investigation arm) because, says USPS Deputy Chief Inspector James Rowan, the Department of Justice had declared the anthrax attack an act of domestic violence with a weapon of mass destruction, an area where the FBI had jurisdiction. The Postal Inspection Service served, however, as a member of the investigative task force. Interview with James Rowan, U.S. Postal Service, Washington, D.C., September 11, 2002. Unless noted, subsequent quotations from Rowan are also from this interview.

[37]The Federal Response Plan was replaced in 2005 by the National Response Plan (NRP), as part of an effort to better coordinate responses to domestic emergencies. The NRP has since been superseded by the National Response Framework, which came into effect in 2008.

[38]Interview with Dennis Baca, Washington, D.C., September 10, 2002. Unless noted, subsequent quotations from Baca are also from this interview.

Another candidate to lead the cleanup effort was EPA, which was already in charge of the AMI building in Florida and had taken responsibility for decontaminating the Hart Senate Office Building. But the majority of the USPS leadership felt that EPA would take too long. Baca speaks specifically to the question of the Brentwood decontamination: "It was my recommendation to senior management that we not turn it over, because [USPS leaders] were interested in getting this facility back for our purpose, which is to move the mail. People in EPA wanted it as a living laboratory. . . . They would have kept us out of there for 3–5 years performing studies." On balance, Willhite recalls, most felt that "it was a Postal Service crisis and that we'd better keep control of it."

By Wednesday evening, USPS was confident it would be the lead agency managing the consequences of the anthrax attacks. But that was not much comfort. As the USPS leadership saw it, at least four daunting tasks needed urgent attention:

- Informing and assisting employees
- Informing the public
- Identifying and decontaminating infected sites
- Delivering the mail

Pursuing all four simultaneously would require some sensitive decision making and the careful balancing of health and safety considerations with the need to continue mail delivery. Of the four tasks, the last one—orchestrating mail delivery—was the most straightforward. That responsibility fell to the National Operations Center (NOC), which had been set up after September 11 to make sure the mail kept moving when aircraft were grounded. Now it was to ensure timely processing and delivery despite the closing of various facilities for anthrax treatment.

The other three jobs were assigned to different groups, with considerable overlap. The Mail Security Task Force formed the nucleus of the crisis management effort. In addition to coordinating all efforts, it took particular responsibility for informing and assisting employees. The Communications Department, which together with NOC maintained a public hotline, took on the job of informing the public. Finally, responsibility for identifying, sampling, and decontaminating sites went to a new subgroup created for the purpose—the Unified Incident Command Center (UICC).[39]

Mail Security Task Force

At the top of the anthrax response pyramid stood the Mail Security Task Force, headed by Chief Postal Inspector Weaver. Its membership included not only top postal management

---

[39]In addition, after September 11 the Postal Inspection Service had started an Inspection Service Command Center, also staffed 24 hours a day, 7 days a week, which continued to operate through December 2001. The Inspection Service was in daily contact with the FBI, and the two agencies exchanged personnel.

but also union representatives and members of management associations. A liaison from the CDC also sat on the Task Force.

The Task Force settled into a grueling but effective routine. Its members met daily at 10:00 a.m., at first for 4 hours per day. They heard reports from all parties working on the anthrax aftermath. Over the weeks, to stay on top of all its responsibilities, the Task Force created seven subcommittees: mail screening, mail preparation, workplace safety, contingency planning, surface transportation, mail center security operations, and communications.

The group saw its principal job as ensuring a constant and reliable flow of information to employees as well as to the public. If sampling showed a site was contaminated, word had to go to field managers and employees, and arrangements had to be made to reassign workers during the cleanup. If a site tested clean, that too was reported. Sometimes as many as three official announcements a day went out to the unions and the public. As Medvidovich learned, "[y]ou cannot communicate too much. Because you can't underestimate the fear."

The Task Force also coordinated communications and logistics with other federal agencies involved in various aspects of managing the anthrax attacks. Willhite twice a day participated in conference calls with her counterparts from Homeland Security, CDC, and EPA. Potter was in close contact with HHS Secretary Thompson, and Jaffer briefed White House spokesman Ari Fleischer or his deputy, Scott McClellan, daily. Jaffer also took part in daily Homeland Security teleconferences, during which "we would all talk about what was going to be said, how we were going to say it, who was going to cover what, and then we basically deployed."[40] Homeland Security, recalls Medvidovich, "really did help. I can't tell you how many times they cleared pathways, they called people, they got us help."

Such cooperation did not necessarily come easy; it required that different institutional cultures mesh. Medvidovich muses, "We had to figure out how our organizations worked together, very quickly. The CDC has a culture that says you investigate, you examine, you make a determination based on the health risk and on evaluating things over a longer period of time. Our culture is do something and do it now."

Informing and Assisting Employees

The Task Force also closely monitored employee welfare. Unusually, the Task Force provided a forum where union members learned critical information at the same time as management. As Jaffer recalls, "It wasn't management telling the labor organizations this is what the deal is. They were sitting at the table with us and if they had questions, they went ahead and fired away."

From the start, as USPS officials remember it, Postmaster General Potter emphasized the health and safety of the employees. As Jaffer recalls, "The Postmaster General made it very clear at the first meeting that we would do what the medical experts asked us to do. If it

---

[40]Jaffer's contacts at Homeland Security were Communications Director Susan K. Neely and her staff.

meant shutting a plant down, we would shut it down." On Monday night, October 22, Potter announced that the standard procedure for cleaning postal machines, known as blow-down, was being revised on the spot. Although there was as yet no proof, there was suspicion that anthrax might have been blown into the air by the powerful jets of pressurized air that cleaned the machinery. Ten days later, on November 2, USPS announced that nationwide it would now clean machinery with vacuums instead of forced air. Postal managers also eliminated the practice of "riffling" envelopes (by running a thumb across the tops) to separate them. In another move directed at public as well as employee confidence, USPS on October 23 announced it would buy ion beam sterilization devices to irradiate the mail.[41]

Medvidovich was keenly aware that the Postal Service's four unions and three management associations "could have had a nationwide walkout" if USPS were seen to be taking anything other than the proper safety and health actions on behalf of its employees.[42] In general, she insists, USPS worried about "people first," and during the first few weeks, the Task Force paid special attention to identifying and treating any postal employee infected with anthrax. It sent out instructions daily that all employees potentially exposed to anthrax should be tested; Jaffer reinforced this message through his mandatory employee stand-up talks. In addition, says Medvidovich, "we literally kept a log of all people who received treatment and we called people who did not receive medication. A few people got called two, three times, and they were mad at us. But we wanted to make sure that everybody got the opportunity to get the medicine."

Logs were maintained for every contaminated facility. Postal inspectors were pulled in to help track employees, and staff from the Employee Assistance Program (EAP) visited sick postal workers and their families. EAP staff also visited postal sites, met with employees, offered counseling, and worked with families. In early November, USPS offered free flu shots to its 800,000 employees so that flu symptoms would not be mistaken for anthrax.[43]

The Task Force focus on employee well-being had at least two powerful motives: to allay health concerns and to reestablish trust. The fact was that a chasm of distrust and anger had opened up between USPS and many of its employees in the wake of the Brentwood deaths.

Second-Class Citizens?

Many Postal Service workers did not feel they were getting adequate protection. Interviews with the (mostly black) postal workers at Brentwood and elsewhere revealed their suspicion

---

[41]Barnaby J. Feder and Andrew C. Revkin, "Post Office to Install Devices to Destroy Deadly Organisms at Mail-Processing Centers," *Washington Post*, October 25, 2001, B5. The decision about just which mail would be irradiated was left until later. USPS could not afford to treat all the mail.

[42]Under the terms of the union contracts with USPS, strikes and walkouts were not permitted—but that might not have prevented such an event.

[43]Michael Janofsky, "Mail Delays Are Minimal, despite Anthrax Problems," *New York Times*, November 2, 2001, B8.

that they had received second-class treatment compared to the (mostly white) staff at the Capitol. "They've been playing this down for us, telling us work was safe," said a Brentwood worker after the plant closed. "And we were asking, 'How do we know that?' The Senate's mail comes through here." [44] William Smith, president of the New York Metro Area Postal Union, insisted that postal workers were subject to a double standard. "When Congress got letters with anthrax, they got checked and got out of town," said Smith. "Our people were left to be the guinea pigs and they feel let down by Congress, the president and the American people." [45] USPS workers in Florida, too, were complaining that emphasis was on getting the mail out rather than on protecting workers.[46] A Brentwood worker agreed. He bitterly rephrased the Postal Service motto about delivering the mail regardless of weather conditions: "Mud, flood, or blood, the mail's got to go," he said. "Anthrax doesn't fit into the rhyme." [47]

It was not easy to explain the chain of events, the science known and unknown as events unfolded, but members of the Task Force tried. On October 22, Willhite clarified at a press conference that USPS had followed CDC advice that testing at Brentwood was unnecessary "until there was an evidence chain that indicated there was anthrax present in the facility." [48] No one knew until Sunday, she emphasized, that a Brentwood worker had inhalation anthrax. CDC's Dr. Mitchell Cohen, who was supervising the D.C. anthrax operation, added that "this is really a new phenomenon. At first, we had no evidence that any of the mail handlers were at risk." [49]

This message was not exactly reassuring to postal workers; it also did not offer the public much comfort. Yet comforting the public by clearly and fully informing the media and citizens was the second task USPS had set itself.

Informing the Public

Reassuring mail-users was a pressing matter. Not only did public hysteria need dampening, but every passing day was costing the Postal Service millions of dollars. USPS could restore much public confidence by providing the public with concise and reliable information. It could also put the crisis in context—of the millions of pieces of mail delivered since September 18, only a handful of letters had contained anthrax.

To handle the deluge of requests from the media and others, Jaffer created a Communications Command Center. He also held daily teleconferences with the D.C. press corps and

---

[44]Quoted in Sheryl Gay Stolberg, "A Nation Challenged: The Government Response," *New York Times,* October 23, 2001, A1.

[45]Dale Russakoff and Michael Powell, "N.J. Postal Worker May Have Anthrax," *Washington Post,* October 24, 2001, A15.

[46]Powell and Russakoff, "Anthrax Fear Billows at Postal Plants."

[47]Fracis X. Clines, "A Nation Challenged," *New York Times,* October 23, 2001, B7.

[48]Quoted in Stolberg, "Quick Response for Politicians," A1.

[49]Ibid.

made available USPS spokespeople to go on camera immediately after the conference calls. But Jaffer decided that he personally would not appear as a spokesman for USPS, telling Postmaster General Potter, "in light of the fact that I've got a name [Azeezaly] that comes from the Middle East, I don't think that I should be out there." Instead he recruited others to do the job: Potter, Chief Inspector Weaver, COO Donahoe, and Vice President Willhite.

Potter, comments Jaffer, "was truly the calming face to the nation." At the same time, the postmaster general had to be careful to preserve his credibility. Thus, during the week of October 22 when postal officials were asked repeatedly if they could guarantee the safety of the mail, Potter (on Jaffer's advice) told a television interviewer that "I can't offer a guarantee." [50] But Jaffer also urged USPS officials to paint a full picture, pointing out, for example, that during the 10 days following the Daschle letter, the Postal Service had delivered 5 million of pieces of mail without incident.

Jaffer's office also put out USPS publications, including the postcards USPS had promised with guidelines on how to handle suspicious letters. By Monday, October 22, the cards were being printed, and by Thursday and Friday, they were being delivered across the country to the 800,000 USPS employees as well as to 120 million homes. Jaffer also made sure that any and all anthrax information went onto the USPS website. In addition, he contributed staff to the anthrax information hotline housed at NOC. The Postal Inspection Service also produced and distributed thousands of mail-security videos and posters to business mailrooms nationwide.

Facing this mountain of tasks, Jaffer called an old friend for assistance, Harold Burson of the New York–based public relations firm Burson, Marsteller. Jaffer was afraid his small staff of eight, working 12-hour shifts, could not long manage the seven hundred to nine hundred phone calls plus six hundred emails per day that were pouring into the Communications Center. During those first weeks, Burson staff helped relieve some of the logistical burden. And as an independent third party, Burson himself, says Jaffer, was invaluable as a barometer of how the media was covering the anthrax events.

Sampling and Decontaminating

The most logistically challenging of the four chief tasks USPS faced was to identify, sample, and decontaminate the infected postal sites. Because the Postal Service had no existing structure to handle this task, Safety Manager Pulcrano and Environmental Manager Baca set out to recruit staff for a new unit.

First to arrive was James Gaffney, who flew in Monday (the day of the Brentwood deaths) from New Jersey, where he worked as an environmental compliance specialist. On Tuesday, Charles Vidich, manager for environmental compliance for the Northeast, was pulled in

---

[50] Quoted in Ben White, "Postmaster General Lauded Despite Mixed Performance," *Washington Post,* October 25, 2001, A29.

from his office in Connecticut. The third member of what became a leadership triumvirate arrived a week later when, realizing they needed an administrator as well as technical expertise, Baca and Pulcrano asked Environmental Programs Analyst Paul Fennewald to run the new unit.

The newly recruited officials immediately sought advice on what kind of structure would get the job done. EPA was the first to recommend that USPS put together a UICC, which would enable all those with jurisdictional or functional responsibility for an incident to manage the situation jointly. Several agencies helped USPS set up the center, including EPA, the U.S. Forest Service, and Homeland Security.

Within weeks, there were fifteen to twenty people (plus contractor representatives) working at the UICC. They came from a variety of agencies, including EPA, CDC, the Occupational Safety and Health Administration (OSHA), and the Postal Inspection Service.[51] Vidich, Gaffney, and Fennewald reported to both Pulcrano and Baca, who reported in turn to Senior Vice President for Human Resources Medvidovich. As for the Task Force, technically UICC reported to it through Pulcrano and Baca. But, in practice, most Task Force members wanted constantly to know what UICC was doing, which created a communications challenge that UICC had to resolve.

But first it had other problems to address. To do its job, UICC needed outside contractors, but it had no authority to negotiate new contracts. Although USPS had existing contracts with four national environmental companies, UICC would need many more. By the end of the first week, UICC had found a solution. It discovered that the USPS Office of Inspector General (OIG) had a standing contract with the U.S. Army Corps of Engineers Rapid Response Group, which in turn had authority to contract out both the sampling and decontamination work that USPS needed done. Corps officer Timothy Gouger became the fourth (unofficial but critical) member of UICC's leadership team. With time, Gaffney emerged as the individual in charge of sampling, while Gouger oversaw the decontamination contractors.[52]

UICC also had to identify *where* to conduct sampling and decontamination. Medvidovich, Pulcrano, Donahoe, and others realized that USPS needed to devise a system for anthrax testing that would clarify the extent of the contamination. There were two theories as to how contamination could occur: from a direct hit (a contaminated letter arrives) or from cross-contamination. So far, USPS had tested only at sites where there were proven infections or through which contaminated letters had been known to transit. By mid-week, the idea of *trading partners* came up, that is, postal facilities with which the contaminated sites traded

---

[51]Some people were more permanent than others. The high turnover in liaisons, especially from OSHA, was a frustration at UICC.

[52]These officials were in charge in theory. In fact, UICC did not manage the sampling or cleanup of Brentwood, Hamilton Township, Morgan Station, or of a mail facility in Indianapolis.

mail. Remembers Medvidovich, "We decided we would test the big plants, and if a big plant was positive, we would go downstream until we all of a sudden started getting negatives."

There were at first only thirty facilities on the list, but as the number of contaminated sites grew, so too did the list of trading partners. Trenton, for example, traded with 151 postal facilities, all of which were tested. Brentwood, meanwhile, sent mail onward to some fifty retail facilities. Many of the Trenton/Brentwood trading partners in turn had their own downstream relationships. On Thursday, October 25, USPS announced that it would expand anthrax testing to more than two hundred facilities across the country.

The Anthrax Crisis and the U.S. Postal Service (B): Terrorism Confirmed

The week of October 21 started on an encouraging note; Congress signaled its resolve that the government would operate as usual by reopening the House of Representatives on Monday—despite the discovery on the previous Saturday of traces of anthrax on mail-bundling machines in the Ford House Office Building, a few blocks from the Capitol. Nonetheless, the week was ultimately marked by a series of discouraging setbacks. On Tuesday, anthrax was discovered on machinery at a military base that sorted mail for the White House. And on Friday, the Supreme Court building was ordered closed for anthrax testing, and a small amount of anthrax was found at CIA headquarters.

Scientific and governmental confusion was palpable; already accusations were flying. Angry words were exchanged in a meeting on Tuesday morning at the office of Secretary Tommy Thompson, Department of Health and Human Services (HHS), because Dr. Anthony S. Fauci, director of the National Institute for Allergy and Infectious Diseases, felt the government had understated the threat in its statements the preceding week.[1] Questions also arose at a Wednesday night meeting chaired by Homeland Security Director Tom Ridge as to whether the FBI had properly shared with CDC and Fort Detrick the results of each agency's testing, with charges made that the potency of the Daschle letter anthrax had been concealed.

By Thursday, October 25, the tenor of the government's message to the public had changed. Ridge confirmed that anthrax from the Daschle letter was highly concentrated, was potent, and could hang suspended in the air (was aerosolized). It was much more finely milled than the NBC and *New York Post* anthrax, and scientists were investigating whether, after all, such weaponized anthrax could escape through a sealed envelope.[2]

Meanwhile, on Monday, October 22, an employee at a Department of State mail-sorting facility fell ill. He was hospitalized on Thursday, and inhalation anthrax was quickly confirmed. On Wednesday, October 24, the Department of State started to hold all mail and instructed embassies to seal and return to Washington, D.C., all mail sent in diplomatic pouches since October 11.

On Tuesday, Hamilton Township postal worker Norma Wallace, 56, was hospitalized with a suspected case of inhalation anthrax. On Wednesday, six postal workers from D.C. were hospitalized on suspicion of anthrax, a *New York Post* mailroom worker was listed as a suspected cutaneous anthrax case, and a second *NBC News* employee, desk assistant Casey

---

[1] Judith Miller and Sheryl Gay Stolberg, "Stung by Criticism, Aides Gather to Coordinate Efforts on Anthrax," *New York Times,* October 25, 2001, A1.

[2] Sheryl Gay Stolberg and Judith Miller, "After a Week of Reassurances, Ridge's Anthrax Message Is Grim," *New York Times,* October 26, 2001, A1.

Chamberlain, was confirmed to have skin anthrax. On Thursday, a Department of State postal worker with no connection to Brentwood was confirmed with inhalation anthrax.

By Thursday, there were thirty-two cases of anthrax exposure, of which thirteen had developed infections: seven cutaneous and six inhaled. The number of Americans taking antibiotics at government urging for possible anthrax exposure was well over 10,000.[3]

Morgan Station, New York City

More anthrax was also found in post offices during the week of October 21. The case that caused U.S. Postal Service (USPS) management the greatest union-related trouble emerged on Thursday, October 25, when anthrax was discovered on four high-speed machines on the third floor of the Morgan Station postal facility in Manhattan.[4] Morgan processed 2 million pieces of mail a day at a site that took up two city blocks, or nearly 2 million square feet. The presumption was that the letters for NBC and the *New York Post,* which would have been sorted at Morgan, had caused the contamination.

Late Wednesday night, USPS had already started Morgan Station employees, as well as workers at five other midtown Manhattan post offices, on 10-day regimes of Cipro.[5] After the Thursday test results, USPS decided not to close the facility but to cordon off and clean the 150,000-square-foot contaminated section.

The union reaction at Morgan was swift. The executive board of the New York Metro Area Postal Union voted on Friday, October 26, to file a lawsuit to close Morgan completely while it was cleaned. In response, David L. Solomon, USPS vice president for operations in the New York area, assured workers that health officials had said there was "no danger for employees to continue working in the building."[6] CDC and local health officials, Sam Pulcrano adds, "went on the workroom floor . . . to talk with employees and explain what was going to happen, what we were going to do, and answer their questions."[7] No Morgan workers had reported anthraxlike symptoms. Morgan used vacuums on the third floor, not blowers, to clean the equipment; contamination was restricted to the third floor. USPS also gave Morgan workers the option of working across the street in a different postal building. Solomon and Mayor Rudolph Giuliani, in a press conference, jointly reiterated that "if in the future a determination is made that the building should be closed, we'll do whatever the health professionals tell us to do."[8]

---

[3]David E. Rosenbaum and Todd S. Purdum, "Another Postal Worker Contracts Inhaled Anthrax," *New York Times,* October 26, 2001, B6.

[4]Morgan Station was located at the corner of 29th Street and 9th Avenue.

[5]The five post offices were the James A. Farley Building, Ansonia Station, Radio City Station, Rockefeller Center Station, and Times Square Station. By Thursday evening, more than 2,500 employees had picked up the antibiotic.

[6]Quoted in Steven Greenhouse, "A Nation Challenged," *New York Times,* October 27, 2001, B6.

[7]Interview with Sam Pulcrano, U.S. Postal Service, Washington, D.C., September 9, 2002. Unless noted, subsequent quotations from Pulcrano are also from this interview.

[8]Quoted in Greenhouse, "A Nation Challenged."

On Friday, November 9, Federal Judge John F. Keenan of the U.S. District Court in Manhattan dismissed the postal union suit, saying that Morgan Station employees had not been shown to have suffered "irreparable harm" and that the peak risk period had been mid- to late September. According to USPS management, the Postal Service had communicated effectively. "We had one union person in New York who tried to stir up the union folks," recalls USPS Senior Vice President for Human Resources Susan Medvidovich, "[but] because we had communicated so well with them, they weren't interested." [9]

New Jersey

On Saturday, October 27, anthrax was newly discovered on a mail bin at the main Princeton, New Jersey, post office in the town of West Windsor. The contamination was judged to have come from the Daschle letter, now identified as a highly potent anthrax source. USPS closed the facility, bringing the number of shuttered central New Jersey postal facilities to three, along with Hamilton and West Trenton. Samples taken at West Trenton had so far yielded no positive results. But at Hamilton, nineteen of fifty-nine samples were positive. Five New Jersey postal workers had developed anthraxlike symptoms; four worked at Hamilton and one at West Trenton. [10] The local health department opened a clinic to dispense antibiotics to all those—as many as 2,500—who had visited Hamilton's public areas since September 18, the day that the NBC and *New York Post* letters were postmarked.

Given these developments, there was intense public and internal pressure on the Unified Incident Command Center (UICC) to get on the job—and quickly. Sampling teams had been going out to identified sites even that first week on a crisis basis. But before the UICC could come up to full speed, it had to put its own house in order.

Ramping Up Efforts at the Unified Incident Command Center

Organizing the Troops

UICC Director Paul Fennewald recognized that his first job was to create a sense of unity and purpose for the ad hoc interagency group that he was overseeing. He had no model to follow, as this was the first UICC to deal with anthrax. He had to create an organizational chart from scratch. To build a common culture, Fennewald asked all UICC staff members "to take off their [institutional] hat and say 'I am here for the organization.'" [11] That was not

---

[9]Interview with Suzanne Medvidovich, U.S. Postal Service, Washington, D.C., September 10, 2002. Unless noted, subsequent quotations from Medvidovich are also from this interview.

[10]Two had skin anthrax and a third had a suspected case, while two others might have had inhalation anthrax.

[11]Interview with Paul Fennewald, Washington, D.C., September 10, 2002. Unless noted, subsequent quotations from Fennewald are also from this interview.

always easy, even for those from within USPS. He recalls that Environmental Management Policy [Dennis Baca's department] "had a very hard time buying into Command Center support" and in the early days often failed to even send a staff member to UICC. But most UICC members, says Fennewald, entered quickly into "the atmosphere of cooperation that was there. It was just happening."

Fennewald also tackled process. He says, "The very first thing that I did is ask: What is the problem we're trying to solve here? And I [realized] it's an information flow problem, it's a communications problem. It's not an anthrax problem." To facilitate the flow of information within UICC, Fennewald began every day with a planning meeting that identified UICC's top five major issues for that day. He then posted a daily operations plan, a schedule of the day's meetings and targets. He also instituted a situation board where staff could post problems as they arose. A log was kept of the problems, how they were resolved, and how quickly.

Fennewald quickly discerned that senior management was hesitant to let the UICC operate as it was designed to do. Some of that stemmed from turf issues; some from lack of information. He notes:

I think there was a reluctance to let go. What we constantly came up against was management's fear of letting the Command Center make the decisions that needed to be made. And so in a time of crisis, the bureaucracy fell back on a very autocratic way of doing business: "I'm going to control this." . . . What I constantly tried to do was to let my management chain know that there were all kinds of capability here.

Interference sometimes hampered operations. Anxious to move things along, leadership would call contractors directly instead of going through UICC or ask for instantaneous test results. So Fennewald tried to educate them. He says, "As soon as we had taken a sample, they wanted results. No one was telling management it takes a while to do this. So I developed little process flow charts to show how long it's going to take to get a sample back."

To further help senior management understand what UICC was doing, Fennewald sent them the daily operations plan. He also "put [himself] on their calendar every day. One o'clock, I would go see Sam Pulcrano. At 1:30, I'd go see Dennis Baca. As opposed to waiting for them to ask for me." And every day at 6 p.m., he sent senior managers a summary report of testing and decontamination results. But the report caused its own problems. Too often, in the last 15 minutes before it was printed, managers would flood UICC with requests that changed the content and delayed the report. Fennewald tried instead to create a website where the status of sampling and decontamination sites could be checked continuously, but it took months to set up due to concerns about cyber-security. Eventually, Fennewald organized a daily teleconference with all senior managers to update them simultaneously.

Testing

Fennewald had logistical problems to resolve as well. If a suspicious powder was found in a letter or package in any postal facility, it was the Postal Service's responsibility to have it tested. Some powders were hoaxes; many were simply false alarms. It hardly mattered. As Medvidovich recalls, "For every hoax, you had to act as if it wasn't a hoax. You had to call the CDC, the health department, get the thing tested, set up the protocol on how to isolate the mail." [12] At the height of the crisis, postal inspectors were responding to six hundred to seven hundred suspicious mail reports each day.

UICC realized quickly that its existing laboratory partner, PathCon, was being overwhelmed by all the samples submitted for testing. By the end of October, it had been deluged with well over 1,000 samples. But, as with the sampling and decontamination contractors, the Postal Service had no authority to contract with other scientific laboratories.

Desperate to find a solution, late on Friday, November 2, UICC organized a conference call with CDC. [13] CDC told the Postal Service officials about the existence of the Association of Public Health Laboratories (APHL), a not-for-profit corporation to which all fifty state laboratories belonged. One contract and one set of protocols could govern all fifty labs. USPS jumped at the opportunity. By Sunday, USPS had a working agreement with APHL to process anthrax samples.

Sampling Plan

UICC simultaneously developed a strategic plan for sampling. There was no protocol for sampling, and creating one was complicated by the continual scientific changes. The technology evolved on a daily basis; as a result, every 3–5 days UICC orders to contractors changed. For example, early testers took thirty-two samples per facility. By mid-November, that number had gone up to fifty-five. Likewise, there were at first no air samples; there was no awareness that anthrax spores could be dispersed in the air.

UICC also had to decide where to sample. The center developed its own checklist but remained open to suggestions. When the unions, for example, asked UICC to sample the small tubs carrying the mail, it added those to the list.

Cleaning Protocols

Then there was the question, once anthrax was found, of how best to clean it up. As soon as it was realized that two types of anthrax, coarse and fine, were in play, different cleanup

---

[12]The Postal Service was not the only agency overwhelmed by anthrax scares. Across the country, police and fire departments were inundated with requests to examine every variety of suspicious white powder. Nonpostal samples went to local laboratories that, as a rule, had never seen anthrax and were just learning how to identify it. From October to December, according to one estimate, the nation's laboratories processed some 121,000 samples.

[13]Charles Vidich was at the airport; Fennewald was in Medvidovich's office.

methods were devised for each. Environmental Manager Baca was in charge of cleaning the two largest sites believed to be contaminated by the finely milled anthrax: Brentwood and Hamilton. There the challenge was how to reach and clean the lofty bays where the aerosolized anthrax had eventually settled. UICC contract teams tackled the remaining, less contaminated sites—those infected either directly by the coarser anthrax or indirectly by cross-contamination from letters containing the finer grade of anthrax.

UICC, together with the U.S. Environmental Protection Agency (EPA), developed protocols for bleaching contaminated surface areas with sodium hypochlorite (a mix of chlorine, sodium hydroxide, and water). But even these procedures kept evolving. At first, the bleach solution was left on for a recommended 5 minutes, then 10 minutes, and later 15 minutes. Eventually, based on World Health Organization (WHO) information, the recommendation increased to 60 minutes of contact time.

Typically, once contamination was found, USPS immediately cordoned off the affected area (if it could be isolated) or closed the building. Then the teleconferencing started. Pulcrano remembers the questions that were posed: "Who's going to go on the floor? Who's going to be the representative? CDC, who are you going to have there? Who's the Department of Health going to have there? How many days do you have? Give us the names of the people. When are they going to be there? When can we start?"

Often a decontamination team came in that same night. Then the area was retested but kept closed until the test results came back negative. Remembers Pulcrano about that time: "There were a dozen linear streams all occurring simultaneously. We were testing and decontaminating multiple facilities, communicating those results."

To codify what the UICC teams were doing in case similar efforts should be needed in the future, Pulcrano and Charles Vidich assembled over a 6-week period a set of interim guidelines. Vidich held meetings nearly around the clock to get comments from other federal agencies and postal unions. As a result, the guidelines were formally adopted in early December. For USPS policy documents, that set a speed record.

Paying for the Crisis

None of these activities came cheap. As early as October 22, the USPS Board of Governors had approved $200 million for new technology to detect anthrax. The next day, USPS spent some of that, signing a $40 million contract with Titan Scan Technologies to supply eight mail sterilizers (with an option for twelve more) to national mail centers.[14] On October 30, Postmaster General Jack Potter told the Senate Governmental Affairs Committee that USPS required "several billion" dollars to recover from the anthrax crisis. On November 8, he told a Senate appropriations subcommittee that USPS needed $5 billion: $2 billion to cover lost

---

[14]Eric Lipton and Kirk Johnson, "Tracking Bioterror's Tangled Course," *New York Times*, December 26, 2001, A1.

revenues (mail volume had dropped 10 percent since the crisis began) and another $3 billion for the anthrax cleanup. Potter did not want to raise postal rates to meet the expenses. "Users of the mail should not be burdened with these extra costs through the price of postage," Potter told the committee.[15] Congress had already granted $175 million for USPS to buy respirators, gloves, and other protective equipment. In late December, USPS won another $500 million in emergency funds for the anthrax cleanup and security measures. But that was all.

Congress sympathized with USPS. But the Postal Service had been struggling financially for years. Congress did not propose to bail out, under the guise of anti-anthrax funding, an organization with systemic problems. The difficulties besetting the Postal Service were fundamental and required thoroughgoing reform. Temporary cash infusions, Congress believed, would only stave off the day of reckoning.

Nonetheless, the anthrax outbreak forced real costs on USPS. No place proved more expensive than Brentwood.

The Brentwood Sorting Center: A Unique Case

From the earliest stages of the crisis, Brentwood was a special case. Although Hamilton was also seriously contaminated, it was at Brentwood that postal workers died. After the sorting facility closed on Sunday, October 21, the first challenge was to figure out what had happened. The test results from the previous Thursday and Friday showed heavy contamination at Brentwood. Where had the Daschle letter gone? Which machines had it touched?

First in line for suspicion were the Advanced Facer Canceller System (AFCS) machines. When a letter arrived, the AFCS looked for a stamp. If it saw the stamp, it cancelled the letter and then sent it through some rollers toward the next station. If the letter was turned facedown, AFCS flipped it and then canceled it. As the letter flipped and went through the rollers, it was twisted and pinched. Letters also went through Delivery Barcode Sorters (DBCSs), whose optical scanners read the name and address and put the letters in the appropriate bins. To reach the bins, the letters traveled down chutes powered by belts moving as quickly as 30 miles per hour, pinching the letters to keep them in place. It seemed likely that at some point during this process, the Daschle letter had released anthrax into the air. The pressured-air blowdown process used to clean the machinery then most likely served to aerosolize the anthrax.

For advice, Baca during that first week contacted the U.S. Army Center for Health Promotion and Preventive Medicine (CHPPM), which provided six people to assist USPS. (CHPPM had experience with anthrax as a potential battlefield weapon, and Baca wanted

---

[15]Quoted in Ellen Nakashima, "Postmaster Asks Senate for Bailout of $5 Billion; Congress Reluctant to Cover Losses," *Washington Post*, November 9, 2001, A30.

to draw on that expertise.) First, the team classified all equipment and mail as either suspect or nonsuspect, with the suspect material treated as a biohazard. All the trucks and trailers that had been inside the Brentwood fence line were included in the suspect category. That meant 529 delivery vehicles and nearly 300 trailers had to be decontaminated. Over the next days and weeks, they were vacuumed using high-efficiency filtration systems and then washed down within constructed containment areas with a chlorine solution.

Cleaning the Mail

Then there was the mail. Three million pieces, or 68 tons, of mail remained on the premises. USPS Vice President for Engineering Thomas Day (Baca's boss) and others had decided that radiation would be the best way to clean the Brentwood mail before delivering it to customers. But first it had to be packaged for transport to a radiation facility. Working with the Armed Forces Radiobiology Research Institute (AFRRI), Baca's team came up with a packaging protocol that allowed efficient mail irradiation. After treatment, the letters would reenter the mail stream.

At Brentwood, the team set up tents labeled "hot zone," "warm zone," and "cold zone." As mail was removed from the periphery of the building and from trailers, it progressed through the zones. First, the trays on which mail rested were wiped down with a chlorine bleach solution. Then the trays of mail were put inside a plastic garbage bag, which was wiped down with chlorine solution. Another bag was placed on the outside. The bags were then placed inside boxes so they would not shift around. Each box was secured, marked with a designation code, and loaded into a trailer. Once the system was up and running, workers could load three to five trailers a day.

USPS contracted with Federal Express Custom Critical for trucks licensed to transport the hazardous materials from Washington, D.C., to Lima, Ohio, where Titan Scan Technologies would irradiate the material. For security, each truck was equipped with an emergency satellite call button on the dashboard. The drivers were certified, the trucks placarded. The first trucks arrived in Lima with packages of Brentwood mail on Friday, October 26.[16] Unfortunately, when the Allen County hazardous materials team examined the first three trucks, it found torn bags inside. Alarmed, they sent the trucks straight back to Washington, D.C., for repackaging, and the members of the hazmat team went on Cipro. But in the days and weeks that followed, trucks—escorted by state troopers the 200 miles to Lima from the Pennsylvania-Ohio border—arrived without further incident.

Protecting the Cleanup Workers

As of early November, Brentwood still had a million pieces of mail left on its machines and nothing inside the building had been touched. That was due to the difficulty of deciding un-

---

[16]Jennifer Lenhart, "City Wants Mail Returned to Sender," *Washington Post*, November 24, 2001, A16.

der which circumstances to permit cleanup workers to enter the building. Contract personnel at Brentwood bagging the suspect mail at first wore Level A personal protective equipment (PPE), requiring the use of double suits with a supplied air system. By early November, the category was downgraded to Level B (one suit). Not until November 7, however, did CDC and OSHA sanction the entry of USPS contract workers into the building to remove the remaining mail and begin to decontaminate the machines.[17]

DBCS 17 was, they determined, the most contaminated machine. Located in the open area of the workroom floor, it had processed the Daschle letter.[18] The deceased Brentwood workers, Thomas Morris and Joseph Curseen, had both worked near DBCS 17. Tests in October showed it had spore colonies in the hundreds of thousands. Contract workers wiped it down three times with a hypochloride solution of chlorine and water, reducing the colonies to fewer than 400 spores. But workers had to wipe down every other piece of equipment and office furniture in the building as well. They also had to clean the walls, remove the ceiling tiles and incinerate them, and remove the carpeting and incinerate it.

Just the experience of removing the mail revealed what a time-consuming project the cleanup would be. The building had been completely sealed with thermal foam board to prevent contamination from leaking out. Its 235 skylights were covered with black plastic, sealed inside and out, and taped. All seventeen HVAC (heating, ventilating, and air conditioning) systems were sealed, as were the gas pipes, water pipes, and electrical conduits. Workers going in wore suits taped all around, sealing gloves and masks. These precautions, coupled with the heat in the building, meant the temperature inside the suits was well over 100° Fahrenheit. Workers at times could remain inside no more than 2 hours before they had to come out, take a shower, rehydrate, and start all over. Baca recalls, "So we've got 150, 200 people generating two suits an entry. By the end of the fourth day, we had eight dumpsters of personal protective equipment and now we have to figure out where do we dispose of it. So we have to go to the EPA."[19]

In early December, EPA's Office of Solid Waste and Emergency Response issued a ruling permitting USPS to dispose of the suits. Next, USPS had to seek State of Virginia Department of Environmental Quality approval to dispose of the suits and other material as medical waste by incinerating them. But the citizens of Virginia protested, so USPS had to obtain permission to transport the hazardous materials through Virginia and other states enroute to Georgia and other states that would accept it. Remarks Baca, "We were trying to figure out the rules and write them at the same time."

---

[17]Justin Blum and Neil Irwin, "Some DC Mail Still Has Not Gone Through," *Washington Post,* November 8, 2001, B1.

[18]It later emerged that the Leahy letter had gone through DBCS 17 as well, not far behind the Daschle letter.

[19]Interview with Dennis Baca, Washington, D.C., September 10, 2002. Unless noted, subsequent quotations from Baca are also from this interview.

Keeping the Records

As Baca was recording these hard-learned rules, he made sure they remained in-house. He and Environmental Coordinator John Bridges had decided from the first day to treat Brentwood as a potential litigation case according to the guidelines set by the National Contingency Plan (NCP). Usually NCP governed hazardous spills, but "[t]here were no specific instructions on how to deal with anthrax," points out Baca, so he modified NCP for anthrax. Using the NCP framework, all information pertaining to the cleanup was restricted as if it were evidence for a court case. Baca wanted to protect any data that could have national security implications. He says, "If we start putting out some of the information that we've generated, and it's made public, then a terrorist will say 'Oh, here's where the holes are in their system.' So everything that we've done, we've pretty much had to keep under wraps."

This secrecy met with some resentment from, among others, UICC. Its members, who were trying to assemble the national protocols for anthrax removal, could learn little about Brentwood (most of the documents, in fact, never left the facility). This did not bother Baca. The experts he needed were at Brentwood field-testing and implementing, as he puts it, "real-time protocols, not hypothetical conditions."

Not surprisingly, as the dimensions of cleaning Brentwood and Hamilton expanded, Baca's role in other decontamination efforts fell off. He rarely attended UICC meetings and, by default, Tim Gouger of the Army Corps of Engineers took over responsibility for all the decontamination except the big two (and Morgan, which had its own command center). At the same time, recalls Baca, he was under pressure from management to reopen Brentwood.

Fortunately, the mail-cleaning operation was proving successful. By November 24, twenty-nine of an expected forty-five trailer-loads from Brentwood had gone through Titan at the rate of two truckloads per week and operations seemed on track to work through the remainder. But there still remained the question of how to clean Brentwood itself, particularly its large open spaces where aerosolized anthrax presumably hung suspended in the air. As Baca and others studied that question, the anthrax outbreak took a turn that was as dramatic as it was difficult to explain.

Late October to November

On Monday, October 29, New York Mayor Giuliani announced that a stockroom worker at the Manhattan Eye, Ear and Throat Hospital was in critical condition with inhalation anthrax. Kathy T. Nguyen, 61, of the Bronx, had felt ill since October 25. The hospital closed, and its hundreds of employees and patients were tested for anthrax starting on October 30. On October 31, Nguyen died. The same day that Nguyen's illness became public, Linda Burch in New Jersey was diagnosed with skin anthrax. The 51-year-old worked as a bookkeeper in an office whose mail bin was found to be infected. The mail to both her office and home was processed at Hamilton.[20] The Nguyen and Burch cases alarmed public health authorities because neither woman worked with the mail. The Nguyen case was especially frustrating because there were no clues indicating how she had become infected, yet somehow she had contracted the more virulent inhalation anthrax.

Three weeks later, the mystery deepened. On November 21, Ottilie Lundgren, a 94-year-old woman from Oxford, Connecticut, died from inhalation anthrax. Mrs. Lundgren had no connection to the media, government, or Postal Service. She rarely left her house. Connecticut health officials, the CDC, and USPS were baffled. Tests at the nearby Wallingford postal facility found anthrax residue on several sorting machines.[21] But no one else was ill. Traces of anthrax were also found on a letter sent to a home 1.5 miles from Lundgren's. Cross-contamination seemed the likely source. But how little anthrax had it taken to kill the elderly Connecticut resident?

The case of Nguyen remained similarly unsolved. There was only circumstantial evidence of cross-contamination—a letter mailed to an address near Nguyen's had passed through the same Hamilton sorting machine that had handled the Daschle letter.[22] "We have no evidence yet that they actually got [anthrax] from the mail," says Medvidovich. "But guess what? We had to act like they got it from the mail and restart our procedures."

There was pressure to close the Wallingford Post Office, but the contamination was light and localized, and so USPS kept it open. Again, the Task Force took pains to communicate fully with the unions and the employees. "We worked with the employees," says Medvidovich. "You can't just dismiss stress. You can't dismiss fear. . . . We had doctors go out on the workroom floor and talk to them about anthrax. . . . The key was, you kept the unions involved."

But union leaders were not particularly reassured. On Thanksgiving Day, November 22, Union President Bill Burrus of the 360,000-member American Postal Workers Union recommended that members refuse to work in buildings where any traces of anthrax remained. "It's a continuing concern that so much uncertainty continues to exist regarding the source of these infections," he said.[23] The unions did not, however, stop mail delivery. Perhaps they, like the USPS leadership, were waiting to see what could be learned from a second anthrax letter bound for Congress—found on November 16.

---

[20]Nicholas Kulish and Jared Sandberg, "Questions of Security: Postal Officials to Face Grilling on Capitol Hill about Anthrax," *Wall Street Journal*, October 30, 2001, A6.

[21]Andrew C. Revkin with Paul Zielbauer, "A Nation Challenged: The Postal Service; Tracking of Anthrax Letter Yields Clues," *New York Times*, December 7, 2001, B1. The anthrax was found on December 2, after numerous tests by both USPS contract teams and the CDC.

[22]Eric Lipton and Judith Miller, "US Says Thousands of Letters May Have Had Anthrax Traces," *New York Times*, December 4, 2001, A1.

[23]Associated Press, "Postal Union Urges Members Not to Work If Anthrax Is Found," *New York Times*, November 23, 2001, B6.

The Leahy Letter

Investigators from the FBI and EPA had believed for weeks that the extent of aerosolized anthrax contamination they were seeing could not have been caused by the Daschle letter alone. They suspected a second letter, perhaps lying among the mountains of quarantined congressional mail. On Monday, November 5, the FBI had moved all the mail received at the Capitol October 12–17 from a congressional building to a General Services Administration warehouse in a northern Virginia suburb.[24] The 600 bags filled 286 sealed 55-gallon barrels.

FBI, EPA, and Fort Detrick investigators had started on Monday, November 12, to go through the barrels of congressional mail. At 5 p.m. on Friday, they struck gold—a heavily taped letter postmarked in Trenton on October 9, with handwriting similar to that on the Daschle letter, addressed to Sen. Patrick Leahy (D-Vt.), chair of the Senate Judiciary Committee. Like the Daschle letter, the return address was the nonexistent "4th Grade, Greendale School, Franklin Park, NJ." [25] Like the Daschle letter, it was loaded with anthrax.

The investigators had been extraordinarily careful handling the quarantined mail. Now that the second letter had been found, scientists, with help from experts around the world, devised an entirely new procedure to handle the Leahy letter. Their efforts were rewarded. Analyzing this plentiful supply of weaponized anthrax, scientists made significant investigative strides over the next couple of weeks. Just one sample from the Leahy letter, the FBI reported shortly after the letter's discovery, contained 23,000 spores.[26] Just 2 weeks later, weapons experts restated that estimate, clarifying that the anthrax sent to Congress contained 1 trillion spores per gram, a degree of fineness inconceivable before the recent events.[27] If a deadly dose was close to 10,000 spores, 1 trillion could potentially kill 100 million people.

The high quality and specific strain of the anthrax led HHS Secretary Thompson to say on November 20 that the anthrax-tainted letters most likely came from a domestic source. Others speculated more explicitly that it must come from a U.S. defense laboratory. Leahy told NBC's *Meet the Press* that the letter addressed to him contained enough anthrax potentially to kill 100,000 people. Armed with this new information, EPA returned to the American Media Inc. (AMI) building in Florida, the site of the first inhalation anthrax cases. New tests showed far wider contamination than had been initially thought; EPA announced

---

[24]Guy Gugliotta, "Senate Delays Plan to Fumigate Its Hart Office Building," *Washington Post,* November 6, 2001, A10.

[25]Judith Miller and David Johnson, "Investigators Liken Anthrax in Leahy Letter to That Sent to Daschle," *New York Times,* November 20, 2001, B1.

[26]Ibid.

[27]William J. Broad, "The Spores: Terror Anthrax Resembles Type Made by US," *New York Times,* December 3, 2001, A1.

on December 5 that 88 of 460 swabs on three floors tested positive.[28] As in the Hart Senate Office building and Brentwood, the anthrax must have spread through the air vents.

For its part, the Postal Inspection Service discovered that the Leahy letter had been mistakenly sent to the Department of State before being rerouted back to Capitol Hill. That explained how some diplomatic mail may have been contaminated. USPS also discovered that the Leahy and Daschle letters were closely spaced during processing. It was the letters in between (plus some in front of and behind them) that most likely had caused most of the cross-contamination.

Fewer Patients

Finding the Leahy letter was not the only good news in November. Apart from the anomalous cases of Nguyen and Lundgren, there were signs that the anthrax outbreak was tapering off. With no new case in more than a week, D.C. Chief Health Officer Dr. Ivan Walks cautiously suggested that the city was "on the downside" of the crisis.[29]

Meanwhile, some of the afflicted were returning home. As early as October 23, Ernesto Blanco, the Florida AMI employee with inhalation anthrax, left the hospital (after 23 days). On November 5, Hamilton postal worker Norma Wallace was released after 2 weeks of hospital treatment for inhalation anthrax.[30] On November 9, a Department of State mail handler with inhalation anthrax and a 56-year-old Brentwood postal worker both went home.[31] On November 19, Leroy Richmond, the first Brentwood worker known to have inhalation anthrax, left the hospital.

Postal Contamination Lessens

But discoveries of contamination continued. On October 30, traces of anthrax were found at several more D.C.-area post offices. On November 2, testers found contamination on two more machines at Morgan Station in Manhattan. On November 3, the South Jersey Processing and Distribution Center in Bellmawr, New Jersey, closed (for a second time) after spores were found on a mail-sorting machine.[32] Spores were found November 5 inside two mailboxes inside the Pentagon. On November 9, authorities announced they had found trace amounts of anthrax in four small post offices that fed into Hamilton. None of the four was closed; they were cleaned overnight.

---

[28]Ceci Connolly and Ellen Nakashima, "CDC Sets 'Tips' on Handling Mail," *Washington Post,* December 6, 2001, A26.

[29]Quoted in Steve Twomey and Avram Goldstein, "Officials Call Off Antibiotics for Many Who Handle Mail," *Washington Post,* November 2, 2001, A13.

[30]Gugliotta, "Senate Delays Plan."

[31]Lipton and Johnson, "Tracking Bioterror's Tangled Course."

[32]"Anthrax Discovery Closes Mail Center," *New York Times,* November 4, 2001, B6.

Encouragingly, however, the new contamination cases exhibited merely light concentrations of anthrax. With the lessened risk, facilities were able to remain open while contaminated areas were cordoned off and cleaned. On a similarly positive note, the UICC sampling teams were finding contamination not because of sick workers but because the UICC was testing facilities according to its trading partners chart. Of the 230 locations on the list by early November, 200 were included as a precaution and only 30 because they were known to have handled contaminated letters or had sick employees. As of November 2, 64 had been tested. Of those, 39 were anthrax-free, 8 had been contaminated and were closed pending cleaning, and the results for 17 were not yet available.[33] Slowly the post offices reopened.

Brentwood Revisited

Brentwood, however, remained definitively closed. With the discovery of the Leahy letter and the analysis of the anthrax it contained, the dimensions of contamination at Brentwood were understood far better. The aerosolized anthrax had by now spread through the ventilation system. Baca and his team had to decide how best to kill those spores. For initial guidance, they observed closely what EPA was doing at the Hart Senate Office Building, where aerosolized anthrax had also spread widely.

To clean Hart's contaminated open spaces, EPA had made a choice. Historically, paraformaldehyde had been used to clean up anthrax, but there were fears that it might be a carcinogen. EPA thus selected instead chlorine dioxide gas, which had been used at the Ames Government Laboratory for anthrax decontamination.

Baca decided that he would select the same cleaning agent for Brentwood that EPA chose for Hart. It was not an easy decision. Since October 22, businesspeople (supported by their congressional representatives) had presented Baca with plenty of options, each salesperson promising his or her product could solve the problem. But Baca felt chlorine dioxide was the right choice, scientifically and politically. He says, "My recommendation to the Postal Service was that we had been characterized as second-class citizens compared to the Hart employees. Well, we were going to use the exact same processes and science that was used at the Hart. Our employees deserved nothing less."

But cleaning Brentwood would be more challenging than cleaning Hart. At 17.5 million cubic feet, the building was 175 times larger than the area that had to be cleaned at Hart. Baca also continued to fend off attempts from EPA to take over the Brentwood decontamination. "EPA could at any time, if we weren't doing what was right, take it away from us," he says. "But we are the lead agency and we were doing it correctly."

As Baca geared up for the Brentwood operation, the rest of the USPS anthrax response team was downshifting from full-bore crisis mode to a more manageable state of emergency.

---

[33]Michael Janofsky, "Mail Delays Are Minimal, despite Anthrax Problems," *New York Times*, November 2, 2001, B8.

A Calmer December

Although false alarms continued to cause occasional scares around the country, by December there had been no new deaths since Lundgren and no new tainted letters since the discovery of the Leahy letter. The crisis seemed to be in retreat. The discovery of anthrax on December 2 at the Wallingford postal facility (after Ms. Lundgren's death) did trigger 2 weeks of fevered activity for UICC. The problem was that contamination was found only after repeated tests by a variety of methods: dry swabs (Q-tips), wet swabs, and wet wipes. Only the wet wipes revealed the presence of anthrax. This disturbed UICC officials because their contract teams, up to then, had used mostly swabs to test for anthrax. The results at Wallingford called into question the validity of all previous tests that had relied on swabbing. With no new illnesses, however, UICC worry diminished. As of mid-December, CDC had confirmed eighteen cases of anthrax infection since the start of the outbreak: eleven cases of inhalation anthrax and seven cases of skin anthrax. Five people had died, all from inhalation anthrax.[34]

USPS senior management began to dare to think they could start to breathe normally again, and by Christmas, UICC had lessened its frenetic pace of October and November.[35] Except for Brentwood and Trenton, UICC teams had bleached and reopened all the infected postal facilities—twenty-one in total.[36] UICC had sampled 284 sites. Postal inspectors had fielded more than 17,000 reports of anthrax. The five hundred to six hundred calls per day from the press and the public to the USPS Communications Center had dwindled by December to a dozen per day. On Friday, December 21, UICC closed its doors—at least temporarily. When it reopened in January, it was as a smaller operation.

Cleaning the large, open buildings proved to be a long-term and costly task. EPA did not finish with the Hart Building until February 2002. The agency reported that the final cost of cleaning up Capitol Hill (thirty buildings) topped $23 million, twice the original estimate.[37] Vice President for Engineering Day said that USPS learned a lot from the Hart building treatment—how much chlorine dioxide gas to use, under what conditions, at what temperature and humidity, and for how long.[38] Still, progress at Brentwood, due to its large size and complex configuration, remained slow, and the building was still closed more than a year later. Despite that, confidence in the mail had rebounded. During the crisis, polls showed it had dropped over 15 percent—only 82 percent of Americans trusted the mail. By March 2002, 96 percent of Americans once again had confidence in their nation's postal service.

---

[34]The deceased were Stevens, Curseen, Morris, Nguyen, and Lundgren.

[35]In late November, Fennewald urgently needed back surgery, and Deputy Incident Commander Vidich took over.

[36]In addition, affected organizations (the Department of State, NBC, and so forth) had independently cleaned up twenty-seven contaminated nonpostal facilities. Of the twenty-seven nonpostal facilities, twenty were in Washington, D.C.

[37]Spencer S. Hsu, "Cost of Anthrax Cleanup on Hill to Top $23 Million, EPA Says," *Washington Post,* March 7, 2002, A7.

[38]Steve Twomey, "Mail Official Predicts Brentwood's Return," *Washington Post,* January 9, 2002, A11.

Key Actors in the Anthrax Crisis and the U.S. Postal Service

U.S. Government Officials

Tommy G. Thompson, secretary of health and human services (HHS)

Thomas Ridge, director of Homeland Security

Sen. Tom Daschle (D-S.D.), Senate Majority Leader

Sen. Patrick Leahy (D-Vt.), chair of the Senate Judiciary Committee

U.S. Postal Service

John "Jack" Potter, postmaster general

Deborah Willhite, U.S. Postal Service (USPS) senior vice president for government relations and public policy

Suzanne Medvidovich, USPS senior vice president for human resources

Patrick Donahoe, USPS chief operating officer

Azeezaly Jaffer, USPS vice president of public affairs and communication

Jon Leonard, USPS internal communications manager

Kenneth Weaver, chief of the U.S. Postal Inspection Service and chair of the Mail Security Task Force

Thomas Day, USPS vice president for engineering

Dennis Baca, USPS manager for environmental management policy

John Bridges, Brentwood environmental coordinator

Sam Pulcrano, USPS manager of safety

Charles Vidich, USPS manager for environmental compliance for the Northeast, responsible for overall coordination at the Unified Incident Command Center (UICC)

Paul Fennewald, environmental programs analyst, became UICC director

James Gaffney, USPS environmental compliance specialist, responsible at UICC for sampling

Timothy Gouger, U.S. Army Corps of Engineers, responsible at UICC for decontamination

Timothy Haney, Brentwood senior plant manager

Medical Officials, U.S. Centers for Disease Control and Prevention

Jeffrey P. Koplan, MD, director of the U.S. Centers for Disease Control and Prevention (CDC)

Julie Gerberding, MD, CDC deputy director for infectious diseases

State and Local Officials

New Jersey

George T. DiFerdinando, MD, New Jersey acting commissioner for health

Washington, D.C.

Anthony A. Williams, mayor of Washington, D.C.

Ivan C. A. Walks, MD, chief health officer, Washington, D.C.

Anthrax Victims (not a complete list)

Deceased

Robert Stevens, photo editor of the American Media Inc. (AMI) tabloid *The Sun,* died October 5

Joseph P. Curseen, Brentwood employee, died October 22

Thomas L. Morris Jr., Brentwood employee, died October 21

Kathy T. Nguyen, stockroom worker at Manhattan Eye, Ear and Throat Hospital, died October 31

Ottilie Lundgren, Oxford, Connecticut, homemaker, died November 21

Recovered Cutaneous Anthrax Cases

Erin O'Connor, assistant to *NBC News* anchor Tom Brokaw, diagnosed October 12

Claire Fletcher, *CBS News* aide, diagnosed October 18

Johanna Huden, *New York Post* editorial page assistant, illness announced October 19

Teresa Heller, West Trenton, New Jersey, letter carrier, illness announced October 18

Patrick O'Donnell, Hamilton, New Jersey, maintenance worker, diagnosed October 19

Casey Chamberlain, *NBC News* desk assistant, diagnosed October 24

Linda Burch, New Jersey bookkeeper, diagnosed October 29

Recovered Inhalation Anthrax Cases

Ernesto Blanco, AMI mailroom employee, admitted to the hospital October 1, diagnosed October 15

Leroy Richmond, Brentwood employee, diagnosed October 21

Norma Wallace, Hamilton Township, New Jersey, postal worker, diagnosed October 23

The Anthrax Crisis, 2001

Chronology of Events

Tuesday, September 18
Envelopes containing letters and granular substances are sent to the *New York Post* and NBC News. Both are mailed from Trenton, New Jersey, and later test positive for anthrax.

Sunday, September 30
Robert Stevens, photo editor of *The Sun,* a tabloid published by American Media Inc. (AMI) in Boca Raton, Florida, begins showing signs of illness.

Monday, October 1
Ernesto Blanco, a mailroom worker at AMI, is hospitalized after feeling ill for several days.

Thursday, October 4
Concerns mount that Stevens has contracted anthrax. Department of Health and Human Services (HHS) Secretary Tommy G. Thompson states, "It is an isolated case, and it is not contagious."

The U.S. Centers for Disease Control and Prevention (CDC) sends a team of scientists to Boca Raton in response to the illnesses at AMI.

Friday, October 5
Stevens dies. His is the first U.S. death from inhaled anthrax since 1976.

Sunday, October 7
AMI closes its Boca Raton headquarters after testing reveals anthrax contamination.

Monday, October 8 (Columbus Day)
The Federal Bureau of Investigation (FBI) takes over the Stevens case.

After seeing a report linking Stevens's death to contaminated mail, U.S. Postal Service (USPS) Vice President Azeezaly Jaffer prepares a memo for employees addressing the anthrax threat.

Tuesday, October 9
Letters postmarked in Trenton, New Jersey, are mailed to Sen. Tom Daschle (D-S.D.), Senate majority leader, and Sen. Patrick Leahy (D-Vt.). Both letters contain high-grade anthrax.

President George W. Bush informs the nation that the Florida case appears to be an isolated incident.

Friday, October 12

NBC's Erin O'Connor is diagnosed with skin (cutaneous) anthrax—the first known case outside Florida.

Sunday, October 14

In Trenton, state health officers inform postal workers that anthrax testing is not necessary.

Monday, October 15

A letter containing anthrax is opened in Senate Majority Leader Tom Daschle's office in the Hart Senate Office Building.

The Washington, D.C., Department of Health (DOH) activates its biohazard response plan and requests CDC's involvement.

Postmaster General John "Jack" Potter announces the formation of a Mail Security Task Force.

AMI's Blanco is diagnosed with anthrax.

Tuesday, October 16

The Hart Senate Office Building closes; hundreds of staffers are tested for anthrax.

CDC confirms that the Daschle letter contains anthrax. CDC sends teams to D.C.

Senator Daschle announces that the letter sent to his office contained a highly potent form of anthrax. Later in the week, however, government officials try to downplay concerns.

Wednesday, October 17

The House of Representatives closes.

Testing of the Hamilton Township, New Jersey, mail processing center identifies thirteen positive anthrax samples.

Thursday, October 18

CBS News aide Claire Fletcher tests positive for cutaneous anthrax.

The House and Senate office complexes close.

FBI and USPS hold a joint press conference at the Brentwood mail processing center in Washington, D.C. They offer $1 million for information leading to the arrest and conviction of those involved with the anthrax mailings.

Concerned that the anthrax threat is greater than originally thought, USPS brings in a private firm to test the Brentwood facility, which processed the Daschle letter.

Teresa Heller, a Trenton letter carrier, is diagnosed with skin anthrax.

USPS closes the Hamilton Township mail processing center.

Friday, October 19
The *New York Post* confirms that Johanna Huden, an editorial page assistant, has skin anthrax. An anthrax-laced letter is found, unopened, near where she works.

The USPS Mail Security Task Force holds its first meeting. As the crisis deepens, the Task Force assumes responsibility for managing the Postal Service's response.

CDC tests Brentwood for anthrax.

The West Trenton, New Jersey, post office closes.

Hamilton Township postal worker Patrick O'Donnell is diagnosed with skin anthrax.

Saturday, October 20
USPS learns that Leroy Richmond, a Brentwood mail sorter, most likely has anthrax—and that D.C. officials are planning on notifying the public.

Sunday, October 21
CDC confirms that Richmond has inhalation anthrax.

Brentwood closes. Test results eventually indicate heavy contamination.

D.C. Mayor Anthony Williams holds a press conference and offers Brentwood workers antibiotics.

Brentwood worker Thomas L. Morris Jr. dies of inhalation anthrax.

Monday, October 22
Brentwood worker Joseph P. Curseen dies of anthrax.

The House of Representatives reopens; the Senate and House office buildings remain closed.

CDC organizes a conference call with the FBI, USPS, Postal Inspection Service, Office of Homeland Security, and local law enforcement officials. They decide to keep USPS running.

James Gaffney arrives in D.C. from the USPS New Jersey district to work at the newly formed Unified Incident Command Center (UICC). The group is assigned the task of identifying and managing anthrax-contaminated sites.

Tuesday, October 23
Charles Vidich, USPS manager for environmental compliance for the Northeast, arrives in D.C. to work at the UICC.

Hamilton Township postal worker Norma Wallace is hospitalized with suspected inhalation anthrax.

Wednesday, October 24

Casey Chamberlain, an NBC desk assistant, is diagnosed with cutaneous anthrax.

A *New York Post* mailroom worker is listed as a suspected cutaneous anthrax case.

Six D.C. postal workers are hospitalized with suspected anthrax.

After an employee at a U.S. Department of State mail sorting facility becomes ill, the Department of State begins holding all mail. (The employee is later hospitalized and diagnosed with inhalation anthrax.)

Thursday, October 25

USPS announces it will expand anthrax contamination testing to more than two hundred facilities.

Homeland Security's Thomas Ridge confirms that the Daschle letter was intended as a weapon.

Anthrax is found at the Morgan Station mail processing facility in Manhattan.

Kathy Nguyen, a stockroom worker at the Manhattan Eye, Ear and Throat Hospital, falls ill.

Friday, October 26

The executive board of the New York Metro Area Postal Union votes to file a suit to close Morgan Station for cleaning.

The first trucks carrying mail from Brentwood arrive in Lima, Ohio, for irradiation by Titan Scan Technologies.

Saturday, October 27

Anthrax is discovered at the West Windsor, New Jersey (Princeton), post office. Like Hamilton and West Trenton, it is closed for decontamination.

Monday, October 29

Lind Burch, a New Jersey bookkeeper, is diagnosed with skin anthrax.

Manhattan Eye, Ear & Throat Hospital closes.

Wednesday, October 31

Nguyen dies from inhalation anthrax.

Sunday, November 4

USPS concludes a working agreement with the Association of Public Health Laboratories (APHL) to process anthrax samples.

Monday, November 5

FBI moves Capitol Hill's quarantined mail—received between October 12 and October 17—in 280 sealed, 55-gallon barrels from D.C. to a Virginia warehouse.

Thursday, November 8

Postmaster General Potter tells the Senate that USPS needs $5 billion: $2 billion to cover lost revenues plus at least $3 billion for anthrax cleanup.

Friday, November 9

A judge dismisses the suit filed by the New York Metro Area Postal Union to close Morgan Station for cleaning.

Friday, November 16

Investigators uncover the anthrax-laden letter addressed to Senator Leahy, which had mistakenly been routed to the Department of State.

Monday, November 19

Brentwood employee Leroy Richmond is released from the hospital.

Wednesday, November 21

Ottilie Lundgren, 94, of Oxford, Connecticut, dies from inhalation anthrax.

Thursday, November 22 (Thanksgiving)

Bill Burrus, president of the 360,000-member American Postal Workers Union, recommends members refuse to work in buildings with any trace of anthrax.

Sunday, December 2

Traces of anthrax are found in the Wallingford, Connecticut, post office near Ms. Lundgren's home.

Wednesday, December 5

The U.S. Environmental Protection Agency (EPA) announces that 88 of 460 swabs obtained during follow-up testing at AMI have tested positive for anthrax, revealing that the contamination is far greater than originally thought.

Friday, December 21

UICC closes down temporarily; it reopens in January as a far smaller operation.

9 Wal-Mart's Response to Hurricane Katrina (A): Striving for a Public-Private Partnership

Susan Rosegrant

When Hurricane Katrina bore down on the U.S. coast in August 2005, Wal-Mart senior officials opened and progressively scaled up the company's Emergency Operations Center (EOC) at corporate headquarters in Bentonville, Arkansas. Before and during the storm and an extended aftermath, the EOC monitored Katrina's threat, coordinated efforts to protect Wal-Mart stores and distribution centers in a multistate region, provided aid and support to employees in storm-affected areas, and collaborated in supplying and reopening stores as quickly as possible to meet customer needs. As the scope of Katrina's destruction became apparent, moreover, an operation that was primarily aimed at the company's own assets, employees, and business operations grew broader: to provide whatever support was possible to public safety workers, government agencies, and the public at large.

Wal-Mart brought formidable capabilities to this task: a proactive, corporate inventory-control system; widespread stocks of goods; a robust supply network; and extensive freight-moving and logistics capacity. Equally important, entrepreneurial regional and local managers were quickly granted and used extraordinary discretion both in protecting company assets and using Wal-Mart resources for the benefit of their communities. Many proved extremely resourceful in coping with the highly unusual degree of disruption that Katrina had caused, particularly in Louisiana and Mississippi.

They also frequently encountered difficulties in meshing their efforts with federal, state, and local government operations. Providing supplies to emergency workers, for example, both by purchase and Wal-Mart donation, was complicated or frustrated by inflexible federal and state procedures, which had not been designed for the exigencies of a catastrophic emergency. An offer to exchange representation at the Department of Homeland Security (DHS) and Wal-Mart EOCs was declined by DHS. While some Wal-Mart managers had preexisting relationships with local and state leaders and emergency managers, many did not, which made it harder to develop mutually appropriate operating practices under the pressure of the widespread disruption caused by Katrina.

In reading this case study, consider how Wal-Mart (and, by extension, other major companies and nonprofit institutions that have substantial operating capabilities) could get ready for future natural disasters or other crises and how they could increase the probability that their efforts would mesh effectively with government response and relief activity. Consider too what government—the Federal Emergency Management Agency (FEMA) and

This is an abridged version of a case written by Susan Rosegrant for Professor Herman B. "Dutch" Leonard, George F. Baker Jr. Professor of Public Management, John F. Kennedy School of Government, Harvard University. Funding was provided by the National Preparedness Leadership Initiative, a project sponsored by the U.S. Centers for Disease Control and Prevention. Kennedy School of Government Case Program, C16-07-1876.0 and C16-07-1876.1. Copyright © 2007 by the President and Fellows of Harvard College.

*other federal agencies, state emergency managers, and local governments—could do to in-
tegrate corporate involvement in disaster response and relief into overall emergency management efforts.*

Discussion Questions

- What factors permitted Wal-Mart to become an effective player in respond-
  ing to Hurricane Katrina?
- What obstacles limited Wal-Mart's effectiveness?
- How might the operational interface between private companies such as Wal-
  Mart and public agencies be improved in planning for and responding to future emergencies?
- Are there inherent limitations in the role that private companies (and major
  nonprofit institutions) can play in disaster response, even if coordination
  with the public sector is improved?
- What might federal, state, and local governments do in advance of a crisis to
  establish relationships with these companies and prepare emergency procedures so that their efforts can mesh under disaster conditions?

On August 28, 2005, as Hurricane Katrina barreled toward the Louisiana and Mississippi
coasts, local law enforcement, state emergency management officials, the National
Guard, and the Federal Emergency Management Agency (FEMA) all feverishly prepared for
what was expected to be a devastating hit. Out of the public eye, the private sector was
undergoing preparations that, in some cases, were even more exhaustive. At Wal-Mart's
Bentonville, Arkansas, headquarters, a comprehensive emergency response was already
underway. Stores in the storm zone had closed early after stocking up on special hurricane
merchandise; teams were stationed near the New Orleans and the Mississippi coast, ready
to sweep in to evaluate damage to stores; and at the centralized emergency operations center (EOC), representatives of all major functional areas were gathered to launch a coordinated effort to find displaced employees, re-open stores as quickly as possible, and help
stricken communities.

After Katrina roared through, Wal-Mart launched a response that it had rolled out many
times before, to good effect. But when the levee system protecting New Orleans began to fail
and the city flooded, the situation grew into something much larger than just the aftermath
of a large hurricane. As government first responders became overwhelmed by the spreading
casualties, public disorder, and chaos, the giant retailer found itself playing a more central
part than anticipated. Indeed, Wal-Mart trucks rolling into New Orleans became an iconic
image of the unfolding response. But questions remained about whether the public sector
could take full advantage of the retailer's strengths and capabilities, and whether it was ready

for Wal-Mart and other companies to carve out a new role for private-sector participation in a national emergency.

Emergency Operations at Wal-Mart

Wal-Mart Stores, Inc., founded its Emergency Management Department in 2003. The department's planning section produced detailed emergency procedures, and a preparedness group trained managers, response teams, and associates in executing the plans they were given. Meanwhile, Alarm Central, a round-the-clock watchdog group of six to eight people, monitored fire and burglar alarms at all 3,218 Wal-Mart stores and 555 Sam's Clubs nationwide; the group also watched CNN, Fox News, and the Weather Channel, scrutinizing world events and weather patterns for developments that could affect store operations.[1]

But perhaps the department's highest profile function was the EOC, which oversaw the coordination, response, and recovery for business disruptions ranging from tornadoes to terrorism to epidemics. Wal-Mart's Director of Business Continuity Jason Jackson, a former Arkansas state trooper/special agent who took over emergency operations in 2004, describes the EOC as a "quasi incident command system" that operated with just a few people to handle small situations, but that could quickly expand as needed.[2]

The EOC operated under three levels of activation. Jackson and his team handled small events from their desks. If from five to fifty Wal-Marts or Sam's Clubs were likely to be affected—for example, by wildfires or a small hurricane—Jackson called a Level Two alert and activated the EOC, a stark, rectangular room in a building on Wal-Mart's Home Office (corporate headquarters) campus. A Level Two response typically involved six to a dozen senior representatives from functional areas, such as emergency merchandise, transportation, logistics, and corporate giving, who coordinated the response along with Jackson's team. Level Three, a large hurricane or other major event, could draw in as many as sixty people from thirty-five to forty different departments.[3]

At the front of the room was a row of computers where Jackson and his crisis management team sat, taking calls from first responders and associates in the field; maintaining an incident management website; producing daily situation updates; making sure that the

---

[1]The Wal-Mart stores included 1,258 general merchandise stores, 1,866 supercenters, and 94 neighborhood markets. Sam's Clubs are Wal-Mart's membership warehouse clubs. Should a situation arise that merited additional attention, Alarm Central used a software tool dubbed Send Word Now to fire off emails or voicemails to various groups, depending on the nature of the event.

[2]Interview with Jason Jackson, Wal-Mart director of business continuity, 2007. Unless noted, subsequent quotations from Jackson are also from this interview. Incident command was a clearly defined and expandable incident management structure designating, among other things, command roles, tasks to be accomplished, and a system to assign responsibility for each task.

[3]Before 2004, departments usually had only one or two people experienced at representing their groups at the EOC. But after the active hurricane season of 2004, Jackson began offering an annual EOC Hurricane Class, initially training 150 managers.

functional representatives in the EOC had the tools they needed; and serving as a bridge to senior officers of the company.[4] The EOC's mandate was three-part, Jackson says: associate welfare, reconstitution of operations, and community support. "If we can take care of our folks, usually we can do number two, which is to get operations back up and running," he explains. "And getting our operations up and running, which is bread and butter for us, is the best way that we can serve the community."

The Calm before the Storm

During the Atlantic hurricane season, which officially ran from June 1 to November 30, Jackson's group intensified its scrutiny of weather systems, using special weather modeling software that pulled from multiple sources, including the U.S. National Weather Service and the U.S. Navy, and calling on private meteorologists. On August 23, 2005, Jackson and his team decided that a storm developing into a tropical depression over the southeastern Bahamas had the potential to disrupt operations in Florida. Jackson called a Level Two alert and activated the EOC, setting off well-organized actions.

A half dozen functional representatives came to the EOC, and Jackson's team called or e-mailed the senior vice presidents and regional managers responsible for the southeast region, including Florida, giving them the latest predictions about when the storm might hit and what its impact might be. (See Exhibit 9A-1 for a Wal-Mart organization chart.) It was then up to the regional managers to pass that information down to their district managers, who in turn communicated with managers at the store and club level.

Next, a number of response teams (typically composed of two people each) were stationed in and near Florida. Loss-prevention teams were first to move in. They were responsible for evaluating the condition of stores and deciding if it was safe for managers and associates to return, often consulting with local law enforcement. Depending on what needed to be done, the EOC would dispatch other teams stationed in the area, including information systems teams, which brought in portable satellite systems to restore phone service and credit and debit card processing capability; generator teams, which trucked in mobile generators to stores without power; and restoration teams, third-party contractors hired to clean merchandise and to provide immediate repairs.

Meanwhile, store operations in Florida began their own structured preparations. A price freeze was already in effect for the region, Jackson says, to avoid any appearance of price gouging. After consulting with store managers, district managers held conference calls with representatives at the Home Office to discuss what emergency products were needed and when. The goal, Jackson says, was to have emergency merchandise in stores before forecasters showed up on TV to announce the storm's imminent arrival. "That's when the community

---

[4]In Wikipedia-like fashion, there could be multiple contributors to the website—from the store manager level on up—so that the EOC didn't bear the full brunt of data entry.

Exhibit 9A-1   Wal-Mart organization chart, 2005

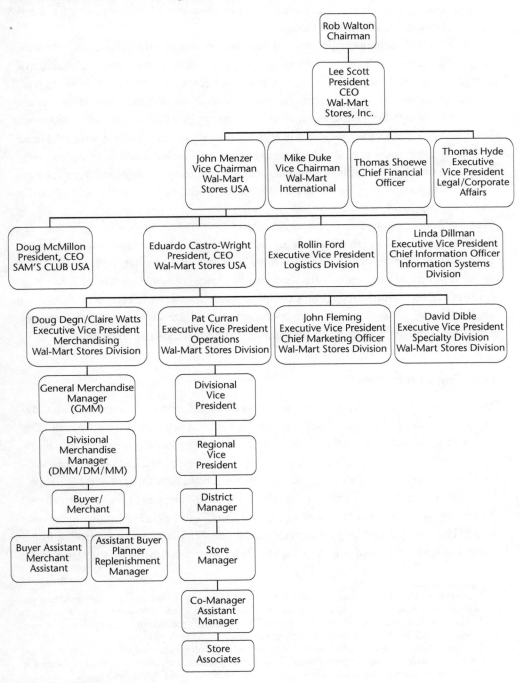

Source: Wal-Mart Stores, Inc.

turns out to buy stuff, and if we're not ready for that, our shelves go dry immediately," Jackson says. The "replenishment" department then placed orders at Wal-Mart's disaster distribution centers, and trucks began to roll.

Wal-Mart had more than one hundred distribution centers nationwide, and eight were designated as disaster distribution centers, with space set aside for some $4.7 million of emergency merchandise. In the Southeast, where hurricanes constituted the main hazard, this included water, batteries, lanterns, lamp oil, and ready-to-eat food.[5] The intent was not to stockpile enough for the biggest emergency; an emergency might never materialize, and even water could not sit long without ill effect.[6] If hurricane merchandise wasn't depleted over the course of the season, Wal-Mart would rotate unused products back into the system, at the same time letting suppliers know that orders would temporarily drop for those items. If, conversely, disaster supplies ran dry during an active season, the system would pull from the regular supply chain to fill demand.[7]

At the individual store level, managers turned to their EOC-provided hurricane preparedness guides and began shutdown procedures: boarding over windows with plywood, storing loose shopping carts, and pre-positioning sandbags and sump pumps. Associates put all frozen food into sealable freezers. Finally, managers stored personnel records up high, out of danger, and brought home computer hard drives as well as contact information for all associates. Store managers were instructed to give local law enforcement a number where they could be reached, although managers admit this didn't always happen.

A Chilling Shift in Direction

On Thursday, August 25, the tropical storm, now dubbed Katrina, was upgraded to a Category 1 hurricane and crossed southern Florida, killing more than a dozen people. The storm's expected path was up the Florida Panhandle. But on Friday, August 26, Hurricane Katrina shifted unexpectedly to the west, toward the Mississippi and Louisiana coasts. Wal-Mart, Jackson says, immediately shifted its response toward New Orleans and Mississippi.

That afternoon, Jackson went to the usual Friday officers' meeting (a group that included all company officers down to the vice president level) and briefed them on the coming storm. "The CEO got up," Jackson recalls, "and he said, 'This company will respond to the level of this disaster. A lot of you are going to have to make decisions above your level. Make

---

[5]In 2005, the top fifteen food items, carefully identified through an ongoing evaluation of buying patterns, included peanut butter, Gatorade, SnackPak puddings, Vienna sausages, Spam, and strawberry Pop Tarts.

[6]Jackson notes that palletized water set on asphalt on a hot day quickly took on an unpleasant flavor, and even under proper storage conditions, water in plastic bottles eventually began tasting like plastic.

[7]Wal-Mart operated under a just-in-time system; except for its disaster merchandise, it kept inventory to a bare minimum by meticulously tracking products sold, sending that information instantly to suppliers, and shipping out replacement products almost as soon as they arrived at its highly automated distribution centers.

the best decision that you can with the information that's available to you at the time, and, above all, do the right thing.' That was it." Jackson says that the edict, which was passed down the line to store managers, was meant to set the tone for how the company should respond.

Concern over the approaching storm was deepening fast. Weather forecasters warned that a direct hit of New Orleans by a powerful hurricane could be catastrophic, given that the city lay below sea level. By Saturday morning, when Hurricane Katrina reached Category 3 intensity, Governor Kathleen Babineaux Blanco had declared a state of emergency and activated 4,000 National Guard troops, and several New Orleans–area parishes had ordered either voluntary or mandatory evacuations.[8]

It was the first hurricane for Ronny Hayes, the regional vice president responsible for all Wal-Mart stores in Louisiana. That Saturday he held his first of what would be daily conference calls with district managers, distribution center managers, and Home Office representatives. Hayes and his Sam's Club counterpart, Mike Turner, began staging teams in Baton Rouge, about 80 miles northwest of New Orleans, and other nearby locations to be ready to move in after the storm.[9] With the hurricane predicted to hit early Monday, August 29, all regional Wal-Mart stores closed at 4:00 p.m. on Saturday. That afternoon, New Orleans Mayor Ray Nagin announced a state of emergency and a voluntary evacuation. Nagin also designated the Louisiana Superdome as a shelter of last resort.[10]

The Wal-Mart EOC had not closed down after Katrina's pass through Florida. Now Jackson jacked up the response to Level Three, bringing in dozens of functional representatives. In addition, Jackson invited an official from the American Red Cross to join the EOC for the first time. For decades, Wal-Mart had had close ties to relief organizations; Wal-Mart gave in-kind and cash donations to the Red Cross to aid relief efforts, and the Red Cross bought supplies from the giant retailer during emergencies.[11] But during the hectic 2004 hurricane season, Jackson says, it had sometimes been hard to coordinate overlapping requests from local Red Cross chapters and the national office; Jackson hoped that having a single person serve as a conduit would reduce that confusion. Lee Siler, executive director of the relief organization's Northwest Arkansas Chapter, was given a seat next to Wal-Mart's corporate giving officer who, among other responsibilities, decided whether the retailer would donate or sell supplies requested by relief agencies and the public sector.

---

[8]The sixty-four parishes in the Louisiana area serve in a capacity similar to counties.

[9]Some teams drew personnel from other states on the assumption that locally based managers and associates would be personally affected by the hurricane and unable to respond.

[10]Although the Louisiana National Guard transported some food and water to the Superdome, Mayor Nagin advised residents going to the Superdome to bring enough water and food to last 3 or 4 days.

[11]As Armond Mascelli notes, "A lot of things that are needed by the Red Cross and other organizations following a disaster rest in the private sector, not necessarily government." Interview with Armond Mascelli, vice president of domestic response operations, American Red Cross, 2007. Unless noted, subsequent quotations from Mascelli are also from this interview.

By Sunday morning, August 28, Katrina was a Category 5 hurricane, with sustained winds of 175 miles per hour. At 10 a.m., Mayor Nagin ordered a mandatory evacuation of New Orleans; President George W. Bush already had declared states of emergency for Louisiana, Mississippi, and Alabama.[12] At the Wal-Mart EOC, Jackson and a few team members called the Louisiana and Mississippi state EOCs and the regional FEMA offices, leaving numbers and offers of help. "It was the most intense hurricane that had been out there in a long time," says Jackson. "Category 5, extremely powerful winds, extremely vast. That was the uh-oh moment for me."

Katrina Hits

On Monday, August 29, Hurricane Katrina, now a Category 3 storm, smashed into the coasts of Louisiana and Mississippi with a devastating storm surge and sustained winds of more than 115 miles per hour. As it moved northward, the massive storm blew roofs and walls off commercial buildings, crushed houses, damaged bridges, knocked over telephone poles and cell phone towers, and blocked roads with trees and debris. Along the Mississippi coast, entire communities largely disappeared.

As soon as the eye of the hurricane passed over New Orleans, Wal-Mart district loss-prevention teams picked their way into the disaster area. Local law enforcement had blocked off many entry points, and debris obstructed others, but the teams managed to reach a number of stores. With phone lines and cell phone towers down, however, they had to drive 1.5 hours back to Baton Rouge before they could report back to the EOC. What they described was alarming. Stores in New Orleans and neighboring parishes were badly battered. Looters already had begun breaking into a few facilities, and police were too busy responding to stranded and injured residents to take control. Worst of all, there was deep water blocking access to some stores, and it seemed to be rising fast.

In fact, a break in the Industrial Canal had been reported Monday morning, and within hours, the Lower Ninth Ward of New Orleans was flooded with 6–8 feet of water and St. Bernard Parish was under at least 10 feet of water. (See Exhibit 9A-2 for a map depicting the impact area of Hurricane Katrina in New Orleans.) At 11 a.m., a levee at the 17th Street Canal was reported breached, and by night, a total of three floodwalls had ruptured, allowing water from Lake Pontchartrain to pour into the city. By Tuesday morning, the extent of the devastation was clear to anyone on the ground; about 80 percent of New Orleans was under water. "We actually had to retreat out of New Orleans," Jackson says. "We never had to do anything like that before."

By Tuesday, the Wal-Mart EOC also had a clearer idea of Katrina's toll. A total of more than 170 Wal-Mart facilities in Louisiana, Mississippi, Florida, and Alabama had been

---

[12]An estimated 90 percent of residents in affected parishes evacuated before Katrina's arrival.

Exhibit 9A-2   Map of New Orleans Hurricane Katrina impact area

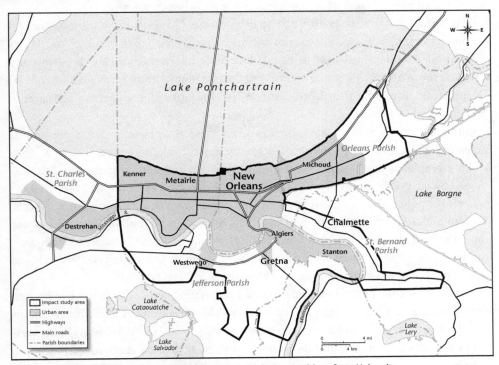

Source: Center for the Study of Public Health Impacts of Hurricanes, Louisiana State University

impacted in some way, and 126 were closed, many because of power outages. The EOC estimated that some 20,000 associates and their families had been displaced or otherwise affected, and thousands of employees were still unaccounted for.[13]

The Response Begins

Back in New Orleans, the loss-prevention teams pressed back into the city on Tuesday morning. At the same time, Regional Vice President Hayes and Deb Hoover, regional manager for Wal-Mart's One-Hour Photo group, flew into the region and then drove to the Boutte Wal-Mart Supercenter, about 28 miles west of New Orleans. Based on accounts of lawlessness in the city, Jackson and his team had designated a red zone of stepped-up security. Now Hayes helped set up a rudimentary command post at the store in Boutte. All Wal-Mart employees

---

[13]The number of impacted associates was later increased to 34,000.

were to register at the command post before entering the red zone and were strongly urged to travel with police escorts when possible, signing out when they emerged.

Hayes and Hoover next set off with sheriff's deputies to visit stores in the red zone and to conduct an initial damage assessment. Although in other parts of the country Wal-Mart's relationship with localities could be contentious, in southern states such as Louisiana and Arkansas the retailer was seen as a mainstay of the community and a generous backer of local initiatives. In part for that reason, Jackson says, law enforcement typically was eager to cooperate with Wal-Mart.

But nothing was normal that day, Hayes says.[14] Road signs were down, cell phones weren't working, and only Hoover's Blackberry got periodic reception. They saw lost-looking people wading through waist-high dirty water, and others, in the distance, marooned by the floods. Stores in Jefferson Parish were damaged or looted, and they couldn't get past the police blockades to reach the Lower Ninth Ward or Chalmette stores.[15] At the Tchoupitoulas Supercenter, people were milling around in the parking lot and pushing shopping carts filled with merchandise. Entering the store, Hayes and Hoover found it overrun with looters, with police simply looking on. The entire gun section had been cleared out.[16] "It became so uncomfortable, we had to just leave," Hayes says.[17]

Deputies took the two to meet Jefferson Parish Sheriff Harry Lee, who was talking with FEMA officials in a Sam's Club parking lot that FEMA was using as a helicopter landing zone.[18] Sheriff Lee had asked volunteers to bring fishing boats and speed boats to help rescue people stranded in trees and on houses. But items such as hatchets, ropes, boots, and sun block were scarce, and conditions were desperate. Hayes explains, "When I went in initially, I was thinking I need to determine the damage to our stores, and find out what's the situation with our associates. But after being there for a couple of hours, it totally shifted from that to, oh my God, what can we do to help these people?"

Hayes told Lee to come down the road to the Harahan Wal-Mart. If Lee's deputies could secure the building from further looting, he said, they could take whatever they needed from the store. That same afternoon, Hayes and Hoover met with Mayor Philip Capitano of Kenner, a community in Jefferson Parish, and struck a similar bargain, asking police to help secure the Kenner Wal-Mart and, in exchange, filling pickup trucks with merchandise for city

---

[14]Interview with Ronny Hayes, Wal-Mart regional vice president, 2007. Unless noted, subsequent information and quotations from Hayes are also from this interview.

[15]Hayes and Hoover later learned that those stores were completely submerged in flood waters.

[16]When Hayes later reported the theft of guns, the EOC directed managers to pull guns out of any store they could get into so that they wouldn't be stolen during future break-ins.

[17]Based on such reports, a security group back at the EOC decided to simply give up certain stores, says Wes Grube. "The store's not worth the safety of our associates." Interview with Wes Grube, regional loss-prevention director, 2007. Unless noted, subsequent quotations from Grube are also from this interview.

[18]That the deputies took the time to escort them in the middle of the chaos might have seemed surprising, Hayes says, but "they viewed us as their only support."

workers and police. "I don't think anybody was worried about being paid for anything," Hoover notes.[19]

But Hayes and Hoover didn't know what else to do, and, with the exception of Sheriff Lee and Mayor Capitano, the public sector wasn't giving them any direction. "At that point, [government officials] were trying to get organized, with Jefferson Parish doing one thing and the city of New Orleans doing another thing and FEMA doing their thing," Hayes recalls. "I was trying to figure out, how do we get these groups together so that they can tell me how we can help them?"

Away from the worst of the destruction, managers scrambled to re-open stores. District Manager Janie McNeil didn't make it to her five stores in the hard-hit area south of Lake Pontchartrain; she lived north of the lake and the bridge was out. But on Tuesday, McNeil, her husband, and a handful of associates began cleaning out the powerless Slidell store. As they worked, a steady stream of residents came to the door, anxiously asking when the store would open. McNeil and the others began handing out diapers, water, formula, and ice. Over the next couple of days, residents and dozens of police officers and firefighters came by for food, sleeping bags, toiletries, socks, and underwear. Some customers paid cash, but for most of the first responders, McNeil adopted a crude credit system—tallying purchases on slips of paper that the buyers then signed.[20]

Meanwhile, in Waveland, Mississippi, a Wal-Mart that was just a stone's throw from the coast had been engulfed by a storm-driven wave estimated at 30 feet. Assistant manager Jessica Lewis decided to salvage what she could. Although she couldn't reach the EOC or any of her superiors to get approval, she and her stepbrother ran a small bulldozer through the ruined store, loading it with items that hadn't been destroyed by the surge of water. These she piled in the parking lot to give away to anyone in need. When a police chief and a local hospital representative told Lewis they were running short of critical drugs, she broke into the store's locked pharmacy.[21] "What Jessica did," Jackson says, "is a good example of autonomy."

Gearing Up at the Emergency Operations Center

At the Home Office, the unexpected scope of the disaster called for a bigger, more expansive response. On Tuesday, August 30, the EOC established a 24-hour toll-free number that associates could call to reach a live operator and publicized the number on radio and television.

---

[19]Interview with Deb Hoover, Wal-Mart regional manager, One-Hour Photo Group, 2007. Unless noted, subsequent quotations from Hoover are also from this interview.

[20]A number of stores that opened without electricity adopted similar systems. McNeil later sent the law enforcement receipts to the Home Office for submittal to FEMA.

[21]Jackson recounts that when an assessment team arrived in Waveland late Tuesday with a satellite phone, Lewis called him. "I talked to her," he laughs, "and she said, 'I'm not going to get in trouble, am I?' And I said, 'Absolutely not.'" Lewis was later promoted to manager of another store.

The original crew of about eight call takers quickly grew to ten operators and then continued expanding to twenty-five, fifty, and finally eighty.[22] The center ultimately received more than 43,000 phone calls from associates. "The calls, especially in the beginning, were things like, 'Where am I going to eat tonight?' 'Where do I shelter?' 'I can't find my children,' " Jackson recalls.

The EOC also quickly grew. Representatives from all affected departments remained in the EOC in order to interact with their counterparts, but Jackson and his team broke off five separate annexes for operations deemed particularly critical to the response: security and safety, health and safety, strategy, information technology, and the associate call center.[23] In addition, Jackson brought in groups not normally represented at the EOC, such as financial services, which needed to address credit card, payroll, and check cashing issues. Instead of the fifty to sixty people who typically responded to a major emergency, the Katrina response expanded to include about two hundred.

To keep CEO H. Lee Scott Jr. and the rest of the company's officers informed and to regularly get their input, Jackson's boss, Ken Senser, vice president for global security, aviation, and travel, organized twice-daily conference calls. The 7:30 a.m. call focused on key developments and actions to be taken that day, while the 5 p.m. call recapped the day's accomplishments and summarized expectations ahead. The retailer's intense focus appeared to produce results. Jackson says that within 48 hours of Katrina's landfall, only fifty-six facilities were still closed and Wal-Mart had completed about 70 percent of its recovery effort.

The EOC also sent out daily situation reports, describing not only the status of store reopenings but police actions, curfew orders, and more. Soon Jackson was sending three updates a day and exchanging reports with the Department of Homeland Security (DHS) National Infrastructure Coordination Center, DHS Homeland Security Operations Center, and state EOCs. Jackson recalls that one DHS report looked eerily familiar. "I pulled up our previous situation report, and I'll be darned if they didn't cut and paste stuff out of our report and put it in theirs!" Jackson says.

Earlier in the week, Wal-Mart had donated $1 million each to the Red Cross and the Salvation Army to aid the response. On Thursday, September 1, the retailer gave $15 million to the newly established Bush-Clinton Katrina Fund.[24] "Wal-Mart has raised the ante for every company in the country," Adam Hanft, chief executive of Hanft Unlimited, Inc., a New York branding and marketing firm, told the *Washington Post*. "This is going to change the face of corporate giving." [25]

---

[22]Employees from across the company volunteered to work the phones and were granted time off from their regular jobs to do so.

[23]The five annexes took over training rooms in a nearby building and linked to the EOC through video teleconferencing.

[24]The Walton Family Foundation soon matched that with a $15 million gift to the relief effort.

[25]Quoted in Michael Barbaro and Justin Gillis, "Wal-Mart at Forefront of Hurricane Relief," *Washington Post*, September 6, 2005, D1.

The Chaos Continues

In New Orleans and the surrounding parishes, however, recovery was still far away. New Orleans police officers had taken over the badly looted Tchoupitoulas Wal-Mart and were using it as a station. The Kenner Wal-Mart continued to hand out merchandise, and the Kenner Sam's Club began supplying troops from the Missouri National Guard bunked down in a hotel across the street. After plugging in a generator at the Marrero Wal-Mart in Jefferson Parish, Hayes opened the store to law enforcement. "What I found was that these police officers had been on the job for three or four days running—no sleep, no food, no change of basic underclothes," Hayes says. "We were able to set up cots for them to sleep, all lined up around the front checkouts, brought in food to cook for them, and gave them basic necessities." Marrero became a command post for local law enforcement and the National Guard, and Hayes and several loss-protection associates also used it as a base.[26] Looting and fires were visible from the store at night, Hayes says, but the show of force kept looters at bay.

Generally, law enforcement asked permission before going into a Wal-Mart. But there were also times when police or the National Guard broke into stores out of desperation. Wal-Mart seemed to accept this as the price of providing community support, but there were some instances of abuse. "If people needed water and they needed food and they couldn't get it anywhere else, let them have it," says Deb Hoover. "When they took the big screen TVs, we had to roll our eyes at that one." Raymond Bracy, senior vice president of corporate affairs for corporate giving, also notes that police sometimes walked into Wal-Marts that weren't in the hardest hit area and asked for donated supplies, and that managers usually handed them over, no questions asked. "Who's to say that wasn't abused?" Bracy asks.[27]

There was a breakthrough of sorts on Wednesday, August 31. With an escort of Kenner police, Wal-Mart brought three truckloads of water in to a shopping center, where officers and city workers helped unload and distribute the merchandise—these were the first trucks Hayes had gotten into the red zone.[28] But Hayes was deeply frustrated by his inability to get food or water into New Orleans proper. One radio station was reporting desperate conditions at the Superdome, where some 23,000 evacuees were estimated to have taken shelter.[29] "We just could not get trucks to them," Hayes says. "It was all flooded around the Dome and

---

[26]By Tuesday, August 30, 1,800 Louisiana National Guard troops had been added to the 4,000 already activated.

[27]Interview with Raymond Bracy, Wal-Mart senior vice president, Corporate Affairs, 2007. Unless noted, subsequent quotations from Bracy are also from this interview.

[28]Wal-Mart already had stationed trucks outside the red zone so that customers could pull up and associates could load water and ice into their cars.

[29]The National Guard had expected to have enough food and water to supply 15,000 people for 3 days at the Superdome, but only 40,000 MREs (meals ready-to-eat) and five trucks of water arrived before Katrina struck. For a comprehensive look at the government's preparation for and response to Hurricane Katrina, see "Hurricane Katrina" (Case 1 in this book).

these people were stranded there." The situation reportedly was even worse at the Ernest N. Morial Convention Center, which became a second shelter on Tuesday and soon filled with more than 20,000 people, despite having no stockpiled food, water, or supplies.

Since Tuesday, Hayes had had thirteen trailers of water waiting at the Boutte command post. Hoover called the DHS outpost in Baton Rouge, but even though the person who took the call was excited and said they would call back with further instructions, no one called back.[30] Hoover also called New Orleans Mayor Ray Nagin's office, spending hours trying to get through.[31] She finally reached a staffer, who told Hoover to send the trucks to a closed-off bridge over the Mississippi River for escort into the city. But the trucks sat for hours Wednesday at the bridge, with Hoover making repeated attempts to call, and no one came or called to tell them where to go. Finally, not wanting to be stuck there after dark, the drivers turned the trucks around and left the city.[32] On Thursday, Hoover sent the trucks to Kenner instead.

By this point, Wal-Mart had even more trucks waiting to enter the city, but the disrupted communications and overall confusion continued to stymie action. Hayes says he met with FEMA representatives more than once to request assistance in making deliveries—since the trucks needed not only a safe place to unload but people and equipment to help with the unloading—but the agency was still trying to get organized and couldn't provide direction. "I had 20 to 25 trailers ready to go, staged outside the city, just trying to get from them [an answer to] 'Where do you want us to take them?' " Hayes recounts. Finally, in desperation, Hayes tried to set up an ad hoc distribution point without police security, parking trucks on a main road into New Orleans and starting to unload them. "It felt good for about 30 minutes," he says. But when the crowd quickly swelled to more than a thousand and people began fighting over food, the trucks pulled out.[33]

Jackson says he was making his own attempts to coordinate efforts through state emergency management officials, but the crisis had exposed serious gaps in those relationships. At the federal level, Jackson had conversations with both DHS's Private Sector Office and FEMA. But neither organization seemed to have thought through how to engage the private sector.[34] DHS had set up an online National Emergency Resource Registry; companies and

---

[30]When the message was finally returned 6 days later, Hoover says, the water had already been delivered.

[31]As it turned out, Mayor Nagin had moved with a number of officials to a Hyatt Regency, concluding it would serve as a better emergency center. But with communications knocked out, the mayor was largely unreachable.

[32]Hoover notes that a police officer on the bridge finally asked them to bring one truck down to a small command post set up in an old wharf. There she met a New Orleans police captain, whom Wal-Mart continued to support over the next few weeks, trucking in pallets of personal supplies, water, and even portable showers. "Everything we did we just tripped on," Hoover says. "It was so disorganized."

[33]The Red Cross, which had a policy of not putting volunteers at risk, had not opened shelters in the red zone because of the perceived danger of doing so.

[34]DHS tended to think of services such as utilities and transportation as critical, for example, Jackson says, without considering the importance of the retail sector.

individuals could list goods or services available and would be contacted if and when the donation was needed. But Jackson concluded it wouldn't work for Wal-Mart. "Wal-Mart's stock and product is in such a dynamic, fast-flowing system that there is no way I could say, 'Here's 5,000 gallons of water, take it whenever you want,' because 2 minutes later, that 5,000 gallons is gone."

Public-sector requests continued to pour in, but Jackson couldn't identify who was in charge. "There was a lot of adversarialism among the governments," Jackson says, "so Louisiana wasn't playing nice with New Orleans, who wasn't playing nice with the feds. FEMA was in there saying one thing and the state was saying another thing and the county parishes were saying something else." Increasingly, the delayed and often ineffective government response was generating widespread criticism from rescue workers, evacuees, the media, and the thousands of residents still stranded in New Orleans.

Hayes eventually was able to stage some trucks right near the Superdome, and by late Thursday, enough National Guard troops had arrived for some supplies to be carried over and for the evacuation of the Superdome to begin in earnest.[35] The floodwater was starting to recede, making access easier, but a large number of troops were needed to maintain order while food was distributed. It took until Saturday, September 3, to remove all the evacuees; the evacuation of the convention center was completed the same day. On the next morning's *Meet the Press* news show, Aaron F. Broussard, president of Jefferson Parish, declared that "if the American government would have responded like Wal-Mart has responded, we wouldn't be in this crisis."[36]

Hayes says a National Guard pilot finally gave him a helicopter ride over the region:

We were able to get a better feel of what was going on in the city, and, logistically, where we could maneuver and stage our trucks better. It also enabled us to visualize the scope of the damage for our other facilities, because at that point we couldn't even get into the Ninth Ward, we couldn't get into Chalmette. And that was the first time I was able to fly over and see that they were basically under water.

Managing the Larger Response

Back at the Home Office, efforts intensified to help displaced employees. Associates who worked at stores that had been closed received 3 days' pay, and many were granted $250 in additional cash assistance. If their houses had been flooded or destroyed, they were eligible for up to $1,000 from an Associate Disaster Relief Fund. Perhaps most significant, CEO Scott announced that displaced associates were guaranteed a job at any Wal-Mart in the country.[37]

---

[35]Within a week, there were 23,500 out-of-state National Guard troops in Louisiana and 11,500 in Mississippi.
[36]Quoted in Barbaro and Gillis, "Wal-Mart at Forefront of Hurricane Relief," D1.
[37]Some 2,400 displaced associates eventually relocated to new work sites.

To help locate employees still unaccounted for, Wal-Mart set up an online message board that allowed anyone at a Wal-Mart photo center to upload a photo of a missing friend or relative into the database with a request for information; the photo requests could be accessed from any Wal-Mart store or by going to the company's website.[38] Wal-Mart also donated 150 Internet-ready computers to Red Cross shelters so that evacuees could check the database and contact those who might be looking for them.

Having Red Cross representative Lee Siler and his staff at the EOC helped Wal-Mart tremendously. Siler took calls from homeless associates who phoned in on the toll-free number and directed them to the nearest Red Cross shelter. And he told Wal-Mart every time the Red Cross opened a new shelter, so that the retailer could ship additional products to the nearest store or club to handle the temporary population bulge. Meanwhile, with merchandising, logistics, and charitable giving representatives all near him, Siler was able to push through Red Cross requests for merchandise quickly and get fast answers as to whether a particular order would be a donation or a purchase.

Given how well the Red Cross collaboration was working, Raymond Bracy, senior vice president, offered to station a Wal-Mart representative at the DHS Homeland Security Operations Center and to have a DHS official based at the Wal-Mart EOC, but the offer wasn't accepted. Similarly, Jackson says, Wal-Mart and Home Depot offered, through the DHS Private Sector Office, to send logistics professionals to help run a FEMA distribution site in Louisiana, but they were told no.

On Friday, September 2, the Slidell store opened, albeit running off a generator and with a sharply reduced staff. In Kenner, the Sam's Club opened on Tuesday, September 6, the first club in the red zone to re-open; the Kenner Wal-Mart opened soon after. "We really became a critical infrastructure element," says Wes Grube, a regional loss-prevention director. "We're not the power company, we're not the water supplier, but we're considered part of the infrastructure in a lot of these places."

As more stores and clubs re-opened, Wal-Mart's distribution system went into high gear. The retailer's normal goal was to deliver goods within 24 hours of when a store placed an order. But that lengthened in some cases to 48 or even 72 hours as merchandising first depleted the disaster distribution centers, then began pulling from regular distribution centers across the country, and finally—for high-demand items such as water—began sending trucks directly to manufacturers for pickup. Orders also were slowed by trucks held up at roadblocks. Credentialing was ad hoc, Jackson says, and not very effective; the best passport seemed to be the big Wal-Mart logo on the side of a truck. Although Wal-Mart gave letters to its third-party carriers who were driving trucks not marked with a logo, police often

---

[38]Although initially meant to target associates, the database was open to the public.

didn't accept them. "They'd sit in this big long line of other trucks while the Wal-Mart trucks were blowing by them," Jackson recalls.

Large orders were also coming in from the public sector. Virginia Higginbotham, senior logistics merchandise manager, assigned two people at the EOC to deal just with those requests. Some sales were to FEMA; even though Wal-Mart was not a federal government supplier, FEMA often bought from Wal-Mart and other large retailers during emergencies.[39] However, FEMA rules governing the purchases often made the sales cumbersome. When Higginbotham got calls from FEMA warning her that certain people weren't authorized to make purchases, she began requiring that FEMA buyers go to a store, pay for the order, and fax the receipt to her before she'd ship it.[40] But probably the largest orders came from various units of the National Guard, which were outfitting large evacuation centers such as the one at Fort Chaffee, Arkansas.

Wal-Mart also continued to get requests for donations. In the first days of the crisis, Jackson says, Wal-Mart wasn't weighing whether it was appropriate to give things away, although from the start, the expectation was that state and federal agencies would purchase supplies rather than solicit donations. After several days, however, Wal-Mart's charitable giving manager began directing most calls asking for donations to FEMA, state emergency management departments, and other official agencies.

Sometimes, the line between donations and sales blurred. A few days after Katrina hit, Bracy received some disturbing reports that National Guard troops were stopping Wal-Mart trucks and driving off with the supply-laden vehicles. But when Bracy complained to Douglas Doan, a liaison in the DHS Private Sector Office, Doan, a former military man and political appointee, cast the events in a different light. In a September 4 e-mail to Bracy, Doan wrote: "Getting emergency supplies into the hands of people that need it most is exactly what we are all about. For us here in Washington, this is a small accounting challenge." Although normal FEMA procurement processes required that an order be placed by a purchasing agent, Doan felt it was possible to bypass the usual procedures, given the pressing need for action and the demonstrated ability of the private sector to help. As Doan says, "Hey, the president said that he wanted the government to cut through layers of bureaucracy to improve the government's response; snip, snip, this is what he meant."[41] Doan told

---

[39]FEMA had standing contracts with wholesalers with large warehousing operations and disaster supply companies that charged more for products but guaranteed they'd be available when needed.

[40]Higginbotham notes that they tracked purchases carefully; during the previous hurricane season, merchandising took a $2 million hit for goods it couldn't account for that had either been donated or not paid for. Interview with Virginia Higginbotham, Wal-Mart senior logistics merchandise manager, 2007. Unless noted, subsequent quotations from Higginbotham are also from this interview.

[41]Interview with Douglas Doan, U.S. Department of Homeland Security, 2007. Unless noted, subsequent quotations from Doan are also from this interview.

Bracy to keep track of any further informal "purchases" by the National Guard or other government agencies and promised that the retailer would eventually be reimbursed.

On Monday, September 5, U.S. Army and U.S. Marine Corps troops began arriving in New Orleans to take over the much criticized disaster response. Wal-Mart offered to help the Department of Defense (DOD) with logistics, Jackson says, but the offer was not accepted. Meanwhile, it was still hard to know who was in control; FEMA head Michael Brown still hadn't set up the Joint Field Office intended to coordinate the federal, state, and local response.[42] "We found ourselves trying to make inroads into a lot of different organizations," Jackson says.

The Ongoing Relief Effort

Over the next several weeks, Wal-Mart continued to provide a broad range of services to communities, government agencies, and associates. (See Exhibit 9A-3 for a list of further Wal-Mart contributions to the relief effort.) Jackson says it was hard to pinpoint when Wal-Mart's Katrina response wound down because the EOC was still active when Hurricane Rita made landfall on September 24 near the Texas-Louisiana border, necessitating another ramped-up response.

In any event, by September 26, 1 month after Katrina hit, a lot had happened. Wal-Mart had located 98.6 percent of its associates.[43] There had been more than 50,000 posts to Wal-Mart's online message board—41,000 of them initiated by associates—and more than 5 million people had accessed the website. Twelve facilities were still closed: two in Mississippi and ten in Jefferson Parish and New Orleans.[44] The Boutte command post was being relocated to Texas to help with the Hurricane Rita response.

According to Jackson, Wal-Mart shipped 2,498 trailers of emergency merchandise in all to aid the Katrina response, including 100 truckloads of donated merchandise. The company gave $3.5 million of merchandise to shelters and command centers in Mississippi, Louisiana, and Texas. In addition, customers and associates at Wal-Mart stores contributed $8.5 million to the relief effort.

But exactly how much the retailer had contributed in supplies handed out to needy residents and first responders may never be known. Even when Wal-Mart tried to get reimbursed for merchandise, it didn't always happen. Government lawyers and procurement officers rejected Doug Doan's arrangement with Bracy that would have allowed Wal-Mart to request payment for informal National Guard "purchases" after the fact. "Their minds

---

[42]The Joint Field Office was finally established 12 days after Katrina hit.

[43]Wal-Mart eventually confirmed the deaths of five associates due to Katrina. The official death toll from Katrina was more than 1,800.

[44]Fourteen stores had suffered losses of more than $1 million, and another sixty-two facilities reported losses ranging from $100,000 to $1 million.

Exhibit 9A-3   Additional Wal-Mart contributions to the Katrina relief effort

- The retailer sent four truckloads of food and water to a community of Native Americans isolated by the storm about 60 miles west of New Orleans and alerted the Red Cross, which set up shelter and kitchen operations for the village.
- About 126 Wal-Mart stores in the disaster area offered free check cashing for government, payroll, insurance, and computer-generated checks for a 2-week period.
- Wal-Mart set up three temporary mobile pharmacies, and its regular pharmacies filled prescriptions for free for evacuees with emergency needs, even when they didn't have copies of their prescriptions.
- To guard against flood-borne illnesses, Wal-Mart established nurse-staffed temporary clinics outside the red zone and provided about 4,000 inoculations to associates, law enforcement officers, and other emergency personnel.
- Wal-Mart opened up and paid the utilities at some twenty-five closed facilities—or "dark stores"—so that they could be used as temporary shelters, food pantries, and other relief facilities.
- The retailer sent a generator and team of electricians to activate a fuel depot in Mississippi that had lost power and couldn't pump fuel for tanker trucks queued up to supply gas stations.[1]
- Wal-Marts and Sam's Clubs across the country set up collection points so that customers and associates could donate to the Katrina relief effort.
- Wal-Mart worked with the Federal Emergency Management Agency (FEMA) to develop an evacuee debit card that hurricane victims could use for emergency purchases. FEMA had never done a debit card program before, and Wal-Mart and other private-sector advisors helped the agency design the card so that it could not be used for firearms, tobacco, or alcohol.
- The retailer converted two facilities to dormitories—one for men and one for women—to house associates who were anxious to return to work but couldn't find housing in the New Orleans area.
- On a site near the devastated store in isolated Waveland, Mississippi, Wal-Mart erected a 16,000-square-foot circus tent and converted it into a store, complete with eighteen pallet positions and generator-run refrigerators.

[1]Initially, a FEMA representative posted at the depot wouldn't let the Wal-Mart team through, claiming they needed special permission. "Sometimes there is a time to throw the protocol out the window," Jackson says, "because you have to save lives, and you have to make decisions right now that may have ripple effects on the area." Interview with Jason Jackson, Wal-Mart's director of business continuity, 2007.

Source: Wal-Mart Stores, Inc.

couldn't get around how to get results and solve the problem," Doan says. "They were still stuck with their bureaucratic processes."[45] Similarly, FEMA disallowed most receipts from store managers who had sold goods to local, state, and federal officials with the understanding that FEMA would pay for the goods. Bracy concedes that Wal-Mart sometimes had

[45]Doan resigned from DHS in September 2005 after procurement officers rejected his proposal to boost the local economy by relying on New Orleans–area chefs and food preparers to feed evacuees.

difficulty substantiating all the purchases, in part because store systems were down and orders were handled manually, but even well-documented orders were denied. "There were times when we gave it away and kept records, but were denied compensation because we did not work with an authorized purchasing agent." He adds, "We wouldn't have done anything different knowing what we know today."

In any event, Wal-Mart's response to Katrina generated remarkable goodwill for the company. For many Wal-Mart managers and associates, the intensity of the experience left them with deep pride at the retailer's ability to contribute during a time of great need. "One of the coolest things that happened was when we were driving down the highway in one of the convoys," recalls Deb Hoover, "and these people were driving by us honking and holding up signs saying, 'We Love Wal-Mart,' and 'Thanks for the Help.' " And regional manager Mike Turner describes a Louisiana state trooper who showed up at the Slidell Sam's Club a day or two after Katrina hit. The trooper, who had been working more than 3 days straight, loaded up with formula, diapers, and water, Turner says. "Then he told me, 'You are going to see a state trooper cry. You've made it so I can take some of this stuff home to my family and be sure they're okay before I go back out for four or five days.' And that makes you feel awesome inside." [46]

---

[46]Interview with Mike Turner, Wal-Mart regional manager, Sam's Club, 2007.

Wal-Mart's Response to Hurricane Katrina (B): Epilogue

Within weeks of Hurricane Katrina's devastating pass through Louisiana and Mississippi, the executive and legislative branches of the U.S. government began examining how the public-sector response had unfurled and what exactly had gone wrong. Wal-Mart Stores, Inc., conducted its own postmortem, but unlike the government, the giant retailer began improving its practices even before the response had ended. By the time Hurricane Rita made landfall near the Texas-Louisiana border on September 24, 2005, Wal-Mart already had instituted a new firearms policy, requiring managers as part of their hurricane preparation to remove guns and gun records from stores, so that they could not be stolen. Gun sales also were restricted in areas neighboring hurricane zones, to discourage criminal behavior in the wake of storms.

In a development that Jason Jackson, the retailer's director of business continuity, saw as particularly significant, Wal-Mart, at the invitation of Texas, stationed two representatives at the Texas state emergency operations center (EOC) in time to help the state respond to Rita.[1] Among other advantages, the collaboration helped Wal-Mart make more informed decisions about where its resources were most needed. In the wake of the successful Texas experiment, Wal-Mart launched discussions with other states, such as Virginia and Missouri, about similar collaborations. Meanwhile, for the 2006 hurricane season, Jackson extended the company's collaboration with the nonprofit sector by inviting a Salvation Army representative to join the American Red Cross in the retailer's EOC.

Perhaps the key weakness that Katrina exposed, Jackson says, was that Wal-Mart's relationships with all levels of government weren't as strong as they needed to be. The company began to insist that store managers and loss-prevention associates meet regularly with local law enforcement and fire chiefs, and Jackson and his team began a purposeful outreach to state and federal contacts. Given the visibility of Wal-Mart's efforts during Katrina, particularly contrasted with what most observers deemed to be a highly flawed government response, reaching out was easy. In fact, Jackson and his team found themselves in high demand.

Although the Department of Defense (DOD) hadn't accepted offers of help during Katrina, Wal-Mart's EOC afterward hosted generals and admirals interested in learning more about Wal-Mart's logistics system, and Jackson and other Wal-Mart officials met with top Department of Homeland Security (DHS) representatives. A flood of other post-Katrina engagements included presentations to the annual National Hurricane Conference, the Red

---

[1]Interview with Jason Jackson, Wal-Mart director of business continuity, 2007. Unless noted, subsequent information and quotations from Jackson are also from this interview.

Cross, the U.S. Coast Guard, the New York City Office of Emergency Services, and several Federal Emergency Management Agency (FEMA) state-sponsored emergency exercises. "Katrina opened the doors for us," reflects Bryan Koon, who joined Wal-Mart's emergency management department in 2006 as senior manager of operations. "People wouldn't have even thought about it before; involving the private sector wasn't a really big thing." [2]

These meetings, combined with Wal-Mart's experiences during Katrina, convinced Jackson that the EOC should concentrate initially on building relationships at the state level. Local jurisdictions, such as cities and parishes, he says, tended to be too narrowly focused on their own residents' needs. For example, Jackson recalls, after Katrina hit, one sheriff seized a convoy of three Wal-Mart trucks passing through to another parish because he wanted the supplies for his own parish. The federal government, meanwhile, experienced huge turnover at both DHS and FEMA after Katrina, Jackson says, and both organizations were "still in a period of trying to figure themselves out." States, by contrast, had a clearly defined constituency, yet could trump some of the more parochial interests in favor of a larger good.

After the productive experience of stationing Wal-Mart representatives at the Texas EOC, Jackson vowed to meet with the emergency management staff of every hurricane-prone state. By early 2007, he and his staff had visited and begun developing relationships with twenty states, including some outside the hurricane zone. Among the concepts that Jackson was pushing for was that states become the main conduit for local emergency requests, so that Wal-Mart and other companies would not be barraged with multiple and sometimes conflicting appeals. Jackson was also offering logistics advice. For example, Louisiana's Emergency Management Office was for the first time implementing a bar code system that would allow it to track supplies rather than physically counting sand bags, pallets of water, and other goods. "We have some of the best people in the world in logistics," Jackson says, "as compared to a state emergency manager who only puts in practice their logistics system when the bell rings. And it may not ring for two years."

Several states initiated meetings, hoping that Wal-Mart would contract with them as an emergency merchandise supplier. But Koon says such a move remains outside Wal-Mart's interest and expertise. "That's not what we do best," he explains. "Our business is taking stuff and moving it somewhere else quickly, instead of letting it sit somewhere for long periods." Moreover, when Texas asked Wal-Mart and Home Depot to be the primary supply anchors for the state, Jackson says, he insisted that the state reach out more broadly. "We said, 'Whoa, wait, you can't just look at us,'" Jackson recounts. "'You need to bring in H-E-B and Brookshire Brothers, our competitors, because they need to help augment the system.'" [3] In part as a result of the broader collaboration that resulted, Jackson says, he was on a first-name

---

[2] Interview with Bryan Koon, Wal-Mart senior manager of operations, 2007. Unless noted, subsequent quotations from Koon are also from this interview.

[3] H-E-B and Brookshire Brothers are Texas-based supermarket chains.

basis with his emergency operations counterparts at several other retailers, and he even gave tours of the EOC to other companies. "Having them be better helps us, because we're all part of the same effort," says Koon.

Although the state collaborations showed real promise, Jackson says, a number of problems remained. The effort to establish a credentialing system that would allow essential private-sector workers into disaster areas had so far not been fruitful. Jackson says Wal-Mart had worked on such a system with federal officials and industry organizations, but many issues remained unresolved, such as which level of government should maintain it, how the system should accommodate employee turnover, and what the credential should look like. "The DOD wants to establish a credentialing system," Jackson says, "the states want to establish a credentialing system, the parishes want to establish a credentialing system, and none of the two shall meet."

Jackson also had discussions with officials at DHS and FEMA about how to design a more effective emergency response registry. Jackson envisioned a kind of "reverse eBay system"—the government could request specific items it needed, and companies could respond with amounts, prices, or donation options, allowing government to pick the best among the offers and move forward quickly. But so far, Jackson says, the idea hadn't generated any excitement.

Perhaps most frustrating, says Jackson, was the fact that the federal government still seemed to feel that the public sector should shoulder the responsibility of preparing for disasters, even when the solutions lay outside its area of expertise. For example, having vowed not to be caught unprepared again, FEMA stockpiled large quantities of food and ice in the Gulf Coast region after the horrors of the 2005 hurricane season. When the predicted 2006 storms failed to materialize, FEMA had to throw out some 279 truckloads of food worth about $43 million. Doug Doan (who formerly worked in the DHS Private Sector Office) laments a chronic "lack of imagination" in government and says, "We can do some great things in government, but it doesn't have to be a complete end-to-end government solution. And, in fact, it probably shouldn't be." [4]

According to Jackson, the biggest shift he was still waiting to see at the federal level was the recognition that the private sector had an important role to play in national emergency responses. "We are not so arrogant as to think that we know it all and can do it all," Jackson says. But, he insists, "The private sector has a lot to offer, and that it needs to offer, and it needs to be an equal partner in emergency and crisis response for communities and the nation." He adds, "Talk to us like we're an adult, and work with us like we're an adult. We can bring a lot of power to bear to help you respond and recover."

---

[4]Interview with Douglas Doan, formerly of U.S. Department of Homeland Security, 2007.

Key Actors in Wal-Mart's Response to Hurricane Katrina

Wal-Mart Personnel

Jason Jackson, director of business
  continuity

Ronny Hayes, regional vice president
  (responsible for Louisiana stores)

Deb Hoover, regional manager, One-Hour
  Photo Group

Raymond Bracy, senior vice president,
  Corporate Affairs

Virginia Higginbotham, senior logistics
  merchandise manager

Mike Turner, regional manager, Sam's
  Club (responsible for Louisiana stores)

Janie McNeil, district manager

Jessica Lewis, assistant manager, Waveland,
  Mississippi

H. Lee Scott Jr., CEO

Louisiana State and Local Government Officials

Kathleen Babineaux Blanco, governor

Aaron F. Broussard, president, Jefferson
  Parish

Philip Capitano, mayor, city of Kenner

Harry Lee, sheriff, Jefferson Parish

Ray Nagin, mayor, New Orleans

Federal Government Officials

Douglas Doan, Private Sector Office, U.S.
  Department of Homeland Security

Michael Brown, director, Federal
  Emergency Management Agency

George W. Bush, president of the United
  States

Other

Lee Siler, executive director, Northwest
  Arkansas Chapter, American Red Cross
  (delegated to the Wal-Mart Emergency
  Operations Center)

Wal-Mart's Response to Hurricane Katrina, 2005

Chronology of Events

Tuesday, August 23, to Wednesday, August 24

With a tropical depression threatening to disrupt store operations in Florida, Jason Jackson, Wal-Mart's director of business continuity, activates the company's emergency operations center (EOC).

Jackson's team briefs senior corporate officers about the storm and hold conference calls with district managers to discuss preparedness activities.

Florida stores begin shut-down procedures. Loss-prevention teams deploy around the state.

Thursday, August 25

Upgraded to a Category 1 hurricane, Katrina crosses southern Florida, killing more than a dozen people.

Friday, August 26

Katrina turns westward, moving toward the Mississippi and Louisiana coasts.

Jackson briefs senior executives on the storm's new course and the anticipated consequences. During the briefing, CEO H. Lee Scott Jr. notes that personnel will have to make decisions beyond their official authority levels.

Saturday, August 27

Katrina reaches Category 3 intensity and is on a path to hit New Orleans directly.

Ronny Hayes, regional vice president for Wal-Mart's Louisiana stores, holds the first of what become daily conference calls with district managers, distribution center managers, and Home Office representatives.

Hayes begins pre-staging teams in Baton Rouge, Louisiana, for poststorm response and recovery efforts.

Afternoon: New Orleans Mayor Ray Nagin announces a state of emergency and a voluntary evacuation. Governor Kathleen Babineaux Blanco has already declared a state of emergency for Louisiana and has begun activating National Guard troops.

4:00 p.m.: All Wal-Mart stores in the Louisiana region close.

Jackson upgrades Wal-Mart's EOC to a Level Three response status. A host of Wal-Mart representatives join the EOC, as does Lee Siler of the Red Cross, who is brought in to serve as a liaison and to help coordinate aid solicitations.

Sunday, August 28

Katrina becomes a Category 5 hurricane.

10:00 a.m.: Mayor Nagin orders a mandatory evacuation of New Orleans.

Jackson's team contacts authorities at the regional Federal Emergency Management Agency (FEMA) office and at the Louisiana and Mississippi state EOCs, offering them assistance on behalf of Wal-Mart.

Monday, August 29

Katrina hits the Mississippi and Louisiana coasts as a Category 3 storm, wreaking havoc on coastal communities.

Wal-Mart's district loss-prevention teams set out from Baton Rouge to assess the damage. They observe extensive property destruction, the looting of stores, and an overwhelmed response effort.

By midday, reports are received of breaches in the Industrial Canal and 17th Street Canal levees. By nightfall, another floodwall has ruptured. The Lower Ninth Ward and St. Bernard Parish are soon inundated as water pours into the area.

Tuesday, August 30

Approximately 80 percent of New Orleans is under water.

Wal-Mart's EOC learns that more than 170 Wal-Mart facilities along the Gulf Coast have been impacted, and 126 have closed, while 20,000 associates and their families have been displaced.

Regional Vice President Hayes, along with Deb Hoover, regional manager for the One-Hour Photo Group, sets up a command post at the Boutte Wal-Mart Supercenter, about 28 miles west of New Orleans.

Hayes and Hoover conduct damage assessments of stores in the red zone surrounding New Orleans, observing stranded residents, damaged stores, and looting as police look on.

Hayes and Hoover meet with the Jefferson Parish sheriff and Kenner's mayor to give access to supplies in return for security assistance.

Wal-Mart managers take the initiative in providing relief supplies in a number of areas.

Wal-Mart establishes a 24-hour hotline for associates. More than 43,000 calls are ultimately received by the call-in center.

The EOC quickly expands to about two hundred people. Separate annexes are established for the most critical response activities.

Wednesday, August 31

Wal-Mart delivers three truckloads of water to a shopping center in Kenner—its first successful foray into the red zone. Access to New Orleans remains blocked, however, even though conditions there remain dire.

After struggling to find someone in New Orleans who will accept thirteen trailers of water, Hoover is told to send the trucks to a bridge over the Mississippi, where an escort will meet them. The escort never arrives, however, and the trucks turn back at nightfall.

Frustrated by the disorganized response, Hayes attempts to create an ad hoc distribution point outside New Orleans. Crowds mob the trucks, forcing Wal-Mart's trucks to pull out.

Thursday, September 1

Late in the day, National Guard troops help deliver Wal-Mart supplies to the Superdome, which they also begin evacuating. It takes a large National Guard presence to maintain order while supplies are distributed.

Friday, September 2

The Slidell, Louisiana, store reopens.

Saturday, September 3

The final groups of Superdome and Convention Center evacuees leave New Orleans.

Monday, September 5

U.S. Army and U.S. Marine Corps troops begin arriving in New Orleans to take over the disaster response. Wal-Mart offers to help the Department of Defense with logistics, but the offer is not accepted.

Tuesday, September 6

The Kenner Sam's Club reopens, becoming the first club in the red zone to do so. As more stores resume operations, the distribution system goes into high gear to meet demand. In all, Wal-Mart ships 2,498 trailers of emergency merchandise as part of its response to Katrina.

Saturday, September 24

Hurricane Rita makes landfall near the Texas-Louisiana border, necessitating another response effort there.

Monday, September 26

In the aftermath of Rita, Wal-Mart's Boutte command post is relocated to Texas.

By now, Wal-Mart has located 98.6% of associates affected by Katrina; twelve facilities remain closed in the Louisiana-Mississippi area.

Part IV   Improving Performance: Dealing with Novelty and Cognitive Bias

In Part III, we examined the distinctive challenges created when rapidly evolving, high-stakes emergency situations produce novel circumstances to which responders must quickly adapt.

The essence of novelty is that it is unfamiliar and, as a consequence, frequently difficult to spot. The eye-brain system tends to be drawn to what it has experienced before. Medical students are taught that "the eye cannot see what the mind does not understand." No doubt this is a useful spur to further study to expand the domain of what the mind understands. But it also implies that when we confront significantly novel events we are not likely to see (or, at least, not likely to see immediately) the important features that are different. In the context of high-stress emergency situations, moreover, familiar elements offer a degree of comfort—a sense of knowing what to do. By contrast, recognizing *unfamiliar* elements confronts us with the discomfort of knowing that we don't know what to do.

Seeing and Recognizing Novelty

If we are to see and appreciate novel elements of crisis situations, given the barriers to recognizing them, we need to recognize this human tendency and develop compensatory mechanisms, both individually and organizationally. There are many methods useful for searching systematically for novelty and taking it into account, including:

- *Focusing attention on the novelties.* Because we are drawn to the familiar, we need to give extra attention to recognizing novelty. Generally, human beings categorize and react to new events on the basis of past personal experience or historical memory. Typically, we mentally apply historical models or analogies, identifying one or two prior events that are like the one being experienced in the moment. These serve as reference points for the current situation. The danger is that the model or analogy may be carelessly applied, thereby masking departures from the norm—that is, the novelty.[1] Deliberately and repeatedly asking the questions, "What is the same? What is different?" is a simple

---

[1] See, for example, Richard Neustadt and Ernest May, *Thinking in Time: The Uses of History for Decision Makers* (New York: Simon and Schuster, 1986).

but powerful form of mental discipline that can help identify the ways in which the current situation departs from experiential models or analogies. These questions can be asked by either an individual or a team examining a new situation.

- *Ensuring that diverse viewpoints are applied.* If a team has people with a variety of backgrounds and experiences, they are less likely to miss elements of a situation that depart from past experience. Collectively, they are more likely to see and appreciate the significance of unfamiliar or unprecedented elements.

- *Systematically requiring additional thought.* Many organizations that have failed to handle crisis situations well have made a similar mistake—they did not consider a large enough set of possibilities early in the event. Often they developed a single dominant (but erroneous) interpretation of the situation and persisted far too long in being guided by it. One mechanism for avoiding this is to force the identification and assessment of one or more *best alternative explanations.* In addition to a primary diagnosis or interpretation of the event, the team (or a subgroup) is forced to postulate that the primary diagnosis is wrong and propose one or more truly plausible alternative possibilities. Two benefits can flow from this practice. First, the team can explicitly ask which information might be secured that would let it decide which explanation is correct; premature closure is less likely if more than one hypothesis is kept alive. Second and highly important, the team can consider whether the alternative explanations imply different courses of action. If the required actions are quite different—or, even worse, in conflict—then caution should be exercised to make sure that confidence in the primary diagnosis is justified. If uncertainty persists, leaders need to seek actions that are robust against both the alternative explanations and the primary diagnosis.

- *Setting operational expectations and tracking actual results against these expectations.* One way to recognize the unexpected is to notice whether the results generated by our actions are tracking with what we expected. Significantly, this requires establishing expectations about how the situation will evolve. We won't notice that we aren't on track if we haven't specified what we think the track will look like.

Perceptual Blinders

Failure or slowness to recognize novelty is not the only perceptual problem that can interfere with effective crisis response. Common modes of thinking, which are usually highly functional in routine emergencies, may not be well-suited to crisis situations.

Many organizations know that there are persistent biases, operating parallel to the problem of recognizing and coping with novelty, built into their cultures, systems, people, and organizational structures. These tend to hold them in a *routine response* frame, preventing them from operating as they need to in the face of *true crises*. These biases are exhibited by some individuals in the organization and often by the organization itself. Some are very general, applying to most individuals and organizations most of the time, while others are particular to specific circumstances. Researchers in psychology, organizational behavior, and economics have studied these patterns of thought, seeking to understand what causes them and how they might be attenuated or eliminated.[2]

One way to think of the persistent forces that shape people's thinking and organizational awareness is to consider them *cognitive biases*. They are cognitive in the sense that they involve the processes of thinking. They are biases *not* in the sense that they are necessarily wrong but in the sense that they persistently operate in one direction, like a wind that blows a ship steadily from one compass point. Cognitive biases are not rare and unusual. To the contrary, they tend to be patterns of thinking or mental habits developed over a long period and frequently applied. Indeed, most of the time, cognitive biases push thinking in the right direction. That is how they came to be patterned habits of thought. When they do not point in the right direction, however, they can be very dangerous. They are powerful, and we are not generally consciously unaware that they exist (because they are mental habits to which we are accustomed). It is thus particularly difficult to spot cognitive biases as they lead us into trouble because it feels perfectly normal to be following our established patterns of thought and behavior.

There are many different characterizations of cognitive biases, and they can be labeled in many different ways. Some of the cognitive biases that appear and are particularly problematic in crisis situations are:

- *Overweighing one's experience.* There is a tendency for individuals to weight their or their organization's own experience more heavily (compared to the data and experiences of other people and organizations) than is appropriate.
- *Illusion of experience.* There is a tendency for individuals to think that they have more experience than they actually do, that their experiential "sample size" is large, and that therefore they can confidently base predictions on that (actually, limited) background rather than seeking a broader range of experience from others that might include outcomes that the individuals have not yet seen.
- *Overconfidence.* There is a tendency for individuals to be overconfident of (1) their powers, capabilities, and influence; (2) their ability to predict the future; and (as a result of these two) (3) their ability to control the future.

---

[2]See, for example, Daniel Kahneman, Paul Slovic, and Amos Tversky, eds., *Judgment under Uncertainty: Heuristics and Biases* (Cambridge, UK: Cambridge University Press, 1982); Max Bazerman and Don Moore, *Judgment in Managerial Decision Making,* 7th ed. (Hoboken, N.J.: John Wiley and Sons, 2008).

- *Failure to observe or believe disconfirming evidence.* There is a tendency for individuals to be unable to observe or unwilling to believe *disconfirming evidence,* data that cast doubt on the prevailing understanding of the situation.
- *Escalation of commitment.* There is a tendency, once individuals do notice that the strategy is not working well, to escalate commitment to the existing strategy rather than to reevaluate and consider alternatives.
- *Migration of objectives.* There is a tendency for objectives to shift—and often to become deeply personal—in the face of strategies that are failing.

These cognitive biases are general. They appear in many individuals, in many organizations, and under many circumstances. Other biases are specific to individuals, organizations, or occupational cultures. For example, law enforcement officials are trained to be skeptical of what they are told by bystanders and witnesses (because these people may have an individual interest or agenda they are trying to advance, or may be co-conspirators with a perpetrator). Firefighters, by contrast, more often receive honest guidance from (and hence believe) citizens gathered at a fire scene. Each of these attitudes constitutes a bias. In most situations, each is professionally functional; these patterns of thinking generally produce useful results. In some cases, however, these cognitive biases may prove harmful—blinding a police officer to a productive tip from a helpful neighborhood resident or misleading a trusting firefighter who has encountered an arsonist. For these reasons, therefore, it is useful to examine the organizational culture, training, socialization, and operating norms of an organization to develop a sense of what its specific cognitive biases are likely to be, in addition to being aware of the general biases common across individuals, organizations, time, and circumstances.

In a crisis, these general cognitive patterns and others, separately or in combination, can have a significant impact on which options seem appropriate and on decisions about priorities, strategy, and tactics. When these biases reinforce positive adaptations to a given situation, they support effective work. *But,* because these biases are largely developed and practiced in routine situations, they often lead in the wrong direction during crisis situations. For example, if a chosen tactic or strategy is not working well in a routine situation, it is quite possible that it is the right approach but just has not been executed sufficiently (because in routine situations a well-practiced organization is likely to make reliable diagnoses). By contrast, if an approach is not working in a highly uncertain and poorly understood crisis situation, it may well be because the approach doesn't fit the situation well. Confidence in a diagnosis should be lower in a situation involving significant novelty. However, the cognitive bias toward escalation of commitment is likely to be equally strong in both cases. In routine situations, it may often be reinforcing a positive action—sticking with it and making it work may well be the right approach. In a crisis situation, however, the bias may prevent an appropriate reexamination of our data, analysis, and solution design.

Counterprogramming

Because these biases are known to be both common and strong—and their essence is that they always push in the same direction, whether or not it is the right direction in particular circumstances—wise leaders and organizations are alert for situations in which these biases might be leading them astray. Because that is most likely in true crisis situations, it is important to be especially vigilant in crisis circumstances about the quality of analysis and decision making. The kind of expertise-enabled, automated, instinctive decision making that can successfully drive action in routine emergencies is likely to be carried along by cognitive biases in crisis situations unless care is taken to examine decisions and reasoning carefully.

We can think of this as *counterprogramming* against the action of cognitive biases. Counterprogramming may be especially important in crises, although it may also sometimes improve decision making in routine circumstances as well. Cognitive biases are viewed as a consistent influence, and the purpose of the counterprogram is to identify the moments when the biases are more likely to be pushing in the wrong direction, and interrupt, attenuate, or counterbalance their action.

There are many approaches that might be used to counter specific cognitive biases, including (1) choosing different leaders or team members from groups less likely to be subject to the same biases, (2) providing training and guidance about cognitive biases and how to avoid them, or (3) developing rules, procedures, and norms that counteract or interrupt cognitive biases. For example, a tendency toward overconfidence might be tempered by having more seasoned people, each with a wide range of experience, involved in consultation with a team leader. Physicians who might mistake an emergent infectious disease for a more common infection can receive special training to alert them to the distinguishing characteristics of the new virus. A bias toward escalation of commitment might be interrupted by a procedure that calls for a complete review every 12 hours.

Two very different kinds of emergency are described in the cases in Part IV. The first case focuses on *transitional fires,* a special category of wildland fires that creates unusually severe danger for firefighting teams. Too often, physically fatigued teams follow cognitive influences that lead them to make choices that seriously endanger them. The case asks how the U.S. Forest Service can create conditions under which improved decision making will occur—and thereby help keep wildland firefighters safer. The second case concerns the U.S. Centers for Disease Control and Prevention (CDC), which must regularly make important decisions about public health threats under conditions of incomplete information, evolving scientific understanding, and severe time pressure. CDC has strong organizational and cultural patterns of thought, which, although often serving it well, could mislead it in dealing with significant public health novelties. In recognition of this possibility, CDC has sought ways of avoiding or minimizing the chance of errors in judgment.

When examining each case, think about the sources of novelty involved in the situation described. What enabled (or blocked) the recognition of this novelty by people in the organizations confronting these situations? What devices or mechanisms can you design that might help them see the important elements of novelty in time to respond in an effective way? Which cognitive biases do you see operating or are you concerned might operate, and what mechanisms can you propose for helping the organization avoid these influences when they are pushing in unproductive directions?

10 The Forest Service and Transitional Fires

Herman B. "Dutch" Leonard and Jerry T. Williams

Wildland or forest fires begin as small events, generally with a single ignition of flammable materials. Many self-extinguish after burning a small area. Every large wildland fire, however, must have started out as a small fire and somehow grew. Most commonly, it will have burned fairly steadily, perhaps with occasional "runs" when fanned by winds or when the fire reached particularly flammable materials. On rare occasions, however, relatively small fires will suddenly "blow up"—that is, rapidly move from being relatively small to being significantly larger and more intense. These are transitional fires.

From long years of experience, U.S. wildland firefighting agencies—prominent among them the U.S. Forest Service—have learned a great deal about how to fight fires and how to protect firefighters under a wide range of conditions. In general, firefighting is relatively safe; occupational injury and fatality rates for all fires taken together (and for small fires or large fires considered separately) indicate that firefighting agencies train their employees to operate reasonably safely in what are obviously dangerous conditions.

General statistics alone, however, mask an important fact—transitional fires are extremely dangerous because of the rate at which their conditions change. This is difficult to discover from looking at the data in broader categories, but excellent analysis of fire injury and fatality data led to the determination that transitional fires are a special category that needs to be thought of and approached differently—and carefully.

In reading this case, think about what makes transitional fires so dangerous. Generally, transitional fires are confronted by teams organized and designed to fight small fires successfully and safely. What are the strengths and weaknesses of these teams when they are facing a small fire on the verge of or in the process of transition? What makes them vulnerable when they encounter transitional fires? Are there organizational means to change the team; its members; their capabilities and inclinations; or their structures, systems, and processes so that they will recognize and successfully respond when the fire they are confronting becomes a transitional fire?

Transitional fires are a real phenomenon, but they can also be a metaphor for analogous circumstances—relatively common, simple, small situations suddenly mushrooming into significant, dangerous events. Often the team or people who are working on the small event suddenly find themselves confronting a situation that is materially transformed. They may not immediately recognize this, and they may not have the resources, skills, and organizational structure to manage the new situation effectively. Will they recognize that and seek

This case was written by Professor Herman B. "Dutch" Leonard at the John F. Kennedy School of Government, Harvard University, and Jerry T. Williams, director of Fire and Aviation Management for the U.S. Forest Service, in consultation with a number of experts in firefighting from the U.S. Forest Service and from other U.S. federal firefighting services. Kennedy School of Government Case Program, CR16-04-1770.0. Copyright © 2004, 2008 by the President and Fellows of Harvard College.

help? Or will they be concerned that they will be seen as having failed and continue to try to get on top of the situation by themselves? What can we learn from firefighting about how to manage such events more successfully in other domains?

Discussion Questions

- What are the key problems that the firefighting agencies need to address in reducing the hazards of fighting transitional fires?
- What would you imagine the state of mind of a firefighter to be as he or she sets out to deal with the typical wildland fire described in this case study?
- What changes would you expect to find in the individual members and in the firefighting team by the time they have been fighting a fire for 24 hours?
- What kinds of changes, if any, in structures, procedures, training, or other aspects of how these fires are addressed might be made to help firefighting agencies address such fires more safely and successfully?

The U.S. Forest Service has a long and proud tradition of fighting wildland fires efficiently, effectively, and safely. During the summer fire season, it fields, together with its sister federal landowning agencies, the largest and best-funded firefighting unit in the world, often simultaneously fighting several large and many small fires scattered widely across the western United States. The Forest Service employs about 7,000 wildland firefighters, and it annually deals with about 10,000 wildfires that in an average year might burn 0.5 million acres and in a bad year might burn 2 million acres. The Forest Service is responsible for protecting 191 million acres of forestland throughout the United States and is engaged in firefighting almost continuously throughout the year.

During the early part of the twentieth century, under a political and social mandate to reduce damage to property from wildland fires, the Forest Service developed an expanding and effective fire-suppression capability, developing and deploying new technologies (including, for example, methods of rapid parachute and helicopter attacks on fires in remote locations) that significantly reduced the prevalence of fire.

Like many well-intentioned interventions to "improve" natural systems—in this case, by protecting the forests—the attempt to suppress wildland fires had major unforeseen consequences, especially in the West's interior long-needle pine forests. These areas are now recognized as *fire-dependent ecosystems*; left in their natural state, they experience relatively frequent low-intensity fires that burn through debris on the forest floor, underbrush, and small trees, leaving the larger trees and the roots of fire-adapted species alive, with large trees spaced far enough apart to reduce the likelihood of major *crown fires* (high-intensity fires that burn entire trees and stands of trees, leaving a path of complete destruction). A principal effect of fire suppression in such ecosystems was that brush and small trees were no longer periodically removed by low-intensity fires that were survivable for the mature trees, so brush and debris and small trees accumulated rapidly. This had a number of increasingly profound effects over time. Forest areas that had historically had 50–100 trees per acre developed hundreds of additional small trees per acre, increasing the amount of burnable fuels on these sites literally by hundreds of tons per acre. The increase in living vegetation on these sites drew up more of the available water from the soil and transpired greater amounts of water into the air; thus, for any given level of rainfall, the fuel in these forests was drier and more burnable than it would have been in its undisturbed state. And, perhaps most damaging, the smaller trees had lower branches that reached almost to the ground, so low-intensity fires burning along the ground could ignite them, carrying fire into the crowns of mature trees and generating stand-destroying high-intensity fires that devastated whole forests. During periodic drought cycles, dense forests become especially predisposed to severe, high-intensity burning.[1]

The changes brought by fire suppression—more and drier fuels, more densely distributed, and ready access for fires to the upper branches of even the largest and most mature trees—fundamentally altered the character of fire on these sites. Fire suppression became increasingly necessary, on the one hand, and increasingly difficult and dangerous, on the other. Today, the most dangerous, most costly, and most damaging wildfires are in these overcrowded forests where before the advent of fire suppression, fires were generally of low intensity. Because the most severely affected forests in the West are on the drier valley bottoms, this problem affects areas that are in close proximity to where people have expanded their homes and vacation retreats into the wildlands. Here, the stakes are high, and there is a high social expectation for protection and a low political tolerance for failure. Although efforts are being directed to reducing fuels in these areas, an important need to control wildfires that threaten lives and property remains. The Forest Service now carries out fuel-reduction treatments on nearly two million acres a year, focusing (under congressional direction) about half of these efforts in the *wildland urban interface* areas, the edge zones between wildland and human habitation that are now increasingly laced with recreational and residential structures.

As a consequence of its facing an increasing number and range of intensities of fires, the Forest Service has developed a systematic approach to fighting a broad spectrum of wildland fires. Its history of fire-suppression efforts provided it with extensive experience in confronting and combating small fires, and it developed well-defined procedures and methods for organizing, rapidly deploying, and managing the small teams sent to attack fires before

---

[1]This is a problem particularly in western states (due to the greater fuel buildup in many western forests) but not only there. Destructive high-intensity fires have taken place in every region of the country.

the fires had a chance to become large. This process came to be known as *initial attack,* and it became a well-defined organizational routine. Teams were organized and trained; team leaders were developed and schooled; procedures were developed and people were trained about their roles within them; equipment was designed, procured, and warehoused; communications, logistics, and financial systems were developed to support them; and rapid deployment systems for both personnel and materiel were designed, built, and kept ready. Various specialized units, often associated with the method by which they were delivered to a fire (by parachute, by helicopter, by foot, by fire engine, and so on), were developed for deployment in different operational situations. An ethos developed within these teams—that they were so effective that, given the appropriate size team for a given fire and access to the fire in the afternoon, they could have a fire line around the fire and have it under control by 10:00 a.m. the next morning. Of the approximately 10,000 fires that the Forest Service deals with in a typical year, over 95 percent are controlled at the initial attack level.

Some fires, of course, become larger. Bad conditions—hot, dry, windy conditions combined with an excess burden of low-humidity fuels in steep terrain—can lead fires to blow up, and when a high-intensity fire is being swept rapidly across a dry, fuel-laden landscape by high winds, there are few useful things that can be done to contain it. Given the buildup of fuels in western forests, this was an increasingly common phenomenon. Only about 1 or 2 percent of wildfires become large "headline" fires, but these few fires account for over 95 percent of the total acres burned and consume 85 percent of the resources expended for fire suppression. Its experience with large fires led the Forest Service to develop routines for deploying and managing much larger teams—on very large fires, numbering in the thousands of line, support, and managerial personnel—and supporting them in the field with food, shelter, equipment, communications, and information, often over the span of weeks or even months.

With long experience to guide it, the Forest Service developed highly effective methods and routines both for the initial attack phase, the deployment of small teams on small fires with the goal of containing them as small fires, and for fighting large fires using large teams (and, on very large fires, deploying multiple large teams and a managerial structure to oversee and coordinate their activities, allocate resources among them, and manage the flow of people and equipment to their operational areas). Given the intrinsic risks of fighting a natural force as powerful as fire in remote locations, the Forest Service's safety record both for small fires and for large fires is very good. Increasing attention to the safety of firefighters, including the development of standard orders that emphasize that the safety of the firefighters themselves is the highest priority, has led to continuing improvement in the safety record over time.

Unfortunately, the same cannot be said of the fires that are passing from being a small-scale fire to becoming a large fire. Because of the massive destruction that can be caused by large fires, extraordinary efforts are expended on fires where initial attack has failed, in order to prevent them from becoming significantly larger. All large fires have passed through this transitional phase; that is, these are fires for which at some point the expectation that they would be controlled in the initial attack phase has been violated. Fires on this scale—between the initial-attack size and a large fire—are called *transitional fires*. Although there is no definition of a transitional fire given in Forest Service policy, one veteran firefighter engaged in revising Forest Service policies and procedures observed:

> Most of us, though, characterize them as fires that are moving from something we thought we controlled and understood to something that is controlling us. . . . In other words, they are fires that are beginning to dominate and define our decision space. Attack is now on the fire's terms, not ours. In time and place, a crew's position on a fire moves from relatively safe to extremely dangerous.[2]

Transitional fires are, indeed, empirically significantly more dangerous (for example, per firefighter-hour of exposure) than either fires in the initial-attack category or large fires. This form of engagement—called *extended attack*—is particularly risky for firefighters. The injury and fatality rate per firefighter-hour during an extended attack may be as much as 10–100 times higher than on either an initial attack or on a large fire. Transitional fires not only produce high risks of injury or fatality—they also create elevated risks of multiple injuries or fatalities, threatening whole teams of firefighters. For example, the Hauser Fire killed eleven Forest Service firefighters in the Cleveland National Forest outside San Diego in 1943. The 1949 Mann Gulch Fire in Montana claimed thirteen lives from a team of sixteen firefighters. At Rattlesnake Creek, California, fifteen lives were lost in 1953. Eleven prison inmates were killed while serving voluntarily as firefighters on the Inaya Fire in 1956. In 1968, twelve died in the Loop Fire, again in the Cleveland National Forest. Four firefighters were overtaken and three were killed on Battlement Mesa, Colorado, in 1976. The 1990 Dude Fire, outside Payson, Arizona, killed six during an intense blowup in which at least two other twenty-person "hotshot" teams were able to get to a safety zone as the fire burned over the area. The fire on Storm King Mountain, again in Colorado, took fourteen lives in 1994. In 1999, two volunteer firefighters lost their lives in the Island Fork Fire near Cranston, Kentucky. And in 2001, the Thirtymile Fire in Washington killed four. In each case, a rapidly moving fire in transition overtook a whole team or one or more portions of a team in close proximity to one another.[3] In transitional fires, not just individual firefighters but whole crews are exposed to heightened danger.

The discovery of this pattern was a product of good data analysis born of an intense interest in figuring out how to produce further improvements in firefighter safety, which led

---

[2]Interview with senior firefighting agency official, 2004.

[3]Many of these fires, together with the safety-guideline changes that have emerged from them, are listed in the National Interagency Fire Center's *The Numbers Tell a Story: 2004 Fireline Safety Refresher Training Student Workbook*, 4, available at www.blm.gov/pgdata/etc/medialib/blm/nifc/training/pdfs/refresher.Par.99870.File.dat/SWB04_cmprsd.pdf [accessed on October 28, 2008].

to a concentration on situations where firefighters were injured and an investigation of what differentiated these situations from those in which people were able to fight fires with fewer injuries. When looked at this way, the data revealed a notable pattern—a surprising number of injuries took place in a relatively small number of fires, a substantial portion of which were in the transitional phase when the injuries occurred.[4]

This discovery immediately raised a series of additional questions. Why were transitional fires so dangerous? What unique elements of these fires—or unique combinations of elements—made them so hazardous?

As senior Forest Service firefighters and researchers reflected on what they knew about transitional fires that might help explain why they presented particularly high risks, they noticed some common features that seemed potentially relevant:

- The firefighting teams deployed on initial attack were generally well trained in the fundamentals, but most members of these teams had not had a chance to accumulate the years and years of experience on the fireline that provided exposure to a wide range of fire situations. Often, the most experienced firefighters had moved on to supervisory jobs, management positions, or the larger management teams deployed on large fires. To the extent that initial attack teams had significant amounts of experience, this was often from their having experienced similar (small fire) situations many times, not from their having experienced a broad range of fire types.

- Initial attack teams largely consisted of relatively young people (college age or a little older), with a team leader (foreman) who was generally a bit older and who had a good bit more experience. As Norman Maclean observed in his brilliant *Young Men and Fire,* about the firefighters who came to grief in Mann Gulch, Montana, in 1949, "They were still so young they hadn't learned to count the odds and to sense that they might owe the universe a tragedy."[5]

- Teams generally consisted mostly of men; women were an increasing and significant presence but still not a majority on most teams.

- If initial attack did not succeed in containing a fire within the first operational cycle, the team generally had already been engaged for many hours. Fatigue had set in.

- Firefighting was grueling work, often involving heavy work with heavy and dangerous implements (chainsaws, fireaxes, and so on) in heavy protective clothing in hot weather near a hot fire, with infrequent rest, inadequate water, and uncertain food.

---

[4]The discovery of this elevated hazard rate by the Forest Service is a good example of the value of careful data analysis. Examining only two categories of fires—initial-attack and large fires—would mask this higher-hazard environment in the border area between them. But a careful focus on the relevant differences between the different fire situations revealed this third, importantly different category.

[5]Norman Maclean, *Young Men and Fire* (Chicago: University of Chicago Press, 1992), 19.

- More than 95 percent of initial attacks succeeded; only a small fraction of fires became transitional fires requiring extended attack, and most of these were successfully contained short of becoming big fires that required massive mobilization.
- Even though most transitional fires did not produce many moderate injuries, severe injuries, or deaths, a high percentage of moderate and severe injuries and a high percentage of firefighter deaths occurred on transitional fires.
- Most initial attack teams had substantial experience on small fires and limited experience on transitional fires. As Norman Maclean observed about the team deployed to fight the 1949 Mann Gulch Fire, "One danger of making almost a sole specialty of dropping on fires as soon as possible is that nearly all such fires will be small fires, and a tragic corollary is that not much about fighting big fires can be learned by fighting small ones." [6]
- Once deployed, initial attack teams (including their foreman, the incident commander) were self-directed in the field; they might request equipment or other resources but rarely sought higher-level (remote) guidance about how to proceed. They had been taught to be self-reliant, and they practiced self-reliance both in training and on real fires.
- From the 1930s until the early 1970s, the Forest Service had a policy that fires engaged through initial attack should be contained by 10:00 in the morning on the day following deployment (hence, the reference to the "10:00 a.m. policy"). Even though this policy had been abolished, it affected the attitudes and behaviors of Fire Service personnel and their firefighting partners into the late 1970s or early 1980s.
- The 10:00 a.m. policy was abolished because the costs of suppression became too great, particularly on backcountry or late-season wildfires where expected damages were minimal and expected losses were insignificant. In the absence of the 10:00 a.m. policy, wildfire control objectives were less clear, opening the door for more subjective assessments that, often, were not clearly articulated nor commonly understood.
- Although the 10:00 a.m. policy emphasis had disappeared, initial attack teams still felt great pressure to "knock down" fires quickly because of the acute awareness that large fires consume extraordinary amounts of resources and create vast damage. All shared the deep-seated aversion to dealing with large fires, and the initial attack team bore the burden of having the last clear chance to contain its assigned fire short of its becoming a large fire and consuming enormous amounts of organizational time, energy, and resources.
- The pressure to contain fires on initial attack was especially acute at the height of the fire season when the Forest Service might already be dealing with several large fires (and, hence, felt even more strongly that it needed to avoid the development of any additional large fires); at the peak of a fire season, a single major lightning storm over

---

[6]Ibid., 31.

Exhibit 10-1   Standard firefighting orders

1. Keep informed on fire weather conditions and forecasts.
2. Know what your fire is doing at all times.
3. Base all actions on current and expected behavior of the fire.
4. Identify escape routes and make them known.
5. Post lookouts when there is possible danger.
6. Be alert. Keep calm. Think clearly. Act decisively.
7. Maintain prompt communications with your forces, your supervisor, and adjoining forces.
8. Give clear instructions and insure they are understood.
9. Maintain control of your forces at all times.
10. Fight fire aggressively, having provided for safety first.

Source: U.S. Forest Service, *Standard Firefighting Orders and 18 Watchout Situations,* available at www.fs.fed.us/fire/safety/10_18/10_18.html [accessed November 6, 2008].

Note: These orders were originally promulgated on June 28, 1957, by Forest Service Chief R. E. McArdle. Subsequently revised to a form that was thought to be easier to remember, the original orders were eventually re-instated and were the orders in force in 2004.

a dry area the size of a large state might produce hundreds of new small fires requiring initial attack.

- Transitional fires did not tend to move linearly and slowly from being potentially controllable to being uncontrollable; instead, they could move from being relatively safe to extremely dangerous when critical but complex (and incompletely understood) thresholds were crossed. Seemingly small changes in fuel type, humidity, temperature, and wind speed, especially in steep terrain, could lead—sometimes in a matter of only a few minutes—to radical transformations in the character and speed of advance of a fire.

- There were many rules to guide firefighters in the field, including the ten *Standard Firefighting Orders,* the most encompassing of which is to "Fight fire aggressively, having provided for safety first." (See Exhibit 10-1 for the Standard Firefighting Orders used in 2004.) Sometimes, due to complacency, inattention, or overconfidence, firefighters overlooked established safe practices. Often, minor violations occurred without major consequences. And some firefighters said that if they followed all the rules all the time they would never be able to put out most fires.

As they developed and analyzed this list, the senior Forest Service team in charge of firefighting and firefighter safety continued to wonder whether these were the most relevant features of transitional fires, what aspects or combinations of these elements created such apparently dangerous situations, and what they could do that would more reliably protect the safety of the firefighters who willingly took up this intrinsically dangerous work.

11 CDC Develops Its "Team B": Keeping an Open Mind in an Emergency

Pamela Varley

The U.S. Centers for Disease Control and Prevention (CDC) is the nation's premiere public health agency and typically the key actor in public health emergencies such as emergent infectious disease. Every such event—the possibility of a swine flu epidemic in the 1970s, outbreaks of West Nile virus starting in 1999, and the appearance of severe acute respiratory syndrome (SARS) in 2003—presents unique conditions and challenges.

Few agencies have thought systematically about how to identify novel elements in emerging crisis situations and about how to process and respond to them effectively. In the face of a series of events with novel challenges, the CDC very deliberately devised and experimented with such methods. "Team B"—named "B" originally for "brainstorming"—was designed to allow the agency to assemble a diverse set of experts who were not caught up in managing or responding to the event but were instead able to take a fresh view. Since its initial deployment, various forms of Team B have been used for different events. Sometimes, new approaches were taken because the events seemed different and required adaptive responses. In other cases, different approaches arose as a way of experimenting to see which methods functioned more effectively.

Discussion Questions

- CDC employed a variety of approaches to Team B at different times and under different circumstances. Which of these seemed most successful and helpful? Why?
- Would it make sense to have different versions of Team B ready for use in different types of situations?
- What do you see as the key success factors (for example, design of the mechanism, who it reports to, nature of its relationship to other parts of the organization, and nature of the circumstances in which it is being employed) that determine whether a Team B approach can make a significant contribution to managing a crisis?
- Consider a different kind of organization with which you are familiar. If you were designing a Team B mechanism for it, what would its characteristics be?

This case was written by Pamela Varley for Herman B. "Dutch" Leonard, George F. Baker Jr. Professor of Public Management, and Arnold M. Howitt, executive director, Taubman Center for State and Local Government. Funding was provided by Harvard's National Preparedness Leadership Initiative, a project sponsored in part by the U.S. Centers for Disease Control and Prevention. The Kennedy School is responsible for the content of this case. Kennedy School of Government Case Program, C16-05-1895.0. Copyright © 2007 by the President and Fellows of Harvard College.

By the early 2000s, the U.S. Centers for Disease Control and Prevention (CDC) had to face a disturbing new reality. One of the agency's most important public protection roles, to investigate and contain disease outbreaks, was becoming progressively more difficult—and, almost certainly, the worst was yet to come.

As recently as the 1970s, public health experts had believed that deadly infectious diseases were very nearly a thing of the past, successfully vanquished by a combination of vaccines, antibiotics, and modern sanitation techniques. But new, resurgent, and drug-resistant pathogens emerged as a serious health threat in the 1980s and 1990s.[1] Global trade and travel allowed for their rapid spread. The September 11, 2001, terror attacks revealed the determination of terrorist enemies of the United States, and the subsequent anthrax attacks demonstrated that, if they chose to do so, terrorists could wreak havoc with the deliberate release of deadly or weaponized pathogens.

In the midst of the CDC's anthrax investigation, and in its immediate aftermath, it became painfully apparent to the CDC leadership that the agency's traditional approach to managing an emergency response, which had served the CDC well for years, was not always well-suited for the new class of public health emergencies—those that involved novel pathogens, that were instigated by terrorists, or that were large and protracted. But CDC leaders were divided about how radical a change was needed and about how to design a new model that preserved the CDC's strengths while increasing its capacity and flexibility.

The CDC's chief response in a public health emergency was to undertake a high-speed scientific investigation—combining epidemiological, clinical, and laboratory data—in order to come up with strategies to prevent, contain, and cure the ailment in question. In the perilous new landscape, the CDC was faced with intense pressure to reach conclusions quickly, without succumbing to the kind of tunnel vision that could lead investigators to miss something unfamiliar in an outbreak—a deliberately altered pathogen, for instance; a simultaneous disease outbreak in animals; or a pathogen that was geographically out-of-place. Traditionally, "we would look at the event and say, 'okay, how does this fit into *what we know?*'" explains one CDC official.[2] But how to make room for the possibility of something new or unforeseen?

Some CDC strategists began to discuss adding a new feature, called "Team B," to emergency investigations, at least in the case of large or unusual incidents. Team B would be made up of people inside the CDC and outside the agency, with expertise in the topic at

---

[1] Disease outbreaks in this period included acquired immunodeficiency disease (AIDS), Lyme disease, legionnaire's disease, ebola, hantavirus, West Nile virus, tuberculosis, and bovine spongiform encephalopathy (BSE) or "mad cow" disease.

[2] All individuals quoted without specific attribution in this case were, at the time of publication, either past or present senior administrators at the CDC.

hand but without significant responsibilities in the investigation itself. This group would convene regularly over the course of the emergency investigation to review the latest developments in the outbreak and, essentially, to brainstorm about them. In particular, the members of Team B would ask themselves whether there were alternative interpretations of the data or concurrent developments that the principal investigating team had missed.

The first Team B was one created midway through the 2002 West Nile outbreak. It was followed, a few months later, by a more elaborate Team B created at the start of the 2003 severe acute respiratory syndrome (SARS) investigation. In the succeeding 18 months, the CDC would convene a Team B in each of two smaller-scale emergencies, as well. But its role and its reception within the agency would vary considerably from one incident to the next. The CDC executive team would ultimately have to decide whether Team B was an idea worth refining or whether another approach would serve the agency better.[3]

No New Thing under the Sun?

The idea of calling in outside experts during a public health emergency was not, per se, new at the CDC; lead scientists had often done so. For example, Jim Hughes, director of the CDC's National Center for Infectious Diseases (NCID) from 1992 to 2005, had led the CDC's 1993 investigation into a mysterious respiratory disease first spotted on a Navajo reservation in New Mexico. In that case, CDC laboratory scientists made a surprising finding: the disease appeared to be a previously unrecognized hantavirus. This was unsettling, as there was no evidence that a hantavirus had ever before caused acute disease anywhere in the Western Hemisphere. Hughes therefore arranged for a 90-minute teleconference with "five or six" internationally recognized hantavirus experts and virologists and presented them with the CDC's data. They listened and agreed with the CDC's conclusions; however unlikely on its face, the cause of this new outbreak did, in fact, show all signs of being a new hantavirus. "It was extremely useful in raising our level of confidence," Hughes recalls.[4]

---

[3]One source of confusion within the CDC was the fact that the term *Team B* was, at different times, used by various agency leaders to refer to different things. "Team B in the CDC is a shape-shifting creature," says Joe Henderson, director of the CDC's Office of Terrorism Preparedness and Response from August 2002 to August 2004. Interview with Joe Henderson, CDC, 2007. Unless noted, subsequent quotations from Henderson are also from this interview. In 2002, for example, Henderson himself used the term *Team B* to refer to the creation, at the start of an emergency response, of a special, short-term group to help the agency make the shift from business-as-usual operations to its emergency management model. This case confines itself to describing the CDC's experiences with Team B when the term referred to a group tasked with maintaining a big-picture view of an emergency while others in the agency were absorbed with the demands of running the emergency investigation.

[4]Interview with Jim Hughes, director, CDC National Center for Infectious Diseases (1992–2005), 2007. Unless noted, subsequent quotations from Hughes are also from this interview.

Deciding when, how, and on what scale to call in outside experts, however, had traditionally been left to the discretion of individual research scientists and response leaders. In retrospect, CDC insiders questioned whether disinterested outside input might have saved responders from making mistakes in certain investigations. West Nile, for example. Or anthrax.

Before its appearance in New York in 1999, the West Nile virus had never been reported in the Western Hemisphere. Based on certain lab findings, CDC scientists initially believed the New York outbreak to be St. Louis encephalitis (SLE). Although SLE had never before appeared in the Northeast, it had appeared in other parts of the country. As the investigators set to work to verify this hypothesis, however, they skated past reasons, apparent in retrospect, to doubt the SLE theory. In addition, the CDC investigators initially paid little attention to a concurrent veterinary investigation into an avian disease outbreak in the same geographical area. Had they been persuaded to pay more attention, some observers believe they would have discovered the true, albeit surprising, virus behind both human and avian outbreaks more quickly.[5]

The CDC made a different kind of misjudgment during the 2001 anthrax attacks[6]—this one more consequential and politically costly for the agency. On October 15, when an anthrax-laced letter arrived in the office of Senate Majority Leader Tom Daschle (D-S.D.), there were immediate concerns about the safety of Senate staff, followed closely by concerns about whether postal workers along the letter's route from Trenton, New Jersey, to Washington, D.C., might have been exposed. The CDC quickly issued an assurance that postal workers were in no danger. Within a few days, however, four postal workers had been diagnosed with inhalation anthrax linked to the letter, and two had died. Another two postal workers were diagnosed with the less serious cutaneous (skin) anthrax.[7]

The CDC's initial judgment had been made without an opportunity to analyze the anthrax sample in the Daschle letter (which was in military custody) and had been based on the prevailing wisdom about anthrax: (1) traces of anthrax were not thought to be a health risk; (2) anthrax spores were thought to be too heavy and sticky to penetrate the pores of an envelope; and (3) heavy taping on the envelope's seams was thought to have kept any of the spores from leaking out around the edges. "There was a lot of dogma about anthrax—what it was, what its characteristics were, and what they weren't—some of which proved to be wrong," says one CDC veteran, in retrospect. Jurisdictional issues certainly complicated the

---

[5]See Esther Scott, *The West Nile Virus Outbreak in New York City (A): On the Trail of a Killer Virus,* KSG Case 16-02-1645.0, 2002.

[6]See Kirsten Lundberg, *Charting a Course in a Storm: US Postal Service and the Anthrax Crisis,* KSG Case C15-03-1692.0, 2003, which appears in this book as Case 8, "The Anthrax Crisis and the U.S. Postal Service."

[7]The other two inhalation anthrax victims in this event, and the two skin anthrax victims, recovered.

case, but could a group of outside experts, sifting through the data, have spared the CDC this mistake? A thoughtful group might have urged caution, he suggests, might have said, "Wait a minute. How do you know? Here's what we think we know—are we sure?"

The CDC created its first Team B during the 2002 West Nile outbreak, but two precursors in the anthrax investigation helped to set the stage.

Precursors to Team B in the 2001 Anthrax Investigation: The Meta-Epi Group and the Critical Training Group

One evening, several weeks into the anthrax emergency, after a long day in the trenches, about a half dozen team leaders in the CDC's investigation gathered together to review what they each had learned over the preceding day or two. Julie Gerberding, then acting deputy director of the CDC's National Center for Infectious Diseases, led the discussion. "As I recall, Dr. Gerberding even went to a board, or a flip chart, and got some things down on paper," says Jay Butler, co-leader of the State Team in the anthrax response.[8] "We all came away saying, 'That was helpful,' because each of us knew something that the others didn't know, and it gave us a bigger understanding of the situation." All agreed to meet periodically for this purpose throughout the remainder of the investigation.

The "Meta-Epi Group," as some called it, did meet several more times, Butler adds, but the meetings were "frequently disrupted because everybody was doing other things. Cell phones were always going off. Julie Gerberding led the meetings, but frequently had to come late and then got called out." In the end, the general consensus of the group was that the exercise was useful, but that, realistically, the leadership team for the investigation was unable to sustain the function. In Butler's words, "You can't be on the ground and up on the observation deck at the same time."

One of the problems that arose during the anthrax attacks was the fact that most practicing physicians did not know how to test patients for anthrax exposure and the associated illnesses. The CDC therefore decided to create a special task group of CDC staff, academics, and physicians to focus on the creation of Web-based instruction to clinicians—the Critical Training Group. In a deliberate move to shelter the task group from the pressures of the larger investigation, the members held their meetings not on the CDC campus but at nearby Emory University.

After the anthrax emergency was over, when the CDC reviewed what had gone well and badly in the anthrax response, this task group stood out as a particular success, according to

---

[8]Interview with Jay Butler, director, CDC Arctic Investigations Program, 2006. Unless noted, subsequent quotations from Butler are also from this interview. The job of the State Team was to field inquiries from state and local health authorities and dispatch research teams to investigate reports of suspected anthrax samples.

Joe Henderson, then assistant director of the Division of Bioterrorism Preparedness and Response in the CDC's National Center for Infectious Diseases.

Team B in West Nile, Summer 2002

A few months later, in spring 2002, the West Nile virus began an ominous spread. Between 1999 and 2001, there had been 149 reported cases of West Nile in the United States altogether, resulting in eighteen deaths. In 2002, there were 4,155 cases, resulting in 284 deaths. The upsurge was apparent in the spring, with cases reported in new locations—Louisiana and Georgia—as well as in the Northeast. The CDC set up an emergency response.

By this point, the CDC was already in the midst of an uncertain transition in the way it organized itself during an emergency. In the past, the CDC's emergency investigations had been managed by whichever center held the appropriate scientific expertise. For disease outbreaks, that usually meant the NCID or one of its divisions. The CDC director was always free to weigh in. Other personnel in other parts of the agency might be recruited to the effort. But as a practical matter, the NCID was in charge. This system had the advantage of allowing personnel who knew each other well and were expert in a particular field to work together, efficiently and with common assumptions, in familiar environs with familiar equipment. But for large, protracted, or complex emergencies, the resources of a single center were insufficient, critics argued; day-to-day work in the center invariably ground to a halt; the system depended too heavily on particular individuals; and it failed to take advantage of significant resources and complementary kinds of expertise elsewhere in the agency. Thus, there was a move afoot to move the CDC toward an agency-wide Incident Management model,[9] in hopes that this approach would do better at tapping the resources of the whole agency.

In the 2002 West Nile outbreak—and for many years afterward—the CDC's emergency response was an amalgam of the old system and the new. In the case of West Nile, that meant that, in the main, the investigation was managed the "old" way, by the NCID's Division of Vector-Borne Infectious Diseases.[10] But a wider cast of characters did participate in the daily emergency operations briefings, including the CDC director and representatives of other complementary research areas within the CDC. New participants, with their different

---

[9]The Incident Management System (IMS) featured a preestablished organizational template that had the advantage of being simple, consistent, and flexible. A basic structure was prescribed, but the pieces of the structure could be expanded, contracted, or eliminated to adapt to emergencies of varying sizes and types. IMS was originally created to eliminate chaotic management of large fires that crossed jurisdictional lines. Whether the template was appropriate for public health emergencies had been a long-standing topic of debate.

[10]A *vector-borne disease* is a disease transmitted by blood-feeding arthropods, such as mosquitoes, ticks, and fleas. West Nile was spread by mosquitoes.

backgrounds and perspectives, had new suggestions. The investigating teams took these "under consideration," but, for the most part, lacked the time, resources, and/or inclination actually to pursue them.

In summer 2002, newly appointed CDC Director Julie Gerberding asked Rima Khabbaz, NCID's associate director of epidemiological science, to play a bigger role in the West Nile investigation. Until this point, Khabbaz had played a peripheral supporting role in the response, but she had attended enough of the emergency response meetings to be well informed about the issues in the investigation. Gerberding asked her to create something she called a "Team B." [11] "I said, 'Wonderful,'" Khabbaz recalls. "'What is a Team B?'" [12]

Gerberding's idea—building on the experiences of the anthrax response—was to pull together a group of people, inside the CDC and outside the agency, with expertise relevant to the West Nile outbreak, to get their thoughts about the outbreak, the investigation, and the new ideas that had come up in the CDC's emergency briefings. It was quite open-ended, Khabbaz recalls, and the director of the 2002 West Nile investigation was initially skeptical, asking, "'Is this group going to second-guess us? Who are you going to bring into it?'" Khabbaz understood the concern and tried to reassure him: "I said, 'Look, my understanding is the idea is to try to help you.'" It might be a way to get a quick outside reading on questions that the investigators had run across but did not have time to explore, she suggested. She also asked his advice about whom to include in the group.

Khabbaz assembled a group of four to five people with expertise in vector-borne illness, virology, and entomology and held weekly teleconferences. At these, she updated the group on the investigation and posed questions raised either in the investigating teams or the emergency operations briefings. "We'd just have a very fluid discussion, and people would give opinions."

It was relatively easy to assemble the group, Khabbaz says, and she believes the team enjoyed the discussions. "I don't think there's any problem getting people to be on Team B." She continues, "They're interested. They're not out there having to [manage the investigation] and put in the long hours, and yet they're kept involved. I sent them little summaries of what was happening week to week—the numbers, the questions, the issues. And they had some good discussions. It was fun."

---

[11] The origins of the name are a little uncertain. According to one report, a former high-level CDC administrator had advocated that the CDC follow the example of the Central Intelligence Agency's Team B, employed selectively to provide agency executives with a second opinion of staff assessments. Most people who worked on the CDC's Team B, however, were reportedly unaware of the CIA's Team B. Some believed the "B" stood for "brainstorming." Others assumed the "B" was meant simply to distinguish the team from the "A" teams that were actually running the response.

[12] Interview with Rima Khabbaz, associate director of epidemiological science, CDC National Center for Infectious Diseases, 2007. Unless noted, subsequent quotations from Khabbaz are also from this interview.

Khabbaz was less sanguine about Team B's impact, however. "It left me thinking [that] it was an interesting exercise, [but] in terms of making a difference in the response—I'm not sure it made a huge difference," she says. After each Team B discussion, Khabbaz wrote up a brief summary, which she gave to the leadership team for the investigation; to Hughes, as infectious disease director; and to Gerberding. "There were a few nice ideas here and there, but I don't think there were any earth-shattering things that people [running the investigation] had overlooked," Khabbaz adds.

A few months later, Team B would get its first full-scale outing.

Team B in Severe Acute Respiratory Syndrome, March 2003 to May 2003

The severe and often deadly respiratory disease that would soon be named SARS appeared in China's Guangdong Province, Hong Kong, and Hanoi in late February and early March 2003. On March 12, the World Health Organization issued a global alert about the new disease, and 2 days later, Canadian authorities announced an apparent SARS cluster in Toronto.[13] The disease was suddenly close to home, and the CDC jumped into the investigation at full-throttle. NCID Director Hughes led the investigation himself. As he assembled his investigative teams, he also called upon two of his nine division directors—Butler, director of the Arctic Investigations Program, and Jon Kaplan, director of the Division of STD, HIV and TB[14] Laboratory Research—to create and manage a Team B for the SARS investigation.

What, exactly, was Hughes looking for? He remembers it this way:

The way I think of Team B is—people with expertise relevant to a particular problem, who are not actively involved in the investigation, so they have the ability to reflect upon the evolving investigation and think about the evidence that's accumulating. And equally important—think about what other things might be going on here that aren't appreciated by people that are caught up in the middle of the investigation. Is there anything that we're missing, or we're not thinking of, that we should be? To me, that's the value of Team B.

Like Khabbaz, Butler and Kaplan found it relatively easy to recruit members to Team B. Within CDC, they asked infectious disease experts without major responsibility for the investigation to participate. In addition, team leaders in the response were welcome to participate whenever they could. From outside the agency, they chose people they knew and respected who were working in academia or in public health systems at the state level. All were well-known in the infectious disease world, and all had associations of long standing with the CDC. As scientific investigators across the world learned more about the nature of

---

[13]See "SARS in Toronto" (Case 2 in this book).
[14]Sexually transmitted disease, human immunodeficiency virus, and tuberculosis.

SARS, the Team B co-leaders added new scientific and technical experts, some as permanent members of the team and some as "guest speakers" for a session or two. For example, once SARS was identified as a corona virus—more common as a cause of disease in cats and birds than in people—the Team B co-leaders pulled in some veterinary virologists. These scientists contributed interesting pieces of information—for example, that there were different patterns of illness depending whether the virus entered an animal's body via airways or the digestive track. This was provocative as there were anomalies in the pattern of symptoms reported in the human version of the disease that scientists were still trying to explain.

On average, about a dozen people joined in the Team B discussions. Those invited were generally more than willing to participate, the co-leaders report. SARS was a compelling medical mystery—a race between a deadly spreading virus and the virologists on its trail. In this high-stakes context, they were eager to help if they could. Also, to serve on Team B was to be "in the loop," where they would hear the latest reports from the front lines.

Early on, Butler was concerned about how to keep Team B well-enough informed about the fast-moving investigation to be of help—and about how to convey the thoughts and perspectives of Team B members back to the CDC investigative teams in a useful form. Within the first few meetings, he, Kaplan, Hughes, and Mitch Cohen (director of the NCID's Division of Bacterial and Mycotic Diseases, who became an active Team B member)[15] settled on a modus operandi similar to Khabbaz's approach during West Nile: one of the Team B co-leaders would attend the daily, and often twice-daily, emergency operations briefings. In this way, the co-leaders would keep abreast of the latest issues in order to report them to Team B. In turn, they would report any relevant contributions from Team B at the emergency operations briefings.[16] The emergency leaders would have the chance to ask followup questions or to ask the team to consider other issues as they arose. The team was also free to decide, on its own, where to focus its attention. One of the things Team B was specifically told *not* to do, however, was to make more work for the investigating teams by proposing new tasks or chores. Team B was to operate at a higher level—analyzing the outbreak and the thinking behind the response.

As in the West Nile experience, the members of Team B were dispersed across the country, so Butler and Kaplan arranged meetings via teleconference three times a week (twice a week in the final month of the investigation). All members of the team were busy professionals, and some were highly placed state officials. Out of respect for their time, the Team B co-leaders agreed to keep the meetings to 1 hour, which meant the discussions had to be

---

[15]A few weeks into the SARS investigation, Kaplan withdrew from Team B to resume his responsibilities as division director and Cohen took his place for the remainder of the investigation.

[16]Notes from each Team B teleconference were also condensed to a concise, one-page summary, using bulletpoints to telegraph the key ideas quickly. These summaries were distributed at the briefings and posted to a secure area of the CDC's computer network, along with other information about the investigation.

focused and disciplined. In addition, they decided not to ask the team members to do any outside reading or preparation, although some did so anyway, on their own.

Each teleconference began with a briefing or update of about 5 minutes, followed by a discussion focused on one or two predetermined questions. One of the co-leaders' responsibilities, Cohen notes, was to set the right atmosphere. The forums were a place to get new ideas out on the table—not a place to subject them to withering scrutiny. For one thing, there was not enough time to pull each idea apart, but, in addition, the co-leaders wanted to create an atmosphere of safety, a brainstorming session in which anyone could throw out an idea without risk to his or her credibility. "Scientists are really sensitive about expressing their lack of knowledge about something," Cohen notes.[17]

The planning and coordination work involved in arranging such teleconferences did take more time than anyone had imagined, Butler says. He estimates that he and the other co-leaders ended up spending "80 to 90 percent" of their time on Team B while the SARS investigation was underway.

Assessing Success or Failure

Participants both in SARS Team B and in the SARS investigation came away with a positive view of the experiment. For one thing, many of the twenty-eight teleconferences were stimulating conversations that fully engaged the participants. One of the most exciting, Butler recalls, was a session that featured a CDC investigator in Hong Kong looking into a confusing development—the rapid spread of SARS, by uncertain means, through the residents of an apartment building called Amoy Gardens. The prevailing hypothesis at the time held that SARS was spread by droplets—relatively good news, if true, as it meant close physical contact was necessary to spread the disease. But the droplet theory did not seem to explain the pattern of transmission at Amoy Gardens. By including an investigator on the ground in Hong Kong, the Team B coordinators were able to create "an opportunity for someone who was very knowledgeable about the situation, and was going to be involved in trying to interpret it and make policy recommendations, to tap into some other opinions and perspectives," Butler says. Some twenty-seven people participated in that session.

Did this or any other Team B conversation provide the investigation with critical insights? Certainly, the team did not come up with any idea so new and radical that it altered the course of the investigation, but was that the appropriate measure of success? "You're not going to hit a home run every time you're at bat," Butler says. Perhaps the importance of Team B was in providing the "at-bat opportunity," he adds. "To me, [the Amoy Gardens discussions, in particular] fit well with what I thought Team B had the potential to do."

---

[17]Interview with Mitchell (Mitch) Cohen, director, CDC Coordinating Center for Infectious Diseases, 2007. Unless noted, subsequent quotations from Cohen are also from this interview.

Team B was one of many sources of input for investigators, notes Khabbaz, who also participated in the SARS Team B; it was probably difficult—maybe impossible—for the investigators to know after the fact how much they were influenced by one source or another, especially if all were pointing in more or less the same direction. For his part, Hughes says that he regarded SARS Team B as a useful addition. Hughes left the CDC in 2005, but says that if he were to lead another SARS-type investigation, he would not hesitate to create another Team B.

A Harbinger of Future Trouble?

There was a nagging concern about one aspect of Team B's job in the SARS outbreak—an issue that had also arisen in the West Nile response and that would come into greater focus when Team B was created again, in subsequent emergency response investigations. Was the team to be fundamentally advisory, answering to the scientific director of the investigation—in this case, Hughes—in the manner of a consultant? Or was the team expected to be more independent than that? Was the team, in fact, being asked to "second guess" Hughes—to challenge him—if the members thought he was off-track? Put another way, was Team B intended to provide Hughes and his team with thoughts and perspectives that they, in turn, were free either to consider or ignore? Or was Team B intended to provide the CDC director with a second opinion that could potentially lead her to overrule the director of the investigation and order a different approach? This distinction was particularly freighted in the context of CDC's shift from a center-centric to an agency-wide emergency response system.

In the SARS investigation, Team B leaned toward the former. Hughes had requested the creation of Team B and had assigned trusted colleagues to assemble the group and oversee it. The CDC director was privy to the Team B reports by virtue of attending the emergency operations briefings. In that sense, Butler says, SARS Team B ended up playing "both roles." But the potential conflict between these two roles never materialized during the SARS investigation—perhaps because, in general, the CDC's conduct of the investigation was not controversial. By all reports, the Team B members, while eager to help in the investigation, were not inclined to take issue with it; their deliberations were characterized by a spirit of collegial goodwill.

Team B and the Flu, December 2003 to January 2004

About 6 months after the SARS Team B was disbanded, in December 2003, the CDC began to receive alarming reports about the seasonal flu. For one, it appeared to be getting an early start. For another, anecdotal reports indicated a high number of pediatric deaths. Further complicating the picture, by early indications, the flu vaccine was not well-matched to the year's prevailing flu strain.[18] Finally, there was an anticipated shortage of inactivated flu vaccine (the "flu shot"). It might be possible to make up for the shortage with live attenuated influenza vaccines (the "nasal spray flu vaccine"), but these were more expensive and, in some recipients, set off symptoms (albeit mild) of the flu itself. The CDC considered them a fine option for healthy, not-pregnant people between the ages of 5 and 49. But for high-risk groups—the same groups for whom flu vaccination was considered most important[19]—the CDC recommended the inactivated flu shot. What should the agency recommend this year, however, if the flu proved more virulent than usual, especially for children; if the vaccine proved less effective than usual; and if the safest version of the vaccine proved less available than usual?

The CDC launched an investigation to get a better handle on the issues. Cohen suggested to Hughes that he convene another Team B to assist in the effort and enlisted Butler's help in running it. The pair reengaged many of the same outside experts who had participated in the SARS investigation. The cast of characters within CDC was different, however, featuring staff with specific expertise in influenza and influenza vaccines.

In retrospect, Butler and Cohen gave this Flu Team B a mixed review. On the one hand, as in the SARS investigation, the team rolled up its sleeves and engaged the issues with energy and dedication, even participating in a teleconference on Christmas Eve. But Butler and Cohen agree that Flu Team B ended up being significantly more disputatious than SARS Team B. Butler notes that there were some basic differences between the two investigations. In the case of SARS, no one knew much about the disease—an inherently humbling state of affairs that perhaps led to more open exchanges. Flu, however, was a different matter. Flu was not mysterious. What's more, in the flu world, there was a set of well-worn and recurring disputes about the illness and the flu vaccine. For instance, should the public be encouraged to get a flu vaccine if it was poorly matched to the flu strains in circulation? Some said yes because even a poorly matched vaccine would offer some measure of protection that might save lives, especially of people in the high-risk groups. Some said no because if people got the vaccine and then came down with the flu anyway, they might lose faith in flu vaccines, generally.

---

[18]Each year, flu experts chose one flu strain in each of three broader categories to include in the vaccine. The vaccine for 2003–2004 protected against A/Panama flu but not against A/Fujian flu, which was emerging as the most prevalent strain in circulation. (A/Fujian was similar enough to A/Panama that experts hoped the vaccine would provide partial protection. In addition, it was possible that, in the course of the year's flu season, A/Fujian would fade and another strain would become more prominent.)

[19]The groups at highest risk for complications from influenza, and therefore most strongly advised to get a yearly flu shot, were children between the ages of 6 months and 5 years, adults older than 49, pregnant women, people of any age with certain chronic medical conditions, and people who resided in long-term care facilities or nursing homes.

Neither Butler nor Cohen recalls the specific points of difference that arose in the Flu Team B discussions, but they do recall that there was a sharp difference of views between the CDC participants, on one side, and one of the outside participants, on the other, over a particular matter of CDC policy. Were the CDC participants overly defensive? One observer notes, "People think [Team B] is an intriguing concept until the first time it tells them something they don't want to hear." On the other hand, was the critical member of Team B out of line? What were the extent and limits of Team B's purview? Butler recalls telling the Team B members, "You know, we haven't been asked to completely *change* [the CDC] approach—we've been asked to *critique* this approach," but he also respected the perspective of the Team B critic. "His answer was, 'Well, it's the *wrong approach!*' " Butler says. The day after this meeting, an article appeared in the *New York Times* reporting the results of an unpublished study (itself controversial) that drew into question the effectiveness of the 2003–2004 flu vaccine.[20] Team B had been privy to the study, and some believed the Team B critic had leaked the story to the press. Tensions escalated—both within Team B and between Team B and the CDC team in charge of the flu response—but fate intervened to ease the strain. By mid-January, it was clear that the 2003–2004 flu season was lifting early; effectively, the concerns over the flu vaccine were moot.

That same month, a few human cases of a particularly worrisome strain of avian flu, H5N1, were diagnosed in Asia. Virologists were concerned that, at some point, this virulent and lethal virus would mutate to a form that could be transmitted from person to person, perhaps leading to the world's next flu pandemic. Butler and Cohen proposed that Team B shift its attention to H5N1. Somewhat to their surprise, however, the team showed little appetite for taking up the question. Perhaps, they later surmised, the combination of people on Team B was not especially well-matched to the issue. Perhaps, in the absence of person-to-person transmission, the threat was too hypothetical. Perhaps the group had grown weary and disaffected by the flu vaccine discussions. In any event, Butler and Cohen disbanded Flu Team B at the end of January, disappointed that it had not gone better yet uncertain what lessons to draw from the experience.

Creating a "Permanent" Team B

Although the Team B model was more formal and structured than past CDC efforts to consult with outside experts during an emergency response, Team B had been, to this point, assembled and disassembled on an ad hoc basis. In any given emergency investigation, large or small, the director of the scientific investigation, the director of one of the CDC centers

---

[20]Lawrence K. Altman, "Vaccine Is Said to Fail to Protect against Flu Strain," *New York Times,* January 15, 2004, A18.

at the heart of the investigation, or the CDC director herself could set up a Team B if it seemed useful.

In spring 2004, however, the CDC began to implement the sweeping agency reorganization known as the Future's Initiative. In addition, Gerberding continued to move the CDC's emergency response model away from the center-centric approach of old and toward the agency-wide Incident Management System (IMS).

As a part of the larger organizational overhaul, Gerberding created a new position: a permanent Team B director. This position was situated within her own executive Office of Strategy and Innovation. The idea was that during an emergency response, the Team B coordinator would assemble and manage a Team B along the lines of those set up during West Nile, SARS, and the 2003–2004 flu. Like the previous Teams B, the new Teams B would walk the delicate line between serving and second-guessing the research teams involved in the investigation and response. Ultimately, however, they would answer to the director's office rather than to the scientific director of the investigation.

Under Gerberding's plan, Team B would also play a role in the agency between major emergencies. At her direction, the Team B coordinator would set up a Team B to offer a second look at significant, nonemergency agency projects. If the agency were to retool its approach to obesity, for example, a Team B might be established to assist, advise, or challenge the CDC public health staff who were working on the issue. If the CDC were to rethink how to handle growing public concern over vaccine safety—a hot political issue for the agency— a Team B might be formed to offer an outside view.

In September 2004, Gerberding appointed Suzanne Smith as the first permanent Team B coordinator. Most recently, Smith had served as acting director of the Public Health and Practice Program Office (PHPPO). PHPPO—the CDC's point of contact for state and local health departments, professional organizations, and academic institutions—had been divided up and redeployed under the reorganization. Before that, Smith had worked in several roles, over a 20-year period, spending greatest time in the areas of injuries and chronic diseases. Smith had not sought the Team B position; like most people in the agency, she had never heard of Team B. She recalls that Gerberding explained the position as "the person who challenges the conventional wisdom."[21] Although uncertain what that would mean, day to day, Smith was ready to roll up her sleeves and figure it out.

As a starting point, Gerberding suggested that she talk to Butler, Cohen, and others in the infectious disease area who had worked on the SARS Team B. Smith listened with interest to their description. She came away with a mixed impression. It seemed clear that those involved had found the SARS Team B to be positive and helpful. The participants already

---

[21]Interview with Suzanne Smith, first permanent CDC Team B coordinator, 2007. Unless noted, subsequent quotations from Smith are also from this interview.

knew and trusted one another. Smith imagined that the sessions—although conducted via teleconference—had had the flavor of a relaxed brainstorming session over a beer with friends. That had some real advantages, she says. "It was a model that was acceptable to the internal scientists and comfortable culturally and there wasn't a lot of dispute." But it did not strike her as a disinterested second look at the outbreak or at CDC's investigation. "Did you get a wide variety of input? Did you have any reactors from the outside, testing or validating what you were saying? Well . . . no."

Smith did some further research and learned that the Central Intelligence Agency (CIA) had created its own version of a Team B several decades earlier. Under the CIA approach, the agency's senior leaders had periodically assembled a group of experts outside the agency to provide a second opinion about the CIA's own in-house assessment of a selected security threat. The most famous CIA Team B, constituted during the cold war, asserted that the Soviet arsenal was a far greater threat than the CIA's own analysts believed. Although influential at the time, this appraisal was, in retrospect, seen by many as suspect, inspired more by anti-Soviet ideology than by a rigorous review of the data. Concerned about this politically loaded association, Smith tried to persuade the CDC executive team to rename Team B, but was unsuccessful. She also looked into a strategy developed in the U.S. Navy to create in-house "red teams," which participated in selected navy operations and reported observations to high-level officers—essentially providing a second opinion to the reports that came up through the traditional chain of command.

Team B and the Vaccine Shortage, October 2004

In September 2004, while Smith was researching the CIA's Team B and the U.S. Navy's red teams, a new vaccine problem was brewing. Authorities in Great Britain announced that, owing to safety concerns, the British pharmaceutical company Chiron, responsible for producing half of the annual U.S. supply of flu vaccine, would be shut down for several months. This meant Chiron would not be able to deliver its flu vaccines to the United States for the 2004–2005 flu season. Other manufacturers might be able to boost their production a little bit to compensate, but it was too late to avert a dramatic shortfall. In early October, when Smith had been in her new job just 9 days, the CDC launched an emergency response to the vaccine shortage. This response effort involved the newly created Coordinating Center for Infectious Diseases and the National Immunization Program (NIP). Gerberding assigned Mitch Cohen, director of the Coordinating Center for Infectious Diseases, to take charge of the response. The goal was to try to make sure the existing vaccines were dispensed across the country to people at the highest risk for hospitalization and death due to the complications of flu. This was easier said than done because the CDC directly controlled only about 10 percent of the vaccine supply. The rest was bought and sold on the private market—and about a third of the vaccine had already been distributed when Chiron's shutdown was announced.

Cohen invited Smith to sit in on his staff meetings for the response, and Gerberding included Smith in the daily emergency response briefings to provide a Team B perspective. At the first emergency response briefing Smith attended, she received Team B's task list, which took her by surprise as it was focused not on the day-to-day response effort per se but on contingency planning. What if, on top of the vaccine shortage, there was an outbreak of avian flu, for example? Or, in event of an exceptionally bad 2004–2005 flu season, how should the CDC think about whether to close schools and businesses? And—although it was too late to affect the present situation—could Team B think about how the CDC should, in future, respond to a manufacturing shortfall? The broad nature of these questions worried Smith. She knew, for instance, that there was already a major effort afoot in the CDC's parent agency, the Department of Health and Human Services, to plan for an avian flu outbreak. Was Team B really supposed to take up this question, starting from scratch?

Smith asked Cohen his thoughts. He suggested that she talk to CDC staff at NIP to see what kind of assistance they thought would be most useful from Team B. The NIP group was most concerned about the distribution of the existing vaccine, Smith says, "The vaccine was sitting in certain pockets and localities. It was particularly rich in places that had had the good fortune not to buy Chiron vaccine—and CDC had no way of knowing where that was," especially with respect to private health-care providers. Might Team B work with the National Association of County and City Health Officials (NACCHO) to see if they could help, the NIP staff wondered? This question was far more specific than the contingency planning questions and, to Smith, more manageable.

Smith's first order of business, however, was to create a Team B. In this respect, she was aware of starting at a disadvantage compared to her predecessors in the 2003 SARS and 2003–2004 flu responses. By virtue of their background and professional contacts, Butler, Kaplan, and Cohen—division directors in the Center for Infectious Diseases—had known, reflexively, whom to recruit for the SARS and Flu Teams B. They were known, personally, in the infectious disease world. They were also acting at the direct behest of Hughes, who was a prominent and powerful figure in the infectious disease world. These facts quickly telegraphed to ranking public health officials that Team B was a distinguished advisory group, worthy of their time.

Smith was supposed to assemble a team—presumably that meant a team of flu and vaccine experts—but she had never worked in these areas at CDC and was not an "insider" in these professional circles. While she did work for Gerberding, she did not report directly to Gerberding and was not part of the CDC executive leadership team. What's more, there were growing tensions between the Coordinating Center for Infectious Diseases, NIP, and Gerberding's office over the reorganization and the shift to an agency-wide Incident

Management model. Smith found that she was not able to persuade CDC staff already busy with the response to participate reliably on the team. "They didn't know me," she says. "I had no currency."

Nor did she know, on her own, which outside experts to recruit for Team B. The people in the best position to advise her were involved in the response, she says, and too busy to help. She therefore sought advice from Butler and others in the infectious disease area, who gave her a list of suggestions. That was a help, but "I had to persuade these people that this was a legitimate effort," she recalls. "Some of them knew me, but they knew I didn't work in this area." Smith did succeed in pulling together a group of about six or eight people for a few sessions, and she did report back on their comments at the emergency response briefings. Her reports, however, were met with silence at the briefings. Meantime, the Team B participants, themselves, grew dubious about the effort, she says: "These are smart people. I think they sorted out quickly that I wasn't really being listened to—that I didn't have a seat at the Big Table." Smith recalls vividly the moment when one prominent member of the group said, " 'Suzanne, I'm just going to call Julie myself.' " She continues, "People wanted to talk to Jim Hughes, or Mitch Cohen, or Julie Gerberding. These are the people they're used to dealing with. They knew that if those three people were serious about their input, they would call and talk to them themselves—that this must be of far less importance or urgency."

After a few sessions, Smith says, "I chucked that approach as futile." But by this time, she had developed some independent thoughts about the nature of the response and about what sort of Team B would be useful. She had come to agree with the perspective of the NIP staff that the key issues were about the location and distribution of the vaccine rather than the vaccine itself. Unlike the SARS outbreak, which had enlisted infectious disease experts worldwide to identify and characterize a mysterious and threatening new disease, the vaccine shortage was, at base, a health systems problem: "It was a health services delivery issue. It was a distribution issue. It was a communications issue," Smith says.

I said, "I'm going to call in my own group of people that I know will actually stay on the calls. I'm not going to pretend to get people who are big players in the infectious disease world. But I will get people who I think can give the response teams a lot of wrap-around experience that, frankly, I think they're missing the boat on, and that [in this situation] is more valuable than the technical information about flu or the vaccine."

Smith's Team B, which held its first teleconference October 21, included about a dozen state health officers, service providers, consultants, and businesspeople. This group talked via teleconference twice a week for about 4–6 weeks, she estimates, and discussed a range of topics that had arisen in the emergency response briefings. For instance, Team B members weighed in with some suggestions about how CDC might piece together information about where the vaccine had already been distributed. The team also raised issues that were not being discussed at CDC, Smith says. A pet peeve from the field, for example, had to do with CDC's communications about the vaccine shortage to the public, which always included the suggestion that citizens take their further questions to their local health department. To small health departments, this was an entirely unmanageable burden. "They were livid," she says, "They would say, 'don't tell them to call us! Tell them to call the CDC!'"

Smith also learned that, in late October, another division of the CDC was sponsoring a meeting in Washington, D.C., for business and labor organizations about how to cultivate a healthier workforce. She was able to "piggy-back" on this event to hold a town hall–style conversation about the vaccine shortage, about how a severe flu season would affect businesses, and about how CDC might work more effectively with businesses with respect to a serious flu outbreak.

Smith reported on this meeting and on the Team B sessions at the daily emergency operations briefings, and she entered her notes in the secure part of the computer network devoted to the vaccine shortage response. But she recalls that these reports were consistently met with silence and that she was not aware that the CDC response teams acted on any of the suggestions.

Cohen, the director of the response, says he does not remember the Team B reports clearly any longer. Although a partisan of the Team B idea, then and later, he does not recall that it was particularly useful in this situation. In retrospect, he thinks a different approach might have been more helpful. For example, once the CDC had identified health-care providers with a relative vaccine "oversupply," the agency wanted to redistribute it to those who had no vaccine. Many providers were willing to do so, in theory, but—as Cohen discovered partway into the response—were barred from doing so by U.S. Food and Drug Administration (FDA) regulations.[22] It would have been helpful, Cohen reflects, if, early on, the Team B coordinator had gathered together a group of knowledgeable regulators to discuss the various hurdles to vaccine redistribution. At the time, however, no one thought of using Team B in this way.

By December, "it hadn't developed into a bad flu year," Smith says. At that point, the vaccine shortage became a less worrisome issue, and "I got to the point where I felt I couldn't any longer use up the time of those on the outside who were participating in these conference calls," she says. "I recognized, after weeks of this, that no one was even reading the reports." Thus, she quietly disbanded the team. In January 2006, however, she did help to set up two different planning groups—one with school officials and one with business officials—to exchange perspectives with CDC officials about the pros, cons, and ramifications of shutting down schools or businesses in the event of a serious influenza outbreak.

---

[22]The FDA did later suspend some of its regulations to permit some vaccine redistribution.

Key Actors in CDC Develops Its "Team B"

U.S. Centers for Disease Control and Prevention (CDC)

Julie Gerberding, director

Jim Hughes, director, National Center for Infectious Diseases (1992–2005)

Suzanne Smith, first permanent Team B coordinator (appointed in 2004)

Jay Butler, director, Arctic Investigations Program, and co-manager of the 2003 SARS (severe acute respiratory syndrome) Team B and the 2003–2004 Flu Team B

Mitchell (Mitch) Cohen, director, Coordinating Center for Infectious Diseases, and co-manager of the 2003 SARS Team B and the 2003–2004 Flu Team B; charged with leading the CDC's response to the 2004 vaccine shortage

Jon Kaplan, director, Division of STD, HIV, and TB (sexually transmitted disease, human immunodeficiency virus, and tuberculosis) Laboratory Research, and co-manager of the 2003 SARS Team B

Rima Khabbaz, associate director of epidemiological science, National Center for Infectious Diseases, and manager of the first CDC Team B, for the 2002 West Nile investigation

CDC Develops Its "Team B"

Chronology of Events

Spring 2002

The West Nile virus spreads rapidly throughout the United States. The U.S. Centers for Disease Control and Prevention (CDC) response is managed by the National Center for Infectious Diseases (NCID).

Summer 2002

CDC Director Julie Gerberding asks Rima Khabbaz, NCID's associate director of epidemiological science, to create a Team B to augment the NCID-managed response to the West Nile outbreak.

Khabbaz assembles the CDC's first Team B, comprising experts from the fields of virology, entomology, and vector-borne illness. Group members conduct engaging discussions, but the team's overall impact is limited.

February and early March 2003

A new disease, later termed severe acute respiratory syndrome (SARS), appears in China, Hong Kong, and Hanoi.

March 12, 2003

The World Health Organization (WHO) issues a global alert about SARS.

March 14, 2003

Canadian authorities announce an apparent SARS cluster in Toronto.

March to May 2003

With SARS at the U.S. border, the CDC opens its own investigation, headed by NCID Director Jim Hughes.

Hughes gives Jay Butler, director of the CDC's Arctic Investigation Programs, and Jon Kaplan, director of the Division of STD, HIV, and TB[23] Laboratory Research, the task of creating and managing a new Team B for the SARS investigation.

Butler and Kaplan gather together infectious disease experts from within and outside CDC. Many of the team members are excited to participate, given the novelty of the disease.

Kaplan withdraws from Team B. He is replaced by Mitch Cohen, director of the NCID's Division of Bacterial and Mycotic Diseases.

---

[23]Sexually transmitted disease, human immunodeficiency virus, and tuberculosis.

The SARS Team B receives positive reviews, although questions remain regarding Team B's role and its authority vis-à-vis the main investigation group.

December 2003 to January 2004

The CDC learns that seasonal flu has gotten an early start and has apparently resulted in an unusually high number of pediatric deaths. In addition, there is an anticipated flu vaccine shortage.

The CDC launches an investigation into the flu issue.

Cohen and Butler gather together a group of experts in influenza and in the influenza vaccine to form a new Team B.

Flu Team B's discussions are much more contentious than those of previous teams, given the fixed (and sometimes conflicting) views of participants on flu and vaccinations.

The *New York Times* publishes a story on an unreleased CDC study. Some wonder whether a disgruntled Team B member has leaked the story.

Tensions escalate within Flu Team B, but with the flu season near an early end by mid-January, the investigation is no longer relevant.

Human cases of the H5N1 strain of avian influenza are identified in Asia. Butler and Cohen propose shifting Flu Team B's focus to H5N1, but team members show little interest.

Flu Team B is disbanded at the end of January.

Spring 2004

CDC begins implementing the Future's Initiative, a sweeping reorganization of the agency. The Incident Management System is adopted as the agency's emergency response model.

CDC Director Gerberding creates the new position of a permanent Team B coordinator, which is based in the executive office of Strategy and Innovation.

September to November 2004

Gerberding appoints Suzanne Smith, previously acting director of the Public Health and Practice Program Office, to the position of permanent Team B coordinator.

Smith researches previous Team B efforts. She talks to Butler, Cohen, and others involved on the SARS Team B.

Smith examines the U.S. Navy's red teams strategy and the Central Intelligence Agency's (CIA's) own Team B program, which had proven politically controversial. Wary of sharing the CIA program's name, Smith seeks to rename the CDC initiative but fails to obtain approval.

The pharmaceutical company Chiron announces that it plans to shut down operations for several months, triggering concerns about flu vaccine availability. (Chiron had been manufacturing half of the U.S. flu vaccine supply.)

CDC launches an emergency response to the vaccine shortage. Gerberding assigns Mitch Cohen, now director of the newly formed Coordinating Center for Infectious Diseases, to manage the response.

Smith attempts to assemble a Team B of flu and vaccine experts, but initially has difficulty forming a team. When she does pull together a small group, her reports on its work are met with silence at emergency response briefings.

Having determined that the main issue is a health systems/delivery problem, Smith reconfigures Team B's membership to include state health officers, service providers, consultants, and businesspeople.

The reconfigured Team B holds its first teleconference on October 21. The group talks about twice a week for a little over a month.

Smith continues to report on Team B's work at daily emergency operations briefings. But, as before, she receives little response.

December 2004

As it becomes clear that the flu season is not particularly severe, the vaccine shortage becomes less of an issue. Smith disbands the team.

Part V   Anticipating Disaster: Event Planning

Many disasters—earthquakes, tsunamis, forest fires, hurricanes, tornadoes, severe transportation accidents, and terrorist attacks, for example—typically occur with relatively little or no advance notice in places and at times that are at best only roughly predictable. Although there is much that can be done to prepare, responders can rarely pinpoint well in advance when and where they must be ready for such calamities.

But emergency response also deals with a category of event that has important dimensions of predictability. These *fixed events* are major public or private activities that are likely to involve large numbers of people; they are scheduled at specific times, ranging from a day to several months, in particular places. Some fixed events, including rock concerts and regular-season major league sporting contests, occur regularly and thus, to some degree, become routine. Others are much rarer, even unique, in the jurisdictions that host them. These include championship games, political rallies, music festivals, conventions and international conferences—for example, the Super Bowl, the Olympic Games, presidential campaign appearances, and major-party political conventions. Although some fixed events have only local importance, the largest and most prominent enjoy significant media visibility, perhaps on a worldwide scale. They attract not only large numbers but also prominent people as participants or spectators: political leaders, leading business executives, and entertainment or sports stars. In addition to the concentration of people and attention, such events frequently have significant symbolic importance to the communities or countries that sponsor them. In the case studies that follow, we look at security planning for several such fixed events: the Summer Olympic Games staged in Atlanta in 1996, the Ministerial Conference of the World Trade Organization (WTO) in Seattle in 1999, the planned millennium celebration in Seattle scheduled for New Year's Eve 1999, and the Democratic National Convention in Boston in 2004 to select that party's presidential nominee.

From an emergency response perspective, high-profile fixed events are a significant part of the job. They can be tempting terrorist targets because they predictably concentrate many vulnerable people in relatively small areas, provide clear notice about the timing of the event, and already command great public attention. Hence, destruction or disruption would endanger many people, be highly visible, and prove economically and symbolically damaging to the community or country in which the event occurs.

But any fixed event poses significant challenges for emergency managers and public safety officials, even when it is notable mainly to the locality in which it occurs and is not especially alluring to terrorists. Public safety officials have to manage the arrival and departure of large numbers of people smoothly enough to prevent injuries and minimize inconvenience or damage to facilities. They must be ready to handle medical emergencies or fires, prevent crime, and manage crowds of potentially unruly or panicky people. They must also be prepared to deal with unexpected occurrences: coincidental natural hazards or major technology failures such as in heating, cooling, lighting, air circulation, and transportation systems.

Advance planning for large-scale fixed events is crucial, both in major jurisdictions that regularly host them and in smaller jurisdictions staging a less visible event. But this planning can be difficult for several reasons.

The complex arrangements necessary to stage and protect atypical events require collaboration among many institutional and individual players. Sufficient expertise, authority, and resources are rarely, if ever, centered in a single public agency or private organization or even in a single jurisdiction. For the largest fixed events, as is true for the large-scale emergencies and disasters discussed in earlier cases in this book, a wide range of professional skills are needed. Law enforcement, fire protection, and emergency medicine are often at the core; but public health, public works, transportation, social services, housing, and many other competencies are frequently needed, especially when an event lasts longer than 1 or 2 days. Moreover, because the social and economic infrastructure to support a large-scale fixed event often lies in more than one political jurisdiction, collaboration among the several governments of these jurisdictions is essential to provide appropriate coverage. But as the Atlanta Olympics case presented in this part well illustrates, often the coordinating structures for such cooperation must be invented or substantially adapted to meet the special needs of an unusual event. Frequently, in fact, more than one level of government must be involved.

Whichever jurisdiction is in the lead in planning, therefore, needs to enlist the cooperation and resources of multiple partners—the surrounding communities and state and federal entities—while managing the collaboration of different agencies and personnel from diverse professions. Past experience or existing organizational structures may provide a starting point, but the unique characteristics of a given event often mean that temporary task forces or other ad hoc structures must be formed. Typically, these are committees, with representatives from each participating agency, that meet periodically to plan for the event's security and review steps taken to date.[1]

---

[1]As such, they are quite different from the *sudden organizations* structured by the incident management system, which are assembled during a major emergency and which are extensively discussed earlier in this book.

Depending on the complexity of the event, the planning structure may need several layers of organization: specialized subcommittees to focus on particular kinds of problems (transportation and emergency medical care, for example), working committees composed of the officials who will supervise the actual response operations, and umbrella policy committees of agency heads and perhaps elected leaders to pull the whole security plan together. When a private "host" committee is taking the lead in planning the event itself (as was the case for the Atlanta Olympics and the Democratic National Convention in Boston), effective coordination between the public agencies and the host committee is crucial.

This process may work smoothly. But it also has the potential for evoking conflict—simmering or more overt—if institutional rivalries, different approaches to planning, or varying interests in the event emerge. One source of conflict is the differing perceptions of the kinds and severity of threat that planners must take into account. The range of possible problems that might beset a major event is enormous, perhaps infinite, but not all these problems are equally likely or potentially consequential. Planners therefore must gauge which risks command attention because of their *likelihood* (for example, individual medical emergencies such as heat exhaustion or heart attack) or *potentially severe consequences* (for example, multiple deaths or injuries or substantial property damage), even if very unlikely (for example, a tornado or a terrorist attack) in the event time frame.

Risk management is difficult because of both high levels of uncertainty and cost constraints. To prepare for a fixed event inevitably means making judgments about the future. Although planners do not have to predict the future precisely, they do have to make at least rough estimates of the probabilities of certain types of problems or, alternatively, the likelihood of having to cope with certain kinds of consequences (injuries, for example), no matter what the cause. But not all of these potential causes or consequences are easy to quantify, even roughly, or, indeed, to identify.[2] As a result, planners both rely on professional norms (that is, experientially or theoretically derived rules of thumb) to suggest good preparedness practices and engage in proactive information gathering about the particular situation. Information gathering methods might range from the consultation of the best and latest weather forecasts to intelligence collection by law enforcement agencies to determine the probability of a terrorist attack or disruptive political demonstrations. As some of the following case studies suggest, however, effective information gathering, as well as the effective assessment of the data collected, can be highly problematic.

In the end, the possible threats or risks involved in any fixed event are likely to exceed the time and financial budgets available to deal with them. Trade-offs and choices therefore

---

[2]These include the "known unknowns" and "unknown unknowns," in former U.S. Defense Secretary Rumsfeld's terminology, that are discussed in the introduction to Part III.

must be made. Planners have to devote their limited resources to the range of problems they consider most likely to arise, trusting or hoping that they will be able to adapt their existing capabilities or improvise effectively "in the moment" to accommodate unexpected threats.

Given the uncertainties involved, there is no fully objective answer. The decisions made must result from either a prevailing dominant judgment or a compromise patched together from the views of multiple participants. This decision making is often complicated by practical matters, political considerations, and competing priorities other than security centering around the following questions:

- Who pays? Private parties sponsoring an event, various agencies within a particular jurisdiction, multiple jurisdictions, and different levels of government all may hope that the costs of security can be pushed off onto another institution or, at least, be shared.
- Who bears the risk? There is a downside to both over- and underpreparation. Who takes the blame if planners overestimate the threat and take what later come to be seen as "unneeded" and expensive protective steps? Alternatively, who is responsible for the outcome if security steps are later seen as inadequate to a threat that unexpectedly materializes?
- Are we sufficiently prepared? Not knowing the future, we can never be sure if the steps taken are adequate for the dangers that could lie ahead. There are also potential trade-offs between security and other values that institutions or the public care about. Could we do with somewhat less security in order to get more of the other values? Inevitably, these trade-offs have a political dimension; judgments depend on stakeholders' varying points of view, shaped by their institutional perspectives and interests. As both the Atlanta Olympics and the Democratic National Convention case studies illustrate, security requirements may compromise other considerations such as convenient spectator or visitor access to the event, the interests of local businesses whose operations are affected, or the convenience of residents who wish to use urban services or transportation facilities whose use security planners want to restrict. On the other hand, the case on the 1999 WTO Ministerial Conference in Seattle reveals that there are also serious social, political, and economic consequences for failing to take adequate security measures in advance of and during large-scale and high-profile events.

As decision makers craft a security plan, their deliberations are thus frequently complicated by the absolute cost and distribution of payments for security, the politics of risk, and competing concerns about how the event will occur and what inconveniences will be placed on those who attend and others who live or work nearby.

Finally, fixed events create significant challenges as *planning* phases into the *implementation* of the security plan. Can the concepts and concerns of the plan be translated into operational capabilities that can be implemented if problems large or small actually occur at the event? Can the judgments and calculations incorporated into any plan survive contact with the real conditions that occur at the time of the event? What happens if they cannot?

The four case studies that follow provide rich opportunities to examine these abstract questions in situations confronted by the people who planned major events and were responsible for implementing the security plans that they and their colleagues devised. The cases provide, moreover, equally rich opportunities for readers to ask whether the planners' efforts were sufficient and, if not, how they might have been improved.

12 Security Preparations for the 1996 Centennial Olympic Games (A): Interagency and Intergovernmental Organization

John Buntin

Hosting the Olympics involves huge challenges for any metropolitan region, and certainly this was the case for Atlanta in planning physical security for the athletes, spectators, venues, and surrounding areas for the Centennial Games of 1996. The issues included the management of the flow of people and traffic into and out of venues and throughout the region; the readiness of emergency services for medical, fire, or other disasters; and law enforcement on alert for individual or organized threats to order and public safety.

Many questions had to be answered. Who would do the planning and how ought it to be organized? With events occurring not only in the city of Atlanta but all across the state of Georgia, a large number of local, state, and federal agencies were involved—137 law enforcement agencies alone. How should responsibility be allotted to specific agencies and communities? How should the coordination across agencies, jurisdictions, and levels of government be managed? Who should be in charge? Who should bear or share the not insignificant costs of providing security? What was the appropriate role for government agencies versus the private-sector Olympic organizing committee, which was staging the Atlanta games?

As security planning got underway, a major difference of perspective divided the officials involved. Were the necessary preparations a familiar exercise except on a larger scale— essentially like hosting the World Series or the Super Bowl but with multiple events occurring simultaneously in venues throughout the region? Or did getting ready for the Olympics pose fundamentally different challenges than such major events?

These were difficult issues, not least because of the uncertain nature of the threats faced. The shadow of Munich in 1972, when terrorists invaded the Olympic Village, kidnapped Israeli athletes, and murdered them in a bloody denouement at the airport, overhung the preparations. But more recent events, some much closer to home, also framed the deliberations of the security planners. The World Trade Center in New York City had been attacked for the first time in 1994; and, within a short period in 1995, the federal building in Oklahoma City was blown up and the Aum Shinrikyo cult had attacked Tokyo subway riders with chemical weapons.

This is an abridged version of a case written by John Buntin for Richard Falkenrath, assistant professor of public policy, and Arnold M. Howitt, executive director, Taubman Center for State and Local Government, for use at the Executive Session on Domestic Preparedness, John F. Kennedy School of Government, Harvard University. Funding was provided by the Office of Justice Programs, U.S. Department of Justice. Kennedy School of Government Case Program, C16-00-1582.0, C16-00-1589.0, and C16-00-1590.0. Copyright © 2000, 2007 by the President and Fellows of Harvard College.

These issues presented themselves in somewhat different ways in Georgia and in Washington, D.C. Georgia's authorities constantly confronted the tensions between staging Olympic Games that, on one hand, would create a festive atmosphere throughout the area and be enjoyable to the participants and spectators at athletic venues and, on the other hand, would provide sufficient security precautions to prevent terrorist targeting of the Olympics. In short, how should they weigh security precautions against restrictions and inconvenience to the spectators and participants? Clinton administration officials, by contrast, gave unambiguous priority to the security dimensions of preparing for the Games. Nonetheless, both state and federal authorities had to pay careful attention to the adequacy of personnel and financial resources needed to carry out their visions of appropriate security measures. Both had to wrestle with questions about the command and control of security forces. Both also had to ask, how much is enough? Facing great uncertainty about what threats might be looming ahead, they had to consider which threats were sufficiently "real" to warrant attention and which had to be given less or no attention because of cost constraints or their perceived low probability. Lurking behind these considerations were two fundamental questions. Could they prevent a terrorist attack on the Games; and, if the worst happened, would they be ready to respond effectively?

Discussion Questions

- Why was it so difficult to develop plans across the many jurisdictions involved in the security preparations for the Games? Would alternative ways of organizing the planning have worked more effectively?
- How can planners determine the range of threats and contingencies for which they should prepare? Where in the continuum from "worst" to "best" cases should planners concentrate? How should resource constraints figure in these determinations?
- Other than security planning, what dimensions of preparedness should animate the efforts of public safety agencies in getting ready for a fixed event such as the Olympics? How well were these aspects of preparedness carried out?

In late November 1995, Vice President Al Gore visited Atlanta to check on the preparations for the 1996 Summer Olympic Games. In 8 months, approximately 15,000 athletes from 197 countries, 20,000 journalists, 8–9 million ticket holders, and 41 heads of state would arrive to attend the biggest Olympic Games of all time. But just 6 months earlier, two terrorist attacks—a nerve gas attack on the Tokyo subway system by the religious cult Aum Shinrikyo and the bombing of the Alfred P. Murrah federal building in Oklahoma City—had demonstrated the growing danger posed by increasingly sophisticated terrorists. The Olympics would require extraordinary security precautions, and Gore wanted to make sure that the organizations responsible for the Games' security were prepared.

When the vice president arrived in Atlanta, however, he was told that security prepa-rations for the Games were in serious disarray. Gore, says one federal law enforcement official, was "bewildered and absolutely in awe that things could be in such a lousy state, roughly nine or ten months before the Games."[1] The Olympics would be held just months before presidential elections; instead of a triumphal Olympics that would make the American people feel good about the country, Gore now saw the possibility of a security catastrophe.

Personal animosities, interagency rivalries, and the perennial tension between the pre-dominantly black city of Atlanta and the predominantly white state of Georgia had all con-tributed to the difficulties of preparing for the Games. The state's vision of security planning for the Games, moreover, was radically different from that of the federal government. Until a decision was made about which vision would prevail, security preparations for the Games remained at an impasse.

Gore was not particularly interested in the origins of Atlanta's problems. He wanted the quick completion of security plans to enable more than 150 federal, state, and local public safety agencies to work together. The centerpiece of any solution would have to be a work-able mechanism of coordination, something that had largely eluded participants in the se-curity planning process for 4 years.

Security Planning Begins, 1990–1992

On September 20, 1990, the International Olympic Committee (IOC) selected Atlanta to host the 1996 Centennial Olympic Games. (See Exhibit 12A-1 for a list of acronyms used in this case.) The task of organizing and financing the Games then fell to the Atlanta Com-mittee for the Olympic Games (ACOG), a group of business and political leaders chaired by Atlanta Mayor Andrew Young and run by Atlanta real estate lawyer William "Billy" Payne.

Although ACOG had vast organizational challenges before it, Olympic security was a priority. Security had been a major concern of Olympic organizers since the 1972 Olympic Games in Munich, when Palestinian commandos took hostage and killed eleven Israeli ath-letes. In addition, Atlanta had one of the highest crime rates in the United States, and its ability to ensure a safe environment was a major IOC concern. To allay IOC concerns, At-lanta's bid committee had promised to assemble 25,000–30,000 security personnel to pro-tect the sixty-odd athletic venues, the Olympic Village, and the 8–9 million visitors that it projected attending the Games.

Yet translating this promise into practice was a major challenge. While most countries could turn to their national police force and military to provide security at special events,

---

[1]All unattributed statements in this case are from interviews conducted by the author, 2000.

Exhibit 12A-1 Acronyms

ACC	Atlanta Command Center
ACOG	Atlanta Committee for the Olympic Games
CDC	U.S. Centers for Disease Control and Prevention
CBIRF	Chemical and Biological Incident Response Force
DOD	U.S. Department of Defense
DOJ	U.S. Department of Justice
EMS	Emergency Medical Services
EOD	Explosive Ordnance Disposal
FBI	Federal Bureau of Investigation
FEMA	Federal Emergency Management Agency
FORSCOM	U.S. Army Forces Command
GBI	Georgia Bureau of Investigation
GEMA	Georgia Emergency Management Agency
IOC	International Olympic Committee
IPG	Integrated Planning Group
JCC	Joint Coordination Center
MARTA	Metropolitan Atlanta Rapid Transportation Authority
OSD	Office of the Secretary of Defense
OSE	Office of Special Events
OSPCC	Olympic Security Planning and Coordinating Committee
OSSG	Olympic Security Support Group
SOLEC	State Olympic Law Enforcement Command
SWAT	Special Weapons and Tactics
UPS	United Parcel Service
WMDs	weapons of mass destruction

the United States had no national police force (with the partial exception of the Federal Bureau of Investigation, FBI), and the *Posse Comitatus Act* of 1878 barred the military from carrying out law enforcement functions; active-duty U.S. military personnel could provide support at a special event but could not make arrests.

Consequently, ACOG had to assemble a team of private security guards and volunteers and coordinate its activities with the law enforcement agencies of the city of Atlanta, the state of Georgia, the federal government, and an array of county and municipal law enforcement agencies, as well as fire, emergency services, and public health agencies. In addition, they all had to work through the tensions that existed between the predominantly black city government and the predominantly white state government and their respective law enforcement agencies. Under the best of circumstances, interagency cooperation among public safety agencies at different levels of government was often difficult; in Atlanta, cooperation would have to take place on an unprecedented scale in an environment characterized by tension and mistrust.

The public safety agencies also had to agree on which preparations would create a secure environment for the Games. This task was complicated by the changing nature of the terrorist threat. In the 1970s and 1980s, Munich was seen as the worst-case scenario. In the 1990s, however, growing concerns about weapons of mass destruction (WMDs)—nuclear, biological, and chemical weapons capable of creating tens if not hundreds of thousands of casualties—forced ACOG and public safety officials in Atlanta to confront threats that had once been only nightmares.

The Atlanta Committee for the Olympic Games Starts the Planning Process

Soon after winning its Olympic bid, ACOG began assembling a security planning structure for the Games. ACOG's first step was to create a security advisory group of important public safety officials to help it make policy decisions about the security effort. It dubbed this group the Olympic Security Support Group (OSSG). Co-chaired by Atlanta Police Chief Eldrin Bell and Georgia State Patrol Commander Ronald Bowman, the OSSG included representatives of the FBI, the Fulton County Sheriff's Office, the Conyers Police Department, and approximately a dozen other agencies. ACOG also asked the city and the state to designate officers who could start working up security plans on a part-time basis. The Atlanta Police Department tapped Deputy Chief W. J. Taylor for this task. The state made a high-ranking state patrol officer, Richard "Stock" Coleman, its Olympic coordinator for security.

The OSSG met for the first time in September 1991. It quickly established two subcommittees. The venue subcommittee, chaired by ACOG, would make final decisions about the locations of the sixty-odd athletic venues. The Olympic Village subcommittee, meanwhile, was chaired by a representative from the Georgia Institute of Technology, whose campus was to be converted into the Olympic Village during the Games.

That fall, Taylor and Coleman began to talk about security planning. It was clear that a major thrust would be to develop security plans for each of the estimated sixty athletic venues. All entry and exit points had to be identified and secured with metal detectors and x-ray machines. Staffing plans for all the venues had to be drawn up; budget estimates had to be developed. In general terms, it was understood that ACOG security personnel would be responsible for enforcing the house rules inside the venues and operating the metal detectors, while law enforcement personnel would secure the perimeter and be on hand to make arrests if necessary. Taylor and Coleman also began to talk about what resources the city had to perform these functions and where the state would need to help out.

Only a few months later in early 1992, however, many public safety agencies had concluded that the planning process so far was lackluster and that the ACOG-led OSSG was inadequate and inappropriate for the task ahead. Anticipating financial benefits from the Olympics, state and local law enforcement agencies had at first been willing to defer to the wealthy, confident, and focused organizing committee. But by 1992 it had become clear, in the words of one law enforcement official, that while ACOG might view the Olympics as a private party, "they couldn't afford to be the only host." Public safety officials continued to expect that ACOG would reimburse them for the costs they would incur during the Games, but it was now clear that the effort would require substantial public resources. Consequently, a growing number of public safety officials felt it was improper to have a private group making decisions about how public safety resources would be used.

To reinvigorate the security planning, law enforcement officials created their own planning group, the Olympic Security Planning and Coordinating Committee (OSPCC), and made W. J. Taylor of the Atlanta Police Department its head. But the OSPCC's purpose and its relationship to the OSSG remained unclear. Stock Coleman and W. J. Taylor, the state and city coordinators, continued to work on the Olympics on only a part-time basis. Many state and local law enforcement officials did not even know how to start planning for the Olympics.

In spring 1992, Roland Vaughan, the police chief of Conyers, Georgia, a small town outside of Atlanta, concluded that the planning process needed a jolt of energy—and money. Vaughn was a friend of then U.S. Attorney General William Barr, and that spring he suggested to Barr that a grant to jumpstart planning for the Olympics would be greatly appreciated in Georgia, a critical swing state in the upcoming presidential elections. Barr embraced the proposal on the spot, and in September 1992, he announced that the Department of Justice (DOJ) was providing $1.7 million to Georgia's criminal justice planning agency to support state and local planning for the Games. In January 1993, Bill Kelley, a fellow at the National Institute of Justice who had previously been the head of Georgia's criminal justice planning agency, returned to Georgia to administer this grant and lead the staff-level planning effort.

A Growing Federal Presence

The FBI was the federal agency most involved in the early planning process.[2] But by fall 1991, the U.S. Department of Defense's Office of Special Events (OSE) had also begun to take an interest in events in Atlanta. Reporting to the secretary of defense, OSE provided materiel support and expert advice for large special events. By virtue of money and expertise, OSE had become an influential player in most special events that it supported. Ann Brooks, the OSE head, felt she had a good idea of what preparations needed to be undertaken for an Olympic Games, and Atlanta wasn't doing them.

In October 1991, Brooks had flown to Atlanta to meet the organizers for the first time. But when Brooks met Billy Payne, the president and chief executive officer of ACOG, she

---

[2]Other federal law enforcement agencies, among them the Secret Service; the Customs Service; the Drug Enforcement Agency; the Bureau of Alcohol, Tobacco, and Firearms; and the Drug Enforcement Agency, sent representatives to OSSG meetings and expected to become more involved in supporting the Olympics as the Games' start date drew nearer.

discovered that he had his own ideas about what the organizing committee needed. According to Brooks, "Billy Payne told me from almost day one . . . '[W]hat if we just bring in the National Guard and tell the Atlanta Police Department we don't need them?'"[3]

Brooks was a bit startled by this comment. While she anticipated that the military would play an important role during the Centennial Games, Brooks did not believe the Atlanta Police Department could be dispensed with. To help Atlanta get its security preparations in order, Brooks brought in Chris Bellavita, an OSE consultant, to help Atlanta develop the planning process.

A Renewed Effort, 1993–1994

By early 1993 most local law enforcement officials were open to the idea of getting outside assistance to help develop a more coherent planning approach process.[4] Many had no idea what needed to be done to prepare for the Olympics, and they were eager to find a template that would help them identify and perform critical tasks. Federal officials, particularly the FBI, made it clear that a new planning structure was needed. By early 1993, both the organizing committee and most of law enforcement agreed on the need to reform and reenergize the planning process.

However, some law enforcement officials reacted poorly to the push for a revamped planning process. Stock Coleman, the state's Olympic security coordinator, resented what he saw as OSE's desire "to come in and pretty much tell everybody what do to."[5] An unmistakable animosity was developing between Coleman and the federal officials. Much of this animosity was personal—Coleman openly disliked Brooks and OSE's law enforcement liaison, Marv Smalley, who soon came to reciprocate these feelings. Coleman disliked the FBI even more.

Disputes over who should control the money that Congress had begun appropriating to the OSE to support the Games also contributed to the strained relations between Coleman and his federal counterparts. Coleman—and many others in Georgia—believed that OSE should provide money and support the state effort. Brooks, however, maintained that Congress was appropriating money to OSE to support Department of Defense (DOD) activities and insisted on maintaining control.

---

[3]Interview with Ann Brooks, DOD Office of Special Events, 2000. Unless noted, subsequent quotations from Brooks are also from this interview.

[4]There was, however, considerable initial skepticism about whether Bellavita, a Berkeley-trained academic whose background did not suggest any apparent affinity for Southern law enforcement personnel, was the person for the job.

[5]Interview with Richard "Stock" Coleman, commanding officer, Georgia State Patrol, 2000. Unless noted, subsequent quotations from Coleman are also from this interview.

Coleman also took issue with one of the basic assumptions that OSE and the FBI were bringing to Atlanta—that putting on the Olympics was qualitatively different from putting on any other big athletic event: "[T]here's a certain group of people who have tried to make the Olympics something unique, and it really isn't. It's just a sporting event. It's crowd management. But you have a group of people who try to make it some kind of mystique, and there's no great mystique to it. You fill a stadium and you empty a stadium; you fill a park and you empty a park. . . ."

Turning to Los Angeles for a Planning Structure

In January 1993 at a retreat facilitated by Chris Bellavita, the OSSG began to discuss seriously how the planning effort should be structured. Bellavita had asked Dallas Police Chief Bill Rathburn, who had directed the Los Angeles Olympic effort in 1984, to make a presentation on his experiences in Los Angeles. Federal officials hoped Rathburn's presentation would push the OSSG toward adopting a similar comprehensive interagency planning process for Atlanta.

In preparation for the 1984 Games, Los Angeles had adopted a three-tiered interagency security planning structure designed to identify and devise solutions to security threats. A small policymaking group of agency heads or deputies oversaw the process and made all final security planning decisions. A middle-tier group was made up of planning managers, the planning chiefs of the most important public safety agencies. They oversaw the work of nearly two dozen subcommittees (the bottom tier). Each subcommittee focused on a specific public safety function and was responsible for assessing and developing a plan to address threats in its area of responsibility. Both the subcommittees and planning managers were supported by an integrated planning group, a small number of full-time staff drawn primarily from the various agencies' planning offices who did everything from arranging meetings to producing documents.

The Los Angeles model appealed to most members of the OSSG. Bill Kelley, who was administering the DOJ grant to jump-start planning for the Olympics, believed the Los Angeles model did at least provide a coherent view of the security jobs other than securing the athletic venues. "There was a template from LA: it was about 18 or 19 special jobs," says Kelley.[6] "It does at least say, 'Well, here are the things you will be doing primarily.' "

A Competing Vision of the Planning Process

Stock Coleman, however, did not share the general admiration for the Los Angeles model. He believed that most of the security planning for the Olympics could be done in 6 or 7

---

[6]Interview with Bill Kelley, fellow, National Justice Institute, 2000. Unless noted, subsequent quotations from Kelley are also from this interview.

months, not several years. Coleman looked at the Games "as 20 ballgames . . . [that] just happen to be going on at the same time." Coleman also questioned the need for an elaborate interagency planning process:

I would never have told the chiefs anything until about six months ahead and then I'd tell them all to rearrange their schedules [and that] I wanted a head count. Then I would have gotten the operational people in, and we would have gone over their head counts, and then I would have told them, "All right, this is your responsibility; this is your venue. I want you to make it safe like you would a sporting event" and maybe add a couple of people to it. And I would have had the operational people identify one operational person for every venue they had, and I would have said, "Now run that son of a bitch and call me when you get a problem, but don't call me till you have problems."

Coleman's ideas about Olympic preparations startled the OSE staff and other Olympics veterans. They believed that the Olympics, by virtue of its size and visibility, required security preparations that were qualitatively different from the preparations required for an event such as the Super Bowl or the World Series, and they dismissed out of hand Coleman's argument that the planning could be done in 6 or 7 months.

Embracing the Los Angeles Model

Sid Miles, Georgia's newly appointed commissioner of public safety, had reaffirmed Coleman's position as the state's Olympic security coordinator and made him the commanding officer of the state patrol. But Coleman chose not to openly fight the proposal in front of the OSSG, and the Atlanta public safety community decided to adopt the Los Angeles model.

In the wake of this decision, the OSSG was given the same responsibilities as the top-level planning group in Los Angeles. Commissioner of Public Safety Sid Miles and Atlanta Police Chief Eldrin Bell became the new co-chairs of the reformulated OSSG. Representatives from forty-odd federal, state, and local public safety agencies rounded out its membership.

The OSPCC, which law enforcement officials had formed as their alternative to the OSSG, was also pressed into the LA model. Its new function was to serve as the equivalent of the group of mid-level planners, who had overseen the work of the various specialized subcommittees in Los Angeles. W. J. Taylor, who had recently retired from the Atlanta Police Department and become an ACOG employee, was put in charge of the reformulated OSPCC. Stock Coleman was also a member of this group. The small office Bill Kelley had assembled to administer the DOJ grant to jump-start security planning was renamed the Integrated Planning Group (IPG) and given the task of providing staff support to the OSPCC. Nineteen subcommittees were created to focus on creating security plans for their specific areas of responsibility. (See Exhibit 12A-2 for a diagram of the new planning structure.)

The decision to reorganize the planning effort along the lines of the Los Angeles Olympics gave security planners a much needed boost. The FBI, OSE, and Bill Rathburn,

Exhibit 12A-2   The new Olympic Support Group planning structure

The state commissioner of public safety and the Atlanta police chief were the co-chairmen of the OSSG. The OSPCC was chaired first by W. J. Taylor and then by Major Jon Gordon of the Atlanta Police Department. Bill Kelley served as the IPG Administrative Coordinator. ACOG, Atlanta Committee for the Olympic Games; EOD, Explosive Ordnance Disposal; EMS, Emergency Medical Services; IPG, Integrated Planning Group; OSPCC, Olympic Security Planning and Coordination Committee; OSSG, Olympic Security Support Group.

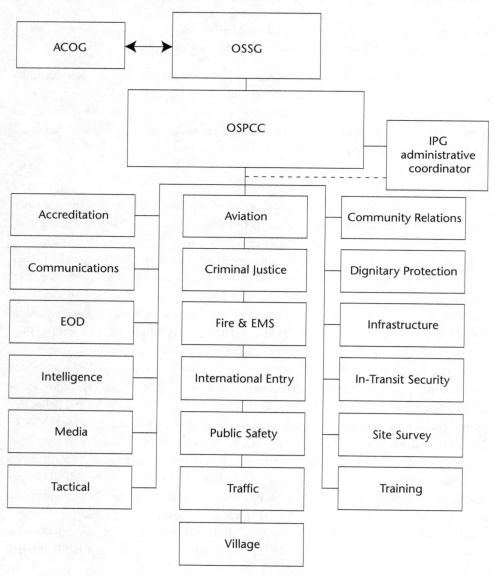

now director of security for ACOG, finally felt optimistic that Atlanta would get organized and develop the detailed security plans they believed were necessary. But this sense of optimism quickly began to disintegrate.

During summer 1993, Milton "Buddy" Nix, the newly appointed head of the Georgia Bureau of Investigation (GBI), the state's small investigative force, went to his first OSSG meeting. He was quite interested in how the group would approach its tasks. But according to Nix, "it became readily apparent that nothing was going to come out of that group: there was not going to be any substantive planning. It was primarily an opportunity to come together periodically for [ACOG] to pass out pins and mementos." [7]

Almost everyone who participated in the reorganized OSSG quickly reached the same conclusion; the "new" OSSG, in the words of David Maples, the FBI's Olympic coordinator, was "uncontrollable from the beginning." [8] In Maples's opinion, it was easy to diagnose the cause of the problem—the OSSG was too big. "In LA, you had about five [law enforcement representatives] on the equivalent of the OSSG," says Maples. "And that's where it ended because everybody realized that, really, once you get beyond about five or six or seven people, it's not a policymaking group anymore. It's a convention. . . . Here, it started with about 40 and went up to about 60. . . ."

To most law enforcement officials, however, it was hard to see how membership in the OSSG could possibly be limited to a dozen agencies, much less six. The state of Georgia was jurisdictionally very fragmented: the state had 159 counties, and many counties had both a police department and a sheriff's office. A total of 137 law enforcement agencies had jurisdiction over some portion of the Games, and they could not simply be ignored. In addition, approximately two dozen federal agencies insisted on having their own representatives at OSSG meetings. Under these circumstances, the limiting of the OSSG's initial membership to forty people seemed like an accomplishment.

The Olympic Security Planning and Coordinating Committee Falters

The OSPCC, which was supposed to supervise the actual planning done by the various subcommittees, was also encountering problems. Soon after the reformulated OSPCC started meeting, the FBI began to express concerns about the group's leadership. The FBI questioned whether W. J. Taylor should be the head of the OSPCC *after* he had retired from the Atlanta Police Department and joined ACOG.

According to David Maples, the FBI's coordinator for the Olympics and a veteran of every Olympic Games since 1984, "the question became, 'If this is a public safety structure,

[7] Interview with Director Milton "Buddy" Nix, Georgia Bureau of Investigation, 2000. Unless noted, subsequent quotations from Nix are also from this interview.

[8] Interview with David Maples, Federal Bureau of Investigation, 2000. Unless noted, subsequent quotations from Maples are also from this interview.

how did you have an employee of ACOG chairing your core committee, your core group?'" In his opinion, you didn't. "In no country I've ever been in has the organizing committee assumed that kind of leadership over government or over the police," says Maples. Maples made it clear that he believed a member of the Atlanta Police Department ought to be in charge of the OSPCC.

The Atlanta Police Department soon adopted this viewpoint as well. Chief Eldrin Bell announced that he wanted one of his close aides, Jon Gordon, to replace Taylor as the chairman of the OSPCC. Although Stock Coleman, a close friend of Taylor, was opposed, the Atlanta Police Department and the FBI carried the argument and forced Taylor out. Gordon became the new chairman of the OSPCC. Bell also put Gordon in charge of the Atlanta Police Department's internal planning.

Gordon inherited a troubled committee. Like the entity to which it reported, the OSPCC had started with a large membership and then gotten larger. But OSPCC had distinctive problems as well. While the Los Angeles planning managers had primarily been hands-on planners from agency planning offices, the OSPCC's members were almost all very high-ranking members of their respective agencies, often agency heads or deputies. Reflecting its origins as an alternative to the ACOG-controlled OSSG, it was not a group of hands-on planners. Indeed, many members of the OSPCC had so many other responsibilities that they could do little more than attend the OSPCC and subcommittee meetings. "The people who were assigned to this level from the departments were way too senior," says Maples. "You don't want a deputy chief, who can look at this ten minutes a month."

The OSPCC's subcommittees also suffered from their size and composition. Some of the subcommittees had such large memberships that they literally could not get through a complicated discussion. Any agency represented in the OSSG could choose to send a representative to any subcommittee. At first, some public safety agencies chose to send representatives to every subcommittee. It quickly became clear that while some of the subcommittees would probably do what they were supposed to do, others would do as little as possible or even nothing at all.

Gordon's task was further complicated by the fact that the city and the state made no real efforts to work out the OSPCC's problems. Stock Coleman, the state's Olympic security coordinator, preferred to push for the transfer of responsibilities from the OSPCC to the IPG, which was more responsive to him.[9] In theory, the IPG was supposed to provide staff support to the OSPCC and its subcommittees. In practice, Kelley, a savvy veteran of Georgia state politics with close personal ties to many of the key players involved in this effort, chafed at his assigned role supporting Gordon's OSPCC.

---

[9]Bill Kelley was both a personal acquaintance of Stock Coleman and a state employee.

The State Asserts Its Authority

As the deficiencies of the OSSG and OSPCC planning structure became increasingly apparent, Stock Coleman began to assert the state's authority over the planning process. At a September 1993 retreat, state Commissioner of Public Safety Sid Miles (Coleman's boss) informed Atlanta Police Chief Eldrin Bell that the state would take responsibility for providing security at all the venues on state-owned property. Chief Bell was visibly upset by this sudden announcement. The Atlanta Police Department had long been eager to take responsibility for as many venues as possible. This enthusiasm was fueled both by pride and by visions of Olympic gold—the more venues the Atlanta Police Department had responsibility for, the more money it could extract from ACOG. But in one fell swoop, the state had determined that it would take lead responsibility for providing the public safety presence for over half of the sixty-one Olympic venues. The city would be responsible for the Olympic Stadium and just three other physical venues.[10] (See Exhibit 12A-3 for a map of Atlanta and the primary venues.)

Federal officials were not worried about the state's decision to take the lead role as the public safety provider for the Games—that decision actually came as something of a relief.[11] However, federal officials were disturbed by what they saw as Coleman's efforts to take control of the planning effort. "In my opinion, he was an obstructionist because it wasn't just [having] a difference of opinion and then working with the group: he was actively working to do it his way," says Maples. "He wanted to be in charge, make no mistake about it."

Progress Is Made

Federal officials recognized that the problems with the OSSG and OSPCC created a vacuum that needed to be filled. In late 1993, David Maples, the FBI's Olympic coordinator, convened a meeting with key planners from the most important agencies, among them Jon Gordon of the Atlanta Police Department, Bill Kelley of IPG, Chris Bellavita of OSE, and representatives from the Conyers Police Department and the GBI, and suggested that this group needed to identify the essential planning tasks and make sure these got done. The formal OSPCC continued to meet, but this informal group soon became a kind of shadow OSPCC.

The existence of an informal planning group greatly facilitated the planning process. Despite the problems with the OSSG and the OSPCC and the growing divide between the city and the state, security planning was getting underway, albeit in a different way than expected. In theory, each subcommittee was supposed to produce a specific security plan for its area of responsibility; the OSPCC was then to take each of the subcommittees' plans and knit them into a single master security plan, which would in turn be approved by the OSSG.

---

[10]Atlanta would also take the lead role in directing traffic during the Games and in securing the marathon and cycling events.

[11]Federal officials believed that traffic management alone would stretch the Atlanta Police Department's capacity to its limits.

Exhibit 12A-3   Map of the Atlanta Olympic ring

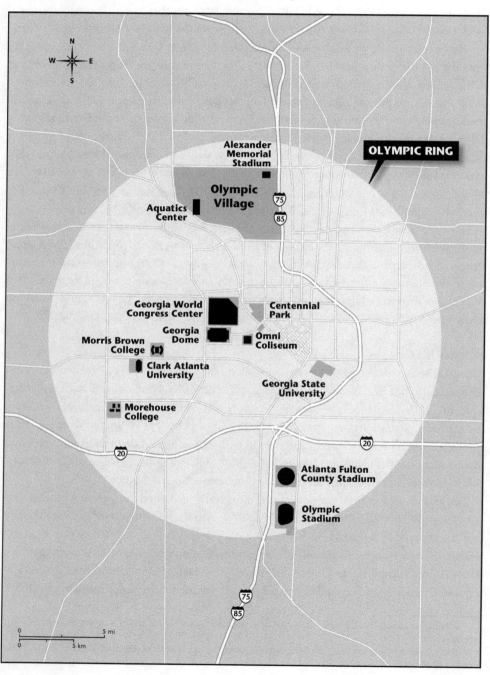

In practice, because many of the subcommittees were essentially stillborn, Gordon and his staff had to draw up a number of the subcommittee security plans on their own. These efforts were complemented by the work of the public safety agencies with the most responsibility for security at the Games—the city, the state, and the FBI, among others—and by the informal planning group first convened by David Maples. Although the process wasn't elegant, Gordon, Kelley, and other members of the informal planning group were identifying vulnerabilities, charting agency capacities, and beginning to develop plans for how agencies would interact during the Games.

Also in late 1993, Stock Coleman made a significant security proposal; he suggested that the FBI be the first responder to *any* major security crisis at a venue or sensitive site during the Olympics. "The state just did not have the assets to address everything that normally would be a state responsibility," explains FBI agent David Maples. The FBI, in contrast, was willing to deploy roughly a thousand officers and bring to Atlanta approximately a dozen heavily armed Special Weapons and Tactics (SWAT) teams. Under Coleman's proposal, if a hostage-taking situation or an incident of similar severity unfolded during the Games, the FBI, not the city or the state, would respond first with FBI personnel. Both the OSPCC and FBI headquarters endorsed this unusual decision.[12]

An Olympic Park Raises New Concerns

In fall 1993, just a week away from city elections, ACOG president Billy Payne unveiled a proposal to create a new Olympic park in a 70-acre swath of downtown Atlanta near the Georgia World Congress Center. (See Exhibit 12A-3 for a map of the Atlanta Olympic ring.) Payne saw the park, which he dubbed Centennial Olympic Park, as a way to create "a magnificent gathering place so our visitors can mix with Southerners and experience firsthand the friendliness of the American South."[13] The plan was immediately embraced by the various mayoral candidates and hailed by the editorial board of the *Atlanta Journal-Constitution*: "This is the missing piece, what Olympic leaders call their 'legacy' to Atlanta. This is what the city's Olympic effort needed."[14]

In addition to providing a place where all Atlantans could gather to share the Olympic spirit, the park would also serve a useful crowd-control function. With its many athletic

---

[12]The FBI worked out detailed memorandums of understanding with both the city and the state that described exactly what circumstances would trigger an FBI takeover of the response effort.

[13]Quoted in "Olympic Facelift: A Master Plan for Downtown; Payne Proposes 'Olympic Legacy,' New Park, New Downtown? It's a Cinderella Tale: Shabby Area May Get Magic Makeover," *Atlanta Journal-Constitution,* November 19, 1993, A1.

[14]"Olympic Watch; Countdown to the Atlanta Games; Centennial Park: Politicians Enthusiastic about Idea, Downtown Development Wins Kudos from Leaders," *Atlanta Journal-Constitution,* November 20, 1993, B10; quotation from "The Missing Olympic Piece," *Atlanta Journal-Constitution,* November 21, 1993, F8. The size of the park was later reduced significantly.

venues, law enforcement officials believed that downtown Atlanta would draw as many as a million visitors during peak periods of the Games. Such huge crowds would overload downtown streets and create transportation nightmares. Centennial Park would be a useful safety valve, a place where people could congregate between athletic events.

But the park presented new security challenges as well. As the major gathering place for the public during the Games, the park would be a natural target for a terrorist attack. And although it was possible to set up metal detectors and secure the athletic venues, it would be difficult, if not impossible, to secure the park. Setting up metal detectors would only push large crowds into the streets where they would still be vulnerable to attack and disrupt traffic to boot. Like the Metropolitan Atlanta Rapid Transportation Authority (MARTA), Atlanta's subway system and another source of great concern to law enforcement officials, Centennial Park would have to be secured in other ways.

Assembling an Adequate Security Force

By the end of 1993, ACOG, federal, state, and local officials were shifting their focus from the planning process to the actual planning itself. ACOG had identified all sixty-one athletic venues for the Games, and the city of Atlanta and the state had determined who would provide the primary law enforcement presence at each venue. ACOG and the law enforcement community had agreed that each athletic venue would have a commander from ACOG and a commander from the law enforcement agency with primary jurisdiction over that venue. ACOG would enforce the house rules, work the metal detectors, and check bags, while law enforcement personnel would protect the perimeter and be on hand to make arrests. Now that the venues were identified and functions were being developed, ACOG and federal, state, and local public safety officials began to focus on their resource needs.

In early 1994, Stock Coleman asked the GBI to provide a venue commander for the Georgia World Congress Center, Atlanta's (state-owned) convention center. ACOG intended to put five athletic venues (which would host eleven athletic events) in the large wing of the World Congress Center. The small wing would house the International Broadcast Center, which would be the base of operations for the 15,000-plus journalists expected to attend the Games. GBI Director Buddy Nix asked agent Mike Eason to take responsibility for this task.

Eason started work that spring. "I met with Major Sutton [who was Stock Coleman's deputy], and they gave me some drawings, and they had some very rough figures about the staffing," recalls Eason. "At that point, I sat down and did some things—worked up some [staffing] numbers and things like that. I soon saw that I was going to be very much more involved in this thing." [15] In fact, Eason was soon working full-time on preparing plans for the World Congress Center. He eventually moved into the office of Coleman's planning team,

---

[15] Interview with Michael Eason, Georgia Bureau of Investigation, 2000. Unless noted, subsequent quotations from Eason are also from this interview.

where he joined another GBI agent, Jim Duff, who was taking a large role in developing the state's security plans.

Coleman, Eason, and others also started meeting with other state agencies to update them on the status of the state planning effort and to give them some sense of what resources Coleman and his team would need during the Olympics. By the end of the year, Eason was working up staffing numbers for all state venues.

Coleman believed that the state of Georgia had sufficient resources to carry out its security obligations during the Games. If state law enforcement officials needed additional security personnel, Coleman believed he could turn to the Georgia National Guard for additional resources. However, ACOG and the Atlanta Police Department weren't so sanguine about their staffing resources; ACOG's efforts to secure additional resources over the course of the next 2 years would have a major effect on the nature of the federal government's involvement in the Games.

By spring 1994, ACOG was acutely concerned about the overall number of security personnel available for the Games. Since the beginning of the planning process, there had been a general agreement that approximately 30,000 security personnel would be needed to secure the Games. But as Bill Rathburn, ACOG security chief, tallied up the number of security personnel available in early 1994, he found that reaching that number would be virtually impossible. Metropolitan Atlanta had a total of approximately 2,500 law enforcement officers; perhaps half of those officers could work on the Olympics.[16] The state of Georgia could conceivably bring as many as 5,000 law enforcement officers to metro Atlanta for the Games.[17] And federal law enforcement agencies could be expected to contribute another 2,000 officers, bringing the total number of law enforcement officers who were available to provide security during the Games to approximately 8,000. ACOG, meanwhile, planned to use about 2,500 private guards and 1,000 law enforcement officers who had volunteered to serve as ACOG security guards to form the backbone of its security effort.[18] They would be supplemented by some 12,500 civilian security volunteers, bringing ACOG's total security force to about 16,000. Together ACOG and law enforcement appeared able to muster 23,000 public safety personnel, 7,000 people fewer than the desired number.[19]

---

[16]Interview with Bill Rathburn, director of security, Atlanta Committee for the Olympic Games, 2000. Unless noted, subsequent quotations and observations from Rathburn are also from this interview.

[17]The state had a total of roughly 9,000 law enforcement officers. Its forces included roughly 7,000 corrections officers, 1,000 state patrol officers, 300 GBI agents, 300 Department of Natural Resources officers, 300 Department of Transportation officers, and some officers from a handful of smaller agencies.

[18]Borg-Warner, the nation's largest private security firm and an Olympic sponsor, had originally committed to provide roughly 5,000 security guards to ACOG; however, soon after making this commitment Borg-Warner began sending signals that it would be hard-pressed to provide even 2,500 private security guards.

[19]These numbers were not as reassuring as they looked. During the 1984 Summer Olympic Games in Los Angeles, private security guards had performed poorly. The 12,500 volunteers ACOG intended to recruit for the Atlanta Games were an unknown; many law enforcement officers worried that once a large number of volunteers learned that they would not be working in venues, they would simply leave. Finally, it was not clear exactly how many law enforcement officials would be available to assist with security during the Games.

ACOG saw only one solution to its security personnel shortfall—the military. From the earliest days of the planning effort, ACOG had envisioned a large Georgia National Guard presence at the Games. But as Rathburn and his staffed crunched the numbers, they became increasingly convinced that a large active-duty U.S. military presence would be the *sine qua non* of a successful Games. Although Rathburn knew that the military could not make arrests or perform law enforcement duties, he believed the very presence of a large number of soldiers would serve as a powerful deterrent to wrong-doing.

In April 1994, ACOG President and CEO Billy Payne wrote a letter to Ann Brooks, the head of the DOD OSE, formally requesting 8,000 soldiers to help ACOG provide security at the Games. OSE was not favorably inclined toward this request—it had supported every large-scale international sporting event in the United States since the 1980 Winter Olympic Games in Lake Placid and had never before provided more than 1,000 military personnel. OSE viewed ACOG as a private group putting on what was ultimately a private event, and the fact that ACOG provided no detailed justification for why it needed 8,000 soldiers did nothing to help its case. Still, OSE passed ACOG's request up the chain of command at the DOD.

The City and State React

ACOG's request for soldiers caught the city of Atlanta off-guard; the organizing committee had not consulted with either the city or the state, much less with the OSSG or OSPCC, before making its request. The Atlanta Police Department was itself planning to request some military backup; it saw ACOG's "stealth" request as a preemptive attempt to lay claim to the U.S. military resources available for the Games.

Stock Coleman, the state's Olympic coordinator, also reacted negatively to the news of ACOG's request. "Why do you want to put 8,000 soldiers on the street? What are they going to do?" he asks. "They can't direct traffic. They can't interact with people. You want to give the look of an armed camp?" Coleman was not averse to having the Georgia National Guard, which had extensive experience working with state law enforcement agencies, provide support to the state, but he thought the idea of bringing in the active-duty U.S. military personnel in large numbers was "crazy."

Others thought so as well. When representatives of the uniformed services met with Bill Rathburn, ACOG security chief, after receiving ACOG's request, they seemed skeptical, if not dismissive. However, neither Rathburn nor ACOG's lobbyists at the law firm of King & Spalding were deterred. They continued to push for U.S. military assistance, even as the attention of other public safety officials turned to other topics.

Problems Emerge, 1995

By the end of 1994, despite some signs of progress, a growing number of public safety officials believed the problems with the OSSG were disrupting the actual security planning.

"Certain areas like the Village—physical security of the athletes' village—were really coming together well, and other areas—like communications—were just floundering," says John Awtrey, the head of OSE's on-the-ground operation in Atlanta.[20] The state, city, and ACOG were developing their own security plans for the various venues, but it was not clear how they would communicate and coordinate their activities when the Games occurred.

Moreover, the amount of work done by subcommittees varied widely. Some, such as the Explosive Ordnance Disposal (EOD) subcommittee, were proceeding smoothly. Preparations to create an interagency bomb management center were well underway. Arrangements were being made to create approximately thirty explosive diagnostic teams that would circulate throughout the various athletic venues and other important locations, such as Centennial Olympic Park, to help ACOG and law enforcement officials ascertain if abandoned bags should be "disrupted" by EOD teams.

But preparations for other specialized functions, such as securing airspace during the Games, seemed to be going nowhere at all. As ACOG's Bill Rathburn puts it:

I don't know how much time I wasted on the issue of air space restrictions. It was a foregone conclusion, I think, with most people that we would have restricted air space over the Olympic sites. Well, it was kind of left to a sergeant in the state patrol to handle this issue. And for whatever reason or reasons—and I can only speculate on what they might be—he decided that it was OK to have banner towers and sightseeing planes and things like that in the restricted air space. I mean [it was] absolutely incredible.[21]

Notwithstanding limited areas of cooperation, it was clear that relations among the city, the state, and ACOG had broken down. Coleman did not hide his lack of respect for the OSPCC or his dislike for OSE and the FBI. Relations between the state and ACOG were also strained. According to Michael Eason, GBI agent, "It got to the point where we had venue plans of where we were going to staff people, and they [ACOG] were supposed to have plans of where they were going to staff people, and they wouldn't show us their plans until we showed them our plans—that sort of stuff."

How Serious a Problem?

The cumulative effect of these planning difficulties was harder to gauge. Federal officials were particularly worried about the status of the state's preparations. Coleman maintained such tight control of state preparations that it was hard to know exactly what the state was doing. Ann Brooks, the head of OSE, was amazed and concerned about what she saw as Coleman's adversarial stance toward the other principal actors in the security planning process. "I got worried when Stock Coleman became so . . . disruptive to the process," says Brooks.

---

[20]Interview with John Awtrey, DOD Office of Special Events, 2000. Unless noted, subsequent quotations from Awtrey are also from this interview.

[21]Not until much later in the planning process was this decision reversed.

State legislators saw a different problem. During the 1994 legislative session and again in early 1995, the chairman of the General Assembly's Public Safety Committee introduced legislation to place all responsibility for Olympic planning in the hands of Public Safety Commissioner Sid Miles and, by extension, in the hands of his chosen Olympic security coordinator, Stock Coleman. Although the bill never made it out of committee, the Atlanta Police Department was outraged by the proposed state takeover.

Others believed that, as messy and slow as the process was, progress was being made. "I thought it was all going pretty well," says Chris Bellavita, the OSE consultant. "I mean, basically planning an Olympics—you need to secure the athletes when they get to the airport; you need to provide them with a way to get to the village and the venues. You need the venues to be secure, and you need the village to be secure. That's about it." [22] Although Bellavita acknowledged that preparations for certain key areas had not progressed very far, he believed state and local agencies had the expertise to draw up the necessary plans if only they could work together.

Bill Rathburn took a pessimistic view. He believed that the breakdown of the OSSG and the OSPCC was a serious problem. Instead of a joint interagency planning effort, security planning had fragmented into separate planning efforts by the state, the city, and various federal agencies. In Rathburn's opinion, some entity needed to make decisions and coordinate the activities of the agencies with primary law enforcement responsibility during the Games—in short, something that could serve the function that the OSSG was originally supposed to have served.

In late 1994, Rathburn quietly contacted the heads of the law enforcement agencies most important to the Olympic security effort—the Georgia Department of Public Safety, the FBI, the Atlanta Police Department, the Fulton County Police Department, the Fulton County Sheriff's Office, the DeKalb County Police Department, and the Conyers Police Department—and invited them to meet over breakfast for an informal discussion of how things were going. By early 1995, the group was meeting weekly. When Marv Smalley, the OSE's law enforcement liaison, got wind of the existence of this group, he dubbed it "the Secret Gang of Seven."

Although the OSSG continued to meet, the Secret Gang of Seven took on many of its functions. [23] Much of the group's work involved simply approving the security plans being prepared for the various venues, but the simple fact of meeting weekly did create a certain

---

[22] Interview with Chris Bellavita, DOD Office of Special Events, 2000. Unless noted, subsequent quotations from Bellavita are also from this interview.

[23] Although the membership of the group did grow, Rathburn defended its small size—sometimes excluding representatives from public safety agencies making major contributions to the security effort. Soon after the Secret Gang of Seven had been formed, Rathburn asked Vernon Keenan, the GBI deputy director of investigations, to leave a meeting when he arrived uninvited. Keenan left, angry that ACOG, a private entity, once again seemed to be making decisions about public safety resources.

sense of familiarity, if not trust, among the members of the group. Workable, if not always smooth, relationships among the various members were being constructed.

Meanwhile, some state law enforcement officials were developing a darker view of ACOG. As GBI Deputy Director of Investigations Vernon Keenan puts it:

[I]t became very plain that many of the security people with ACOG, they're looking at saving money because that's going to be a bigger bonus for them at the end of the Olympics. It doesn't have anything to do with the mission; it has to do with [the fact that] this is a money-making operation for them. Here they are, taking the role of government officials, and this is a money-making operation![24]

Not all state law enforcement officials were surprised by this discovery. "This is not a security affair," says Bill Kelley, the head of the IPG. "It's not a war. It's not a mobilization. Security is the butt-heel of the event. This is about athletes and people making megabucks. And they look at cops as dispensable servants. They do not look at them as in charge of the event."

The Atlanta Committee for the Olympic Games Angles for the Military

While Bill Rathburn was pleased at the progress that the Gang of Seven was making, the upper echelons of ACOG were becoming increasingly concerned about how it would provide—and pay for—security for the Games. As 1995 got underway, ACOG and its lobbyists at King & Spaulding redoubled their efforts to win substantial military assistance.

ACOG's ace in the hole was Georgia's senior U.S. senator, Sam Nunn (D-Ga.), the ranking minority member of the Senate Armed Services Committee. Nunn and his staff were naturally eager to do everything they could to make the Atlanta Games a success, and King & Spaulding made sure that they were kept fully up to date on ACOG's needs.

ACOG also worked hard to cultivate good relations with the military. It had hired a retired three-star army general, Gen. Michael Spigelmire, to oversee its venue planning effort, and to OSE's annoyance, Spigelmire took full advantage of his military connections. "Myself and one of the other people I worked with, our job was to go out to the military installations and just find out who the players were and kind of let them know what's coming up," says Marv Smalley, the OSE's law enforcement liaison. "And almost to a point, Spigelmire had been there before us . . . touching base, making contacts, renewing old acquaintances, and identifying resources—just making himself known."[25]

Ann Brooks believed OSE was being squeezed to be more openhanded with ACOG. Nevertheless, she felt confident that she could resist the pressure. Brooks believed that her efforts to defend her budget and to force ACOG to pare back its troop request were so reasonable that even Senator Nunn's staff would accept her positions.

---

[24]Interview with Vernon Keenan, Georgia Bureau of Investigation, 2000. Unless noted, subsequent quotations from Keenan are also from this interview.

[25]Interview with Marv Smalley, DOD Office of Special Events, 2000. Unless noted, subsequent quotations from Smalley are also from this interview.

But Brooks was unaware of the full extent of the resistance she had stirred up. Her astringent demeanor and her insistence on maintaining a tight grip on OSE resources had annoyed many Georgia law enforcement officials. These officials also believed that to gain leverage over the planning effort, OSE had made big promises it was now unwilling to keep. ACOG's leadership echoed these criticisms and together with some state officials concluded that they would be better off without Brooks. They quietly let their desire for a change be known.

Meanwhile, Brooks's tough line seemed to be paying off. By the end of August 1995, Rathburn and OSE had negotiated ACOG's troop request down from 8,000 to approximately 4,400 soldiers. OSE and the Atlanta Police Department had also reached an agreement on how many soldiers the Atlanta Police Department would need during the Games to supplement its force—1,097 soldiers, mainly military police officers who could help direct traffic.

Brooks passed the revised troop requests of ACOG and the Atlanta Police Department up her chain of command, as well as to Senator Nunn's office.[26] However, there was no immediate response to her request. "The package kind of went on hold," says Brooks.

The Pentagon Takes Notice

When OSE forwarded a draft of its plans for the Olympics and its military resources request to Secretary of Defense William Perry in late summer 1995, the department's top officials took notice. Brooks had regularly reported on her activities, but OSE, which was just one of many entities within the Office of the Secretary of Defense (OSD), had not really captured the department's attention. One of the reasons for the newfound attentiveness of the DOD top officials was the sheer size of the Olympic request—4,000-plus soldiers. A deployment that large invariably raised questions about how the command and control structure would work.

The second reason was the intersection of two hitherto separate concerns: the well-established fear of terrorism and new worries about the possible proliferation of chemical, biological, and nuclear weapons, WMDs. The intersection of these two concerns gave birth to a new fear—catastrophic terrorism. After the Persian Gulf War, U.S. intelligence agencies had uncovered disturbing evidence that Iraq had been engaged in an elaborate effort to develop WMDs. To informed policymakers, the possibility that a rogue state could threaten the United States with such weapons seemed increasingly plausible.

A variation on this danger materialized in spring 1995 as OSE was negotiating troop numbers with ACOG and with the Atlanta Police Department. On March 20, 1995, Aum Shinrikyo, a Japanese religious cult, carried out an attack on the Tokyo subway system using

---

[26]The state refused to submit a troop request to OSE. Coleman preferred to work directly with the adjutant general of the Georgia National Guard, Gen. William Bland.

the nerve gas sarin. More than 1,000 people were injured; 12 were killed. The attack marked the first time a terrorist group had attempted to use a WMD to cause death on a massive scale.

The threat of a large-scale terrorist attack did not center entirely on foreign terrorists. On April 19, 1995, 1 month after the Aum Shinrikyo attack, a rental truck packed with explosives blew up in front of the Alfred P. Murrah Federal Building in Oklahoma City. The explosion destroyed most of the nine-story building, killed 168 people, and injured more than 500. The FBI, which had been focused on the threats posed by international terrorist groups or "the individual nut case," now had to take into account the potential dangers posed by domestic militias.[27]

Attention Turns to Atlanta

Now that the Olympics were only a year away, DOD officials realized that the DOD was being asked to commit a large amount of resources to what could well be the most high-profile event of the world in 1996. This realization was very unsettling. "It doesn't take you long when you finally sit down and focus on it to say, 'Oh, this could be a very big problem,'" says then Deputy Secretary of Defense John White. "As you looked at that, you thought, 'Boy, I need a command structure. I need to put the money some place. I need to make sure we've got some logic in terms of how we're doing things.'"[28]

OSE had considered the question of what the chain of command should be, and when OSE had passed along the revised request for troops that it had negotiated with ACOG, it included organization charts explaining a proposed chain of command. Essentially, OSE planned to coordinate troop activities with the Georgia National Guard. The Georgia National Guard would command all of the National Guard troops, both Georgian and out-of-state; active-duty U.S. military colonels under the supervision of Ann Brooks would command the active-duty military officers.

But this solution did not have much appeal in the upper echelons of the DOD. If the DOD was going to be accountable for what happened in Atlanta, it wanted authority over the military assets that would be used there. OSE had never supervised more than a thousand troops before; White felt certain that OSE was not up to the much bigger command challenges posed by the Atlanta Olympics.

The fact that OSE was located in the OSD also posed potential problems. Because of OSE's location, politicians who wanted to overrule OSE's decisions could simply call OSD directly. As the Games drew closer and requests for assistance escalated, the last thing White

---

[27]"Olympic Weekly; 448 Days; Security; Team Rethinking Plans in Wake of Oklahoma Bombing," *Atlanta Journal-Constitution,* April 28, 1995, B3.

[28]Interview with John White, deputy secretary of defense, 2000. Unless noted, subsequent quotations from White are also from this interview.

wanted to deal with were requests for favors from powerful politicians such as Sen. Sam Nunn (D-Ga.) or Representative Newt Gingrich (R-Ga.), Speaker of the House of Representatives. White needed to find a way both to address the command issues that would arise from having several thousand troops in the field and provide a little insulation from political pressures.

Bringing in the Army

White did not have to look far for such an arrangement. Atlanta was already the home of a major army command, U.S. Forces Command (FORSCOM), the headquarters for the Third U.S. Army. White thought highly of FORSCOM's commander and considered him more fit than OSE to command large numbers of troops. Putting FORSCOM in charge of the military support effort seemed to White to have clear advantages: "They have a field structure, and they're organized, and they communicate. . . . So I have a command-and-control system; I already have an organization in place; I have people who work with other people; I have a system of communication; I've got all the stuff I need. I don't have to *ad hoc*, which I'd have to do if I was going to do it in something like the special events office."

Putting FORSCOM in charge would also have political advantages. With FORSCOM in command, White would be able to tell politicians and officials that decisions about military assistance for the Games were being made not in the OSD but in the Office of the Director of Military Support.

In August 1995, the DOD announced that it was giving FORSCOM operational authority over all U.S. military assets that would be used during the Games. The OSE was stunned by this decision. However, there was nothing that Ann Brooks could do. OSE would continue to support the Games, but it would no longer be the DOD's lead support agency.

The Atlanta Police Department was surprised and dismayed by the military shakeup as well. So was Bill Rathburn, ACOG's head of security. Rathburn had not been consulted about ACOG's efforts to ease Brooks out in the hope of getting a more open-handed replacement. And although working with Brooks could at times be difficult, Rathburn did not relish the prospect of working with the army.

Most state law enforcement officials were also surprised, even stunned, by the Pentagon's reorganization of the Olympic support effort. The possibility that FORSCOM, an active-duty military command, might take control of the effort had never even crossed state law enforcement officials' minds. To most law enforcement officials, it was a dismaying turn of events. "We routinely work with the National Guard; we've been on major civil disturbance operations where they've had 2,000 troops in the field that we worked with," says Vernon Keenan, the GBI's deputy director of investigations. "That's why, from our perspective, it's very important that law enforcement support come from the National Guard, which has a very clear understanding of the role of local and state law enforcement."

Another Change Is Sought

Meanwhile, another coalition had been forming around the common goal of ousting Stock Coleman, the state's Olympic security coordinator. In early 1995, a group of law enforcement officials asked Roland Vaughan, the former police chief of Conyers, Georgia (now the Conyers city manager), to relay their concerns about Coleman to A. D. Frazier, ACOG's chief operating officer, and to ask Frazier to take up the issue with Zell Miller, governor of Georgia. The FBI also began to lobby vigorously for Coleman's ouster. Even the GBI offered some circumspect criticisms of the current state planning effort; a 1995 memo to the Governor's Office even went so far as to recommend the creation of a new state entity whose entire *raison d'être* would be to plan and coordinate the state security effort for the Olympics.

It was not clear that this push to oust Coleman would succeed. Coleman seemed very entrenched; some believed that because Coleman's brother was the chairman of the Appropriations Committee in the General Assembly he was unassailable. Neither Governor Zell Miller nor Coleman's immediate superior, Public Safety Commissioner Sid Miles, had shown any inclination to rein Coleman in, much less oust him. In addition, Coleman seemed to have a good relationship with Billy Payne, ACOG's president.

Yet even Coleman's supporters believed that the state planning effort had to change, that it could not continue to be the self-contained, tightly held concern it had been under Coleman. A growing number of influential participants and observers had come to believe that state security preparations had to become an all-encompassing effort. They believed that to go into the operational phase of the Games without having comprehensive state security plans and a clear sense of how the state would interact with ACOG and with federal and city public safety officials would amount to courting disaster.

Public or Private?

Meanwhile, Bill Rathburn was worried about the Centennial Olympic Park. The park had originally been envisioned as a safety valve for the crowds drawn to downtown by the many athletic venues at the Georgia World Congress Center. However, the organizing committee's changing plans for the park had made it a major destination in its own right; ACOG had decided to allow its five largest corporate sponsors to create elaborate pavilions there, thus creating a theme park–like environment. Rathburn worried that the huge crowds the park was expected to attract would cause traffic disruptions if members of the public dashed back and forth across the streets surrounding the park. The result might well be a logistical breakdown that would prevent athletes from arriving at their venues on time.

In an interview with the *Atlanta Journal-Constitution* in early September 1995, Rathburn proposed that Centennial Park be fenced off. Rathburn also suggested that Olympic sponsors

474   *Anticipating Disaster*

and VIPs would have special access to the park. "This will not be a public park," said Rathburn. "There will be conditions of admission." [29]

The outcry was immediate. The *Atlanta Journal-Constitution* recalled ACOG chief Billy Payne's original conception of the park as a place for visitors "to mix with Southerners and experience firsthand the friendliness of the American South" and lambasted Rathburn for taking the view that "visitors must be protected from those friendly Southerners—especially if they are not well-heeled enough or lucky enough to have tickets to the sporting events." It called on Payne to "get Rathburn straightened out." [30] Payne quickly announced that Centennial Park would be open to the public.

ACOG could ill afford another spat with the city. Little if any progress had been made on how ACOG would reimburse the city for the extra services the city would provide during the Games, and by late 1995, the city was making it clear that ACOG would suffer from its stonewalling. That fall, the city announced its intention to issue licenses for street vendors to operate around Centennial Park. This outraged the IOC, which zealously guarded the marketing of the Olympic name and feared the vendors would sully the Olympic image. As the Games drew nearer, ACOG's relationship with the city seemed likely to worsen.

The tense relationship between the city and ACOG's top leadership contrasted with Coleman's apparently good relationship with ACOG's higher-ups, President and CEO Billy Payne and Chief Operating Office A. D. Frazier. Unlike the city, the state had taken no steps to draw up a contract. "The city was looking for somebody to pay their bills," says Coleman. "The state took the [position] that they were responsible for the safety and well-being of the visitors. . . ." Yet, despite the absence of a contract, state law enforcement officials assumed that ACOG would provide basic support functions such as paying overtime for state law enforcement personnel involved in security for the Games and providing food, housing, and transportation.

The Vice President's Visit

In late November 1995, Vice President Al Gore arrived in Atlanta and stepped into this feverish environment. One day in Atlanta was enough to convince him that disaster was imminent unless the federal government poured resources into Georgia and took control of the effort. Flying back to Washington, Gore hit on a solution—Atlanta needed a federal Olympic "czar," someone who would take overall responsibility for security arrangements at the Games and who would have the authority to make sure that all the agencies involved did what needed to be done.

---

[29]Quoted in "Building Fences; Barrier Will Limit Size of Crowds at Park," *Atlanta Journal-Constitution*, September 15, 1995, A1.

[30]"Open Park in Spirit of Olympics," *Atlanta Journal-Constitution*, September 18, 1995, A6.

Although word of Gore's reaction to the Olympic planning effort reached Atlanta quickly, law enforcement agencies were not aware of Gore's proposed solution to the problem. The GBI continued to believe that the best way to address the state's planning problems would be to create a new interagency entity, "an organization that [in the words of Vernon Keenan, the GBI's deputy director of investigations] was above pettiness . . . an organization that was going to exist to get the mission done and everything else was secondary." However, GBI had circumspectly suggested the creation of such an entity before, to a resounding silence.

At the end of 1995, it was clear that if changes were made they would have to be made quickly. The Centennial Olympic Games would formally begin with a grand opening ceremony in the new Olympic Stadium in just 7 months, on July 19, 1996.

Security Preparations for the 1996 Centennial Olympic Games (B): Seeking a Structural Fix

Vice President Al Gore believed a substantial increase in federal resources, overseen by a federal Olympic "czar" on the ground in Atlanta, would be necessary to ensure the safety of the Games.[1] Gore first asked Thomas "Mack" McLarty, President Bill Clinton's former chief of staff, if he would take on this job. But McLarty declined, saying he didn't believe he had the security expertise that the federal Olympic "czar" would need. Gore next asked Deputy Attorney General Jamie Gorelick if she could find an appropriate person for the assignment. Gorelick eventually decided to ask Gilmore Childers, who had been the lead prosecutor in the World Trade Center bombing trial; Childers enthusiastically accepted this assignment.

In early January, Childers went to Washington, D.C., for several weeks to prepare for his relocation to Atlanta. In Washington, Childers discovered that although there was a general sense of what his mission in Atlanta was ("Mack" McLarty told him his job was "basically to make the Games safe"[2]), no one had a very clear idea of exactly what he was supposed to do. Childers didn't have a very clear idea either. He did conclude, however, that he could not parachute into Atlanta and take over the security planning process. "I couldn't imagine that a bunch of folks in Atlanta, Georgia and other parts of Georgia were going to take kindly to having someone being imposed upon them from above in Washington—and by the way what is worse is that this guy is actually from New York," says Childers.

Childers and Gorelick ultimately settled on a different approach. "[W]e sort of decided that this 'czar' idea is not the right way to go and that the right way to go in is to go in very softly and quietly and not as somebody who is in charge," says Childers. This was not just a tactical choice. Childers felt that he had no authority to do more; he could not order state or local governments to do anything.

Childers did have one major source of power—access to the federal government's checkbook. But because his mission was somehow to save the Games from disaster by providing whatever federal resources were needed, Childers felt he couldn't easily threaten to withhold money. Consequently, he decided to go in quietly and conduct himself more like a facilitator than a "czar."

---

[1] Several participants in the security planning process believed that this was just the conclusion that ACOG had wanted Gore to reach. "To say, 'Oh, Gore came down here and saw trouble in River City'—that's false," says Bill Kelley, the head of the Integrated Planning Group (IPG.) "There were hundreds of people working to make that happen. . . . That really does not capture . . . what was going on or the sophistication of ACOG [and its lobbyists]. They saw a way to make this occur. . . ." Interview with Bill Kelley, fellow, National Justice Institute, 2000. Unless noted, subsequent quotations from Kelley are also from this interview.

[2] Interview with Gilmore Childers, the Clinton administration's Olympic "czar," 2000. Unless noted, subsequent quotations from Childers are also from this interview.

Up and Out

In early January, a delegation of federal law enforcement and government officials met with Governor Zell Miller to urge him to remove Stock Coleman from his position as head of the state-level planning effort. In addition, the White House called Miller to express its deep concerns about the state of the planning process.

The White House intervention proved decisive. In mid-January, Governor Miller called Gary McConnell, the head of the Georgia Emergency Management Agency (GEMA), into his office and asked him how he thought the Olympic preparations were going. As the head of the OSPCC infrastructure subcommittee, McConnell was well-positioned to answer this question. "I said, 'Governor, do you really want to know?'" McConnell recalls. "And he said, 'Yeah, I want to know.' And I told him what I thought the problems were. He kind of laughed and he said, 'Well, I'm going to give you a chance to fix all that.'"[3]

On January 19, 1996, Governor Miller put McConnell in charge of the Georgia security planning effort. Stock Coleman was "promoted" and put in charge of security for the Olympic torch. Three days later, Governor Miller signed an executive order that created a new state entity, the State Olympic Law Enforcement Command (SOLEC), and placed the twenty-nine state agencies with responsibility for the Games under SOLEC's command. SOLEC would be responsible for both the final security preparations and for the operations of all state agencies during the Games. Governor Miller made Gary McConnell SOLEC's chief of staff and de facto head.[4] Miller's executive order gave SOLEC the legal authority to draw on all of Georgia's law enforcement resources for the Atlanta Games; the knowledge that McConnell was close to the governor gave McConnell additional informal clout. McConnell had received what Coleman had always wanted—a formal, unified command.[5]

Reaction to McConnell's Appointment

McConnell was something of an unknown to the people most involved in security planning for the Olympics. Like many agency heads, McConnell had carried out his agency's Olympic obligations while trying to stay clear of conflict and making sure that neither he nor his agency could be blamed for the increasingly obvious problems afflicting the Olympic Security Support Group (OSSG).

Nevertheless, most people involved in the planning process were relieved at the change in command. "I thought it was the salvation of the state's effort," says Federal Bureau of

---

[3]Interview with Director Gary McConnell, Georgia Emergency Management Agency, 2000. Unless noted, subsequent quotations from McConnell are also from this interview.

[4]The executive order also created a SOLEC advisory board that consisted of Sid Miles, the head of the Georgia Department of Public Safety; Buddy Nix, the head of GBI; and William Bland, the adjutant general of the Georgia National Guard.

[5]SOLEC would not, however, exercise any command authority over the Atlanta Police Department or over city agencies.

Investigation (FBI) agent David Maples.[6] "Coleman was such a disruptive force that everybody was sort of pleased. They were willing to give Gary more opportunity than they would have if he had been put in under different circumstances," says Marv Smalley, Office of Special Events (OSE) law enforcement liaison.[7]

Others had a more nuanced reaction. "Not in terms of the Coleman removal but in terms of the governor getting interested in doing something, I thought it was about time," says Bill Kelley, the head of the Integrated Planning Group (IPG). "My reaction was that organizations are artifacts," says OSE facilitator Chris Bellavita. "I want to know who the people involved are. When the organization changed, the question I had in my mind was, 'Okay, what happens to [Mike] Eason and [Jim] Duff,' "[8] the two Georgia Bureau of Investigation (GBI) agents who had done the bulk of the actual hands-on planning under Coleman.

Gilmore Childers arrived in Atlanta the same day Governor Miller created SOLEC. Soon thereafter, Childers met McConnell for the first time. McConnell greeted Childers warmly but with a warning. "I think Gil and my conversation went something like, 'Yeah, we're glad to have you down here; we want to welcome you to our state; and the last time the federal government came here and tried to take over, you were not welcome and we still remember it,' " says McConnell. But by the end of the evening, Childers and McConnell had come to an understanding; Childers's primary responsibility would be to facilitate the flow of federal resources into Atlanta.

The State Olympic Law Enforcement Command Starts Work

Now that the responsibility for the Olympic Games was his, McConnell moved quickly to ascertain the state's readiness. One of his first steps was to sit down with Jim Duff and Mike Eason, the two GBI agents who had drawn up the security plans for most of the venues. Duff and Eason gave McConnell a candid report on the planning effort, in Eason's words, "what needed to be done; who was good; who was bad as far as planners. . . ."[9]

SOLEC faced huge challenges. In 6 months, Georgia would be bringing 5,500 state officers (from twenty-nine agencies) into metropolitan Atlanta to support the Games. Many of the logistics of this deployment had yet to be worked out. "There was a lot of stuff already in place that OSSG had done; but there were a lot of issues they had not addressed at all,

---

[6]Interview with David Maples, Federal Bureau of Investigation, 2000. Unless noted, subsequent quotations from Maples are also from this interview.

[7]Interview with Marv Smalley, DOD Office of Special Events, 2000. Unless noted, subsequent quotations from Smalley are also from this interview.

[8]Interview with Chris Bellavita, DOD Office of Special Events, 2000. Unless noted, subsequent quotations from Bellavita are also from this interview.

[9]Interview with Michael Eason, Georgia Bureau of Investigation, 2000. Unless noted, subsequent quotations from Eason are also from this interview.

such as housing and feeding and transportation of our state people," says McConnell. "The plans were a long way from being completed."

The renewed state vigor and increased effectiveness became clear within days of McConnell's appointment. McConnell opened the entire process up; he gave his key operations planners more latitude and authority and encouraged interaction with other important players in the security planning process. "Down at the operational level . . . what it did was it let Duff and Eason come out from underneath the gag order [that Coleman had imposed]," says John Awtrey, head of OSE's on-the-ground effort in Atlanta. "All of a sudden we could sit together in public or in their office and hammer out the details of what needed to be done. . . ."[10]

In addition, McConnell was seen as a person who enjoyed the full support of Governor Miller, a significant advantage that Stock Coleman, who at times had struggled to get resources out of even the Department of Public Safety, had never had. "We started getting resources," says Duff. "And McConnell had the strength from the Governor's Office to get things done. If he needed 100 people from a department, he got it."[11]

Security Collaboration: From Bad to Worse

The relationship between the Atlanta Committee for the Olympic Games (ACOG) and SOLEC was taking a turn for the worse, however. With the Games rapidly approaching, SOLEC began demanding to know how ACOG would assist with such urgent tasks as billeting, transporting, and feeding the state's 5,500 law enforcement officers. The answers from the organizing committee soon came back—ACOG would not be able to provide any transportation for the roughly 5,500 officers that the state was providing to the Olympic effort. Nor would ACOG be able to feed and house law enforcement officers. ACOG's refusal to provide the expected support infuriated SOLEC officials, but they felt there was nothing they could do. SOLEC would now have to find transportation, housing, and food for its officers on its own.[12]

SOLEC wasn't the only one having a difficult time with ACOG. In early February, A. D. Frazier, ACOG's chief operating officer, informed Gil Childers that ACOG would not only be unable to feed or provide transportation for any federal law enforcement or military personnel, it desperately needed the U.S. military to provide drivers and buses for the Games. Childers was dismayed by this request and by ACOG's general approach to getting

---

[10]Interview with John Awtrey, DOD Office of Special Events, 2000. Unless noted, subsequent quotations from Awtrey are also from this interview.

[11]Interview with Jim Duff, Georgia Bureau of Investigation, 2000. Unless noted, subsequent quotations from Duff are also from this interview.

[12]Fortunately for SOLEC, the state legislature had budgeted $26.7 million for state expenditures on Olympic-related projects. However, even with this funding, SOLEC was also forced to draw on a special discretionary spending fund available to Governor Miller and take substantial bites from state agencies' training budgets.

federal resources. He says, "There was no question, they made calculated gambles and calculated decisions that . . . the federal government won't let this sink so we'll toss the ball to them. . . ." But he felt he was in no position to call ACOG's bluff. The military would provide buses and drivers and unarmed security escorts.

Bill Rathburn insisted that his security operations were not being cut back to save money, but few believed this. "Anybody observing his operation from the outside and anybody talking to anybody on his staff would know that his budget was being cut every month," says David Maples, who was heading up the FBI's Olympic preparations. "ACOG started balancing their budget on the back of security," says McConnell.

Childers took a slightly more charitable view of the situation. "There's no question that ACOG consistently looked for someone else to foot the bill—sort of at every turn," says Childers. "By the same token, I know right up until the Games, they were running well over budget, and they were really hurting."

SOLEC didn't have time to complain. It had too much work to do. In order to house the roughly 5,500 state officers it planned to bring to metro Atlanta, SOLEC supervised the construction of a five-hundred-unit mobile home park and rented a brand-new six-hundred-unit apartment complex downtown. It scrambled to find 150 school buses to transport its personnel to and from the venues where they would be deployed. It also drew up plans to feed its officers and to bring in food inspectors, building inspectors, mental health counselors, victims' rights advocates, and others. It even built its own court and hired a part-time judge so that it could quickly process any arrests it made. The state was also in charge of running 450,000 criminal background checks so that ACOG could issue accreditation badges for the Games.

Atlanta Hangs Tough

Unlike the state of Georgia or the federal government, the city of Atlanta seemed determined to extract a sizable payment from ACOG to cover the additional costs that the Olympics would impose on the city during the Games, including the costs the Atlanta Police Department would incur. Atlanta Mayor Bill Campbell also seemed prepared to deny ACOG these services if ACOG did not come up with the money. In early 1996, ACOG gave in. Under the terms of the contract, ACOG offered to pay Atlanta $23 million to reimburse it for the additional costs that the Atlanta Police Department would incur during the Games.

Atlanta Chief of Police Beverly Harvard was determined to make her force's experience at the Olympics as comfortable as possible, and the contract with ACOG gave her the cash to carry out this desire. Atlanta Police officers would receive special overtime pay for their work on the Olympics. They would be transported in air-conditioned buses, in sharp distinction to state law enforcement. And while state officers were forbidden from working any off-duty jobs during the Games, the Atlanta Police Department allowed its officers to do so. The stark contrast between how ACOG was providing money and support to the Atlanta Police Department and how it left the state to bear all the costs of its Olympics deployment further rankled SOLEC members.

Yet a common enemy did not make the state and city friends. In early March at a press conference called to discuss a January crime report, Georgia Attorney General Mike Bowers expressed his belief that "it is safer to walk the streets of Sarajevo [then under violent siege by Serbian-backed armed forces] than to walk the streets of my hometown [i.e., Atlanta]."[13]

Mayor Bill Campbell denounced Bowers's claim as "reckless, irresponsible, and inaccurate." Billy Payne and Bill Rathburn promised that with tens of thousands of security personnel in place during the Games, "Atlanta will be the safest place on earth."[14] But many state law enforcement officials had a very low opinion of the Atlanta Police Department and worried that it would not be able to carry out even its limited responsibilities during the Games. Many federal officials shared these reservations. In early 1996, Atlanta had about 1,200 officers—300 fewer than when Atlanta won its Olympic bid. "I don't think the Atlanta Police Department was anywhere close to being up to what they should have been up to for this," says Childers.

Working with U.S. Army Forces Command

The October 1995 Department of Defense (DOD) decision to give U.S. Army Forces Command (FORSCOM) primary responsibility for managing the troops it was sending to Atlanta made FORSCOM one of the most important factors in the Games' security operations. By early 1996, the decision had been made to deploy approximately 11,000 troops during the Olympics—a number far larger than the figures being considered by the OSE.[15] Yet, despite this increase in military support, public safety officials soon regretted their decision to push for OSE's ouster.

OSE was an organization with a relatively flat organizational structure and an informal culture. When law enforcement agencies had wanted equipment or resources from OSE, they had typically approached Marv Smalley with an oral request. If Smalley thought the request was reasonable, he asked the agency to put its request in writing. In contrast, one of FORSCOM's first decisions was to require that all requests for military assistance be put in

---

[13]Simon Barnes, "Streets of Ire," *Times* (London), March 16, 1996.

[14]Simon Barnes, "Streets of Ire."

[15]Approximately 9,000 of those soldiers were from the National Guard (primarily but not exclusively the Georgia National Guard). Roughly 2,000 of the troops were active-duty U.S. military officers. Other forces, such as the U.S. Army's special operations forces based in Fort Bragg, would be on alert during the Games. In addition, a considerable number of the 11,000 troops being sent to Atlanta would be support personnel.

writing so that they could be formally tracked. The result was a breakdown that forced the U.S. Army to reverse course.

Law enforcement officials soon made another dismaying discovery—the army was even less open-handed with money and resources than OSE. The Pentagon needed to use most of the money Congress had appropriated for the Games to support its large troop deployment. As the flow of materiel from OSE dwindled, law enforcement officials who had once looked forward to Ann Brooks's ouster now fumed that ACOG had gotten its troops at the state's expense. Later that fall when FORSCOM refused to let ACOG revise its military staffing request, Bill Rathburn, the head of ACOG's security effort, joined the ranks of public safety officials dissatisfied with FORSCOM.

Yet, despite its obvious importance, in the months leading up to the Games law enforcement officials had little to do with FORSCOM. Most law enforcement officials had far more interaction with the OSE personnel who continued to work on many of the specific projects that most concerned law enforcement officials than with the constantly changing officers at FORSCOM. The result: FORSCOM remained unknown to most law enforcement officers.

The Federal Focus

The federal government had already made extensive preparations for detecting any terrorist threat to the Games. For the previous 2 years, the intelligence community had been looking for any indications of a pending attack; and in the wake of the Oklahoma City bombing in April 1995, the FBI had increased surveillance of domestic militia groups. (See Exhibit 12B-1 for a list of terrorist attacks preceding the Olympic Games.) The FBI was planning to deploy approximately a thousand officers in Atlanta during the Games; other federal law enforcement agencies would provide another 1,000.

But many federal officials were jittery. Officials were increasingly worried about the U.S. vulnerability to a terrorist attack that employed weapons of mass destruction (WMDs). The sarin gas attack on the Tokyo subway system by the Japanese religious cult Aum Shinrikyo 1 year earlier had come as an unpleasant shock to the United States. The lesson was clear and unnerving—a completely unknown terrorist group could emerge from nowhere and inflict catastrophic damage on its target.

In fall 1995, federal officials began developing detailed contingency plans for how they would react to a chemical or biological terrorist attack in Atlanta. The U.S. surgeon general, the Pentagon's director of military support, and the FBI agreed to create an interagency unit with the expertise to analyze and recommend the response to a biological attack. This Science and Technology Center would consist of fifty to seventy-five government chemists and biologists and would be based at the U.S. Centers for Disease Control and Prevention (CDC) in Atlanta. In the event of a chemical or biological attack, the Public Health Service

Exhibit 12B-1   Timeline of terrorist attacks preceding the Olympics, 1993–1996

February 1993	World Trade Center bombing kills six people and injures more than a thousand.
March 1995	Aum Shinrikyo members mount a sarin nerve gas attack on the Tokyo subway system, killing twelve people.
April 1995	Bomb explodes at the Alfred P. Murrah building in Oklahoma City, killing 168 people.
June 1995	Presidential Decision Directive 39 is issued. The Federal Bureau of Investigation is designated the lead federal agency for responding to any terrorist attack and the Federal Emergency Management Agency is put in charge of consequence management.
November 1995	Five Americans are killed in bombing attack on National Guard training center at Riyadh, Saudi Arabia.
June 1996	Khobar Towers housing complex for U.S. Air Force is bombed in Dharan, killing nineteen and wounding more than five hundred.
July 1996	TWA Flight #800 to Paris explodes off the coast of Long Island.

would direct the treatment of casualties, using special disaster medical assistance teams and the U.S. Marine Corps's Chemical and Biological Incident Response Force (CBIRF).[16]

The federal government also created a tactical unit known as the Chemical/Biological Response team to support the center's work. Headed by the FBI and stationed at Dobbins Air Force Base in Marietta, Georgia, this unit consisted of FBI laboratory and response team specialists, as well as members of the U.S. Army's Technical Escort Unit, a specialized unit with the capacity to respond to and neutralize toxic materials. This unit would be on stand-by 24 hours per day for the duration of the Games. If an incident occurred, team members would don full protective gear and fly to the scene in helicopters, where they would assess the situation and collect and preserve evidence that could be analyzed back at the Science and Technology Center.[17]

---

[16]The Public Health Service's disaster medical assistance teams, as well as disaster mortuary teams, could deploy to the scene of a disaster within 12 hours. If local hospitals were overwhelmed, casualties would be evacuated to hospitals in major metropolitan areas around the country that had enrolled in the Public Health Service's National Disaster Medical System. The system theoretically included 118,000 private-sector hospital beds, a number that did not count military health facilities. See "Science Center to Handle Terrorism at Olympics," *C&EN*, July 15, 1996, 11; J. B. Tucker, "National Health and Medical Services Response to Incidents of Chemical and Biological Terrorism," *Journal of the American Medical Association* 278, no. 5 (1997): 362–368.

[17]Tucker, "National Health and Medical Services Response," 353.

Back in Washington, D.C., Deputy Attorney General Jamie Gorelick and Deputy Secretary of Defense John White were also in close contact. In keeping with the role that Gore had asked her to assume, Gorelick called White often to push the DOD to provide more resources for the Games. In addition, the Department of Justice (DOJ) and the DOD began determining exactly how the FBI and FORSCOM would interact in the event of a terrorist attack. Even though the FBI would be the lead responder to any terrorist attack, it was clear that only the military had the assets to handle a truly worst-case scenario. Consequently, DOD and DOJ began to develop detailed organization charts that laid out exactly how DOD and DOJ assets would interact in a wide range of hypothetical scenarios.

The U.S. Public Health Service was also busy finalizing its preparations. It pre-positioned enhanced disaster medical assistance teams in Atlanta, which, together with a small group of medical doctors in the specialized marine unit CBIRF, would treat casualties in the event of a chemical attack. It stockpiled a large number of antidotes to chemical weapons in the Atlanta area. In addition, the Public Health Service and other federal agencies worked with Atlanta's fire department and other emergency medical services (EMS) personnel to prepare for a possible chemical or biological attack.[18]

A Renewed Effort

As the Games drew near, the federal government stepped up its already considerable efforts to ensure their safety. In April, Vice President Al Gore promised to increase the federal security commitment to Atlanta and urged Governor Miller and Mayor Bill Campbell to do more.[19] Because federal officers had very limited authority to respond to common crimes (assault, robbery, and the like), the state decided to swear in federal officers as GBI agents. All told, the federal government was providing approximately 2,500 federal law enforcement officers to support the Games. In May, U.S. Attorney General Janet Reno announced that 1,000 employees from federal agencies throughout Atlanta would also be available to assist with security tasks.[20]

The huge federal presence in Atlanta was not without its risks. A large military presence might aggravate domestic militias. "Obviously, one of the precepts of militia types is . . .

---

[18]Federal agencies were more concerned about preparing first responders to respond to a chemical attack, which would cause immediate casualties, than to a biological attack, which had delayed effects and might not be detected until people started going to hospitals. The state of Georgia did have a monitoring program in which state hospitals were supposed to report any unusual rash of illnesses, but no major efforts were made to upgrade that system in preparation for the Olympics Games.

[19]"Gore: Security Is Top Federal Concern; State, Federal, and City Agencies Pressed for More Personnel to 'Walk the Beats,'" *Atlanta Journal-Constitution*, April 13, 1996, E8. Gore ultimately found another seven hundred federal agents and persuaded Miller and Campbell to find another eight hundred officers. "Security System at the Olympics to Be Gigantic," *New York Times*, July 12, 1996, A1.

[20]"Federal Employees to Boost Security Force for Olympics; 1,000 Non-law Enforcement Workers to Lend a Hand in Atlanta," *Washington Post*, May 23, 1996, A19.

the increasing military presence and loss of freedom in America and stuff like that, and here we are doing in some ways exactly that," notes Childers. "So there was a definite concern about that."

Who's in Charge?

That spring, Gil Childers flew to Washington to attend a briefing on the state of the Olympic planning. Vice President Gore was also in attendance. According to Childers, in the middle of one of the presentations, Gore said, "Excuse me, I've got a question." The flustered FBI agent who was presenting paused. "Who's in charge?" Gore asked. It depends on the situation, Gore was told. Memoranda of understanding among the various law enforcement agencies involved in the Games had sketched out law enforcement agencies' various roles, and tabletop exercises to test agencies' understanding of their roles would soon begin. But there was no single person in charge.

There had been some consideration of how federal, state, and local public safety agencies and ACOG would interact operationally during the Games. The sixty-one athletic venues would have dual ACOG and law enforcement commanders who would work together to address routine problems; however, if the venue commanders needed extra resources, they would have to appeal up through a chain of command. There the picture became more complicated.

At OSE's urging, public safety agencies had agreed to create a Joint Coordination Center (JCC) for the Games where all of the federal, state, and local agencies with significant responsibility for the Olympics would station personnel 24 hours per day, 7 days per week for the duration of the Games. The JCC was not, however, a joint command center—ACOG, the Atlanta Police Department, FBI, and Georgia each intended to have its own command center. Instead, its purpose was to collect and disseminate information. If, for instance, an explosion went off at the equestrian center in Conyers outside of Atlanta, the Conyers Police Department would call the JCC, which would immediately disseminate the news to other law enforcement agencies.

The View on the Ground

Less than 4 months before the Centennial Olympic Games were scheduled to begin, Atlanta was a city under construction. Contractors were still finishing work on the Olympic cauldron that would sit atop the new stadium. Centennial Park, the central public gathering place for the Games, was still little more than a red clay pit.[21]

Nevertheless, the external chaos masked a growing internal cohesiveness on security matters. SOLEC had come together quickly and was moving forward with the remaining

---

[21]"100 Days to Atlanta 1996; Anxiety for Atlantans, but Officials Are Upbeat," *New York Times*, April 10, 1996, B4.

planning for state venues with remarkable speed. The FBI had already conducted several field exercises involving a number of public safety agencies, which seemed, for the most part, well prepared. The Atlanta Police Department, although it continued to be viewed as a weak link by many of the other agencies, seemed to have done a thorough planning job. The Secret "Gang of Seven," formed by Bill Rathburn in late 1994 and consisting of representatives from the agencies most involved in security planning for the Games, was also functioning well and performing many of the functions that had originally been envisioned for the OSSG.

Threat Perceptions

In the run-up to the Games, law enforcement officials identified thirty-five venues and locations as potentially attractive targets for terrorist attack. Several stood out as subjects of particular concern.

The Olympic Village

At the top of the list was the Olympic Village (on the Georgia Tech campus), where the 15,000 athletes coming to the Games would reside. It was a state venue, and security preparations had gotten off to a slow start. In fact, McConnell had been startled to discover that no security plans for the Village had been put on paper. SOLEC had frantically drawn up a venue security plan, and by April the security plans for the Village were complete. Nevertheless, the Village remained a source of considerable anxiety.[22] Not only would public safety personnel have to maintain perimeter security for the Village, they would also have to monitor vehicle entry. Any vehicle entering the Village would have to be thoroughly inspected and "sanitized," and all deliveries would also have to be inspected.

Several measures were designed to protect the Village from a terrorist attack. OSE personnel were planning to install a high-tech perimeter fence around the Village. The FBI would pre-position two Special Weapons and Tactics (SWAT) teams in the Village. And Governor Miller had declared a limited state of emergency at the Olympic Village, thus allowing the Georgia National Guard to keep approximately three hundred armed soldiers on duty along the perimeter at all times. For its part, ACOG planned to use the contingent of volunteer law enforcement officials it had recruited for the Games within the Village.

The Olympic Stadium

The Olympic Stadium, particularly during the Opening and Closing Ceremonies, was also a source of great concern. Childers says, "That's the single biggest venue. . . . It's also right

---

[22]The Georgia Tech campus also housed a research nuclear reactor, which became a source of concern and a target of civilian protesters.

smack in the heart of Atlanta. If you did some sort of large bomb [there], that could have devastating effects." Childers and other federal officials knew that terrorists could potentially cause hundreds of thousands of casualties if they used a nuclear, biological, or chemical weapon. GEMA and the Federal Emergency Management Agency (FEMA) also began to consider seriously how they would respond to a successful attack. How many hospital beds did Atlanta have? How would victims be transported there? How many body bags did GEMA have on hand?

Metropolitan Atlanta Rapid Transportation Authority

ACOG was relying on Atlanta's transit system, the Metropolitan Atlanta Rapid Transportation Authority (MARTA), to serve as the primary means of transportation during the Games. MARTA carried roughly 200,000 passengers on a normal day. During the Games, MARTA was expected to provide transportation to roughly three times that number every day. "MARTA was everybody's problem because it is the heart of everything," says Childers.

Let's not even talk about a bomb or some terrorist event. Let's talk about something that is probably a 50–50 chance of happening. It's late July, August in Atlanta. The temperature is 100 degrees, 95 degrees—very uncomfortable. People are hot waiting. You have a train break down. The platforms are going to be completely full. People will be standing on the streets waiting to get into the station. . . . There's an announcement that there's been a breakdown . . . [and] because of that the next train won't be here for 20 minutes or so. You've got maybe 5,000 people at that MARTA station holding tickets that they've paid several hundred dollars for that have now become possibly worthless. You're going to have 5,000 angry people . . . on your streets. . . .

It had long been clear that the 120-person MARTA police force would not be able to provide an adequate security presence during the Games and would have to be supplemented by other law enforcement personnel. However, the March 1995 sarin nerve gas attack on the Tokyo subway system ratcheted up anxieties about MARTA to a new level. MARTA's elite Special Police Unit was sent to the U.S. Army Chemical School to receive special training for responding to a chemical or biological attack. The FBI put on a full-scale exercise simulating a gas attack in a MARTA station, and planners explored other MARTA problem scenarios in a series of tabletop exercises. MARTA's security force was bolstered by additional members.

Centennial Park

Early in the planning process, Centennial Park had been envisioned as a safety valve for the crowds the Georgia World Congress Center and the other venues in the area would draw to downtown. The park had gradually been transformed into a destination in its own right, yet the park would not be treated like a venue. People would be able to enter and exit Centennial Park freely, in accordance with the demands of the public.

Although more security could have been put in place, there was generally a high level of comfort with the security plans for the park. Law enforcement officers would patrol the park at all times. ACOG and the pavilion sponsors would provide private security, and ACOG surveillance cameras would observe and document the crowd's activities. Although fencing off the park would have allowed law enforcement officers to observe the people entering and exiting the park more closely, it would also have risked creating long lines that could disrupt traffic and that might themselves be vulnerable to attack. In short, both the course of action that ACOG and SOLEC had adopted and the course of action that Rathburn had proposed in fall 1995 had their pros and cons.

Differing Threat Perceptions Going into the Games

As the Games approached, different agencies were worried about different issues. SOLEC and the Atlanta Police Department were primarily concerned with such mundane but essential subjects as transportation. Federal officials seemed more concerned about the possibility of a terrorist attack, particularly a bombing, and planned accordingly. "Probably a pretty good percentage of the national assets to respond to bombings were here," says FBI Olympic coordinator David Maples.

State and local law enforcement officials thought it unlikely terrorists would attack Atlanta during the Games, particularly foreign terrorists. They did worry, however, about the danger of homegrown terrorism. On the day the Olympic torch arrived in Los Angeles, law enforcement officers had discovered a cache of explosive devices in the town of Macon, just 60 miles away from Atlanta. But there was only so much law enforcement officials could do about such an attack. The FBI already kept potentially violent domestic groups under observation, and SOLEC could only encourage law enforcement throughout Georgia to be particularly alert to potential threats against the Olympics.

"You know, we did everything we possibly could to ensure nobody drove a truck bomb up into a venue, things like that," says GBI agent Mike Eason. "[But] if a guy was going to fly a small airplane over and crash it into your venue, there's nothing you can do about it. We're not going to shoot him down. We're just going to pick up the pieces."

Even though state and local officials downplayed the threat of a major terrorist attack, they were relieved that the feds were taking responsibility for preparing for the worst. However, exactly how they would react to a terrorist attack remained unclear. "We knew that the federal government had resources staged to react to that, but what those resources were, we did not know," says GBI Director of Operations Vernon Keenan.[23]

---

[23]Interview with Vernon Keenan, Georgia Bureau of Investigation, 2000. Unless noted, subsequent quotations from Keenan are also from this interview.

Preparing for the Worst

Much of the push to prepare for worst-case scenarios came from the military.[24] "The people from our special operations and low intensity conflict [unit] were all worried about the terrorism side of the world," recalls John Awtrey, the head of OSE's on-the-ground effort in Atlanta. "All they wanted to talk about was the 'Black Sunday' scenario," a reference to the eponymous 1975 best-selling book (and 1976 movie) in which a demented Vietnam veteran controlled by a beautiful Palestinian terrorist decides to mount an attack from the Goodyear blimp on the Super Bowl and its 80,000 spectators, including the president of the United States. An aerial attack on the Olympics would be even more harmful than the fictional attack on the Super Bowl; President Bill Clinton planned to attend the Opening Ceremonies, and 2 billion people were expected to tune in. "That's all those guys wanted to talk about—nothing less than that," says Awtrey. "You have to sort of back them down and say, 'There are levels of threat and there are probabilities of those kinds of things happening'" and only so many resources.

Although some law enforcement officials doubted that much could be done about an aerial attack, the military thought otherwise. Plans were made to keep four aerial interceptors within 7 minutes of downtown Atlanta at all times to respond to aerial intruders.

And if disaster could not be averted, public safety officials were prepared to manage the consequences. "On the consequence management side . . . an incredible amount of resources were put on the ground down there," says Awtrey. "[If] five kiloton low airbursts went off over the stadium, we had enough stuff there to take care of it."

Rathburn found the intensity of the federal government's preparations almost disconcerting:

> We went to Washington in April of '96 and Vice President Gore and "Mack" McClarty kind of co-chaired this big meeting there. And we had deputy secretaries in departments and some secretaries themselves at the meeting—I mean, really a very high level meeting. Gore was very, very well informed, very personally involved in the whole process. I was absolutely astounded. . . . I mean it was a little frightening to me.[25]

When Rathburn got back from Washington, he immediately called Woody Johnson, the FBI special agent-in-charge for Atlanta, and asked Johnson if the federal government knew something he didn't. Was there any intelligence pointing to a possible terrorist attack? Johnson

---

[24]Even the FBI, the designated first responder in the event of a terrorist attack, had only a limited sense of the preparations that the military was making.

[25]Interview with Bill Rathburn, director of security, Atlanta Committee for the Olympic Games, 2000. Unless noted, subsequent quotations and observations from Rathburn are also from this interview.

assured him that the FBI was merely preparing for every contingency.[26] But Rathburn continued to worry. "[T]o keep getting this concern from the National Security Council about the safety of air space, of the vulnerability from the air. I tell you, I really got worried," says Rathburn.

From Traffic Congestion to Chlorine Gas

As the Games approached, a wide range of security issues began hitting law enforcement officials' radar screens. "It was not just the intentional [attack], it was also potentially the accidental problem you've got to deal with," says Childers. For instance, the Georgia World Congress Center straddled a railway line that served as a shipping route for chlorine and other hazardous materials. If a chlorine spill occurred while the Georgia World Congress Center was full, the number of casualties could reach into the thousands. The shipper was ultimately persuaded not to send chlorine through that route for the duration of the Olympics.

Worst-case-scenario thinking did not always drive security preparations; OSE refused a request to provide 40 miles of fencing for the equestrian venue in Conyers because, Marv Smalley says, "the risk wasn't there." But such a quick dismissal of a threat was rare. "What we do in this country—we have so many people, so many resources, and so much money, we can 'worst-case scenario' everything we do," says Smalley. "We don't really do the work necessary to identify what the true risk is."

Indicative of the heightened level of precautions was law enforcement's preparation for the rowing event at Lake Lanier outside of Atlanta. "There was concern because the grandstands were out on the water, built on floating docks basically, so there was some real vulnerability there," says Childers. "You're talking about a relatively sophisticated attack involving frogmen and things like that, but you can't completely discount that." However, it was hard to know how to assess such threats. "You don't go crazy trying to prevent that but you take reasonable precautions, and hopefully if nothing happens then your precautions were reasonable," says Childers. "If something happens, they were unreasonable."

Although other low-probability, high-consequence security concerns did occasionally arise, law enforcement officials worried most about mundane problems: gridlock, logistical problems, bad weather, and transportation. Even Gilmore Childers, who had come to Atlanta with the expectation that his primary work would be to help the city and state prepare for the possibility of a terrorist attack, found himself spending most of his time on logistical issues such as lining up buses for the organizing committee.

---

[26]"The problem you run into with an event like this is that you can't wait until there's an articulated threat to commit [resources]," says Maples. "So even if there's no threat or no inference of a threat, you've got to go through all the same steps and planning and putting people in place that you would if there were a threat."

The Transition from Planning to Operations

In the months leading up to the Games, the FBI mounted several major field exercises to test security preparations for the Games. The exercises involved both ACOG security personnel and the law enforcement agencies that would be present at these venues and were designed to test their interaction with the FBI in a crisis. Although the exercises revealed some critical misunderstandings, that fact contributed to the widespread feeling that they were useful and successful operations.

But despite the general agreement that such exercises were helpful, no other agency mounted full-scale field exercises. This was unusual. OSE had never before supported a special event that did not include such an exercise in its preparations. Instead, agencies relied on tabletop exercises, conducted by OSE consultant Chris Bellavita, as often as three times per week. In these exercises, Bellavita assembled public safety officials with command responsibility from a wide variety of agencies, presented them with an unfolding crisis, and pushed them to describe how they would interact with each other under these circumstances. While the FBI field exercises revolved around situations where the FBI would be the lead responder, Bellavita's tabletop exercises explored a wider range of crises. Together, these field and tabletop exercises constituted the primary tests of the readiness of the public safety force assembled for the Games.

On June 18, Bellavita assembled representatives from a dozen metro Atlanta public safety agencies for a final command-post exercise that was designed to test how the various commands—SOLEC, FBI, the Atlanta Police Department, and ACOG foremost among them—interacted with one another. Bellavita's assessment of Atlanta's readiness was cautiously optimistic.

"Most agencies seem close to being ready internally for the Olympics," Bellavita concluded. "However, at the command post level, there has been very little testing yet of integration among agencies. Most of that integration will probably come together after July 19th [i.e., after the Games begin]. Police are good at reacting. If the Olympics are like other major events, the first few days will be busy, confusing, and perhaps frustrating. But they will provide a lot of opportunities for learning how to do things better." [27]

Renewed Concerns

On June 26, a gasoline truck loaded with approximately 5,000 pounds of TNT blew up outside a U.S. military housing complex in the Saudi Arabian city of Dhahran. The explosion, which occurred within 100 feet of the Khobar Towers apartment building, sheared off the

---

[27]Office of Special Events, *1996 Olympics After Action Report,* OUSD (Personnel and Readiness), August 22, 1997, 108.

front of the building, killing nineteen American soldiers and injuring more than four hundred. Ominously, the Khobar Towers bombing was the second major attack against the U.S. military in Saudi Arabia in less than a year.

The bombing in Dharan had an immediate impact on security planning in Atlanta. Some security experts thought that the unprecedented size of the Khobar Towers bomb called into question the security of several venues in Atlanta, most notably the Olympic Village itself. Interstate I-75, the north-south connector through downtown Atlanta, passed directly by a corner of the Olympic Village at Georgia Tech. Although the interstate was recessed and separated from the Village by a tall concrete wall, the explosion of a Khobar Towers–size truck bomb at that point would almost certainly cause tremendous damage. One proposed solution was to close the connector entirely. However, SOLEC rejected this suggestion; the traffic disruptions created by the Games would already be significant enough without entirely shutting down one of the city's major arteries. Ultimately, the state decided to keep several State Patrol officers—and a big-rig tow truck—at the scene 24 hours per day in the hope of deterring any would-be car bombers.

Operations Begin

By late June, security planning had come to an end. On July 4, 1996, the SOLEC command center went operational. In 2 weeks, 8–9 million ticket holders, 15,000 athletes from 191 countries, 15,000–30,000 reporters, and 41 heads of state would be on their way to the 1996 Centennial Olympic Games. Approximately 30,000 security personnel drawn from more than one hundred federal, state, and local agencies, as well as ACOG and the U.S. military, would be on hand to protect them.

Despite their concerns, state officials were cautiously optimistic that they were ready for the Games. "My sense was that people would rise to the occasion," says Bill Kelley, the head of the IPG. "That was not just a blind faith. The plans were in place. . . . we had looked at eventualities and problems. The only problems we were going to face were those of different jurisdictions and trying to deal with the lack of command, which every place in America has to deal with."

The planning was over. On July 19, the Centennial Olympic Games would begin.

Security Preparations for the 1996 Centennial Olympic Games (C): The Games Begin

On the evening of July 4, 1996, just hours after the State Olympic Law Enforcement Command (SOLEC) command center went operational, a soldier stationed at the gates of the Olympic Village was shot.[1] The shooting was the first in a series of last-minute challenges faced by public safety officials. On July 5, the Secret Service announced that it was considering banning all nongovernmental aircraft from air space near the Games venues. The uproar was immediate: the Atlanta Committee for the Olympic Games (ACOG) vehemently objected that the measure would prevent it from conducting aerial tours, and United Parcel Service (UPS) objected that such restrictions would prevent it from making helicopter deliveries to downtown Atlanta (a temporary solution to the traffic problems expected during the Games). Eventually, the Federal Aviation Administration brokered an agreement that allowed aircraft equipped with special tracking devices to enter airspace near athletic venues and other sensitive sites.

Meanwhile, federal law enforcement officials prepared to move into Atlanta en masse. The Federal Bureau of Investigation (FBI) was bringing more than a thousand agents into Atlanta for the Games, including a dozen Special Weapons and Tactics (SWAT) teams. It was also putting the final touches on its Science and Technology Center. Other federal law enforcement agencies, including the Secret Service; the Bureau of Alcohol, Tobacco, and Firearms; and the Drug Enforcement Administration, were also moving an estimated 1,500 officers into Atlanta.

The U.S. military was also moving assets into Atlanta. U.S. Army Forces Command (FORSCOM) was bringing in roughly 2,000 active-duty military personnel for the Games. The Georgia National Guard and other state national guards were contributing another 9,000 personnel. Army Special Forces were standing by at Fort Bragg. Coast Guard boats would be on hand at the sailing venue in Savannah. The U.S. Marine Corps's newly created Chemical and Biological Incident Response Force (CBIRF) was also moving into position at a vacated winery in central Atlanta that they had disguised as a military depot.

The Threat Made Real

On Wednesday, July 17, 2 days before the Opening Ceremonies, TWA Flight #800 exploded off the coast of Long Island, New York, on its way to Paris, killing all 230 people on board. Despite the dearth of evidence, the explosion was generally viewed as a terrorist attack. As

---

[1]Investigators later determined that the soldier had been hit by a round fired up into the air at random from an AK-47 to celebrate Independence Day.

such, it brought home the consequences of a security failure at the Olympics. A poll of downtown office workers conducted by the *Atlanta Journal-Constitution* found that 71 percent worried that terrorists would target the Centennial Olympic Games.[2]

The day of the TWA explosion, ACOG and the Atlanta Police Department staged a dress rehearsal of the Opening Ceremonies. According to Georgia Bureau of Investigation (GBI) Director Buddy Nix, the rehearsal was "a disaster."[3] Perimeter fencing was still not in place, ACOG did not have enough volunteers on hand to run the metal detectors, and the chaos was obvious to state law enforcement officials and presumably to the large group of prominent government and International Olympic Committee (IOC) officials that ACOG had invited as observers.

Moreover, on Thursday, July 18, ACOG faced a crisis of its own. ACOG had recruited 1,000 law enforcement officers from the United States and other countries to work at the Games as volunteer security guards. ACOG planned to use part of this experienced multilingual force in the Olympic Village. However, when these volunteers arrived, they found that ACOG had done virtually nothing to prepare for their arrival, save securing accommodations that most of the volunteers found unacceptable. The situation was so bad that the volunteers threatened to turn around and leave. State law enforcement officials stepped in to mediate and after an evening of discussions, the volunteers and ACOG reached an agreement—in exchange for the volunteers' staying, ACOG allowed them to select their own commanders and exercise considerable autonomy in performing their duties at the Village.

Problems and Glitches

Opening Ceremonies

The Opening Ceremonies were scheduled to begin Friday evening, July 19, at the new Olympic Stadium. Some 83,000 spectators would be on hand to witness the festivities, including President Bill Clinton and First Lady Hillary Rodham Clinton, plus a television audience of approximately 2 billion people. Some 15,000 accredited journalists would also be on hand.

Because the Opening Ceremonies were expected be the highest-profile moment of the Games, they were a potentially spectacular target. The presence of so many heads of state also complicated matters, and ACOG had to beat back a last-minute attempt by the Secret Service to tighten stadium security arrangements. Yet, despite the obvious importance of the Opening Ceremonies, the installation of the perimeter fence, which was supposed to have been put

---

[2]"Atlanta Games; 9 Days to Go; Olympic City; Close Up; Security; An Arena for Terrorism; 'Atlanta Will Be the Safest Place in the World this Summer'; Mantra May Sound Like a Challenge to Every Militant Group Seeking an International Stage for Murder and Mayhem to Advance a Cause," *Atlanta Journal-Constitution*, July 10, 1996, 15S.

[3]Interview with Director Milton "Buddy" Nix, Georgia Bureau of Investigation, 2000. Unless noted, subsequent quotations from Nix are also from this interview.

in place days before the Games, was not actually completed until just hours before the ceremonies were to begin. Ninety minutes before the ceremonies began, an Atlanta Police Department officer discovered a man dressed as a security guard sitting in one of the spectator sections. The man turned out to have a .45-millimeter handgun and a knife. He was quickly arrested and removed from the scene.[4] The Opening Ceremonies went on as scheduled.

State Olympic Law Enforcement Command–Atlanta Committee for the Olympic Games Relations

With the beginning of the Games, the security dynamic at the Games changed. Planning had been a top-down process in which important security decisions were made at a high level. Now that the Games were beginning, most of the security decisions would be made by law enforcement and ACOG venue commanders. The role of the various agency command centers was to monitor venue operations and respond quickly to questions or requests for help.

All the venues had joint venue commanders: an ACOG commander and a law enforcement commander. For the venues to operate smoothly, it was critical that the ACOG and law enforcement commanders work well together. For the most part, they did. The two security forces, however, were not integrated. Even the military support personnel were divided up. "We had our military; they had their military," says Mike Eason, the GBI agent who oversaw the state's venue security effort. "In every venue you had that—ours and theirs."[5]

But the relatively harmonious relationship between law enforcement and ACOG venue commanders was not replicated at the command level. The relationship between SOLEC and ACOG had already been strained by what SOLEC saw as ACOG's failure to support SOLEC. It did not improve once the Games began. ACOG approached SOLEC with a request to reposition the perimeter fence at the Olympic Village so that IOC officials would have easier access to the Village. GBI adamantly objected to this request, which it estimated would cost almost $1 million, and Gary McConnell refused to make the adjustments. ACOG chief Billy Payne responded by suggesting that the decision was above McConnell's pay grade. McConnell called Governor Miller on the spot, quickly explained the situation, and handed the phone to Payne, who was promptly told the fence would not be moved.

ACOG and SOLEC disagreed on other substantive issues. One continual irritant was the issue of metal detector settings. In theory, ACOG set its metal detectors at the level used by the Federal Aviation Administration. SOLEC officials charged that in practice ACOG personnel operating the metal detectors turned the metal detectors down even lower—or turned them off completely. State officials were so upset by this practice that Mike Eason

---

[4]At a press conference the next day, ACOG Security Chief Bill Rathburn was forced to concede that he had no idea how the man had penetrated what was supposedly a secure area. Officials later speculated that the man had slipped into the stadium before the perimeter fences were erected.

[5]Interview with Michael Eason, Georgia Bureau of Investigation, 2000. Unless noted, subsequent quotations from Eason are also from this interview.

ordered state personnel to check metal detectors settings every 4 hours. "[W]e wanted security, and ACOG didn't," he says, an opinion shared by many state officials.

Although he could understand how some of ACOG's decisions in the months leading up to the Games might have annoyed SOLEC, Bill Rathburn felt that SOLEC was responding by adopting a ridiculously inflexible attitude. While state officials fumed at IOC officials entering venues without being screened, Rathburn felt confident that no IOC official or federal law enforcement officer was going to pull out a weapon and open fire at an athletic venue. "I think it's ridiculous to waste time screening FBI agents' cars," says Rathburn.[6]

The Military in Action

Relations among the organizing committee, law enforcement, and FORSCOM were somewhat better. The primary purpose of the soldiers, "armed only with a radio and a smile," was to provide a security presence; even though the troops themselves would be unable to make arrests, the mere presence of uniformed troops was expected to deter wrongdoing. Military personnel also supported a number of more specific missions, from directing traffic to maintaining perimeter lines.

Once the Games began, most troops on the ground were competent and flexible, within certain parameters. "The troops and military police that were here in the trenches, they worked terrifically," says Jon Gordon of the Atlanta Police Department.[7] However, some law enforcement officers continued to perceive FORSCOM itself as rigid and inflexible. ACOG security personnel shared many of these frustrations. "We couldn't even move troops between venues," notes Gene Brown, the head of ACOG's security effort outside of Atlanta.[8] And law enforcement officials were frustrated by their lack of authority over military personnel. "My biggest gripe, and I think I'm speaking for everybody, is the lack of control we had over the military," says GBI director Buddy Nix.

Other Problems

Soon after the Games began, ACOG encountered another major problem—its 12,000 volunteers. Rathburn had estimated that about 10 percent of these volunteers would not show up on any given day,[9] but the actual volunteer absentee rate turned out to be more than 20 percent, leaving ACOG continually improvising to compensate for short staffing.

---

[6]Interview with Bill Rathburn, director of security, Atlanta Committee for the Olympic Games, 2000. Unless noted, subsequent quotations from Rathburn are also from this interview.

[7]Interview with Jon Gordon, Atlanta Police Department, 2000. Unless noted, subsequent quotations from Gordon are also from this interview.

[8]Interview Gene Brown, Atlanta Committee for the Olympic Games, 2000. Unless noted, subsequent quotations from Brown are also from this interview.

[9]He had not, however, planned to have enough volunteers to offset these shortfalls. Because of the costs of providing training, uniforms, and meals, even volunteers were quite expensive.

The Atlanta Police Department was also experiencing problems. Despite its efforts, traffic in Atlanta near the venues was a snarl. State and federal law enforcement officers ultimately had to assist the Atlanta Police Department in directing traffic.

The Games also experienced a number of technical and logistical glitches. Some of them, such as the problems with IBM's electronic system for providing the results of athletic contests, affected the media, which thoroughly drubbed Atlanta for perceived shortcomings: logistical, climatological, commercial, and otherwise. A high-tech incident tracking system intended to help law enforcement agencies track incidents of crime and disorder was also glitch-prone. Other support problems also surfaced. Early in the Games, SOLEC realized that it had dramatically underestimated the number of people it would need to provide administrative support to its law enforcement officers in the field; it had to scramble to find state employees to do these tasks.

A Triumph in the Making

Yet, despite these problems, at the end of the first week organizers and law enforcement officials shared the belief that the Centennial Olympic Games were well on their way to being a tremendous success. Security arrangements at the Village were working well; law enforcement officials were delighted with the high-tech perimeter fence erected by OSE. Athletes in the Village reportedly felt safe. Venue plans were also working well. The security glitches with the metal detectors had not resulted in major incidents (with the exception of the armed "security officer" who slipped into the Olympic Stadium before the Opening Ceremonies). For the most part, ACOG and law enforcement officials were cooperating with one another. Venue commanders had shown great flexibility in working around staffing shortfalls. "I can't tell you how cooperative these guys were," says GBI agent Mike Eason. "When I would call them at 10 o'clock in the morning and say, 'We've been tasked to come up with 100 people for the Atlanta Police Department, and I need 15 from your venue.' . . . I mean, they did it."

Centennial Park had also proved wildly popular. When querulous reporters pressed Billy Payne about technical shortcomings, the traffic tie-ups, the "gross" commercialism of the Games, or other perceived problems, Payne walked them to his window and pointed to the throngs of people gathered in Centennial Park as evidence that the Games were a hit with the public.

The popularity of Centennial Park was a highlight of the Games. The public had flocked there to trade Olympic pins, tour the high-tech pavilions of Olympic sponsors, cool off in the Olympic fountain, and watch events on big-screen televisions. Authorities estimated that several hundred thousand were visiting Centennial Park every day, and the park was a popular destination from the beginning of athletic events in the morning to late at night when bars and free concerts kept fans in the area.

On July 26, Governor Zell Miller hosted a reception at the Governor's Mansion to thank public safety officials for the work they had done on the Olympics. Miller was reportedly "ecstatic" about how well things were going, and law enforcement officials were feeling pretty good too. "It was going very smoothly," says GBI Director Nix. After a week of unexpected problems and improvisation, the security operation seemed to have found its groove.

An Explosion in Centennial Park

Late Saturday evening, July 27, Mike Eason, the GBI agent who oversaw the development of the security plans for SOLEC's venues, walked over to Centennial Park to see how things were going. As it had been since day one of the Games, Centennial Park was a hub of activity. About 60,000 people were jammed into the park, listening to live music and hanging out. At about 12:30 a.m., Eason went back to his nearby room and went to bed. All seemed well.

Approximately an hour later, Eason's cell phone, pager, and the hotel phone started ringing simultaneously. He immediately called in to the SOLEC operational center and was told that an explosion had gone off in Centennial Park. Eason called the state venue commander of the Olympic Village at once to tell him to shift to a red status—the highest level of alert, which effectively locked down the Village. The venue commander had already done so. Eason dressed and rushed off to the SOLEC command center.

At 1:24 a.m., SOLEC chief Gary McConnell, who was sleeping in the small bedroom adjacent to the SOLEC command room in the Georgia Emergency Management Agency (GEMA) building, was awakened with the report that a bomb had gone off at Centennial Park and that one person was dead and a hundred-plus people injured. McConnell immediately got up and called Governor Zell Miller.

Meanwhile, the roughly 60,000 people in Centennial Park were pouring out on to the city streets.[10] State, city, and federal law enforcement officers on the scene were now trying to care for the injured, secure the crime scene, and direct the exodus—a complicated task that they were handling well. It seemed clear that there had been a terrorist attack, possibly the first in a series of attacks. News agencies were broadcasting the pandemonium live.

Reacting to an Unknown Attack

Although the state venue commander first secured the scene—Centennial Park was a state responsibility—the FBI quickly took control of the situation, working on the assumption that Centennial Park had experienced a terrorist attack. All venues were locked down. No one and nothing were allowed to enter or exit. But in the first minutes after the explosion,

---

[10]Jim Duff estimates that there were another 100,000 people in the immediate vicinity of the park at the time of the explosion. Interview with Jim Duff, Georgia Bureau of Investigation, 2000. Unless noted, subsequent quotations from Duff are also from this interview.

the nature of the attack remained unclear. Initial reports indicated that shrapnel from an explosion had injured roughly a hundred people. However, there were also reports of respiratory problems among some of the casualties, and the possibility that the attack had a chemical component could not be ruled out.

The only way to make sure that the explosion had not released toxic chemicals was to send in the joint FBI–U.S. Army Chemical/Biological Response team to collect shrapnel, soil, and clothing samples that could be analyzed at the FBI's Science and Technology Center. Given the possibility, however slim, that the explosion might have released deadly chemicals, it was only logical that the team go in wearing full protective gear.

Within minutes of the explosion in Centennial Park, both the Chemical-Biological Response team and the CBIRF had been informed of the apparent attack and readied for deployment. The FBI, however, hesitated to dispatch units in full protective gear. It feared that the appearance of men in "moon suits" would create panic in downtown Atlanta. Ultimately, the decision was made to send in a sample team from the Chemical/Biological Response team without protective gear. The risk of creating a public panic seemed to outweigh the remote risk of sending personnel into a "hot zone."

After briefing Governor Miller, Gary McConnell called Georgia's two U.S. senators, Sen. Sam Nunn (D-Ga.) and Sen. Paul Coverdell (R-Ga.), both of whom were in town. Both immediately decided to come to the SOLEC command center. At 1:45 a.m., McConnell and Governor Miller briefed President Clinton.

By 1:50 a.m., emergency medical service (EMS) personnel had transported all forty-three people who had been seriously wounded in the explosion to the Grady Memorial Hospital emergency room. Two people had died in the explosion: a woman from Albany, Georgia, was killed by the shrapnel, and a Turkish cameraman had a heart attack immediately after the explosion.

According to McConnell, there was no serious discussion of calling off the Games. He recalls, "We're going to continue with the Games. We're going to continue to provide security. We're going to bring enough extra personnel to open the park back up. And basically there's no group going to tell us in Georgia that we cannot put on the Games." [11] Both the federal and state governments began looking for ways to bulk up security forces at the Games. [12]

By this time, law enforcement officials had a clear picture of what had happened. At 12:57 a.m., Richard Jewell, a private security guard, noticed an unattended knapsack near the base of a sound tower at the AT&T pavilion, where a concert was underway. Since the beginning of

---

[11] Interview with Director Gary McConnell, Georgia Emergency Management Agency, 2000. Unless noted, subsequent quotations from McConnell are also from this interview. Juan Antonio Samaranch, the president of the IOC, and Billy Payne, the president of ACOG, were also included in these conversations.

[12] The federal government soon decided to empty out a nearby Border Patrol training academy to increase the number of federal officers at the Games, and the state began to scour the state in search of several hundred additional law enforcement officers that they could bring into Atlanta.

the Games, law enforcement officials had found on average three or four suspicious packages a day that required them to call in an Explosive Ordnance Disposal (EOD) team. The police had also received roughly a hundred bomb threats by telephone.[13] None of the packages turned out to be a bomb. But Jewell, the security guard who spotted this knapsack, thought it looked suspicious. He immediately flagged down a GBI agent, who in turn called over two explosives ordnance experts, part of an explosives diagnostic team (composed of FBI; Bureau of Alcohol, Tobacco, and Firearms; and military bomb experts) that was assigned to the park. This team examined the knapsack and, seeing wires and what appeared to be a pipe, identified it as a possible bomb. State and federal officers had moved the crowd approximately 25 feet away from the knapsack when the bomb exploded, blasting to the ground scores of spectators, as well as eleven of the law enforcement officers who had been moving the crowd back.[14]

Of the people farther back in the crowd, some initially thought the explosion was part of the concert, while others thought it was a large firecracker. However, reality soon became apparent. "I was right near the stage and I heard a big boom and I saw people drop to the ground," said one bystander. "There was shrapnel flying. The guy next to me was bleeding and people were running like crazy. People were hitting the ground. It was pandemonium." [15]

The Public Safety Reaction

By 2:30 a.m., state law enforcement officers and the FBI had, with the assistance of personnel from the Atlanta Police Department and other federal law enforcement agencies, secured the crime scene. The FBI's sampling team had collected soil, shrapnel, and clothing samples and rushed them to its lab at the U.S. Centers for Disease Control and Prevention (CDC). As police officers blocked off the main thoroughfares around the park and ambulances raced through the streets, thousands of stunned visitors, many of them weeping, roamed the surrounding streets, pursued by journalists.[16]

Meanwhile, Eason was focusing on how to ensure that the Games did not grind to a halt. As soon as the explosion occurred, all state venues were put on red alert, the highest level of security. Nothing could go into or out of these state venues. Eason realized, however, that a prolonged condition red would make it impossible to resume the Games quickly. Even though athletic events were not scheduled to resume until Sunday afternoon, that would prove impossible if supplies could not be delivered and garbage could not be removed. McConnell allowed Eason to move parts of several essential state venues, such as the Georgia World Congress Center, from red to yellow alert.

---

[13]"Patchwork of Agencies Can Slow Communication, Officials Say," *Washington Post,* July 28, 1996, A23.

[14]"Special Report; Chronology; Federal Agents Tried to Prevent Disaster," *Atlanta Journal-Constitution,* July 28, 1996, 10S.

[15]Quoted in "Atlanta Games Special Report; Explosion in Centennial Park; Eyewitness Accounts," *Atlanta Journal-Constitution,* July 28, 1996, 2S.

[16]"Bomb at the Olympics; the Overview; Olympics Park Blast Kills One, Hurts 111; Atlanta Games Go On," *New York Times,* July 28, 1996, 1.

Exhibit 12C-1   Timeline of the 911 call (abridged transcript), July 28, 1996

12:58 a.m.	911 operator receives the following call: "There is a bomb in Centennial Park. You have 30 minutes."
1:01	Operator cannot find the address for Centennial Park. She is unable to send a message to the Atlanta Police Department's Agency Command Center without including an address. 911 operator calls Atlanta Command Center (ACC) but no one is answering the phone.
1:02	911 operator calls Atlanta Police Department dispatcher for zone 5 and asks, "You know the address of Centennial Park?"
	Dispatcher: "Girl, don't ask me to lie to you."
	Operator: "I tried to call the ACC but ain't nobody answering the phone. . . . But I just got this man talking about there's a bomb set to go off in 30 minutes in Centennial Park."
	911 operator calls Atlanta Command Center again and gets through, but has a bad connection and is told to call again. She calls back and asks for the address of Centennial Park. Man at Atlanta Command Center replies that he does not have the park's address, asks "What y'all think I am?" Man does give the dispatcher Centennial Park's main telephone number.
1:05	911 operator calls Centennial Park and is put on hold for two minutes. She finally gets the address. The 911 operator does not mention the bomb threat.
1:08	911 calls dispatcher with address.
1:11	Dispatcher calls patrol car and says there is a bomb threat "at 145 International Boulevard. It came from the pay phone at the Day's Inn."
1:12	Patrol car acknowledges the call and says he'll go to the Days Inn to look for the call. Patrol officer tells the dispatcher to "advise the state police, they police that park."
1:18	Patrol officer repeats request for dispatcher to call the state police. The dispatcher responds, "I'm doing that now." (The transcript has no record of that call. SOLEC also has no record of that call.)
1:20	An officer calls in and says "Be advised that something just blew up at Olympic Park."
3:30	Atlanta Police Department informs SOLEC of the 911 call.

Source: Chronology compiled from "A Menace Mishandled; Confusion after the Bomb Warning, 'Got No Address to Centennial Park,'" *Atlanta Journal-Constitution,* August 9, 1996, 1B; "Errors Delayed Warning to Police of Atlanta Bomb," *Guardian* (London), August 10, 1996, 16.

At about 3:30 in the morning, the Atlanta Police Department informed SOLEC that it had gotten a 911 call warning of a bomb in Centennial Park just minutes before it had exploded. (See Exhibit 12C-1 for a timeline of the 911 bomb report.) The Atlanta Police Department said it had called SOLEC to report the threat at 1:19 a.m., 1 minute before the explosion. However, SOLEC had no record of such a call. Regardless, a minute's warning would likely have made no difference, and in the aftermath, law enforcement officials were too busy searching for more personnel and dealing with the unfolding crisis to worry about a phantom 911 call.

At 5:15 a.m., Olympic officials made a formal announcement that the Games would continue. Although Sunday morning events would be postponed, athletic events would resume Sunday afternoon.

At roughly 6:00 a.m., the FBI's interagency Science and Technology Center confirmed what most people already believed: a single, relatively crude pipe bomb packed with nails had caused the explosion. This was not the type of weapon a sophisticated international terrorist group was likely to opt for, and indeed the preliminary analysis of the 911 call received by the Atlanta Police Department had tagged the caller as a Caucasian male without a pronounced regional accent. The evidence pointed to an act of domestic terrorism, possibly by a solo operator.

The Morning After

On Sunday morning, approximately 85 percent of ACOG's security volunteers failed to appear, and law enforcement officials were forced to fill the gaps as best they could. Law enforcement personnel also took over the operation of all the metal detectors. Meanwhile, EOD personnel were in the process of checking all athletic venues for bombs.

In addition to the severe shortfall in ACOG security personnel, security and law enforcement officials had to deal with an immediate upsurge in suspicious-package reports. After an unattended package at Underground Atlanta, a shopping center four blocks away from Centennial Park and adjacent to the Five Points Metropolitan Atlanta Rapid Transportation Authority (MARTA) station, was identified as a possible bomb, the mall was evacuated and the subway station closed. An EOD team detonated the bag and discovered that the object had been a clothes iron. Other bomb scares forced authorities to briefly close the Greyhound bus station and to delay a performance of the Atlanta Symphony Orchestra for an hour and a half.[17] For the remainder of the Games, law enforcement and security personnel received a suspicious-package call every 10 minutes (on average) from hypervigilant citizens and hoaxers. By the end of the Games, law enforcement officials at the Olympics had logged 691 calls about suspicious packages and EOD teams had examined over 600 suspicious items and x-rayed or destroyed 450 of those packages. None turned out to be a bomb.

The Games did resume Sunday afternoon, and 90 percent of the tickets available were sold out. By Monday, most of ACOG's volunteers had returned to work. In the aftermath of

---

[17]"Special Report Park Bombing Coverage; Fans Crowd City; Search Continues; More Threats Cause Underground Atlanta to Be Evacuated; Probe Delays Reopening of Centennial Park," *Atlanta Journal-Constitution,* July 28, 1996, 1S.

the bombing, law enforcement agencies held the upper hand in their arguments with ACOG. "[T]he power struggles over who was going to control the military . . . a lot of that went away, and it went to law enforcement," says GBI agent Mike Eason. "There wasn't any bickering or, you know, just ignoring the fact that you have your six military guys walking this way and mine are walking this way. They all [came under] the same umbrella and more control of that took place, which is what should have happened from the day they walked in[to] the venue."

But according to some law enforcement interviews, even after the bombing, ACOG continued to be a difficult security partner. "They did everything that they could to try to force us to go along with them on authorizing and directing that the metal detectors be turned down—this was after the bombing," says GBI director Buddy Nix. "The only thing they were concerned about was getting people in[to] the venues and out of the venues and not doing anything that would inconvenience the Olympic family. I mean, it was embarrassing."

A Bungled Warning

At a press conference on Monday morning, reporters quizzed Atlanta Police Chief Beverly Harvard about reports that the 911 call warning of a bomb had actually been received much earlier than the department had originally reported. Harvard vehemently denied that there had been any delay in responding to the threat.[18]

Yet the account of how the 911 call was handled that later emerged largely bore out these early rumors. At 12:58 a.m. (1 minute after Richard Jewell first noticed the suspicious knapsack) an Atlanta Police Department 911 operator had picked up a call and heard the following: "There is a bomb in Centennial Park. You have 30 minutes." The 911 operator attempted to enter *Centennial Park* into her computer but without success—the address of the park was not in the dispatch system. Not until 1:11 were Atlanta Police Department officers dispatched to Centennial Park. No effort was made to notify SOLEC of the bomb threat until 1:18 (and even then it was not clear whether the Atlanta Police Department did in fact manage to contact SOLEC). (See Exhibit 12C-1 for a timeline of the 911 bomb report and the dispatcher's actions.)

The Atlanta Police Department stoutly defended the conduct of the 911 dispatcher after the transcript was released. Some officers even argued that the failure to relay the bomb warning might actually have saved lives—the bomb had exploded in 22, not 30, minutes, a discrepancy that might have been an attempt to lure law enforcement officers to the scene to maximize casualties.

---

[18]"Targeting the Terrorism; Crucial Half Hour Examined; Took 27 Minutes to Notify Experts," *Atlanta Journal-Constitution,* July 30, 1996, A4.

The Games Resume

On Tuesday, July 30, Centennial Park reopened to the public after a short memorial ceremony. An additional 150 deputy sheriffs and law enforcement officials from around Georgia were on hand to help with security and to search the bags of every person entering the park.[19] Visitors were also informed that upon entering the park they could be subjected to random searches. Approximately 30,000 people returned to Centennial Park the day it reopened.[20] In the days that followed, attendance figures rose to 250,000 visitors a day.

On Tuesday afternoon, the *Atlanta Journal-Constitution* reported that the FBI had identified Richard Jewell, the security guard who first discovered the bomb, as the primary suspect in the bombing.[21] Although doubts about Jewell's guilt remained, the news that the FBI had already identified a suspect created a palpable relief in Atlanta.[22]

The last athletic event of the Centennial Games was held on August 5. Despite the Centennial Park bombing, most Atlantans and visitors to the Games viewed the Games as a resounding success. Many members of the press, particularly members of the international press, took a more skeptical view, faulting the Atlanta Games for its technical and logistical problems and for the crass commercialism of the Games. The IOC seemed to share this critical viewpoint. At the Closing Ceremonies on August 6, with Vice President Al Gore in attendance, IOC President Juan Antonio Samaranch damned the Centennial Olympic Games with faint praise by congratulating Atlanta for a "most exceptional" Games instead of offering his customary congratulations for hosting the best Games ever.

After the Closing Ceremonies, Gore left Atlanta to return to Washington. Although full security measures remained in place for another day (and high levels of security were maintained for the Paralympics Games that began soon afterward), law enforcement officers heaved a tremendous sigh of relief after the vice president's departure. From a security standpoint, the 1996 Centennial Olympics Games were at an end.

---

[19]Another 550 deputy sheriffs and other law enforcement personnel from around the state were dispatched to other venues and locations around Atlanta.

[20]"Tens of Thousands Gather as Park Makes Comeback," *Washington Post*, July 31, 1996, A1.

[21]"Atlanta Extra; FBI Suspects 'Hero' Guard May Have Planted Bomb," *Atlanta Journal-Constitution*, July 30, 1996, 1X.

[22]But it soon became clear that the FBI's suspicions about Jewell were not well founded and that the FBI's conduct toward Jewell had at best been questionable. In October, DOJ took the unusual step of formally notifying Jewell that he was no longer a suspect. In October 1998, DOJ formally indicted Eric Rudolph, who was already on the FBI's Ten Most Wanted list for a series of bomb attacks across the southeastern United States, for the Centennial Park bombing.

Key Actors in Security Preparations for the 1996 Centennial Olympic Games

Federal Officials

William Barr, U.S. attorney general

Gilmore Childers, Clinton administration's Olympic "czar"

Al Gore, vice president of the United States

Jamie Gorelick, deputy attorney general

Woody Johnson, special-agent-in-charge for Atlanta, Federal Bureau of Investigation (FBI)

Bill Kelley, fellow, National Justice Institute, and head of the Integrated Planning Group

David Maples, Olympic coordinator, FBI

U.S. Department of Defense

John Awtrey, head of U.S. Department of Defense (DOD) Office of Special Events (OSE) on-ground operations in Atlanta

Chris Bellavita, OSE consultant/planning facilitator

Ann Brooks, director, OSE

Marv Smalley, OSE liaison to Georgia law enforcement agencies

John White, deputy secretary of defense

State of Georgia Officials

Richard "Stock" Coleman, commanding officer, Georgia State Patrol, and state Olympic security coordinator (reassigned in early 1996)

Gary McConnell, director, Georgia Emergency Management Agency (GEMA), and chief of staff, State

Olympic Law Enforcement Command (SOLEC)

Sid Miles, commissioner, Georgia Department of Public Safety, and co-chair, Olympic Security Support Group (OSSG)

Zell Miller, governor

Georgia Bureau of Investigation

Jim Duff, Georgia Bureau of Investigation (GBI) agent, involved in state Olympic security planning

Michael (Mike) Eason, GBI agent, in charge of state athletic venue staffing plans

Vernon Keenan, GBI deputy director of investigations

Milton "Buddy" Nix, GBI director

City of Atlanta Officials

Eldrin Bell, chief, Atlanta Police Department (during early planning stages), and co-chair, OSSG

Bill Campbell, mayor of Atlanta

Jon Gordon, Atlanta Police Department, and chairman, Olympic Security Planning and Coordinating Committee (OSPCC) (succeeded W. J. Taylor)

Beverly Harvard, chief, Atlanta Police Department (succeeded Eldrin Bell)

W. J. Taylor, deputy chief, Atlanta Police Department; head of OSPCC, and head of Atlanta Committee for the Olympic Games (ACOG) security in Atlanta (on retirement from the Atlanta Police Department)

Atlanta Committee for the Olympic Games

A.D. Frazier, chief operating officer

William "Billy" Payne, president and CEO

Bill Rathburn, director of security

Other

Richard Jewell, private security guard, discovered Centennial Park bomb

Roland Vaughan, chief of police, Conyers, Georgia, and OSSG member

Security Preparations for the 1996 Olympic Games

Chronology of Events

1990
Thursday, September 20
Atlanta, Georgia, is selected to host the 1996 Centennial Olympic Games. The Atlanta Committee for the Olympic Games (ACOG) assumes responsibility for organizing and financing the Games.

1991
September
ACOG's security advisory body, the Olympic Security Support Group (OSSG), meets for the first time.

Fall
Deputy Chief W. J. Taylor of the Atlanta Police Department and Georgia State Patrol Officer Richard "Stock" Coleman begin discussing security plans on behalf of the city and state.

October
Worried about the state of security planning, Ann Brooks, head of the Department of Defense (DOD) Office of Special Events (OSE), brings in OSE consultant Chris Bellavita to advise organizers.

1992
Early 1992
Public law enforcement officials establish their own planning group, the Olympic Security Planning and Coordinating Committee (OSPCC), with Deputy Chief Taylor as its head.

September
U.S. Attorney General William Barr announces that the Department of Justice (DOJ) will provide $1.7 million to support state and local planning for the Olympics.

1993
Early 1993
Bill Kelley, a fellow at the National Institute of Justice, is sent to Georgia to administer the DOJ grant.

OSSG members discuss how to structure the security planning process. They subsequently adopt a planning structure similar to that used during the 1984 Los Angeles Olympics.

OSSG is given top-level planning responsibilities, while OSPCC is reconceived as a group of mid-level planners, overseeing specialized subcommittees.

Kelley's office is renamed the Integrated Planning Group (IPG) and is assigned to provide staff support to the OSPCC.

The Federal Bureau of Investigation (FBI) and others question whether W. J. Taylor (now retired from the Atlanta Police Department and an ACOG employee) should continue leading the OSPCC. He is replaced by Jon Gordon of the Atlanta Police Department, who inherits a dysfunctional group.

September

Georgia Public Safety Commissioner Sid Miles announces that the state will take responsibility for security at all state-owned venues, raising concerns that the state's Olympic security coordinator, Stock Coleman (perceived by many as less than cooperative), will have even more control over planning efforts.

Late 1993

Worried about continued problems within the OSSG and OSPCC, David Maples, the FBI's Olympic coordinator, gathers a core group of key planners. He suggests they assume some essential planning tasks. The group soon becomes an informal "shadow" OSPCC.

ACOG President Billy Payne unveils plans for a Centennial Olympic Park, which will be located in downtown Atlanta. Although quickly embraced, the idea presents serious security challenges.

Olympic organizers begin allocating law enforcement resources to specific sports venues.

1994
April

Billy Payne writes a letter to OSE head Ann Brooks requesting 8,000 soldiers to help bolster security forces. OSE considers the request excessive but passes it up the DOD chain of command.

Late 1994

Worried about the progress of security planning efforts, ACOG's Director of Security Bill Rathburn convenes representatives from key law enforcement agencies. The group takes on many of OSSG's functions.

1995

August

Rathburn and OSE negotiate ACOG's troop request down from 8,000 to 4,400 soldiers.

September

ACOG's Bill Rathburn, worried about the security situation, proposes fencing off Centennial Park. His proposal sparks an immediate outcry.

October

DOD announces that it will give the U.S. Forces Command (FORSCOM) operational authority over all military assets used for the Games.

November

Vice President Al Gore visits Atlanta. Determining that the planning process is in bad shape, he decides to appoint a federal Olympic "czar" to take control of security arrangements.

1996

Early January

Gilmore Childers, Gore's Olympic "czar," prepares for his relocation to Atlanta. He determines that it is best for him to take a facilitative, low-key approach.

A delegation of federal law enforcement and government officials meet with Georgia Governor Zell Miller to urge him to remove Stock Coleman from his position as head of the state's security planning effort.

The White House contacts Governor Miller about the planning process.

Friday, January 19

Governor Miller puts Gary McConnell, head of the Georgia Emergency Management Agency (GEMA), in charge of state security planning. Coleman is reassigned.

Monday, January 22

Governor Miller creates the State Olympic Law Enforcement Command (SOLEC) and places the twenty-nine state agencies with responsibility for the Games under its command. McConnell is named chief of staff of SOLEC.

Late winter to early spring

ACOG agrees to pay the city of Atlanta $23 million to reimburse it for costs incurred by its police department during the Games. No such agreement is made with the state, which is left to bear all costs for its Olympics deployment.

FORSCOM decides to deploy around 11,000 troops for the Olympics, far more than OSE had ever considered.

April

Gore co-chairs a high-level meeting on Olympic security preparations. The scale of the meeting alarms Bill Rathburn, who wonders whether the federal government knows of security threats, particularly terrorism-related ones, that planners in Atlanta do not.

Late spring to early summer

The FBI mounts several large field exercises involving security personnel from ACOG and law enforcement agencies.

Following a June 18 exercise, OSE consultant Bellavita determines that most agencies appear prepared for the Games, but he remains worried about interagency coordination.

Wednesday, June 26

An explosion at the Khobar Towers, a U.S. military housing complex in Saudi Arabia, kills nineteen American soldiers, heightening security concerns as the Olympics approach.

Thursday, July 4

SOLEC's command center goes operational.

Wednesday, July 17

TWA Flight #800 explodes off the coast of Long Island, killing all 230 people on board. Some suspect terrorism, which again raises worries that a security failure could occur at the Olympics.

ACOG and the Atlanta Police Department stage a dress rehearsal for the Opening Ceremonies. Observers characterize it as chaotic, even disastrous.

Friday, July 19

The Centennial Olympic Games commence.

Ninety minutes before the Opening Ceremonies are to begin, a man carrying a knife and handgun is arrested in the spectator section of the Olympic Stadium.

Friday, July 26

Governor Miller hosts a reception to thank public safety officials for their work. Overall, things appear to be going well—no major incidents have occurred and law enforcement agencies and ACOG are cooperating.

Saturday, July 27

Late in the evening, Georgia Bureau of Investigation Agent Mike Eason checks on the scene at Centennial Park. It is a hub of activity, filled with 60,000 people.

Sunday, July 28

12:57 a.m.: Richard Jewell, a private security guard, discovers a suspicious knapsack at Centennial Park. An explosives diagnostic team soon determines that the knapsack contains what looks like a bomb. Law enforcement officers begin moving people away from the knapsack.

12:58 a.m.: An Atlanta Police Department 911 operator receives a call warning of a bomb at Centennial Park. The operator is unable to enter *Centennial Park* into her computer, however, because it is not part of the dispatch system. Dispatch is delayed.

1:11 a.m.: Atlanta police officers are dispatched to Centennial Park.

1:20 a.m.: The bomb in Centennial Park explodes, blasting scores of spectators to the ground.

1:24 a.m.: SOLEC Chief Gary McConnell is awakened and told that there has been an explosion at Centennial Park. McConnell immediately contacts Governor Miller.

1:30 a.m.: Eason learns of the explosion. He orders the commander of the Olympic Village to shift to red status (lock-down mode) and rushes to SOLEC's command center.

People pour from Centennial Park into the streets while law enforcement officials attempt to treat the injured and secure the crime scene. News agencies broadcast the pandemonium live.

The FBI takes control, assuming that the explosion is a terrorist attack. All venues go into lock-down mode.

The FBI hesitates to dispatch chemical and biological response units, worried that the appearance of men in hazmat suits could trigger panic. Eventually, a sample team is sent in without protective gear.

1:45 a.m.: McConnell and Governor Miller brief President Bill Clinton.

1:50 a.m.: All seriously wounded victims are now at Grady Memorial Hospital. Two people are confirmed dead: a woman killed by shrapnel and a Turkish cameraman who had suffered a heart attack.

2:30 a.m.: State law enforcement officers and the FBI finish securing the crime scene.

Eason begins moving parts of several sports venues from red to yellow alert.

3:30 a.m.: The Atlanta Police Department informs SOLEC that at 1:19 a.m. it had reported receiving a 911 call warning of the bomb, but SOLEC has no record of the call.

5:15 a.m.: Officials announce that the Games will continue.

6:00 a.m.: The FBI's Interagency Science and Technology Center confirms that a crude pipe bomb caused the explosion. Evidence points to an act of domestic terrorism.

Morning: Around 85 percent of ACOG's security volunteers fail to appear. An upsurge in reports of suspicious packages further stretches law enforcement capacity.

Afternoon: The Games resume.

Monday, July 29
Most ACOG security volunteers return to work.

At a press conference, Atlanta Police Chief Beverly Harvard denies any delay in responding to the bomb threat, but accounts later reveal the delay caused by the confusion during dispatch.

Tuesday, July 30
Centennial Park reopens.

The *Atlanta Journal-Constitution* reports that the FBI has identified Richard Jewell as the primary suspect in the bombing. Jewell's guilt is doubted, but the public is relieved to hear that the FBI has identified a suspect.

Tuesday, August 6
At the Closing Ceremonies, International Olympic Committee (IOC) President Juan Antonio Samaranch praises the Games, but less enthusiastically than in prior years.

13 Protecting the WTO Ministerial Conference of 1999 (A): Security Preparations

David Tannenwald

The World Trade Organization (WTO), an international body that sets rules for and adjudicates trade disputes among nations, holds ministerial conferences at least every 2 years. In January 1999, the WTO selected Seattle, Washington, as the site for its next ministerial conference of 129 member countries, scheduled for late November of that year. It was a very high-profile event; President Bill Clinton and UN Secretary-General Kofi Annan, among other world leaders, were expected to attend.

From the time of the site-selection announcement to the beginning of the event itself, two sets of actors engaged in serious planning. On one side, a loosely linked network of protesters developed strategies to dramatize opposition to trade practices that they deemed damaging to industrial workers, farmers, and poor people throughout the world. Some of these activists, affiliated with the American Federation of Labor–Congress of Industrial Organizations (AFL-CIO) and other labor unions, sought to organize large-scale protest demonstrations at the meeting to focus public attention on their views. Other groups, connected through the Direct Action Network (DAN), also planned WTO protests, but they were prepared to go further by committing acts of civil disobedience to disrupt the meetings. Even more disruptive tactics were being readied by the self-styled "black bloc" of anarchists—a very secretive, far less formally organized group only minimally coupled to the other protest groups.

At the same time, public safety agencies—led by the Seattle Police Department but also including representatives from the city's fire department, the King County Sheriff's Office, the Washington State Patrol (the state police), and the FBI and federal Secret Service, among others—began working together on the security arrangements for the streets and public spaces near the locus of the ministerial meetings. (Federal agencies, led by the Secret Service, were separately responsible for security inside the meeting site.) The public safety agencies' goals were to make sure that the meeting occurred in orderly fashion, ensure the safety of the world leaders and other people attending, and permit any activists to exercise their constitutional rights to protest.

Although there had been increasingly aggressive protest activities at previous international meetings, including riots at the previous year's WTO Ministerial Conference in Geneva, Switzerland, local leaders strongly felt that the European experience was not predictive of what would happen in Seattle. The views of Seattle's mayor and the police leadership were framed by the last major international meeting held in Seattle, the Asia Pacific Economic Cooperation (APEC) conference in 1993. At that meeting, there had been no

This case was written by David Tannenwald, research assistant, Taubman Center for State and Local Government, for Herman B. "Dutch" Leonard, George F. Baker Jr. Professor of Public Management, and Arnold M. Howitt, executive director of the Taubman Center for State and Local Government, John F. Kennedy School of Government, Harvard University. Funding was provided by the Taubman Center. Kennedy School of Government Case Program, CR16-08-1897.0 and CR16-08-1897.1. Copyright © 2005, 2008 by the President and Fellows of Harvard College.

disruptive protests, and local leaders believed that the tolerant ethos of the Pacific Northwest would again prevail for the WTO ministerial meeting in Seattle.

As planning proceeded, there were some signals of potential trouble to come in intelligence reports gathered in Seattle and gleaned by federal law enforcement from their own sources; but little specific information came to light from traditional sources about what might occur in Seattle. During the event, however, the behavior of some of the protesters far exceeded what public safety officials expected, outnumbered law enforcement officials lost control of the crowds outside the meeting venue, violence erupted, police overreacted, and video of these troubles was beamed across the world.

In reading this case, consider how the security planners might have thought differently about how to prepare for the WTO Ministerial Conference. What levels of trouble should security planners be ready for even if they expect less to materialize? For what contingencies should they have been planning? How can the probability of bad outcomes be assessed in advance of an event? How can planners avoid becoming the prisoners of their own expectations? By what means should security planners obtain information about potential disruptions? When resources are too scarce to cover every contingency, how should security plans be made?

Discussion Questions

- To what extent should security planners have understood in advance the nature of the challenges they would face during the WTO meeting?
- What impeded security planners' ability to reach a better understanding of the challenges?
- What procedures or behaviors might have made it more likely that they would have developed a more complete and accurate assessment of the situation?

"We may not know what is going to happen, but we are prepared."
Vivian Phillips, Seattle communications director, November 9, 1999[1]

When the World Trade Organization (WTO), the international body that sets the rules for trade and adjudicates trade disputes among its member nations, announced in late January 1999 that the city of Seattle would host the Third WTO Ministerial Conference that coming fall, it seemed to have made an excellent choice.[2] The city had long-standing ties to international trade and enjoyed a reputation for having a relaxed atmosphere and a picturesque natural setting.

---

[1]Quoted in Stephen Dunphy, "We're Ready for Anything, Officials Say," *Seattle Times,* November 10, 1999, available at http://web.lexis-nexis.com [accessed April 29, 2005].

[2]World Trade Organization, "Seattle: What's at Stake?" available at www.wto.org/english/thewto_e/ minist_ e/min99_e/english/book_e/stak_e_2.htm [accessed April 28, 2005]; World Trade Organization, "Office of the United States Trade Representative in Washington D.C.," available at www.wto.org/english/thewto_e/ minist_e/ min99_e/english/press_e/ustr_e.htm [accessed April 28, 2005].

The Ministerial Conference, the WTO's highest decision-making body, generally met once every 2 years. Scheduled to take place from Tuesday, November 30, through Friday, December 3, 1999, the Seattle Ministerial was supposed to launch a major new round of trade negotiations "to further liberalize international trade"[3] and to review rules regarding services, agriculture, tariffs, and dumping (among other issues). With many prominent leaders, including U.S. President Bill Clinton and UN Secretary-General Kofi Annan, planning to attend, a secure setting was essential.[4]

Within weeks of the announcement that Seattle would host the Ministerial, two very different groups began to plan for the events that would occur in the streets outside the conference. On the one side, a diverse group of protesters began to plan how they could best voice their anti-WTO agenda. On the other side and at the same time, law enforcement officials started to gather intelligence and frame a plan that would protect trade officials and dignitaries while allowing protesters to exercise their constitutional rights of assembly, free speech, and protest.

The Early Planning among Protest Groups

Anti-WTO groups had, in fact, begun mobilizing even before the WTO announced that Seattle would host the Ministerial, thanks in large part to the vigilance of Michael Dolan, a leading activist who had been following the WTO's plans carefully.[5] In January 1999, Dolan identified Seattle and San Diego as the leading host-city candidates, and he notified activists in both communities that an announcement was imminent.[6]

Once Seattle was named the official host, Dolan flew to the city and started to organize. He met with Sally Soriano, the coordinator of the Washington Fair Trade Campaign, and David Korten, a leader in the antiglobalization movement with strong ties to Washington state.[7] Together, they organized a rally that took place on January 20, 1999, at Seattle's Labor Temple and was attended by about eighty people. There, a "self-selected . . . steering committee"[8] emerged and agreed to meet once a week. The groups also agreed to continue

---

[3]World Trade Organization, "Press Pack: World Trade Organization: 3rd Ministerial Conference Seattle," available at www.wto.org/english/thewto_e/minist_e/min99_e/english/about_e/presspack_english.pdf [accessed March 1, 2005], 3.

[4]Ibid., 3–4.

[5]Dolan was the deputy director of Public Citizen's Global Trade Watch and the field director of the Citizens Trade Campaign (an environmental-trade-labor coalition). Margaret Levi and Gillian Murphy, "Coalitions of Contention: The Case of the WTO Protests in Seattle," *Political Studies* 54, no. 4 (2006): 658–659.

[6]Michael Dolan, interview by Steven Pfaff and Gillian Murphy, WTO History Project, Harry Bridges Center for Labor Studies (University of Washington), November 10, 1999, available at http://depts.washington.edu/wtohist/interviews/Dolan-Pfaff%20Murphy.pdf, 3 [accessed April 28, 2005] (hereafter, 1999 interview).

[7]"David Korten," Wikipedia, available at http://en.wikipedia.org/wiki/David_Korten [accessed April 29, 2005].

[8]Dolan, 1999 interview, 4.

to hold a series of rallies at the Labor Temple; these eventually became meetings that were held about once a month. By nightfall on January 20, the protesters' early organizational structure was in place.

It quickly became apparent, however, that this nascent coalition of protest groups spanned a wide range of ideologies. The debate over what to name the committee provides a case in point. As Dolan painfully recalls,

We spent several months just deciding on the name for this effort. Some people wanted it to be called People for Fair Trade and to reach out to the moderate middle that needed to be educated about the WTO, and People for Fair Trade sounded innocuous and harmless, but some people wanted the more militant, No2WTO, which stands for Network Opposed to the World Trade Organization.[9]

Unable to resolve their differences, they called themselves People for Fair Trade/Network Opposed to WTO (PFT).

Driven in part—and, to some extent, *a*part—by their ideological diversity, those involved in the original meeting formed a loose coalition of many groups, the most prominent of which were the Direct Action Network (DAN; itself an amalgam of many groups), labor, and PFT; other groups, including the "black bloc," a shadowy group of anarchists, also eventually became part of this informal association.[10]

Over the next few months, DAN gradually coalesced. A letter to activists by Art and Revolution, "a San Francisco-based group devoted to developing creative protests,"[11] led to the formation of a network by the end of the spring. The group applied for and received funding from Global Exchange, the Rainforest Action Network, and the Ruckus Society. And at a meeting in August, DAN decided on a strategy that, according to Professor Margaret Levi and Gillian Murphy (contributors to the WTO History Project at the University of Washington), emphasized "coordinated but autonomous actions" by its various affinity groups.[12]

Like DAN, labor spent the first half of 1999 mobilizing support and formulating its strategy. During the winter, Dolan had lobbied labor to organize for the WTO. Although labor leaders were receptive, tensions existed between the American Federation of Labor–Congress of Industrial Organizations (AFL-CIO) national leadership, which advocated reforming the WTO, and more militant local organizers.[13] An event at the Washington State Labor Council Convention in August provides a case in point. Because minimal WTO-related activity was

---

[9]Ibid.

[10]The "black bloc" is variously referred to, sometimes as a group and sometimes as a tactical approach to protest. Consistent with the group's anarchist roots, the label is often not capitalized even when used as a proper noun, a convention that we follow here.

[11]Levi and Murphy, "Coalitions of Contention," 660.

[12]Ibid.

[13]Dolan, 1999 interview, 11; Geov Parrish, "Will Labor Fight?" *Seattle Weekly*, September 30, 1999, available at http://web.lexis-nexis.com/scholastic [accessed February 24, 2005].

planned for the conference, several labor activists convinced a delegate to put an anti-WTO resolution on the agenda. The resolution passed. But, according to Levi and Murphy, "Its passage was a source of tension between King County Labor Council head [Ron] Judd and AFL-CIO President John Sweeney, who accused Judd of not being able to control his own people." [14] Soon thereafter, Judd removed Martha Baskin, a local labor leader who had pushed for the resolution, from her position as the King County Labor Council fair trade representative.

Despite these tensions, by the end of August, the AFL-CIO had two full-time organizers working to coordinate a major rally and march planned for November 30 (the Ministerial's opening day). Simultaneously, other labor organizations were "mobilizing" their own forces (a term used by the *Seattle Weekly*). Although far from unified, labor began to look as though it would be a major factor during the Ministerial. [15]

The umbrella group PFT, meanwhile, evolved from a steering committee to a more robust organization run by Dolan, with an office and a staff. [16] In addition to lobbying nongovernmental organizations (NGOs), "it ran a speakers bureau, held large public informational meetings, did outreach to student groups, and supplied local activists with background materials." [17] PFT was especially helpful for labor because it recruited people to participate in the labor march. Levi and Murphy, however, describe a nuanced relationship between PFT (and Dolan), on the one hand, and DAN, on the other: "Publicly, Dolan distanced himself and PFT from DAN. Privately, he continued to cooperate sporadically with DAN, even providing some of the cash for the lease on the warehouse space in Seattle where DAN trained and fed activists." [18] Dolan thus served as an unofficial intermediary between labor and DAN.

Once these groups had formed into a loose coalition, they spent the summer months laying the foundations for their efforts. This included both coordination and a great deal of logistical work. PFT, for instance, organized extensive conference calls with NGO leaders. Dolan described the sometimes comical coordination challenges: "My God, when we do these international conference calls, just the time difference alone. I mean, it is 7 am in Malaysia, it's 9 pm in Paris, you know, . . . I've gotten people out of bed on the West Coast in the U.S. at 5 am. I've woken Agnes Bertrand in France at 2 am." [19]

Dolan also made a host of local arrangements, booking hotel rooms and holding various educational events. [20] During this period, many of the protest groups also engaged in educational drives, holding talks, symposia, and teach-ins in and around Seattle. The main

---

[14] Levi and Murphy, "Coalitions of Contention," 662.

[15] Parrish, "Will Labor Fight?"

[16] Levi and Murphy, "Coalitions of Contention," 659.

[17] Ibid.

[18] Ibid., 660.

[19] Dolan, 1999 interview, 12.

[20] Levi and Murphy, "Coalitions of Contention," 659.

objectives of these events were to discuss major issues, to increase general understanding of the WTO's power and importance, and, especially, to raise awareness that the WTO's next major meeting would take place in Seattle immediately after Thanksgiving.

The "black bloc" may at this time already have been planning to engage in more aggressive action at the protests. Few details are known about the group's formal preparations, but David Postman of the *Seattle Times* reported, "From the earliest days of planning for protests, there was talk that young, tough anarchists would make a showing during the World Trade Organization."[21]

A major protest in London on June 18, 1999, may have provided a catalyst for the preparations of violent anarchists. J18, "a previously unknown anarchist umbrella group," had organized what it called on its website a "carnival against capitalism" with events in forty-three countries on June 18, the same day as the opening of the G-8 Summit in Cologne, Germany.[22] The *London Financial Times* painted a frightening picture of the protests in London, where "police were attacked with bricks and metal pipes by groups of activists, and protesters forced the evacuation of the London International Financial Futures and Options Exchange."[23] In a harbinger of the impressive application of technology that N30 protesters (the term *N30* signifying November 30, the opening day of the Ministerial) would use in Seattle, J18 used Internet-based communications to coordinate events worldwide.[24]

Closer to Seattle, the protests on June 18 may have galvanized a violent group of anarchists in Eugene, Oregon. A town with a reputation for tolerating fringe groups, Eugene was one of the many places that witnessed protests on June 18. The situation there took a violent turn when, in the midst of preplanned speeches and demonstrations, "a breakaway mob in hoods and masks began marching through downtown, throwing rocks, smashing storefronts and jumping on cars."[25] Although it was impossible to know exactly which anarchists participated in the violence, followers of John Zerzan, an anarchist who had advocated property destruction, appeared to have played a major role.[26] The J18 incident in Eugene received extensive news coverage, and twenty people were arrested. A number of anarchists from Eugene were believed to be among those who later gathered in Seattle.

What some saw as a harsh sentence for one Eugene anarchist who was arrested on June 18 appears to have increased group members' agitation. Robert Lee Thaxton received a 7-year

---

[21]David Postman, "Group Rejects Others' Pleas of No Violence'—Black-Clad Anarchists Target Cars, Windows," *Seattle Times,* December 1, 1999, available at http://web.lexis-nexis.com [accessed February 22, 2005].

[22]Ibid.

[23]Samantha Sanghera, Michael Peel, and Jimmy Burns, "Anti-capitalists Lay Siege to the City of London," *London Financial Times,* June 19, 1999, available at http://web.lexis-nexis.com [accessed February 28, 2005].

[24]Adam Sherwin and Tracy Connor, "Internet Message Was Invitation to Protest," *Times* (London), June 19, 1999.

[25]Terrence Foley, "Riot Tests College Town's Tie-Dyed Ideals of Tolerance," Associated Press State & Local Wire, July 2, 1999, available at http://web.lexis-nexis.com [accessed March 1, 2005].

[26]Ibid.

prison sentence for throwing a rock at a police officer during the June 18 rioting in Eugene. Zerzan declared, "What they're trying to do is intimidate people. But I don't think it's going to stop us from trying to get across our point of view." [27] Other anarchists were less polite. Posting on an Internet message board for anarchists, "Duff" said, "Thaxton is a Political Prisoner and deserves our full support. . . . (expletive) the police." "Jeff," another protester, added, "and the press." [28]

The J18 protests also appear to have increased international coordination among potentially violent anarchists. The London *Sunday Times* reported on September 12 that anarchists involved in the June 18 protests were using international coordination to plan a similar global riot on November 30, including violence in Seattle. [29]

The protesters opposed the WTO for a variety of reasons. Labor groups were angry about job loss to overseas contractors and argued that international labor standards should be established, including the right to form unions and prohibitions against child labor, forced labor, and discrimination in the workplace. [30] Environmentalists argued that, among other things, trade was increasing deforestation. [31] Animal rights activists were outraged over a WTO ruling that weakened a U.S. law that required shrimp boats to have nets from which sea turtles can escape. [32] Others simply opposed capitalism. Most protesters agreed, however, that the WTO was undemocratic and favored corporate interests over average people. More generally, as the *Seattle Times* suggested in late November, protesters "made [WTO] a kind of metaphor for all their fears of globalization." [33]

Security Planning

As the protest groups continued to organize, the Seattle Police Department (SPD) and affiliated agencies started to develop their own plans to ensure that the event proceeded smoothly. The SPD, as the law enforcement authority in the host jurisdiction, would have the lead, particularly for safety and law enforcement in the streets outside the meeting venues (as well as

---

[27]Quoted in Cristine Gonzalez, "Anarchists Denounce Rioter's Seven-Year Sentence for Throwing Rock," Associated Press State & Local Wire, October 15, 1999, available at http://web.lexis-nexis.com [accessed March 1, 2005].

[28]Quoted in "Anarchist Gets Sentenced to 7 Years in Eugene Oregon US for J18 Activity," A-Infos, October, 16, 1999, available at www.ainfos.ca/99/oct/ainfos0048.html [accessed March 1, 2005].

[29]Mark Macaskill and Jessica Berry, "Anti-City Anarchists Plot Global Riot," *Sunday Times* (London), September 12, 1999, available at http://web.lexis-nexis.com [accessed March 9, 2005].

[30]Tyrone Beason, "The WTO/The Opposition," *Seattle Times*, November 7, 1999, available at http://web.lexis-nexis.com [accessed February 24, 2005].

[31]Robert McClure, "Critics of WTO Launch Ad Blitz," *Seattle Post-Intelligencer*, November 12, 1999, available at http://web.lexis-nexis.com [accessed February 24, 2005].

[32]Ibid.

[33]Stephen Dunphy, David Postman, and Helen Jung, "The Lines Have Been Drawn—Battle in Seattle Pits Free-Trade Backers against Those Who Vow to Protest Greed," *Seattle Times*, November 28, 1999, available at http://web.lexis-nexis.com [accessed April 29, 2005].

elsewhere in the city).[34] The planners were at a disadvantage from the beginning, however, because of the relatively short notice. (According to the SPD, lead time for such high-profile events is ordinarily 14–24 months; planners in Seattle had only about 10 months.[35])

As in most security plans, gathering sound intelligence was a key part of Seattle's approach. In late spring 1999, the WTO Information Management Subcommittee was formed by the Public Safety Committee (PSC), "an interjurisdictional organization established to coordinate the public safety planning for the Conference," [36] Led by the SPD, the Information Management Subcommittee also included officials from the Federal Bureau of Investigation (FBI), the King County Sheriff's Office, and the Washington State Patrol.

Seattle and Washington state law enforcement personnel, in fact, had begun receiving intelligence several months prior to the subcommittee's establishment. In February 1999, the FBI briefed the SPD about the major riots that had occurred at the WTO meeting in Geneva in 1998.[37] Many in the SPD downplayed the relevance of these prior events; in the words of the SPD's *After Action Report*, the protests in Geneva were "viewed as unique to Europe and highly unlikely to migrate to the U.S. Moreover, the use of physical barricades and razor wire to secure the ministerial conference in Geneva was viewed as inflammatory, leading to the assumption that Seattle's more open and facilitative approach to demonstrations would lessen the chances of violence and property destruction." [38]

The King County Sheriff's Department, in a February 16 internal assessment, was less optimistic, concluding:

An estimated 10,000 demonstrators, representing a wide variety of viewpoints and causes, appeared on each of several days during the [Geneva] conference. This fact is particularly noteworthy because the people of Switzerland are noted for their reserve, orderly behavior and tradition of non-participation in such events. Reasonable speculation is that we will experience some protests and/or demonstrations. . . . Even a peaceful and orderly conference would tax local law enforcement resources. Dealing with 10,000 plus demonstrators in the core area of Seattle would be a significant challenge.[39]

---

[34]Reflecting the main purview of the SPD and its primary law enforcement partner agencies, this case focuses on citywide security planning and enforcement efforts, not on the venue-specific security arrangements.

[35]Linda Pierce, "The Seattle Police Department After Action Report: World Trade Organization Ministerial Conference Seattle, Washington November 29, 1999–December 3, 1999," Seattle Police Department, available at www.ci.seattle.wa.us/Police/Publications/WTO/WTO_AAR.PDF [accessed April 29, 2005], 51.

[36]Ibid., 13.

[37]City of Seattle, "Panel 2 Final Report: Report to the Seattle City Council WTO Accountability Committee by the Citizens' Panel on WTO Operations," WTO Accountability Review Committee, City of Seattle, available at www.cityofseattle.net/wtocommittee/panel2_report2.htm [accessed February 7, 2005].

[38]Pierce, "Seattle Police Department After Action Report," 18.

[39]"Memo from a King County Officer to Sheriff Reichert," February 16, 1999, quoted in City of Seattle, "Panel 2 Final Report," App. D.

Given the many meetings at which members of the Sheriff's Department and the SPD interacted over this period, it seems likely that at least the sense of this assessment was shared with the SPD.

Although no major new intelligence surfaced during the spring, the incidence and seriousness of threat warnings gradually increased during the summer. On July 7, the FBI issued a "threat assessment [which] stated there was a 'strong indication' considerable protest activity will be directed at the [Conference] . . . but concluded that there was 'no credible information' to suggest that 'violence or significant property damage' should be expected."[40] However, during August, reports of potentially disruptive acts increased in frequency. All the same, the SPD appears to have disregarded much of this information, explaining in its *After Action Report* that "Events like the WTO invariably attract doomsayers and extremist rhetoric. The challenge of intelligence gathering is to separate disinformation and fallacious reports from potentially authentic data."[41]

The SPD also appears to have lacked the expertise to interpret these data. In its *After Action Report*, the SPD identifies the use of the Internet by protesters as a critical issue and suggests that "focus and expertise needs to be developed and dedicated to the use of the Internet and other technologies as a communication and intelligence tool."[42] By the end of the summer, a significant body of evidence suggested that protesters were mobilizing, many with the explicit intent of interfering with the WTO.

Parallel to the ongoing intelligence-gathering effort, security planning for the meetings began with the establishment of the Public Safety Executive Committee (PSEC), which consisted of command representatives from the SPD, King County Sheriff's Office, Seattle Fire Department, Washington State Patrol, FBI, and U.S. Secret Service. From the beginning, the Seattle-based representatives to the PSEC (the SPD representatives, in particular) took the lead in the committee's security planning efforts, with federal member agencies playing a somewhat more limited role.[43]

The PSEC, in turn, established the Public Safety Committee (PSC), which convened semimonthly until mid-September and weekly thereafter. The PSC was formed "to coordinate the

---

[40]Pierce, "Seattle Police Department After Action Report," 18.

[41]Ibid.

[42]Ibid., 54.

[43]This dynamic seems to have carried over into security for the talks themselves. For instance, although the presence of high-level officials from the United States and other nations implied that federal law enforcement agencies would have responsibility for planning and providing public safety and law enforcement inside official venues, the WTO Accountability Review Committee found that in other instances, "officials from a variety of federal agencies had only a limited, sporadic, and sometimes conflicting role." WTO Accountability Committee, "Panel Three Final Report," available at www.cityofseattle.net/wtocommittee/panel3_report2.htm [accessed 30 September 2007].

public safety planning for the Conference." [44] In addition to the members of the PSEC, the PSC included the Bellevue, Tukwila, and Port of Seattle police departments, the Federal Aviation Administration, and the U.S. Department of State Bureau of Diplomatic Security. Below the PSC lay public safety subcommittees that dealt with issues such as intelligence and venue security.

As the lead agency for security planning efforts, the SPD formed a full-time unit to be a liaison with the PSC and to coordinate the PSC's subcommittees. [45] Several foundational assumptions guided the SPD's preparations. First, it based its security model on what it regarded as a "reasonable premise" that security needs for the WTO Ministerial would be comparable to those at the Asia Pacific Economic Cooperation (APEC) talks that Seattle had hosted in 1993. [46] Like the WTO, the APEC talks focused on broad economic issues and were attended by major world leaders. The APEC talks had not attracted major protests. In addition, the SPD was optimistic because of Seattle's history of peaceful protests. [47] Early security plans did not, therefore, call for a large show of force.

On May 13, Seattle's Mayor Paul Schell sent a letter to "forty-one city and county executives . . . asking them to identify law enforcement resources that would be available for staffing the conference." [48] The majority of those who were solicited could not commit forces either because of already inadequate staffing levels or because the city of Seattle could not guarantee reimbursement (or, in some cases, both). However, the Washington State Patrol, King County Sheriff's Office, Port of Seattle Police, and Bellevue Police offered some support. [49]

In response to the July 7 FBI bulletin, the SPD bolstered its Demonstration Management Team (which was to be responsible for controlling the protests), increasing the planned number of officers to be deployed from 90 to 180. [50] The SPD initially planned to use its existing Special Weapons and Tactics (SWAT) teams to police the demonstrations, but in mid-July it set up a Demonstration Management Subcommittee and formed special-purpose demonstration management teams. Some officers were scheduled to perform other specified tasks during the conference, including working on chemical agent response teams (CARTs), guarding the hotels, and managing traffic. By contrast, the demonstration management teams were focused on controlling the protests. Nevertheless, planners maintained their fundamental assumptions about the APEC model and the peaceful tendencies of the

---

[44]Pierce, "Seattle Police Department After Action Report," 13.
[45]Ibid., 14.
[46]Ibid., 4.
[47]Ibid.
[48]Ibid., 29.
[49]Ibid., 29–30.
[50]Ibid., 18.

people of Seattle. In spite of the rising levels of media attention and Internet threats, few alterations were made in the deployment plan over the course of the rest of the summer.

Protest Plans Gel

By the fall, the major protest groups had developed and, in many cases, broadcasted clear strategies. The AFL-CIO, for instance, planned a massive rally and march for November 30, the opening day of the conference. Their stated intent was not interfering with the conference but, instead, "supporting and legitimizing President Clinton's actions at the conference through purely symbolic displays as a loyal opposition."[51] DAN, on the other hand, planned on the same day to engage in civil disobedience in an attempt to shut down the WTO meetings.[52]

In preparing their respective plans, both groups had sophisticated organizations. Labor, led by the AFL-CIO, focused on recruiting people to participate in its march through a full-time team of roughly twenty organizers. DAN, meanwhile, focused on training for nonviolent civil protest and disobedience as well as recruitment. Various groups within DAN held training workshops for protesters, the most notable of which was a camp held in the Cascade Mountains in mid-September by the Ruckus Society.[53]

Although Dolan ensured some coordination between the groups, communication between labor and DAN was at best uneven. As Levi and Murphy explain, "According to Dolan, both organized labor and DAN maintained contact with him but not with each other, and they used him to coordinate with each other."[54]

---

[51]Paul de Armond, "Netwar in the Emerald City: WTO Protest Strategy and Tactics," in *Networks and Netwars: The Future of Terror, Crime, and Militancy,* ed. John Arquilla and David Ronfeldt, available at www.rand.org/publications/MR/MR1382/MR1382.ch7.pdf, 204. [accessed April 29, 2005].

[52]Michael Dolan, interview by Jeremy Simer, WTO History Project, March 3 2000, available at http://depts.washington.edu/wtohist/interviews/Dolan_Simer.pdf. [accessed April 29, 2005] (hereafter, 2000 interview).

[53]Judd Slivka, "Ruckus Society Getting Set to Disrupt WTO Conference," *Seattle Post-Intelligencer,* September 15, 1999, available at http://forests.org/archive/general/rucsocgs.htm [accessed February 22, 2005].

[54]Levi and Murphy, "Coalitions of Contention," 661. In an interview following the Minsterial, Dolan relayed an interesting story that illustrates the poor communication and coordination among the various parties. "So, the DAN people were trying to figure out—they weren't even called DAN yet—trying to figure out when they should do their action—some direct action against the World Trade Organization. . . . One weekend, this must have been in July, David Solnit [from Art and Revolution] called me and said 'When is Labor wanting to do their thing and what's their feeling about when we do our . . . direct action, cause we want to do our thing the morning of the 30th . . . at the opening ceremonies to shut it down. Will Labor have a hard time with that?' And I said, 'We'll get back to you, I'll let you know.' So I called Labor and I said, 'The Direct Action people want to do something on Tuesday morning the 30th. I need to get right back to them because they're going to be having a big conference call to decide this to make a decision and if you have a serious objection, they need to know it soon.' . . . Labor didn't get back to me. So, I called David and I said, 'You know, they didn't get back to me. So, I guess you have the tacit . . . agreement.' . . . and then the following week Labor got back to me to say, 'No, we don't think that's a good idea.' And I said, 'Labor, it's too late, all right?' " Dolan, 2000 interview, 11–12.

The "black bloc's" preparation appears to have been both more secretive and less thorough. At the very least, some preparations were under way; in a communiqué released several days after the November 30 protest, the "black bloc" noted "we've all been working on this convergence in Seattle for months."[55] In addition, media reports indicated that militant British anarchists were coordinating with their American counterparts to mount a campaign of property destruction similar to the J18 London protest.[56]

During the fall, media and Internet reports about protest activity continued to increase in frequency and increasingly predicted dangerous protests. Throughout the spring and summer, however, the SPD had been restricted from conducting its own direct surveillance of any of the protest groups as a result of Seattle's Investigations Ordinance, which requires approval for law enforcement to collect information about any group and for the disclosure of any such surveillance (generally not more than 6 months later). In late September, the SPD finally received clearance to engage in its own direct surveillance of protest groups.

Despite the increased reports of threats, the SPD did not significantly change its strategy. Rather, it continued to develop the details of its implementation plan. For instance, it designated protest zones near major sites, which were communicated to protest groups, and met with protest groups to discuss the expected events.[57] At these meetings, Dolan says he warned the SPD that things might get out of control: "Every single meeting I had with the police, I made it very clear that there were lots of groups coming to Seattle, many of which I wouldn't have any control over. . . . The police told us they would actually wait until the cameras were rolling to allow for the choreography of the confrontation to unfold in a dramatic way."[58]

The police also prepared for potential confrontations with crowds by purchasing chemical irritants. With eight launchers and $8,100 of munitions, the police were confident that they had a sufficient supply of crowd-control agents "to last through two days of moderate usage or one day of heavy usage."[59] But in the event that supplies ran low, the police set up contingency plans to get additional tear gas and pepper spray from nearby towns and, if necessary, from Wyoming.[60] However, according to one observer, "a police consultant

[55]ACME Collective, "N30 Black Bloc Communique," WTO History Project, Harry Bridges Center for Labor Studies (University of Washington), available at http://depts.washington.edu/wtohist/documents/black_bloc_communique.htm [accessed February 9, 2005].

[56]Macaskill and Berry, "Anti-City Anarchists Plot Global Riot."

[57]Pierce, "Seattle Police Department After Action Report," 21, 23.

[58]Quoted in David Postman and Mike Carter, "Police Switch to a New Strategy—They Say Rough Protest Caught Them off Guard," *Seattle Times,* December 1, 1999, available at http://web.lexis-nexis.com [accessed February 7, 2005].

[59]Pierce, "Seattle Police Department After Action Report," 28.

[60]Ibid., 28, 72.

recommended that $100,000 be spent to purchase tear gas and other crowd control agents, but this was cut to $20,000." [61]

In parallel with the logistical planning, Seattle leaders projected themselves calmly and confidently to the public. In a letter to Seattle business leaders at the end of October, Mayor Schell observed, "Seattle has a long history of level-headed citizen expression and demonstrations. As the city did prior to the APEC conference, we have been meeting regularly with protesting organizations to support their right to free speech. . . . We expect everything to flow peacefully during the event, but we are fully prepared to respond to emerging situations if need be." [62] As protesters continued to organize and mobilize, the police and mayor remained confident in their own preparations.

A well-planned takeover of the Plum Creek Timber Company offices in Seattle on October 28 and an arson attack at the city's downtown GAP store on November 1, however, increased concerns that violence and vandalism would occur at the WTO Ministerial. At Plum Creek, a security guard was assaulted and a key card security system was foiled, giving an unknown number of intruders access to the premises. Door locks were taped, apparently in an attempt to permit later reentry. [63] At the GAP, a front window was broken, and three firebombs were thrown into the store. An *A* (an anarchist symbol, sometimes also used by the Animal Liberation Front) was spray-painted on several parts of the store, and anti-WTO literature was left behind. [64]

Still, Mayor Schell continued to appear calm and confident. In a letter mailed on November 2 to Seattle business owners, who were concerned about losing business during the conference, he proclaimed, "This event is a momentous, exciting affair for Seattle. It speaks to the growing stature of Seattle's place on the world stage, and it shows impressive confidence in our ability to serve as gracious and competent hosts for international dialogues." [65] He frequently reiterated this theme, often using the same words, in the days before the Ministerial began.

[61]Quoted in David Wilma, "What about Security?" HistoryLink.org: The Online Encyclopedia of Washington State History, available at www.historylink.org/essays/output.cfm?file_id=2137 [accessed January 18, 2005].

[62]Quoted in David Wilma, "Mayor Schell Advises Seattle Business Owners on October 29, 1999, of Plans to Handle Protests during the Upcoming WTO Meeting," HistoryLink.org: The Online Encyclopedia of Washington State History, available at www.historylink.org/essays/printer_friendly/index.cfm?file_id=2137 [accessed January 18, 2005].

[63]City of Seattle, "Report to the Seattle City Council by the Citizens' Panel on WTO Operations," WTO Accountability Review Committee, City of Seattle, available at www.cityofseattle.net/wtocommittee/panel3 final.pdf, 17 [accessed April 29, 2005].

[64]U.S. Department of Justice, "Terrorism in the United States 1999," Federal Bureau of Investigation, available at www.fbi.gov/publications/terror/terror99.pdf, 7 [accessed August 30, 2005].

[65]Quoted in Judd Slivka, "Downtown Traffic Will Be a Mess; Streets Will Be Closed for WTO and Protests," *Seattle Post-Intelligencer,* November 2, 1999, available at http://web.lexis-nexis.com [accessed April 29, 2005].

The most noteworthy additional official intelligence received during the fall, the second FBI threat assessment, came in briefings 3 weeks prior to the conference and in a written FBI report to the SPD on November 17.[66] According to the *Seattle Times,* the FBI assessed "the threat of terrorism and violent protest activity . . . as low to medium," an apparently intentionally vague and broad range encompassing anything "from simple civil disobedience to an Oklahoma City-style terrorist bombing." [67]

Concerns about potentially violent protests continued to emerge in the press in late November. As Geov Parrish, a columnist for the *Seattle Weekly,* summarized, "The West Coast network that is organizing WTO anarchist protests has agreed to abide by the nonviolence code being promulgated by Seattle direct action organizers—but that won't necessarily stop individuals or small affinity groups from acting on their own outside the mainstream protests." [68]

So, while it appears that many of the anarchists were preparing for nonviolent action, a small group, at the very least, remained open to engaging in property destruction—or worse.

The Final 2 Weeks

During the 2 weeks leading up to the Ministerial, the protest organizations set up their official headquarters in Seattle to complete preparations. DAN established its headquarters at 420 East Denny Way, about ten blocks from the convention center where the Ministerial was to be held. With teach-ins, training sessions, street theater, and housing, the headquarters provided support for protesters coming into town. It also provided the venue at which DAN could finalize its plans to shut down the WTO. There, organizers identified key intersections that they needed to block to prevent delegates and dignitaries from entering the convention center.

By the night before the conference, DAN members had organized themselves into "affinity groups," small cells of roughly three to ten people each. They had also determined a protest strategy. In a first wave of action, members were to cluster themselves into groups of two hundred to three hundred, risking arrest as they locked themselves together at key intersections. In a second wave, thousands of people were to surround these clusters, making it more difficult for the police to arrest the protesters.[69] DAN was also well-equipped with

---

[66]Pierce, "Seattle Police Department After Action Report," 18.

[67]Mike Carter, "Police Had WTO Alert—FBI Warning of Violence Came Well before Event," *Seattle Times,* December 11, 1999, available at http://web.lexis-nexis.com [accessed January 28, 2005].

[68]Geov Parrish, "The High Cost of Throwing Rocks," *Seattle Weekly,* November 4, 1999, available at http://web.lexis-nexis.com [accessed April 29, 2005].

[69]Armond, "Netwar in the Emerald City," 209–210.

a "communications network of cell phones, radios, police scanners, and portable computers."[70] On the night before the protests, DAN, its constituent groups, and the many people in those groups were organized, motivated, and ready.

Meanwhile, labor spent the final 2 weeks gearing up for its rally and march. Anticipating a crowd as large as 50,000 people, the AFL-CIO initially thought its march would essentially push the DAN protesters out of the downtown area, apparently believing that the DAN protesters would be absorbed by the larger AFL-CIO march as it passed them by.[71] According to commentator Paul de Armond,

The AFL-CIO strategy was to hold a rally at the Seattle Center and then march downtown (but not too far). Central to the AFL-CIO strategy was the notion that they could contain the majority of the demonstrators and keep them out of the downtown area. All the AFL-CIO had to do was prevent any effective protests by groups not under their control and allow the media to spin the tale of how labor caused a sudden change in national policy.[72]

The anarchists used the final 2 weeks to organize as well. Some set up a headquarters called The Squat at 918 Virginia Street, about six blocks from the convention area.[73] *Time* magazine describes the house as:

A largely vacant building on the edge of downtown Seattle. The 'squat' . . . [is] a protesters' crash pad. About 100 people a night sleep there. There's no power or water, but organizers have set up a kitchen and security and toilet systems. House rules hang on one wall: **"NO ILLEGAL DRUGS, NO ALCOHOL, NO WEAPONS"** and so on, ending with **"NO VIOLENCE."**[74]

Like DAN, the "black bloc" organized into small operating groups.[75]

It remains unclear whether any, some, or a substantial number of the anarchists actively planned and intended to engage in property destruction and violent protest[76] or, instead, were simply prepared to see events evolve in that direction as the circumstances might dictate. Either way, many arrived in Seattle in the days before November 30 with "crowbars, hammers, [and] acid-filled eggs."[77] Moreover, the London *Sunday Times* reported the week before the protests that:

---

[70]Ibid., 210.

[71]Ibid.

[72]Ibid., 209.

[73]This distance is an estimate from maps available at www.mapquest.com.

[74]Michael Krantz, "How Organized Anarchists Led Seattle into Chaos," *Time,* December 13, 1999, available at http://web2.infotrac.galegroup.com, 38 [accessed January 31, 2005].

[75]ACME Collective, "N30 Black Bloc Communique."

[76]Many anarchists make a distinction between violence and property destruction.

[77]Paul Hawken, "N30: What Skeleton Woman Told the WTO in Seattle," Natural Capital Institute, available at www.ratical.org/co-globalize/PaulHawken.pdf [accessed August 30, 2005].

The FBI has identified up to seven British "organisers" who have travelled to the so-called N30 demonstration. Agents fear that the activists who led rioting that caused £2m of damage during the J18 riots in June, setting buildings alight, overturning cars and attacking police, have been drafted to ensure that similar scenes occur at the World Trade Organization meeting in Seattle.[78]

With the protesters ready to proceed, the PSC's Information Management Subcommittee produced "a series of comprehensive oral and written briefings" for security officials.[79] According to the SPD's subsequent *After Action Report,* the subcommittee warned of

a strong likelihood that groups of organized extremists were planning to use a variety of specific tactics to "shut down the WTO." In these briefings, a number of potential tactics were identified . . . [including] the use of blockades, property destruction, the hanging of banners, "arrest-a-thons" and non-cooperation aimed at overwhelming the criminal justice system, "street theater", and simultaneous disruption and/or property damage aimed at multiple targets.[80]

Media reports contained comparable descriptions of the threats. Security planners noted these reports, but they could not, at this stage, easily bring in extra forces to increase security. All of the SPD's forces had been scheduled in for shifts, and the SPD did not have the financial resources to pay for officers from surrounding towns. Consequently, it intended, if necessary, to rely on requests for mutual aid services, which could be called on in the event of an emergency.[81] Although the SPD contacted nearby law enforcement services before the conference, they did not plan crucial details, including what the specific responsibilities of mutual aid groups would be.[82]

The SPD also discovered that it had overestimated the number of its own officers who would be available. The SPD *After Action Report* explains,

the *initial* staffing estimate of available personnel was greater than the *actual* number of available personnel due to inaccurate data. Additionally, special event vacation approval procedures were not in place for the Conference until April 22. Any vacations approved before that date were retained in the unit of origin and were not forwarded to the staffing unit until October.[83]

As events began to unfold, the SPD thus found itself needing more but having fewer officers than it initially expected. In lieu of calling in more officers, the SPD reallocated the officers it had. Two weeks before the event, it added a fifth demonstration management platoon and

---

[78]James Clarke and Tom Rhodes, "British Anarchists Plan Seattle Riot," *Sunday Times* (London), November 28, 1999, available at http://web.lexis-nexis.com [accessed February 23, 2005].

[79]Pierce, "Seattle Police Department After Action Report," 18. These reports were released during the 3 weeks before the Ministerial, so some of them were produced before the start of the 2-week period examined in this section.

[80]Ibid., 18–19.

[81]Ibid., 19.

[82]Ibid., 5.

[83]Ibid., 31.

created a "flying squad," a special team "formed to identify and arrest individuals attempting to engage in property destruction."[84]

While Seattle had trouble securing commitments of forces from other local jurisdictions, Governor Gary Locke did offer to send in the National Guard, and U.S. Attorney General Janet Reno also offered the week before the WTO meeting to send in federal law enforcement officers. (Mayor Schell later said that he did not recall receiving these offers.[85])

The adaptation of operational plans also continued in the weeks immediately preceding the event. The SPD had planned a security perimeter around the convention center and other key sites, but in response to intelligence that the protesters wanted to shut down the WTO opening ceremony, the SPD decided to take added precautions. According to its own *After Action Report,* the "SPD hardened the perimeter around [the Paramount and Convention Center], created corridors through the placement of metro busses, and [took] other prudent operational measures."[86] But overall, planners remained confident in their strategy, and in spite of the increased protest predictions, the police did not increase deployment. In addition, Seattle leaders, starting with the mayor—who had himself been an activist and protester in the 1960s—were dedicated to protecting the peaceful protesters' freedom of speech.

Although there were some officials involved in the planning process who felt that the SPD plans did not constitute full or adequate preparation for what might take place, there appears to have been relatively little dissent formally expressed during planning meetings. The SPD *After Action Report* explains that "(t)he process of planning review was informal. While allied agencies were represented on the planning subcommittees, there was no formal process for plan acceptance. Consequently, acceptance or objections to the plan were not documented."[87]

Moreover, as the conference drew near, it became obvious that some elements of the previously developed plans were unrealistic. As the Seattle City Council WTO Accountability Review Committee report explains,

Large numbers of protesters expected to be arrested for civil disobedience during the WTO meetings. Prior to the WTO Ministerial, SPD, Seattle Mayor's Office and city council representatives held several meetings with the leaders of various protest groups, including representatives from the Ruckus Society and Direct Action Network. At these meetings, according to one participant, some protest group representatives stated that they would be engaging in civil disobedience, and SPD warned that anyone who broke the law would be "picked up and carried away."[88]

[84]Ibid., 24.

[85]Mike Barber, "City Rejected Offers of Help Even as Tear Gas Filled Streets," *Seattle Post-Intelligencer,* December 4, 1999, available at http://web.lexis-nexis.com [accessed August 31, 2005].

[86]Pierce, "Seattle Police Department After Action Report," 20.

[87]Ibid., 52.

[88]City of Seattle, "Panel 2 Final Report," Recommendation B-7.

On November 29, the SPD reversed its stance regarding these arrests, realizing that it lacked the resources to make them. The "Panel 2 Final Report" of the WTO Accountability Review Committee adds:

On Sunday night (November 28th) Ruckus Society representatives met with SPD representatives to express their desire to have 500–1,500 civil disobedience arrests on Tuesday November 30th, to which the demonstration management commander was unable to commit. Finally, late on Monday night SPD stated that they would not in fact be able to accommodate mass arrests to one protest group representative, but there appears to have been no effort made to warn other groups that SPD was unable to uphold its part of the mass arrests.[89]

Immediately before the events were set to begin, the protesters and police were thus on completely different wavelengths about how the protests would unfold and how they would be managed. Hundreds of protesters were apparently expecting to be peacefully arrested and carried away; police were apparently expecting that protesters would either voluntarily leave when asked or allow themselves easily to be pushed out of the way.

In the hours before the Ministerial was scheduled to open, all sides appeared confident. DAN, labor, and anarchists each believed they had strong organization and a good game plan. The police thought they, too, had a good and sufficient plan, especially in light of Seattle's history of peaceful protest. As the event grew near, Schell continued to appear confident, suggesting that Seattle is "not a city that shrinks from a challenge. We're probably the best place in the world to host this meeting."[90] On the night before the largest scheduled demonstrations, he addressed a group of protesters. "Be tough on your issues, but be gentle on my town," he said.[91]

At about 5:00 a.m. on November 30, State Patrol Chief Annette Sandberg walked from her downtown hotel and observed that protesters were "moving into strategic positions"— in places where no police had yet deployed.[92]

---

[89]Ibid.

[90]Quoted in Patrick McMahon, "Protesters Prepare to Make Views Known as Trade Summit Billboards Go Up, Demonstrations Scheduled to Get Point Across," *USA Today*, November 12, 1999, available at http://web.lexis-nexis.com [accessed March 1, 2005].

[91]Quoted in David Wilma, "Protests against the World Trade Organization (WTO) Begin on November 29, 1999," HistoryLink.org: The Online Encyclopedia of Washington State History, available at www.history link.org/essays/output.cfm?file_id=2143 [accessed January 18, 2005].

[92]Quoted in Mike Carter and David Postman, "There Was Unrest Even at the Top during WTO Riots," *Seattle Times*, December 16, 1999, available at www.worldministries.org/prophecynewsarticles/america/wto_riots 12-16-99.html [accessed February 22, 2005].

Protecting the WTO Ministerial Conference of 1999 (B): Epilogue

The expectation that Seattle would provide a beautiful, problem-free environment in which to host a major gathering of trade representatives from around the world could hardly have been further from the eventual reality. Local activists, working in conjunction with protesters from around the world, effectively disrupted the World Trade Organization (WTO) Ministerial Conference. Seattle experienced aftershocks for months, ranging from a heated public confrontation between Mayor Paul Schell and King County Sheriff Dave Reichert to the cancellation of a major part of the city's millennium celebration. In the long term, experience from and analysis of the riots have produced critical lessons for law enforcement officials, but those lessons are a small silver lining in a dark cloud hovering over a normally picturesque city.

The Protests Themselves

Problems immediately surfaced on Tuesday, November 30, the opening day of the Ministerial. Even though protesters had been massing in areas around key WTO sites, including the site of the opening ceremony, since before dawn, the police did not plan to arrive until after 7 a.m., which gave members of the Direct Action Network (DAN) unobstructed time and opportunity to block key intersections.[1] At 8 a.m., Reichert received a phone call from a county detective at the Sheraton hotel who cried, "Sheriff, we're trapped. . . . We have no back-up."[2] Reichert painfully remembered, "I had officers barricaded in the hotel with a mob literally pounding on the glass, and there was nobody there to help them. Nobody."[3]

The "black bloc" and organized labor were active as well. Between 8:45 a.m. and noon, a group of people dressed entirely in black (presumably members of the "black bloc") engaged in various forms of vandalism, including throwing garbage cans into the street and breaking storefront windows.[4] They acted with virtual impunity, in part because the police

---

[1] Daniel Jack Chasan and Christianne Walker, "Out of Control: Seattle's Flawed Response to Protests against the World Trade Organization," American Civil Liberties Union of Washington, American Civil Liberties Union, available at www.aclu-wa.org/Issues/police/WTO-Report.html [accessed March 3, 2005].

[2] Quoted in Mike Carter and David Postman, "There Was Unrest Even at the Top during WTO Riots," *Seattle Times,* December 16, 1999, available at www.worldministries.org/prophecynewsarticles/america/wto_ riots12-16-99.html [accessed February 22, 2005].

[3] Quoted in ibid.

[4] David Wilma, "Mayor Schell Reacts to Protests and Vandalism against the WTO by Declaring a State of Emergency on November 30, 1999," HistoryLink.org: The Online Encyclopedia of Washington State History, available at www.historylink.org/essays/printer_friendly/index.cfm?file_id=2142 [accessed August 30, 2005].

"flying squad" (which had been designed and set up precisely to counter these kinds of activities) had been redeployed to control demonstrators who were preventing delegates from attending the opening ceremony.[5] Meanwhile, "25,000 union members . . . rall[ied] in Memorial Stadium preparing for a noontime march through downtown."[6]

As a result of multiple disruptions, the WTO Opening Ceremony was postponed. Few delegates had arrived at the official venue. Officials told the delegates who had not reached the theater to stay in their hotels while, in the streets, the police fired their first rounds of tear gas, to little avail. The WTO Ministerial was off to a very tenuous start.

With the situation sliding out of control in the view of many, the Seattle Police Department (SPD) had to make a critical decision at 11:00 a.m.: whether to allow the labor march to proceed. Assistant Chief John Pirak, who was monitoring the situation at the city's emergency operations center, recommended canceling the march and declaring a state of emergency. Assistant Chief Ed Joiner, the senior officer in charge at the Multiple Agency Command Center (MACC), the highest-level command center overseeing and managing law enforcement for the event, however, apparently reasoned (according to a later account by two journalists) that "the march would actually work in favor of his stretched police lines. The strategy, he said, was for the peaceful march to sweep the other demonstrators into its ranks and deposit them several blocks away."[7] Although faced with events unfolding adversely, Joiner nonetheless chose to stick to the original plan.

Many present at the time—and many others later—disagreed with Joiner's decision. Ronald Legan, the special agent in charge of the Seattle office of the Secret Service, who has extensive experience with security at international events, later observed, "I would never have brought 50,000 protesters within a block of my venue. There were some people naïve as to what that would look like."[8] Legan made this statement after the protests, but others communicated their concerns at the time. One law enforcement official who was in the MACC recalled, "We all were looking at one another and saying, 'Is that the plan to get us out of this?'. . . It was denying that more resources were needed. People were shaking their heads and wondering how could anybody believe that would [work] based on what had happened so far."[9] Joiner was decidedly in the minority—but he was also in charge.

Allowing the labor march to proceed proved to be somewhere between highly problematic and disastrous. The labor marchers became entangled with the DAN protesters, resulting in as many as 50,000 people in the vicinity of the Ministerial's main sites. Chaos ensued

---

[5]Linda Pierce, "The Seattle Police Department After Action Report: World Trade Organization Ministerial Conference Seattle, Washington November 29, 1999–December 3, 1999," Seattle Police Department, City of Seattle, available at www.ci.seattle.wa.us/Police/Publications/WTO/WTO_AAR.PDF, 6 [accessed April 29, 2005].

[6]Chasan and Walker, "Out of Control."

[7]Carter and Postman, "There Was Unrest."

[8]Quoted in ibid.

[9]Quoted in ibid.

as protesters started bonfires, anarchists vandalized stores, and police fired more tear gas. By 3 p.m., the police were out of pepper spray, and the opening ceremony had been cancelled.[10]

As the SPD became stretched, federal and state officials began to take actions of their own. The *Seattle Times* described a flurry of activity:

At 11:20 a.m. [Washington State Patrol Chief Annette] Sandberg ordered State Patrol troopers in Eastern Washington on higher alert. Twenty minutes later, she ordered a 22-member Civil Disturbance Team from Spokane to drive to Seattle. . . . At 12:45 p.m., the governor told his chief of staff to begin preparing to call-up the National Guard. . . . About 1:00 p.m., the telephone at Locke's Olympia office rang. The staffer who picked up the line was confronted by a furious Secretary of State Madeleine Albright. [Meanwhile,] the MACC began filling with top-ranking officials. Sandberg characterized the federal officials as in a "kind of panicky mode."[11]

SPD officers in the field adapted as best they could. Police officers followed the contingency plan to go to Wyoming to obtain more tear gas, and plain-clothes officers carried tear gas in duffel bags through the crowds to deliver it to the officers on the front lines.[12] Heavily outnumbered, substantially outmaneuvered, and placed at a disadvantage by protesters' novel street tactics and by planning that had now been completely overtaken by events, most police field units demonstrated resourcefulness and adaptability. There were, however, also a number of instances of use of excessive force by some police officers and units. A number of these were captured on video by some of the many reporters present to cover the talks (and the protests) and were widely replayed on newscasts around the nation and around the world.[13]

At about 3 p.m., Mayor Schell entered the MACC. The *Seattle Times* described the intense meeting that followed: "Officials from the SPD, Secret Service, FBI, State Patrol, Department of Justice, State Department, King County, the governor's office and the White House moved into a back room, where they spread out city maps and engaged in a heated discussion."[14] Legan, as the senior Secret Service official present, said categorically "that unless we get control of the streets, we would recommend that [President Bill Clinton] not come," but, according to the *Seattle Times*, "at least three participants [in the meeting] said Schell was reluctant to admit the city had lost control of the streets."[15] At the same time the meeting

---

[10] Wilma, "Mayor Schell Reacts to Protests."

[11] Carter and Postman, "There Was Unrest."

[12] J. Martin McOmber, Mike Carter, and Steve Miletich, "Police Caught Short at WTO; Officers Went to Wyoming for Tear Gas," *Seattle Times*, March 8, 2000, available at http://web.lexis-nexis.com [accessed February 2, 2005].

[13] Mark Rahner, "Man Kicked in Groin Calls His Fame 'Humiliating,'" *Seattle Times*, December 15, 1999, B1; "Horror Stories from Protesters, Police—Officers Saw It as Life and Death, Others Saw Brutality," *Seattle Times*, December 7, 1999, A2; Rick Anderson, "Protesters Riot, Police Riot," *Seattle Weekly*, December 9, 1999, 17; Michele Matassa Flores, "WTO: A Turning Point; Seattle Left Less Naïve as It Counts Costs, Both Physical and Psychological," *Seattle Times*, December 5, 1999, A1.

[14] Carter and Postman, "There Was Unrest."

[15] Ibid.

was going on, Attorney General Janet Reno "called the Governor['s office] to insist that the National Guard be called up." [16] Finally, at 3:24 p.m., the mayor "issued an emergency declaration, the trigger allowing him to request National Guard assistance, ban protests and the use of gas masks by demonstrators, and set a curfew." [17] Schell also instituted a curfew from 7 p.m. to daybreak that covered a large swath of the downtown area. [18]

Even these efforts were, initially, not very successful. Demonstrators broke storefront windows and looted shops. Protests continued, with demonstrators using their cell phones to coordinate with one another and maintain an advantage in situational awareness over police units in the rapidly evolving circumstances. For their part, police continued to make arrests and use concussion grenades and tear gas. [19] Confrontations between the police and protesters continued late into the night.

And although the curfew helped enable President Clinton's safe arrival early Wednesday morning (Clinton was, in the end, the only head of state to attend the talks), the protests extended into that day as well. [20] The situation finally began to deescalate on Thursday, when 1,000 demonstrators marched with a police escort to the King County Jail where 500 protesters were being held on WTO-protest-related charges. That evening, after hearing that an attorney and protest organizer would be able to meet with those in jail, the protesters departed peacefully. [21] On Friday, some additional demonstrations occurred, and the WTO conference ended without achieving its goal of setting an agenda for future action. As Don Bonker, a former member of Congress who worked for a trade consulting group, explained, "What was happening on the street had a powerful influence on what was going on inside. . . . The WTO has been politicized as never before." [22]

The Aftermath

In the days after the Ministerial, the most visible damage was the broken glass and windows in shops throughout downtown Seattle. [23] The financial toll, however, loomed larger. By

---

[16] Ibid.

[17] Ibid.

[18] Wilma, "Mayor Schell Reacts to Protests."

[19] Chasan and Walker, "Out of Control"; Paul de Armond, "Netwar in the Emerald City: WTO Protest Strategy and Tactics," in *Networks and Netwars: The Future of Terror, Crime, and Militancy,* ed. John Arquilla and David Ronfeldt, available at www.rand.org/publications/MR/MR1382/MR1382.ch7.pdf, 204 [accessed April 29, 2005].

[20] Charles Babington and John Burgess, "Clinton Defends Open Trade; President Condemns Violence; 400 Arrested as Response Toughens," *Washington Post,* December 2, 1999, A01.

[21] David Wilma, "WTO Protesters Shift Focus to Police and Arrest Demonstrators on December 2, 1999," HistoryLink.org: The Online Encyclopedia of Washington State History, available at www.historylink.org/essays/output.cfm?file_id=2140 [accessed August 23, 2005].

[22] Quoted in Stephen Dunphy, "Talks Collapse; Meeting Ends—Group Will Leave Here without an Agreement," *Seattle Times,* December 4, 1999, available at http://web.lexis-nexis.com [accessed May 6, 2005].

[23] Flores, "WTO."

December 5, the Downtown Seattle Association had already estimated that lost sales and property damage had cost Seattle businesses over $14.5 million.[24] The city faced a large, although still undetermined, tab for "police overtime, riot equipment, clean-up, lost parking revenue, and lost sales tax."[25] Add to that state spending for National Guard troops, Seattle Metro's expenses, and overtime for other work, and the financial impact was substantial.[26]

Along with these tangible losses, the city suffered a blow to its self-esteem. Seattle had a reputation for being tranquil, but now its citizens were confronted by the violent images that dominated the media, including a police officer kicking a young man in the groin.[27] One *Seattle Times* article asked the question that was on the minds of many Seattle citizens: "Was this Los Angeles? New York? Detroit? Chicago?"[28] The events challenged Seattle's sense of itself as a genteel city.

Seattle also faced international humiliation. Some of the criticism was good-natured and humorous. Comedian Jay Leno poked fun: "Seattle, being such a yuppie town, did you notice the police were using only fresh-ground pepper spray?"[29] Other criticism was more pointed. The *Sydney Morning Herald* ran a story under the headline "Grunge City v. World Greed: Restless in Seattle," while *Washington Post* columnist Joel Achenbach wrote that "Seattle had hoped, in what may be a case of extreme civic hubris, to corral the protests into a kind of feel-good, cappuccino-sipping encounter session."[30] For a city trying to prove that it ranked among the world's elite, such words stung.

After the fact, it seemed to many that the authorities should have been able to figure out in advance more of what the protests might look like and how large they would be and that they could and should have been able to make more effective preparations for them. Looking back, certainly, the emerging pattern was easy to spot: the 1998 Geneva riots and the J18 protests that had taken place just a few months earlier were precursors, not aberrations; the *Sunday Times* in London had been right in September when it said there was coordinated global action developing; the Ruckus Society's summer training camp in the Cascades was real preparation for real events, not a self-indulgent fantasy on the part of disaffected, over-privileged adolescents; and the break-in at Plum Creek and the arson at the GAP were preludes. All this, of course, had the clarity of hindsight, but many felt that more of it could have been seen and understood in real time in the months before the protests. It seemed to be a situation resulting from not so much an absence of intelligence but a failure to apply intelligence effectively.

---

[24]Ibid.
[25]Ibid.
[26]Ibid.
[27]Ibid.
[28]Ibid.
[29]Quoted in ibid.
[30]Quoted in ibid.

And, therefore, along with assessing the damage, people sought accountability from leaders, especially from Mayor Paul Schell and Police Chief Norm Stamper. As observed in the *Seattle Times,* Schell had "enraged his strong allies, the powerful downtown business community; alienated police and firefighter unions already critical of Schell's leadership; and turned a rocky relationship with the City Council into a downright hostile one."[31] Common complaints included that he minimized security expenditures to maintain city council support for the event[32] and that he allowed the labor march to proceed because he fondly recalled his own days as a protester. A less frequent but nevertheless significant criticism was that he had stifled the police. State Patrol Chief Sandberg said, "a police chief needs a certain amount of autonomy to run a department from political leadership and it was apparent that SPD's managers did not have that kind of autonomy."[33]

Schell had difficulty mending bridges. His heated public confrontation with Sheriff Reichert is a case in point. Schell was angry about Reichert's public criticism of him and conveyed his anger when he saw Reichert at a reception for Nelson Mandela at Boeing Field on December 8, 1999. Schell "threatened to personally derail Reichert's political career if he [ran] for re-election in 2001 . . . [and] also accused the sheriff of staging a pursuit of downtown looters last week. . . . When Reichert attempted to end the conversation, the mayor blocked his path twice."[34] Even though the two met later in the day to mend fences, the unusually confrontational actions of the normally calm Schell give some insight into the intensity of the emotional aftermath of the WTO events.

Schell never fully recovered from the WTO crisis. While running for reelection in 2001, he became "the first mayor since 1936 to lose in a primary campaign."[35] City Attorney Mark Sidran, one of Schell's opponents, links the results to the WTO: "I think what the voters are telling him is [that] despite the positives in his record he ran on . . . voters found it very hard to forgive Mardi Gras [a situation subsequent to the WTO that many thought Schell also mishandled[36]], and there also were perhaps some residues of WTO."[37]

---

[31]J. Martin McOmber, "WTO: A Turning Point—Scrutiny of Schell's Leadership Is Just Beginning as Council Schedules Meetings," *Seattle Times,* December 5, 1999, available at http://web.lexis-nexis.com [accessed February 7, 2005].

[32]WTO Accountability Review Committee, "Accountability Review Committee Final Report," City of Seattle, available at www.cityofseattle.net/wtocommittee/arcfinal_report2.htm [accessed August 31, 2005].

[33]Quoted in Mike Carter and Jim Brunner, "Patrol Accounts say Schell Hurt WTO Response," *Seattle Times,* May 23, 2000, available at http://web.lexis-nexis.com/scholastic [accessed January 28, 2005].

[34]J. Martin McOmber, Dave Birkland, Mike Carter, and Brian Dudley, "Another WTO Clash: Mayor Gets in the Sheriff's Face—Schell Confronts Reichert over Public Criticism," *Seattle Times,* December 10, 1999, available at http://web.lexis-nexis.com [accessed May 5, 2005].

[35]Jim Brunner, "Lame-Duck Schell Pledges Cooperation," *Seattle Times,* September 20, 2001, available at http://web.lexis-nexis.com [accessed May 5, 2005].

[36]Beth Kaiman and Ian Ith, "Police Shoulder Blame for Melee," *Seattle Times,* August 2, 2001, available at http://web.lexis-nexis.com [accessed August 23, 2005].

[37]Brunner, "Lame-Duck Schell Pledges Cooperation."

While Schell felt the ramifications of the WTO over an extended period, the negative results for Police Chief Norm Stamper were more immediate. He announced his retirement on December 6, 1999, just 3 days after the talks ended and earlier than he had originally planned. Mayor Schell made it clear that the early retirement announcement was linked to the WTO riots, noting that "Given the current climate, he [Chief Stamper] would be unable to be effective in his job. Everything he said would be viewed as trying to save his job. This way, he can ensure that the facts get out for a change, and he has every reason to hold his head high." [38]

Events, as well as careers, were derailed in the aftermath of the WTO crisis. In late December, the Algerian tourist Ahmed Ressam was arrested on a ferry dock in Puget Sound, having just crossed the border from Canada near Seattle, with a trunkload of explosives in his car; this raised the specter of a terrorist attack. The recent painful experience of the WTO riots added to the pressure to cancel the city's planned millennium celebration. A headline in the *Seattle Times* conveyed the city's anxiety and fatigue: "No Party Mood after WTO Hangover; Riots Big Factor in Dropping Y2K Bash." [39] Port of Seattle Commissioner Pat Davis, who had played an integral role in bringing the WTO to Seattle, highlighted the proximity of the two events by likening the situation to "giving birth. You wouldn't want to do it again a month later, but a year later you'd think about it." [40]

Along with questioning the actions of individual leaders and canceling events, the city cast a wide investigatory net through a series of hearings and investigations. The city council held the first of two public hearings on December 8, 1999. After over 8 hours of testimony and with more people waiting to speak, a second set of hearings had to be scheduled for December 14, 1999. [41] At the second meeting, more than two hundred people spoke, and testimony lasted for 10 hours. The meeting did not adjourn until 1:55 a.m. [42]

The city council continued its probe through the creation of the WTO Accountability Review Committee, led by three council members, that analyzed what went wrong. The committee's work culminated with the release of its final report in September 2000. Other groups, including the American Civil Liberties Union and the SPD, also thoroughly analyzed the actions prior to and during the WTO.

---

[38]Quoted in J. Martin McOmber, Mike Carter, Steve Miletich, Charles Brown, and Jack Broom, "I Don't Feel Like the Fall Guy—in Wake of WTO, Police Chief Stamper Announces He'll Retire," *Seattle Times,* December 7, 1999, available at http://web.lexis-nexis.com [accessed May 5, 2005].

[39]Alex Fryer and J. Martin McOmber, "No Party Mood after WTO Hangover; Riots Big Factor in Dropping Y2K Bash," *Seattle Times,* December 29, 1999, available at http://web.lexis-nexis.com [accessed August 30, 2005].

[40]Quoted in ibid. For a detailed account of how Ressam's arrest affected the city's planned millennium celebration, see "The Seattle Millennium Security Threat" (Case 14).

[41]J. Martin McOmber, "Eight Hours of Outrage—Council Hears Marathon of WTO Horror Stories," *Seattle Times,* December 9, 1999, available at http://web.lexis-nexis.com [accessed May 6, 2005].

[42]Jeff Hodson, "Anger Erupts Again over WTO Events," *Seattle Times,* December 15, 1999, available at http://web.lexis-nexis.com [accessed May 6, 2005].

Key Actors in Protecting the WTO Ministerial Conference of 1999

Anti-trade Organizers

Michael Dolan, head, People for Fair Trade/
   Network Opposed to WTO (PFT)
David Korten, leader in the
   antiglobalization movement
Sally Soriano, coordinator, Washington
   Fair Trade Campaign

Labor Leaders

Martha Baskin, fair trade representative,
   King County Labor Council
Ron Judd, head, King County Labor Council
John Sweeney, president, American
   Federation of Labor–Congress of
   Industrial Organizations (AFL-CIO)

Government Officials

Madeleine Albright, U.S. secretary of state
Bill Clinton, president of the United States
Gary Locke, governor of Washington
Janet Reno, U.S. attorney general
Paul Schell, mayor of Seattle, Washington

Law Enforcement Officials:

Ed Joiner, assistant chief, Seattle Police
   Department
Ronald Legan, special agent in charge,
   Seattle Office, U.S. Secret Service
John Pirak, assistant chief, Seattle Police
   Department
Dave Reichert, sheriff, King County
Annette Sandberg, chief, Washington State
   Patrol
Norm Stamper, chief, Seattle Police
   Department

Others

Robert Lee Thaxton, protester at June 18
   riots in Eugene, Oregon
John Zerzan, radical anarchist leader

Protecting the WTO Ministerial Conference of 1999

Chronology of Events

1999
Early January

The World Trade Organization (WTO) announces that Seattle, Washington, will host the Third WTO Ministerial Conference, scheduled to meet from Tuesday, November 30, through Friday, December 3.

Michael Dolan, a leading anti-WTO activist, arrives in Seattle and begins organizing activities in opposition to the Ministerial.

Wednesday, January 20

A rally organized by Dolan and other activists takes place at Seattle's Labor Temple. Participants form a loose coalition, the People for Fair Trade/Network Opposed to WTO (PFT).

Late winter and spring

PFT evolves into a robust organization. It and its chief partners, the Direct Action Network (DAN) and organized labor, begin mobilizing support and formulating strategy.

Security planning intensifies. The Public Safety Committee (PSC), formed to coordinate public safety planning efforts for the Ministerial, establishes the WTO Information Management Subcommittee to gather security intelligence.

Thursday, May 13

Seattle Mayor Paul Schell asks other jurisdictions to provide law enforcement resources to help staff the Ministerial. Only a few are willing to do so.

June

Delegates at the Washington State Labor Convention approve an anti-WTO resolution, causing tension between King County Labor Council head Ron Judd and AFL-CIO President John Sweeney.

Friday, June 18

The anarchist umbrella group J18 organizes global anticapitalism protests. Twenty people are arrested at a violent protest in Eugene, Oregon.

Wednesday, July 7

A Federal Bureau of Investigation (FBI) threat assessment finds "no credible information" that "violence or significant property damage" will occur at the Ministerial in Seattle.

August

Reports that potentially disruptive acts may take place at the Ministerial increase in frequency, but they are apparently disregarded by the Seattle Police Department (SPD) and other law enforcement agencies.

The AFL-CIO works on organizing the rally and march that it has scheduled for the opening day of the Ministerial.

Mid-September

The Ruckus Society holds a training camp for protesters in the Cascade Mountains.

Late October

Mayor Schell writes to business leaders, assuring them that Seattle is well prepared for the Ministerial.

Thursday, October 28

The Plum Creek Timber Company's Seattle offices are broken into.

Monday, November 1

Vandals firebomb the downtown Seattle GAP store. Along with the Plum Creek break-in, the attack on the GAP store heightens security concerns in advance of the Ministerial.

Tuesday, November 2

Mayor Schell sends another letter to business owners, stressing the value of hosting the Ministerial.

Wednesday, November 17

The FBI submits a written report to the SPD, assessing the threat of violent protest as "low to medium."

Late November

DAN establishes its headquarters about ten blocks from Seattle's convention center, where the Ministerial is to take place. It finalizes its protest plans there.

Labor prepares for its rally and march, which are expected to attract thousands of participants.

Anarchist groups set up a headquarters known as The Squat, about six blocks from the convention center.

The WTO Information Management Subcommittee warns security officials that extremists plan to disrupt WTO proceedings.

The SPD hardens the security perimeter around the convention center and adds another demonstration management platoon to help control the protests, but authorities remain largely confident in their security plans.

Monday, November 29

The SPD decides that it will not be able to make mass civil disobedience arrests, as it had planned. This decision is not conveyed to most protest groups, however.

Tuesday, November 30

5:00 a.m.: With the Ministerial about to begin, State Patrol Chief Annette Sandberg notices that protesters have already started taking up positions—well in advance of the police.

8:00 a.m.: King County Sheriff Dave Reichert is informed that some of his officers have been trapped by demonstrators inside the Seattle Sheraton.

8:45 a.m.–12:00 p.m.: A group of people dressed entirely in black (most likely members of the "black bloc") vandalize storefronts and take over streets. Security forces do little to stop the vandalism, focusing instead on trying to help delegates reach the opening ceremony.

In Memorial Stadium, 25,000 union members rally in advance of their planned march through downtown Seattle.

11:00 a.m.: SPD Assistant Chief Ed Joiner, senior officer in charge at the Multiple Agency Command Center (MACC), decides against canceling the labor march, arguing that it would help blunt the more violent demonstrations by absorbing protestors and carrying them away from key sites. Many security officials disagree with Joiner's decision, which eventually proves disastrous. Labor marchers become entangled with DAN protesters, and the chaos and violence escalate.

11:20 a.m.: With the SPD stretched thin, State Patrol Chief Sandberg places state troopers in eastern Washington on high alert.

11:40 a.m.: Chief Sandberg orders a twenty-two-member civil disturbance team to deploy to Seattle.

12:45 p.m.: Washington Governor Gary Locke directs his chief of staff to make preparations for calling up the National Guard.

1:00 p.m.: U.S. Secretary of State Madeleine Albright, furious over the situation in Seattle, calls Locke's Olympia office.

High-level officials begin flocking to the MACC.

3:00 p.m.: The Ministerial opening ceremony is cancelled.

Mayor Schell enters the MACC, and federal, state, and local officials engage in a heated discussion about how to deal with the crisis. Schell is reluctant to admit the situation is out of control, but Ronald Legan of the U.S. Secret Service insists that unless order is reestablished, he will continue to recommend that President Bill Clinton not come to the city.

U.S. Attorney General Janet Reno calls Governor Locke's office and insists that he call up the National Guard.

3:24 p.m.: Mayor Schell issues an emergency declaration and institutes a curfew lasting from 7:00 p.m. to daybreak.

Demonstrators continue to wreak havoc while police continue to make arrests. Confrontations continue late into the night.

Wednesday, December 1
President Clinton arrives early in the morning. Protests continue throughout the day.

Thursday, December 2
The crisis begins to deescalate when demonstrators who had gathered at King County Jail are told that five hundred arrested protesters can meet with an attorney and a protest organizer.

Friday, December 3
The Ministerial concludes without achieving its main goals.

Monday, December 6
Police Chief Norm Stamper announces his retirement. Mayor Schell makes it clear that Stamper's retirement is linked to the security failures during the Ministerial.

Wednesday, December 8
Schell and Reichert have a heated and public confrontation at an event honoring Nelson Mandela. Schell threatens to derail Reichert's political career for having criticized his handling of the riots.

The city council holds its first public hearing on the WTO riots. The meeting lasts over 8 hours.

Tuesday, December 14
The city council holds a second hearing on the riots, at which more than two hundred people speak. The meeting lasts 10 hours.

Late December

Algerian tourist Ahmed Ressam is arrested after crossing into Washington from Canada with a trunkload of explosives. Ressam's arrest and the lingering effects of the WTO riots raise concerns about the city's planned millennium celebrations.

2000

September

The city council's WTO Accountability Review Committee releases its final report.

2001

September

Schell loses his bid for reelection.

14 The Seattle Millennium Security Threat (A): Weighing Public Safety in Seattle

Kirsten Lundberg

Only 10 days after the traumatic events surrounding the World Trade Organization (WTO) Ministerial Conference in December 1999,[1] Seattle officials confronted another high-stakes decision. Seeking entry to Washington state across the U.S.-Canadian border, Ahmed Ressam was arrested by an alert customs officer. His car was laden with bomb-making materials that easily could have exploded if mishandled. His intended destination and purpose were unknown, but circumstantial evidence suggested the possibility that he was a terrorist intent on attacking the Seattle Center and its Space Needle, perhaps at the moment of a planned New Year's Eve 2000 millennium celebration that would attract upward of 50,000 people. The concern only increased when, 5 days after Ressam's arrest, two Algerians were arrested at the Vermont-Canadian border because a bomb-sniffing dog detected explosives residue in their car trunk. Whether they were connected to Ressam was unknown, but all three had Montreal connections.

Seattle Mayor Paul Schell, advised by senior administrators in the Mayor's Office, police and fire departments, and Seattle Center, had the sobering responsibility of deciding whether the city could go ahead with its millennium celebration plans or whether proper regard for public safety demanded that he cancel the event. The great uncertainty made it extremely difficult to judge the degree of risk. Should the once-in-many-lifetimes millennium celebration be cancelled because of a possible threat of terrorism? Although there was ample reason to worry, there was no firm evidence that Seattle was the target at all and, if it was so, whether the arrests in Washington and Vermont had disrupted the plot. Local Federal Bureau of Investigation (FBI) officials and the U.S. attorney insisted that although they had no specific information that Seattle was a terrorist target, they could not definitively rule it out. Notwithstanding these assurances, some Seattle officials feared that they were not getting the full story. To cancel the celebration, however, would be particularly poignant for Seattle, so recently bruised and embarrassed by worldwide publicity about the disturbances at the WTO Ministerial Conference.

As you mull over Mayor Schell's decision-making dilemma, also consider the more general questions about risk that the case raises. In any uncertain situation, decision makers face very tough choices, but this is especially the case when great harm might occur but incomplete information makes it very difficult to gauge the risk. Under these conditions, decision makers can make serious errors in two general ways. If they are overly cautious, they

This is an abridged version of a case written by Kirsten Lundberg for Arnold M. Howitt, executive director of the Taubman Center for State and Local Government, John F. Kennedy School of Government, Harvard University for use at Executive Session on Domestic Preparedness. Funding was provided by the Office of Justice Programs, U.S. Department of Justice. Kennedy School of Government Case Program, C15-02-1648.0 and C15-02-1648.1. Copyright © 2002, 2007 by the President and Fellows of Harvard College.

[1]See "Protecting the WTO Ministerial Conference of 1999" (Case 13).

may forgo significant opportunities and benefits. But if they are insufficiently wary, they may be held responsible for bad outcomes: lives lost, injuries, property damage, and ruined reputations. The burden of decision weighs heavily, as it did for Mayor Schell.

Discussion Questions

- Should Mayor Schell have gone ahead with the millennium celebration at Seattle Center or cancelled it? Why or why not?
- Was Seattle's decision making on this issue effectively organized? Could it have been improved or, even, approached in a different way?
- How should the benefits, costs, and degree of risk of proceeding (or not proceeding) be determined and weighed?

On December 27, 1999, Seattle Mayor Paul Schell called a meeting in the small conference room adjacent to his office. In only 4 days, on New Year's Eve, Seattle Center (a 74-acre public recreation and cultural facility in the heart of the city) was expecting upward of 50,000 visitors to celebrate the beginning of a new millennium. Yet on December 14, U.S. Customs authorities had detained Algerian Ahmed Ressam crossing into the United States from Canada just north of Seattle with a trunkload of explosives—enough, the Federal Bureau of Investigation (FBI) told the mayor, to topple a multistory building. Ressam held a motel reservation for December 14 just blocks from Seattle Center and its internationally recognized landmark, the Space Needle.

Among the meeting participants were several members of the City Council, the head of the Seattle FBI office, the director of the Seattle Center, and representatives from the Seattle police. Their task: to decide whether to cancel the millennium celebration. Ressam was in custody, and there was no hard evidence that Seattle was his target. But no one could assure Schell that the city was *not* a target, and an accomplice of Ressam was still at large. Moreover, just 3 weeks earlier the city had endured one of its most grueling experiences in history. Protesters had turned a World Trade Organization (WTO) conference into a riot scene, with television broadcasting pictures worldwide of an out-of-control downtown Seattle.

The mayor and his advisers did not want to appear weak in the face of terrorist threats. New York and Washington, D.C., planning much bigger celebrations, seemed to be on track with their plans. Yet it was plain to all at the table that the FBI had information it could not share with the public officials. The FBI chief assured those present that they had all the *relevant* information; and, he said, the FBI would not tell the mayor—by law Seattle's chief law enforcement officer—what decision to make. It was his call.

The World Trade Organization Conference

The need for Mayor Schell to decide whether to hold Seattle's millennium celebration arose amid outspoken criticism of his handling of the WTO event. The meeting of the WTO Third Ministerial Conference from November 29 through December 3, 1999, had been intended to establish Seattle as a global political player. Unparalleled prosperity in the 1990s—largely driven by technology leader Microsoft Corporation and airplane manufacturer Boeing—had catapulted the Pacific Northwest city into the first ranks economically; it was hoped that the WTO conference would accomplish the same politically.

It did not. Breaking a cherished Seattle tradition of peaceful demonstrations, the protesters turned violent. Antiglobalization protesters used tactics that police had not seen before, such as blocking intersections by chaining themselves together under sleeves of concrete, making it difficult to separate them. They threw objects through plate-glass windows, starting with those of the internationally recognized Starbucks coffee-store chain. They succeeded in closing a portion of downtown and prevented WTO delegates from attending opening ceremonies.

Mayor Schell and Seattle police ultimately changed their tactics to meet the situation. Comments Charles Mandigo, special-agent-in-charge of the Seattle FBI office, "[Schell] had to make some decisions that were unpleasant and, politically I'm sure, not what he would have liked to have done. But in a sense, he had no option at a certain point."[2] Police appeared in battle gear, the National Guard was mobilized, and extra supplies of tear gas were airlifted in and directed against the protesters. Over six hundred protesters were arrested (although most of the charges were eventually dropped). By the time the WTO delegates went home, protesters had caused over $20 million worth of damage.

Blame trading began immediately. Police charged that the FBI had not prepared them adequately; the FBI responded that police had never taken its warnings seriously. Public figures and the press criticized the mayor as too keen to project an image of a "gentle Seattle," where civilized parties could agree to disagree. This had led, they charged, to a disastrous decision to minimize the show of force on opening day and the failure to have in place easily deployed backup police. The City Council, which already had a rocky relationship with the mayor, held hearings and appointed a committee to investigate the security preparations for the WTO conference. Although Schell attempted to highlight the positive elements of the

---

[2]Interview with Charles Mandigo, FBI Seattle special-agent-in-charge, Seattle, November 29, 2001. Unless noted, subsequent quotations from Mandigo are also from this interview. Mandigo arrived in Seattle in November 1994 as assistant special-agent-in-charge and took over the office in August 1999.

WTO conference protests—free speech had been preserved, and no one was seriously injured or killed—a newspaper poll ranked Schell's performance just above that of the lawless
demonstrators.[3]

Ressam Arrested

Just ten days after the WTO conference wrapped up, on December 14, 1999, the last ferry
from Victoria, British Columbia, pulled into Port Angeles, Washington—a modest-size
border-crossing city—at 5:30 p.m.[4] (See Exhibit 14A-1 for a map of the Seattle and Vancouver area, showing Port Angeles.) The last car in line was driven by a small man who appeared to be in his early thirties. His driver's license said he was Benni Antoine Noris of
Montreal (although he later proved to be Ahmed Ressam). U.S. Customs Service Agent Diana Dean noticed that the man's hands were shaking and that he was perspiring. Dean also
could not figure out why he had taken such a roundabout route to get from Vancouver,
where he had been staying, to Seattle; an interstate highway linked the two cities. She ordered him out for an inspection.

In the wheel well of the car's trunk, agents found ten green plastic trash bags filled with
white crystals, two glass jars full of a golden liquid packed in sawdust, four black boxes, and
two pill-size bottles. When Dean's colleague Mark Johnson went to pat down Ressam, the
man ran. After a chase of several blocks, he was caught, handcuffed, and taken into custody.
The inspectors examined the bottles and the bags, which they thought contained drugs.

Only after more sophisticated tests by an FBI lab and the U.S. Bureau of Alcohol, Tobacco, and Firearms (ATF) did local authorities learn what they had actually found. The
bags contained 118 pounds of urea fertilizer and 14 pounds of sulfate powder. The jars had
50 ounces of ethylene glycol dinitrate (EGDN),[5] chemically related to nitroglycerin. EGDN
is sensitive to shock, heat, and friction. The two small bottles held explosives.[6] Had Johnson
unscrewed any of them, they could have exploded. The black boxes were four timing devices. Combined, the ingredients could create a powerful bomb (or bombs). All that was

[3]J. Martin Mcomber, "Paul Schell: Midnight at Midterm?" *Seattle Times,* December 26, 1999, A1.

[4]Paula Bock, "An Otherwise Ordinary Day," *Pacific Northwest Magazine, Seattle Times,* November 25, 2001, 16.
Several of the details described here come from this account. See also Josh Meyer, "Border Arrest Stirs Fear of Terrorist Cells in US," *Los Angeles Times,* March 11, 2001, A1.

[5]The first test that determined the brown liquid was EGDN was done by the Washington State Patrol Crime
Lab and was confirmed by the FBI within 24 hours.

[6]A Tylenol bottle held a military-grade explosive known as cyclotrimethylenetrinitramine (RDX). The other
small bottle contained the explosive hexamethylentriperoxodiamin (HMTD). HMTD is so unstable that it is not
made commercially.

Exhibit 14A-1   The Seattle and Vancouver area

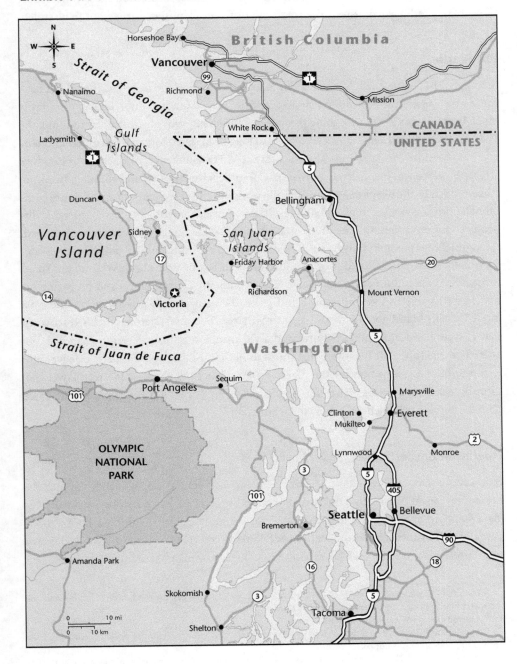

lacking were common batteries to power the timing devices.[7] Moreover, Ressam's passport proved fake, and his two driver's licenses (with different identities) turned out to be stolen.

FBI Seattle

Mandigo, FBI Seattle chief, learned about Ressam's detention the next day. It couldn't have come at a worse time. On the psychological front, says Mandigo, "our people were fairly much beat up after WTO, just going through it emotionally and physically." In addition, the FBI office was, literally, in chaos. The office had long been slated to move to a different building, but the move had been put off until after the WTO conference. At the time of Ressam's arrest, the office was just halfway moved in. Computers were not up and running, furniture had gone astray, the telephones were not fully working, and the system for some secure communications was not yet in place.[8] As a result, Port Angeles and others had considerable difficulty communicating with the FBI Seattle office in the first hours after Ressam was stopped.

As quickly as possible, however, FBI Seattle opened a criminal investigation into Ressam. Eventually some 50 agents (out of an office of 80 in Seattle and 120 in Washington state) worked the case full time, chasing down leads, conducting surveillance, and preparing for searches and arrests. "We were on a full press, 24-hour, 7-days-a-week command post mode," recalls Mandigo, FBI special-agent-in-charge. The investigators quickly discovered that Ressam had California brochures and a videocamera in his car, recalls Mandigo, but judged "at the time that they were just props to make him look like a tourist." He was also found to have a reservation for the night of December 14 at the Best Western Loyal Inn, three blocks from Seattle's Space Needle. He had in his pocket a scrap of paper with three phone numbers scribbled on it, plus the word *Gani*.[9]

Operation Borderbom

FBI headquarters in Washington, D.C., recognizing its potential scope, quickly adopted the Ressam investigation, which it dubbed Operation Borderbom. Ressam's case went from being a standard criminal case to a counterterrorism investigation. Within 48 hours, thousands of FBI agents fanned out nationwide looking for clues to Ressam's past. Eighteen counterterrorism task forces were mobilized.[10] The Strategic Information Operations Cen-

---

[7]When the FBI exploded 5 pounds of Ressam's materials under an old car, the car vanished, leaving only ash and metal shards. Bock, "An Otherwise Ordinary Day."

[8]These problems were resolved within 3–5 days.

[9]Reports, which have persistently survived in press accounts, said Ressam had in his pocket a ticket from Los Angeles to London. This is not correct.

[10]Lorraine Adams, "The Other Man: For Months the Feds Contended That Abdel Ghani Meskini Was the Key to Unlocking the Millennial Terrorist Bomb Plot. But Was He a Mastermind or a Dupe?" *Washington Post Magazine*, May 20, 2001, W10. Several details described here of the national investigation are from this article.

ter at FBI headquarters in Washington functioned as the command post. Dale Watson, FBI counterterrorism chief, was in charge, along with Michael E. Rolince, head of the international terrorism section for the FBI. The Central Intelligence Agency (CIA) and National Security Agency were notified. At the White House, National Security Adviser Alexander "Sandy" Berger convened a meeting of the Principals' Committee, which oversees national intelligence matters.

Federal officials knew there had been multiple threats of terrorism against millennium celebrations worldwide. In fact, U.S. counterterrorism authorities had been apprehensive since the 1993 bombing of New York's World Trade Center and the deadly 1998 attacks on U.S. embassies in Kenya and Tanzania, the latter ascribed to Islamic militant Osama bin Laden and his Al Qaeda network. In 1998, bin Laden had declared it "the individual duty for every Muslim" to kill Americans.[11] The day after Ressam's arrest, authorities in Jordan broke up an Al Qaeda cell plotting attacks against Americans and Israelis in the Middle East. Investigators wanted to know whether Ressam had any connection to this network. Was Ressam working alone? What was his target? Had another bomb-equipped car slipped across the border elsewhere?

Retracing Ressam's steps, the FBI discovered that the 32-year-old Algerian had been living in Montreal for 5 years, where he belonged to a cell of the Armed Islamic Group, Algerians seeking to transform their country into a Muslim theocracy. Before he surfaced in Port Angeles, Ressam had spent 3 weeks in Vancouver, British Columbia, with an associate, Abdelmajid Dahoumane. In a hotel room there, the two men assembled the chemicals for up to four bombs. They presumably then separated; police could not now locate Dahoumane. Ressam drove southwest to Victoria, going well out of his way if his destination was Seattle, presumably because the border crossing using the direct-link interstate was much bigger than sleepy Port Angeles. From Victoria, he phoned ahead to reserve at Seattle's Best Western.

One of the New York telephone numbers in Ressam's pocket turned out to belong to Abdelghani Meskini (explaining the word *Gani* in the note). The FBI obtained an electronic surveillance warrant for Meskini under the Foreign Intelligence Surveillance Act (FISA), which governs cases where international espionage or terrorism is suspected.[12] The phone tap on Meskini paid off. On Christmas Day, the FBI learned that he and Ressam were part of a well-organized group. On December 11, Meskini had flown to Seattle, where he was to provide Ressam with money, help him as a translator, and drive him to "meet with people." But the two never met; Meskini left on December 16 after Ressam failed to surface.

---

[11]Osama bin Laden, "World Islamic Front on Jihad Against Jews and Crusaders," *Al-Quds Al-Arabi* (London), February 23, 1998, 3; English translation available at www.fas.org/irp/world/para/docs/980223-fatwa.htm.

[12]The 1978 Foreign Intelligence Surveillance Act was passed to ensure that the FBI used secret wiretaps only in cases with a foreign connection; it was meant to curb FBI surveillance of legitimate domestic groups. FISA wiretaps were approved by a special court that heard requests exclusively from the Department of Justice.

Walls and Secrets

In Seattle, the elevation of Ressam's case from a criminal to a counterterrorism investigation caused a change in case management and bred considerable resentment. As practice had evolved, no one involved with the criminal side of an investigation could know what was discovered through FISA surveillance.[13] Thus, the FBI Seattle agent already assigned to the criminal case, the Seattle police, U.S. Customs agents, and even prosecutors in the U.S. Attorney's Office were not privy to information gathered under the FISA warrant.

This proved logistically awkward. The command post for the case had been established on the twelfth floor of the FBI building; officials lacking clearance for FISA information were now banned from accessing it. Seattle law enforcement officials came to believe they were being denied vital information. Although the U.S. attorney for western Washington, Kate Pflaumer, had clearance to receive FISA information, other prosecutors in the U.S. Attorney's Office did not and were likewise offended. "People in the Police Department and some other people believed that what we were doing was throwing them out of the case, and it caused a little bit of friction," Mandigo, FBI special-agent-in-charge, observes with understatement.

The FISA restrictions also influenced how much Mandigo and U.S. Attorney Pflaumer could tell Seattle's elected officials. Pflaumer emphasizes, "We had permission to share everything that could affect security plans about the event."[14] The difficulty lay in persuading public officials that this was so.

The Mayor's Office

Mayor Schell and his office learned about Ressam's detention 3 days later, along with the rest of the nation, from the newspapers. On December 17, 1999, Ressam's arrest became national news when he was flown to Seattle and arraigned.[15] President Bill Clinton assured the nation that "we're taking extraordinary efforts in the government to act based on the incident out in the Pacific Northwest."[16] The mayor's immediate concern was to learn what Ressam's apprehension meant for Seattle.

---

[13]At the time of the Ressam case, a FISA warrant was granted specifically to uncover foreign espionage or terrorism, not to contribute evidence to a criminal case (for which a different kind of warrant was required). By Department of Justice policy, the FBI had to prevent the "contamination" of an espionage or counterterrorism case by separating criminal investigators from those working on an intelligence case. This practice was changed significantly in the aftermath of 9/11 with the enactment of the PATRIOT Act in late 2001 and subsequent refinements. (For further details, see Richard A. Best, *Sharing Law Enforcement and Intelligence Information: The Congressional Role* [Washington, D.C.: Congressional Research Service, February 13, 2007].)

[14]Interview with Kate Pflaumer, U.S. attorney for western Washington, Seattle, November 28, 2001. Unless noted, subsequent quotations from Pflaumer are also from this interview.

[15]He was indicted December 22 on five charges, including smuggling explosives.

[16]Quoted in Meyer, "Border Arrest Stirs Fear," A1.

Seattle Deputy Mayor Maud Smith Daudon recalls that she initiated a call to U.S. Attorney Pflaumer to find out what was going on. Pflaumer provided what details she could: that Ressam was stopped thanks to one customs officer's vigilance and great good luck, that he had an accomplice, that he had bomb-making chemicals in his trunk, that he had a reservation at a Seattle motel, and that California brochures were found in the car. "What they didn't know," recalls Daudon, "was what was the intent of this person to begin with. . . . I said, 'Do you think the target could be the Space Needle?' And she said, 'We just don't know.' " [17]

Meanwhile, on December 19 at the U.S.-Canadian border in Bellows Falls, Vermont, authorities detained an Algerian man and the wife of another Algerian, whose car was singled out by bomb-sniffing dogs. Only explosives residue was found in the trunk, but the two were held without bond on immigration violations.[18] No one knew whether these two were working with Ressam, but they all had Montreal connections.

Daudon advised the mayor to call a meeting of city officials, including members of the City Council, and invite Mandigo and Pflaumer to report on the Ressam incident. It was nearly Christmas, and on December 31 Seattle was expecting more than 50,000 people to congregate for a lavish New Year's Eve celebration at the Seattle Center, with the Space Needle at its heart.

The Millennium Preparations

Mayor Schell had long had grand plans for how Seattle would celebrate the millennium. A week's festivities at Seattle Center would be the capstone of a year of civic improvements. He wanted to light up the city, including its bridges. That vision was abbreviated when citizens complained the light would bother their sleep. But the city did plant 30,000 new trees, and national TV networks were lined up to photograph fireworks at the Space Needle as the symbol of New Year's on the West Coast.

At Seattle Center, preparations for the millennium celebration had been underway for 18 months. John Merner, director of Seattle Center Productions, had enlisted some thirty staff members to work on millennium events; Center Director Virginia Anderson was enthusiastically involved. The centerpiece of the celebration, "At the Crossroads," featured seventeen different sculptures, five of them fully 25 feet tall. Throughout the year, visitors were encouraged to write their dreams for the next millennium on slips of paper and place them inside the sculptures. On New Year's Eve, a bonfire of the statues would symbolically release the accumulated dreams to the heavens in accordance with traditions from countries such as Japan, China, and Spain.

---

[17]Interview with Maud Smith Daudon, Seattle deputy mayor, Seattle, November 29, 2001. Unless noted, subsequent quotations from Daudon are also from this interview.

[18]The two were Bouabide Chemmach and Lucia Garofalo.

Bonfire Out

The proposed bonfire celebration ran into criticism after a bonfire killed several students in Texas. There were also fears it might invite trouble from radical protestors. Ressam's arrest proved the last straw, and the event was cancelled. Although Merner's team was disappointed,[19] plenty of scheduled activities for New Year's Eve remained—from a big band dance to a concert, an exhibition, and a series of cultural entertainments.

Space Needle Booked

The Space Needle, a private enterprise, had its own plans. The Space Needle was a private enterprise located in the middle of Seattle Center's public grounds. In the early 1990s, a family from Portland, Oregon, arranged to rent the 605-foot tower, which featured an observation deck and the SkyCity restaurant, for the millennial New Year's Eve. They planned to invite some 1,000 friends and relations to party the night away.

Traditionally, the Space Needle Corporation had also funded and arranged for an annual New Year's Eve fireworks display. The news of Ressam's arrest, says Space Needle CEO Dean Nelson, "was unnerving, to say the least,"[20] but he adds that "we would get a bomb threat almost every New Year's Eve. . . . If every time that there were a threat, if you closed your business, you'd be closed a lot." In this instance, he says, the FBI was able to confirm that "there was no specific threat directed at either the Space Needle or Seattle." Therefore, he says, "we were fully prepared to go ahead" with both the private party and the fireworks.

Seattle Center Meetings

Seattle Center held a couple of informational meetings after Ressam's detention, including one on December 21 for local community and business people that reviewed the security plans for New Year's Eve. Although the center knew of no specific threat against the general area, it had decided to fence its perimeter by December 29 and erect ten gates where security officials could inspect visitors and bags. At another meeting of some 150 staff members from Seattle Center plus other organizations based on the campus, Director Anderson reiterated what she knew about Ressam—which was not much. Anderson also made it clear that Seattle Center intended to go forward with its plans for New Year's Eve. However, on December 23, she was invited to attend a meeting in the Mayor's Office to consider that very question from a citywide perspective.

---

[19]Interview with John Merner, director of Seattle Center Productions, Seattle, November 29, 2001. Unless noted, subsequent quotations and material from Merner are also from this interview.

[20]Interview with Dean Nelson, chief executive officer, Space Needle Corporation, Seattle, November 27, 2001. Unless noted, subsequent quotations from Nelson are also from this interview.

The First Meeting

Mayor Schell had been criticized after the WTO conference disaster for failing to solicit the City Council's advice on how to manage the event. For the millennium celebration decision, he did things differently. On Thursday, December 23, 1999, he convened about twenty-five people to brief city officials about the Ressam situation, make sure all parties involved had a chance to speak, and collaboratively consider options.

Among those at the table were Mayor Schell, Deputy Mayor Daudon, Deputy Mayor Tom Byers, the fire chief, FBI Special-Agent-in-Charge Mandigo, U.S. Attorney Pflaumer, Seattle Center Director Anderson, and—coming and going—members of the City Council. Under state law, no more than four City Council members at a time could be in the room simultaneously or it would qualify as an official public meeting and require advance advertising. So as one City Council member departed, another would come in.

There were also several senior police department officials at the meeting: assistant chiefs Edward Joiner, John Pirak, and Daniel Bryant, as well as Captain James Pugel, whose West Precinct included several downtown neighborhoods and the Seattle Center. Chief Norm Stamper, who had announced his resignation (effective in early 2000) following the WTO Ministerial, stopped in but did not contribute. A key missing figure was a permanent mayoral public relations officer; the previous one had resigned for personal reasons in November and the Mayor's Office was functioning with interim staff.

Schell opened with a request to Mandigo and Pflaumer to help the group assess the threat and plan appropriate security. Mandigo described what had been found in Ressam's car and the circumstances of his arrest. Mandigo recalls that he and Pflaumer "gave assurances from a federal point of view that we had no knowledge of any specific information that would indicate that Seattle or the Space Needle was a target of terrorist activity."

As Council President Sue Donaldson remembers it, "The thing that made an impression on me was when we learned something to the effect that had [the Port Angeles agents] actually unscrewed this container, everybody would have blown up. . . . It was details like that where you got a sense of the seriousness of it." [21] At the same time, Donaldson had the distinct impression that Mandigo "just couldn't share things. We had this sense that he knew so much more than we did. And yet he couldn't tell us."

Deputy Mayor Daudon agrees: "I felt they knew more than they could tell us." Council member Jim Compton echoes the same theme: "I remember my frustration that Kate [Pflaumer], who is just a wonderful person, was unable to say anything beyond 'you're on your own on this. We can't really advise you. We can't tell you what to do.' " [22]

---

[21]Interview with Susan Donaldson, president, Seattle City Council, Seattle, November 28, 2001. Unless noted, subsequent quotations from Donaldson are also from this interview.

[22]Interview with James Compton, council member, Seattle City Council, Seattle, November 27, 2001. Unless noted, subsequent quotations from Compton are also from this interview.

Council President Donaldson thought she saw a way to, as she terms it, "break the code, so we could at least get a toehold to make a decision." She asked bluntly, "Would you let your children go to Seattle Center at midnight to watch the fireworks, if we let this go ahead?" [23] Pflaumer answered without hesitation, "No." [24] "It really surprised me, when Kate said that," comments Mandigo. But Pflaumer felt that the facts on which she based her judgment were those the whole group had heard: Ressam came across the border with explosives, he had a reservation near the Space Needle, the Space Needle would be featured in New Year's television coverage as the symbol of the western United States, Ressam had an accomplice in Vancouver who had not been located, there were four timing devices (whether for redundancy or for four targets, no one knew), and no one would want to drive long distances with the volatile chemicals found in the trunk of Ressam's car.

At the same time, she wanted to make it crystal clear that there was no specific threat; federal officials had no privileged facts. Sensing skepticism from the group, Pflaumer observed, "I'm getting the impression that you all feel we are sitting on some dragon's horde of information that we don't think you are entitled to know, or that we can't give you for some reason." She continued, "That is not true. We do not know. . . . We have gotten permission to give you everything relevant. You know as much as we do. The difficulty here is that none of us knows enough."

Police Are Split

After presenting their points, Mandigo and Pflaumer left the meeting. The police were next to submit their views. Although not united on how to handle the Seattle Center celebration, they generally felt that the police could not rely on the FBI for complete information. There was a history of distrust between the police and the FBI, stemming in part from a Seattle law known as the Intelligence Ordinance,[25] which barred police from collecting information about any individual "who is active in politics or community affairs" unless such information "shall reasonably appear relevant to the performance of an authorized police function." As the police understood the regulation, "information" included even such public records as newspaper articles.

The ordinance, moreover, provided that every 180 days an auditor would review all authorizations and provide a written report to the mayor, City Council, and other officials as a public record. Over time the unintended consequence of this legislation was a perception among Seattle police that federal law enforcement agencies routinely withheld information

---

[23]Donaldson remembers putting the question to Mandigo; Pflaumer remembers answering it. Perhaps Donaldson intended the question for Mandigo; in any event, he remained silent.

[24]Pflaumer, who is single, recalls that Police Chief Stamper caught her eye with a skeptical expression, to which she responded: "I know, Norm, I don't have any children. But if I did, I wouldn't let them go!"

[25]Collection of Information for Law Enforcement Purposes, Seattle Municipal Code (SMC), Chapter 14.12.

for fear the information would be made public. Deputy Mayor Daudon says the police frequently invoked the Intelligence Ordinance to justify a lack of information and that the Mayor's Office had consistently directed the department "to disregard that if necessary to ensure public safety. . . . Let us take the heat. But they have raised it all the time."

Then came the embarrassment and indignity of the WTO conference. After the event, accusations were traded among the police, the Mayor's Office, and the FBI over who had adequately warned whom about the new breed of protesters bound for Seattle. Police insisted that the FBI had not given them full information, while the FBI claimed its warnings had been specific and on target. But Assistant Chief Pugel (in 1999, Captain Pugel) says that the FBI had warned against "the traditional black cloak, black helicopters, weapons of mass destruction, hazardous materials, Hollywood-type terrorist attack. Not these unplanned or never-seen-for-25-years demonstrations that take over a city. . . . They did not tell us what occurred at the WTO [conference] was going to happen. Afterwards, they said they did." [26] Assistant Chief Bryant concurs: "The [FBI] threat assessment of the WTO event before it happened was low to medium—and whether or not they changed that shortly before the event, that's what we actually had in hand." [27]

The result was a certain lack of faith in FBI security diagnoses of the millennium celebration. Given this context, Pugel was "leaning toward canceling. . . . Based on what I had just been through, I didn't think the city could stand another [trauma]." He continues, add to that the FBI "mystique that they know stuff that we don't. Quite often, you find out they had no idea what was going on [but] it's a subjective thing that plays into your decision making in that okay, what did they uncover at the border in subsequent searches and debriefing Ressam, and how much are they telling us?"

Assistant Chief Bryant, by contrast, argued for going ahead with the New Year's plans. Bryant had served as nighttime director of the Emergency Operations Center during the WTO conference and was in charge of the Year 2000 security planning. "When it came to the millennium event," remembers Bryant, "it was my feeling that maybe [the FBI] were holding back from us, or maybe they weren't. But at least they weren't giving us anything tangible to say there is a threat." If the city decided to cancel, Bryant felt it would set a poor precedent.

---

[26]Interview with Assistant Chief James Pugel, Seattle Police Department, Seattle, November 29, 2001. Unless noted, subsequent quotations from Pugel are also from this interview. Pugel became assistant chief after the events recounted here.

[27]Interview with Assistant Chief Daniel Bryant, Seattle Police Department, 2001. Unless noted, subsequent quotations from Bryant are also from this interview. The low-to-medium threat assessment had referred, however, specifically to terrorist activity; police were also responsible for "public disorder-riot" situations, and the FBI had assessed the potential for that as high—and its report was circulated and discussed. The police recollections reflect the kind of misconstructions that arose between police and FBI.

For their part, the Seattle Center officials were persuaded they would be able to hold the event as scheduled, safely. As a spokesperson told the press, "[p]eople don't want to be held hostage to rumors and speculations. They don't want us to shut down."[28]

The police department, meanwhile, made clear it would take a full week with the Seattle Center completely closed to ensure that all the buildings, tunnels, old swimming pools, and other structures could be verified danger-free. Closing Seattle Center for that period would be impossible. The police, however, had already intended to ramp up security for New Year's Eve. Ordinarily, only six officers patrolled the campus on a daily basis. For the millennium, the department planned to field some 850 officers throughout Seattle, including 100 at Seattle Center, plus four roving platoons of 40–60 officers downtown.

Conversation also turned to the possible perception that Seattle was caving in to terrorists. The line between prudence and capitulation, they agreed, was thin. "There are always going to be some risks," says Mayor Schell. "You can't live in fear of them, and yet you take each one of them seriously."[29] The specter of the WTO protests also played a role. As Council President Donaldson recalls, "WTO was clearly the 600-pound gorilla in the room. It was very much raised that if we cancel this, will people think we can't manage WTO, we can't manage this, the city is not functioning?"

The participants agreed they would not try for a decision just yet but hope that more information would become available over the Christmas weekend; then they would reconvene. Says Schell, "I was mulling it. There were clear differences of view, and we were hoping there would be more information."

What We Don't Know

Given his early commitment to a splendid millennium show in Seattle, Mayor Schell was loathe to contemplate any curtailment: "It was the last thing I wanted to do." But he adds, "It's what you don't know that's frightening. . . . Were there more weapons? How many more people were involved? Who were they? Then it was felt that we had a very short time frame to understand [the scope of the threat]." Schell says his first concern was public safety: "I just don't think you take any risks with the public safety. . . . [But] you can't win. If nothing happens, you didn't need to do that. The only way you can win is if somebody blows up something. . . . [Otherwise] you can never be proven right."

Schell recognized that, as the city's chief law enforcement officer, the final decision to continue or cancel would be his. But he was frustrated that so many of the security decisions were being forced on to his office. Assistant Mayor Daudon attributes that in part to Police

---

[28]Quoted in Christine Clarridge, "So Far, Show Going On Despite Rumors, Alerts," *Seattle Times*, December 23, 1999, A1.

[29]Interview with Mayor Paul Schell, Seattle, November 29, 2001. Unless noted, subsequent quotations from Schell are also from this interview.

Chief Stamper's pending resignation and the resulting temporary vacuum at the top of the police department. At one point, she recalls, "I caught myself and said, why am I sitting here thinking of ways to protect the Space Needle? Isn't this the police chief's job?" She says, "There was no leadership there to say let's go this way, let's go that way. It was going to be thrust upon the mayor to ultimately have to make a lot of very detailed decisions about how to manage this event."

As for the FBI, observes Schell, Mandigo "made a real point of saying we're not telling you what to do. . . . That was very frustrating. . . . How do I make a judgment when they have the information?" Mandigo responds that "our belief was [that] it was a decision that the city had to make. . . . If I had specific information, then maybe it would be 'Mr. Mayor, I'm advising you not to do this because. . . .' But I didn't have any [information]."

The Terror Context

Over Christmas weekend, Mayor Schell and other Seattle officials contemplated how to proceed. As the millennium drew closer, warnings of related terrorism grew. On December 22, a TV network broadcast what it admitted was an unsubstantiated report that Ressam's confederates might be planning to bomb six or more U.S. sites.[30] Among the possible targets mentioned were the New Year's celebrations in New York; Washington, D.C.; and Seattle. Government agencies took the mounting warnings seriously. The U.S. Customs Service deployed an additional three hundred inspectors to the borders with Mexico and Canada and placed all entry points on high alert. President Clinton requested that Americans be vigilant and report to authorities if they "see something that's suspicious."[31] The U.S. Department of State issued a warning that terrorists could be planning attacks on New Year's revels around the world. The FBI planned to keep open all fifty-six field offices on New Year's Eve. In Washington, D.C.; New York; and Los Angeles, teams would be ready for instant deployment.[32]

Other cities were taking elaborate security precautions for New Year's Eve but, so far, none had exhibited any hesitation about proceeding as planned. New York City expected upward of 2 million people in Times Square. The city's security operation, dubbed Archangel, called for more than 8,000 police officers to work that night.[33] Additional security measures included clearing cars from midtown Manhattan and screwing down manhole covers. In Washington, D.C., officials prepared for a celebration at the Lincoln Memorial and the mall, culminating in midnight fireworks started by President Clinton. National Guard troops

---

[30]Clarridge, "So Far, Show Going On."
[31]Quoted in ibid., A1.
[32]Massimo Calabresi, "The Terror Countdown," *Time,* December 27, 1999, 126.
[33]Neil King Jr., "Cities Are Stepping Up Security before New Year's Celebrations," *Wall Street Journal,* December 29, 1999, A4.

would supplement the 3,500 officers assigned to patrol that evening. And in Las Vegas, which was expecting about 250,000 visitors, authorities were planning to close several miles of the Strip to car traffic and deploy some eight hundred police.[34]

An equally urgent concern was the threat of technological sabotage. For a couple of years, governments, businesses, universities, and private citizens worldwide had raced against time to eliminate a potentially crippling computer glitch, known as Y2K, which would cause computers to misread the date, leading to disastrous consequences. While authorities struggled to bring their computer systems into compliance with the technological requirements of the Year 2000, law enforcement agencies focused on the potential for willful sabotage of the nation's computer-driven infrastructure, such as electricity grids, water reservoirs, and transportation and communication systems.

In Seattle, U.S. Attorney Pflaumer struck a note of calm with vigilance when she told a Seattle newspaper on December 23 that "I think we all need to be careful and concerned as we reach the end of this century." [35] Washington state had slated 400 troopers to work New Year's Eve, and 1,000 National Guard troops were on standby should the governor declare a state of emergency. Seattle-Tacoma International Airport had been on high alert (security level three) since the August 1998 embassy bombings and intended to remain so.

It was hardly reassuring to the group that had met in Schell's office, however, to read in the newspapers that, over the Christmas weekend, the FBI in Seattle had detained three Algerians who had hosted Ressam's collaborator, Meskini, even though all three were quickly cleared of terrorist connections. On Monday, December 27, the mayor called a second meeting to reach a decision on Seattle's millennium celebration. There were only 4 days until the planned events.

The Second Meeting

Some ten to fifteen people congregated in a small room off the Mayor's Office. The participants included Mayor Schell, assistant police chiefs Dan Bryant and John Pirak, Seattle Center Director Anderson and her colleague Merner, City Council members Donaldson, Compton and Jan Drago, a representative from the fire department, and Mandigo from the FBI.

Again the mayor asked Mandigo for his assessment. The FBI chief confirmed that three Algerians had been detained and cleared; he could not discuss the details because the three had been identified using FISA warrants. He asserted, however, that "we were fairly satisfied that we did not have any known presence of somebody associated with Ressam left, or any known activity about any planned terrorist acts or anything in Seattle." He concedes that due

---

[34]Timothy Egan, "Citing Security, Seattle Cancels a New Year's Eve Party," *New York Times*, December 29, 1999, A16.
[35]Clarridge, "So Far, Show Going On," A1.

to the restrictions on what he could say, "it was kind of me giving an oral representation that, although this Ressam came across with all this bomb-making material on the 14th, and although we've since arrested three additional Algerians, there is nothing to worry about."

At this point, the mayor decided to reiterate the question that Donaldson had put to Pflaumer; he asked Mandigo straight out whether he would take his children to Seattle Center on New Year's Eve. "My answer was well, I wouldn't take my children to that in any event, [meaning] this isn't the kind of thing that I would normally take my children to," recalls Mandigo. He commented that he could see the Space Needle from his house and fully expected to see it still there on January 1. The message that the assembled officials clearly heard, however, was that he would keep his family away.[36]

Mandigo, as before, left the meeting before it was over. At that point, the mayor started to go around the table, soliciting the view of each person there. Assistant Police Chief Pirak, a coordinator in the city's Emergency Operations Center who had advised early during the WTO conference that Seattle declare a state of emergency (but had been overruled), was one of the first to speak. Pirak says the mayor had a tough decision to make: "It was either promote the city, and show everybody that we're proud to be here and we're going to celebrate—or public safety."[37] Looking at the facts they had, Pirak had no doubt about the decision that the mayor should make. He remembers, "I'm thinking that this was a perfect opportunity to hurt a whole bunch of people. . . . To me, it was a much bigger risk for people from a public safety standpoint than it was from a public relations standpoint. My recommendation was: 'As hard as it is, I think that public safety needs to take precedence.' "

His colleague, Assistant Chief Bryant, voiced his dissenting view that police could ensure the security of the event and that it should continue. Seattle Center Director Anderson, remembers Merner, "said we manage risk all the time. We are prepared to go forward. We don't know of a specific threat to the organization and we would go forward." But City Council members Donaldson, Drago, and Compton were dead set against it. The fire chief abstained. It was time for Mayor Schell to make his decision.

---

[36]"The answer," admits Mandigo in retrospect, "wasn't well formulated."

[37]Interview with Assistant Chief John Pirak, Seattle Police Department, Tacoma, Washington, November 30, 2001.

The Seattle Millennium Security Threat (B): Epilogue

On Monday, December 27, 1999, Mayor Schell announced that Seattle's New Year's Eve extravaganza would be cancelled—but only the evening activities. Seattle Center would remain open as scheduled until 6:00 p.m., but then the entire campus would be cleared. There would be no dance, concerts, or other evening performances. The Space Needle's fireworks would proceed, but spectators would have to gather outside the Seattle Center to watch them. Although the Space Needle remained prepared to hold its private party, the client canceled for private reasons.

"This is already an unprecedented, unpredictable New Year, and we did not want to take chances with public safety, no matter how remote the threat might seem," Mayor Schell said in a statement on Monday evening. On Tuesday, he amplified to the press that the Federal Bureau of Investigation (FBI) "can't assure us there is no risk." He continued, "At a time when the city is recovering from WTO [World Trade Organization Conference] and heightened anxiety, adding another layer of uncertainty was not a prudent thing to do. Obviously there are those who would say we are caving in to terrorism, but I'm concerned with the safety of our citizens." [1]

City Council member James Compton applauded the mayor publicly, saying that "no one will give the city credit if 12 people don't die at Seattle Center. The city made a good decision." [2] City Council President Sue Donaldson recalls that "it was very much an intuitive decision in the end. I don't think we ever made a decision with so little information." [3]

Within days, however, a public chorus of criticism had risen against the mayor. Radio hosts ragged him unmercifully. Jay Leno, on the *Tonight Show,* made fun of Seattle for its alleged cowardice. Even New York Mayor Rudolph W. Giuliani implied disapproval in comments to the *New York Times:* "I would urge people not to let the psychology of fear infect the way they act, otherwise we have let the terrorist win without anybody striking a blow. No mayor, no governor, can offer anyone perfect security. Life involves a level of risk." [4]

Seattle citizens were split on whether Schell had decided wisely. "It is far better to be cautious than to put people in jeopardy," wrote a supporter in a *Seattle Times* poll. But a critic said, "The WTO fiasco was bad enough, when Schell's fond memories of '60s protests led

---

[1] All three statements quoted in Steve Miletich, J. Martin Mcomber, and Anne Koch, "How City Party Was Canceled," *Seattle Times,* December 28, 1999, A16.

[2] Quoted in ibid.

[3] Interview with Susan Donaldson, Seattle, November 28, 2001. Unless noted, subsequent quotations from Donaldson are also from this interview.

[4] Quoted in Timothy Egan, "Citing Security, Seattle Cancels a New Year's Eve Party," *New York Times,* December 29, 1999, A16.

him to ignore the need for better preparations. To turn around and cancel the new millennium's eve celebration in overreaction to the WTO disaster just shows that Schell and the City Council are floundering."[5]

The mayor was wounded when the *Seattle Times,* which had supported him on its editorial page, ran a headline January 2, 2000, that read: "Schell: 'I'm Not a Wuss.' "[6] But he insists he has never regretted his decision: "I never lost any sleep over making that decision. I thought it was the right choice."[7] Moreover, emphasizes Schell, he would have made the same decision on the millennium celebration even if the WTO Ministerial had never happened. The WTO, he says, "did not enter into it."

The millennium passed with no terrorist attack on any U.S. city. It was never demonstrated that Seattle had been a target (nor was it definitively disproven). When Algerian Ahmed Ressam went on trial in spring 2001, he claimed that Los Angeles airport had been the target. The intensive investigation that followed Ressam's arrest on December 14, 1999, revealed a far-flung network of operatives—organized into sleeper cells—under the direction of Saudi-born terrorist Osama bin Laden and dedicated to bringing terror to the United States. Ressam himself proved to have ties to bin Laden; in 1998, he had trained in the use of explosives at one of bin Laden's Afghan terrorism camps.[8]

As a result of the Ressam investigation, the FBI nearly doubled the number of its metropolitan-level multiagency joint terrorism task forces, from sixteen to twenty-nine. Nonetheless, in October 2000, suicide bombers blew up the U.S. destroyer *Cole* in a Yemen port, killing seventeen U.S. sailors. In February 2001, Central Intelligence Agency (CIA) Director George Tenet testified to Congress that bin Laden's adherents pose the most "immediate and serious threat" to U.S. security. And on September 11, 2001, bin Laden–trained terrorists commandeered four airplanes leaving U.S. airports and flew two of them into New York's World Trade Center and one into the Pentagon (the fourth plane crashed).

In Seattle after September 11, talk show hosts who had lampooned Mayor Schell in the wake of his decision to cancel Seattle's millennium celebration called him, says Schell, to offer "lots of private apologies." The City Council president said at a press conference that Schell had taken a lot of heat in December 1999 for what proved to be the right decision. But all of it was too late for Schell. On September 18, 2001, voters had ignominiously ousted him in the primary election during his race for a second term—one of the issues that commentators highlighted as contributing to his political demise: the decision to cancel Seattle's millennium party.

---

[5] Quoted in Frank Vinluna, "Public: Schell's 'Wise,' 'a Wimp,' " *Seattle Times,* December 30, 1999, A22.

[6] Jack Broom, Susan Gilmore, et al., "Schell: 'I'm Not a Wuss'; Cancelled Celebration Puts Focus on What Kind of City We Are, Our Appetite for Risk," *Seattle Times,* January 2, 2000, A1.

[7] Interview with Mayor Paul Schell, Seattle, November 29, 2001. Unless noted, subsequent quotations from Schell are also from this interview.

[8] Josh Meyer, "Border Arrest Stirs Fear of Terrorist Cells in US," *Los Angeles Times,* March 11, 2001, A1.

Key Actors in the Seattle Millennium Security Threat

Seattle, Washington, Officials

Mayor's Office
Paul Schell, mayor
Maud Smith Daudon, deputy mayor
Tom Byers, deputy mayor

Seattle City Council
Sue Donaldson, president
James (Jim) Compton, council member
Jan Drago, council member

Seattle Police Department
Norm Stamper, chief of police
Daniel (Dan) Bryant, assistant chief
Edward Joiner, assistant chief
John Pirak, assistant chief
James Pugel, captain

Seattle Center and the Space Needle Corporation
Virginia Anderson, director, Seattle Center
John Merner, director, Seattle Center
　　Productions
Dean Nelson, CEO, Space Needle
　　Corporation

Federal Government Officials
Charles Mandigo, special-agent-in-charge,
　　Seattle Office, Federal Bureau of
　　Investigation (FBI)
Kate Pflaumer, U.S. attorney, western
　　Washington
Diana Dean, U.S. Customs Service,
　　Port Angeles, Washington
Mark Johnson, U.S. Customs Service,
　　Port Angeles, Washington

Suspected Terrorists
Ahmed Ressam, member of the Armed
　　Islamic Group; arrested for
　　transporting explosives into the
　　United States
Abdelmajid Dahoumane, Ressam associate
Abdelghani Meskini, Ressam associate

The Seattle Millennium Security Threat, 1999

Chronology of Events

Tuesday, December 14

U.S. Customs authorities in Port Angeles, Washington, detain Algerian-born Ahmed Ressam as he attempts to cross the U.S.-Canadian border with a trunkload of explosives. The Federal Bureau of Investigation (FBI) subsequently launches Operation Borderbom to investigate Ressam and his possible connections to terrorist organizations.

Friday, December 17

Ressam is flown to Seattle and arraigned. The case quickly attracts national media attention.

Seattle Mayor Paul Schell learns of Ressam's detention through media reports.

Seattle Deputy Mayor Maud Smith Daudon contacts Kate Pflaumer, the U.S. attorney for western Washington, to learn more about the case. Pflaumer tells Daudon that investigators know that Ressam had planned to make a stop in Seattle, but admits that his intended target remains unknown.

Sunday, December 19

Authorities detain two individuals at the U.S.-Canadian border in Bellows Falls, Vermont, after bomb-sniffing dogs identify explosives residue in their car. Whether they are connected to Ressam is unclear.

Tuesday, December 21

The Seattle Center, the designated hub of the city's millennium celebration, holds a community meeting to review security plans. Center Director Virginia Anderson subsequently announces that festivities will take place as planned, but the center implements additional security measures.

Thursday, December 23

Mayor Schell convenes a meeting to brief city officials on the Ressam investigation and to discuss canceling the city's New Year's Eve plans. Participants hold off on making a decision.

Over the Christmas weekend, reports and warnings of terrorist threats intensify across the country. Seattle officials contemplate how to proceed.

Saturday, December 25
Through a wiretap on Ressam associate Abdelghani Meskini, the FBI confirms that Ressam is part of a well-organized group.

Monday, December 27
Mayor Schell calls a second meeting to consider canceling the city's millennium celebrations. The meeting participants are divided as to whether or not to go forward. The decision is left to Mayor Schell. He ultimately chooses to cancel the evening activities.

15   Security Planning for the 2004 Democratic National Convention (A): The Stakeholders Get Started

Esther Scott

The jetliner assaults of September 11, 2001, closely followed by the anthrax letter attacks, gave increased urgency to security planning for major public events, particularly those likely to capture the nation's or the world's attention. Throughout the United States, security planning became more organized, professionalized, and centralized—and the role of the federal government relative to that of the state and local governments became more pronounced.

Carrying out security planning for a major event is no easy task, however. This case, focusing on security preparations for the 2004 Democratic National Convention (DNC) in Boston that nominated Senator John F. Kerry (D-Mass.) for president, describes the planning process in detail and illustrates some of the key dilemmas that planners face in getting ready for such major events in the post-9/11 world.

One important change was how the DNC planners managed the interactions among the stakeholders that needed to play roles in decision making and the implementation of the security plan. The U.S. Secret Service, now part of the newly organized federal Department of Homeland Security, took the lead in security planning for the DNC both inside and outside the FleetCenter, the arena in which the convention would take place.

The DNC planning process involved a complex process of identifying risks, protective tasks, and capabilities for response that needed to be in place during the DNC. It required assignments of responsibility to each participating agency and the mobilization of the financial, human, and technical resources that would be needed to get the job done. Detailed operational plans had to be put in place, probed and tested through tabletop simulations, and exercised by the agency personnel who would be on the front lines when the DNC occurred. Finally, the security planning process required the development of a set of personal relationships among leaders of the key agencies involved to bring paper plans to life; create confidence that their partners could and would fulfill their responsibilities; and facilitate smooth, rivalry-free implementation of the security plan, especially if horrible contingencies required a rapid effective response.

The Secret Service team assigned to the DNC, led by Special Agent Scott Sheafe, brought well-practiced expertise to bear on the security planning process, but its skills went beyond the technical dimensions of security planning. The planning process regularly brought participants face to face with tough trade-offs between security and other values and interests, such as the economic impact of the convention on Boston and the extent to which protection

This is an abridged version of a case written by Esther Scott for Arnold M. Howitt, executive director of the Taubman Center for State and Local Government, for use at the John F. Kennedy School of Government, Harvard University. Funding for the case was provided by the U.S. Centers for Disease Control and Prevention through the National Preparedness Leadership Initiative. Kennedy School of Government Case Program, C16-05-1807.0, C16-05-1808.0, and C16-05-1808.1. Copyright © 2005, 2007 by the President and Fellows of Harvard C

required curtailing the normal movement of commuters and shoppers via major modes of transportation that passed near the convention venue. The sense of danger was palpable, but the likelihood of attack, and its potential means and location, could be only imperfectly estimated and thus was potentially debatable. Managing the complex interrelationships of stakeholders with differing interests and expectations was a challenging assignment that typifies the pressures operating on event planners in the post-9/11 world.

Discussion Questions

- What strengths and weaknesses did the security planning process for the 2004 Democratic National Convention in Boston exhibit?
- How well would the security plan for the DNC have worked had there been a crisis?

When the Democratic National Committee announced in November 2002 that it had selected Boston, Massachusetts, to host its July 2004 convention, the city's leaders and political allies jubilantly hailed their hard-fought victory. Boston had beaten out much larger cities to win the convention, which would formally nominate the Democratic challenger to President George W. Bush in the upcoming 2004 election. The city hoped to reap significant economic benefits from the many thousands expected to gather for the event, and it expected to showcase its historical and contemporary attractions to a large national and international television audience. It was little wonder that the city's popular Democratic mayor, Thomas Menino, who had long sought to bring the convention to Boston, was likened in the press to the proverbial "grinning . . . cat that had swallowed the canary" when news of the award was made public.[1]

But the city's joy would soon be tempered by the somber realities of hosting the first major political event in the United States since the September 11 terrorist attacks. Nominating conventions had long been a magnet for a range of domestic protesters, many of them seeking to disrupt the proceedings, but they were now also seen as a possible target for terrorist groups eager to capitalize on the opportunity to attack an important symbol of the nation's democratic process. In these more threatening times, the task of devising a comprehensive security plan that would protect conventioneers was a daunting—and expensive—one, with no exact precedent to act as guide. The city could, however, draw on a major source of experience and expertise—the U.S. Secret Service. It sought to have the Department of Homeland Security (DHS) designate the convention a National Special Security Event, thereby giving that agency lead responsibility for security planning.

---

[1] Scot Lehigh, "Is This the Start of a New Boston Attitude?" *Boston Globe*, November 15, 2002, A19.

Thus it was that Secret Service Special Agent Scott Sheafe arrived in Boston in June 2003 to take on the role of coordinator of the security arrangements for the Democratic National Convention (DNC), still a little over a year away. To do his job, he needed to enlist the cooperation and participation of over thirty federal, state, and local agencies, as well as the support of city and state political leaders. Under any circumstances, this would be demanding work, but the convention site—the FleetCenter, a sports and entertainment facility—posed special challenges. It was situated directly over a busy public transit station and right next to a key interstate highway; it was bordered by a bustling commercial district and was close to the city's harbor and downtown. From a security point of view, the FleetCenter was, in Sheafe's words, "a very sick patient," [2] and the medicine he prescribed to make it well was harsh. It was Sheafe's task not only to prescribe but to convince the patient to take the medicine.

Background: The Democratic National Convention Comes to Boston

It was no secret that Mayor Menino, who would mark his tenth year in office in 2003, ardently wished to bring the DNC to Boston. The convention, notes Julie Burns, a former deputy chief of staff for Menino and organizer of the city's 2004 bid for the DNC, was not in itself "a large event." [3] Only about 35,000 were expected to attend the event—a trifling figure compared to the hundreds of thousands that turned out for the Patriots's Super Bowl parade or to view the Tall Ships in Boston Harbor—but roughly 15,000 of that number would be members of the press. "You've got 15,000 members of the media in your city," Burns points out, "for somewhere between six days and two to three weeks, because the planners come early; so in that sense, it's just an incredible opportunity to highlight your city." Moreover, the convention was expected to bring business to the city in the short term—organizers had estimated that the event would pump $154 million into the local economy—and attract investment in the long term.

Once the long-sought prize had been won, the huge job of planning for the DNC, which would take place July 26–29, 2004, quickly got underway. The overall responsibility for organizing the event fell to Boston 2004, the convention's host committee, headed by two former Menino aides: David Passafaro, the committee's president, and Julie Burns, its executive director. Among other things, the committee was responsible for raising the $49.5 million that the city had budgeted for the convention in its bid.[4] Even as the city basked in the glow

---

[2] Sarah D. Scalet, "Is This Any Place to Hold a Convention?" *CSO Magazine,* September 2004, available at www.csoonline.com/read/090104/convention.html.

[3] Interview with Julie Burns, Boston 2004 Democratic National Convention Host Committee, 2005. Unless noted, subsequent quotations from Burns are also from this interview.

[4] The host committee expected the majority of funds to come from private donors, but hoped to secure $17.5 million from public sources, either in cash or in-kind services.

of its victory, questions arose as to whether this sum would cover the costs of the convention and, in particular, an item that loomed increasingly large in importance—security.

The Security Issue

Boston had submitted its proposal for the DNC in April 2001. Its bid package, Burns notes, included a section on security, detailing the city's "ability to deal with large-scale protests, ability to deal with political events, dignitary protection. . . . It was not at all focused on anti-terrorism." But by the time Boston's bid was accepted, September 11 had happened, and concerns about a terrorist attack cast a long shadow over the coming presidential race. Such concerns moved security to the front of the line of issues demanding the attention of the host committee. "Security was [only] one of the things we thought of" in preparing the bid, Burns says. "Post-9/11, it was the first thing." The city had budgeted $10 million for security in its winning bid. Even without the added worry of a terrorist attack, that figure had seemed low to some; Los Angeles, which had hosted the 2000 DNC, had spent over twice that amount to handle the massive demonstrations around the convention center there.[5] After September 11, there was general agreement that the need to protect against terrorism would add significantly to the cost—and the complexity—of security planning for the 2004 convention. Cognizant of the new challenges facing it, the host committee moved quickly to avail itself of an important source of help from the federal government by seeking to be designated a National Special Security Event (NSSE).

NSSE was created in May 1998 by presidential directive during the Bill Clinton administration in the aftermath of earlier terrorist incidents, such as the first World Trade Center attack and the bombing of the Murrah Federal Building in Oklahoma City.[6] Under the terms of the directive, the governor of a state in which an event of national significance was planned could request an NSSE designation; after the passage of the Homeland Security Act in 2002, such requests were directed to the Department of Homeland Security (DHS). Previous NSSEs included, among others, the 1999 World Trade Organization meetings in Seattle; the 2000 Democratic and Republican National Conventions in Los Angeles and Philadelphia, respectively; and the 2002 Winter Olympics in Salt Lake City. The NSSE designation provided no funding, but it did authorize the participation of federal agencies in the security planning process. Specifically, the NSSE designation stipulated the roles and re-

---

[5]Ralph Ranalli, "Critics Say $10M Budget Not Enough to Protect Convention," *Boston Globe*, November 14, 2002, A29; Yvonne Abraham, "DNC Has Price Tags, Details Galore for '04," *Boston Globe*, December 17, 2002, A1.

[6]In 1993, Islamic extremists detonated a truck filled with explosives in the underground garage of the North Tower of the World Trade Center, killing 6 and injuring over 1,000 people. Two years later, Timothy McVeigh parked an explosives-packed truck in front of the Murrah Federal Building in Oklahoma City; the resulting explosion killed 168.

sponsibilities of three federal agencies: the Secret Service, the lead agency for preparing and implementing a security plan; the Federal Bureau of Investigation (FBI), the lead for crisis management, which included responsibility for preparing for and resolving any crisis that might arise; and the Federal Emergency Management Agency (FEMA), the lead in consequence management, which included responsibility for dealing with the aftermath of any incident that might occur.

It was this federal involvement that the Boston 2004 committee eagerly sought. "We were actually very proactive," Burns recalls, "working with the governor [newly elected Republican Mitt Romney] and with [DHS] Secretary [Tom] Ridge to get our certification early, so that the Secret Service would come on board" early in the planning process. Governor Romney submitted his request to have the DNC designated an NSSE in February 2003; 3 months later, on May 27, Ridge wrote to Romney informing him that his request had been approved. The Secret Service was on its way.

The Secret Service Steps In

The U.S. Secret Service was charged with two missions: to investigate counterfeiting and other financial crimes, and (better known) to protect the president, the vice president, their families, and other dignitaries from the United States and abroad. The job of planning the security for an event, as opposed to an individual, as the NSSE directive required it to do, was a novel one for the Secret Service, but, as Steven Ricciardi, special-agent-in-charge of the Secret Service field office in Boston, notes, it was "a good fit" for the agency. "When you're on the president's detail [as Ricciardi had been], you're involved in planning his security, which is a large-type event every time he leaves the White House."[7] Moreover, Ricciardi adds, "when you do presidential security, you cannot . . . do it alone. You have to rely on other folks [and their] expertise [in] their jurisdictions." Special Agent Scott Sheafe agrees: "Every day somewhere there is an advance team from the Secret Service in a city either domestic or foreign that's building a coalition of partners to prepare for a protectee visit."[8] This was precisely the kind of collaborative effort that managing an NSSE required.

In 2003, Sheafe, a 12-year veteran of the Secret Service, applied for and got the assignment of coordinator for the DNC in Boston. Once the NSSE designation was made official in late May and Sheafe had taken care of his last responsibilities as a member of the presidential detail, he and his family moved to Boston, "a place I've never been to," he notes. "I know no one. But here I am."

---

[7]Interview with Steven Ricciardi, U.S. Secret Service, 2005. Unless noted, subsequent quotations from Ricciardi are also from this interview.

[8]Interview with Scott Sheafe, U.S. Secret Service, 2005. Unless noted, subsequent quotations from Sheafe are also from this interview.

The Boston field office, which was staffed by about fifty people and headed by Ricciardi, would work with Sheafe on security planning; Sheafe, however, would officially report to the Major Events Division[9] in the agency's headquarters in Washington, D.C. It was up to Sheafe to establish cooperative relationships with the state and local agencies that would be involved in providing security for the DNC. He was acutely aware of his outsider status. "Boston, I come to find out," Sheafe says, "is a tight-knit community, and [local agencies] I think were very much expecting this coordinator to come from within the [field] office." The Secret Service's decision to assign "somebody from out of town" made sense to Sheafe, "because it gives you a fresh perspective when you don't owe anybody anything." Still, Sheafe felt that his task had to be handled with some delicacy to preserve the field office's good relations with local officials.

The Planning Mechanism

Although Sheafe was starting almost from scratch in Boston, he did have the benefit of a procedure that Secret Service headquarters had established to organize planning for any NSSE, based on the agency's "core strategy" of "forming partnerships" with other law enforcement, security, and public safety agencies.[10] The procedure called for the establishment of an intergovernmental apparatus that brought together federal, state, and local agencies to work cooperatively on security planning and on resolving any issues that arose in the process. Its basic components were (1) a steering committee (a kind of "board of directors," in Sheafe's words) composed of the heads of agencies that would have a role in the NSSE and (2) subcommittees co-chaired by a member of the Secret Service and the local police department whose task was to devise operational and tactical plans for specific parts of the overall security plan.[11] The membership of the steering committee, as well as the number and makeup of the subcommittees, depended on the type of event being planned.

The group that Sheafe ultimately settled on for the steering committee encompassed the heads of eleven different agencies, including the commissioners of the Boston Police and Fire departments, the special-agent-in-charge of the Boston division of the FBI, the superintendent of the Massachusetts State Police, the secretary of the state Executive Office of Public Safety, the director of the regional FEMA office, and the general manager of the FleetCenter.[12] (See Exhibit 15A-1 for a complete list of the organizations represented on the steering committee.) Having agency leaders on the committee was considered a crucial in-

---

[9]The Major Events Division was later merged with the agency's Dignitary Protective Division.

[10]From the U.S. Secret Service website, www.secretservice.gov/nsse.shtml.

[11]There were actually three plans: the Secret Service's, for venue and dignitary protection; the FBI's, for crisis management; and FEMA's, for consequence management. Subcommittee plans were subsumed into whichever of the three was appropriate.

[12]Other senior managers of the agencies also sat in on some steering committee meetings.

Exhibit 15A-1   Boston Democratic National Convention Steering Committee members and subcommittees

Steering Committee Members	Subcommittees for Security Planning
Boston Police Department	Venues
Boston Fire Department	Consequence Management
Federal Bureau of Investigation	Crisis Management
Federal Emergency Management Agency	Intelligence and Counterterrorism
Boston Emergency Medical Services	Airspace Security
FleetCenter Management	Legal
Massachusetts State Police	Public Affairs
U.S. Attorney	Explosive Ordnance Disposal/K-9
U.S. Secret Service	Civil Disturbance/Prisoner Processing
Massachusetts Executive Office of	Transportation/Traffic
Public Safety	Dignitary/VIP Protection
U.S. Coast Guard	Credentialing
	Interagency Communication
	Critical Infrastructure
	Training
	Fire/Life Safety/HazMat
	Tactical and Counter-Surveillance

Source: Scott W. Sheafe (U.S. Secret Service), "2004 Boston DNC," presentation at Harvard University, Cambridge, Mass., September 29, 2005.

Note: HazMat, Hazardous Materials.

gredient to its effectiveness. "The steering committee is not going to work," Sheafe points out, "if you have the designee of the U.S. attorney or the designee of the commissioner of police. We needed to create a body . . . that had the players that were going to be involved—the decision-makers."

Sheafe also put together a roster of "what the subcommittees should be and who should be on them." As was the case with the steering committee, there would be some additions and some rearrangements, but the final list comprised seventeen subcommittees in all, each with responsibility for an area of security planning, such as venues, transportation and traffic, intelligence and counterterrorism, and consequence management. (See Exhibit 15A-1 for a complete list of subcommittees.) Each subcommittee would be chaired by a member of the Secret Service (some of whom came up from headquarters in Washington) and a member of the Boston Police Department; a number of subcommittees had one or more additional co-chairs, the representatives of agencies that would play a major role in that particular group's work. The size of the subcommittees varied, but some were quite large: the medical subgroup of the Consequence Management Subcommittee, for example, had thirty-nine member agencies. Together, the subcommittees worked on creating highly detailed plans that would protect the FleetCenter from an attack of any kind; ensure the safety of delegates and dignitaries as they shuttled from their hotels to the events at the FleetCenter and other venues; keep protesters from getting out of hand while allowing them adequate opportunities to demonstrate; and respond to a range of possible emergencies, including chemical or biological attacks, explosions, fires, and simple human illness.

Building Partnerships

While he was assembling his lists of committee and subcommittee members, Sheafe also sought to introduce himself to key officials whose cooperation would be crucial to the success of his mission. Chief among these was Superintendent Robert Dunford, a respected veteran of the Boston Police Department (BPD). While the Secret Service would be responsible for the protection of the actual venue of the convention (the FleetCenter) as well as a handful of individual dignitaries in attendance, the BPD was expected to provide security for the surrounding area and the rest of the city, including dozens of hotels and other sites where delegates and dignitaries would be gathering. Dunford had been chosen by then Police Commissioner Paul Evans to take charge of the security arrangements for the BPD and had been hard at work on plans since November 2002. From Sheafe's point of view, the decision to make Dunford the BPD's "point person" for the convention "made all the difference in the world." The superintendent, Sheafe notes, "was just extremely kind, willing to explain to me the plans that he had established to date; I got the impression from him right away that he was willing to work it as a partnership."

In June, Sheafe was ready for the official launch of the planning process. He sent out letters, over the signature of an assistant director from Secret Service headquarters, to the heads of the agencies he had selected, inviting them to the inaugural meeting of the steering committee on June 20, 2003, 13 months before the kickoff of the DNC. When the group convened, Sheafe recalls, "everybody [was] obviously a little bit nervous, [wondering] where the hell is this going to go and who am I and how is this going to be set up." He had given some thought to the seating arrangements, placing Dunford "right next to me," with Ken Kaiser, FBI special-agent-in-charge, "very, very close as well. I wanted everybody to see that it was my hope that Mr. Kaiser . . . and us could build a coalition also," as he had with Dunford.

Steve Ricciardi served as the committee chairman, but he generally let Sheafe set the agenda and guide the meetings.[13] At that first meeting, after Ricciardi introduced him to the assembled agency leaders, Sheafe set out the ground rules for the committee and the sub-

---

[13]Later, in March 2004, Ricciardi was named *principal federal official* (PFO) for the convention. The PFO (a new position created by DHS as part of its National Response Plan), Ricciardi explains, "facilitate[s] any type of federal response that would be needed in the event of a crisis." Once he assumed his new role, he adds, he became less directly involved in the work of the steering committee.

committees. The steering committee, he told them, would meet every 2 months at first, more often as the convention drew near; subcommittees would meet according to whatever time frame worked best for them. Only the co-chairs of the subcommittees, Sheafe said, would report back to the steering committee. When Sheafe finished outlining his goals, the first person to respond, as he recalls, was U.S. Attorney Michael Sullivan. "Basically, what he said was '. . . We're fully supportive and we're going to do anything we can to make this work for you.' . . . And that really kind of set the [tone]. . . ."

The Planning Process

As they settled into their novel and complex task, some committee and subcommittee members felt the benefit of having worked together, in some cases for many years, in a relatively small community of law enforcement and public safety agencies. "All of the relationships that we built over time," reflects Richard Serino, chief of Emergency Medical Services (EMS) in Boston, "and over the years for all these other events . . . helped us when we were developing the plan for the DNC. . . . So when it comes time for a special event [like the DNC], it's not going to be introductions for the first time; we're not exchanging business cards. . . . [We're] on a first-name basis."[14] This was especially true in the law enforcement area, where a Joint Terrorism Task Force—a consortium of about twenty-two federal, state, and local agencies responsible for conducting counterterrorism investigations—had brought officials into frequent contact with one another.

Where that was not the case, the early going took some adjusting. FEMA, for example, had little experience in working with some of the key participants involved in the security planning effort. It was, says Ken Horak, acting director of FEMA's regional office in Boston, "the first time we have had meaningful interaction with the Secret Service," and, as well, "the first time we were working with a number of city agencies."[15] It took some time for the agencies to come to an understanding of one another's perspectives and priorities.

It was, perhaps, the clarity of the Secret Service's role under the NSSE directive that kept any differences that arose from becoming disruptive. "There was no argument about who was in charge," says Carlo Boccia, director of the Mayor's Office of Homeland Security, "because that was designated—the Secret Service was in charge."[16] Many also praised Scott Sheafe for his efforts to keep traditional rivalries and animosities to a minimum. The FBI and the Secret Service had, for example, long been rivals, which is not surprising, Sheafe

---

[14]Interview with Richard Serino, Boston Emergency Medical Services, 2005. Unless noted, subsequent quotations from Serino are also from this interview.

[15]Interview with Ken Horak, Federal Emergency Management Agency, 2005. Unless noted, subsequent quotations from Horak are also from this interview.

[16]Interview with Director Carlo Boccia, Mayor's Office of Homeland Security, 2005. Unless noted, subsequent quotations from Boccia are also from this interview.

notes, because "you have these two big kids on the block" whose jurisdictions sometimes overlapped. "Quite honestly," says Boccia, who had recently retired from the Drug Enforcement Administration, "most of the difficulty always comes from the law enforcement agencies, because they are always very thin-skinned when it comes to turf. . . . But the strategic ability of [Sheafe] really overcame all of those." Sheafe himself credited Dunford with helping to lend legitimacy to the Secret Service's role in security planning and implementation for the DNC. "[Dunford] would constantly say, 'Tell me what you need and I'll help you find it.' He didn't try to dictate what was happening; he had a grasp of his role and my role, and how to complement each other."

Several participants noted that in a small city such as Boston, the interdependence of law enforcement and public safety agencies in handling a large event such as the DNC was an asset in building positive relationships within the security planning group. "We had to work together," Ken Kaiser, FBI special-agent-in-charge, points out, "because if we didn't work well . . . we wouldn't possibly have enough personnel to cover [the event]."[17] Kaiser and Sheafe both contrasted the situation in Boston with that in New York City, where the massive police force of about 38,000 (Boston's was only a little over 2,000) was virtually self-sufficient. "They can do just about anything they want with 38,000 police officers," Kaiser says. "They don't need us."

Getting the Work Done

For the most part, Sheafe let the subcommittees work independently, relying on their technical expertise and their familiarity with the city to produce viable plans for their particular area of concern. After their meetings, subcommittee co-chairs submitted worksheets to Sheafe, detailing "what their main issues were at the meeting, and how they felt they were resolved and [whether they] needed help from me." Not all the subcommittees were working from an entirely blank slate. The BPD had begun formulating its own security plans back in November 2002, shortly before the city's winning bid for the convention was made public. When, months later, Sheafe set up the NSSE subcommittees, "we just transferred our . . . structure over to theirs," says Dunford, "so it worked very, very smoothly."[18]

In other cases, the subcommittees were starting from scratch. After the first meeting of the steering committee, Sheafe belatedly realized that, in Boston, EMS was an independent agency and not part of the fire department, as it was in many cities. He called EMS Chief Richard Serino to invite him to join the steering committee and participate in the planning effort. In response, Serino created a thirty-nine-member subgroup of the Consequence Management Subcommittee that included local public and private hospitals as well as gov-

---

[17]Interview with Ken Kaiser, Federal Bureau of Investigation, 2005. Unless noted, subsequent quotations from Kaiser are also from this interview.

[18]Interview with Superintendent Robert Dunford, Boston Police Department, 2005. Unless noted, subsequent quotations from Dunford are also from this interview.

ernment agencies and that set about drawing up plans to cover the full range of medical and health aspects of the security plan. "He really took a lot of ownership," Sheafe notes.

Periodically, the various subcommittees made presentations before the steering committee, but these were primarily briefing sessions. The steering committee, says John Wentzell, senior vice president and general manager of the FleetCenter, was not a "critical decision-making body. . . . I would say it was a validating group; it was a group that empowered their staff."[19] The meetings of the steering committee were essentially choreographed by Sheafe to run smoothly. "I didn't want any surprises," he says. He consulted frequently with local officials, particularly Dunford, over potentially thorny matters "because I knew that, no matter what, when I sit at that table, two heads are going to be going up and down: mine and the superintendent's." When there were unresolved issues or differences within a subcommittee that might surface during steering committee briefings, Sheafe sought to "have a private meeting with the agencies that I thought were going to be affected," in the hope of forestalling a larger conversation that could veer out of control.

This tactic extended as well to questions that Sheafe himself had about security arrangements. After observing some tabletop exercises, for example, Sheafe became "very concerned" that some Boston Fire Department officials were "very quick to want to completely evacuate the [FleetCenter]." From Sheafe's perspective, "better safe than sorry doesn't always work" where evacuation was concerned. If it proved to be a false alarm, then thousands of people would need to be screened again before being allowed back into the building; or the alarm could prove to be "a ploy to get [people] outside" and therefore vulnerable to attack. Sheafe took the matter to Fire Commissioner Paul Christian in a private meeting, where he proposed that the Secret Service should "take that responsibility for [evacuations] from off your shoulders." Initially, the fire commissioner was dubious. It was "a big issue," Christian says, "because I have statutory responsibility [for evacuation] . . . and I was reluctant to give it up."[20] At the same time, he acknowledges, some chiefs "will do maybe more than they should, to err on the side of safety" in ordering evacuations. Ultimately, he and Sheafe hammered out an agreement, in writing, that gave the Secret Service authority over evacuation decisions at the FleetCenter but in consultation with the fire department's on-site commander. "I had no problem with it," says Christian, "after discussing it with Scott. . . ."

Keeping the City Apprised

There was no official representative from the Mayor's Office on the steering committee, although, Sheafe says, when he talked with Dunford, in effect he was talking as well "to the

---

[19]Interview with John Wentzell, FleetCenter, 2005. Unless noted, subsequent quotations from Wentzell are also from this interview.

[20]Interview with Paul Christian, Boston fire commissioner, 2005. Unless noted, subsequent quotations from Christian are also from this interview.

police commissioner, the mayor, Julie Burns—all in one person. . . . He knows the city well." Still, Sheafe kept in close touch with the host committee—and, by extension, the city—by making sure that either he or a deputy sat in on the Monday morning public agency working group meetings that Burns organized to help manage the complex logistics of the convention.

It was in the discussions with the Monday morning group and in private meetings that the most consequential security issues of the convention were raised. While the various sub-committees were working on their plans, Sheafe, in conjunction with the Venues Subcommittee, was tackling the Secret Service's major direct responsibility for the DNC—the security of the FleetCenter itself. About a month after arriving in Boston, he recalls, he had met privately with Burns, who "was concerned that the Secret Service would be making decisions that could have a negative political impact on the mayor, because he had done such hard work to get this event here [and] he didn't want to get burned as a result of that." Sheafe's response was hardly reassuring. "I said to her in a truthful manner, I'm not looking to do anything but what's right here, but I've got a public safety issue—a security issue—and a political issue, and I've got to balance the two. . . . But I will be frank with you on what I'm going to decide to do, and let you know about it so you can make whatever decisions you think are appropriate."

In the months to follow, it became clear that Burns had reason to worry. The measures that Sheafe and his superiors at Secret Service headquarters were contemplating to secure the FleetCenter would affect not only the area immediately surrounding it but potentially the entire metropolitan region, disrupting local and interstate traffic, the commutes of thousands of people, the conduct of business, and even the medical care of patients as far away as New Hampshire and Rhode Island.

Securing the FleetCenter

A privately owned facility, the FleetCenter was home to two Boston sports teams—the Bruins and the Celtics—and host to numerous concerts and other indoor events. It was ideally located for the thousands of people who flocked to it from all parts of the city and its suburbs and even from neighboring states; it was within walking distance of the city's downtown and easily accessible by public transit or car. But the very features that made the FleetCenter a virtue for sports fans and concert-goers made it a liability to those concerned with protecting it from harm during the convention. "From a security perspective at least," wrote one observer caustically, "the Democrats couldn't have chosen a worse site." [21]

---

[21] Quoted in Scalet, "Is This Any Place?"

The FleetCenter was a highly porous venue, located directly over North Station, a major public transit nexus. Every day roughly 24,000 commuters passed through the ground level of the facility on their way to or from the four commuter rail lines that had their terminus at North Station—the trains actually pulled in beneath the building's cantilevered over-hang—where they often mingled with crowds entering the FleetCenter to attend one of its events. Another 13,200 subway commuters used the Orange and Green subway lines, which made stops one level below, in a newly renovated superstation scheduled to open in June 2004, 1 month before the DNC began. Moreover, Interstate 93 (I-93), a major north-south artery, passed within 40 feet of the building's glass facade; Boston's inner harbor was visible from the FleetCenter, and Logan International Airport was a couple of miles away.[22] In short, it was vulnerable to attack from any number of angles. (See Exhibit 15A-2 for a map of the FleetCenter and the Boston area.)

The Threat

In the post–September 11 era, the danger of an attack on the convention was associated in most people's minds with Al Qaeda or other international terrorist organization, but security officials believed the more likely threat would come from domestic protest groups—most notably, anarchists—whose sometimes violent tactics had disrupted the 2000 Republican and Democratic National conventions in Philadelphia and Los Angeles. DNC organizers feared Boston would suffer the same fate or worse. Law enforcement officials monitoring anarchist and other protest-group websites saw signs of an intention to circumvent security measures and wreak havoc at the FleetCenter and its environs. From the evidence, says Dunford, it appeared that "we were going to get hammered."

But even though officials "felt the most probable source of a violent attack or major disruption was a domestic threat," says Thomas Powers, assistant special-agent-in-charge of the Boston FBI office, "we never, ever discounted the Al Qaeda threat or any other international terrorism threat that, if they did attack, would probably be a major attack."[23] Such an attack could, for example, take the form of a truck loaded with explosives speeding down the highway or a bomb planted on a commuter rail train—which was precisely what happened in March 2004 in Madrid, shortly before elections in Spain, when a series of train bombings killed almost two hundred passengers. Such incidents ratcheted up the fear that terrorists would strike at some point in the U.S. presidential election cycle, possibly during a convention.[24]

---

[22]Ibid.

[23]Interview with Thomas Powers, Federal Bureau of Investigation, 2005. Unless noted, subsequent quotations from Powers are also from this interview.

[24]In early July 2004, just a few weeks before the DNC began, DHS Secretary Tom Ridge issued a warning that Al Qaeda terrorists were "moving forward" with plans to launch an attack on the United States sometime during the election. Charlie Savage, "Al Qaeda Planning Attack, Ridge Says," *Boston Globe,* July 9, 2004, A1.

Exhibit 15A-2   FleetCenter and the Boston area

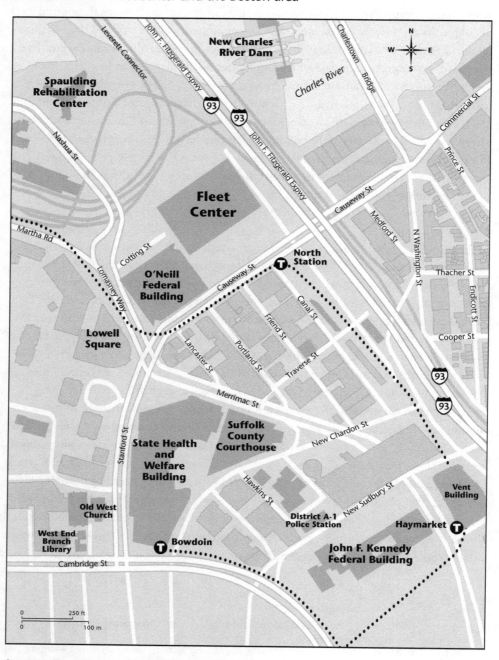

Source: Based on a map provided by the U.S. Secret Service.

Despite the FleetCenter's vulnerabilities, the Secret Service was prepared to work with what it had. Says Sheafe, "I told Rod O'Connor [CEO of the DNC] flat out: 'You decide what you want to do, and I'll figure out how to make it safe.'" For the city, however, Sheafe's message was tougher. "The [analogy] I use," he explains, "[is] somebody rang the doorbell at the doctor's office and said, 'Look, I feel awful. Can you make me better?' We said, 'Sure, . . . but it's going to take some lifestyle changes to get you better.'"

The Solution

As the agency charged with protecting the president and other high officials, the Secret Service had developed and refined an effective technique for ensuring the safety of its charges. The job of the Secret Service, Sheafe says, "is not to do bodyguarding. Physical protection is going to fail." Instead, the agency relied on "advance work"—or, as Sheafe puts it, "environmental manipulation"—to protect the dignitaries under its care. Admittedly, this was a "very expensive . . . and time-consuming" approach, but it had a long history of success.

As Sheafe recalls, he had been in Boston only "about a week and a half, and [already] knew how I wanted it to look," that is, how he wanted to go about making the FleetCenter secure. Essentially, it meant employing the Secret Service's practice of isolating a site, searching it thoroughly, and then allowing only those who had been screened to pass through. It also meant ensuring that the now-secured venue would remain uncontaminated by anyone or anything that was not authorized to come into it or even near it. In turn, this meant keeping subway and rail commuters from mingling with conventioneers and keeping vehicles from passing close enough to do damage to the facility.

The Station

Some of the precautions that the Secret Service required had been anticipated. During the DNC bidding process, says Michael Mulhern, who was then general manager of the Massachusetts Bay Transportation Authority (MBTA), "it was clearly understood that we would be adjusting the stopping locations and the lengths of some of our [commuter rail] trains so we could . . . stay out from underneath the cantilevered overhang."[25] The MBTA planned to have Orange- and Green-line passengers disembark at stops before North Station, a difference of just a few blocks, so that the subway trains could pass beneath the FleetCenter without stopping. In addition, it would build a temporary platform about 100 feet away from the facility where commuter trains could stop and let passengers on and off; instead of entering the FleetCenter, passengers would be directed to the side streets east or west of the building

---

[25]Interview with Michael Mulhern, MBTA, 2005. Unless noted, subsequent quotations from Mulhern are also from this interview. Mulhern stepped down as MBTA general manager for a private-sector job in May 2005.

and out on to Causeway Street, the thoroughfare that separated the FleetCenter and North Station from a commercial and business area known as the Bullfinch Triangle.

But it soon became apparent that there were problems with this last scenario. The Secret Service wanted its secure perimeter (what was later called the "hard zone") to include the streets bordering the FleetCenter. This area would be under the tightest control. "We sweep the entire area—the Secret Service, [the Boston police], bomb-sniffing dogs—the whole thing," Dunford explains. "We [sweep] the building, then out into the streets, sweep the entire streets, move everyone that is in there. . . . And then we seal it. Once we seal it, the only way we could maintain security is that everyone who comes there goes through a magnetometer as an authorized person." After all this painstaking effort, it would not be acceptable, says Sheafe, to have hordes of commuters walking "right into my venue, right into my secure area." The best solution, from a security perspective, would be to close North Station to commuter rail altogether.

Not surprisingly, Mulhern strongly resisted the idea. "He was determined," Sheafe says, "to keep the train station open" for commuters. And the MBTA general manager was not the only one with reservations about closing North Station. Governor Mitt Romney, a conservative Republican who took office in January 2003, was opposed to the idea, according to Mulhern. "The governor," Mulhern recalls, "was pushing back, saying not to close it . . . because we can't be inconveniencing all those [commuters] coming from the north just because the Democrats want to have a party." Romney was himself familiar with the workings of an NSSE from his experience running the 2002 Winter Olympics in Salt Lake City. He had welcomed the DNC to Boston but made it clear that he frowned on spending state taxpayer dollars on political events; and some in his administration thought, as Mulhern puts it, that "the MBTA went too far in our commitments" to the convention.[26]

Mulhern describes himself as an enthusiastic supporter of the city's bid for the DNC, pledging services that he estimated would cost the MBTA about $1.5–2 million (a figure that eventually more than doubled). "I have a pretty good relationship with the mayor," he says, "and I believed in everything the mayor was trying to do. And quite frankly, I looked at [the DNC] as not only a big advertisement for the city of Boston, but a big advertisement for our transit system. I always felt [there] was going to be a huge return on our investment." Now, however, Mulhern found himself being "second-guessed left and right," as he puts it, as it became clear that security requirements would drive up the cost to the transit authority. The controversy over the closure of North Station came to a head in early 2004 at a meeting in Mayor Menino's office that included Mulhern, Dunford, and Julie Burns. Dunford (who was

---

[26]The MBTA was an independent authority, but the secretary of transportation, a gubernatorial appointee, chaired its board.

Sheafe's strongest ally in the issue)[27] "was saying, 'You've got to do it [close the station],'" Mulhern recalls, "I was very concerned. . . . I said, 'I need to be convinced.' . . . And the mayor said, 'Listen, until we decide [what to do], I don't want to hear any more arguing, any more sparring.'" At that point, the parties agreed to try to hammer out a solution that would be satisfactory on all sides. It was a challenging task; as word got out that the Secret Service was contemplating closing down the Orange line platform at North Station (the possibility of a complete closure of the station had not yet surfaced publicly) the *Boston Globe* weighed in on the debate. The Secret Service, it wrote in an August 23, 2003 editorial, "ought to remember that the FleetCenter is a desirable site for a convention precisely because of its location at a transit nexus. Security should enhance the safety of delegates and others without walling off the convention from its lively host city."[28] For those who were concerned about walling off the convention from the city, however, there was worse news to come.

The Interstate

I-93, one of the busiest roads in Massachusetts, ran from Vermont, through New Hampshire, and through the heart of Boston on its way to the junction with I-95, the major north-south highway along the eastern seaboard. It was heavily used by commuters from north and south of Boston and was a major truck route for the region. On an average weekday, an estimated 200,000 vehicles traveled the road.[29] The southbound lanes of I-93 passed within 40 feet of the glass façade of the FleetCenter—much too close for the Secret Service's comfort. "Security specialists," the *Boston Globe* reported, "recommend a 150-foot buffer zone between the building being protected and the first point where an explosives-laden vehicle can have access." Even the northbound lanes, the paper pointed out, fell within the 150-foot radius.[30]

Sheafe had been eyeing the highway since he first arrived in Boston. "I'm looking at this, and I'm saying to myself, okay, I need offset. I need reasonable distance to secure [the Fleet-Center]." At his request, the technical security division of the Secret Service sent experts to do blast surveys of the area; the Secret Service also hired an outside contractor to do independent research on the site's vulnerability to explosives. In addition, he asked three assistant directors from headquarters to tour the site with him about 6 months before the start of the convention in July. Ultimately, he explains, the senior agency officials would "be making the final decisions" on closures and making the case for these closures to city and state political leaders.

---

[27]In fact, says Sheafe, Dunford had written a memo "suggesting what needed to be done [to secure the site] very early on, even before I showed up. You don't have to be a Secret Service agent to figure out a secure site."

[28]"Editorial," *Boston Globe*, August 23, 2003, A12.

[29]Scalet, "Is This Any Place?"

[30]Rick Klein and Anthony Flint, "Security for DNC to Snarl X-Way," *Boston Globe*, October 30, 2003, B1.

The findings of the blast surveys confirmed Sheafe's initial assessment—the FleetCenter could not be safeguarded from a vehicle packed with explosives traveling on I-93. "If you just use a regular sedan," Dunford notes, "you're probably talking 120–125 feet standoff distance that you need. . . . You start getting into a truck or an 18-wheeler, you need thousands of feet standoff distance." That someone might try to detonate a car or truck bomb from I-93 during the convention did not seem a remote possibility to those in charge of security for the convention. "The issue for the Secret Service," Sheafe explains, "is that you can't tell me that this [the FleetCenter] isn't a target. I cannot be convinced that this [wouldn't be] a target 24 hours a day for the four days [of the DNC]."

Under the circumstances, the ideal solution was clear, at least to the Secret Service; "to do this right," Sheafe says, "that road should be closed . . . for four straight days, period. End of discussion. Close it, never open it, and don't let any cars on it." But, as Sheafe was aware, the ideal solution did not take into account the high price it would extract from the city and its environs.

The Cost of Closure

The impact of closing any portion of I-93 would be hard to overestimate. For commuters from the north in particular, who already faced disruptions if North Station (the terminus for commuter rail lines serving the northern suburbs) were to close as well, the shutdown of I-93 would most likely mean long backups on alternative roads into the city. Truckers serving the region would face similar traffic jams and delays. Businesses might be harmed if goods were not delivered in a timely fashion or if workers found it difficult to get to their jobs or if customers stayed home rather than facing congested highways and streets. Even medical care could be compromised—I-93 was the main route from north and south for patients as far away as New Hampshire and Rhode Island seeking care at one of Boston's major teaching hospitals, most notably Massachusetts General Hospital, which was nearest the FleetCenter.

There were other costs as well. Shutting down I-93 would make enormous logistical demands on the state police, who would be responsible for managing any kind of highway closure. Even estimating the effect of closing a major artery was difficult. "The state police had an incredibly big challenge in trying to model it," Burns notes. "There was no data that they could use to say what would happen to traffic if the highway was closed for four days, because it had never happened." Moreover, the workforce needed to divert traffic from the closed highway would severely tax the state police force of 2,300 officers. As it was, police forces throughout the state would be stretched thin by convention-related duties. There "weren't enough bodies to go around to secure all the events," both on-site and off, says Burns. The BPD was planning to borrow heavily from other forces: the state police, the Suffolk County Sheriff's Office, the Massachusetts Department of Corrections, the Boston

Municipal Police, and the Massachusetts National Guard, as well as police departments in neighboring cities and towns.[31] The state police already had responsibility for law enforcement in one of eight security zones in the city created by the BPD for the duration of the convention, as well as its usual policing duties for the rest of the state; how it would find the officers to manage traffic on I-93 was an open question.

Creating Options

Sometime in fall 2003, Sheafe began discussions with both the BPD and the state police, in part to share his concerns about the highway and in part to get "fully educated on what the road meant to the region." These talks led to a kind of shuttle diplomacy for Sheafe, in which various scenarios for dealing with I-93 were considered by both sides in the discussion. "We would talk issues and game it out, and then [I] would fly out to [Secret Service headquarters in] Washington, D.C., and brief the assistant director," Sheafe says; the assistant director also traveled to Boston to meet with the state police superintendent. Ultimately, four options for I-93 emerged, ranging from complete closure to closure only on certain days or for certain hours.

Discussions of the pros and cons of these scenarios were still underway when the BPD circulated a document outlining the four options during an October 2003 meeting of Burns's Monday morning group, where, according to Sheafe, they created quite a stir. For some of those present, this was the first time they were learning that a complete shutdown of I-93 was one of the options under consideration. The revelation elicited some strongly negative reactions. Sheafe recalls one official from the state highway department whose "basic assertion to us was that it's impossible to do that; it cannot happen. . . . There were people who said this will absolutely cripple the city of Boston. The financial repercussions will be so obscene and damaging that there will be no recovery from it."

Burns, too, recalls the consternation among Monday morning group members when they saw the options. "Our response was," she says, " 'Absolutely not. You're not closing I-93.' " For the city, the ramifications of closing the road were politically awkward as well as logistically staggering. It meant, Burns explains, "the city going to the state and saying, 'Okay, we bid for this; it's our event and it's your road and, oh, by the way, you have to close it.' " Although the Secret Service could frame the road closing "in terms of law enforcement, myself and the host committee and . . . the politicians had to talk about it in much more political terms— what are you doing to businesses, what are you doing to commuters, what are you doing to

---

[31]To pay for the skyrocketing costs of security for the Democratic and Republican conventions, most of it for overtime pay for law enforcement and emergency response personnel, the cities of Boston and New York (which was hosting the Republican convention) together sought additional funds from Washington, D.C. In late 2003, Congress appropriated $25 million for each city for security-related expenses. Later, in June 2004, the mayors of both cities asked for, and received, an additional $25 million in federal funds.

residents? Can people even function around the FleetCenter?" The state's response was equally emphatic. Colonel Thomas Robbins, superintendent of the state police, recalls meetings in which "the state police and all the other state entities and local entities were saying to the Secret Service, 'You cannot close down 93; you just can't do it. I don't know what you're thinking.'" The state's foremost concern, according to Robert Haas, undersecretary of public safety in the Romney administration, was the ripple effect it would have on the struggling regional economy. Although Governor Romney readily acknowledged that "it's fine to host an event like this," Haas says, he questioned whether "we can afford to shut down our largest city for a week, and what kind of economic impact [it was] going to have, not just for the city, but for the entire region, because you have commerce that's passing through all the time."[32] Burns also recalls a meeting with some members of the governor's cabinet in which there were "diatribes about if we close the highway, the entire region is going to shut down, and [people were asking] is there any other way to do this?"

In the Mayor's Office, the same question was being asked as well. When he first learned in fall 2003 that closure of I-93 was being contemplated, Mayor Menino recalls, he thought the idea was "very extreme," although, he acknowledges, the Secret Service had to "protect their own interests also. . . . They were the lead agency. If something happened, they'd get their heads kicked in."[33] But whatever his personal opinion in the matter, Menino did not want to pick a public fight with the Secret Service—or any law enforcement agency. Instead, he says, he told Burns and David Passafaro, president of the host committee, "that we'd better negotiate this thing. . . . It can't be in cement. Let's figure this out, how we [can] work it out."

This approach suited Sheafe, at least for the time being. "I think everyone wanted to give the issue the proper amount of time before the final decision was made." He continued to explore the four scenarios in meetings with city and state police, and to consult with Secret Service headquarters in Washington. Periodically, he would get together with Menino and other city officials to go over a variety of security issues, including I-93. The mayor, Sheafe recalls, was supportive of the work that Dunford and others were doing to ensure the public safety during the convention, but "he's not going to address an issue before it specifically needs to be addressed. . . . So we let some issues slide down the line to be addressed at the proper time. . . . [But] the mayor knows it's coming."

As the new year began and the convention loomed nearer, however, the issues of I-93 and North Station moved inexorably to the forefront. While negotiations continued behind the scenes, Governor Romney offered what the *Boston Globe* called "some unsolicited advice"[34]

---

[32]Interview with Robert Haas, Massachusetts undersecretary of public safety, 2005. Unless noted, subsequent quotations from Haas are also from this interview.

[33]Interview with Mayor Thomas Menino, 2005. Unless noted, subsequent quotations from Menino are also from this interview.

[34]Rick Klein and Frank Phillips, "Romney Says Convention Should Move," *Boston Globe,* March 17, 2004, A1.

to Democrats. In March 2004, he suggested—provocatively, in the eyes of some—that the city move the DNC from the FleetCenter to the new Boston Convention and Exhibition Center (which was still under construction but scheduled to open in June) located in South Boston, a safe remove from interstate highways and major public transit hubs. The governor hinted broadly at the political damage to Democrats from having the DNC at the FleetCenter. "I anticipate that when people find it difficult to come in and out of the city," he told reporters, "they're going to ask a question: 'Why wasn't this held at the new convention center?' And the answer is, 'This is where the [Democratic] party chose to have their convention.'"[35]

Democrats quickly accused the governor of making political mischief, although some commuters, concerned over reports of possible closures that had begun filtering into the press, voiced support for the idea.[36] But, says Burns, there was no possibility of switching venues. The Democratic National Committee, she points out, had specified that the convention site "had to be a bowl," which would provide the right "sightlines" for delegates and for television cameras. Not only was the South Boston facility still under construction, with no guarantee of a firm completion date, at the time the city had been preparing its bid, Burns notes, but the site could not be configured to meet the committee's specifications for stadium-style seating. Moreover, Boston 2004 had signed a $3.5 million lease agreement with the FleetCenter and could not back out of its contract without a huge financial penalty.

But if the convention was to stay in the FleetCenter, a solution had to be found to the security problems posed by North Station and I-93, and to the political and logistical problems posed by their closure. For the Secret Service, the public's reaction to security-related disruptions was not the central concern. "That's totally outside my purview," Sheafe told a reporter. "It doesn't affect me in the job that we do one way or another. Our mandate is clear; our responsibilities are clear. The politics of the local reception for the event doesn't affect our way of thinking at all."[37] But for city and state officials, the politics was a serious matter. Snarled traffic, frustrated commuters, and stranded businesses could lead to serious backlash locally and to ugly publicity nationwide. Sheafe and his superiors at Secret Service needed to decide how—and whether—they could meet their goal of securing the FleetCenter without wreaking economic and political havoc on the region.

---

[35]Quoted in ibid.

[36]Disgruntled commuters noted that there were no plans to shut down New York's Pennsylvania Station, a major commuter rail terminus that was directly under Madison Square Garden, the site of the upcoming Republican National Convention. Penn Station, however, lay several levels below Madison Square Garden—whereas commuter rail trains in North Station pulled in at the ground level of the FleetCenter—and there were exits that led passengers to streets farther away from the Garden.

[37]Quoted in Scalet, "Is This Any Place?"

Security Planning for the 2004 Democratic National Convention (B): Resolving the Security Trade-Offs

Throughout February and March 2004, Secret Service Special Agent Scott Sheafe continued to work with city and state officials, and with the Massachusetts Bay Transportation Authority (MBTA), on the issue of closing Interstate 93 (I-93) and North Station while the Democratic National Convention (DNC) was in session in late July. In essence, his method was the same in both cases—generating options for each and weighing the pros and cons. "How we approached decision-making," explains Boston Police Superintendent Robert Dunford, "was we wrote scenarios and then wrote options; and then we [asked], what . . . [are] the strength, weakness, threat, and opportunity of each of those."[1] But while the various scenarios were being discussed and winnowed out by city, state, and federal law enforcement officials, Sheafe was aware that the top political leaders would ultimately determine, if not which options were chosen, at least how smoothly and cooperatively they would be implemented. "I didn't doubt," he says, "that the final decisions on these things [were] going to be made between law enforcement, the mayor, and the governor. It [was] going to be a very small pool of people who [were] going to be able to make a decision of that magnitude."[2]

Closing North Station

In the case of North Station, MBTA General Manager Michael Mulhern, who fought hard to keep the transit hub open, was presented with a scenario that granted him his wish. "We went through a process," Mulhern recalls, "where the Secret Service actually devised a plan where we could keep [the station] open. . . . They said, 'Okay, we'll keep it open, but here's what it's going to look like.'"[3]

What it looked like proved to be unpalatable. For one thing, passengers would have to take a long and circuitous route to and from subway or commuter rail trains to avoid passing through the secure perimeter around the FleetCenter, a detour that would mean a walk of about a mile and a half. For another, Mulhern realized, there would be no guarantee that the station would not be abruptly shut down by security forces in the event of an incident.

---

[1] Interview with Superintendent Robert Dunford, Boston Police Department, 2005. Unless noted, subsequent quotations from Dunford are also from this interview.

[2] Interview with Scott Sheafe, U.S. Secret Service, 2005. Unless noted, subsequent quotations from Sheafe are also from this interview.

[3] Interview with Michael Mulhern, MBTA, 2005. Unless noted, subsequent quotations from Mulhern are also from this interview.

"Now I began to get educated for the first time on what it means to run a national convention," Mulhern reflects. "The MBTA was always very proud of its [ability] to move the masses . . . [but] we didn't understand the security concerns, especially post-9/11—how those concerns had increased over that period of time." If, for example, protesters managed to make their way into North Station—the closest, Mulhern points out, that they "could have gotten to the actual convention"—the Secret Service and Boston police "would act unilaterally to close the station. . . . Then I'd have all my resources deployed in the wrong place, [I'd] have to implement a substitute service plan—and that would be a crisis for us." After reviewing this scenario, Mulhern conceded the wisdom of closing North Station. Sheafe, Mulhern wryly notes, "turned out to be a very wise man who understood [that we] are going to have to figure it out on our own. . . . I think he effectively managed me in terms of getting us where we needed to be."

But, as Mulhern recalls it, he found it difficult initially to "get the word out" that North Station would be closed during the 4 days of the convention. "Nobody wanted to take responsibility for getting the story out," he maintains. Governor Mitt Romney's administration, Mulhern continues, had not "been convinced at that point that that was the way to go."[4] Mayor Thomas Menino was more "where I was," as Mulhern puts it, reluctantly bowing to the necessity of closing the station.

Early on, we [both] thought . . . we were going to be able to just do some adjustments down at North Station to keep it open. . . . I don't think he understood how serious an implication the security zone would have [for] the transportation infrastructure. So it became an issue for us to deal with. And it's like you go through the stages of grief. . . . There was the storming phase, there was the angry phase, and then we went to the figure-it-out phase.

Eventually, feeling that the public "needed a head start to plan their summer vacations"—possibly timing them to avoid a difficult commute—Mulhern decided to take matters into his own hands by planting "a strategic leak" with the *Boston Globe*. On March 3, 2004, the paper reported that "MBTA officials want to shut down North Station to all commuter rail and subway traffic [during the DNC]. . . . The officials said they made the decision in part because even if they elected to keep North Station open, a security problem during the convention, such as a bomb threat or violent protest, could compel the Secret Service to shut it down, causing commuter chaos." City Hall, however, remained noncommittal, at least publicly. Asked for a response, a spokesman for Menino "said the mayor still considers the matter open for discussion," the March 3 article reported, although, the spokesman

---

[4]Undersecretary of Public Safety Robert Haas, however, maintains that the Romney administration recognized the security problems posed by keeping North Station open. "There really was no choice," he says, "in terms of what you do with North Station." Interview with Robert Haas, Massachusetts undersecretary of public safety, 2005. Unless noted, subsequent quotations from Haas are also from this interview.

added, "Obviously, the mayor will abide by whatever public safety determination is created."[5] A few days later, on March 6, Mulhern again spoke to the *Globe,* this time for attribution, telling the paper that the MBTA was "leaning toward closing commuter rail access to North Station."[6]

The effort to persuade Mulhern was "tedious and time-consuming," says Sheafe, but he viewed the planning process philosophically as "a marathon, not a sprint." Moreover, once the MBTA general manager was convinced, he became an ally. "I remember [Mulhern] saying, 'I've been looking at this [the closure of North Station] the wrong way; this is what I think we need to do.' Then once he did that, people began to realize that this is going to take some major muscle movement on behalf of the city. And I really give him a lot of credit because he was the first one to kind of step out and say, 'Okay, we'll take our lumps.' "

Closing Interstate 93

The issue of North Station was settled in early March (albeit to the dismay of the commuting public), but the fate of I-93 continued unresolved for a few more weeks. Over the course of their meetings in early 2004, the Secret Service and the city and state police reviewed and debated the merits of the four options under consideration, which ranged from complete to partial shutdown of the highway. Some of the less severe options for I-93 did not seem workable to the Secret Service. One scenario called for shutting down the highway only on the last night of the convention (Thursday, July 29) when Senator John Kerry would formally accept the Democratic Party's nomination. But that made little sense to Sheafe. "The people that are looking to inflict harm," he reasons, "aren't looking to do damage to Senator Kerry—they're looking to do damage to democracy" and could strike any of the four days the DNC was in session.

But another of the scenarios appeared more workable—to close I-93 in the evenings, when the main events of the convention would be staged. There was a flaw in this scenario, too, because, Sheafe notes, the FleetCenter was going to be "almost as full during the day as it [was] at night." Nonetheless, he concedes, "you could make the argument that somebody who was . . . less sophisticated than an Al Qaeda may look to do damage at the highest threshold of people, when the most spotlight is on." Accordingly, he continues, "we came to a compromise." Under the terms of that compromise, I-93 would be completely closed only during evening hours for all 4 days of the convention. "And during the time [the road] was open," Sheafe adds, "we would leave one lane [reserved] for emergency vehicles, so if there is a grid-

---

[5]Raphael Lewis, "North Station May Shut for Parley," *Boston Globe,* March 3, 2004, A1.
[6]Quoted in Andrea Estes, "T's Pledge to Convention Is in Jeopardy," *Boston Globe,* March 6, 2004, B1.

lock situation, we can always get emergency vehicles in and out. And we're going to divert certain size vehicles off the road at all times." Police officials said, Sheafe recalls, " 'It's going to be tough for us, but [we] think we can figure it out.' And there was some give and take, and then I took it back to Washington and [Secret Service officials] said, 'There's an acceptable level of risk there that we can live with.' And then we took it to the governor and the mayor."

Two Briefings

On March 25, Sheafe, two assistant directors from Secret Service headquarters, and a blast expert met separately with Mayor Menino and with Governor Romney. "The briefings were identical," Sheafe recalls. "We briefed the threat. We briefed options for mitigation. . . ." Julie Burns, executive director of the Boston 2004 committee, who was present at the mayor's briefing, as was Dunford, notes that the session was "more for the mayor to understand the potential of an incident on I-93. [It] was not so much about closing it . . . [or] the logistics of closing it. It was the impact of what could happen if there was an incident." [7] "We said to them," Dunford recalls, " 'All we can do is tell you what the threat is and what the risk is, what the vulnerabilities are. You have to make the decision. But we're telling you that if someone came down this highway with a truckload of explosives, you would have thousands and thousands of casualties.' "

By this time, an "evolutionary process," as Burns puts it, that took place over months of conversations and meetings, made the prospect of some kind of closure of I-93 seem, if not palatable, at least unavoidable. Menino, Dunford recalls, "knew the challenges and obstacles we were facing. And I think the best thing is he had confidence in us that we could do the job. [When] he was made the presentation, [he] said, 'Okay, if that's the way it's got to be,' and he made it without hesitation." The Secret Service, Burns notes, "really did their homework before they came to the [mayor]," and given the potential threat, the mayor's acquiescence was in a sense a foregone conclusion. "No elected official," she maintains, "or no public servant—or actually no really sane person—is going to say, 'I don't like this. I'm going to tell you no,' and then be responsible for the outcome." This did not necessarily mean, however, that the mayor saw eye to eye with the Secret Service on which measures were needed to protect the FleetCenter. "My persuasion point," Menino reflects, "was really [that] I couldn't step in the way of the Secret Service. Security was number one. I didn't agree with them, but they had a better view, and they knew security much better than I did. [But] I thought we were going to an extreme." [8]

---

[7]Interview with Julie Burns, Boston 2004 Democratic National Convention Host Committee, 2005. Unless noted, subsequent quotations from Burns are also from this interview.

[8]Interview with Mayor Thomas Menino, 2005. Unless noted, subsequent quotations from Menino are also from this interview.

The same could perhaps be said for Governor Romney. Concerned about the possibly severe economic repercussions from any kind of shutdown of I-93, as well as the burden it would put on the state police force, Romney sought a clear justification from the Secret Service for taking such drastic action. As Undersecretary of Public Safety Robert Haas puts it:

[The governor] wanted an emphatic statement from the Secret Service that this had to be done, because [the argument being made] was kind of, this is a good thing to do, or this is a prudent thing to do. The governor wanted something a little bit more definitive than that. If he was about to disrupt traffic and people's lives to this degree, he wanted to know that there was a good and proper reason to do so.

This was, in essence, the message that the governor heard during his March 25 briefing with the Secret Service. Along with providing graphic data from the blast surveys, Secret Service officials were at pains to make clear that the approach they were recommending was a compromise for the Secret Service as well as for the police. Secret Service officials "were blunt," Sheafe recalls. "They said, 'We feel strongly enough about this threat that we were initially thinking of suggesting that the roads be closed in all directions at all times for the duration of the [DNC]. But when we take into consideration your region and your public, we think we've come to [a workable compromise].'" The briefing, according to Sheafe, "wasn't a hard sell. We restated the facts; we stated some options; we came to a conclusion. Everybody shook hands, and we went on our way."

The following day, March 26, a larger, more public meeting was held in the Parkman House in Boston, with both Mayor Menino and Governor Romney in attendance, along with other state and local officials and representatives from Secret Service headquarters. Sheafe distributed "a white paper," as he puts it, with "three bullets representing the things the mayor had agreed to and the governor had agreed to": that portions of I-93, north and south, would be "closed during certain evening hours to be determined" for the 4 days of the convention; that commuter rail service to North Station would be halted; and that subway service to North Station would likewise be suspended. The meeting, according to the *Globe*'s account the following day, was cordial and ended in pledges of cooperation.[9]

The Parkman House meeting, and the two briefings that preceded it, Sheafe reflects, were "a defining moment for me." Although Menino and Romney did not have "a whole lot of options" where matters of terrorist threats were concerned, he acknowledges, they could have made things harder for him and the Secret Service. At the worst, they could have resisted the closure recommendations, which "would have put us in a difficult place of having then to try to use some sort of political pressure to accomplish that." Or they could have ac-

[9]Frank Phillips and Rick Klein, "Governor and Mayor Meet about Convention," *Boston Globe*, March 27, 2004, B1.

quiesced but made it clear to the public that the Secret Service had forced their hand, and left it for the agency to deliver the bad news. Instead, Sheafe notes, "They said, 'We are all in this together.'"

Still, there was perhaps a tacit agreement about who would ultimately be seen to be the driving force behind the I-93 and North Station closures. The mayor and the governor "were both supportive," Sheafe observes, "but they're also very politically astute, in that they say, 'You're the experts, and if that's what you're telling us needs to happen, then I guess that's what needs to happen.' . . . So I felt like everybody got what they needed." A few days later, shortly before a March 31 public briefing to announce the broad outlines of the plan to close North Station and I-93, a spokesman for the state secretary of transportation told reporters, "This is the Secret Service's show at this point. We have to defer to the folks with the earpieces and the microphones in their sleeves."[10]

Planning for Closure

The March 31 briefing on the closures of I-93 and North Station provided few specifics, but managed nonetheless to generate waves of prospective anxiety and anger among the public over the impact that the shutdowns would have. "I just think it's crazy that they're going to shut down the main vein of the city just to please all these Democrats," one aggrieved commuter told the *Globe*. "To inconvenience that many people is absolutely crazy."[11] Political leaders voiced their unhappiness as well. U.S. Representative Stephen Lynch (D-Mass.), a Democrat from South Boston, grumbled that in Washington, D.C., a city that had "a lot of . . . high-value targets for a terrorist attack, . . . we don't shut down the expressways. There's got to be a better way to handle this. I can be persuaded that this is necessary, but I'm not there yet."[12] Businesses worried about how workers would get to their jobs; workers worried likewise. Hospitals—particularly Massachusetts General, a major tertiary-care institution located only a few blocks from the FleetCenter—worried about how both medical staff and patients would make their way in. In the subcommittees set up by Sheafe and the agencies that were charged with traffic management, officials began laying plans to cope with the massive dislocation of traffic and commuters that the closures would bring. The MBTA had already announced its alternative routes for the roughly 24,000 commuter-rail passengers who would be affected each day by the closing of North Station. Where possible, passengers would detrain at rapid transit stops outside Boston and take the subway into the

---

[10]Anthony Flint and Michael Rosenwald, "Shutdowns Set for Convention; North Station, I-93 Are Affected," *Boston Globe,* March 31, 2004, A1.

[11]Quoted in Rick Klein, "Downtown Businesses Scramble to Make Plans," *Boston Globe,* April 1, 2004, A1.

[12]Anthony Flint and Kevin Joy, "Safety Precautions Draw Complaints," *Boston Globe,* April 1, 2004, A30.

city; where no such connections were available, they would have to transfer to buses for the remainder of their commute.[13]

Meanwhile, the medical subgroup of the Consequence Management Subcommittee worked on finding ways to mitigate the impact of the shut-down of I-93 which, according to Boston Emergency Medical Services Chief Richard Serino, "had huge consequences for the medical community."[14] Among the many dilemmas created by the road closure was the question of what to do about the ambulances that came into the city every day carrying sometimes desperately ill patients from the suburbs and neighboring states to Boston's world-famous hospitals. Ambulances, Serino points out, had been used to "deliver bombs in the Middle East," so devising a secure way to allow them access to Boston's top medical facilities would take some ingenuity. Eventually, after working with the Massachusetts State Police, the State Office of Medical Services, local hospitals, and "every ambulance service in New England," Serino and his group put together an elaborate security procedure—involving advance radio contacts and identity checks, checkpoints, and security sweeps of the vehicles with bomb-sniffing dogs—that would permit ambulances to come through on I-93 even when the road was "closed, period, final, end of statement," even to state troopers.

But similar accommodation could not be made for the approximately 200,000 commuters and truckers who traveled each day on I-93 or for those who used the "vast network of roads," as the *Boston Globe* put it, that fed into it. In order to prevent long lines of traffic from stacking up at entrance ramps to the highway near the FleetCenter, planners determined that almost 40 miles of roads, bridges, and tunnels would have to be closed; signs and warnings would have to be posted as far away as New Hampshire and Vermont.[15] What's more, because of the complex nature of the road-closure plan, some ancillary roads would begin shutting down at 4:00 p.m., just as the evening rush hour was beginning and 3 hours earlier than anticipated.[16] Even with these precautions, however, analytical models prepared by traffic consultants forecast a grim scenario. "We had projections," says Haas, "[of] six to eight hours of back-up" under normal traffic flow conditions; some predicted that southbound traffic would back up all the way to the New Hampshire border.

It was the specter of the region's roadways grinding to a standstill that led state officials to conclude that the public should be urged to avoid Boston altogether during the convention. This ran sharply counter to the mayor's and the host committee's vision of the DNC

---

[13]Sheafe did, however, arrange for MBTA buses carrying commuter-rail passengers to use I-93 after it was closed to general traffic.

[14]Interview with Richard Serino, Boston Emergency Medical Services, 2005. Unless noted, subsequent quotations from Serino are also from this interview.

[15]Anthony Flint, "Road Closures Make Sense, Engineers Say," *Boston Globe,* May 23, 2004, B1.

[16]I-93 itself would not be completely shut down until 7:00 p.m.; it would reopen at 11:00 p.m.

as a time to showcase the city not just to delegates and the press but to area residents and tourists as well. The host committee had planned free concerts and other events as part of a citywide celebration during the convention. "We really wanted people to come into town and experience it," says Burns. Governor Romney, however, who had firsthand experience in running a National Special Security Event (NSSE), the 2002 Winter Olympics in Salt Lake City, viewed the DNC in a different light—as the sole draw to the city, a single event intended only for those with tickets or some official form of entrée. The governor "kept saying over and over again . . . ," Haas recalls, "that what they did out in Utah was . . . they just convinced the public that you don't want to be coming into the city unless you're coming in for [an Olympic] event, and that saved them an awful lot of trouble."

These divergent visions of the DNC led to "discussions back and forth," Haas says, "between Boston and the governor in terms of how this should be played out." In the end, as Haas remembers it, "we just agreed that, given the fact that we're going to be shutting down North Station, given the fact that we're going to shut down 93, it wasn't viable to have people trying to get into the city." Burns recalls it somewhat differently. "The host committee," she says, "never told people to stay home. That message was definitely getting out, but it was definitely not a message of the host committee."

Unveiling the Plan

On May 20, 2004, 2 months before the kickoff of the convention, the public got its first detailed look at the security precautions that would be in place during the 4-day event. In a presentation hosted by the Greater Boston Chamber of Commerce and the Boston 2004 committee, city and state officials unveiled to local businesses and the media what the *Boston Globe* called the "staggering scope of the security measures," which, it maintained, "surpassed the worst fears of many residents and businesses." [17]

Under the security plan, a "hard zone" would be established around the FleetCenter, encompassing not only that facility but the adjacent O'Neill Federal Building as well. A staging area for delegates' buses across Causeway Street from the FleetCenter—essentially, the upper right-hand side of the Bullfinch Triangle—was also included in the secure perimeter.[18] Anyone entering the hard zone would be required to have credentials, issued by the Secret Service, and to be screened by metal detectors and x-ray machines. In addition, there would be a "soft zone," south of Causeway Street, extending from Merrimac Street eastward

---

[17]Anthony Flint, "Massive Closings of Roads Set for Convention Week," *Boston Globe,* May 21, 2004, A1.

[18]From the Boston Police Department, Democratic National Convention Operating Plan. The hard zone was bounded by Martha Way and Lomasney Way to the west, Causeway Street to the south, the North Washington Street Bridge to the east, and the Charles River to the north. (See Exhibit 15A-2.)

to Canal Street. (See Exhibit 15A-2 for a map.) Pedestrians could enter this area without credentials or security checks, but no vehicles would be allowed. Delivery truck drivers serving the area would have to park outside the perimeter and wheel their goods into businesses and offices; no deliveries would be permitted after 2:00 p.m.

The restrictions around the immediate vicinity of the FleetCenter paled in comparison to the ripple effects they would have on traffic patterns in the area. Almost all modes of transportation would be affected: private noncommercial jets would be banned from the airspace around the FleetCenter, and sections of Boston Harbor and the Charles River would be closed to all boat traffic. But it was the road closings that raised eyebrows and generated the most negative response during and after the briefing. In particular, the revelation that not just a section of I-93 but nearly 40 miles of ancillary roads as well would begin shutting down as early as 4:00 p.m. "drew gasps, grimaces, and gallows humor," according to the *Globe*.[19]

State police outlined a grim scenario for commuters. "This is going to be a serious traffic condition that we're trying to manage," said Major Michael Mucci, who was in charge of traffic management during the convention. "If everybody decides to have traffic as normal, we will back up to New Hampshire. It's as simple as that."[20] To Menino and Burns, such statements, and the accompanying press coverage, were needlessly alarmist and drowned out the more "can-do" message they were trying to convey. The mayor urged employers to allow workers to telecommute or to reschedule their hours so that they could leave the city before the road closings began or to help organize car pools to reduce traffic volume. He also announced the launching of a Let's Work Around It campaign that would provide maps and information for businesses and commuters on changes in the traffic and transit routes during the convention.[21] The campaign slogan was instantly lampooned in the press, with the *Boston Herald* suggesting alternative catchphrases, such as "Let's just get it over with" or "Let's get outta here."[22] The city's efforts notwithstanding, however, what seemed to be largely conveyed was a sense that the open invitation to come to the city was being withdrawn. "The dominant message," a May 21 *Boston Globe* editorial declared, "is to stay out of town."[23]

That message seemed to cast a pall over the upcoming convention, once seen as a source of civic pride. The crowds of tourists that local businesses had expected to flock to the city for convention-related events now seemed unlikely to materialize; worse still, it seemed possible that even regular customers would stay away as well. Instead of the $154 million eco-

[19]Flint, "Massive Closings of Roads," A1.

[20]Quoted in Rick Klein, "Boston's 'Party' Gets a New Spin," *Boston Globe*, May 21, 2004, B4.

[21]Kimberly Blanton, "Firms See Traffic-Plan Headaches," *Boston Globe*, May 21, 2004, C1; Flint, "Massive Closings of Roads."

[22]Cosmo Macero Jr., "DNC Mess; Unconventional Honesty Precedes DNC Hassles," *Boston Herald*, May 21, 2004, 35.

[23]"Editorial: Detours and Damages," *Boston Globe*, May 21, 2004, A18.

nomic benefit that the mayor's office had predicted, some were now forecasting losses of anywhere from $34 million to almost $50 million.[24] In a blistering May 26 piece on the security arrangements, *Globe* business columnist Steve Bailey castigated the mayor, Senator Ted Kennedy, and others for having "sold the Democratic Party an impossible venue in this post-9/11 world, the FleetCenter, ground zero for the city's transportation network. Our best hope for avoiding complete gridlock is to scare the pants off 250,000 daily commuters and persuade half of them to stay home. Some plan."[25] But Scott Sheafe offered a different perspective on the convention and the tight security surrounding it. "What is about to happen in Boston," he said at the May 20 briefing, "is the continuation of the democratic process and the American way, at a time when the country is at war."[26]

Going Down to the Wire

While the press and the general public continued to stew about the closings, city, state, and federal officials put the finishing touches on their security plans for the convention. In addition to the three federal plans—for implementation of an operational security plan (primarily for securing the FleetCenter), for crisis management, and for consequence management—some agencies produced their own plans outlining in detail the deployment of their personnel and supplies and, where pertinent, their response to a wide array of incidents. The most comprehensive of these came from the Boston Police Department (BPD), which was responsible for security outside the hard zone. For the BPD, the most serious concern was the prospect of violent demonstrations from anarchists and other groups, who had managed to disrupt previous conventions and who were expected to show up in numbers for the DNC, ready for trouble. "Experts across the country," recalls Kathleen O'Toole, who was named police commissioner in February 2004, "predicted we'd have between 1,500 and 2,000 arrests."[27]

The experience of Seattle during the 1999 World Trade Organization meeting, when demonstrations led to violent clashes between protesters and an overwhelmed police force, was much on the mind of police officials, says Dunford, as they prepared their operational plan. There was, as well, the specter of recent conventions, such as the 2000 DNC in Los Angeles, where police, according to Sheafe, resorted to rubber bullets and tear gas to subdue

---

[24]Kimberly Blanton and Andrew Caffrey, "Convention Bust May Reach $50m," *Boston Globe,* May 22, 2004, A1.

[25]Steve Bailey, "The DNC Train Wreck," *Boston Globe,* May 26, 2004, available at www.boston.com/news/politics/conventions/articles/2004/05/26/the_dnc_train_wreck.

[26]Quoted in Flint, "Massive Closings of Roads," A1.

[27]Interview with Kathleen O'Toole, Boston police commissioner, 2005. Unless noted, subsequent quotations from O'Toole are also from this interview.

unruly crowds. It was the kind of ugly scene that the BPD hoped to avoid. O'Toole had been a member of a commission in Northern Ireland that had developed "a new framework for policing," a less confrontational approach that she believed would be effective in dealing with protesters at the convention. "I think that's probably the thing that I felt most strongly about," she says, "because I'd witnessed it in Northern Ireland . . . and saw how dramatically different the results could be if the police engaged in a different approach." Under this "soft approach," as Dunford calls it, the police would present a less aggressive face to protesters. Demonstrators "would see police officers everywhere," he explains, "but [they] would be in the normal uniform of the day, which in July was short-sleeved uniforms." Should a demonstration threaten to escalate, there would be a three-tiered response of specially trained units that could be called in to handle the situation, starting with a small "quick response squad" and ending, if necessary, with a "public order platoon," equipped with "full Ninja suits" and riot gear. But although the tiered response had proven successful in Northern Ireland, it was untried in Boston and, as O'Toole recalls, some of the police officers who would be out in shirtsleeves were apprehensive. She explains:

[They were] so concerned about some of the predictions [of violent demonstrations] that they wanted to wear protective clothing . . . battle dress uniforms and helmets. . . . I had to meet with the Health and Safety Committee of the union and convince them that we needed to approach this from a different perspective, and that their gear would be staged in close proximity if they needed it, and we'd have tactical teams strategically placed throughout the city. . . .

Training

The detailed planning was accompanied by intensive training, both within and among agencies at all levels of government. In addition, Boston police cross-trained with state police, as well as with officers from other cities and towns who were brought in to supplement the city's thinly stretched force. The Secret Service, meanwhile, was doing "some grander-scheme training," in Sheafe's words. This included multiple tabletop exercises involving the steering committee members, in which a wide range of incidents was presented. Ken Kaiser, FBI special-agent-in-charge, jokes that "the only thing they didn't exercise for was a tsunami."[28] As the convention drew nearer, the Secret Service staged a major exercise at "an old airbase," Sheafe recalls, where participants "did a lot of robust training. . . . We actually brought in motorcade vehicles and motorcycles and pyrotechnics and were blowing things up and [staging] simulations [of] attacks and biochem[ical] attacks, and things like that."

---

[28]Interview with Ken Kaiser, Federal Bureau of Investigation, 2005. Unless noted, subsequent quotations from Kaiser are also from this interview.

Eventually, however, Sheafe concluded that it was time to stop preparing. "I would go to these tabletop exercises," he says, "and everybody would be very high-strung, . . . very cautious about what they should say." Participants, he noticed, were losing confidence in their ability to handle an event as freighted with significance as an NSSE. "We planned for so long," Sheafe says, "that people began to plan themselves out of their comfort zone." He reminded participants that "this is a community that handles events, big and small, all the time," and that they were well-trained and prepared for any eventuality. "And I started telling people about six weeks out that we're ready."

D-Day Approaches

On the eve of the convention, after 18 months of planning in some cases, officials were ready to launch what the *Boston Globe* called "the most ambitious security operations ever mounted in New England." An estimated 3,000 law enforcement officers from almost one hundred federal, state, and local agencies had been mustered for the event, along with the "biggest concentration of bomb-sniffing dogs ever assembled in a city."[29] Over half of the state police force—about 1,400 officers, out of a total of 2,300—was assigned to convention-related duties, along with about 400 members of the Massachusetts National Guard. Contingents of state troopers from the five other New England states were on duty as well to help with traffic, at the request of Massachusetts State Police Superintendent Thomas Robbins.[30] Both state police and BPD officers would work 12-hour shifts for the duration of the convention; all vacation leaves were cancelled. Hundreds of additional Secret Service and FBI agents were on hand; the U.S. Coast Guard was patrolling the waters of Boston Harbor near the FleetCenter; hospitals and ambulance companies were on alert to handle patient "surges"; special Disaster Medical Assistance Teams, part of the Federal Emergency Management Agency (FEMA), had been deployed to the area; and the U.S. Centers for Disease Control and Prevention had expedited a shipment of antidotes in the event of a chemical attack.

The Secret Service activated its expensive new Multi-Agency Communications Center at the Volpe Transportation Building in Cambridge, where seventy-five agencies and companies (such as Verizon) could gather before incident monitors to keep tabs on developments. The BPD established a Unified Command Center and a Tactical Operations Center at its headquarters. The FBI readied its Joint Operations Center for counterterrorism and investigations at its office in Boston and opened an intelligence operations center at the Volpe

---

[29]Kevin Cullen, "Convention Gears for Top Security; US, State, and Local Officers Set for Boston," *Boston Globe,* July 11, 2004, A1.

[30]The out-of-state troopers were provided after Robbins asked the governors of the New England states to invoke the New England State Police Administrator Compact.

Exhibit 15B-1　Partial list of operational platforms

	Lead agency	Site
Multi-Agency Communications Center	U.S. Secret Service	Volpe National Transportation Center
DNC Coordinating Center	U.S. Secret Service	O'Neill Federal Building
Intelligence Division Coordinating Center	U.S. Secret Service	O'Neill Federal Building
Intelligence Operations Center	FBI	Volpe National Transportation Center
Joint Operations Center	FBI	FBI Boston Division Headquarters
Joint Information Center	U.S. Secret Service/ Boston Police Department	Boston Police Headquarters
Unified Command Center	Boston Police Department	Boston Police Headquarters
Bomb Management Center	U.S. Secret Service/Boston Police Department/FBI	South Boston
Fusion Center	Democratic National Convention Committee	FleetCenter
Emergency Operations Center	Multiple agencies	Multiple locations

Note: DNC, Democratic National Convention; FBI, Federal Bureau of Investigation

building as well. Other agencies set up command posts and emergency operations centers throughout the area. (See Exhibit 15B-1 for a partial list of these centers.)

As the delegates (and protesters) began arriving in Boston for the start of the convention on July 26, no one was sure what to expect—devastating terrorist attacks, violent and disruptive demonstrations, or paralyzing traffic jams—or whether the complex security arrangements that required the cooperation of so many different agencies would work seamlessly. Officials, the *Boston Globe* reported on July 11, seemed "confident, and realistic."[31] "I'm too much of a fatalist and Irish Catholic to say we are ready for anything at any time," State Public Safety Secretary Edward Flynn told the paper. "We've tried to anticipate as many scenarios as possible."[32]

[31]Cullen, "Convention Gears for Top Security," A1.

[32]Quoted in ibid.

Security Planning for the 2004 Democratic National Convention (C): Epilogue

On July 29, 2004, Sen. John Kerry (D-Mass.) formally accepted the nomination of the Democratic Party as its candidate in the upcoming presidential election before throngs of cheering delegates in Boston's FleetCenter. It was a galvanizing moment for the party faithful and, for the officials who had been responsible for security planning for the convention, a time of triumph—and relief. The Democratic National Convention (DNC) had gone off virtually without a hitch from a security standpoint. There had been no major incidents, and few minor ones, involving protesters. Terrorist threats had not materialized; even the traffic had flowed smoothly. As workers began dismantling the security fence surrounding the hard zone and city life resumed its normal rhythms, the consensus was that the event had been a success and had produced some lasting benefits for the city—but at a steep cost.

Civil Disturbances

Possibly the most visible success, from a security standpoint, was in the policing of the convention. Protesters had not appeared in the numbers that had been anticipated, but many officials credited the heavy police presence with deterring those who did show up from engaging in the kind of disruptive activities that had marred previous conventions. But when they did try something, Boston Police Commissioner Kathleen O'Toole notes, they were met with a "very non-confrontational approach" that gave demonstrators some leeway. "Rather than have riot cops in full gear respond to demonstrations where people were getting a bit disorderly," she says, "we sent in cops on mountain bikes. Even the anarchists were impressed." [1] The reduced numbers of protesters and the "soft approach" of the police resulted in only six arrests—far fewer than the 1,500–2,000 originally expected. "We got tremendous publicity here in the city," Boston Police Superintendent Robert Dunford says. "If you looked around, everything was peaceful and quiet." [2]

Traffic

The anticipated snarls on the region's major roads and highways never materialized, as commuters stayed away in droves. Overall, traffic was down by an estimated 40 percent—and by

---

[1] Interview with Kathleen O'Toole, Boston police commissioner, 2005. Unless noted, subsequent quotations from O'Toole are also from this interview.

[2] Interview with Superintendent Robert Dunford, Boston Police Department, 2005. Unless noted, subsequent quotations from Dunford are also from this interview.

a whopping 90 percent at 4:00 p.m., when the first road closures had been scheduled to begin. As a result of the unusually light traffic, state police discovered that there was no need for an early shutdown of the ancillary roads; it took "only a few minutes," according to the *Boston Globe,* to close down a nearly deserted Interstate 93 (I-93) at 7:00 p.m.[3]

For those who commuted into the city during the convention, it was, as one *Globe* columnist wrote, a "week of bliss," as they zipped into and out of the city on what normally were congested roads.[4] For some retail businesses, particularly those in the area near the FleetCenter, however, it was a week of disappointment. The normally bustling Bullfinch Triangle—site of the soft zone established by the Secret Service—was "like a ghost town," says FleetCenter Vice President and General Manager John Wentzell.[5] In Boston's North End—a food and dining mecca—bakeries and restaurants were reporting that business was down by over 50 percent. Some "faulted Mayor Thomas Menino," the *Boston Globe* reported, "for agreeing to security measures they thought were too extreme, and the media for hyping the extensive road closures."[6] The mayor himself points to comments made by State Police Major Michael Mucci on the extent of the closures and the likelihood of traffic jams, which, he argues, scared people away from the city.[7] Nonetheless, state officials were unapologetic about their role in warning the public away from the city. "We wanted to get [traffic] volumes down 50 percent," a Massachusetts Turnpike Authority official told the *Globe,* "and we succeeded beyond our wildest dreams. This wasn't a conspiracy to lie to the public. If we didn't knock those volumes down, it would have been Armageddon around here."[8] But Julie Burns, executive director of the Boston 2004 committee, lamented the decision of so many to stay away from the city during what had been conceived of as a time of public celebration. "We really wanted people to come and take part," she says. ". . .That was a big disappointment for us."[9]

Still, although acknowledging that some businesses may have been hurt, Burns maintains that "the hospitality industry did well. It could have done better, had it not been for the

---

[3]Andrea Estes and Anthony Flint, "Officials Defend Traffic Measures," *Boston Globe,* July 31, 2004, B4. Traffic was, however, reported to be heavier than normal in the early morning hours because some commuters adjusted their work schedules so that they could leave work before the scheduled closings began at 4:00 p.m. According to a July 30 *Globe* article, ridership on the four commuter rail lines that normally terminated at North Station was down by over 50 percent. Michael Paulson, "Convention Leaves Costs, Prospects of Gain for City," *Boston Globe,* July 30, 2004, A1.

[4]Mac Daniel, "Welcome Back! You Missed Our Week of Bliss," *Boston Globe,* August 1, 2004, B2.

[5]Interview with John Wentzell, FleetCenter, 2005. Unless noted, subsequent quotations from Wentzell are also from this interview.

[6]Stephen Smith and Benjamin Gedan, "Shops' Dreams Don't Pan Out," *Boston Globe,* July 28, 2004, A1.

[7]Interview with Mayor Thomas Menino, 2005. Unless noted, subsequent quotations from Menino are also from this interview.

[8]Quoted in Estes and Flint, "Officials Defend Traffic Measures," B4.

[9]Interview with Julie Burns, Boston 2004 Democratic National Convention Host Committee, 2005. Unless noted, subsequent quotations from Burns are also from this interview.

security, but it did do well." Although the city did not realize its initial estimate of a $154 million benefit, neither did it suffer the economic losses some had predicted. According to one study, the DNC pumped $14.8 million into the local economy—a figure that Mayor Menino argued understated the "total scope of benefits." [10]

Security Plan Implementation

Among those responsible for security, there was general agreement that their long efforts at planning had paid off, although the security plans had not been put to a severe test. "Everybody understood the plan," says Secret Service Special Agent Scott Sheafe, "and the implementation of it was outstanding." [11]

The chief criticism from participants concerned the proliferation of command centers—twenty-nine in all, according to Emergency Medical Services Chief Richard Serino. There were several major communications and command centers (or operational platforms, as the Secret Service termed them), most of them run by the Secret Service, the Federal Bureau of Investigation (FBI), or the Boston Police Department (BPD). (See Exhibit 15B-1 for a partial list.) But there were, as well, a number of smaller centers set up by other agencies whose mission and function were ill-defined, according to Serino. "A lot of people put up their own command centers," he says, "and they all called them command posts, and they all called them emergency operations centers [EOCs]. Everybody had their EOC, and everybody said they're in charge. . . ." [12] Still, he notes, there were no major coordination problems among the command centers "that mattered," and in most regards communications ran smoothly. The elaborate system he had set up to allow ambulances on I-93 when it was closed, for example, "worked flawlessly" 180 times, he says, "[for] ambulances from Maine to New Hampshire [and] Rhode Island."

Participants noted that the planning effort had helped improve law enforcement and emergency response for strictly local events. "We developed a plan that can be used for other events going forward," Serino points out. ". . . We got a lot of good training that we've used subsequently. . . . A lot of the equipment we had [for the DNC] we were able to utilize [in other events]." But it was not only in plans and equipment that Serino felt the benefit of the DNC security planning process. "I can't say enough how the relationships we built [with public and private hospitals and public health agencies]," he says, "paid dividends" in later incidents.

---

[10]Quoted in Andrew Caffrey, "Convention Benefit 'Negligible,' Study Finds," *Boston Globe*, August 10, 2004, A1.

[11]Interview with Scott Sheafe, U.S. Secret Service, 2005. Unless noted, subsequent quotations from Sheafe are also from this interview.

[12]Interview with Richard Serino, Boston Emergency Medical Services, 2005. Unless noted, subsequent quotations from Serino are also from this interview.

Group Harmony

Many who participated in the security planning remarked on the cooperative and cordial relations that had developed over the long months of meetings of the steering committee and the subcommittees. Although there had been some friction among federal, state, and local agencies, it did not bog down the planning process. Disagreements or problem areas were worked out between agencies or by agency leaders who used informal contacts to talk over any issues that had arisen. A number of participants also believed that the security planning effort had cemented relationships among officials who had had little or no previous experience of working together. "I got to know Michael Sullivan, the United States Attorney," says Boston Fire Commissioner Paul Christian. "I got to know people in the FBI who I wouldn't [otherwise] run into. I go to meet Scott Sheafe, Steve Ricciardi [of the] Secret Service. These are people [who are usually] just ships passing in the night." [13] Ken Horak, acting director of the regional Federal Emergency Management Agency (FEMA) office, notes that despite differences that arose during security planning, "the relationships, the contacts we made were really the net positive of this experience. It's something that should be happening all the time, but here was an event that clearly got everybody's attention and focus for a year and a half . . . and it paid off." [14]

Perhaps most surprising, in view of the many agencies involved, the turf issues that traditionally plagued the law enforcement community proved not to be a major problem in either the security planning or the implementation phase. Many attributed this to the personalities of the officials heading up the different agencies, as well as to their history of working together on security issues, particularly since September 11. Others also noted that the structure of a National Special Security Event (NSSE) left no ambiguities as to who was ultimately in charge. "It was," says Ken Kaiser of the FBI, "[the Secret Service's] show." [15] But, Dunford notes, the agency was careful not to be seen to exert too much direct control. "The Secret Service," he observes, "is excellent at getting what they want without making you feel like they just twisted your arm, because they talk, they listen, they do a lot of persuading." Many also praised Scott Sheafe for his organizing skills and his tact in dealing with local agencies. Whatever the precise cause, the general consensus was that the DNC was a model of cooperative behavior. "We jokingly refer to the Democratic National Convention here among the law enforcement community," says Kaiser, "as the summer of love."

---

[13]Interview with Paul Christian, Boston fire commissioner, 2005. Unless noted, subsequent quotations from Christian are also from this interview.

[14]Interview with Ken Horak, Federal Emergency Management Agency, 2005. Unless noted, subsequent quotations from Horak are also from this interview.

[15]Interview with Ken Kaiser, Federal Bureau of Investigation, 2005. Unless noted, subsequent quotations from Kaiser are also from this interview.

Final Assessments

Most observers agreed that for all the controversy and complaints it generated, the convention had shown Boston in a highly favorable light to the delegates and to the TV viewing public. Even the *Boston Globe,* which had been critical of the tight security imposed for the convention, acknowledged in an August 2 editorial that while "some security preparations were excessive," the DNC itself "ran smoothly and safely, and Boston received a boost in the national perception as a diverse, welcoming, and mature city." [16] The mayor also got a vote of confidence from his constituents: 63 percent of Bostonians polled by the *Globe* said that Menino had done "an excellent or a good job overseeing the convention." [17]

Despite the generally positive reviews for both the convention and the security planning, however, few in the city evinced any appetite for a repeat. "I don't think you'll have another [political] convention in a city like Boston or New York," Menino says. "Maybe New York will want to try it again, but it's just so much work. It really is a full-time job for the police, staff, everyone." Both Menino and David Passafaro, president of the host committee, pointed to the cost of security arrangements, in time and money. [18] "I would find it very difficult to believe that either party will go to a downtown setting again," Passafaro told the *Boston Globe.* "I guess we never anticipated the impact of [security requirements] early on." [19] In fact, Dunford notes, he had a good suggestion for what kind of place might be most suitable for a political convention or any kind of NSSE, based on his visit to Sea Island, Georgia, in June 2004 to observe security preparations for the upcoming G-8 summit. "We would recommend," he says, "that if you have any special events now, you have them on an island."

[16]"Editorial: Was It Worth It?" *Boston Globe,* August 2, 2004, A10.

[17]Scott Greenberger, "Menino, Convention Get Favorable Reviews," *Boston Globe,* August 23, 2004, A1.

[18]The host committee did not, however, spend the entire $50 million in funds appropriated to it by Congress for security-related expenses. According to Burns, roughly $30 million was spent; the rest was returned to the federal government.

[19]Quoted in Rick Klein, "Convention Must Change, Planner Says; Urban Site Is Less Likely to Be Chosen," *Boston Globe,* August 1, 2004, A1.

Key Actors in the Security Planning for the 2004 Democratic National Convention

Boston, Massachusetts, City Officials

Carlo Boccia, director, Mayor's Office of Homeland Security

Paul Christian, fire commissioner

Robert Dunford, superintendent, Boston Police Department

Paul Evans, police commissioner (until 2003)

Thomas Menino, mayor

Kathleen O'Toole, police commissioner (beginning February 2004)

Richard Serino, chief of department, Boston Emergency Medical Services

Commonwealth of Massachusetts Officials

Edward Flynn, secretary of public safety

Robert Haas, undersecretary of public safety

Michael Mucci, major, Massachusetts State Police

Thomas Robbins, colonel and superintendent, Massachusetts State Police

Mitt Romney, governor

Federal Officials

Ken Horak, acting director, Federal Emergency Management Agency (FEMA) Region 1

Ken Kaiser, special-agent-in-charge, Federal Bureau of Investigation (FBI)

John Kerry, U.S. senator (D-Mass.) and 2004 Democratic candidate for president of the United States

Steven Ricciardi, special-agent-in-charge, U.S. Secret Service Boston Field Office

Tom Ridge, secretary, U.S. Department of Homeland Security

Scott Sheafe, special agent, U.S. Secret Service; coordinated security arrangements for the convention

Others

Julie Burns, executive director, Boston 2004 Democratic National Convention Host Committee

Michael Mulhern, general manager, Massachusetts Bay Transportation Authority (MBTA)

David Passafaro, president, Boston 2004 Democratic National Convention Host Committee

John Wentzell, senior vice president and general manager, FleetCenter

Security Planning for the 2004 Democratic National Convention

Chronology of Events

2002
November
The Democratic National Committee announces that Boston, Massachusetts, will host its July 2004 convention.

2003
February
Massachusetts Governor Mitt Romney requests that the convention be designated a National Special Security Event (NSSE).

May 27
The convention is officially granted NSSE status, triggering the involvement of several federal agencies, including the U.S. Secret Service (the lead agency for NSSE security planning).

June
Secret Service Special Agent Scott Sheafe arrives in Boston to coordinate security arrangements for the convention.

Sheafe works on developing relationships with key officials, especially at the Boston Police Department (BPD), which has retained responsibility for citywide security during the convention.

June 20
An interagency steering committee, established by Sheafe to help coordinate security planning, meets for the first time.

July
At a private meeting with Sheafe, Julie Burns, executive director of Boston 2004, the convention's host committee, expresses concerns that the Secret Service might make security decisions that could have negative political ramifications for Boston Mayor Thomas Menino.

The FleetCenter, where the convention is to take place, emerges as a major security concern.

Fall
Sheafe begins talking with Boston and Massachusetts police about the security threat presented by Interstate 93 (I-93), a major transportation artery that runs alongside the FleetCenter.

October

At a meeting organized by Julie Burns, the BPD circulates a memo detailing four different scenarios for dealing with I-93 (ranging from complete to partial shutdown). The memo provokes protest from some participants, but negotiations proceed behind the scenes.

2004

Early 2004

Law enforcement officials argue for closing North Station, the transportation hub at the FleetCenter. The Mayor's Office is reluctant to make an immediate decision, and (as with I-93) negotiations continue behind the scenes.

March

Governor Romney suggests moving the convention to the Boston Convention and Exhibition Center. The suggestion gains little traction because the convention center is not yet completed and Boston 2004 has already signed a lease agreement with the FleetCenter.

Train bombings in Madrid kill almost two hundred passengers, raising concerns that terrorists might strike at the convention.

After some initial reluctance, Michael Mulhern, general manager of the Massachusetts Bay Transportation Authority, agrees with the Secret Service about the need for closing North Station.

March 25

Sheafe and two assistant directors of the Secret Service meet with Mayor Menino and Governor Romney to brief them on the possible consequences of an incident occurring on I-93 near the FleetCenter.

March 26

At a meeting at the Parkman House, Sheafe summarizes the understanding he has reached with Mayor Menino and Governor Romney—portions of I-93 will be closed during evening hours and commuter rail and subway service to North Station will be suspended.

March 31

Officials publicly outline plans for closing North Station and I-93, sparking a public outcry.

May 20

City and state officials detail security plans to the public. The plans include establishing a "hard zone" around the FleetCenter, accessible to credentialed people only, and shutting down 40 miles of ancillary roads to mange the evening closures of I-93.

Late spring to early summer

The BPD finalizes its security plans for areas beyond the "hard zone." Police Commissioner Kathleen O'Toole calls for a large but nonconfrontational police presence.

Agencies at all levels of government conduct training exercises.

Command posts and emergency operations centers (EOCs) are activated.

July 26

The convention begins. Around 3,000 law enforcement officers from federal, state, and local agencies provide security over the course of the event.

July 29

U.S. Sen. John Kerry (D-Mass.) accepts the Democratic Party's nomination as its candidate for president of the United States.

The convention ends without any major incidents, but parts of Boston resemble a ghost town, thanks to the extensive security measures taken. All the same, the convention pumps almost $15 million into the local economy.

Conclusion

High Performance in Emergencies: Two Modes of Operation

Herman B. "Dutch" Leonard and Arnold M. Howitt

A round the world, emergency management professionals, governments, and citizens alike are asking crucial questions.[1] How can they ensure that, when disaster threatens lives, property, professional reputations, government credibility, and even ways of life, they will be ready? How can they build on basic emergency response capabilities so they can act effectively in a moment of extreme crisis?

The case studies in this book describe a wide range of emergency situations. All emergencies have high stakes and major uncertainties about what will happen. Nearly always, they involve rapidly evolving events and correspondingly great time pressure on decision-makers. Emergencies are highly "contingent"—the ultimate consequences depend in important ways on the actions taken by those affected and by public agencies, nongovernmental organizations, and business firms with an interest in the outcomes. They create fear and stress, so that the people managing them must operate in a climate in which, at a minimum, many of the participants are afraid. Often, they themselves must operate in the face of their own fears and uncertainties.

Looking across the wide array of examples, we have made a fundamental distinction between those events that are *routine emergencies* and those that are *crisis emergencies* involving significant elements of novelty. These are significantly different in terms of the responses they require. They differ in appropriate forms of advance preparation, the organizational structures through which they should be addressed, and the actions that must be carried out in the moment. Organizations handling emergency situations thus must be able to operate in two distinct modes of action, neither of which is the best method in all situations. They must master the art of deploying each mode effectively and learn to recognize the circumstances in which each is likely to be more beneficial. Both are essential components of emergency management's repertoire.

Mode R for Routine Emergencies

The first mode of response is the more familiar one. When a particular type of emergency happens frequently in a location where people have the resources to organize and prepare,

---

[1]This chapter draws on Herman B. "Dutch" Leonard and Arnold M. Howitt, " 'Routine' or 'Crisis'—The Search for Excellence," *Crisis/Response Journal* 4, no. 3 (June 2008): 32–35; "Against Desperate Peril: High Performance in Emergency Preparation and Response," in *Communicable Crises*, ed. Deborah Gibbons (Charlotte, N.C.: Information Age Publishing, 2007), 1–24.

it becomes a routine event. These are *routine emergencies,* even when quite severe, because regularity creates the opportunity for organized preparation and practiced response. Familiarity makes a severe residential or commercial fire or a typical hurricane manageable for experienced responders.

By calling such events "routine," we do not imply that they are unimportant or that their consequences are minor. We mean only that they involve largely familiar phenomena, consequences, and associated responses. By virtue of familiarity with a range of otherwise potentially severe events, emergency organizations have developed templates and scripts through which they can respond effectively and efficiently, keeping associated losses and damage to a minimum. They develop organizational routines, cultures, training, staffing, systems, and procedures to support their efforts. These response organizations deserve great credit for the professionalism and dedication that make this possible. Indeed, their success in addressing routine emergencies is one of the more compelling practical accomplishments of modern societies.

To illustrate, imagine a serious highway accident in which three passenger cars collide with a jackknifing tractor-trailer on a freeway, injuring six people—three severely—and disrupting traffic for miles in both directions. Emergency calls go out to highway police, the fire department, the ambulance service, a nearby hospital, the highway department, and a private towing company. Each group responds and takes care of different dimensions of the emergency. Police officers take command of traffic flow, routing lines of vehicles past the accident site, and maintain security around the crash scene. Emergency medical personnel minister to the victims, quickly assessing which ones should receive which kinds of attention in which order of priority. Firefighters douse the flames enveloping an auto. Hospital emergency staff members, alerted by the emergency medical technicians, ready teams to treat the specific medical needs of the most severely injured victims. Highway department personnel oversee private wrecking crews that remove damaged vehicles from the site. Within a few hours, the injured have been cared for, damaged vehicles have been removed from the accident scene, and traffic is once more flowing. While each highway accident differs in key particulars, the fact that similar situations have been faced many times before means that expertise is embedded in these organizations in the knowledge, training, and experience of key leaders and line responders.

Operating in what we might call *Mode R* (for routine emergencies), responders take advantage of such deep expertise to make "recognitionally primed" decisions, swiftly determining what is required and carrying out appropriate measures with practiced precision. Because of their experience, they do not have to analyze and deliberate about decisions and actions.[2] Such response organizations develop routines, scripts, and templates for action for

---

[2] See Gary Klein, *Sources of Power: How People Make Decisions* (Cambridge, Mass.: MIT Press, 1999) for a pathbreaking analysis of this form of decision making in emergency response organizations.

their most common deployments; and they are equipped and staffed to carry out actions up to a scale that it is sufficiently unlikely that it doesn't make economic sense to maintain the standing capacity to address it.[3] These organizations have cultures that attract, socialize, and retain people whose general inclinations and capabilities are well suited to the important types of actions that are standard in their responses. And they tend to have an authority-driven hierarchical structure that allows them to operate efficiently and smoothly, moving rapidly from assessment to execution. Most of their emergency work is organized and deployed in the Mode R form of action, and, if they are highly proficient, they are appropriately celebrated for carrying it out effectively.

The key elements of Mode R that produce excellent response in routine emergencies are:

- **High awareness and embedded expertise:** A detailed understanding of the nature of this kind of situation has been developed, along with an understanding of its key elements, so that the organization knows which facts and observations are relevant and, therefore, which to collect.
- **Rapid assessment and recognition-primed decisions:** Through training, practice, and operational experience, the ability to recognize patterns of circumstances rapidly and trigger appropriate, nearly autonomic responses has been developed.
- **Comprehensive scripts:** There are well-engineered general routines that provide the step-by-step assignment of roles and responsibilities for dealing with the emergency.
- **Modest customization:** Well-defined methods have been developed for adapting the general routine to the specific instance.
- **Well-defined, highly developed skills:** Training is given in the skills necessary to customize and execute the routines.
- **Scalability:** The organization and its response can adapt, quickly and easily, to routine emergencies of the same type but at different scales, organizing and coordinating the execution of appropriately larger response activities for larger events.
- **Leadership:** Leaders are trained in the knowledge and methods of the situation and response; practiced at organizing, deciding, and directing their execution in this type of situation; and selected on the basis of their prior training, experience, and performance as better able than others to organize and direct responses of this kind.
- **Command presence:** A leadership approach is adopted (generally through an authority-based command and control structure) that performs well in directing the customization and execution of the routines.

---

[3]This scale may encompass events that can be handled only with help from other responders through mutual aid agreements; but mutual aid in this form—characteristic of urban and wildland firefighting, for example—is part of the routine handling of such events.

- **Hierarchical structure:** An organizational structure is adopted (generally, a hierarchical system) that is well suited to customizing the general routines to specific circumstances and executing them effectively.
- **Precision execution:** Well-designed and practiced routines are implemented precisely and accurately.

In short, organizations that perform well in a routine emergency environment are based on a well-defined, well-developed, and ingrained expertise about the nature of emergencies of this type, on the knowledge of how to handle them, and on the skills necessary to deploy that knowledge. This expertise is at once substantive, procedural, and organizational. It involves factual knowledge of how situations of this kind evolve and what the key factors are, an understanding of and ability to deploy the relevant response actions and routines, and an ability to operate effectively in a well-defined organizational setting.

Mode C for Crisis Emergencies

As we have seen in many of the cases studies in this book, however, some emergencies are *not* like those previously experienced. Because of unusual scale, a previously unknown cause, or an atypical combination of causes, responders face novel challenges, the facts and implications of which cannot be completely assimilated in the moment of crisis. Some such events involve major elements or combinations of elements that are novel to the organizations involved and possibly unprecedented anywhere.

These *crisis emergencies* are defined by significant novelty, which ensures that an understanding of the situation, at least at the outset, will be relatively low. There will be no executable script that provides a comprehensive, reliable, and fully adequate response. Existing routines will be inadequate to the demands of the moment and may even be counterproductive given the novel circumstances faced. Dealing with a crisis emergency, therefore, means that the response must operate beyond the boundary of plans, existing capabilities, and readily available resources. Response will necessarily be *incompletely* planned, and resources and capabilities will generally be (or seem) inadequate. Improvisation will be of the essence. In true crisis emergency situations, effective leadership will have to organize and carry out rapid and effective innovation, under high stress, in the context of fear. Operating strictly according to the preestablished procedures appropriate for dealing with routine situations is unlikely to produce good results in crisis emergency situations. Instead, organizations must be able to operate in *Mode C,* a distinctive style for crisis conditions.

Taken as a whole, the Mode C response has three necessary phases: (1) the *establishment of awareness,* during an understanding phase; (2) the *development of a design for action,* during a design phase; and (3) the *implementation of the chosen actions,* during an execution phase characterized by the implementation of unpracticed actions that go well beyond our existing plans and resources. This process then recycles as observations of the results of the actions build an understanding of the new situation as it continues to evolve.

In Mode C, organizations need to think and learn their way forward—they need to invent new approaches or combinations of approaches to take account of the novelty. They need to be creative, inventive, and innovative under time pressure, under stress, and even in the face of their own fears that they will not be able to cope with the unfamiliar. Operating in the realm of "unknown unknowns,"[4] they need to create an orderly process for determining which data they need, and then gathering and analyzing it, all the while being open to the possibility that they have missed something significant that requires collecting additional inputs. In successive data determination and collection phases, they need to be open to a disparate range of sources and observations and to figure out how to amalgamate and interpret potentially inconsistent or contradictory views of what is happening. They then need to develop creative options for approaching the unfolding situation. The team of people involved in developing response options may well be a much smaller group than those collecting data, but it needs to be diverse enough to bring different kinds of experience and expertise to bear in assessing the novel features of the situation. Given the likely incomplete and confusing information obtained in the early stages of a crisis, this team should not lock on to a primary explanation for the emerging situation (even a highly plausible one based on its best current assessment). It should also develop at least one next-best alternative explanation of the ongoing events and consider which actions would be appropriate to respond to that state of affairs. This is essential in order to test whether the options developed to deal with the presumed nature of the events will be appropriate if the primary understanding proves incorrect.

In Mode C, a response organization quite likely needs to reach beyond the group of people who would normally fit the organization's mold for acting in routine situations. These people may well come from sister response organizations or perhaps from beyond the boundaries of the emergency community. Almost certainly, the group assembled needs to be eclectic, diverse, and provocative—people who have training and experience in dealing with highly uncertain, poorly understood, and therefore intrinsically chaotic events.

Excellence in coping with crisis emergencies, therefore, means dealing effectively with the specific challenges that novel circumstances generate.

- **Low awareness and limited expertise:** By definition, the novelty of the situation implies that there is a less than complete comprehension of the circumstances or even of which facts are relevant. No one is an expert on what is happening. Those enmeshed in the crisis do not have a comprehensive checklist outlining the data they need to collect to have a good understanding of the situation. Often different people will have

---

[4] See our introduction to Part III, note 1.

been exposed to different aspects of the crisis and will therefore have different relevant observations and data that need to be captured, assembled, and interpreted so that a robust picture of the whole event can be developed.

- **Openness to recognizing novelty:** Given the uncertainties born of novelty and the corresponding lack of available comprehensive routines, decisions cannot reliably be driven by pattern recognition (because, by definition, the patterns are not available). Leaders and others in the organization must actively look for and be able to notice ways in which a particular event differs significantly from familiar events of the past, not becoming so focused on the familiar elements of a situation that they become blind to the ways in which it is novel.

- **Cognitively driven decisions:** Decision making must proceed through a standard analytical process: the identification of objectives, the development of alternatives, the prediction of the likely results from different approaches, and the choice of a best action.

- **Lack of comprehensive scripts:** Scripts developed for routine situations may be applicable, but they may prove inadequate in scale or even counterproductive as a result of conditions not previously encountered in tandem. By definition, there is no comprehensive playbook from which the response can be directed.

- **Creativity to improvise new approaches:** The existence of significant novelty implies that significant customization or improvisation is likely to be needed. Creativity—the ability to imagine and invent new options and combinations of actions quickly—is a key organizational asset. Although existing routines may provide useful elements of the response, they probably have to be adapted or melded in unusual and unpracticed ways. As a result, a crisis team should have broad familiarity with as wide an array of existing capabilities as is reasonably feasible, so that it can quickly imagine new approaches that may be needed.

- **Incompletely specified skills:** Because new actions may be taken, skills will not have been comprehensively developed for either the design or the execution of the required response. Although existing skills will be useful, the relevant skill base for components of the new approach that is being invented and improvised cannot reasonably have been foreseen and may not be available.

- **Leadership:** Leaders are adaptive; comfortable sharing authority and responsibility; and able to elicit information, ideas, and proposed solutions from their teams.

- **Muted command presence:** A leadership approach must be generally oriented to producing effective collaboration. It will seek to facilitate the development of understanding and the design of a new approach through invention and improvisation, followed by a more authority-driven approach during the execution phase.

- **Variably flattened structure:** An organizational structure is needed that is well suited to collecting a broad range of information (because, at least in the early phases, it will not necessarily be clear which information is relevant) and to absorbing and processing it and developing a range of alternatives. This initially calls for a "flattened" structure; but in the later phases, a more hierarchical structure is probably necessary to execute the chosen approach reasonably efficiently.

- **Ability to execute new, largely untested approaches and a tolerance for errors:** Because newly improvised and unrehearsed approaches or previously untried combinations of existing routines may be implemented—frequently by organizations that have not previously worked together—execution is likely to be much less precise than in routine circumstances. This may well require more tolerance of imperfections and errors in execution than is the case in routine operations that have been practiced and repeated in prior implementations.

The essence of an effective response to novel or crisis emergencies thus lies in a very different form of expertise than that required for routine emergencies. In the face of novelty, no one is a substantive expert—no one knows precisely what to do. The response leaders, under stress, have to think their way through, developing an understanding of a situation with potentially great and unknown uncertainties; analyzing possible courses of action; and then executing untried, untested, and unperfected sequences of actions. Leading people and organizations through such an intrinsically chaotic experience requires a leadership expertise, *adaptive leadership*,[5] that is very different from that used by successful leaders in routine emergencies.

The Special Challenges of Emergent Crises

Many crisis situations occur suddenly and are unavoidably noticeable: a major earthquake, the landfall of a major hurricane, or a severe bomb blast. We may make incorrect judgments about which mode of response is required,[6] but we are not in doubt that there is some type of emergency underway.

But some forms of crisis do not arrive suddenly. They fester and grow, arising from more ordinary circumstances that often mask their appearance. We term such situations *emergent*

---

[5]See Ronald A. Heifetz, "Mobilizing Adaptive Work," in *Leadership without Easy Answers* (Cambridge, Mass.: Harvard University Press, 1994), Chap. 4; Martin Linsky and Ronald A. Heifetz, *Leadership on the Line: Staying Alive through the Dangers of Leading* (Boston, Mass.: Harvard Business School Press, 2002).

[6]Most commonly, when there is a mistake, the error is to miss some of the novel elements and activate a routine response to the event instead of recognizing the need for a more creative and improvisational approach.

crises, a special and especially difficult category. When severe acute respiratory syndrome (SARS) emerged in south China in winter 2002–2003, it initially appeared as a series of deaths from respiratory infections in a region that annually experiences many such deaths; thus, at first, it was not easily distinguishable from the routine emergency of an influenza outbreak. The famous 1979 nuclear accident at the Three Mile Island power plant in Pennsylvania started as a simple pump failure, out of which spun an escalating series of failures and mistakes until a major crisis was underway.[7]

What makes emergent crises problematic? First, they arise from normally variable operating conditions, making emerging problems difficult to spot as a break from typical operating and response patterns. There had been previous pump failures at Three Mile Island, and these had always responded to the routine procedures that were applied at the time of the crisis. But two other challenges also arise in recognizing emergent crises.

When and if an emergency or potential emergency situation is spotted, an individual or group with technical expertise in the issue (as it is understood at the time) is generally assigned to address it. Firefighters are dispatched to a fire, police to the scene of a crime in progress or an accident, and emergency medical technicians to help injured or seriously ill people. These responders are likely to take "ownership" of the problem and its resolution. Generally, this will work. The situation will be correctly diagnosed, the team chosen because of its capacity to address situations of this type, and the response sized appropriately to address the problem. But what if the diagnosis is not correct? If the standard approach doesn't work? If the response is too small or too late?

A second major challenge of coping with emerging crisis situations, therefore, is that the leaders of the initial response, if not immediately successful, may either fail to diagnose their inadequacies or resist calling for additional help. Often, experts are not adept at recognizing that their approach is not working. Often, they ignore disconfirming evidence (that is, the flow of data tending to show that what they are doing is not working) and escalate commitment to their existing approach.[8] The person or team working on the situation may not only believe that it is about to succeed (with just a little more effort and time) but also feel pressure not to lose face if it fails to handle the assigned situation. The response leaders involved may feel embarrassed; they don't want to call for additional help because that would signal shortcomings in their professional competence. Moreover, as experts (which is why they were dispatched in the first place), they may have difficulty imagining who else might be better qualified to handle the situation. As they may see it, someone else—a high-level super-

---

[7]See Charles Perrow, *Normal Accidents: Living with High-Risk Technologies,* rev. ed. (Princeton, N.J.: Princeton University Press, 1999).

[8]See, for example, Daniel Kahneman, Paul Slovic, and Amos Tvesky, eds., *Judgment under Uncertainty: Heuristics and Biases* (Cambridge, UK: Cambridge University Press, 1982); Max Bazerman and Don Moore, *Judgment in Managerial Decision Making,* 7th ed. (Hoboken, N.J.: John Wiley and Sons, 2008).

visor or a different type of professional team—might be even less likely to succeed. When we look at situations that started as small issues and eventually became significant crises, this is often their history. At the beginning, the team sent to resolve the matter did not perceive that its approach was not working; the situation worsened; and by the time the team did realize that circumstances were not improving, it hesitated to seek additional help and instead continued to try to handle it, escalating its commitment to the existing approach.

From the perspective of crisis managers, there is a third reason that emergent crises are challenging—they present all of the challenges of managing the crisis, but these now arise when organizations and teams have already been deployed and are working on the situation in terms of standard practice. Teams may find it quite difficult to change modes of operation in the midst of extremely challenging circumstances. In a sudden crisis, obvious to all as a crisis, the response organizations may not be as resistant to engagement with others (for example, senior political officials or teams from other professional disciplines) because they see immediately that the situation makes extraordinary demands and is not "business as usual." But in an emergent crisis rank and file responders, operating under field conditions, are less likely to see the novelty and more likely to resent the intrusion of those they may regard as unneeded, inappropriately trained, or even lacking the competence to deal with the situation. Even when their leaders are collaborating, responders at the scene may not mesh effectively with individuals from different agencies or professional disciplines who arrive at later stages of an emergent crisis. They may experience great difficulty in switching from their normal mode of operation to a hastily improvised method that they may perceive as unjustified, untried, and perhaps dangerous.

Managing Emergency Response: Both Mode R and Mode C Are Essential

Emergencies thus fall into three distinct categories. First, some emergencies, even quite serious ones, are routine events for the response organizations involved. These situations arise more or less suddenly but are clearly emergencies and are correctly identified as situations that the organization has anticipated and for which it is prepared. These emergencies will generally be handled successfully because the responders have professional knowledge, experience, and appropriate organizational preparation. Second, some major events occur suddenly and are clearly recognized as containing significant elements of novelty. These situations demand very different skills and organizational capabilities, and they may require collaboration with people from different professional backgrounds, organizations, jurisdictions, and levels of government. And third, some events start as routine emergencies and evolve into even more serious problems, eventually becoming true crises. In some ways, these may pose the most difficult organizational challenges: *recognizing* that an emergency is migrating from being a routine event to being a true crisis event, *admitting* that this

Exhibit C-1 Comparison of response modes for routine emergencies and crises

Characteristics	Response mode	
	Mode R (routine emergencies)	Mode C (crises)
Situational awareness and expertise	High	Low, but openness to recognizing novelty is necessary
Decision making	Rapid and recognition-primed	Cognitively driven, analytic
Scripts	Comprehensive	Unavailable
Customization	Modest	Extensive
Skills required	Well-defined, highly developed	Incompletely specified, but creativity and improvisational ability are important
Leadership	Trained, practiced, and selected for prior training and performance	Adaptive, comfortable sharing authority, skilled in eliciting ideas from the team, and innovative
Command presence	Authority-based, directive	Muted, oriented toward collaboration in developing solutions; more hierarchical in execution
Organizational structure	Hierarchical	Flattened for solution development; more hierarchical for design; hierarchical for execution
Execution	Aims for precision through repeated opportunities for application of routine practices	Must be fault-tolerant because solutions have been improvised and are thus not fully tested or practiced

implies that the response needs to shift modes, and then actually *switching* to a true crisis emergency response mode.

Exhibit C-1 summarizes the differences between excellence in routine and crisis responses. The critical point, however, is that neither mode of emergency response is the best approach to all situations. On one hand, the ability to routinize emergency response is an enormous organizational strength that permits responders, through experience and advance planning, to deal quickly and effectively with a host of critical circumstances. Moreover, the ability to look ahead—to imagine future challenges—and make effective plans, assemble necessary resources, and train personnel in advance of the occurrence of an emergency can transform a potential crisis into a more manageable (and thus routine) event. Preparation now under way in many nations for a potential influenza pandemic can be thought of in this vein. On the other hand, confronting novel events is inevitable in a rapidly changing world. An organization that can only execute detailed plans or operate in strict hierarchical fashion will not be able to cope with the novel features of a true crisis. Unless it can improvise effectively and operate flexibly, it will be trapped in routines that can prove inadequate or even counterproductive.

We are thus definitely not arguing that organizations should switch completely from Mode R to Mode C. As we have shown, they need to have both repertoires available to them to be able reliably to distinguish which kind of situation they are in, and, when emergent crises arise, to switch effectively from Mode R to Mode C. Response organizations must develop the capability of operating in both modes and, quite critically, of recognizing under the pressure of unfolding events when each is appropriate. This is extremely difficult under the best of conditions and even more so if the need for excellence in both modes of operation is not explicitly addressed.

Many emergency response organizations are not prepared to operate in both Mode R and Mode C or to switch effectively from one to the other. What is true of these organizations is more emphatically the case for other kinds of organizations that, even though not seeing themselves in the "emergency business," may well need to function as such during and after a major disaster or emergency. We are thinking here, for example, of transportation or public works agencies, which provide critical support for emergency responders in a catastrophic situation, and of health-care, social service, and education agencies, which inevitably play key roles in caring for people injured or displaced by the disaster or emergency.

What kinds of leadership, decision making, organizational structure, and training will improve the chances of success in operating in both modes of emergency response? Preparing for both Mode R and Mode C is no simple matter. First, organizations that typically handle routine emergencies may experience difficulty in organizing themselves for response to true crises. Emergency organizations that are designed to cope with routine emergencies tend to have strong hierarchies, with expertise that is well but relatively narrowly defined. They may be creative in adapting routine practices to the situations they regularly encounter, but they are not generally attracted to adopting untested innovations or improvising in the face of dangerous situations. Such measures, they believe (with considerable justification), could put their lives at risk if unsuccessful. They often resist entanglements with other agencies that may not understand their special rules and procedures, preferring to operate independently in their assigned space. By contrast, the hallmark of effective response in a novel situation is the ability to get a reasonable fix on the situation and then to rapidly and creatively design new approaches to it, reaching across agencies to tap the capabilities of different professional disciplines, and creatively combining them to produce new but untested solutions that hold the promise of dealing with the crisis.

Second, organizations confronting true crises have to think and invent their way through the situation. They cannot rely on their scripts and templates because novelty undermines and may completely invalidate elements of the existing scripts on which response organizations typically rely. The organizations may have deep expertise and robust capabilities, but they will not have comprehensive expertise about the novel situation; by definition, no one is an expert on these happenings. This implies that they cannot rely on the same forms of decision making (pattern recognition and near-instinctive, trained reactions) that work in routine situations. Indeed, they may actively have to keep themselves from following their instinctive reactions because these instincts are not likely to be well informed if the event is unfamiliar. They will need to set priorities, collect data, develop options, predict consequences that will flow from different choices, and choose options that seem likely to best serve the established priorities; they then need to repeat this analytical cycle again and again as the events evolve.

Third, preparing in advance to confront true crisis situations requires capabilities-based (rather than threat-based) planning. In planning the response to a routine situation, agencies have a more or less specific threat or challenge in mind, and they can directly optimize their capacity to perform against that specific threat. For example, urban firefighting organizations repeatedly confront a relatively small array of threats, and they can prepare directly to cope with each of them. By contrast, when preparing for the next novel or unprecedented event, we do not know in advance the precise nature of the threat. We are forced, therefore, to organize a set of capabilities—for example, equipment and training for search and rescue; medical care for injured people or those suffering from exposure; and emergency shelter, sanitation, and food supply—that are robust across a wide range of known threats and potentially useful for unknown ones. If these capabilities are available, they can be rapidly and creatively combined and deployed to meet the novel demands of a crisis.

Finally, organizations facing true crises may need to exhibit different organizational forms in different parts of the response. At the outset, when they are trying to understand a new situation, they may need to be more collaborative and more open to input from many more sources than most hierarchical organizations typically are. They need to become a relatively "flat" organization when they are trying to understand the situation because, in the early stages of a novel event, many individuals are each likely to know a little bit about it (and to know different things). Later, when these organizations begin to improvise their response, they will probably need a smaller but diverse and flexible planning and decision-making group; this group has to be open to various design possibilities, broadly knowledgeable about the operational capabilities potentially available, and ready to work collaboratively to design and develop different options. Finally, when the organizations turn to executing the approach they have developed, they will probably need to function in a more hierarchical, authority-driven manner in order to coordinate the implementation effectively and efficiently.

In closing, we hope that the case studies in this book not only inform but inspire. Thoughtful analysis of the situations described here can provide insight into the nature of crises and the difficulties of effectively protecting society from disasters small and large. Every citizen should have at least some degree of appreciation for the organizational capabilities that such protection requires. But some readers may also be encouraged to think about participating in the system more personally. The challenges of improving emergency response and crisis management in the United States and in other countries are great, but the potential benefits of improvement to individuals, society, and the economy are also large. The emergency management system has multitudes of brave and dedicated individuals who have committed their lives to protecting others; the rewards of choosing a career that could contribute to improving that system in the future are substantial.

Index